THE MEANING OF DIFFERENCE

American Constructions of Race,
Sex and Gender,
Social Class,
and Sexual Orientation

THE MEANING OF DIFFERENCE

**American Constructions of Race,
Sex and Gender,
Social Class,
and Sexual Orientation**

Karen E. Rosenblum
George Mason University

Toni-Michelle C. Travis
George Mason University

The McGraw-Hill Companies, Inc.

New York   St. Louis   San Francisco   Auckland   Bogotá   Caracas
Lisbon   London   Madrid   Mexico City   Milan   Montreal   New Delhi
San Juan   Singapore   Sydney   Tokyo   Toronto

This book was set in Times Roman by The Clarinda Company.
The editors were Jill S. Gordon and Katherine Blake;
the production supervisor was Paula Keller.
The cover was designed by Edward Butler.
Project Supervision was done by Tage Publishing Service, Inc.
Quebecor Printing/Fairfield was printer and binder.

THE MEANING OF DIFFERENCE
American Constructions of Race, Sex and Gender, Social Class, and Sexual Orientation

Acknowledgments appear on pages 433–435, and on this page by reference.

This book is printed on acid-free paper.

5 6 7 8 9 0   FGR   FGR   9 0 9 8 7

ISBN 0-07-053962-6

Library of Congress Cataloging-in-Publication Data
The meaning of difference: American constructions of race, sex, and gender, social class, and sexual orientation / Karen E. Rosenblum, Toni-Michelle Travis.
    p.   cm.
   Includes bibliographical references (p.   ).
   ISBN 0-07-053962-6
    1. United States—Social conditions—1980–   2. Pluralism (Social sciences)—
    United States.   I. Rosenblum, Karen Elaine.   II. Travis, Toni-Michelle, (date).
HN59.2.M44   1996
306′.0973—dc20   95-36974

ABOUT THE
AUTHORS

Karen E. Rosenblum is Associate Professor of Sociology and Director of Women's Studies at George Mason University in Fairfax, Virginia. She is also a faculty member in American Studies and Cultural Studies. Professor Rosenblum received her Ph.D. in Sociology from the University of Colorado, Boulder. Her areas of research and teaching include sex and gender, language, and deviance. Professor Rosenblum's work has appeared in many scholarly collections and in journals such as *The British Journal of Sociology, The Journal of Family Issues, Semiotica, Sociological Forum, Sociological Inquiry, and Women's Studies International Forum.*

Toni-Michelle C. Travis is Associate Professor of Government and Politics at George Mason University in Fairfax, Virginia. She is also a faculty member in the Women's Studies and African American Studies Programs. Professor Travis received her Ph.D. in Political Science from the University of Chicago. Her areas of research and teaching include race and gender in political participation, women and politics, and interest group politics. Professor Travis' work has appeared in numerous scholarly collections. She has served as the President of the National Capital Area Political Science Association and the Women's Caucus of the American Political Science Association, is on the editorial board of *Urban Affairs Quarterly* and *Women & Politics*, has served as a grant reviewer for the American Council of Learned Societies, and is a frequent news commentator on Virginia politics.

CONTENTS

vii

SECTION 3

The Meaning of Difference

PREFACE

This book examines the contemporary American constructions of race, sex and gender, social class, and sexual orientation. It is premised on the idea that while each of these statuses is distinctive in many ways, an understanding of their shared features provides conceptual and practical insights that are useful for all of us.

The volume combines the features of both a textbook and a reader. It is divided into three main sections. Each section begins with a Framework Essay that offers a "generic" conceptual frame and is followed by a set of readings that illustrate and extend the points made in the essay. The readings have been specifically selected for the generalizability of their analyses to race, sex, class, and sexual orientation statuses. For example, Deborah Tannen's article on women as a "marked category" can be extended to consider how people of color, gays, and those who are poor are also "marked." The Framework Essays are not introductions to the readings in the usual sense. Rather, they are intended to frame and supplement the selections; generally they offer material *not* addressed in the readings. Thus, the Framework Essays and readings may be used jointly or independently of one another, just as the book's three main sections may be treated as freestanding units.

The volume has especially been designed with an eye toward the pedagogic difficulties that accompany the topics of race, sex and gender, social class, and sexual orientation. Our aim has been to provide a fresh look at a set of issues that many say they are tired of talking about. Thus, we have included several original accounts written by students (and presented here as boxed inserts) and a chapter explaining the historical and legal context of ten key Supreme Court cases affecting America's race, sex, social class, sexual orientation, and language minorities. To move beyond what are often well-entrenched positions, we have also tried to minimize use of the terminology that currently predominates in campus discussions of racism, sexism, and homophobia.

Many colleagues and friends have helped us clarify the ideas we present here. David Haines provided a thoughtful critique of the Framework Essays and was an endless source of conceptual and technical insight. Theodore W. Travis provided insight on Supreme Court decisions, their relationship to social values, and their impact on American society. Our colleague Victoria Rader reviewed several versions of the manuscript, lending us the vision and encouragement of a master teacher on these topics. We also owe special thanks to our George Mason students who shared with us their understanding of American constructions of difference, and to Sheila Barrows, Mark Colvin, Cybele Eidenschenk, Kathi George, Beth Gordon, Joshua Haines, Lois Horton, Elaine Hyams, Susan Kent, Barbara Knight, Michelle Massé, Paul McLaughlin, Rose Pascarell, Louise Rosenblum, and John Stone for their review and comments on the material. The support provided by Katherine Blake, Jill Boggs, Phil Butcher, and Jill Gordon at McGraw-Hill was much appreciated. Finally, it was the work of Joan Lester and the Equity Institute in Emeryville, California that convinced us of the progress that could be made through a comparison of race, sex, class, and sexual orientation.

The review process conducted by McGraw-Hill reaffirmed our faith in the publishers of textbooks. McGraw-Hill provided a panel of accomplished scholars with broad expertise, thus allowing us a chance to tap the range of fields a volume such as this addresses. Joe Feagin, Linda Grant, Allan Johnson, Mari Molseed, Joyce Nielsen, Brenda Phillips, Suey Spivey, Becky Thompson, and several anonymous reviewers offered excellent suggestions for readings as well as a vision of the project as a whole. Becky Thompson in particular reviewed multiple versions of this material. Her enthusiasm and inspired suggestions for improvement gave us hope that a volume such as this would be useful.

Karen E. Rosenblum
Toni-Michelle C. Travis

THE MEANING OF DIFFERENCE

**American Constructions of Race,
Sex and Gender,
Social Class, and
Sexual Orientation**

CONSTRUCTING CATEGORIES OF DIFFERENCE

FRAMEWORK ESSAY

This text explores the contemporary American construction of race, sex, social class, and sexual orientation. Although these are categories most of us have taken for granted, in this book they will be critically examined.

Race, sex, class, and sexual orientation may be described as "master statuses." In common usage "status" means prestige, but in this volume and in most social science literature status is understood as a position within a social structure, for example, a kinship or occupational status. Any individual simultaneously occupies a number of statuses, but their master status "in most or all social situations, will overpower or dominate all other statuses. . . . Master status influences every other aspect of life, including personal identity" (Marshall, 1994:315).

In this text we argue that there are important similarities in how the master statuses of race, sex, social class, and sexual orientation operate—examining the American construction of race reveals processes that also operate in the construction of sex, class, and sexual orientation. This is not to say that these master statuses operate identically, or that people in these categories have had interchangeable experiences. The past and present circumstances of African American, Latino, and Asian American men and women are distinctive on innumerable counts; they cannot easily be compared to the experience of white women. Gay and lesbian members of America's racial minorities face circumstances different from those faced by white Americans who are gay or lesbian. The impact of race, sex, and sexual orientation unfolds quite differently in the upper, middle, working, and poor classes. Nonetheless, there are also important similarities in the way these master statuses are currently constructed and in their impact on individual lives. Indeed, only space limitations have kept us from extending our discussion to the master statuses of age, physical ability, and religion.

1

As we prepared this volume, we were struck by how frequently the topics of race and racism, sex and sexism, sexual orientation, homophobia,[1] and poverty appeared in the news, as themes in popular films and music, as the subject of talk shows and soap operas, as research themes in scholarly journals and monographs, in sermons, as issues of practical concern in work and educational settings, and as simply topics of everyday conversation. There is much intensity evident around these subjects; that intensity inevitably promotes both the desire to talk about these topics and the desire to avoid them.

As a consequence, readers may have strong reactions to the material included here. Whatever the reaction, however, it provides key analytic information. In broadest terms, one is likely to discover oneself taking either an "essentialist" or "constructionist" approach to this material.

The Essentialist and Constructionist Orientations

The difference between the constructionist and essentialist orientations is illustrated in the tale of the three umpires, first apparently told by social psychologist Hadley Cantril:

> Hadley Cantril relates the story of three baseball umpires discussing their profession. The first umpire said, 'Some are balls and some are strikes, and I call them as they are.' The second replied, 'Some's balls and some's strikes, and I call 'em as I sees 'em.' The third thought about it and said, 'Some's balls and some's strikes, but they ain't nothing 'till I calls 'em' (Henshel and Silverman, 1975:26).

The first umpire takes an essentialist position. In arguing that "I call them as they are," he indicates his assumption that balls and strikes are entities that exist in the world independent of his perception of them. For this umpire, "balls" and "strikes" are distinct, easily identified, mutually exclusive categories, and he is a neutral and relatively powerless observer of them. In all, he "regards knowledge as objective and independent of mind, and himself as the impartial reporter of things 'as they are'" (Pfuhl, 1986:5). For this essentialist umpire, balls and strikes exist in the world; he simply observes their presence.

Thus, the essentialist orientation presumes that the items in a category all share some "essential" quality, their "ball-ness" or "strike-ness." For essentialists, the categories of race, sex, sexual orientation, and social class identify significant, empirically verifiable similarities among and differences between people. From the essentialist perspective, for example, racial categories exist apart from any social or cultural processes; they are objective categories of essential difference between people.

---

[1]The term homophobia was coined in 1973 by psychologist George Weinberg to describe an irrational fear of, or anger toward, homosexuals. While the psychological application has been abandoned, the word remains in common usage as describing a strong opposition to or rejection of same-sex relationships. The term leaves much to be desired, but the alternative that has emerged, heterosexism, is not yet in conventional usage. Heterosexism has been defined as the presumption that all people are heterosexual and that heterosexuality is the only acceptable form of sexual expression.

Though somewhat removed from pure essentialism, the second umpire still affirms that there is an independent, objective reality, though it is one which is subject to *interpretation*. For him, balls and strikes exist in the world, but individuals might have different perceptions of which is which.

The third umpire, who argues "they ain't nothing till I call 'em," is unabashedly constructionist. He argues that "conceptions such as 'strikes' and 'balls' have no meaning except that given them by the observer" (Pfuhl, 1986:5); balls and strikes do not exist until an umpire names them as such. While the essentialist presumes an external world with distinct categories existing independent of observation, the constructionist argues that reality cannot be separated from the way that a culture makes sense of it. From the constructionist perspective *social* processes determine that one set of differences is more important than another, just as social processes shape our understanding of what those differences *mean*. The constructionist assumes that "essential" similarities are conferred and created rather than intrinsic to the phenomenon, that the way that a society identifies its members tells us more about the society than about the individuals so classified. Thus, the constructionist perspective treats classifications such as race as socially constructed through political, legal, economic, scientific, and religious institutions. Although individuals do not on their own create such classifications, macro-level social processes and institutions do. That this textbook asks *how* we have arrived at our race, sex, sexual orientation, and social class categories signals our use of the constructionist perspective.

Few of us have grown up as constructionists, however. More likely, we were raised as essentialists who believe that master statuses such as race or sex encompass clear-cut, immutable, and in some way meaningful differences. From an essentialist perspective, one simply *is* what one *is:* someone with African ancestry is black, and a person with male genitalia is male even if he does not feel like a male. It is fairly unsettling to have these bedrock classifications questioned—which is what the constructionist perspective does.

However, not all of us have grown up as essentialists. Those from mixed racial or religious backgrounds are likely to be familiar with the ways in which identity is not clear cut. They grow up understanding how definitions of self vary with the context; how others try to define one as belonging in a particular category; and how in many ways, one's very presence calls prevailing classification systems into question. For example, being asked "What are you?" is a common experience among mixed-race people. Such experiences make evident the social constructedness of racial identity.

Still, few of us are likely to take either an essentialist or constructionist perspective exclusively. Our own perspective as authors has been constructionist, and our goal in this book—to examine the social processes that create the categories of race, sex, sexual orientation, and class—is a constructionist one. Nonetheless, we have sometimes had to rely on essentialist terms we ourselves find problematic. The irony of simultaneously questioning the idea of race, but still talking about "blacks," "whites," and "Asians"; or of rejecting a dualistic approach to sexual identity, while still using the terms "gay" and "straight" has not escaped us. Indeed, throughout our discussion we have used the currently favored essentialist phrase "sexual orientation" over the more constructionist "sexual preference" (a topic to which we will return shortly).[2]

Further, there is a serious risk that a text such as this falsely identifies people on the basis of either their sex, or race, or sexual orientation, or social class, despite the fact that master statuses are not parts of a person that can simply be broken off from one another like the segments of a Tootsie Roll (Spelman, 1988). Each of us is always simultaneously all of our master statuses, and it is that complex package that exists in the world. While Section I of the readings may make it seem as if these were separable statuses, they are not. Indeed, even the concept of master status suggests that there can be only one dominating status, though we would reject that position.

Both constructionism and essentialism are used in the social sciences. While we are offering constructionism here as a useful approach to contemporary master status formulations, essentialism has nonetheless been a critical element in the development of modern science. It has been the basis of probability theory and statistics (Hilts, 1973) and forms the bedrock for most social scientific research. While in its common uses, essentialism carries static, ahistoric, and determinist connotations, these are not inevitable parts of the perspective (McLaughlin, 1994; Sober, 1980).

Essentialism and constructionism can be found both among the proponents of contemporary social movements and among those who criticize those movements. For example, some feminists argue that women are essentially different from men, as do those critical of feminism. Similarly, constructionism dominated the gay rights movement of the 1970s, but now characterizes the perspective of those opposed to gay relationships. During the 1970s many took a constructionist approach to sexuality, arguing especially that women could choose same-sex relationships (Faderman, 1991); some in the women's movement debated whether one could be a good feminist and be a practicing heterosexual. The phrase common among both gay and heterosexual people at the time was a constructionist one: "sexual preference."

Over the years, however, "sexual preference" has been replaced by "sexual orientation." Thus, an essentialist perspective has come to dominate both the heterosexual and gay communities. Whereas "preference" conveyed active, human decision-making with the possibility of change, "orientation" is understood as something people are "born with," something that is constant over time. While many religious groups opposed to same-sex relationships maintain a constructionist approach—arguing that sexuality exists within the realm of personal control—the prevailing view in both the popular culture and among gay activists now appears to be essentialist.

One explanation for this shift is that essentialist explanations emerge as a defense when levels of prejudice are high (Faderman, 1991). Journalist and gay activist Darryl Rist makes the appeal of essentialist explanations clear in this description:

---

[2]"Sexual identity" may now be replacing sexual orientation. It could be used in either an essentialist or constructionist way.

[Chris Yates's parents were] . . . Pentecostal ministers who had tortured his adolescence with Christian cures for sexual perversity. Shock and aversion therapies under born-again doctors and gruesome exorcisms of sexual demons by spirit-filled preachers had culminated in a plan to have him castrated by a Mexican surgeon who touted the procedure as a way to make the boy, if not straight, at least sexless. Only then had the terrified son rebelled.

Then, in the summer of 1991, the journal *Science* reported anatomical differences between the brains of homosexual and heterosexual men. . . . The euphoric media—those great purveyors of cultural myths—drove the story wildly. Every major paper in the country headlined the discovery smack on the front page. . . . Like many others, I suspect, Chris Yates's family saw in this newly reported sexual science a way out of its wrenching impasse. After years of virtual silence between them and their son, Chris's parents drove several hundred miles to visit him and ask for reconciliation. Whatever faded guilt they might have felt for the family's faulty genes was nothing next to the reassurance that neither by a perverse upbringing nor by his own iniquity was Chris or the family culpable for his urges and actions. "We could never have condoned this if you could do something to change it. But when we finally understood that you were *born* that way, we knew we'd been wrong. We had to ask your forgiveness" (Rist, 1992:425–26).

It is understandable that those under attack would find essentialist orientations appealing, just as the expansiveness of constructionist approaches would be appealing in more tolerant eras.

Why have we spent so much time describing the essentialist and constructionist perspectives? Discussions about racism, sexism, homophobia, and poverty generate the intensity they do partly because they involve the clash of essentialist and constructionist assumptions. Essentialists are likely to view categories of people as in some important way "essentially" different; constructionists are likely to see these differences as socially created and arbitrary. An essentialist asks what causes people to be different; a constructionist asks about the origin and consequence of the categorization system itself. While arguments about the nature and cause of racism, sexism, homophobia, and poverty are disputes about power and justice, from the perspective of essentialism and constructionism they are also disputes about what differences in sex, color, sexuality, and social class *mean*.

Both perspectives may be used as a justification for discrimination, but there is one clear advantage to the constructionist approach: It is from that perspective that one understands that all the talk about race, sex, sexual orientation, and social class has a profound significance. These are conversations about what it means to be a particular kind of person, a member of a particular category. The topics carry the intensity that they do because they are about who we *are*. This talk is not simply *about* difference and similarity; it is itself the *creation* of difference and similarity. In the sections that follow, we will examine how categories of people are named, aggregated, dichotomized, and stigmatized—all toward the construction of difference.

Naming and Aggregating

Classification schemes are by definition systems for *naming* categories of people; thus constructionists pay special attention to the names people use to refer to themselves and others—particularly the points at which new names are asserted, the negotiations that surround the use of particular names, and those occasions when categories of people are grouped together or separated out.

Asserting a Name   The issues surrounding the assertion of a name are similar whether we are talking about individuals or categories of people. A change of name involves, to some extent, the claim of a new identity. For example, one of our colleagues decided that she wanted to be called by her full first name, rather than by its abbreviated version because the diminutive had come to seem childish to her. It took a few rounds of reminding people that this was her new name, and with most that was adequate. One colleague, however, argued that he simply could not adapt to the new name; she would just have to tolerate his continuing with the previous version. This was a small but public battle about who had the power to name whom. Did she have the power to enforce her own naming, or did he have the power to name her despite her wishes? (Eventually, she won.) A more disturbing example was provided by a young woman who wanted to keep her "maiden" name after she married. Her fiancé agreed with her decision, recognizing how reluctant he would be to give up his name were the tables turned. When her prospective mother-in-law heard of this possibility, however, she was outraged. In her mind, a rejection of her family's name was a rejection of her family: she urged her son and his fiancé to reconsider getting married. (We do not know how this story ended.)

Thus, the assertion of a name can yield some degree of social conflict. On both the personal and a societal level, naming can involve the claim of a particular identity and the rejection of others' power to impose a name. All of this applies to individual preferences. For example, is one Chicano, Mexican American, Mexican, Latino, Hispanic, Spanish-American, or Hispaño; Native American, American Indian, or Sioux; African American or black; girl or woman; Asian American or Japanese American; gay or homosexual? This list does not begin to cover the full range of possibilities, or include geographic and historical variations.

> Geographically, *Hispanic* is preferred in the Southeast and much of Texas. New Yorkers use both *Hispanic* and *Latino.* Chicago, where no nationality has attained a majority, prefers *Latino.* In California, the word *Hispanic* has been barred from the Los Angeles *Times,* in keeping with the strong feelings of people in the community. Some people in New Mexico prefer *Hispaño.* Politically, *Hispanic* belongs to the right and some of the center, while *Latino* belongs to the left and the center. Historically, the choice went from *Spanish* or *Spanish-speaking* to *Latin American, Latino,* and *Hispanic* (Shorris, 1992:xvi–xvii).

Thus, determining the appropriate name by which to refer to a category of people is no easy task. It is unlikely that all members of the category prefer the same name; the name members use for one another may not be acceptable when used by those outside the group; nor is it always advisable to ask what name a person prefers. We once saw an old friend become visibly angry when asked whether he preferred the term "black" or "African American." "Either one is fine with me," he replied, "*I* know what *I* am." To him, such a question indicated that he was being seen as a member of a category rather than as an individual.

As we have said, on both the individual and collective level naming may involve a redefinition of self, an assertion of power, and a rejection of others' ability to impose an identity. For this reason, social movements often claim a new name, just as those who continue to use the old name may do so as a way to indicate opposition to the movement. For example, in the current American setting, we may be in the midst of a change from "black" to "African American." "Black" emerged in opposition to "Negro" as the Black Power movement of the Black Panthers, Black Muslims, and the Student Nonviolent Coordinating Committee (SNCC) came to distinguish itself from the more mainstream Martin Luther King wing of the civil rights movement (Smith, 1992).

The term "Negro" had itself been born of a rejection of the term "colored" that dominated the mid- to late-nineteenth century. The term "African" had preceeded "colored," and was used as late as the 1820s. Led by influential leaders such as W. E. B. Du Bois and Booker T. Washington, " 'Negro' was seen as a 'stronger' term [than "colored"] . . . despite its association with racial epithets. 'Negro' was defined to stand for a new way of thinking about Blacks" (Smith, 1992:497–8).

On the same grounds, president of the National Urban Coalition Ramona H. Edelin, proposed in 1988 using "African American" instead of "black." The campaign to adopt the term, led by Coalition spokesman Jessie Jackson, met with immediate success among black leaders and now both terms are in use (Smith, 1992).[3]

Ironically, the phrase "people of color" is emerging now as a reference encompassing all non-white Americans. White students unfamiliar with the historical background of "colored" will sometimes use that term interchangeably with "people of color." Unaware of the historical distinction, they are surprised by the anger with which they are met.

Each of these changes—from "Negro" to "black" to "African American"—was first promoted by activists as a way to demonstrate their commitment to change and militance. Many of the same themes are reflected in the history of the terms "Chicano," and "Chicanismo." As reporter Ruben Salazar wrote in the 1960s, "a chicano is a Mexican-American with a non-Anglo image of himself" (Shorris, 1992:101).

> [Chicanismo] had no official beginning. It may have started in the mid-sixties with the Brown Berets or in 1967 with the publication of the epic poem *I Am Joaquin* by the former professional boxer, Rudolfo 'Corky' Gonzales. The chicanos showed their power for the first time in Los Angeles in March of 1968, when ten thousand students walked out of barrio high schools. . . . Chicano students protested in Colorado, Texas, and Arizona. The complaints were always the same: poor facilities, racism, cultural bias, and a tracking system that prepared Latino students for the worst, lowest-paying jobs (Shorris, 1992:103).

Presently, it is unclear whether "Chicano" continues as a favored name among Mexican Americans (or Mexicans as many prefer to call themselves).

---

[3]One can find Black Studies, Afro-American Studies, and African American Studies programs in universities across the country.

Similar themes emerge in the history of the gay rights movement. As Peter Conrad and Joseph Schneider describe in selection 30, the term "homosexual" was coined in 1869 by a Hungarian physician in an effort to thwart the criminalization of same-sex relationships. The term dominated the medical and psychological literature until the emergence of the contemporary gay rights movement, which argued for rejecting the term homosexual as a way to reject the medico-psychological treatment of same-sex relations as pathological. Presently "gay" is used both as a generic term encompassing men and women and as a specific reference to men.[4]

The 1990 founding of Queer Nation (which grew out of the AIDS activist organization, ACT UP) may signal the eventual demise of "gay," however. This use of "queer"—as for example in the slogan "We're here. We're queer. Get used to it."—attempts to transform an epithet into a label of pride and militance. Nonetheless, use of the word is also much debated within the gay community: Those against it argue that it reflects the internalization of homophobic imagery, those who favor it argue that it offers an appropriate defiance of straight culture.

Just as each of these social movements has involved a public renaming that proclaims pride and a changed attitude, the women's movement has asserted "woman" as a replacement for "girl." The significance of these two terms is revealed in the account of a student who described a running feud with her roommate. The student preferred the word "woman" rather than "girl," arguing that the application of the word "girl" to females past adolescence was insulting. Her roommate, who was also female, just as strongly preferred the term "girl" and just as regularly applied it to the females she knew. Finally, they tried to "agree to disagree," but each of them had such strong feelings on the matter it was clear they could not be roommates much longer.

How could these two words destroy their relationship? It appears that English speakers use the terms "girl" and "woman" to refer to quite different qualities. "Woman" (like "man") is understood to convey adulthood, power, and sexuality; "girl" (like "boy") connotes youth, powerlessness, and irresponsibility (Richardson, 1988). Thus, the two roommates were asserting quite different places for themselves in the world. One claimed adulthood; the other saw herself as not having achieved that. This is the explanation offered by many females: It is not so much that they like being "girls," as that they value youth and/or do not yet feel justified in calling themselves "women." Yet this is precisely the identity the women's movement has put forward: "We cannot be girls any more, we must be women."

---

[4]In the seventeenth century *gay* became associated with an addiction to social pleasure, dissipation, and loose morality and was used to refer to female prostitutes (e.g., gay girl). The term was apparently first used in reference to a male homosexual in 1925 in Australia. "It may have been both the connotations of femininity and those of immorality that led American homosexuals to adopt the title 'gay' with some self-irony in the 1920s. The slogan 'Glad to be Gay,' adopted by both female and male homosexuals, and the naming of the Gay Liberation Front, which was born from the Stonewall resistance riots following police raids on homosexual bars in New York in 1969, bear witness to a greater self-confidence" (Mills, 1989:102).

The Negotiation and Control of Names   While individuals and social movements may assert a name for themselves, government agencies also control access to such categorizations. Still, these agencies are not impervious to social movements and social change. The recent history of U.S. Census Bureau classifications offers an example of the negotiation of a categorization system.

Census classifications and census data are significant for a variety of reasons. The census determines the apportionment of seats (among states) in the U.S. House of Representatives, and it affects the distribution of federal monies to states, counties, and cities for "everything from feeding the poor to running mass transit systems" (Espiritu, 1992:116). Since the census is conducted only once every ten years, its results shape policy for a decade.

Most important to our discussion, events in the 1960s and 1970s elevated the importance of census data:

> There were the civil rights movement and its offshoots such as the Mexican-American Brown Power movement. In addition, the federal government initiated the War Against Poverty and the Great Society programs. These movements and programs stated clearly that poor minority groups [specifically, Hispanics, Native Americans, blacks, and Asian or Pacific Islanders] had a legitimate claim to better conditions in cities. Several of the social welfare programs of President Johnson's Great Society distributed dollars by means of statistically driven grant-in-aid formulas. The proliferation of federal grants programs and the cities' increasing dependence upon them tended to heighten the political salience of census statistics. Such formulas often incorporated population size, as measured or estimated by the Census Bureau, as a major factor. By 1978 there were more than one hundred such programs, covering a wide range of concerns, from preschool education (Headstart) to urban mass transportation (U.S. Congress 1978). . . . [T]he single most commonly used data source was the decennial census (Choldin, 1994:27–8).

The census offered an important source of information by which the courts, Congress, and local entities could gauge the extent of discrimination. "Groups had to prove that they had been discriminated against in order to qualify for federal help under the Voting Rights Act. . . . To receive help in the form of an affirmative action plan from the newly established Equal Employment Opportunity Commission, each minority had to demonstrate its disproportionate absence from certain categories of employment" (Choldin, 1986: 406). As legislation raised the stakes involved in census data, disputes regarding its structure escalated. In response, the Census Bureau—for the first time ever—established minority committees to advise the government on the content and implementation of the 1980 census (Choldin, 1986).

On the Hispanic Advisory Committee, representatives argued strongly that the census "differentially undercounted" the Hispanic population, i.e., that the census missed more Hispanics than it did those in other categories. Undercounting primarily affects those who are low-income, non-English speaking, and live in inner cities—those who are poor often lack stable residences and are thus difficult to reach; those who cannot read English cannot answer the questions (only in 1990 did the census provide for Spanish-language surveys); those who are illegal immigrants may be unwilling to respond to the questionnaire. (The Constitution requires a count of all the people in the United States, not just those who are legal residents.)

While the Census Bureau might use birth and death records to determine the undercount of blacks, representatives on the Hispanic Advisory Committee pointed out that the Latino undercount could not be determined by this method since birth and death records did not record Hispanic ancestry. As a way to correct for an undercount, the advisory committee argued for the introduction of a Spanish/Hispanic origin *self-identification* question in the 1980 census. Thus, negotiation produced a new census category. (Figure 1 shows the 1990 version of this question.)

But self-identification is also a problematic way to classify a population. It lacks scientific validity because people may classify themselves by different criteria or use inconsistent criteria over time. Nonetheless, the census actually began moving toward the self-identification of race as early as 1960. By 1980, it fully relied on that approach.

Thus, while many treat census classifications as if they were fixed categorizations grounded in scientifically valid distinctions, that is not the case as even the Census Bureau admits: "The concept of race as used by the Census Bureau reflects self-identification, it does not denote any clear-cut scientific definition of biological stock . . . the categories of the race item include both racial and national origin or sociocultural groups" (U.S. Bureau of the Census, 1990). Indeed, the federal guidelines that regulate research and policy-making in health, education, employment, civil rights compliance, school desegregation, and voting rights are similarly clear that the classifications "should not be interpreted as being scientific or anthropological in nature" (Overbey, 1994).

Still, when we consider "official counts" of the population, we risk believing that what is counted must be real. While the Census Bureau and other federal agencies operate from explicit constructionist premises, the data they produce may

FIGURE 1

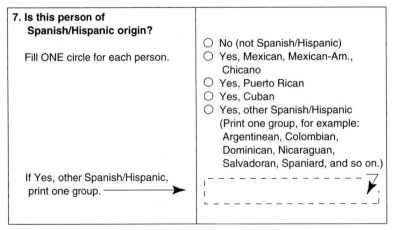

be used toward an essentialist worldview in which racial categories are presumed to reflect real and abiding differences between people. Indeed, the Census Bureau is now conducting a review of its classification system, considering especially the possibility of adding a "multiracial" classification, changing terminology (black to African American, American Indian to Native American, Hispanic to Latino), adding a "Middle Eastern" category, and including Latino as a *racial* category (Overbey, 1994; Harrison, 1994). (For the 1990 census question on race, see Figure 2.)

The Spanish/Hispanic origin question provides an example of the negotiation of a categorization. By contrast, assignment to the category "Native American" was not initially open to negotiation by those it affected: Native Americans were not allowed to define who was included within that classification, only the federal government could do that.

Historically, federal definitions relied on the idea of "blood quantum," which was a measure of how much of one's ancestry could be traced to Native Americans. This standard was established in the 1887 General Allotment Act, which redistributed collectively held reservation land as individually deeded parcels. In order to qualify for a land parcel, Native Americans had to document that they possessed one-half or more Native American ancestry. The General Allotment Act left a considerable portion of land unallocated. That land (along with its mineral, water, and fishing rights) was then declared "surplus," becoming available to the federal government for lease to non-Indians (Jaimes, 1992). Despite an ongoing debate about abandoning blood quantum, the standard persists for access to federal and some state services (one-quarter ancestry is now the usual requirement). Though individual tribes now define their own criteria for tribal membership, many still rely on the blood quantum standard.

FIGURE 2

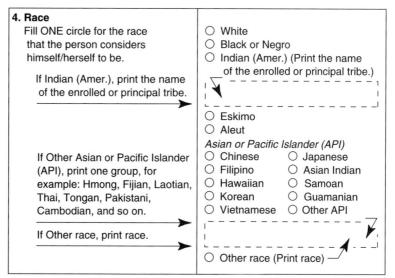

Aggregating and Disaggregating   The naming or labeling processes we have described serve both to aggregate and disaggregate categories of people. On the one hand, the federal identification of categories of disadvantaged Americans collapsed various national-origin groups into four headings—Hispanics, Native Americans, Blacks, and Asian or Pacific Islanders (Lowry, 1982). Thus, Puerto Ricans, Mexican Americans, and Cuban Americans all became "Hispanic" in some way. On the other hand, the groups which comprised these aggregates had historically regarded one another as different and thus the aggregate category was likely to "disaggregate" or decompose back into its constituent national-origin elements.

While one might think that "Hispanic" or "Asian American" are terms used for self-identification, that does not appear to be often the case. In the U.S. "Mexicans, Puerto Ricans, and Cubans have little interaction with each other, most do not recognize that they have much in common culturally, and they do not profess strong affection for each other" (de la Garza, et al., 1992:14). Thus, it is not surprising that a survey of the Latino population concludes that "respondents do not primarily identify as members of an Hispanic or Latino community. . . . [Rather, they] overwhelmingly prefer to identify by national origin . . ." (de la Garza, et al., 1992:13). While members of these groups share common positions on many domestic policy issues, they do not appear to share a commitment to Spanish language maintenance, common cultural traditions, or religiosity (de la Garza, et al., 1992). In short, the category "Latino/Hispanic" exists primarily, but not exclusively, from the perspective of non-Latinos.

The same can be said about the aggregate census category "Asian or Pacific Islander," which encompasses about fifty different nationalities. While the classification "Hispanic" offers at least a commonality in Spanish as a shared language in the country of origin, "Asian American" encompasses groups with unique languages, cultures, and religions; different racial groupings; and several centuries of congenial and/or hostile contact with members of other groups with whom they now share the category "Asian American." In all, the category "Asian American" aggregates on the basis of geography rather than any cultural, racial, linguistic, or religious commonalities. "Asian Americans are those who come from a region of the world that *the rest of the world* has defined as Asia" (Hu-Dehart, 1994).[5]

---

[5]In Census classifications, "Asian" includes Chinese, Filipino, Japanese, Asian Indian, Korean, Vietnamese, Cambodian, Hmong, Laotian, Thai; "Other Asian" includes Bangladeshi, Bhutanese, Borneo, Burmese, Celebesian, Ceram, Indochinese, Indonesian, Iwo-Jiman, Javanese, Malayan, Maldivian, Nepali, Okinawan, Pakistani, Sikkim, Singaporean, Sri Lankan, and Sumatran. The category "Pacific Islander" includes Hawaiian, Samoan, and Guamian; "Other Pacific Islander" includes Carolinian, Fijan, Kosraean, Melanesian, Micronesinan, Northern Mariana Islander, Palauan, Papua New Guinean, Ponapean, Polynesian, Solomon Islander, Tahitian, Tarawa Islander, Tokelauan, Tongan, Trukese, and Yapese (U.S. Census Bureau, 1990).

In 1980, Asian Indians successfully lobbied to change their census classification from white to Asian American by reminding Congress that historically immigrants from India had been classed as Asian. With other Asians, those from India had been barred from immigration by the 1917 Immigration Act, prohibited from becoming naturalized citizens until 1946, and denied the right to own land by the 1920 Alien Land Law. Indeed, in 1923 the U.S. Supreme Court (in *Thind*) ruled that Asian Indians were non-white, and could therefore have their U.S. citizenship nullified (Espiritu, 1992:124–125). Thus, in the bulk of their experience in the U.S., Asian Indians had been classed as Asian.

Aggregate classifications like "Latino," "Hispanic," or "Asian American" were not simply the result of federal classifications, however. These terms were first proposed by student activists following the lead of the Black Power and Civil Rights movements, and they continue to be used, although by a small proportion of people. As Yen Le Espiritu describes in selection 3, college students coined the pan-ethnic identifier Asian American in response to "the similarity of [their] experiences and treatment." As we saw earlier, when participants in social change movements forge new social identities and alliances, they also assert new names for themselves. In all, people use both aggregating pan-ethnic terms like "Asian American" and disaggregating national origin identifiers like Japanese American—each is used at particular moments, for particular reasons.

For two categories, however, Native and African Americans, the submerging of differences into an aggregate classification was the direct result of conquest and enslavement.

> The "Indian," like the European, is an idea. The notion of "Indians" was invented to distinguish the indigenous peoples of the New World from Europeans. The "Indian" is the person on shore, outside of the boat. . . . There [were] hundreds of cultures, languages, ways of living in Native America. The place was a model of diversity at the time of Columbus's arrival. Yet Europeans did not see this diversity. They created the concept of the "Indian" to give what they did see some kind of unification, to make it a single entity they could deal with, because they could not cope with the reality of 400 different cultures (Mohawk, 1992: 440).[6]

Conquest made "Indians" out of a heterogeneity of tribes and nations distinctive on linguistic, religious, and economic grounds. It was not only that Europeans had the unifying concept of "Indian" in mind—after all, they were sufficiently cognizant of tribal differences to generate an extensive body of tribally specific treaties. It was also that conquest itself—encompassing as it did the usurpation of land, the forging and violation of treaties, and the implementation of policies that forced relocation and concentration—structured the life of Native Americans along common lines. While contemporary Native Americans still identify themselves by tribal ancestry, just as those called Asian American and Latino identify themselves by national origin, their shared experience of conquest also forged the common identity reflected in the aggregate name, Native American.

Similarly, the capture, purchase, forced and often fatal relocation of Africans, and their experience of being moved from place to place when they were sold as property, created the category now called African American. This experience forged a single people from those who had been culturally diverse; it produced an "oppositional racial consciousness," i.e., a unity-in-opposition (Omi and Winant, 1994). "Just as the conquest created the 'native' where once there had been

---

[6]The idea of "Europe" and the "European" is also a constructed category. "Physically, Europe is not a continent. Where is the water separating Europe from Asia? It is culture that separates Europe from Asia. Western Europe roughly comprises the countries that in the Middle Ages were Latin Christendom, and Eastern Europe consists of those countries that in the Middle Ages were Eastern Orthodox Christendom. It was about 1257 A.D. when the Pope claimed hegemony over the secular emperors in Western Europe and formulated the idea that Europeans, that Christians, were a unified ethnicity even though they spoke many different languages" (Mohawk, 1992:439–440).

Pequot, Iroquois, or Tutelo, so too it created the 'black' where once there had been Asante or Ovimbundu, Yoruba or Bakongo" (Omi and Winant, 1994:66).

Even the categories of gay and straight, male and female, poor and middle class are aggregations that presume a commonality by virtue of shared master status. For example, the category "gay and lesbian" assumes that sharing a sexual orientation binds people together despite all the issues that might divide them as men and women, people of different colors, or people of different social classes. And, just as in the cases we have previously discussed, alliances of gay and lesbian people can be expected to come together and separate out in response to social circumstances.

Still, there is a category of people our analysis has so far ignored. From whose perspective do the categories of Native American, Asian American, African American, and Latino/Hispanic exist? Since "difference" is always "difference *from*," from whose perspective is "difference" determined? Who has the power to define "difference"? If "we" are in the boat looking at "them," who precisely are "we?"

Every perspective on the social world emerges from a particular vantage point, a particular social location. Ignoring who the "us" is in the boat, risks treating that place as if it were anywhere and nowhere, as if it were just the view "anyone" would take. Historically, the people in the boat were European, contemporarily they are white Americans. As Ruth Frankenberg frames it in selection 4, in America "whites are the nondefined definers of other people," "the unmarked marker of others' differentness." Failing to identify the "us" in the boat, means that "white culture [becomes] the unspoken norm," a category that is powerful enough to define others while itself remaining invisible. Indeed, as Frankenberg argues, those with the most power in a society are best positioned to have their own identities left unnamed, thus masking their power.

The term androcentrism describes the world as seen from a male-centered perspective. By analogy, one may also describe a Eurocentric and heterocentric perspective. To some extent, regardless of their sex, race, or sexual orientation all Americans operate from an andro-, Euro-, and heterocentric perspective since these are the guiding assumptions of the culture. Recognizing these as historically and culturally located perspectives makes it possible to evaluate their adequacy.

Dichotomization

As we have seen, many factors promote the construction of aggregate categories of people. Often aggregation yields dichotomization, that is, the sense that there are two and only two categories, that everyone fits easily in one or the other, and that the categories stand in opposition to one another. This has particularly been the case for the master statuses that are the focus of this book. In contemporary American culture we appear to treat race, sex, class, and sexual orientation as if each embodied "us" and "them"—as if people could be sorted into two mutually exclusive, opposed groupings.[7]

---

[7]Springer and Deutsch (1981) coined the term dichotomania to describe current belief that there are male and female sides of the brain. We think that term also fits our discussion here.

Dichotomizing Race Perhaps the clearest example of dichotomization is provided by the "one-drop rule," discussed by F. James Davis in selection 1. The one-drop rule describes the set of social practices whereby someone with any traceable African heritage is judged to be "black" by both American blacks and whites. As Davis makes clear, in American society this rule is applied only to blacks—no other category of people is defined by only "one drop." This is not simply an informal social practice; it was a principle reaffirmed in 1986 by the Supreme Court in *Jane Doe v. the State of Louisiana,* a case discussed by Davis in the selection included here.

The one-drop rule explains why some American racial classifications are so confounding to many immigrant and even native-born Americans. Several years ago, Marion Barry, then mayor of Washington, D.C. and his wife, Effie, often appeared on local television. Effie Barry looked white—prompting many to ask why she wasn't considered white since she looked white. The answer to that question is that in contemporary American culture, assignment to the status of black is not based on appearance or even the preponderance of racial heritage. Rather, social custom and law hold that a person with as little as $\frac{1}{32}$ African ancestry is black. While in other cultures people of mixed racial ancestry might be defined specifically as "mixed," the American one-drop rule precisely denied the possibility of being mixed; instead, it defined a child born to black and white parents as black.

While the black/white dichotomy may well be the most abiding and rigidly enforced racial distinction in American society, different regions and historical periods have also produced their own splits: In the southwest the divide has been between Anglos and Latinos; in parts of the west coast it is between Asian Americans and whites. Still, each of these distinctions is embedded in the country's historic dichotomy of "whites" and "non-whites." That distinction was stressed early in the nation's history: "Congress's first attempt to define American citizenship, the Naturalization Law of 1790, declared that only free 'white' immigrants could qualify" for citizenship (Omi and Winant, 1994:81). That position was reaffirmed in 1922, when the Supreme Court held that a Japanese immigrant could not become a naturalized U.S. citizen because he was not white, a position the Court reiterated a year later in terms of Asian Indians (Espiritu, 1992; Takaki, 1993). In this way, needed labor could be recruited to the country, while minimizing the risk that immigrants would become permanent residents and an economic threat (Steinberg, 1989). Not until 1952 were all immigrants eligible for naturalization, though the children of immigrants born on U.S. soil were always considered U.S. citizens.

Thus, while three racial categories—"white," "Negro," and "Indian"—were identified throughout the nineteenth century (Omi and Winant, 1994), all were located within the white/non-white dichotomy. In 1854, the California Supreme Court in *People v. Hall* held that blacks, mulattos, Native Americans, and Chinese were "not white" and therefore could not testify for or against a white man in court. (Takaki, 1993:205–6.) (Hall, a white man, had been convicted of killing a Chinese man on the testimony of one white and three Chinese witnesses; the Supreme Court overturned the conviction.) By contrast, Mexican residents of the Southwest territories ceded to the United States in the 1848 Treaty of Guadalupe

Hidalgo "were defined as a white population and accorded the political-legal status of 'free white persons'" (Omi and Winant, 1994). As historian David Roediger argues, even European immigrants were initially treated as non-white, or at least not-yet-white. In turn, they lobbied for their own inclusion in American society on the basis of the white/non-white distinction.

> [Immigrants struggled to] equate whiteness with Americanism in order to turn arguments over immigration from the question of who was foreign to the question of who was white. . . . Immigrants could not win on the question of who was foreign. . . . But if the issue somehow became defending "white man's jobs" or "white man's government" . . . [they] could gain space by deflecting debate from nativity, a hopeless issue, to race, an ambiguous one. . . . After the Civil War, the new-coming Irish would help lead the movement to bar the relatively established Chinese from California, with their agitation for a "white man's government," serving to make race, and not nativity, the center of the debate and to prove the Irish white (Roediger, 1994:189–90).

Thus, historically "American" has meant white, as many Asian Americans are casually reminded when they are complimented for speaking such good English—a compliment which presumes that someone who is Asian could not be a native-born American.[8] Historian Ronald Takaki frames it succinctly in this story:

> A white woman from New Jersey once raved to William Wong of the *Oakland Tribune* about a wonderful new Vietnamese restaurant in her town: "We were there the other night and we were the only Americans there." Wong noted with regret: "She probably meant the only white people" (Takaki, 1989:6).

Novelist Toni Morrison would describe this as a story about "how American means white":

> Deep within the word "American" is its association with race. To identify someone as South African is to say very little; we need the adjective "white" or "black" or "colored" to make our meaning clear. In this country it is quite the reverse. American means white, and Africanist people struggle to make the term applicable to themselves with . . . hyphen after hyphen after hyphen (Morrison, 1992:47).

Because American means white, those who are not white are presumed to be recent arrivals and are regularly told to go "back where they came from." In short, in America we appear to operate within the dichotomized *racial* categories of American/non-American—these are racial categories, because they effectively mean white/non-white.

But what exactly *is* race? First, we need to distinguish race from ethnicity. Social scientists define ethnic groups as categories of people who are distinctive on the basis of national origin, language, and cultural practices. As Robert Blauner explains in selection 13, "members of an ethnic group hold a set of common memories that make them feel that their customs, culture, and outlook are distinctive." Thus, racial categories encompass diverse ethnic groups; e.g., in America the racial

---

[8]Since the historic American ban on Asian immigration remained effectively in place until 1965, it is nonetheless the case that a high proportion of Asian Americans are foreign born. As of 1980, 62.1 percent of Asian Americans were foreign born (U.S. Civil Rights Commission, 1992:14).

category "white" encompasses ethnic groups such as Irish, Italian, and Polish Americans. Unfortunately, many fail to recognize ethnic distinctions among people of color. For example, not all American blacks are African American, some are Haitian, Jamaican, or Nigerian; African American is an ethnic group identification that does not encompass all American blacks.

Returning to the concept of race, the term most likely first appeared in the Romance languages of Europe in the Middle Ages where it was used to refer to breeding stock (Smedley, 1993). A "race" of horses, for example, would describe common ancestry and a distinctive appearance or behavior. "Race" appears to have been first applied to humans by the Spanish in the sixteenth century in reference to the New World populations they discovered. It was later adopted by the English, again in reference to people of the New World, and generally came to mean "people," "nation," or "variety." By the late eighteenth century, "when scholars became more actively engaged in investigations, classifications, and definitions of human populations, the term 'race' was elevated as the one major symbol and mode of human group differentiation employed extensively for non-European groups and even those in Europe who varied in some way from the subjective norm" (Smedley, 1993:39).

Though elevated to the level of science, the concept of race continued to reflect its origins in animal husbandry. Farmers and herders had used the concept to describe stock bred for particular qualities; scholars used it to suggest that human behaviors could also be inherited. "Unlike other terms for classifying people . . . the term 'race' places emphasis on innateness, on the inbred nature of whatever is being judged" (Smedley, 1993:39). Like animal breeders, scholars also presumed that appearance revealed something about potential behavior, that among humans race signified something more than just difference of color. Just as the selective breeding of animals entailed the ranking of stock by some criteria, scholarly use of the concept of race involved the ranking of human "races" along a variety of dimensions. Thus, differences in skin color, hair texture, and the shape of head, eyes, nose, lips, and body were developed into an elaborate system for classifying humans into discrete categories. These categories were then ranked as to their merit and potential for "civilization." Although the conquered peoples of the world were the objects of this classification system, they did not participate in its invention.

The idea of race emerged among all the European colonial powers (although their conceptions of it varied), but only the British in North America (and South Africa) constructed a system of rigid, exclusive racial categories and a social order *based on race,* a "racialized social structure" (Omi and Winant, 1994).

> [S]kin color variations in many regions of the world and in many societies have been imbued with some degree of social value or significance, but color prejudice or preferences do not of themselves amount to a fully evolved racial worldview. There are many societies, past and contemporary, in which the range of skin color variation is quite large, but all such societies have not imposed on themselves worldviews with the specific ideological components of race that we experience in North America or South Africa (Smedley, 1993:25).

This racialized social structure—which in America produced a race-based system of slavery and later a race-based distribution of political, legal, and social rights—was an historical first. "Expansion, conquest, exploitation, and enslavement have characterized much of human history over the past five thousand years or so, but none of these events before the modern era resulted in the development of ideologies or social systems based on race" (Smedley, 1993:15). While differences of color had long been noted, social structures had never before been built on those differences.

Thus, it is not surprising that scientists have assumed that race difference involves more than simply skin color or hair texture and have sought the biological distinctiveness of racial categories—but with little success. In the early twentieth century, anthropologists looked to physical features such as height, stature, and head shape to distinguish the races, only to learn that these are affected by environment and nutrition. Later, the search turned to genetic traits carried in the blood, only to find that those cannot be correlated with conventional racial classifications. Even efforts to reach a consensus about how many races there are or what specific features distinguish them from one another are problematic.

If our eyes could perceive more than the superficial, we might find race in chromosome 11: there lies the gene for hemoglobin. If you divide humankind by which of two forms of the gene each person has, than equatorial Africans, Italians and Greeks fall into the "sickle-cell race"; Swedes and South Africa's Xhosas (Nelson Mandela's ethnic group) are in the healthy hemoglobin race. Or do you prefer to group people by whether they have epicanthic eye folds, which produce the "Asian" eye? Then the !Kung San (Bushmen) belong with the Japanese and Chinese. . . . [D]epending on which traits you pick, you can form very surprising races. Take the scooped-out shape of the back of the front teeth, a standard "Asian" trait. Native Americans and Swedes have these shovel-shaped incisors, too, and so would fall in the same race. Is biochemistry better? Norwegians, Arabians, north Indians and the Fulani of northern Nigeria . . . fall into the "lactase race" (the lactase enzyme digests milk sugar). Everyone else—other Africans, Japanese, Native Americans—form the "lactase-deprived race" (their ancestors did not drink milk from cows or goats and hence never evolved the lactase gene). How about blood types, the familiar A, B, and O groups? Then Germans and New Guineans, populations that have the same percentages of each type, are in one race; Estonians and Japanese comprise a separate one for the same reason. . . . The dark skin of Somalis and Ghanaians, for instance, indicates that they evolved under the same selective force (a sunny climate). But that's all it shows. It does *not* show that they are any more closely related in the sense of sharing more genes than either is to Greeks. Calling Somalis and Ghanaians "black" therefore sheds no further light on their evolutionary history and implies—wrongly—that they are more closely related to each other than either is to someone of a different "race." . . . If you pick at random any two "blacks" walking along the street, and analyze their 23 pairs of chromosomes, you will probably find that their genes have less in common than do the genes of one of them with that of a random "white" person [because the genetic variation within one race is greater than the average difference between races] (Begley, 1995: 67, 68).

Thus, since the 1960s an increasing number of physical anthropologists have adopted what is called the "no-race" position (Littlefield, Lieberman, and Reynolds, 1982). This perspective argues that "(1) Biological variability exists but this variability does not conform to the discrete packages labeled races. (2) So-called racial characteristics are not transmitted as complexes. (3) Races do not exist because isolation of groups has been infrequent; populations have always interbred" (Lieberman, 1968:128). While some scholars continue to argue for the utility of the concept of race, it appears that the no-race position is becoming dominant in the field of anthropology. Still, few beyond anthropology are aware of this change.

> [I]t does not appear that this debate [about the existence of race] has had widespread impact on professionals in the fields of medicine, psychology, sociology, history, or political science. . . . it will suffice to point out that virtually all scholars who write about "race and intelligence" assume that the "races" which they study are distinguished on the basis of biologically relevant criteria. So accepted is this fact that most scholars engaged in such research never consider it necessary to justify their assignment of individuals to this or that "race". . . . [Thus], the layman who reads the literature on race and racial groupings is justified in assuming that the existent typologies have been derived through the application of theories and methods current in disciplines concerned with the biological study of human variation. Since the scientific racial classifications which a layman finds in the literature are not too different from popular ones, he can be expected to feel justified in the maintenance of his views on race (Marshall 1993; 117, 121).

In all, the primary significance of race is as a *social* concept: We "see" it, we expect it to tell us something significant about a person, we organize social policy, law, and the distribution of wealth, power and prestige around it. From the essentialist position, race is assumed to exist independent of our perception of it; it is assumed to significantly distinguish people from one another. From the constructionist perspective, race exists because we have created it as a meaningful category of difference between people.

Dichotomizing Sexual Orientation   Just as the complexities of race appear to have been distilled into mutually exclusive categories and then dichotomized into black and white or white and non-white, the range and complexity of human sexual experience appears to have been refined into two categories, gay and straight. In sexuality as in race, we generally assume there are only two categories, that everyone can be easily classed as one or the other, and that the people who comprise each category are in important ways different from each other.

As with "race," "sexual orientation" sounds straightforward, but its reference is actually quite unclear. Sexuality encompasses physical, social, and emotional attraction, as well as actual sexual behavior, fantasies, and self-identity (Klein, 1978). Because these different features of sexuality need not be consistent with one another, determining one's sexual orientation may involve emphasizing one of these features over the others. Just as the system of racial classification appears to require that people of mixed ancestry pick *one* classification, the system of sexual orientation classification appears to require that all the different aspects of sexuality be distilled into one of two possible choices.

For example, an acquaintance described the process by which he came to self-identify as gay. In high school and college he had dated and been sexually active with women, but his relations with men had always been more important to him. He looked to men for emotional and social gratification and for relief from the "gender games" he felt required to play with women. He had been engaged to be married, but when that ended he spent his time exclusively with other men. Eventually he established a sexual relationship with another man and came to identify himself as gay. While his experience reflects the varied dimensions of sexuality described above, it also shows the resolution of those differences by choosing a single sexual identity.

Not only is sexuality itself comprised of many different components, human sexual activity is manifested in a fairly wide range of behaviors. In selection 10, Barbara Heyl describes Alfred Kinsey's landmark 1948 survey of American sexual practices.[9] Kinsey's data showed that same-sex experience was more prevalent than had been assumed, that people's sexual practices were quite variable, and that sexual practices could change over the lifespan. He suggested that instead of thinking about "homosexuals" and "heterosexuals" as if these were two discrete categories of people, we should recognize that sexual behavior exists along a continuum from those who are exclusively heterosexual to those who are exclusively gay.

Further, there is no necessary correspondence between sexual identity and sexual behavior. Someone who identifies as gay is still likely to have had some heterosexual experience; someone who identifies as straight may have had some same-sex experience. Identity is not always directly tied to behavior. Indeed, a person who identifies as gay may have had quantitatively *more* heterosexual experience than someone who identifies as straight. This distinction between identity and experience was underscored by the results of a 1994 survey, the most comprehensive American sex survey since Kinsey's: Although 2.8 percent of the men and 1.4 percent of the women surveyed identified as gay, 10.1 percent and 8.6 percent respectively either identified as gay or had had a same-sex experience or attraction at some point since puberty (Michael, 1994).

In all, sexuality is comprised of many different elements which can themselves be differently weighted. Nonetheless, in a remarkable social consensus, this complexity is distilled into two mutually exclusive possibilities—gay and straight. Even people who are not sexually active are still likely to be cast by themselves and others as either gay or straight. Thus, it is not surprising that adolescents sometimes engage in heterosexual activity to prove they are straight (Elze, 1992).

Although there is increasing discussion of bisexuality (when sexual possibilities include both sexes) and many gay and lesbian organizations now have added the term bisexual to their title, it is unclear whether the category will gain wide social support. At present, many heterosexuals assume bisexuals are really gay (Pope and Reynolds, 1991), and many gays assume bisexuals are heterosexuals experimenting with same-sex relationships or gays unwilling to commit to a gay identity—in any case the options are still only gay or straight.

The essentialist assumption that one can straightforwardly classify people into two mutually exclusive sexual-orientation categories plagues scientific research as

---

[9]Heyl's article is titled "Homosexuality: A Social Phenomenon." The subtitle conveys Heyl's constructionist orientation, since in sociological theory the term *phenomenon* emphasizes the constructed dimension of social life. Heyl is not using the term to indicate something extraordinary or unusual.

well as commonsense understanding. For example, in 1991 neurobiologist Simon LeVay published findings from his dissection of the brain tissue of forty-one cadavers; his research argued that between gay and straight men there was a difference in the size of a small group of neurons in the hypothalamus. LeVay's findings were widely publicized by the popular press as demonstrating a biological basis to homosexuality. Yet, how did LeVay decide which cadavers were gay and which straight? Below, gay activist Darryl Rist critiques LeVay's research from the constructionist perspective.

> What criteria, other than self-identification, could [LeVay] possibly have relied upon to categorize his cadavers? How did he account for the frequent dissonance between sexual self-definitions and what men actually want and do? In the best of circumstances, how would he measure degrees of desire and draw the inexorable line between gay and straight? Does he actually believe that most American men (including his study's presumed heterosexuals) will confess to homoerotic urges? Or that self-identified gay men, by nature, experience no heterosexual longing? All these men, alas, were *dead* by the time [LeVay] met them! (Rist, 1992:426).

The search for biological difference not only presumes that it is possible to easily distinguish gay and straight people, but it is also based on the unlikely possibility that there is some physiological structure or process that *all* gay people share but *no* straight people have (as Barbara Heyl makes clear in selection 10).

The treatment of sexual orientation is problematic in other ways as well. For example, for most Americans this sentence makes sense: "Tom has been monogamously married for thirty years and had a dozen children, but I know he's *really* gay." In a real-life illustration of the same logic, a young man and woman were often seen "making out" on our campus. When this became the subject of a class discussion, an interesting ripple of laughter went through the room: Everyone "knew" that the young man was really gay.

How could they "know" that? For such conclusions to make sense, we must believe that someone could be gay irrespective of their actual behavior. Just as it is possible in this culture for someone to be "black" even if they look "white," apparently one may be gay despite acting straight. Just as "black" can be established by any African heritage (or, in the past, by even the presumption of that heritage), "gay" is apparently established in the display of any behavior thought to be associated with gays. Indeed, "gay" can be "established" by reputation alone, by a failure to demonstrate heterosexuality, or even by the demonstration of too aggressive a heterosexuality. In all, gay can be assigned no matter what one actually does. Sociologist Jack Katz (1975) explains this as the imposition of an "essential identity," that is, when an identity is assigned to an individual *irrespective of their actual behavior,* as in "I know she's a genius even though she's flunking all her courses." Because gay is understood as an essential identity in our culture, it can be assigned no matter what one's behavior. Because no behavior can ever prove one *not* gay, this label is an extremely effective mechanism of social control.

In all, there are several parallels between race and sexual orientation classifications. With both, we assume there are a limited number of possibilities— usually two but no more than three—and we assume individuals can be easily fit into one or another of these options. We treat both race and sexual orientation categories as encompassing populations that are internally homogeneous and profoundly dissimilar from one another. For both, this presumption of difference has prompted a wide-ranging search for the biological distinctiveness of the categories. Different races or sexual orientations are judged superior and inferior to one another and members of each category have historically been provided unequal legal and social rights. Finally, we assume that sexual orientation, like color, tells us something meaningful about a person.

Dichotomizing Class Although the case is less clear-cut, in the realm of social class it appears that the full range of classes is often reduced to a dichotomy between the poor and the middle class, or between the "deserving" and "undeserving" poor as Michael Katz describes in selection 9.

Americans more than people of other nationalities explain success and failure in terms of *individual merit* rather than economic or social forces (Morris and Williamson, 1982). Indeed, the "culture of poverty" thesis authored by anthropologist Oscar Lewis in the 1960s, which argued that about 20 percent of the poor were in poverty because of their own actions and attitudes, quickly became a characterization applied to most of those who are poor (M. Katz, 1989). "In one way or another, most of the terms used to describe poor people stressed the behavioral and cultural aspects of poverty" not the lack of jobs (M. Katz, 1989:38).

Thus, Americans are likely to conclude that those who are financially successful have become so on the basis of their merit and that those who fail do so by virtue of their faults. Indeed, many talk about social class as if it were just the result of personal values or attitudes. Surveys taken in 1984 and 1989 "found that 64 percent and 55 percent of the public, respectively, believed that lack of effort by the poor was the principal reason for poverty, or a reason at least equal to any that was beyond a person's control. . . . Popular majorities did not consider any other factor to be a very important cause of poverty—not low wages, or a scarcity of jobs, or discrimination, or even sickness" (Schwarz and Volgy, 1992:11).

This attribution of poverty and wealth to individual merit hides the complex reality of American social class. It ignores the working poor whose income places them below the poverty line—a group estimated to be as high as 12 million workers (Schwarz and Volgy, 1992); it also defines those in the highest income brackets as "really just like the rest of us," i.e., middle class. Although Americans are aware of a broad range of social class differences (Jackman and Jackman, 1983; Vanneman and Cannon, 1987), the widespread conviction that one's station in life reflects one's merit in many ways overwhelms this awareness. In a strikingly essentialist formulation, social class standing is taken to reveal one's essential nature and merit. Two presumably homogeneous and distinct categories are constructed, the poor and the rest of us.

Because social class is seldom discussed in American society, the vocabulary for talking about it is not well-developed. Indeed, it appears that we often substitute race for class. For example, the common assumption that people of color are poor and whites well-off simply applies the dichotomy of race to the arena of social class. Just as the American/non-American distinction functions to mean white/non-white, the middle class/poor dichotomy is often understood to mean white/non-white.

Dichotomizing Sex   First, the terms "sex" and "gender" require clarification. "Sex" refers to females and males, i.e., to chromosomal, hormonal, anatomical, and physiological differences. By contrast, "gender" describes the socially constructed roles associated with sex. Gender is learned; it is the culturally and historically specific acting out of "masculinity" and "femininity." Increasingly, however, the term gender is used synonymously with sex; for example, newspapers now describe sex differences in voting as "gender" differences. In these Framework Essays, however, the distinction between the terms will be maintained.

While the approach may be unsettling, sex can be understood as a socially created dichotomy much like race, sexual orientation, or gender. As selections 5 and 6 by developmental geneticist Anne Fausto-Sterling and anthropologist Walter Williams make clear, Western culture has an abiding commitment to the belief that there are two and only two sexes and that all individuals can be clearly identified as one or the other (Kessler and McKenna, 1978). But, like sexual orientation, sex refers to a complex set of attributes—anatomical, chromosomal, hormonal, physiological—that may sometimes be inconsistent with one another or with an individual's sense of their own identity. This is illustrated in the recent case of a Spanish athlete who is anatomically female, but in a pre-game genetic test was classified as male. On the basis of that test, she was excluded from the 1985 World University Games. She was then reclassed as female in 1991, when the governing body for track-and-field contests abandoned genetic testing and returned to physical inspection. As the gynecologist for the sports federation noted, "about 1 in 20,000 people has genes that conflict with his or her apparent gender" (Lemonick, 1992).

Nonetheless, just as with race and sexual orientation, membership is assigned to one or the other of the sex categories irrespective of inconsistent or ambiguous evidence. Indeed, the conviction that there ought to be consistency between the physical and psychological dimensions of sex propels some people into sex change surgery in an effort to produce a body consistent with their self-identity. Others will pursue psychotherapy seeking an identity consistent with their body. In either case, it makes more sense to us to use surgery and therapy to create consistency than to accept inconsistency: a man who feels like a woman must become a woman rather than just being a man who feels like a woman.

Constructing the "Other"

We have so far considered how the full range and complexity of a population may be reduced to aggregates, and then to a simplistic dichotomy. Aggregation and dichotomization essentialize a population by implying that sharing a master status effectively binds a set of people together, by treating membership in a particular status as revealing an individual's "essential" or most important characteristic, and by ignoring the multiple and conflicting statuses an individual inevitably occupies.

As we will see in the next sections, dichotomization especially promotes the image of a mythical "Other" who is not at all like "us." Whether in race, sex, sexual orientation, or social class, dichotomization yields a vision of "them" as profoundly different and promotes the leveling of sanctions against those who associate with "them." Ultimately, dichotomization results in the stigmatization of those in the less powerful category, i.e., it provides the grounds by which whole categories of people may be made the objects of contempt.

Constructing "Others" as Profoundly Different The expectation that Others are profoundly different can be seen most clearly in the significance that has historically been attached to sex differences. In this case, biological differences between males and females have been the grounds from which to infer an extensive range of non-biological differences. Thus, women and men are assumed to differ from one another in behavior, perception, and personality, and such differences are used to argue for different legal, social, and economic roles and rights. The expectation that men and women are not at all alike is so widespread that we often talk about them as members of the "opposite" sex; indeed, it is not unusual to talk about the "war" between the sexes. Because they differ in reproductive systems, it is assumed that men and women must also differ in a host of other ways (Thorne, 1993).

While this assumption of difference undergirds everyday life as well as scientific research, few significant differences in behavior, personality, or even physical ability have actually been found between men and women of any age, as described by Susan Basow in selection 7. The lack of difference between women and men is especially striking given the degree to which we are all socialized to produce gender difference. Thus, while boys and girls, men and women, are often encouraged to be different as well as treated differently, this does not mean that they inevitably become different. Even though decades of research have confirmed few differences, the search for difference continues and, as Basow suggests, may even have been intensified by the failure to find many differences.

The same expectation that the Other differs in personality or behavior emerges in race, class, and sexual orientation classifications. Race differences are expected to involve more than just differences of color, those who are "gay" or "straight" are expected to differ in more ways than just their sexual orientation, the categorizations of poor and middle class are expected to speak to more than just economic standing. In each case, scientific resources are directed toward finding such differences.

Sanctioning Those Who Associate With the "Other" There are also similarities in the sanctions leveled at those who cross race, sex, class, or sexual orientation boundaries. Parents sometimes disown children who marry outside of their racial or social class group, just as they often sever connections with children who are gay. More generally, it appears that those who associate with the Other are in danger of being labeled a member of that category.

For example, during Reconstruction the fear of an invisible black ancestry was pervasive among Southern whites, since that heritage would subject them to the emerging system of segregation. "Concern about people passing as white became so great that even behaving like blacks or willingly associating with them were often treated as more important than any proof of actual black ancestry" (Davis, 1991:56). Thus, Southern whites who associated with blacks ran the risk of being defined as black.

A contemporary parallel can be found in gay/straight relations: Those who associate with gays and lesbians or defend gay rights are often presumed—by gays and straights alike—to be gay. Many men report that when they object to homophobic remarks, they simply become the target of them; many women avoid calling themselves feminists for similar reasons. Indeed, the prestige of young men in fraternities and other all-male groups often rests on a willingness to disparage women and gays (Sanday, 1990).

Similarly, few contemporary reactions are as strongly negative as that against men who appear feminine. Because acting like a woman is so disparaged, boys learn at an early age to control their behavior or suffer public humiliation. These injunctions have their greatest affect on young men; the power and prestige usually available to older men reduces their susceptibility to such accusations. A list of all the behaviors young men must avoid for fear of being called feminine or gay is considerable: don't be too emotional, watch how you sit, don't move your hips when you walk, take long strides, don't put your hands on your hips, don't talk too much, don't let your voice show emotion, don't be too compliant or eager to please, etc., etc.

Because effeminate men are also often assumed to be gay, they become targets for verbal and physical abuse. The popular linkage of effeminate behavior with a gay sexual orientation is so strong that it may be the primary criterion most people use to decide which men are gay and which are straight: a "masculine" man must be straight, a "feminine" man must be gay. But as Marshall Kirk and Hunter Madsen explain in selection 33, this linkage is misguided. Gender and sexual orientation are *separate* phenomena. Knowing that someone is a masculine man or feminine woman does not tell us what their sexual orientation is—indeed, our guesses are most likely to be "false negatives," i.e., we are most likely to falsely identify someone as straight. Since we do not know who around us is gay, we cannot accurately judge how gay people behave.

In the world of mutual Othering, being labeled one of "them" is a remarkably effective social control mechanism. Boys and men control their behavior so that they are not called gay. Heterosexuals avoid alliances with gays and lesbians for the same reason. Members of racial and ethnic groups maintain distance from one another to avoid the criticism that might be leveled by members of their own and other groups (a subject to which we will return in Framework Essay II). These social controls are effective because all parties are willing to enforce them.

Stigma

While conceiving of people as Others can take place from either side of the dichotomies we have described, categories of people differ in their access to power and in their ability to affect one another's lives. Thus, we turn now to those Others who are less powerful and who therefore can be stigmatized. Although those in stigmatized master statuses are not powerless, they do have relatively less power than those on the other side of the dichotomy.

The term *stigma* in its Greek origin meant a "bodily sign designed to expose something unusual and bad about the moral status of [an individual]" (Goffman, 1963:1). Such signs were "cut or burnt into the body to advertise that the bearer was a slave, a criminal, or a blemished person, ritually polluted, to be avoided, especially in public places" (Goffman, 1963:1). The contemporary usage of stigma also links external sign and internal worth; it involves the condemnation of individuals because they possess a particular set of attributes. Stigmatized individuals are the "subjects of categorical devaluation" (Schur, 1984); they are devalued precisely because of the categories they belong to. Those who are stigmatized are seen first in terms of their stigma and only later in terms of their individual characteristics. Stigma is always negative.

The core assumption of stigma—that one can infer internal worth from an external sign—is pervasive. For example, people of all ages think that those they find physically attractive are likely to be "poised, kind, and flexible," "sociable, outgoing, and likable," educated, well-employed, and to overall "possess more socially desirable personality dispositions" (Adams, 1982:265). While physical attractiveness is also associated with egocentrism and snobbery, this still links external appearance with internal worth.

Such judgments of worth based on membership in certain categories have a self-fulfilling potential. Those who are judged superior by virtue of their membership in some category are given more opportunity to prove their worth; those who are judged less worthy by virtue of membership in a stigmatized category have a difficult time establishing their merit no matter what they do. For example, experimental evidence from social psychology indicates that many whites are likely to perceive blacks as incompetent, regardless of evidence to the contrary: White subjects were "reluctant or unable to recognize that a black person is higher or equal in intelligence compared to themselves" (Gaertner and Dovidio, 1986:75). This would explain why many whites react negatively to affirmative action programs. If they cannot conceive of black applicants as being more qualified than whites, they will see such programs as mandates to hire the less qualified.

Stigma involves objectification as well as devaluation. Objectification means treating people as if they were objects, as if they were only members of a category rather than possessors of individual characteristics. In objectification, the "living, breathing, complex individual" ceases to be seen or valued (Allport, 1958:175). In its extreme, those who are objectified are "viewed as having no other noteworthy status or identity. When that point is reached a person becomes *nothing* but 'a delinquent,' 'a cripple,' 'a homosexual,' 'a black,' 'a woman.' The indefinite article 'a' underlines the depersonalized nature of such response" (Schur, 1984:30–31).

We have purposefully used the term stigma here in lieu of talking about prejudice and discrimination. As Robert Blauner describes in selection 13, the latter terms are often understood to mean only individual attitudes or behaviors—thus they mask the institutional and systematic nature of inequalities. Stigma instead conveys a categorization that is not simply the product of individual behavior, but is rather the outcome of large-scale social and historical forces, stigma cannot be conferred by individual attitude. For example, one of the problems with the word homophobia is that it implies that the treatment of gays is simply the result of individual prejudice rather than systematic institutional practices.

Examples of Stigmatized Master Statuses: Women and the Poor   Sociologist Edwin Schur argues that since women are subject to both objectification and devaluation, they are a stigmatized category. We will examine the operation of each of these, objectification and devaluation, separately.

First, considering objectification, Schur argues that women are seen

> as all alike, and therefore substitutable for one another; as innately passive and object-like; as easily ignored, dismissed, trivialized, treated as childlike, and even as a nonperson; as having a social standing only through their attachments to men (or other non-stigmatized groups); and as a group which can be easily victimized through harassment, violence, and discrimination (Schur, 1984:33).

Objectification takes place when women are thought of as generally indistinguishable from one another, as for example when someone says "Let's get the woman's angle on this story"; or "My girlfriend didn't think it was sexist, so I don't know what that woman's complaining about"; or "Tonight I'm going to get one of these women in bed with me." In all of these, one woman stands for "any woman"; they are all the same, interchangeable.[10]

Black Americans, Latinos, Asian Americans, and gay and lesbian people are often similarly treated as indistinguishable from one another. Indeed, hate crimes have been defined by this quality of interchangeability, e.g., the attack on any black family that moves into a neighborhood, or the assault on any woman or man who looks gay. Hate crimes are also marked by excessive brutality, personal violence rather than property destruction, and are likely to have been perpetrated by multiple offenders—all of which indicate that the victims have been objectified (Levin and McDevitt, 1993).

There is much encouragement for members of stigmatized categories to objectify themselves in the same ways that they are objectified by others. Thus, women are encouraged to evaluate their own worth in terms of physical appearance. In the process of self-objectification, a woman "joins the spectators of herself," i.e., she views her self as if from the outside, as if she were nothing more than what she looked like (Berger, 1963:50). This sense of making an object of oneself was recently conveyed by a cereal commercial in which a bikini-clad woman stands in front of a mirror. She has apparently lost weight for an upcoming vacation and is now trying out different poses, viewing herself as a stranger on the beach might see her. Thus, she has succeeded in making an object of herself. While physical appearance is also valued for men, it rarely takes precedence over all other qualities. Rather, men are more likely to be objectified in terms of wealth and power.

As we said earlier, stigmatization involves both objectification and devaluation. Considering the latter, there is a strong case that American women as a category

---

[10]Heterosexuals sometimes assume that gay men objectify straight men much as many straight men objectify women. Thus, many straight men fear being treated as sexual objects by gay men.

are still devalued, a conclusion drawn from the characteristics most frequently attributed to men and women. Research conducted over the last forty years has documented a remarkable consistency in those attributes. While both sexes are described as possessing valued qualities, the characteristics attributed to men are the ones more valued in the culture as a whole. For example, female-valued characteristics include being talkative, gentle, quiet, religious, aware of the feelings of others, security oriented, and attentive to personal appearance. Male-valued traits include being aggressive, independent, unemotional, objective, dominant, active, competitive, logical, adventurous, and direct (Basow, 1992).[11] (Note that these attributes are only people's beliefs about sex differences.) As Patricia Hill Collins makes clear in selection 19, these characteristics are more likely to be attributed to whites than to people of color.

In many ways, the characteristics attributed to women are inconsistent with core American values. While American culture values achievement, individualism, and action—all understood as male attributes—women are expected to subordinate their personal interests to the family and to be passive and patient (Richardson, 1977). In all, "women are asked to become the kind of people that this culture does not value" (Richardson, 1977:11). Thus, it is more acceptable for women to display masculine traits, since these are culturally valued, than it is for men to display the less-valued feminine characteristics. Men who are talkative, gentle, quiet, religious, aware of the feelings of others, security oriented, and attentive to personal appearance are much maligned. By contrast, women may be independent, unemotional, objective, dominant, active, competitive, logical, adventurous, and direct, with less negative consequence. The characteristics we attribute to women are not valued for everyone, unlike the characteristics attributed to men.

The sex classification system we have sketched in this and previous sections offers a striking parallel to the system of race classification. As in the case of race, we operate within a dichotomized conception of sex in which the two categories are ranked as superior and inferior to one another; membership in a category is taken to mean something significant about one's behavior, abilities, perceptions, etc.; physical differences prompt an extensive and generally unsuccessful search for other manifestations of difference. Just as we earlier described a racialized social structure, i.e., a society structured in terms of race differences, societies structured in terms of sex differences—with political, legal, and social rights, power, prestige, and wealth based on membership in sex categories—have been historically and cross-culturally pervasive. While women have been subject to such sex-based social structures, they have not generally been party to their development.

---

[11]"Compared with White women, Black women are viewed as less passive, dependent, status conscious, emotional and concerned about their appearance. . . . Hispanic women tend to be viewed as more 'feminine' than White women in terms of submissiveness and dependence. . . . a similar stereotype holds for Asian women, but with the addition of exotic sexuality. . . . Native-American women typically are stereotyped as faceless . . . drudges without any personality. . . . Jewish women are stereotyped as either pushy, vain 'princesses' or overprotective, manipulative 'Jewish mothers'. . . . working-class women are stereotyped as more hostile, confused, inconsiderate and irresponsible than middle-class women. . . . and lesbians are stereotyped as possessing masculine traits" (Basow, 1992:4).

Much of what we have described about the stigmatization of women applies to the poor as well. Indeed, being poor is a much more obviously shameful status than being female. The category "poor" is intrinsically devalued; it is not presumed that there is much commendable to be said about poor people; "they" are primarily constructed as a "problem." Poor people are also objectified; they are described as "*the* poor," as if they were all alike, substitutable for and interchangeable with one another.

> Most of the writing about poor people, even by sympathetic observers, tells us that they are different, truly strangers in our midst: Poor people think, feel, and act in ways unlike middle-class Americans. . . .
>
> We can think about poor people as "them" or as "us." For the most part, Americans have talked about "them." Even in the language of social science, as well as in ordinary conversation and political rhetoric, poor people usually remain outsiders, strangers to be pitied or despised, helped or punished, ignored or studied, but rarely full citizens, members of a larger community on the same terms as the rest of us. They are . . . "those people," objects of curiosity, analysis, prurience, or compassion, not subjects who construct their own lives and history. Poor people seem cardboard cutouts, figures in single dimension, members of inferior categories, rarely complex, multifaceted, even contradictory in the manner of other persons (M. Katz, 1989:6 and 126).

Like women, poor people are not expected to display attributes valued in the culture as a whole.

Stereotypes About Those Who are Stigmatized   Finally, in an effort to capture the general features of what "we" say about "them," let us consider five common stereotypes about those in stigmatized master statuses. (Framework Essay III examines the difference between a stereotype and a description.)

We have already mentioned the first stereotype about those in stigmatized categories: They are presumed to lack the values the culture holds dear. Neither women, nor those who are poor, gay, black, Asian American, or Hispanic are expected to be independent, unemotional, objective, dominant, active, competitive, logical, adventurous, or direct. Stigmatized Others are presumed to lack precisely those values that non-stigmatized categories of people are expected to possess.

Second, those who are stigmatized are likely to be seen as a problem (Adam, 1978; Wilson and Gutierrez, 1985). Certainly black, Latino, and Native American men and women, gay and lesbian people of all colors, white women, and those who are poor, are constructed both as *having* problems and *being* problems—often the implication is that they are responsible for all of "our" problems. While there are occasions for the celebration of the historic contributions of such groups to the culture, little in the public discourse lauds current contributions. Those in stigmatized categories are often constructed as nothing but a problem; as if they had no life or existence apart from those problems. As one black student framed it, she thought she lived in a pleasant neighborhood of middle-class homeowners until the white students in her school described her neighborhood as a "ghetto."

Ironically, this depiction of stigmatized Others as nothing but a problem is accompanied by trivialization of those problems. For example, the Civil Rights

Commission Report notes that "a majority of voting Americans believe that Asian Americans are not discriminated against" despite evidence to that effect. Despite the annual participation of hundreds of thousands of people in Gay Pride marches throughout the country, television footage typically focuses on the small number in drag. Whites' opinion that blacks prefer welfare to supporting themselves (a 1992 poll showed 78 percent of whites affirming that view), similarly trivializes the experience of poverty (Thornton and Whitman, 1992). The pervasive belief that women and men are now treated equally in employment, dismisses the wage gap that continues to characterize male/female earnings. Thus, the problems that stigmatized categories of people create for those in privileged statuses are highlighted, while the problems they experience are discounted.

Third, those in stigmatized master statuses are stereotyped as lacking self-control; they are characterized as being uncontrollably lustful, immoral, and carriers of disease (Gilman, 1985, 1991). Currently, such accusations hold center stage in the depictions of gay men; historically, African American, Latino, and Asian American men (e.g., Chinese immigrants in the late nineteenth century) were expected to be sexually dangerous to white women; poor women and women of color have been and continue to be depicted as promiscuous (as evidenced in the contemporary debate about welfare and unwed mothers); poor men and women are presumed morally irresponsible.

Fourth, those in stigmatized categories are often marked as having too much or too little intelligence, and in either case as tending to deception or criminality. Many stigmatized categories of people have been assumed to use their "excessive" intelligence to unfair advantage. This was historically the case for Jews, and now appears to be the case for Asian American college students.

> Between 1976 and 1982, Asian American undergraduate enrollment climbed 62 percent while Hispanic enrollment grew 32 percent, white enrollment grew 5 percent, and black enrollment rose 1.3 percent. . . . But the educational achievement of Asian American students was, and continues to be, followed by a wave of reaction. The image of Asian Americans as diligent super-students has often kindled resentment in other students. Sometimes called "damned curve raisers," a term applied first to Jewish students at elite East Coast colleges during the 1920s and 1930s, Asian American students have increasingly found themselves taking the brunt of campus racial jokes. . . . On many college campuses, college seniors only half-jokingly advised freshmen to avoid classes with high Asian enrollments. Their advice was based on the belief that white students "don't have a chance" against all that Asian American "unfair competition" (Takagi, 1992:20, 60).

Fifth, those in stigmatized categories are often depicted as simultaneously childlike and savagely brutal. Historically, characterizations of Native Americans, enslaved Africans, and Chinese immigrants reflected both of these conceptions. The same is true currently for the poor in their representation as both pervasively violent and irresponsible. A related depiction of women as both "virgins and whores" has been well documented in historical and contemporary scholarship.

Perhaps because people in stigmatized master statuses are stereotyped as violent, it appears that those who commit violence against them are unlikely to be punished. As Schur argues in terms of women, "major offenses *against* women which we *profess* to consider deviant, in practice have been responded to with much ambivalence" (Schur, 1984:7). For example, in the case of sexual assault, "in fewer than half of reported rape cases is anyone arrested, and only 5 percent of those arrested are convicted" (Gordon and Riger, 1989:45). If the example is race, "of the 16,000 executions in U.S. history, only thirty cases involved a white sentenced for killing a black" (Smolowe, 1991:68). Sociologist Schur argues that one way to recognize a stigmatized category of people is that the violence directed at them is not treated seriously (Schur, 1984).

Overall, those in stigmatized master statuses are represented as not only physically distinctive but in their behavior and attitudes the antithesis of the culture's desired attributes: They do not operate from cultural values; they are problems; they are immoral and disease ridden; their intelligence is questionable; they are childlike and savage. Such characterizations serve to dismiss claims of discrimination and unfair treatment; they affirm that those in stigmatized categories deserve such treatment, that they are themselves responsible for their plight. Indeed, many of these stereotypes are now applied to teenagers, who in the media are depicted as violent, reckless, hypersexed, ignorant, out of control, and the cause of society's problems (Males, 1994).

A Final Comment

It is disheartening to think of oneself as a member of a stigmatized group just as it is disheartening to think of oneself as thoughtlessly perpetuating stigma. Still, there are at least two important points of hopefulness here. First, the characteristics attributed to stigmatized groups are similar across a great variety of master statuses and thus should carry the relief of impersonality—they are not tied to the actual characteristics of any particular group. Second, those who are stigmatized—often in alliance with those who are not stigmatized—have regularly and successfully lobbied against these attributions.

As we said at the outset of this essay, our hope was to provide you with a framework by which to make sense of what sex, race, social class, and sexual orientation mean in contemporary American society. Clearly, these categorizations are fraught with complexity; they are tied to issues of emotional intensity that are in many ways uniquely American; and they have consequences which are both mundane and dramatic. From naming, to aggregating, to dichotomizing, and ultimately to stigmatizing, difference has a meaning for us. The readings in Section I will explore the construction of these categorizations; the readings in Section II will examine how we experience them; and the readings in Section III will address the meaning that is attributed to difference.

REFERENCES

Adam, Barry. 1978. *The Survival of Domination.* New York: Elsevier.

Adams, Gerald R. 1982. Physical Attractiveness. *In the Eye of the Beholder: Contemporary Issues in Stereotyping,* edited by A. G. Miller, 253–304. New York: Praeger.

Allport, Gordon. 1958. *The Nature of Prejudice.* Garden City, New York: Doubleday Anchor.

Basow, Susan A. 1992. *Gender: Stereotypes and Roles.* 3d ed. Pacific Grove, California: Brooks/Cole Publishing.

Begley, Sharon. 1995. Three is Not Enough. *Newsweek,* February 13, 1995, 67–69.

Berger, Peter L. 1963. *Invitation to Sociology: A Humanistic Perspective.* Garden City, New York: Doubleday Anchor.

Choldin, Harvey M. 1986. Statistics and Politics: The "Hispanic Issue" in the 1980 Census. *Demography,* 23:403–418.

Choldin, Harvey M. 1994. *Looking for the Last Percent: The Controversy Over Census Undercounts.* New Brunswick, New Jersey: Rutgers University Press.

Davis, F. James. 1991. *Who is Black? One Nation's Rule.* University Park, Pennsylvania: Pennsylvania State Press.

de la Garza, Rudolfo O., Louis DeSipio, F. Chris Garcia, John Garcia, and Angelo Falcon. 1992. *Latino Voices: Mexican, Puerto Rican, and Cuban Perspectives on American Politics.* Boulder, Colorado: Westview Press.

Elze, Diane. 1992. It Has Nothing to Do With Me. *Homophobia: How We All Pay the Price,* edited by Warren J. Blumenfeld, 95–113. Boston: Beacon Press.

Espiritu, Yen Le. 1992. *Asian American Panethnicity: Bridging Institutions and Identities.* Philadelphia: Temple University Press.

Faderman, Lillian. 1991. *Odd Girls and Twilight Lovers: A History of Lesbian Life in Twentieth-Century America.* New York: Penguin Books.

Gaertner, Samuel L., and John F. Dovidio. 1986. The Aversive Form of Racism. *Prejudice, Discrimination, and Racism,* edited by John F. Dovidio and Samuel L. Gaertner, 61–89. Orlando, Florida: Academic Press.

Gilman, Sander. 1991. *The Jew's Body.* New York: Routledge.

———. 1985. *Difference and Pathology: Stereotypes of Sexuality, Race, and Madness.* Ithaca, New York: Cornell University Press.

Goffman, Erving. 1963. *Stigma: Notes on the Management of Spoiled Identity.* Englewood Cliffs, New Jersey: Prentice-Hall.

Gordon, Margaret T., and Stephanie Riger. 1989. *The Female Fear.* New York: The Free Press.

Harrison, Rodrick. 1994. Rethinking Race and Ethnic Categories in Federal Statistics. Paper presented at the annual meeting of the *American Anthropological Association,* Atlanta, 1994.

Henshel, Richard L., and Robert A. Silverman. 1975. *Perceptions in Criminology.* New York: Columbia University Press.

Hilts, V. 1973. Statistics and Social Science. *Foundations of Scientific Method in the Nineteenth Century,* edited by R. Giere and R. Westfall, 206–33. Bloomington: Indiana University Press.

Hu-Dehart, Evelyn. 1994. Asian/Pacific American Issues in American Education. Presentation at the 7th Annual National Conference on Race and Ethnicity in American Higher Education, Atlanta, sponsored by The Southwest Center for Human Relations Studies, University of Oklahoma, College of Continuing Education.

Jackman, Mary R., and Robert W. Jackman. 1983. *Class Awareness in the United States.* Berkeley, California: University of California Press.

Jaimes, M. Annette. 1992. Federal Indian Identification Policy: A Usurpation of Indigenous Sovereignty in North America. *The State of Native America: Genocide, Colonization, and Resistance,* edited by M. Annette Jaimes, 123–38. Boston: South End Press.

Katz, Jack. 1975. Essences as Moral Identities: Verifiability and Responsibility in Imputations of Deviance and Charisma. *American Journal of Sociology,* 80:1369–90.

Katz, Michael B. 1989. *The Undeserving Poor: From the War on Poverty to the War on Welfare.* New York: Pantheon Books.

Kessler, Suzanne J., and Wendy McKenna. 1978. *Gender: An Ethnomethodological Approach.* New York: John Wiley & Sons.

Kinsey, Alfred, Wardell Pomeroy, and Clyde Martin. 1948. *Sexual Behavior in the Human Male.* Philadelphia: W. B. Saunders.

Klein, Fritz. 1978. *The Bisexual Option.* New York: Arbor House.

Lemonick, Michael. 1992. Genetic Tests Under Fire. *Time,* February 24, 65.

LeVay, Simon. 1991. A Difference in Hypothalmic Structure between Heterosexual and Homosexual Men. *Science,* 253:1034-7.

Levin, Jack, and Jack McDevitt. 1993. *Hate Crimes.* New York: Plenum Press.

Lieberman, Leonard. 1968. A Debate Over Race: A Study in the Sociology of Knowledge. *Phylon* 29:127–141.

Littlefield, Alice, Leonard Lieberman, and Larry T. Reynolds. 1982. Redefining Race: The Potential Demise of a Concept in Anthropology. *Current Anthropology* 23:641–647.

Lowry, Ira S. 1982. The Science and Politics of Ethnic Enumeration. *Ethnicity and Public Policy,* edited by Winston A. Van Horne, 42–61. Madison: University of Wisconsin Press.

Males, Mike. 1994. Bashing Youth: Media Myths about Teenagers. *Extra!,* March/April, 8–11.

Marshall, Gloria. 1993. Racial Classifications: Popular and Scientific. *The "Racial" Economy of Science: Toward a Democratic Future,* edited by Sandra Harding, 116–27. Bloomington: Indiana University Press, (Originally published 1968)

Marshall, Gordon. 1994. *The Concise Oxford Dictionary of Sociology.* Oxford: Oxford University Press.

McLaughlin, Paul. 1994. Essentialism, Nominalism and Population Thinking: Towards a New Organizational Ecology. Paper presented at the annual meeting of the American Sociological Association, Los Angeles, 1994. (Also personal communication.)

Michael, Robert T. 1994. *Sex in America: A Definitive Survey.* Boston: Little Brown.

Mills, Jane. 1989. *Womanwords: A Dictionary of Words about Women.* New York: Henry Holt.

Mohawk, John. 1992. Looking for Columbus: Thoughts on the Past, Present and Future of Humanity. *The State of Native America: Genocide, Colonization, and Resistance,* edited by M. Annette Jaimes, 439–44. Boston: South End Press.

Morris, Michael and John B. Williamson. 1982. Stereotypes and Social Class: A Focus on Poverty. *In the Eye of the Beholder,* edited by Arthur G. Miller, 411–465. New York: Praeger.

Morrison, Toni. 1992. *Playing in the Dark.* New York: Vintage.

Omi, Michael, and Howard Winant. 1994. *Racial Formation in the United States.* New York: Routledge.

Overbey, Mary Margaret. 1994. Notes from Washington. *Anthropology Newsletter,* December, 31. Washington, D.C.: American Anthropological Association.

Pfuhl, Erdwin H. 1986. *The Deviance Process.* 2d ed. Belmont, California: Wadsworth.

Pope, Raechele L., and Amy L. Reynolds. 1991. Including Bisexuality: It's More Than Just a Label. *Beyond Tolerance: Gays, Lesbians, and Bisexuals on Campus,* edited by Nancy J. Evans and Vernon A. Wall, 205–11. Alexandria, Virginia: American College Personnel Association.

Richardson, Laurel. 1977. *The Dynamics of Sex and Gender: A Sociological Perspective.* 1st ed. New York: Harper and Row.

Richardson, Laurel. 1988. *The Dynamics of Sex and Gender: A Sociological Perspective.* 3d ed. New York: Harper and Row.

Rist, Darrell Yates. 1992. Are Homosexuals Born That Way? *The Nation,* 255:424-9.

Roediger, David. 1994. *Towards the Abolition of Whiteness.* London: Verso.

Sanday, Peggy Reeves. 1990. *Fraternity Gang Rape.* New York: New York University Press.

Schur, Edwin. 1984. *Labeling Women Deviant: Gender, Stigma, and Social Control.* New York: Random House.

Schwarz, John E., and Thomas J. Volgy. 1992. *The Forgotten Americans.* New York: W. W. Norton.

Shipman, Pat. 1994. *The Evolution of Racism: Human Differences and the Use and Abuse of Science.* New York: Simon and Schuster.

Shorris, Earl. 1992. *Latinos: A Biography of the People.* New York: W. W. Norton.

Smedley, Audrey. 1993. *Race in North America: Origin and Evolution of a Worldview.* Boulder: Westview Press.

Smith, Tom W. 1992. Changing Racial Labels: From "Colored" to "Negro" to "Black" to "African American." *Public Opinion Quarterly* 56:496–514.

Smolowe, Jill. 1991. Race and the Death Penalty. *Time,* April 29, 68–69.

Sober, E. 1980. Evolution, Population Thinking, and Essentialism. *Philosophy of Science* 47:350–83.

Spelman, Elizabeth. 1988. *Inessential Woman.* Boston: Beacon Press.

Springer, S. P., and G. Deutsch. 1981. *Left Brain, Right Brain.* San Francisco: Freeman.

Steinberg, Stephen. 1989. *The Ethnic Myth: Race, Ethnicity, and Class in America.* Boston: Beacon Press.

Takagi, Dana Y. 1992. *The Retreat from Race: Asian-American Admission and Racial Politics.* New Brunswick, New Jersey: Rutgers University Press.

Takaki, Ronald. 1989. *Strangers from a Different Shore: A History of Asian Americans.* New York: Penguin.

Takaki, Ronald. 1990. *Iron Cages: Race and Culture in 19th-Century America.* New York: Oxford University Press.

Takaki, Ronald. 1993. *A Different Mirror.* Boston: Little Brown.

Thorne, Barrie. 1993. *Gender Play: Girls and Boys in School.* New Brunswick, New Jersey: Rutgers University Press.

Thornton, Jeannye, and David Whitman. 1992. Whites' Myths about Blacks. *U.S. News and World Report,* November 9, 41–44.

United States Bureau of the Census. 1990. *Definitions of Subject Characteristics,* 1990 Census of Population and Housing. Washington, D.C.: U.S. Government Printing Office.

United States Commission on Civil Rights. 1992. *Civil Rights Issues Facing Asian Americans in the 1990s.* Washington, D.C.: U.S. Government Printing Office.

Vanneman, Reeve, and Lynn Weber Cannon. 1987. *The American Perception of Class.* Philadelphia: Temple University Press.

Weinberg, George. 1973. *Society and the Healthy Homosexual.* Garden City, New York: Anchor.

Wilson, II, Clint, and Felix Gutierrez. 1985. *Minorities and the Media.* Beverly Hills: Sage.

What Is Race?

Who Is Black? One Nation's Definition

F. James Davis

In a taped interview conducted by a blind, black anthropologist, a black man nearly ninety years old said: "Now you must understand that this is just a name we have. I am not black and you are not black either, if you go by the evidence of your eyes. . . . Anyway, black people are all colors. White people don't look all the same way, but there are more different kinds of us than there are of them. Then too, there is a certain stage [at] which you cannot tell who is white and who is black. Many of the people I see who are thought of as black could just as well be white in their appearance. Many of the white people I see are black as far as I can tell by the way they look. Now, that's it for looks. Looks don't mean much. The things that makes us different is how we think. What we believe is important, the ways we look at life" (Gwaltney, 1980:96).

How does a person get defined as a black, both socially and legally, in the United States? What is the nation's rule for who is black, and how did it come to be? And so what? Don't we all know who is black, and isn't the most important issue what opportunities the group has? Let us start with some experiences of three well-known American blacks—actress and beauty pageant winner Vanessa Williams, U.S. Representative Adam Clayton Powell, Jr., and entertainer Lena Horne.

For three decades after the first Miss America Pageant in 1921, black women were barred from competing. The first black winner was Vanessa Williams of Millwood, New York, crowned Miss America in 1984. In the same year the first runner-up—Suzette Charles of Mays Landing, New Jersey—was also black. The viewing public was charmed by the television images and magazine pictures of the beautiful and musically talented Williams, but many people were also puzzled. Why was she being called black when she appeared to be white? Suzette Charles, whose ancestry appeared to be more European than African, at least looked like many of the "lighter blacks." Notoriety followed when Vanessa Williams resigned because of the impending publication of some nude photographs of her taken before the pageant, and Suzette Charles became Miss America for the balance of 1984. Beyond the troubling question of whether these young women could have won if they had looked "more black," the publicity dramatized the nation's definition of a black person.

Some blacks complained that the Rev. Adam Clayton Powell, Jr., was so light that he was a stranger in their midst. In the words of Roi Ottley, "He was white to all appearances, having blue eyes, an aquiline nose, and light, almost blond, hair" (1943:220), yet he became a bold, effective black leader—first as minister of the Abyssinian Baptist Church of Harlem, then as a New York city councilman, and finally as a U.S. congressman from the state of New York. Early in his activist career he led 6,000 blacks in a march on New York City Hall. He used his power in Congress to fight for civil rights legislation and other black causes. In 1966, in Washington, D.C., he convened the first black power conference.

In his autobiography, Powell recounts some experiences with racial classification in his youth that left a lasting impression on him. During Powell's freshman year at Colgate University, his roommate did not know that he was a black until his father, Adam Clayton Powell, Sr., was invited to give a chapel talk on Negro rights and problems, after which the roommate announced that because Adam was a Negro they could no longer be roommates or friends.

Another experience that affected Powell deeply occurred one summer during his Colgate years. He was working as a bellhop at a summer resort in Manchester, Vermont, when Abraham Lincoln's aging son Robert was a guest there. Robert Lincoln disliked blacks so much that he refused to let them wait on him or touch his luggage, car, or any of his possessions. Blacks who did got their knuckles whacked with his cane. To the great amusement of the other bellhops, Lincoln took young Powell for a white man and accepted his services (Powell, 1971:31–33).

Lena Horne's parents were both very light in color and came from black upper-middle-class families in Brooklyn (Horne and Schickel, 1965; Buckley, 1986). Lena lived with her father's parents until she was about seven years old. Her grandfather was very light and blue-eyed. Her fair-skinned grandmother was the daughter of a slave woman and her white owner, from the family of John C. Calhoun, well-known defender of slavery. One of her father's great-grandmothers was a Blackfoot Indian, to whom Lena Horne has attributed her somewhat coppery skin color. One of her mother's grandmothers was a French-speaking black woman from Senegal and never a slave. Her mother's father was a "Portuguese Negro," and two women in his family had passed as white and become entertainers.

Lena Horne's parents had separated, and when she was seven her entertainer mother began placing her in a succession of homes in different states. Her favorite place was in the home of her Uncle Frank, her father's brother, a red-haired, blue-eyed teacher in a black school in Georgia. The black children in that community asked her why she was so light and called her a "yellow bastard." She learned that when satisfactory evidence of respectable black parents is lacking, being light-skinned implies illegitimacy and having an underclass white parent and is thus a disgrace in the black community. When her mother married a white Cuban, Lena also learned that blacks can be very hostile to the white spouse, especially when the "black" mate is very light. At this time she began to blame the confused color line for her childhood troubles. She later endured much hostility from blacks and whites alike when her own second marriage, to white composer-

arranger Lennie Hayton, was finally made public in 1950 after three years of keeping it secret.

Early in Lena Horne's career there were complaints that she did not fit the desired image of a black entertainer for white audiences, either physically or in her style. She sang white love songs, not the blues. Noting her brunette-white beauty, one white agent tried to get her to take a Spanish name, learn some Spanish songs, and pass as a Latin white, but she had learned to have a horror of passing and never considered it, although Hollywood blacks accused her of trying to pass after she played her first bit part in a film. After she failed her first screen test because she looked like a white girl trying to play blackface, the directors tried making her up with a shade called "Light Egyptian" to make her look darker. The whole procedure embarrassed and hurt her deeply. . . .

Other light mulatto entertainers have also had painful experiences because of their light skin and other caucasoid features. Starting an acting career is never easy, but actress Jane White's difficulties in the 1940s were compounded by her lightness. Her father was NAACP leader Walter White. Even with dark makeup on her ivory skin, she did not look like a black person on the stage, but she was not allowed to try out for white roles because blacks were barred from playing them. When she auditioned for the part of a young girl from India, the director was enthusiastic, although her skin color was too light, but higher management decreed that it was unthinkable for a Negro to play the part of an Asian Indian (White, 1948:338). Only after great perseverance did Jane White make her debut as the educated mulatto maid Nonnie in the stage version of Lillian Smith's *Strange Fruit* (1944). . . .

THE ONE-DROP RULE DEFINED

As the above cases illustrate, to be considered black in the United States not even half of one's ancestry must be African black. But will one-fourth do, or one-eighth, or less? The nation's answer to the question "Who is black?" has long been that a black is any person with *any* known African black ancestry (Myrdal, 1944:113–18; Berry and Tischler, 1978:97–98; Williamson, 1980:1–2). This definition reflects the long experience with slavery and later with Jim Crow segregation. In the South it became known as the "one-drop rule," meaning that a single drop of "black blood" makes a person a black. It is also known as the "one black ancestor rule," some courts have called it the "traceable amount rule," and anthropologists call it the "hypo-descent rule," meaning that racially mixed persons are assigned the status of the subordinate group (Harris, 1964:56). This definition emerged from the American South to become the nation's definition, generally accepted by whites and blacks alike (Bahr, Chadwick, and Stauss, 1979:27–28). Blacks had no other choice. This American cultural definition of blacks is taken for granted as readily by judges, affirmative action officers, and black protesters as it is by Ku Klux Klansmen.

Let us not be confused by terminology. At present the usual statement of the one-drop rule is in terms of "black blood" or black ancestry, while not so long ago it referred to "Negro blood" or ancestry. The term "black" rapidly replaced "Negro" in general usage in the United States as the black power movement peaked at the end of the 1960s, but the black and Negro populations are the same. The term "black" is used [here] for persons with any black African lineage, not just for unmixed members of populations from sub-Saharan Africa. The term "Negro," which is used in certain historical contexts, means the same thing. Terms such as "African black," "unmixed Negro," and "all black" are used here to refer to unmixed blacks descended from African populations.

We must also pay attention to the terms "mulatto" and "colored." The term "mulatto" was originally used to mean the offspring of a "pure African Negro" and a "pure white." Although the root meaning of mulatto, in Spanish, is "hybrid," "mulatto" came to include the children of unions between whites and so-called "mixed Negroes."

For example, Booker T. Washington and Frederick Douglass, with slave mothers and white fathers, were referred to as mulattoes (Bennett, 1962:255). To whatever extent their mothers were part white, these men were more than half white. Douglass was evidently part Indian as well, and he looked it (Preston, 1980:9–10). Washington had reddish hair and gray eyes. At the time of the American Revolution, many of the founding fathers had some very light slaves, including some who appeared to be white. The term "colored" seemed for a time to refer only to mulattoes, especially lighter ones, but later it became a euphemism for darker Negroes, even including unmixed blacks. With widespread racial mixture, "Negro" came to mean any slave or descendant of a slave, no matter how much mixed. Eventually in the United States, the terms mulatto, colored, Negro, black, and African American all came to mean people with any known black African ancestry. Mulattoes are racially mixed, to whatever degree, while the terms black, Negro, African American, and colored include both mulattoes and unmixed blacks. These terms have quite different meanings in other countries.

Whites in the United States need some help envisioning the American black experience with ancestral fractions. At the beginning of miscegenation between two populations presumed to be racially pure, quadroons appear in the second generation of continuing mixing with whites, and octoroons in the third. A quadroon is one-fourth African black and thus easily classed as black in the United States, yet three of this person's four grandparents are white. An octoroon has seven white great-grandparents out of eight and usually looks white or almost so. Most parents of black American children in recent decades have themselves been racially mixed, but often the fractions get complicated because the earlier details of the mixing were obscured generations ago. Like so many white Americans, black people are forced to speculate about some of the fractions—one-eighth this, three-sixteenths that, and so on. . . .

PLESSY, PHIPPS, AND OTHER CHALLENGES IN THE COURTS

Homer Plessy was the plaintiff in the 1896 precedent-setting "separate-but-equal" case of *Plessy v. Ferguson* (163 U.S. 537). This case challenged the Jim Crow statute that required racially segregated seating on trains in interstate commerce in the state of Louisiana. The U.S. Supreme Court quickly dispensed with Plessy's contention that because he was only one-eighth Negro and could pass as white he was entitled to ride in the seats reserved for whites. Without ruling directly on the definition of a Negro, the Supreme Court briefly took what is called "judicial notice" of what it assumed to be common knowledge: that a Negro or black is any person with any black ancestry. (Judges often take explicit "judicial notice" not only of scientific or scholarly conclusions, or of opinion surveys or other systematic investigations, but also of something they just assume to be so, including customary practices or common knowledge.) This has consistently been the ruling in the federal courts, and often when the black ancestry was even less than one-eighth. The federal courts have thus taken judicial notice of the customary boundary between two sociocultural groups that differ, on the average, in physical traits, not between two discrete genetic categories. In the absence of proof of a specific black ancestor, merely being known as a black in the community has usually been accepted by the courts as evidence of black ancestry. The separate-but-equal doctrine established in the Plessy case is no longer the law, as a result of the judicial and legislative successes of the civil rights movement, but the nation's legal definition of who is black remains unchanged.

State courts have generally upheld the one-drop rule. For instance, in a 1948 Mississippi case a young man, Davis Knight, was sentenced to five years in jail for violating the anti-miscegenation statute. Less than one-sixteenth black, Knight said he was not aware that he had any black lineage, but the state proved his great-grandmother was a slave girl. In some states the operating definition of black has been limited by statute to particular fractions, yet the social definition—the one-drop rule—has generally prevailed in case of doubt. Mississippi, Missouri, and five other states have had the criterion of one-eighth. Virginia changed from one-fourth to one-eighth in 1910, then in 1930 forbade white intermarriage with a person with any black ancestry. Persons in Virginia who are one-fourth or more Indian and less than one-sixteenth African black are defined as Indians while on the reservation but as blacks when they leave (Berry, 1965:26). While some states have had general race classification statutes, at least for a time, others have legislated a definition of black only for particular purposes, such as marriage or education. In a few states there have even been varying definitions for different situations (Mangum, 1940:38–48). All states require a designation of race on birth certificates, but there are no clear guidelines to help physicians and midwives do the classifying.

Louisiana's latest race classification statute became highly controversial and was finally repealed in 1983 (Trillin, 1986:77). Until 1970, a Louisiana statute had embraced the one-drop rule, defining a Negro as anyone with a "trace of black ancestry." This law was challenged in court a number of times from the 1920s on, including an unsuccessful attempt in 1957 by boxer Ralph Dupas, who asked to be declared white so that a law banning "interracial sports" (since repealed) would not prevent him from boxing in the state. In 1970 a lawsuit was brought on behalf of a child whose ancestry was allegedly only one two-hundred-fifty-sixth black, and the legislature revised its law. The 1970 Louisiana statute defined a black as someone whose ancestry is more than one thirty-second black (La. Rev. Stat. 42:267). Adverse publicity about this law was widely disseminated during the Phipps trial in 1983 (discussed below), filed as *Jane Doe v. State of Louisiana*. This case was decided in a district court in May 1983, and in June the legislature abolished its one thirty-second statute and gave parents the right to designate the race of newborns, and even to change classifications on birth certificates if they can prove the child is white by a "preponderance of the evidence." However, the new statute in 1983 did not abolish the "traceable amount rule" (the one-drop rule), as demonstrated by the outcomes when the Phipps decision was appealed to higher courts in 1985 and 1986.

The history in the Phipps (Jane Doe) case goes as far back as 1770, when a French planter named Jean Gregoire Guillory took his wife's slave, Margarita, as his mistress (Model, 1983:3–4). More than two centuries and two decades later, their great-great-great-great-granddaughter, Susie Guillory Phipps, asked the Louisiana courts to change the classification on her deceased parents' birth certificates to "white" so she and her brothers and sisters could be designated white. They all looked white, and some were blue-eyed blonds. Mrs. Susie Phipps had been denied a passport because she had checked "white" on her application although her birth certificate designated her race as "colored." This designation was based on information supplied by a midwife, who presumably relied on the parents or on the family's status in the community. Mrs. Phipps claimed that this classification came as a shock, since she had always thought she was white, had lived as white, and had twice married as white. Some of her relatives, however, gave depositions saying they considered themselves "colored," and the lawyers for the state claimed to have proof that Mrs. Phipps is three-thirty-seconds black (Trillin, 1986:62–63, 71–74). That was more than enough "blackness" for the district court in 1983 to declare her parents, and thus Mrs. Phipps and her siblings, to be legally black.

In October and again in December 1985, the state's Fourth Circuit Court of Appeals upheld the district court's decision, saying that no one can change the racial designation of his or her parents or anyone else's (479 So. 2d 369). Said the majority of the court in its opinion: "That appellants might today describe themselves as white does not prove error in a document which designates their parents as colored" (479 So. 2d 371). Of course, if the parents' designation as "colored"

cannot be disturbed, their descendants must be defined as black by the "traceable amount rule." The court also concluded that the preponderance of the evidence clearly showed that the Guillory parents were "colored." Although noting expert testimony to the effect that the race of an individual cannot be determined with scientific accuracy, the court said the law of racial designation is not based on science, that "individual race designations are purely social and cultural perceptions and the evidence conclusively proves those subjective perspectives were correctly recorded at the time the appellants' birth certificates were recorded" (479 So. 2d 372). At the rehearing in December 1985, the appellate court also affirmed the necessity of designating race on birth certificates for public health, affirmative action, and other important public programs and held that equal protection of the law has not been denied so long as the designation is treated as confidential.

When this case was appealed to the Louisiana Supreme Court in 1986, that court declined to review the decision, saying only that the court "concurs in the denial for the reasons assigned by the court of appeals on rehearing" (485 So. 2d 60). In December 1986 the U.S. Supreme Court was equally brief in stating its reason for refusing to review the decision: "The appeal is dismissed for want of a substantial federal question" (107 Sup. Ct. Reporter, interim ed. 638). Thus, both the final court of appeals in Louisiana and the highest court of the United States saw no reason to disturb the application of the one-drop rule in the lawsuit brought by Susie Guillory Phipps and her siblings.

CENSUS ENUMERATION OF BLACKS

When the U.S. Bureau of the Census enumerates blacks (always counted as Negroes until 1980), it does not use a scientific definition, but rather the one accepted by the general public and by the courts. The Census Bureau counts what the nation wants counted. Although various operational instructions have been tried, the definition of black used by the Census Bureau has been the nation's cultural and legal definition: all persons with any known black ancestry. Other nations define and count blacks differently, so international comparisons of census data on blacks can be extremely misleading. For example, Latin American countries generally count as black only unmixed African blacks, those only slightly mixed, and the very poorest mulattoes. If they used the U.S. definition, they would count far more blacks than they do, and if Americans used their definition, millions in the black community in the United States would be counted either as white or as "coloreds" of different descriptions, not as black.

Instructions to our census enumerators in 1840, 1850, and 1860 provided "mulatto" as a category but did not define the term. In 1870 and 1880, mulattoes were officially defined to include "quadroons, octoroons, and all persons having any perceptible trace of African blood." In 1890 enumerators were told to record the *exact* proportion of the "African blood," again relying on visibility. In 1900 the Census Bureau specified that "pure Negroes" be counted separately from mulattoes, the latter to mean "all persons with some trace of black blood." In 1920 the mulatto category was dropped, and black was defined to mean any person with any black ancestry, as it has been ever since.

In 1960 the practice of self-definition began, with the head of household indicating the race of its members. This did not seem to introduce any noticeable fluctuation in the number of blacks, thus indicating that black Americans generally apply the one-drop rule to themselves. One exception is that Spanish-speaking Americans who have black ancestry but were considered white, or some designation other than black, in their place of origin generally reject the one-drop rule if they can. American Indians with some black ancestry also generally try to avoid the rule, but those who leave the reservation are often treated as black. At any rate, the 1980 census count showed that self-designated blacks made up about 12 percent of the population of the United States.

No other ethnic population in the nation, including those with visibly non-caucasoid features, is defined and counted according to a one-drop rule. For example, persons whose ancestry is one-fourth or less American Indian are not generally defined as Indian unless they want to be, and they are considered assimilating Americans who may even be proud of having some Indian ancestry. The same implicit rule appears to apply to Japanese Americans, Filipinos, or other peoples from East Asian nations and also to Mexican Americans who have Central American Indian ancestry, as a large majority do. For instance, a person whose ancestry is one-eighth Chinese is not defined as just Chinese, or East Asian, or a member of the mongoloid race. The United States certainly does not apply a one-drop rule to its white ethnic populations either, which include both national and religious groups. Ethnicity has often been confused with racial biology and not just in Nazi Germany. Americans do not insist that an American with a small fraction of Polish ancestry be classified as a Pole, or that someone with a single remote Greek ancestor be designated Greek, or that someone with any trace of Jewish lineage is a Jew and nothing else.

It is interesting that, in *The Passing of the Great Race* (1916), Madison Grant maintained that the one-drop rule should be applied not only to blacks but also to all the other ethnic groups he considered biologically inferior "races," such as Hindus, Asians in general, Jews, Italians, and other Southern and Eastern European peoples. Grant's book went through four editions, and he and others succeeded in getting Congress to pass the national origins quota laws of the early 1920s. This racist quota legislation sharply curtailed immigration from everywhere in the world except Northern and Western Europe and the Western Hemisphere, until it was repealed in 1965. Grant and other believers in the racial superiority of their own group have confused race with ethnicity. They consider miscegenation with any "inferior" people to be the ultimate danger to the survival of their own group and have often seen the one-drop rule as a crucial component in their line of defense. Americans in general, however, while finding other ways to discriminate against immigrant groups, have rejected the application of the drastic one-drop rule to all groups but blacks.

UNIQUENESS OF THE ONE-DROP RULE

Not only does the one-drop rule apply to no other group than American blacks, but apparently the rule is unique in that it is found only in the United States and not in any other nation in the world. In fact, definitions of who is black vary quite sharply from country to country, and for this reason people in other countries often express consternation about our definition. James Baldwin relates a revealing incident that occurred in 1956 at the Conference of Negro-African Writers and Artists held in Paris. The head of the delegation of writers and artists from the United States was John Davis. The French chairperson introduced Davis and then asked him why he considered himself Negro, since he certainly did not look like one. Baldwin wrote, "He *is* a Negro, of course, from the remarkable legal point of view which obtains in the United States, but more importantly, as he tried to make clear to his interlocutor, he was a Negro by choice and by depth of involvement—by experience, in fact" (1962:19).

The phenomenon known as "passing as white" is difficult to explain in other countries or to foreign students. Typical questions are: "Shouldn't Americans say that a person who is passing as white *is* white, or nearly all white, and has previously been passing as black?" or "To be consistent, shouldn't you say that someone who is one-eighth white is passing as black?" or "Why is there so much concern, since the so-called blacks who pass take so little negroid ancestry with them?" Those who ask such questions need to realize that "passing" is so much more a social phenomenon than a biological one, reflecting the nation's unique definition of what makes a person black. The concept of "passing" rests on the one-drop rule and on folk beliefs about race and miscegenation, not on biological or historical fact.

The black experience with passing as white in the United States contrasts with the experience of other ethnic minorities that have features that are clearly non-caucasoid. The concept of passing applies only to blacks—consistent with the nation's unique definition of the group. A person who is one-fourth or less American Indian or Korean or Filipino is not regarded as passing if he or she intermarries and joins fully the life of the dominant community, so the minority ancestry need not be hidden. It is often suggested that the key reason for this is that the physical differences between these other groups and whites are less pronounced than the physical differences between African blacks and whites, and therefore are less threatening to whites. However, keep in mind that the one-drop rule and anxiety about passing originated during slavery and later received powerful reinforcement under the Jim Crow system.

For the physically visible groups other than blacks, miscegenation promotes assimilation, despite barriers of prejudice and discrimination during two or more generations of racial mixing. As noted above, when ancestry in one of these racial minority groups does not exceed one-fourth, a person is not defined solely as a member of that group. Masses of white European immigrants have climbed the class ladder not only through education but also with the help of close personal relationships in the dominant community, intermarriage, and ultimately full cultural and social assimilation. Young people tend to marry people they meet in the same informal social circles (Gordon, 1964:70–81). For visibly noncaucasoid minorities other than blacks in the United States, this entire route to full assimilation is slow but possible.

For all persons of any known black lineage, however, assimilation is blocked and is not promoted by miscegenation. Barriers to full opportunity and participation for blacks are still formidable, and a fractionally black person cannot escape these obstacles without passing as white and cutting off all ties to the black family and community. The pain of this separation, and condemnation by the black family and community, are major reasons why many or most of those who could pass as white choose not to. Loss of security within the minority community, and fear and distrust of the white world are also factors.

It should now be apparent that the definition of a black person as one with any trace at all of black African ancestry is inextricably woven into the history of the United States. It incorporates beliefs once used to justify slavery and later used to buttress the castelike Jim Crow system of segregation. Developed in the South, the definition of "Negro" (now black) spread and became the nation's social and legal definition. Because blacks are defined according to the one-drop rule, they are a socially constructed category in which there is wide variation in racial traits and therefore not a race group in the scientific sense. However, because that category has a definite status position in the society it has become a self-conscious social group with an ethnic identity.

The one-drop rule has long been taken for granted throughout the United States by whites and blacks alike, and the federal courts have taken "judicial notice" of it as being a matter of common knowledge. State courts have generally upheld the one-drop rule, but some have limited the definition to one thirty-second or one-sixteenth or one-eighth black ancestry, or made other limited exceptions for persons with both Indian and black ancestry. Most Americans seem unaware that this definition of blacks is extremely unusual in other countries, perhaps even unique to the United States, and that Americans define no other minority group in a similar way. . . .

REFERENCES

Bahr, Howard M., Bruce A. Chadwick, and Joseph H. Stauss. 1979. *American Ethnicity.* Lexington, Mass.: D.C. Heath & Co.

Baldwin, James. 1962. *Nobody Knows My Name.* New York: Dell Publishing Co.

Bennett, Lerone, Jr. 1962. *Before the Mayflower: A History of the Negro in America 1619–1962.* Chicago: Johnson Publishing Co.

Berry, Brewton. 1965. *Race and Ethnic Relations.* 3rd ed. Boston: Houghton Mifflin Co.

Berry, Brewton, and Henry L. Tischler. 1978. *Race and Ethnic Relations.* 4th ed. Boston: Houghton Mifflin Co.

Buckley, Gail Lumet. 1986. *The Hornes: An American Family.* New York: Alfred A. Knopf.

Gordon, Milton M. 1964. *Assimilation in American Life.* New York: Oxford University Press.

Grant, Madison. 1916. *The Passing of the Great Race.* New York: Scribner.

Gwaltney, John Langston. 1980. *Drylongso: A Self-Portrait of Black America.* New York: Vintage Books.

Harris, Melvin. 1964. *Patterns of Race in the Americas.* New York: W. W. Norton.

Horne, Lena, and Richard Schickel. 1965. *Lena.* Garden City, N.Y.: Doubleday & Co.

Mangum, Charles Staples, Jr. 1940. *The Legal Status of the Negro in the United States.* Chapel Hill: University of North Carolina Press.

Model, F. Peter, ed. 1983. "Apartheid in the Bayou." *Perspectives: The Civil Rights Quarterly* 15 (Winter– Spring), 3–4.

Myrdal, Gunnar, assisted by Richard Sterner and Arnold M. Rose. 1944. *An American Dilemma.* New York: Harper & Bros.

Ottley, Roi. 1943. *New World A-Coming.* Cleveland: World Publishing Co.

Powell, Adam Clayton, Jr. 1971. *Adam by Adam: The Autobiography of Adam Clayton Powell, Jr.* New York: Dial Press.

Preston, Dickson J. 1980. *Young Frederick Douglass: the Maryland Years.* Baltimore: Johns Hopkins University Press.

Trillin, Calvin. 1986. "American Chronicles: Black or White." *New Yorker,* April 14, 1986, pp. 62–78.

White, Walter. 1948. *A Man Called White: The Autobiography of Walter White.* New York: Viking Press.

Williamson, Joel. 1980. *New People: Miscegenation and Mulattoes in the United States.* New York: The Free Press.

A Wonderful Opportunity

I was one among many—growing up and being educated in a stable, loving, supportive Black community—who was informed of a wonderful opportunity that lay ahead for me.

My neighborhood school would be closed and I, and others like me, would have the "honor" and "privilege" of being transported to the suburbs to go to school where everything would be "bigger and better": bigger gym, bigger lunchroom, better teachers, better equipment, better books, "better" people. It would be a great opportunity for me, and others like me, to "better" ourselves.

This land of "bigger and better" was located atop one of the many hills surrounding the city of Pittsburgh, Pennsylvania, a hill pregnant with fear, ignorance, and hate. It was not long after my arrival in this land that I, and others like me, would be greeted, verbally and visually, with that welcoming term of endearment, "nigger."

During my stay in this land of "bigger and better" (midseventies through early eighties, grades 6 through 12) this hill gave birth, on several occasions, to a human wall of hate brandishing weapons of intimidation: lead pipes, baseball bats, vicious dogs, and vicious racial epithets. Those of us who were targets of this intimidation did what anyone would do when an assault against one's humanity is launched. We masked our fear with anger-bravado-

attitude and defiance. A hostile confrontation ensued. Some of us were chased by dogs, some were attacked with pipes and chains, some were injured when buses were turned over while occupied, some were hit and cut by rocks being thrown at buses as they attempted to descend the hill.

No one effectively intervened on our behalf. Our parents' response was to be defiant, to send us back up the hill determined not to have their children denied access to that "wonderful opportunity." The parents of our combatants responded by aligning themselves on the hills with their children. Thus, busing for integration was transformed into busing for confrontation. . . . Welcome to the Suburbs.

I would have liked for both groups of parents (Black and White) to have realized that the political, ideological, and social battle for and against integration left in the middle a group of kids battling (literally) each other. This physical battle strained and/or dissolved newly formed friendships. The mental battle shattered a child's sense of self and fostered feelings of inadequacy, inferiority, and hatred of others (and self) in a young person previously insulated from such a penetrating and devastating psychological ambush. What an "opportunity."

R.M.A.

La Raza and the Melting Pot: A Comparative Look at Multiethnicity

Carlos A. Fernández

LATIN AMERICA: LA RAZA CÓSMICA[1]

. . . The year 1992 marks the 500th anniversary of the accidental discovery of the Americas by Columbus under the sponsorship of the Catholic Spanish monarchs Isabella and Fernando. In the United States, we refer to the commemoration of this discovery as Columbus Day. In parts of Latin America, however, they celebrate El Día de la

Raza (the Day of the [New Mixed] Race). The different names for the same observance illustrate one of the most fundamental cultural, historical, and even philosophical differences between the United States and Latin America, namely, the way we view race and interracial mixture.[2]

Many Americans are unaware of the "racial" history of Latin America. Evidence for this can be found in the fact that people of Latin American origin or ancestry are included as "Whites" in the U.S. Census, and since about 1980 have come to be referred to as "Hispanic," that is, European (Muñoz, 1989). What is the truth of the matter?

Mexico and Mexicans

By far the largest number of "Hispanics" in the United States today are Mexican American. Historically as well as currently, the majority of Mexican Americans have concentrated in the southwestern part of the United States, the annexed northern territory of Mexico, primarily in California and Texas. Mexican Americans make up the second largest non-White ethnic group in the United States (estimated at 6%, based on survey rates in March 1982 and March 1989; all Hispanics are 9%, African Americans, 12.1%), and are among the fastest growing of all groups (53% all Hispanics). Contrary to popular images, more than 90% of Hispanics are urban; less than 10% are farm workers (U.S. Bureau of the Census, 1990, 1991).

According to the Mexican American Legal Defense and Education Fund (MALDEF), the majority of Mexican Americans speak English and are U.S. citizens. Los Angeles, America's second-largest city, may have the largest urban concentration of Mexicans after Mexico City, which by now may be the largest city in the world. Upward of 60% of all the children enrolled in the Los Angeles public schools today are Hispanic, primarily Mexican Americans (A. Vargas, MALDEF, personal communication, February 1991).

The racial history of Mexico out of which Mexican Americans have emerged starts with Native Americans. An estimated 25 million Native Americans, the largest concentration in the hemisphere, lived in the region of Mexico and Central America at the time of the Spanish invasion (MacLachlan & Rodríguez O, 1980). The Spanish eventually conquered the Mexica[3] (Aztec) capital city, Tenochtitlán, in 1522, not by superior arms, nor by disease, which took its heavy toll later, but by their ability to muster a huge army of non-Mexica indigenous peoples eager to rid themselves of their reputedly oppressive overlords. The conquest of the Aztec empire was not just a Spanish conquest, but also a Spanish-led indigenous revolt (White, 1971).

Upon the Spanish-Indian alliance's success, the Spanish soldiery and the Native American ruling classes, including what remained of the Mexicas, established mutually agreeable social and political ties, secured in many cases by intermarriage with noble families. The first mestizos born of these relationships were not products of rape; they were acknowledged as "Spanish" or "Creoles" by their Spanish fathers. Of course, the ordinary Native Americans who constituted the masses of the people were not privy to any of these transactions. Indeed, rape and concubinage befell many indigenous commoner women; their children became the first "illegitimate" mestizos. During this early era, the "purely" Spanish constituted approximately 3-5% of the total population, and never grew beyond an estimated 10% throughout the subsequent history of Mexico (MacLachlan & Rodríguez O, 1980; Morner, 1970).

From the beginning of Spanish colonialism, Indian slaves in large numbers were employed in the silver mines. In 1523, the first foreign-origin slaves were introduced to Mexico, mainly as servants. These first slaves were a collection of Spanish Moslems—Arabs, Berbers, Moors (a mixed people of Arab, Berber, and Black African ancestry)—and *ladino* Blacks, that is, Blacks who had been slaves in Spain or one of its colonies prior to arriving in Mexico (MacLachlan & Rodríguez O, 1980). With the opening up of the large coastal plantations, however, the Spanish turned to the principal region in the world where slaves were being offered for sale in significant numbers at the time, the coast of Africa.

The number of African slaves increased dramatically in Mexico between 1530 and 1700. By the middle of the eighteenth century, African and part-African people were the second largest component of the Mexican population. Only the Native Americans had a larger population. Several individuals of acknowledged part-African ancestry played prominent roles in Mexican history; for example, the Independence hero Vicente Guerrero, for whom a state is named (MacLachlan & Rodríguez O, 1980).

Toward the end of the eighteenth century, the mestizo population began to increase more rapidly. By 1800, it overtook the African and part-

African groups, who were increasingly absorbed into the mestizo population. By 1900, the mestizos had become the largest ethnic group in Mexico.

Although the 1921 census was the last in which racial classifications were used in Mexico, some estimates are that mestizos (which in practice became a catchall term for all mixtures) today constitute some 85-90% of the Mexican population and Native Americans some 8-10%, with Europeans, mainly Spanish, making up the rest of the total (Morner, 1970). These estimates are highly suspect, however, a fact generally acknowledged by Mexican demographers, because *Indian* has come to mean "someone who speaks an Indian language" or who "lives like an Indian," that is, who is poor. The fact is, many biological Indians have become cultural mestizos who speak Spanish, and hence are regarded as mestizos. There are also many "Indians" and "Spanish" who are actually of mixed ancestry (Morner, 1970). This ambiguity serves to highlight the absurdity and practical irrelevance of racial categories in Mexico today. . . .

LA RAZA CÓSMICA VERSUS THE MELTING POT

The prevailing attitude toward race among the masses throughout Latin America might be summarized as comparative indifference. Of course, this is far from concluding that the region is the exaggerated stereotype of a "racial paradise." Indeed, by observing the disproportion of darker people in the lower classes and of lighter people in the upper classes, one might be led to conclude that race is at least as much of an active principle in Latin America as it is in the United States. But this is not quite true. For example, how is it that the Mexicans could elect a full-blooded Indian, Benito Juárez, as their president around the time of the U.S. Civil War? How is it that Peruvians of today elected an Asian their president? Many Mexican and other Latin American leaders have been and are of mixed blood. Then what explains the apparent tie between race and class in Latin America?

Many sociologists have long noted that in the absence of effective countermeasures, poverty and wealth alike tend to be inherited (Harris, 1971, chap. 18). Thus in Latin America the caste form of racism that was the hallmark of its colonial past has become ensconced, even though legal racial discrimination has long since been done away with. Add to this the blurring of racial lines on a large scale over hundreds of years, such that customary forms of discrimination based on actual ancestry have been rendered impotent. Taken together, these factors are what is usually meant by the observation that the race question in Latin America has by and large been transformed into a socioeconomic issue (Morner, 1970).

It needs to be said, however, that active remnants of attitudinal racism persist. One of these presents itself as "colorism" or even "featurism," neither of which requires proof of actual ancestry to be operative. Professor G. Reginald Daniel of the University of California, Los Angeles, very aptly terms this phenomenon a "recapitulation of racism" (personal communication, February 1991). To what extent this attitude affects whatever social mobility is available to poor people of any phenotype in Latin America remains to be definitively measured. Some evidence for it can be seen in the disproportion of European-looking models and actors in the Latin American media, although another, probably coexistent, explanation for this is that, for socioeconomic reasons, access to the media is easier for the predominantly lighter elite. There is also a conservative tendency to ape the European and U.S. media.

Another remnant of racism can be heard in many derogatory expressions that include the term *indio* (or other, usually vulgar, terms for Black). Though originally directed at *indios,* these epithets have become generalized insults often used even by their supposed objects, the purely racist feeling having been muted or lost (as, for instance, we might use the expression "welshed"). However, in those districts where Native American communities remain relatively intact, such as in the Yucatán, the Andes, and the many isolated mountain settlements throughout

Latin America, these expressions still carry their hard edge and reflect a real, present-day situation of unresolved interethnic conflict and outright oppression.

In the United States, it is the biological aspect of race and racial mixture that is essential to racist thinking, quite apart from any other consideration. This attitude finds expression in the failure of our society and its institutions officially to acknowledge racial mixture, potentially the basis for a unifying national identity and a crucial step for breaking down traditional lines of social separation. Such an important omission unnecessarily contributes to the perpetuation of ethnic divisiveness in U.S. society.

HISTORICALLY EVOLVED CULTURAL FACTORS

Since both the United States and Latin America came into existence from the same expansionary impulse of a Europe reawakening out of medievalism, what might explain the contrasting attitudes regarding race and race mixture?

Sex Ratio Differences

An important difference between the Anglo-dominated colonization of North America and the Iberian conquest of Central and South America was that the Spanish and Portuguese came primarily as soldiers and priests, while the British (and Dutch) came as religious rebels and farmers. That is to say, the Iberians had proportionally fewer of their countrywomen with them than did the Anglos. Thus sexual relations occurred more frequently between the Iberians and the indigenous and African slave women, and, consequently, the numbers of "mixed" people began to increase in Latin America relative to Anglo America right from the outset.

Because interracial unions were less common in Anglo America, their rare occurrence was regarded as aberrational and, hence, in a religiously puritanical milieu where anything unusual was cause for alarm, deeply sinful. On the other hand, while the Catholic church was not at all tolerant of any sexual relations outside of marriage, interracial sexual relations within the bounds of marriage were permitted and at times even encouraged. Nevertheless, the vast majority of interracial sexual relations occurred outside of marriage in Latin America, to the extent that the very terms for a mixed person, *mestizo* and *mulato,* became synonyms for *bastard.*[4] In Mexico, use of the term *mestizo* was not really legitimized until the Revolution of 1910. Today it is regarded by most Mexicans as an honorable badge of national identity (if it is given any thought at all) (Páz, 1950/1961).

Racial Classifications

Another striking difference between Anglo and Latin America can be seen in the systems of racial classification. In Anglo America, no mixed category has ever existed officially, except as a means for assigning all people of any discernible African ancestry to the status of "Negro." This principle of classifying Blacks has been referred to as the "one-drop rule." In common parlance, terms such as *mulatto, Eurasian,* and *half-breed* (or simply *breed*) have been used, but never adopted as ongoing racial categories.[5] This institutional refusal to make a place for a racially mixed identity is strong evidence for the visceral abhorrence of race mixture in U.S. culture. Further evidence can be seen in that peculiar rule of "check one box only" with which multiethnic children and adults are constantly confronted (which parent and heritage shall be denied today?)

In Latin America, on the other hand, elaborate racial taxonomies gained official recognition from the outset, drawing on Spain's own national experience. Some of these have already been mentioned. In the Spanish colonies, these *casta* designations became distinct identities unto themselves, with legal rights as well as disabilities attaching to each.[6] Most, if not all, of Spain's colonies abolished the *casta* system upon their independence. Classifications based on race persisted in some official documents, but discriminatory application of laws based on race was forbidden, something that did not occur in the United States until the middle of the twentieth century. Today, given the large degree of mixture in the Latin American countries, racial classifications are virtually meaningless and hence, for the most part, are no longer used. . . .

The Native Americans, North and South

The difference in the size and nature of the Native American populations in Anglo and Latin America also helps account for the emergence of different attitudes about race. In that part of North America in which the English, Dutch, and others settled, the indigenous peoples were by and large nomadic or seminomadic and not very numerous. Moreover, the socioeconomic and technological distance between the settlers and the indigenous peoples they encountered allowed the settlers from England and other parts of Northwestern Europe to regard surviving Native Americans as savages, mere objects of the wilderness to be moved out of the way. The Anglos, for the most part, felt they had little reason to respect Native Americans (notwithstanding later maudlin stories about the "noble savage"), nor did they feel any need to compromise with them, or to abide by the few compromises that were made.

Entire peoples were segregated, forcibly removed, or exterminated. The occasional exceptions to this history of genocide are few and far between. Although some intermarriage occurred, and some native peoples managed to survive in various desperate, ingenious, and often fortuitous ways, the major outcome was the virtual disappearance of Native Americans as a significant part of North American society.

In those parts of the Americas to which the Spanish came, particularly Mexico and Peru, the indigenous peoples lived a settled, advanced (even by European standards) agricultural life with large cities and developed class systems. They were also very numerous, despite the estimated disease mortality rate of nearly 90% following the first contacts with Europeans. Eliminating them, even if the idea had occurred to the Spanish, would probably have been impossible.

Instead, the Spanish found it advantageous to graft their feudal society onto the semifeudal structures of the Native American civilizations already in place. Spaniards, in the absence of their countrywomen, married into Indian ruling-class families, thereby acquiring key kinship ties to the various peoples composing the Mexican and Incan empires. In short, the Spanish integrated themselves and their culture into communities of civilized (defined as above, in terms of relative technological and socioeconomic development) peoples. Instead of genocide, they opted for a more profitable (and brutally exploitative) *modus vivendi.*

In contrast to the Anglo settlers, many, though not all, of the Spanish came to regard the Native Americans as people rather than savages.[7] The Catholic church itself eventually recognized this and, in theory at least, maintained that an Indian could become the spiritual equal of a Spaniard, if only he or she converted to Christianity. Of course, there was no question about who was superior in secular life, but the very idea of making a place for the Native American in Spanish colonial society demonstrated an attitude far different from the outright genocidal policies carried out further to the north. This difference resulted in a greater permissiveness in the Iberians regarding miscegenation, an attitude that was to some extent generalized to include Africans.

Race Consciousness and "Scientific" Racism

A major ideological difference between the United States and Latin America respecting race and race consciousness is a result of the development of "race theory," a pseudoscientific expression of social Darwinism in the nineteenth century. It is this theory and concept of race to which most Americans have become accustomed, particularly in the form of the "three-race theory" (King, 1981; Stepan, 1982). It is also the basis of modern racism.[8]

Whereas the idea that the human species might be divided up into distinct subspecies marked by skin color or other superficial features had occurred before, it was not until the scientific revolution that accompanied the Industrial Revolution in Europe and North America that such divisions were elevated to the status of "science." The first outstanding proponent of the race theory was the Count Gobineau, a petty French noble among whose occupations had been an ambassadorship in Rio de Janeiro from 1868 to 1870. Of that stay, he once wrote, revealingly: "This is not a country to my taste. An entirely Mulatto population, corrupted in body and soul, ugly to a terrifying degree" (quoted in Morner, 1967). His *Essay on the Inequality of the Human Races* became the starting point for a long line of intellectual racists, culminating in the atrocities of the Nazi death camps (Biddess, 1970). Other Europeans and Americans of European ancestry took up the race theory with relish, perhaps noting how conveniently it displaced onto "nature" human responsibility for discriminatory laws and practices, the drawing of territorial borders, the annexation and government of non-Europeans in the interests of overseas commercial empires, and so forth.

Today, most anthropologists reject traditional race theory, though their continued occasional use of its terminology betrays its stubborn influence, and remains a source of ongoing debate. Reputable anthropologists will typically use the alternative term *population* to refer to groupings of humans having various genetic frequencies. But these groups are predefined by the researcher, their boundaries changing depending on what it is that he or she wishes to study. When discussing the very real sociocultural distinctions that exist among human societies, terms such as *tribe, ethnic group, class,* and *religion* are preferred. These labels do not suffer from the disabilities of the term *race* because they are acknowledged to be artifices of humankind, with no pretense or implication of being "natural."

In the nineteenth century, pseudoscientific concepts of race had a decisive influence on the public mind in Europe and the United States, an influence that continues right down to the present. On the other hand, though race theory was disseminated and discussed among the intelligentsia in Latin America, it never caught on among the masses of the people in the same way as it did here. The reasons for this different receptivity have much to do with the various historically evolved cultural factors reviewed above.

Demographic Differences

The outcome of the differing conditions outlined above brings us finally to the most important difference between Latin and Anglo America with regard to race: the fact that people of mixed racial ancestry came to form a much greater proportion of the population in Latin America than in Anglo America. This simple fact meant that, in varying degrees, race was neutralized as a significant social issue (or at least transformed into a class issue) throughout much of Latin America while it remains one of the most salient features of North American life.

Mexican Americans in the Melting Pot

The United States is poised to integrate the greatest diversity of ethnic groups across all traditional "race" lines that the world has yet seen. As the "browning of America" accelerates through the course of the next few decades, the question of race in all its dimensions will have to be resolved. With their numbers rapidly growing, Mexican Americans, together with their Latino cousins, will undoubtedly exercise an increasing influence on the future development of U.S. culture. Indeed, that influence has already occurred in our folk culture—witness the all-American cowboy, originally the *vaquero,* the Mexican mestizo ranch hand of what is now the American Southwest.

But perhaps the most important contribution is yet to come, that is, in the reshaping of our attitudes about race and especially about race mixture. As the bearers of Latin America's historico-cultural experience and familiar with the ways of U.S. society, Mexican Americans are uniquely positioned to upset the traditional Anglo-American taboo against "race mixing" by merely reaffirming their heritage. Concretely, Chicanos and their Latino cousins are also favorably positioned to mediate alliances among the various racial and ethnic groups that make up the U.S. population, something the African American group, for all its accomplishments, could not do, defined as it was (and is still) by the dominant White culture. Latinos, and especially Mexican Americans, have been conditioned by their history, however imperfectly and unevenly, to accept racial ambiguity and mixture as "normal." This attitude might be of enormous benefit to all of us in the United States. First, the race question may be neutralized and energies redirected to other pressing socioeconomic issues. Second, the principle of *mestizaje,* or "multicultural synthesis," as a social norm, a truer expression of the old melting-pot thesis, can free us all from the limits of ethnocentrism by opening us up to a wider repertoire of cultural elements, thereby stimulating our creativity to the fullest. From this, we can reap economic as well as psychological benefits. As a society, we will then be especially well suited to shape the ongoing emergence of a truly global community.

Unfortunately, it must be noted here that the pervasiveness of U.S. culture in Latin America as well as the assimilation of Latin American immigrants into it within this country has had some effect of instilling U.S.-style race consciousness. Thus some Latin Americans will adopt views against intermarriage or repeat what racist Whites say about African and Asian Americans, or even Latin Americans of nationalities different from their own.[9] There are also some who will insist on the purity of their Spanish ancestry and culture, by which they mean White, European ancestry, especially if they are phenotypically light-skinned, even though, for most, such hoped-for purity is extremely dubious.[10] The self-proclaimed "Hispanic" who has definite African or Native American features is particularly absurd and foolish.

Which way will the Latino community go? Nonracial ethnocentrism? Anglo conformity? *Hispanidad? Indigenismo?* Afrocentrism? Or *mestizaje?* The decision must be made. In this society, deeply scarred by racism, evading the issue will prove useless. Latinos cannot avoid the reality of their mixed identity without losing themselves. In the process of asserting their mixed identity, Mexican Americans and other Latinos will have little choice but to challenge traditional American race thinking.[11]

CONCLUSION

Whether we in the United States change our attitudes as a society or not, the numbers of "mixed," "blended," "brown," "cosmic," "melded," or simply *multiethnic* people will grow, in both numbers and complexity. Moreover, our global society is rapidly becoming a union of all cultures, the old cultures not dying, but living on in new forms. It is in the minds of the multiethnic children that the new culture of the future world society is being synthesized. There will be no place for racism or ethnocentrism in this new world, because the multiethnic children cannot hate or disrespect their parents and their heritage without sacrificing their own personal integrity and peace of mind.

What will happen in this future world of race or ethnic irrelevance? As many have speculated, national cultures may indeed disappear as independent entities, to be replaced not by the homogeneous-monotony specter we often hear about (really what narrow cultural nationalism is about —rigid, forced conformity to an ideal, monolithic cultural standard), but by a society that recognizes and respects diversity at the level of the individual.

The fulfillment of the melting-pot and *La Raza Cósmica*—ideals and realities on the continents of the Western Hemisphere—these will form the real New World for all humankind.

NOTES

1. *La Raza Cósmica* is the title of an essay by the Mexican philosopher and educator Jose Vasconcelos (1925/1979), in which he proclaims and extolls the spiritual virtues that may ensue from the fact that America—in particular, Latin America—has become the site of the first large-scale mixture of "races" in the world. As Minister of Education he

took every opportunity to foster a unified Mexican identity. Vasconcelos was responsible for the motto of the National Autonomous University of Mexico (my father's alma mater): "Por mi raza, el espíritu se hablará" (Through my race [the mixed race], the spirit shall speak).

2. Of course, any discussion of race or racial mixing presumes the existence of "race" or, more specifically, the existence of the particular concept of race that holds sway in the popular consciousness.

3. *Mexica* (pronounced meshEEca), besides being the origin of the name for the country of Mexico, is also the probable origin of *Chicano,* a slang term for Mexican Americans popularized in the 1960s. In colonial times, many in the Spanish upper class did not consider themselves "Mexican," that is, Indian or mestizo. Thus they might refer to ordinary Mexicans derogatorily as *xicanos.* The usage was carried over into the United States, where Mexican American youths transformed *Chicano* into a term of pride and defiance.

4. The number of terms for the various mixtures of peoples in Latin America far exceeds the two mentioned here. In fact, the race terminology in popular usage and adopted into law by many states in the United States is directly derived from the Spanish: *Negro* (from the Spanish word for *black*), *mulatto* (from the Spanish *mulato,* which means mule, meaning half Black and half White), *quadroon* (from the Spanish *cuarterón,* or one-quarter Black), *octoroon* (from the Spanish *octorón,* or one-eighth Black), *zambo* (from the Spanish *zambo,* or Black and Indian), and *maroon* (from the Spanish *cimarrón,* or runaway Black slave). Many other terms were also used, including *coyote, pardo, castizo, morisco, lobo,* and *chino.* Collectively, the mixed groups were called *castas* (castes). See O'Crouley (1774/1972) and Woodbridge (1948).

5. The U.S. Census, for example, included mulatto and quadroon during some censuses, but not consistently, and certainly with no bearing on the legal rights of the people so designated.

6. *Casta* was a term midway in meaning between "estate" and "race." To the extent it meant race it had a spiritual or ethnic sense rather than the genetic sense to which we are accustomed (Castro, 1971).

7. The question of Native American humanity was the subject of a famous debate in Valladolid, Spain, between Bartolomé de las Casas and Juan Ginés de Sepúlveda during the sixteenth century. Sepúlveda invoked Aristotle's thesis that some people are naturally slaves. Las Casas argued that slavery and generally brutal treatment of Native Americans violated Christian principles. Las Casas won the debate, and the Laws of the Indies resulted. Unfortunately, Las Casas's solution to Native American slavery was African slavery, a view that he later apparently recanted. That any controversy existed at all during this early period says much about Spanish attitudes regarding race compared with those of other Europeans (including their fellow Iberians, the Portuguese) of that or subsequent times. For an excellent examination of this famous debate, see Hanke (1959/1970).

8. I contend that in its most essential sense, racism is a system of thinking, an *ideology,* based on the concept of race.

9. In March 1989, 82% of "Hispanic" men who got married married Hispanic women, while 85% of "Hispanic" women married Hispanic men. The Mexican intermarriage rate was nearly the same as the overall "Hispanic" rate, while it was actually higher (28%) for Puerto Rican men (see U.S. Bureau of the Census, 1990).

10. Even if this is true in any given instance, Spaniards and Spanish culture are a mixture anyway, including the ancestry of Black Africans, Gypsies (from India), and Semites (Jews, Arabs, and Phoenicians), as well as Romans, Celts, Germans, Greeks, Berbers, Basques, and probably more. Today, there are even many mestizo and *mulato* immigrants from Latin America resident in Spain.

11. Interestingly, more than 96% of the 9.8 million people who declined to choose a particular race by checking the "other race" box on the 1990 census forms were "Hispanics" (J. García, demographic analyst, U.S. Bureau of the Census, Ethnic and Hispanic Branch, personal communication, May 1991).

REFERENCES

Biddess, M. D. (1970). *Father of racist ideology: The social and political thought of Count Gobineau.* New York: Weybright & Talley.

Castro, A. (1971). *The Spaniards: An introduction to their history.* Berkeley: University of California Press.

Hanke, L. (1970). *Aristotle and the American Indians: A study in race prejudice in the modern world.* Bloomington: Indiana University Press. (Original work published 1959).

Harris, M. (1971). *Culture, man and nature.* New York: Thomas Y. Crowell.

King, J. C. (1981). *The biology of race.* Berkeley: University of California Press.

MacLachlan, C. M., & Rodríguez O, J. E. (1980). *The forging of the cosmic race: A reinterpretation of colonial Mexico.* Berkeley: University of California Press.

Morner, M. (1967). *Race Mixture in the History of Latin America.* Boston: Little, Brown

Morner, M. (Ed.). (1970). *Race and class in Latin America.* New York: Columbia University Press.

Muñoz, C., Jr. (1989). *Youth, identity, power: The Chicano movement.* London: Verso.

O'Crouley, P. (1972). *A description of the kingdom of New Spain in 1774.* San Francisco: John Howell. (Original work published 1774).

Páz, O. (1961). *The labyrinth of solitude: Life and thought in Mexico* (L. Kemp, Trans.). New York: Grove. (Original work published 1950).

Stepan, N. (1982). *The idea of race in science.* Hamden, CT: Archon.

U.S. Bureau of the Census. (1990). *The Hispanic population in the United States: March 1989* (Current Population Reports, Series P-20, No. 444). Washington DC: Government Printing Office.

U.S. Bureau of the Census. (1991, March 11). *U.S. Department of Commerce news* (Publication No. CB91-100). Washington, DC: Government Printing Office.

Vasconcelos, J. (1979). *La raza cósmica* (D. T. Jaen, Trans.). Los Angeles: California State University, Centro de Publicaciones. (Original work published 1925)

White, J. M. (1971). *Cortés and the downfall of the Aztec empire.* New York: St. Martin's.

Woodbridge, H. C. (1948). Glossary of names in colonial Latin America for crosses among Indians, Negros and Whites. *Journal of the Washington Academy of Sciences, 38,* 353–362.

Asian American Panethnicity

Yen Le Espiritu

Arriving in the United States, nineteenth-century immigrants from Asian countries did not think of themselves as "Asians." Coming from specific districts in provinces in different nations, Asian immigrant groups did not even consider themselves Chinese, Japanese, Korean, and so forth, but rather people from Toisan, Hoiping, or some other district in Guandong Province in China or from Hiroshima, Yamaguchi, or some other prefecture in Japan. Members of each group considered themselves culturally and politically distinct. Historical enmities between their mother countries further separated the groups even after their arrival in the United States. Writing about early Asian immigrant communities, Eliot Mears (1928:4) reported that "it is exceptional when one learns of any entente between these Orientals." However, non-Asians had little understanding or appreciation of these distinctions. For the most part, outsiders accorded to Asian peoples certain common characteristics and traits that were essentially supranational (Browne 1985:8–9). Indeed, the exclusion acts and quotas limiting Asian immigration to the United States relied upon racialist constructions of Asians as homogeneous (Lowe 1991:28).

Mindful that whites generally lump all Asians together, early Asian immigrant communities sought to "keep their images discrete and were not above denigrating, or at least approving the denigration of, other Asian groups" (Daniels 1988:113). It was not until the late 1960s, with the advent of the Asian American movement, that a pan-Asian consciousness and constituency were first formed. To build political unity, college students of Asian ancestry heralded their common fate—the similarity of experiences and treatment that Asian groups endured in the United States (Omi and Winant 1986:105). In other words, the pan-Asian concept, originally imposed by non-Asians, became a symbol of pride and a rallying point for mass mobilization by later generations. This [discussion] examines the social, political, and demographic factors that allowed pan-Asianism to take root in the 1960s and not earlier.

ETHNIC "DISIDENTIFICATION"

Before the 1960s, Asians in this country frequently practiced ethnic disidentification, the act of distancing one's group from another group so as not to be mistaken and suffer the blame for the presumed misdeeds of that group (Hayano 1981:162). Faced with external threats, group members can either intensify their solidarity or they can distance themselves from the stigmatized segment. Instead of uniting to fight anti-Asian forces, early Asian immigrant communities often disassociated themselves from the targeted group so as not to be mistaken for members of it and suffer any possible negative consequences (Hayano 1981:161; Daniels 1988:113). Two examples of ethnic disidentification among Asians in this country occurred during the various anti-Asian exclusion movements and during World War II. These incidents are instructive not only as evidence of ethnic disidentification but also as documentation of the pervasiveness of racial lumping. Precisely because of racial lumping, persons of Asian ancestry found it necessary to disassociate themselves from other Asian groups.

Exclusion Movements

Beginning with the first student laborers in the late nineteenth century, Japanese immigrants always differentiated themselves from Chinese immigrants. Almost uniformly, Japanese immigrants perceived their Chinese counterparts in an "unsympathetic, negative light, and often repeated harsh American criticisms of the Chinese" (Ichioka 1988:191). In their opinion, the Chinese came from an inferior nation; they also were lower-class laborers, who had not adapted themselves to American society. In 1892, a Japanese student laborer described San Francisco's China-

town as "a world of beasts in which . . . exists every imaginable depravity, crime, and vice" (cited in Ichioka 1988:191).

Indeed, the Japanese immigrants were a more select group than their Chinese counterparts. The Japanese government viewed overseas Japanese as representatives of their homeland. Therefore, it screened prospective emigrants to ensure that they were healthy and literate and would uphold Japan's national honor (Takaki 1989:46).

More important, Japanese immigrants distanced themselves from the Chinese because they feared that Americans would lump them together. Aware of Chinese exclusion, Japanese immigrant leaders had always dreaded the thought of Japanese exclusion. To counteract any negative association, Japanese immigrant leaders did everything possible to distinguish themselves from the Chinese immigrants (Ichioka 1988:250). For example, to separate themselves from the unassimilable Chinese laborers, some Japanese immigrant leaders insisted that their Japanese workers wear American work clothes and even eat American food (Ichioka 1988:185). In 1901, the Japanese in California distributed leaflets requesting that they be differentiated from the Chinese (tenBroek, Barnhart, and Matson 1970:23).

However, under the general rubric Asiatic, the Japanese inherited the painful experiences of the Chinese.[1] All the vices attributed to the Chinese were transferred to these newest Asian immigrants (Browne 1985). Having successfully excluded Chinese laborers, organized labor once again led the campaign to drive out the Japanese immigrants. In 1904, the American Federation of Labor adopted its first anti-Japanese resolution. Charging that the Japanese immigrants were as undesirable as the Chinese, the unions' resolution called for the expansion of the 1902 Chinese Exclusion Act to include Japanese and other Asian laborers. By mid-1905, the labor unions of California had joined forces to establish the Asiatic Exclusion League (Hill 1973:52–54; Ichioka 1988:191–192).

Since the Japanese immigrants considered themselves superior to the Chinese, they felt indignant and insulted whenever they were lumped together with them. In 1892, a Japanese immigrant wrote in the *Oakland Enquirer* that he wished "to inveigh with all my power" against American newspapers that compared the Japanese to "the truly ignorant class of Chinese laborers and condemned them as bearers of some mischievous Oriental evils" (cited in Ichioka 1988:192). Instead of joining with the Chinese to fight the anti-Asian exclusion movement, some Japanese leaders went so far as to condone publicly the exclusion of the Chinese while insisting that the Japanese were the equals of Americans (Daniels 1988:113). Above all else, Japanese immigrant leaders wanted Japanese immigration to be treated on the same footing as European immigration (Ichioka 1988:250).

In the end, Japanese attempts at disidentification failed. With the passage of the 1924 Immigration Act, Japanese immigration was effectively halted. This act contained two provisions designed to stop Japanese immigration. The first barred the immigration of Japanese wives even if their husbands were United States citizens. The second prohibited the immigration of aliens ineligible for citizenship. Because the Supreme Court had ruled in 1922 that persons of Japanese ancestry could not become naturalized citizens, this provision effectively closed the door on Japanese and most other Asian immigration (U.S. Commission on Civil Rights 1986:8–9). The Japanese immigrants felt doubly affronted by the 1924 act because it ranked them, not as the equals of Europeans, but on the same level as the lowly Chinese, the very people whom they themselves considered inferior (Ichioka 1988:250). Thus, despite all their attempts to disassociate themselves from the Chinese, with the passage of the act, the Japanese joined the Chinese as a people deemed unworthy of becoming Americans. Little did they foresee that, in less than two decades, other Asian groups in America would disassociate themselves from the Japanese.

World War II and Japanese Internment

Immediately after the bombing of Pearl Harbor, the incarceration of Japanese Americans began. On the night of December 7, the Federal Bureau of Investigation (FBI) began taking into custody persons of Japanese ancestry who had connections to the Japanese government. Working on the principle of guilt by association, the security agencies simply rounded up most of the Issei (first-generation) leaders of the Japanese community. Initially, the federal government differentiated between alien and citizen Japanese Americans, but this distinction gradually disappeared. In the end, the government evacuated more than 100,000 persons of Japanese ancestry into concentration camps, approximately two-thirds of whom were American-born citizens. It was during this period that the Japanese community discovered that the legal distinction between citizen and alien was not nearly so important as the distinction between white and yellow (Daniels 1988:ch. 6).

Like the Japanese, the Chinese understood the importance of the distinction between white and yellow. Fearful that they would be targets of anti-Japanese activities, many persons of Chinese ancestry, especially in the West, took to wearing buttons that proclaimed positively "I'm Chinese." Similarly, many Chinese shopkeepers displayed signs announcing, "This is a Chinese shop." Some Chinese immigrants even joined the white persecution with buttons that added "I hate Japs worse than you do" (Daniels 1988:205; Takaki 1989: 370–371). The small Korean and Filipino communities took similar actions. Because of Japan's occupation of Korea at the time, being mistaken as Japanese particularly angered Koreans in the United States. Cognizant of Asian lumping, the United Korean Committee prepared identification cards proclaiming "I am Korean." During the early months of the war, women wore Korean dresses regularly to distinguish themselves from the Japanese (Melendy 1977:158; Takaki 1989:365–366). Similarly, persons of Filipino ancestry wore buttons proclaiming "I am a Filipino" (Takaki 1989:363).

Given the wars between their mother countries and Japan, it is not surprising that the Chinese, Koreans, and Filipinos distanced themselves from the Japanese. But their reactions are instructive not only as examples of ethnic disidentification but also as testimonies to the pervasiveness of racial lumping. Popular confusion of the various Asian groups was so prevalent that it was necessary for Chinese, Filipinos, and Koreans to don ethnic clothing and identification buttons to differentiate themselves from the Japanese. Without these *visible* signs of ethnicity, these three Asian groups would probably have been mistaken for Japanese by anti-Japanese forces. As Ronald Takaki (1989:370) reported, Asian groups "remembered how they had previously been called 'Japs' and how many whites had lumped all Asians together." But there are also examples of how Asian groups united when inter-Asian cooperation advanced their common interests.

Inter-Asian Labor Movements

The most notable example of inter-Asian solidarity was the 1920 collaboration of Japanese and Filipino plantation laborers in Hawaii. In the beginning, plantation workers had organized in terms of national origins. Thus, the Japanese belonged to the Japanese union and the Filipinos to the Filipino union. In the early 1900s, an ethnically based strike seemed sensible to Japanese plantation laborers because they represented about 70 percent of the entire work force. Filipinos constituted less than 1 percent. However, by 1920, Japanese workers represented only 44 percent of the labor force, while Filipino workers represented 30 percent. Japanese and Filipino union leaders understood that they would have to combine to be politically and economically effective (Johanessen 1950:75–83; Takaki 1989:152).

Because together they constituted more than 70 percent of the work force in Oahu, the 1920 Japanese-Filipino strike brought plantation operations to a sudden stop. Although the workers were eventually defeated, the 1920 strike was the "first major interethnic working-class struggle in Hawaii" (Takaki 1989:154).[2] Subsequently, the Japanese Federation of Labor elected to become an interethnic union. To promote a multiethnic class solidarity, the new union called itself the Hawaii Laborers Association (Takaki 1989:154–155).

Although the 1920 strike was a de facto example of pan-Asian cooperation, this cooperation needs to be distinguished from the post-1960 pan-Asian solidarity. The purported unifying factor in 1920 was a common class status, not a shared cultural or racial background (Takaki 1989:154). This class solidarity is different from the large-scale organization of ethnicity that emerged in the late 1960s. For most Asian Americans, the more recent development represents an enlargement of their identity system, a circle beyond their previous national markers of identity. True, like working-class unions, panethnic groups are interest groups with material demands (Glazer and Moynihan 1963; Bonacich and Modell 1980). However, unlike labor unions, panethnic groups couch their demands in ethnic or racial terms—not purely in class terms. In other words, their ethnicity is used as a basis for the assertion of collective claims, many but not all of which are class based.

SOCIAL AND DEMOGRAPHIC CHANGES: SETTING THE CONTEXT

. . . Before 1940, the Asian population in the United States was primarily an immigrant population. Immigrant Asians faced practical barriers to pan-Asian unity. Foremost was their lack of a common language. Old national rivalries were another obstacle, as many early Asian immigrants carried the political memories and outlook of their homelands. For example, Japan's occupation of Korea resulted in pervasive anti-Japanese sentiments among Koreans in the United States. According to Brett Melendy (1977:155), "Fear and hatred of the Japanese appeared to be the only unifying force among the various Korean groups through the years." Moreover, these historical enmities and linguistic and cultural differences reinforced one another as divisive agents.

During the postwar period, due to immigration restrictions and the growing dominance of the second and third generations, American-born Asians outnumbered immigrants. The demographic changes of the 1940s were pronounced. During this decade, nearly twenty thousand Chinese American babies were born. For the first time, the largest five-year cohort of Chinese Americans was under five years of age (Kitano and Daniels 1988:37). By 1960, approximately two-thirds of the Asian population in California had been born in the United States (Ong 1989:5–8). As the Asian population became a native-born community, linguistic and cultural differences began to blur. Although they had attended Asian-language schools, most American-born Asians possessed only a limited knowledge of their ethnic language (Chan 1991:115). By 1960, with English as the common language, persons from different Asian backgrounds were able to communicate with one another (Ling 1984:73), and in so doing create a common identity associated with the United States.

Moreover, unlike their immigrant parents, native-born and American-educated Asians could muster only scant loyalties to old world ties. Historical antagonisms between their mother countries thus receded in importance (Wong 1972:34). For example, growing up in America, second-generation Koreans "had difficulty feeling the painful loss of the homeland and understanding the indignity of Japanese domination" (Takaki 1989:292). Thus, while the older generation of Koreans hated all Japanese, "their children were much less hostile or had no concern at all" (Melendy 1977:156). As a native-born Japanese American community advocate explained, "By 1968, we had a second generation. We could speak English; so there was no language problem. And we had little feelings of historical animosity" (Kokubun interview).

As national differences receded in subjective importance, generational differences widened. For the most part, American-born Asians considered themselves to have more in common with other American-born Asians than they did with foreign-born compatriots.[3] According to a third-generation Japanese American who is married to a Chinese American, "As far as our experiences in America, I have more things in common than differences with a Chinese American. Being born and raised here gives us something in common. We have more in common with each other than

with a Japanese from Japan, or a Chinese from China" (Ichioka interview). Much to their parents' dismay, young Asian Americans began to choose their friends and spouses from other Asian groups. . . .

Before World War II, Asian immigrant communities were quite distinct entities, isolated from one another and from the larger society. Because of language difficulties, prejudice, and lack of business opportunities elsewhere, there was little chance for Asians in the United States to live outside their ethnic enclaves (Yuan 1966:331). Shut out of the mainstream of American society, the various immigrant groups struggled separately in their respective Chinatowns, Little Tokyos, or Manilatowns. Stanford Lyman (1970:57–63) reported that the early Chinese and Japanese communities in the western states had little to do with one another—either socially or politically. . .

Economic and residential barriers began to crumble after World War II. The war against Nazism called attention to racism at home and discredited the notions of white superiority. The fifteen years after the war was a period of largely positive change as civil rights statutes outlawed racial discrimination in employment as well as housing (Daniels 1988:ch. 7). Popular attitudes were also changing. Polls taken during World War II showed a distinct hostility toward Japan: 74 percent of the respondents favored either killing off all Japanese, destroying Japan as a political entity, or supervising it. On the West Coast, 97 percent of the people polled approved of the relocation of Japanese Americans. In contrast, by 1949, 64 percent of those polled were either friendly or neutral toward Japan (Feraru 1950).

During the postwar years, Asian American residential patterns changed significantly. Because of the lack of statistical data,[4] a longitudinal study of the changing residential patterns of Asian Americans cannot be made. However, descriptive accounts of Asian American communities indicate that these enclaves declined in the postwar years. Edwin Hoyt (1974:94) reported that in the 1940s, second-generation Chinese Americans moved out of the Chinatowns. Although they still came back to shop or to see friends, they lived elsewhere. In 1940, Rose Hum Lee found twenty-eight cities with an area called Chinatown in the United States. By 1955, Peter Sih found only sixteen (Sung 1967:143–144). New York's Chinatown exemplifies the declining significance of Asian ethnic enclaves. In 1940, 50 percent of the Chinese in New York City lived in its Chinatown; by 1960, less than one-third lived there (Yuan 1966:331). Similarly, many returning Japanese Americans abandoned their prewar settlement in old central cities and joined the migration to suburbia (Daniels 1988:294). In the early 1970s, Little Tokyo in Los Angeles remained a bustling Japanese American center, "but at night the shop owners [went] home to the houses in the suburbs" (Hoyt 1974:84). . . .

Moreover, recent research on suburban segregation indicates that the level of segregation between certain Asian American groups is often less than that between them and non-Asians. . . . Though not comprehensive, these studies together suggest that Asian residential segregation declined in the postwar years.

As various Asian groups in the United States interacted, they became aware of common problems and goals that transcended parochial interests and historical antagonisms. One recurrent problem was employment discrimination. According to a 1965 report published by the California Fair Employment Practices Commission, for every $51 earned by a white male Californian, Japanese males earned $43 and Chinese males $38—even though Chinese and Japanese American men had become slightly better educated than the white majority (Daniels 1988:315). Moreover, although the postwar period marked the first time that well-trained Chinese and Japanese Americans could find suitable employment with relative ease, they continued to be passed over for promotion to administrative and supervisory positions (Kitano and Daniels 1988:47). Asians in the United States began to see themselves as a group that shared important common experiences: exploitation, oppression, and discrimination (Uyematsu 1971).

Because inter-Asian contact and communication were greatest on college campuses, pan-Asianism was strongest there (Wong 1972:33–34). Exposure to one another and to the mainstream society led some young Asian Americans to feel that they were fundamentally different from whites. Disillusioned with the white society and alienated from their traditional communities, many Asian American student activists turned to the alternative strategy of pan-Asian unification (Weiss 1974:69–70).

THE CONSTRUCTION OF PAN-ASIAN ETHNICITY

Although broader social struggles and internal demographic changes provided the impetus for the Asian American movement, it was the group's politics—confrontational and explicitly pan-Asian—that shaped the movement's content. Influenced by the internal colonial model, which stresses the commonalities among "colonized groups," college students of Asian ancestry declared solidarity with fellow Asian Americans—and with other Third World[5] minorities (Blauner 1972:ch. 2). Rejecting the label "Oriental," they proclaimed themselves "Asian American." Through pan-Asian organizations, publications, and Asian American studies programs, Asian American activists built pan-Asian solidarity by pointing out their common fate in American society. The pan-Asian concept enabled diverse Asian American groups to understand their "unequal circumstances and histories as being related" (Lowe 1991:30).

From "Yellow" to "Asian American"

Following the example of the Black Power movement, Asian American activists spearheaded their own Yellow Power movement to seek "freedom from racial oppression through the power of a consolidated yellow people" (Uyematsu 1971:12). In the summer of 1968, more than one hundred students of diverse Asian backgrounds attended an "Are You Yellow?" conference at UCLA to discuss issues of Yellow Power, identity, and the war in Vietnam (Ling 1989:53). In 1970, a new pan-Asian organization in northern California called itself the "Yellow Seed" because "Yellow [is] the common bond between Asian-Americans and Seed symboliz[es] growth as an individual and as an alliance" (Masada 1970). This "yellow" reference was dropped when Filipino Americans rejected the term, claiming that they were brown, not yellow (Rabaya 1971:110; Ignacio 1976:84). At the first Asian American national conference in 1972, Filipino Americans "made it clear to the conferees that we were 'Brown Asians'" by forming a Brown Asian Caucus (Ignacio 1976:139–141). It is important to note, however, that Filipino American activists did not reject the term "yellow" because they objected to the pan-Asian framework. Quite the contrary, they rejected it because it allegedly excluded them from that grouping (Rabaya 1971:110).

. . . Asian American activists also rejected *Oriental* because the term conjures up images of "the sexy Susie Wong, the wily Charlie Chan, and the evil Fu Manchu" (Weiss 1974:234). It is also a term that smacks of European colonialism and imperialism: *Oriental* means "East"; Asia is "east" only in relationship to Europe, which was taken as the point of reference (Browne 1985). To define their own image and to claim an *American* identity, college students of Asian ancestry coined the term *Asian American* to "stand for all of us Americans of Asian descent" (Ichioka interview). While *Oriental* suggests passivity and acquiescence, *Asian Americans* connotes political activism because an Asian American "gives a damn about his life, his work, his beliefs, and is willing to do almost anything to help Orientals become Asian Americans" (cited in Weiss 1974:234).

The account above suggests that the creation of a new name is a significant symbolic move in constructing an ethnic identity. In their attempt to forge a pan-Asian identity, Asian American activists first had to coin a composite term that would unify and encompass the constituent groups. Filipino Americans' rejection of the term "yellow" and the activists' objection to the cliché-ridden *Oriental* forced the group to change its name to Asian American. . . .

Pan-Asian Organizations

Influenced by the political tempo of the 1960s, young Asian Americans began to join such organizations as the Free Speech Movement at the University of California at Berkeley, Students for a Democratic Society, and the Progressive Labor Party. However, these young activists "had no organization or coalition to draw attention to themselves as a distinct group" (Wong 1972:33). Instead, they participated as individuals—often at the invitation of their white or black friends (Chin 1971:285; Nakano 1984:3–4). While Asian American activists subscribed to the integrationist ideology of the 1960s and 1970s social movements, they also felt impotent and alienated. There was no structure to uphold their own identity. As an example, when the Peace and Freedom Party was formed on the basis of black and white coalitions, Asian American activists felt excluded because they were neither black nor white (Wong 1972:34; Yoshimura 1989:107).

In the late 1960s, linking their political views with the growth of racial pride among their ranks, Asian Americans already active in various political movements came together to form their own organizations (Nakano 1984:3–4). Most of the early pan-Asian organizations were college based. In 1968, activists at the University of California, Berkeley founded one of the first pan-Asian political organizations: the Asian American Political Alliance (AAPA). According to a co-founder of the organization, its establishment marked the first time that the term "Asian American" was used nationally to mobilize people of Asian descent (Ichioka interview). . . .

By the mid-1970s, *Asian American* had become a familiar term (Lott 1976:30). Although first coined by college activists, the pan-Asian concept began to be used extensively by professional and community spokespersons to lobby for the health and welfare of Americans of Asian descent. In addition to the local and single-ethnic organizations of an earlier era, Asian American professionals and community activists formed national and pan-Asian organizations such as the Pacific/Asian Coalition and the Asian American Social Workers (Ignacio 1976:162; Kuo 1979:283–284). Also, Asian American caucuses could be found in national professional organizations such as the American Public Health Association, the American Sociological Association, the American Psychological Association, the American Psychiatric Association, and the American Librarians Association (Lott 1976:31). Commenting on the "literally scores of pan-Asian organizations" in the mid-1970s, William Liu (1976:6) asserted that "the idea of pan-Asian cooperation [was] viable and ripe for development." . . .

THE LIMITS OF PAN-ASIANISM

Although pan-Asian consolidation certainly has occurred, it has been by no means universal. For those who wanted a broader political agenda, the pan-Asian scope was too narrow and its racial orientation too segregative (Wong 1972:33; Lowe 1991:39). For others who wanted to preserve ethnic particularism, the pan-Asian agenda threatened to remove second- and third-generation Asians "from their conceptual ties to their community" (R. Tanaka 1976:47). These competing levels of organization mitigated the impact of pan-Asianism.

Moreover, pan-Asianism has been primarily the ideology of native-born, American-educated, and middle-class Asians. Embraced by students, artists, professionals, and political activists, pan-Asian consciousness thrived on college campuses and in urban settings. However, it barely touched the Asian ethnic enclaves. When the middle-class student activists carried the enlarged and politicized Asian American consciousness to the ethnic communities, they encountered apprehension, if not outright hostility (Chan 1991:175). Conscious of their national origins and overburdened with their day-to-day struggles for survival, most community residents ignored or spurned the movement's political agenda (P.

Wong 1972:34). Chin (1971:287) reported that few Chinatown residents participated in any of the pan-Asian political events. Similarly, members of the Nisei-dominated Japanese American Citizens League "were determined to keep a closed mind and maintain their negative stereotype" of the members of the Asian American Political Alliance (J. Matsui 1968:6). For their part, young Asian American activists accused their elders of having been so whitewashed that they had deleted their experiences of prejudice and discrimination from their history (Weiss 1974:238). Because these young activists were not rooted in the community, their base of support was narrow and their impact upon the larger society often limited (Wong 1972:37; Nishio 1982:37).

Even among those who were involved in the Asian American movement, divisions arose from conflicting sets of interests as subgroups decided what and whose interests would be addressed. Oftentimes, conflicts over material interests took on ethnic coloration, with participants from smaller subgroups charging that "Asian American" primarily meant Chinese and Japanese American, the two largest and most acculturated Asian American groups at the time (Ignacio 1976:220; Ling 1984:193–195). For example, most Asian American Studies programs did not include courses on other Asian groups, but only on Chinese and Japanese. Similarly, the Asian American women's movement often subsumed the needs of their Korean and Filipina members under those of Chinese and Japanese women (Ling 1984:193–195). Chinese and Japanese Americans also were the instructors of Asian American ethnic studies directors and staff members of many Asian American projects,[6] and advisory and panel members in many governmental agencies (Ignacio 1976:223–224).

The ethnic and class inequality within the pan-Asian structure has continued to be a source of friction and mistrust, with participants from the less dominant groups feeling shortchanged and excluded. The influx of the post-1965 immigrants and the tightening of public funding resources have further deepened the ethnic and class cleavages among Asian American subgroups.

CONCLUSION

The development of a pan-Asian consciousness and constituency reflected broader societal developments and demographic changes, as well as the group's political agenda. By the late 1960s, pan-Asianism was possible because of the more amicable relationships among the Asian countries, the declining residential segregation among diverse Asian groups in America, and the large number of native-born, American-educated political actors. Disillusioned with the larger society and estranged from their traditional communities, third- and fourth-generation Asian Americans turned to the alternative strategy of pan-Asian unification. Through pan-Asian organizations, media, and Asian American Studies programs, these political activists assumed the role of "cultural entrepreneurs" consciously creating a community of culture out of diverse Asian peoples.[7] This process of pan-Asian consolidation did not proceed smoothly nor did it encompass all Asian Americans. Ethnic chauvinism, competition for scarce resources, and class cleavages continued to divide the subgroups. However, once established, the pan-Asian structure not only reinforced the cohesiveness of already existing networks but also expanded these networks. Although first conceived by young Asian American activists, the pan-Asian concept was subsequently institutionalized by professionals and community groups, as well as government agencies. The confrontational politics of the activists eventually gave way to the conventional and electoral politics of the politicians, lobbyists, and professionals, as Asian Americans continued to rely on the pan-Asian framework to enlarge their political capacities.

NOTES

1. On the other hand, due to the relative strength of Japan in the world order, Japanese immigrants at times received more favorable treatment than other Asian immigrants. For example, in 1905, wary of offending Japan, national politicians blocked an attempt by the San Francisco Board of Education to transfer Japanese students from the public schools reserved for white children to the "Oriental" school serving the Chinese (Chan 1991: 59).

2. Although many Korean laborers were sympathetic to the 1920 strike, because of their hatred for the Japanese, they did not participate. As the Korean National Association announced, "We do not wish to be looked upon as strikebreakers, but we shall continue to work in the plantation and we are opposed to the Japanese in everything" (cited in Melendy 1977: 164).

3. The same is true with other racial groups. For example, American-born Haitians are more like their African American peers than like their Haitian parents (Woldemikael 1989: 166).

4. Ideally, residential patterns should be analyzed at the census tract level. However, this analysis cannot be done because Asians were not tabulated by census tracts until the 1980 census.

5. During the late 1960s, in radical circles, the term *third world* referred to the nation's racially oppressed people.

6. For example, the staff of the movement publication *Gidra* were predominantly Japanese Americans.

7. For a discussion of the role of "cultural entrepreneurs," see Cornell (1988b).

REFERENCES

Blauner, Robert. 1972. *Racial Oppression in America.* New York: Harper & Row.

Bonacich, Edna, and John Modell. 1980. *The Economic Basis of Ethnic Solidarity: A Study of Japanese Americans.* Berkeley: University of California Press.

Browne, Blaine T. 1985. "A Common Thread: American Images of the Chinese and Japanese, 1930–1960." Ph.D. dissertation, University of Oklahoma.

Chan, Sucheng. 1991. *Asian Americans: An Interpretive History.* Boston: Twayne.

Chin, Rocky. 1971. "NY Chinatown Today: Community in Crisis." Pp. 282-295 in *Roots: An Asian American Reader,* edited by Amy Tachiki, Eddie Wong, and Franklin Odo. Los Angeles: UCLA Asian American Studies Center.

Cornell, Stephen. 1988*a*. *The Return of the Native: American Indian Political Resurgence.* New York: Oxford University Press.

———. 1988*b*. "Structure, Content, and Logic in Ethnic Group Formation." Working Paper series, Center for Research on Politics and Social Organization, Department of Sociology, Harvard University.

Daniels, Roger. 1971. *Concentration Camps USA: Japanese Americans and World War II.* Hinsdale, Ill.: Dryden Press.

———. 1988. *Asian America: Chinese and Japanese in the United States since 1850.* Seattle: University of Washington Press.

Feraru, Arthur N. 1950. "Public Opinions Polls on Japan." *Far Eastern Survey* 19 (10): 101–103.

Glazer, Nathan, and Daniel Patrick Moynihan. 1963. *Beyond the Melting Pot: The Negroes, Puerto Ricans, Jews, Italians, and Irish of New York City.* Cambridge, Mass.: M.I.T. Press.

Hayano, David M. 1981. "Ethnic Identification and Disidentification: Japanese-American Views of Chinese-Americans." *Ethnic Groups* 3 (2): 157–171.

Hill, Herbert. 1973. "Anti-Oriental Agitation and the Rise of Working-Class Racism." *Society* 10 (2): 43–54.

Hoyt, Edwin P. 1974. *Asians in the West.* New York: Thomas Nelson.

Ichioka, Yuji. 1988. *The Issei: The World of the First Generation Japanese Americans, 1885–1924.* New York: Free Press.

Ignacio, Lemuel F. 1976. *Asian Americans and Pacific Islanders (Is There Such an Ethnic Group?)* San Jose: Pilipino Development Associates.

Johanessen, Edward L. H. 1950. *The Labor Movement in the Territory of Hawaii.* M.A. thesis, University of California, Berkeley.

Kitano, Harry H. L., and Roger Daniels. 1988. *Asian Americans: Emerging Minorities.* Englewood Cliffs, N.J.: Prentice-Hall.

Kuo, Wen H. 1979. "On the Study of Asian-Americans: Its Current State and Agenda." *Sociological Quarterly* 20 (Spring): 279–290.

Ling, Susie Hsiuhan. 1984. "The Mountain Movers: Asian American Women's Movement in Los Angeles." M.A. thesis, University of California, Los Angeles.

———. 1989. "The Mountain Movers: Asian American Women's Movement in Los Angeles." *Amerasia Journal* 15 (1): 51–67.

Liu, William. 1976. "Asian American Research: Views of a Sociologist." *Asian Studies Occasional Report,* no. 2.

Lott, Juanita Tamayo. 1976. "The Asian American Concept: In Quest of Identity." *Bridge,* November, pp. 30–34.

Lowe, Lisa. 1991. "Heterogeneity, Hybridity, Multiplicity: Marking Asian American Differences." *Diaspora* 1: 24–44.

Lyman, Stanford M. 1970. *The Asian in the West.* Reno and Las Vegas: Desert Research Institute, University of Nevada.

Masada, Saburo. 1970. "Stockton's Yellow Seed." *Pacific Citizen,* 9 October.

Massey, Douglas S., and Nancy A. Denton. 1987. "Trends in the Residential Segregation of Blacks, Hispanics, and Asians, 1970–1980." *American Sociological Review* 52 (December): 802–825.

Matsui, Jeffrey. 1968. "Asian Americans." *Pacific Citizen,* 6 September.

Mears, Eliot Grinnell. 1928. *Resident Orientals on the American Pacific Coast.* New York: Arno Press.

Melendy, H. Brett. 1977. *Asians in America: Filipinos, Koreans, and East Indians.* Boston: Twayne.

Nakano, Roy. 1984. "Marxist Leninist Organization in the Asian American Community: Los Angeles, 1969–79." Unpublished student paper, UCLA

Nishio, Alan. 1982. "Personal Reflections on the Asian National Movements." *East Wind,* Spring/Summer, pp. 36-38

Omi, Michael, and Howard Winant. 1986. *Racial Formation in the United States: From the 1960s to the 1980s.* New York: Routledge and Kegan Paul.

Ong, Paul. 1989. "California's Asian Population: Past Trends and Projections for the Year 2000." Los Angeles: Graduate School of Architecture and Urban Planning.

Rabaya, Violet. 1971. "I Am Curious (Yellow?)." Pp. 110–111 in *Roots: An Asian American Reader,* edited by Amy Tachiki, Eddie Wong, and Franklin Odo. Los Angeles: UCLA Asian American Studies Center.

Sung, Betty Lee. 1967. *Mountain of Gold: The Story of the Chinese in America.* New York: Macmillan.

Takaki, Ronald. 1989. *Strangers from a Different Shore: A History of Asian Americans.* Boston: Little, Brown.

Tanaka, Ron. 1976. "Culture, Communication, and the Asian Movement in Perspective." *Journal of Ethnic Studies* 4 (1): 37–52.

tenBrock, J., E. N. Barnhart, and F. W. Matson. 1970. *Prejudice, War, and the Constitution.* Berkeley: University of California Press.

U.S. Commission on Civil Rights. 1986. *Recent Activities against Citizens and Residents of Asian Descent.* Washington, D.C.: U.S. Government Printing Office.

Uyematsu, Amy. 1971. "The Emergence of Yellow Power in America." Pp. 9–13 in *Roots: An Asian American Reader,* edited by Amy Tachiki, Eddie Wong, and Franklin Odo. Los Angeles: UCLA Asian American Studies Center.

Weiss, Melford S. 1974. *Valley City: A Chinese Community in America.* Cambridge, Mass.: Schenkman.

Woldemikael, Tekle Mariam. 1989. *Becoming Black Americans: Haitians and American Institutions in Evanston, Illinois.* New York: AMS Press.

Wong, Paul. 1972. "The Emergence of the Asian-American Movement." *Bridge* 2 (1): 33–39.

Yoshimura, Evelyn. 1989. "How I Became an Activist and What It All Means to Me." *Amerasia Journal* 15 (I): 106-109

Yuan, D. Y. 1966. "Chinatown and Beyond: The Chinese Population in Metropolitan New York." *Phylon* 23 (4): 321–332.

PERSONAL ACCOUNT

I Thought My Race Was Invisible

In a conversation with a close friend, I noticed that I am, to her, a representative of my entire racial category. To put things in perspective, my friend Janet and I have been friends for eight years. During this period, it has come up that I am a third-generation Japanese-American who has no ties to being Japanese other than a couple of sushi dishes I learned how to make from my grandmother. Nonetheless, whenever a question regarding "Asians" comes up, she comes to me as if I can provide the definitive answer to every Asian mystery.

Yesterday Janet asked me if there is a cultural reason why Asians "always drive so slow." Not having noticed that Asians drive slowly (in fact, I have noticed a number of Asians who actually exceed the speed limit), I commented that perhaps they are law-abiding citizens. She said that must explain it: "They are used to following the law." I thought, "Am I one of 'they'?" but didn't comment further. Before we switched subjects, she noted that she "knew there had to be a cultural reason" for their driving.

Janet then told me about a Vietnamese woman at the Hair Cuttery who cut her husband's hair. As is normal, her husband talked to the woman as she worked on his hair; he asked her what she did before working at the Hair Cuttery. She said that she used to work in the fields in California (i.e., she was a field hand). Janet told me of the healthy respect that she and her husband had for a woman who worked in the fields, put herself through cosmetology school, moved East,

and became a professional hair stylist. She commented that "Blacks" should follow her example and work instead of complaining of their lot in life.

This conversation was interesting and a bit startling. Janet is a good friend who shares many interests with me. What I realized from this conversation, and in remembering others that were similar, is that she feels that I am a representative of the whole Asian race. Not only is this unrealistic, but it is surprising that she would imagine I could answer for my race given my lack of real cultural exposure. In relaying the story of the Vietnamese woman, I had a sense that she was complimenting me, and my race, for the industriousness "we" demonstrate. It seems to me that she approved of the "typically" Asian way of working (quietly, so as not to insult or offend), even though this woman was probably underpaid and overworked in her field hand job. While she approved of her reticence, Janet did not approve of "Black" complaints.

I realize that to Janet, I will always be Asian. I had not really thought about it before, but I never think of Janet as White; her race is invisible to me. I had thought that my race was invisible too; however, I realize now that I will always be the "marked" friend. This saddens me a bit, but I accept it with the knowledge that she is a close friend. Nonetheless, it is unfortunate to think that even between friends, race is an issue.

Sherri H. Pereira

Whiteness as an "Unmarked" Cultural Category

Ruth Frankenberg

America's supposed to be the melting pot. I know that I've got a huge number of nationalities in my blood, but how do I—what do I call myself? And hating this country as I do, I don't like to say I'm an American. Even though it is what I am. I hate identifying myself as only an American, because I have so much objections to Americans' place in the world. I don't know how I felt about that when I was growing up, but I never—I didn't like to pledge allegiance to the flag. . . . Still, at this point in my life, I wonder what it is that somebody with all this melting pot blood can call their own. . . .

Especially growing up in the sixties, when people *did* say "I'm proud to be Black," "I'm proud to be Hispanic," you know, and it became very popular to be proud of your ethnicity. And even feminists, you know, you could say, "I'm a woman," and be proud of it. But there's still a majority of the country that can't say they are proud of anything!

Suzie Roberts's words powerfully illustrate the key themes . . . that stirred the women I interviewed as they examined their own identities: what had formed them, what they counted as (their own or others') cultural practice(s), and what constituted identities of which they could be proud.* This [discussion] explores perceptions of whiteness as a location of culture and identity, focusing mainly on white feminist . . . women's views and contrasting their voices with those of more politically conservative women. . . .

[M]any of the women I interviewed, including even some of the conservative ones, appeared to be self-conscious about white power and racial inequality. In part because of their sense of the

---

*Between 1984 and 1986 I interviewed 30 white women, diverse in age, class, region of origin, sexuality, family situation and political orientation, all living in California at the time of the interviews.

links and parallels between white racial dominance in the United States and U.S. domination on a global scale, there was a complex interweaving of questions about race and nation—whiteness and Americanness—in these women's thoughts about white culture. Similarly, conceptions of racial, national, and cultural belonging frequently leaked into one another.

On the one hand, then, these women's views of white culture seemed to be distinctively modern. But at the same time, their words drew on much earlier historical moments and participated in long-established modes of cultural description. In the broadest sense, Western colonial discourses on the white self, the nonwhite Other, and the white Other too, were very much in evidence. These discourses produced dualistic conceptualizations of whiteness versus other cultural forms. The women thus often spoke about culture in ways that reworked, and yet remained tied to, "older" forms of racism.

For a significant number of young white women, being white felt like being cultureless. Cathy Thomas, in the following description of whiteness, raised many of the themes alluded to by other feminist and race-cognizant women. She described what she saw as a lack of form and substance:

> . . . the formlessness of being white. Now if I was a middle western girl, or a New Yorker, if I had a fixed regional identity that was something palpable, then I'd be a white New Yorker, no doubt, but I'd still be a New Yorker. . . . Being a Californian, I'm sure it has its hallmarks, but to me they were invisible. . . . If I had an ethnic base to identify from, if I was even Irish American, that would have been something formed, if I was a working-class woman, that would have been something formed. But to be a Heinz 57 American, a white, class-confused American, land of the Kleenex type American, is so formless in and of itself. It only takes shape in relation to other people.

Whiteness as a cultural space is represented here as amorphous and indescribable, in contrast with a range of other identities marked by race, ethnicity, region, and class. Further, white culture is viewed here as "bad" culture. In fact, the extent to which identities can be named seems to show an inverse relationship to power in the U.S. social structure. The elisions, parallels, and differences between characterizations of white people, Americans, people of color, and so-called white ethnic groups will be explored [here] .

Cathy's own cultural positioning seemed to her impossible to grasp, shapeless and unnameable. It was easier to know others and to know, with certainty, what one was *not*. Providing a clue to one of the mechanisms operating here is the fact that, while Cathy viewed New Yorkers and midwesterners as having a cultural shape or identity, women from the East Coast and the Midwest also described or mourned their own seeming lack of culture. The self, where it is part of a dominant cultural group, does not have to name itself. In this regard, Chris Patterson hit the nail on the head, linking the power of white culture with the privilege not to be named:

I'm probably at the stage where I'm beginning to see that you can come up with a definition of white. Before, I didn't know that you could turn it around and say, "Well what *does* white mean?" One thing is, it's taken for granted. . . . [To be white means to] have some sort of advantage or privilege, even if it's something as simple as not having a definition.

The notion of "turning it around" indicates Chris's realization that, most often, whites are the nondefined definers of other people. Or, to put it another way, whiteness comes to be an unmarked or neutral category, whereas other cultures are specifically marked "cultural."

Many of the women shared the habit of turning to elements of white culture as the unspoken norm. This assumption of a white norm was so prevalent that even Sandy Alvarez and Louise Glebocki, who were acutely aware of racial inequality as well as being members of racially mixed families, referred to "Mexican" music versus "regular" music, and regular meant "white."

Similarly, discussions of race difference and cultural diversity at times revealed a view in which people of color actually embodied differ-ence and whites stood for sameness. Hence, Margaret Phillips said of her Jamaican daughter-in-law that: "She *really* comes with diversity." In spite of its brevity, and because of its curious structure, this short statement says a great deal. It implicitly designates whiteness as norm, and Jamaicans as having or bearing with them "differentness." At the risk of being crass, one might say that in this view, diversity is to the daughter-in-law as "the works" is to a hamburger—added on, adding color and flavor, but not exactly essential. Whiteness, seen by many of these women as boring, but nonetheless definitive, could also follow this analogy. This mode of thinking about "difference" expresses clearly the double-edged sword of a color- and power-evasive repertoire, apparently valorizing cultural difference but doing so in a way that leaves racial and cultural hierarchies intact.

For a seemingly formless entity, then, white culture had a great deal of power, difficult to dislodge from its place in white consciousness as a point of reference for the measuring of others. Whiteness served simultaneously to eclipse and marginalize others (two modes of making the other inessential). Helen Standish's description of her growing-up years in a small New England town captured these processes well. Since the community was all white, the differences at issue were differences between whites. (This also enables an assessment of the links between white and nonwhite "marked" cultures.) Asked about her own cultural identity, Helen explained that "it didn't seem like a culture because everyone else was the same." She had, however, previously mentioned Italian Americans in the town, so I asked about their status. She responded as follows, adopting at first the voice of childhood:

They are different, but I'm the same as everybody else. They speak Italian, but everybody else in the U.S. speaks English. They eat strange, different food, but I eat the same kind of food as everybody else in the U.S. . . . The way I was brought up was to think that everybody who was the same as me were "Americans," and the other people were of "such and such descent."

Viewing the Italian Americans as different and oneself as "same" serves, first, to marginalize, to push from the center, the former group. At the same time, claiming to be the same as *everyone* else makes other cultural groups invisible or eclipses them. Finally, there is a marginalizing of all those who are not like Helen's own family, leaving a residual, core or normative group who are the true Americans. The category of "American" represents simultaneously the normative and the residual, the dominant culture and a nonculture.

Although Helen talked here about whites, it is safe to guess that people of color would not have counted among the "same" group but among the communities of "such and such descent" (Mexican American, for example). Whites, within this discursive repertoire, became conceptually the real Americans, and only certain kinds of whites actually qualified. Whiteness and Americanness both stood as normative and exclusive categories in relation to which other cultures were identified and marginalized. And this clarifies that there are two kinds of whites, just as there are two kinds of Americans: those who are truly or only white, and those who are white but also something more—or is it something less?

In sum, whiteness often stood as an unmarked marker of others' differentness—whiteness not so much void or formlessness as norm. I associate this construction with colonialism and with the more recent assymetrical dualisms of liberal humanist views of culture, race, and identity. For the most part, this construction views nonwhite cultures as lesser, deviant, or pathological. However, another trajectory has been the inverse: conceptualizations of the cultures of peoples of color as somehow better than the dominant culture, perhaps more natural or more spiritual. These are positive evaluations of a sort, but they are equally dualistic. Many of the women I interviewed saw white culture as less appealing and found the cultures of the "different" people more interesting. As Helen Standish put it:

> [We had] Wonder bread, white bread. I'm more interested in, you know, "What's a bagel?" in other people's cultures rather than my own.

The claim that whiteness lacks form and content says more about the definitions of culture being used than it does about the content of whiteness. However, I would suggest that in describing themselves as cultureless these women are in fact identifying specific kinds of unwanted absences or presences in their own culture(s) as a generalized lack or nonexistence. It thus becomes important to look at what they *did* say about the cultural content of whiteness.

Descriptions of the content of white culture were thin, to say the least. But despite the paucity of signifiers, there was a great deal of consistency across the narratives. First, there was naming based on color, the linking of white culture with white objects—the clichéd white bread and mayonnaise, for example. Freida Kazen's identification of whiteness as "bland," together with Helen Standish's "blah," also signified paleness or neutrality. The images connote several things—color itself (although exaggerated, and besides, bagels are usually white inside, too), lack of vitality (Wonder bread is highly processed), and homogeneity. However, these images are perched on a slippery slope, at once suggesting "white" identified as a color (though an unappealing one) and as an absence of color, that is, white as the unmarked marker.

Whiteness was often signified in these narratives by commodities and brands: Wonder bread, Kleenex, Heinz 57. In this identification whiteness came to be seen as spoiled by capitalism, and as being linked with capitalism in a way that other cultures supposedly are not. Another set of signifiers that constructed whiteness as uniquely tainted by capitalism had to do with the "modern condition": Dot Humphrey described white neighborhoods as "more privatized," and Cathy Thomas used "alienated" to describe her cultural condition. Clare Traverso added to this theme, mourning her own feeling of lack of identity, in contrast with images of her husband's Italian American background (and here, Clare is again talking about perceived differences between whites):

> Food, old country, mama. Stories about a grandmother who can't speak English. . . . Candles,

adobe houses, arts, music. [It] has emotion, feeling, belongingness that to me is unique.

In linking whiteness to capitalism and viewing nonwhite cultures as untainted by it, these women were again drawing on a colonial discourse in which progress and industrialization were seen as synonymous with Westernization, while the rest of the world is seen as caught up in tradition and "culture." In addition, one can identify, in white women's mourning over whiteness, elements of what Raymond Williams has called "pastoralism," or nostalgia for a golden era now gone by (but in fact, says Williams, one that never existed).[1]

The image of whiteness as corrupted and impoverished by capitalism is but one of a series of ways in which white culture was seen as impure or tainted. White culture was also seen as tainted by its relationship to power. For example, Clare Traverso clearly counterposed white culture and white power, finding it difficult to value the former because of the overwhelming weight of the latter:

> The good things about whites are to do with folk arts, music. Because other things have power associated with them.

For many race-cognizant white women, white culture was also made impure by its very efforts to maintain race purity. Dot Humphrey, for example, characterized white neighborhoods as places in which people were segregated by choice. For her, this was a good reason to avoid living in them.

The link between whiteness and domination, however, was frequently made in ways that both artificially isolated culture from other factors and obscured economics. For at times, the traits the women envied in Other cultures were in fact at least in part the product of poverty or other dimensions of oppression. Lack of money, for example, often means lack of privacy or space, and it can be valorized as "more street life, less alienation." Cathy Thomas's notion of Chicanas' relationship to the kitchen ("the hearth of the home") as a cultural "good" might be an ideal-

ized one that disregards the reality of intensive labor.

Another link between class and culture emerged in Louise Glebocki's reference to the working-class Chicanos she met as a child as less pretentious, "closer to the truth," more "down to earth." And Marjorie Hoffman spoke of the "earthy humor" of Black people, which she interpreted as, in the words of Langston Hughes, a means of "laughing to keep from crying." On the one hand, as has been pointed out especially by Black scholars and activists, the positions of people of color at the bottom of a social and economic hierarchy create the potential for a critique of the system as a whole and consciousness of the need to resist.[2] From the standpoint of race privilege, the system of racism is thus made structurally invisible. On the other hand, descriptions of this kind leave in place a troubling dichotomy that can be appropriated as easily by the right as by the left. For example, there is an inadvertent affinity between the image of Black people as "earthy" and the conservative racist view that African American culture leaves African American people ill equipped for advancement in the modern age. Here, echoing essentialist racism, both Chicanos and African Americans are placed on the borders of "nature" and "culture."

By the same token, often what was criticized as "white" was as much the product of middle-class status as of whiteness as such. Louise Glebocki's image of her fate had she married a white man was an image of a white-collar, nuclear family:

> Him saying, 'I'm home, dear,' and me with an apron on—ugh!

The intersections of class, race, and culture were obscured in other ways. Patricia Bowen was angry with some of her white feminist friends who, she felt, embraced as "cultural" certain aspects of African American, Chicano, and Native American cultures (including, for example, artwork or dance performances) but would reject as "tacky" (her term) those aspects of daily life that communities of color shared with working-class whites, such as the stores and supermarkets of poor neighborhoods. This, she felt, was tantamount to a selective expansion of middle-class aesthetic horizons, but not to true antiracism or to comprehension of the cultures of people of color. Having herself grown up in a white working-class family, Pat also felt that middle-class white feminists were able to use selective engagement to avoid addressing their class privilege.

I have already indicated some of the problems inherent in this kind of conceptualization, suggesting that it tends to keep in place dichotomous constructions of "white" versus Other cultures, to separate "culture" from other dimensions of daily life, and to reify or strip of history *all* cultural forms. There are, then, a range of issues that need to be disentangled if we are to understand the location of "whiteness" in the terrain of culture. It is, I believe, useful to approach this question by means of a reconceptualization of the concept of culture itself. A culture, in the sense of the set of rules and practices by means of which a group organizes itself and its values, manners, and worldview—in other words, culture as "a field articulating the life-world of subjects . . . and the structures created by human activity"[3]—is an indispensable precondition to any individual's existence in the world. It is nonsensical in terms of this kind of definition to suggest that anyone could actually have "no culture." But this is not, as I have suggested, the mode of thinking about culture that these women are employing.

Whiteness emerges here as inextricably tied to domination partly as an effect of a discursive "draining process" applied to both whiteness and Americanness. In this process, any cultural practice engaged in by a white person that is not identical to the dominant culture is automatically counted as either "not really white"—and, for that matter, not really American, either—(but rather of such and such descent), or as "not really cultural" (but rather "economic"). There is a slipperiness to whiteness here: it shifts from "no culture" to "normal culture" to "bad culture" and back again. Simultaneously, a range of marginal or, in Trinh T. Minh-ha's terminology, "bounded" cultures are generated. These are viewed as envi-

able spaces, separate and untainted by relations of dominance or by linkage to other structures or systems. By contrast, whiteness is conceived as axiomatically tied to dominance, to economics, to political structures. In this process, both whiteness and nonwhiteness are reified, made into objects rather than processes, and robbed of historical context and human agency. As long as the discussion remains couched in these terms, a critique of whiteness remains a double-edged sword: for one thing, whiteness remains normative because there is no way to name the cultural practices associated with it *as* cultural. Moreover, as I have suggested, whether whiteness is viewed as artificial and dominating (and therefore "bad") or civilized (and therefore "good"), whiteness and all varieties of nonwhiteness continue to be viewed as ontologically different from one another.

A genuine sadness and frustration about the meaning of whiteness at this moment in history motivated these women to decry white culture. It becomes important, then, to recognize the grains of truth in their views of white culture. It is important to acknowledge their anger and frustration about the meaning of whiteness as we reach toward a politicized analysis of culture that is freer of colonial and pastoral legacies.

The terms "white" and "American" as these women used them signified domination in international and domestic terms. This link is both accurate and inaccurate. While it is true that, by and large, those in power in the United States are white, it is also true that not all those who are white are in power. Nor is the axiomatic linkage between Americanness and power accurate, because not all Americans have the same access to power. At the same time, the link between whiteness, Americanness, and power *are* accurate because, as we have seen, the terms "white" and "American" both function discursively to exclude people from normativity—including white people "of such and such descent." But here we need to distinguish between the fates of people of color and those of white people. Notwithstanding a complicated history, the boundaries of Americanness and whiteness have been much more fluid for "white ethnic" groups than for people of color.

There have been border skirmishes over the meaning of whiteness and Americanness since the inception of those terms. For white people, however, those skirmishes have been resolved through processes of assimilation, not exclusion. The late nineteenth and early twentieth centuries in the United States saw a systematic push toward the cultural homogenization of whites carried out through social reform movements and the schools. This push took place alongside the expansion of industrial capitalism, giving rise to the sense that whiteness signifies the production and consumption of commodities under capitalism.[4] But recognition of this history should not be translated into an assertion that whites were stripped of culture (for to do that would be to continue to adhere to a colonial view of "culture"). Instead one must argue that certain cultural practices replaced others. Were one to undertake a history of this "generic" white culture, it would fragment into a thousand tributary elements, culturally specific religious observances, and class survival mechanisms as well as mass-produced commodities and mass media.

There are a number of dangers inherent in continuing to view white culture as no culture. Whiteness appeared in the narratives to function as both norm or core, that against which everything else is measured, and as residue, that which is left after everything else has been named. A far-reaching danger of whiteness coded as "no culture" is that it leaves in place whiteness as defining a set of normative cultural practices against which all are measured and into which all are expected to fit. This normativity has underwritten oppression from the beginning of colonial expansion and has had impact in multiple ways: from the American pioneers' assumption of a norm of private property used to justify appropriation of land that within their worldview did not have an owner, and the ideological construction of nations like Britain as white,[5] to Western feminism's Eurocentric shaping of its movements and

institutions. It is important for white feminists not to continue to participate in these processes.

And if whiteness has a history, so do the cultures of people of color, which are worked on, crafted, and created, rather than just "there." For peoples of color in the United States, this work has gone on as much in the context of relationships to imperialism and capitalism as has the production of whiteness, though it has been premised on exclusion and resistance to exclusion more than on assimilation. Although not always or only forged in resistance, the visibility and recognition of the cultures of U.S. peoples of color in recent times *is* the product of individual and collective struggle. Only a short time has elapsed since those struggles made possible the introduction into public discourse of celebration and valorization of their cultural forms. In short, it is important not to reify any culture by failing to acknowledge its createdness, and not to view it as always having been there in unchanging form.

Rather than feeling "cultureless," white women need to become conscious of the histories and specificities of our cultural positions, and of the political, economic, and creative fusions that form all cultures. The purpose of such an exercise is not, of course, to reinvent the dualisms and valorize whiteness so much as to develop a clearer sense of where and who we are.

NOTES

1. Raymond Williams, *The Country and the City* (New York: Oxford University Press, 1978).
2. The classic statement of this position is W. E. B. Du Bois's concept of the "double consciousness" of Americans of African descent. Two recent feminist statements of similar positions are Patricia Hill Collins, *Black Feminist Thought: Knowledge, Consciousness, and the Politics of Empowerment* (Boston: Unwin Hyman, 1990); and Aida Hurtado, "Relating to Privilege: Seduction and Rejection in the Subordination of White Women and Women of Color," *Signs* 14, no. 4:833–55.
3. Paul Gilroy, *There Ain't No Black In The Union Jack.* London: Hutchinson, 1987.

4. See, for example, Winthrop Talbot, ed., *American-ization* (New York: H. W. Wilson, 1917), esp. Sophonisba P. Breckinridge, "The Immigrant Family," 251–52; Olivia Howard Dunbar, "Teaching the Immigrant Woman," 252–56, and North American Civic League for Immigrants, "Domestic Education among Immigrants," 256–58; and Kathie Friedman Kasaba, " 'To Become a Person': The Experience of Gender, Ethnicity and Work in the Lives of Immigrant Women, New York City, 1870–1940," doctoral dissertation. Department of Sociology, State University of New York, Binghamton, 1991. I am indebted to Katie Friedman Kasaba for these references and for her discussions with me about working-class European immigrants to the United States at the turn of this century.

5. Gilroy, *There Ain't No Black In The Union Jack.*

What Is Sex? What Is Gender?

The Five Sexes

Why Male and Female Are Not Enough

Anne Fausto-Sterling

In 1843 Levi Suydam, a twenty-three-year-old resident of Salisbury, Connecticut, asked the town board of selectmen to validate his right to vote as a Whig in a hotly contested local election. The request raised a flurry of objections from the opposition party, for reasons that must be rare in the annals of American democracy: it was said that Suydam was more female than male and thus (some eighty years before suffrage was extended to women) could not be allowed to cast a ballot. To settle the dispute a physician, one William James Barry, was brought in to examine Suydam. And, presumably upon encountering a phallus, the good doctor declared the prospective voter male. With Suydam safely in their column the Whigs won the election by a majority of one.

Barry's diagnosis, however, turned out to be somewhat premature. Within a few days he discovered that, phallus notwithstanding, Suydam menstruated regularly and had a vaginal opening. Both his/her physique and his/her mental predispositions were more complex than was first suspected. S/he had narrow shoulders and broad hips and felt occasional sexual yearnings for women. Suydam's "feminine propensities, such as a fond-ness for gay colors, for pieces of calico, comparing and placing them together, and an aversion for bodily labor, and an inability to perform the same, were remarked by many," Barry later wrote. It is not clear whether Suydam lost or retained the vote, or whether the election results were reversed.

Western culture is deeply committed to the idea that there are only two sexes. Even language refuses other possibilities; thus to write about Levi Suydam I have had to invent conventions— s/he and his/her—to denote someone who is clearly neither male nor female or who is perhaps both sexes at once. Legally, too, every adult is either man or woman, and the difference, of course, is not trivial. For Suydam it meant the franchise; today it means being available for, or exempt from, draft registration, as well as being subject, in various ways, to a number of laws governing marriage, the family and human intimacy. In many parts of the United States, for instance, two people legally registered as men cannot have sexual relations without violating anti-sodomy statutes.

But if the state and the legal system have an interest in maintaining a two-party sexual system, they are in defiance of nature. For biologically speaking, there are many gradations running from female to male; and depending on how one calls the shots, one can argue that along that spectrum lie at least five sexes—and perhaps even more.

For some time medical investigators have recognized the concept of the intersexual body. But the standard medical literature uses the term *intersex* as a catch-all for three major subgroups with some mixture of male and female characteristics: the so-called true hermaphrodites, whom I call herms, who possess one testis and one ovary (the sperm- and egg-producing vessels, or gonads); the male pseudohermaphrodites (the "merms"), who have testes and some aspects of the female genitalia but no ovaries; and the female pseudohermaphrodites (the "ferms"), who have ovaries and some aspects of the male genitalia but lack testes. Each of those categories is in itself complex; the percentage of male and female characteristics, for instance, can vary enormously among members of the same subgroup. Moreover, the inner lives of the people in each subgroup—their special needs and their problems, attractions and repulsions—have gone unexplored by science. But on the basis of what is known about them I suggest that the three intersexes, herm, merm and ferm, deserve to be considered additional sexes each in its own right. Indeed, I would argue further that sex is a vast, infinitely malleable continuum that defies the constraints of even five categories.

Not surprisingly, it is extremely difficult to estimate the frequency of intersexuality, much less the frequency of each of the three additional sexes: it is not the sort of information one volunteers on a job application. The psychologist John Money of Johns Hopkins University, a specialist in the study of congenital sexual-organ defects, suggests intersexuals may constitute as many as 4 percent of births. As I point out to my students at Brown University, in a student body of about 6,000 that fraction, if correct, implies there may be as many as 240 intersexuals on campus—surely enough to form a minority caucus of some kind.

In reality though, few such students would make it as far as Brown in sexually diverse form. Recent advances in physiology and surgical technology now enable physicians to catch most intersexuals at the moment of birth. Almost at once such infants are entered into a program of hormonal and surgical management so that they can slip quietly into society as "normal" heterosexual males or females. I emphasize that the motive is in no way conspiratorial. The aims of the policy are genuinely humanitarian, reflecting the wish that people be able to "fit in" both physically and psychologically. In the medical community, however, the assumptions behind that wish—that there be only two sexes, that heterosexuality alone is normal, that there is one true model of psychological health—have gone virtually unexamined.

The word *hermaphrodite* comes from the Greek names Hermes, variously known as the messenger of the gods, the patron of music, the controller of dreams or the protector of livestock, and Aphrodite, the goddess of sexual love and beauty. According to Greek mythology, those two gods parented Hermaphroditus, who at age fifteen became half male and half female when his body fused with the body of a nymph he fell in love with. In some true hermaphrodites the testis and the ovary grow separately but bilaterally; in others they grow together within the same organ, forming an ovo-testis. Not infrequently, at least one of the gonads functions quite well, producing either sperm cells or eggs, as well as functional levels of the sex hormones—androgens or estrogens. Although in theory it might be possible for a true hermaphrodite to become both father and mother to a child, in practice the appropriate ducts and tubes are not configured so that egg and sperm can meet.

In contrast with the true hermaphrodites, the pseudohermaphrodites possess two gonads of the same kind along with the usual male (XY) or female (XX) chromosomal makeup. But their external genitalia and secondary sex characteristics do not match their chromosomes. Thus merms have testes and XY chromosomes, yet they also have a vagina and a clitoris, and at puberty they often develop breasts. They do not menstruate, however. Ferms have ovaries, two X chromosomes and sometimes a uterus, but they also have at least partly masculine external genitalia. Without medical intervention they can develop beards, deep voices and adult-size penises. . . .

Intersexuality itself is old news. Hermaphrodites, for instance, are often featured in stories about human origins. Early biblical scholars believed Adam began life as a hermaphrodite and later divided into two people—a male and a female—after falling from grace. According to Plato there once were three sexes—male, female and hermaphrodite—but the third sex was lost with time.

Both the Talmud and the Tosefta, the Jewish books of law, list extensive regulations for people of mixed sex. The Tosefta expressly forbids hermaphrodites to inherit their fathers' estates (like daughters), to seclude themselves with women (like sons) or to shave (like men). When hermaphrodites menstruate they must be isolated from men (like women); they are disqualified from serving as witnesses or as priests (like women), but the laws of pederasty apply to them.

In Europe a pattern emerged by the end of the Middle Ages that, in a sense, has lasted to the present day: hermaphrodites were compelled to choose an established gender role and stick with it. The penalty for transgression was often death. Thus in the 1600s a Scottish hermaphrodite living as a woman was buried alive after impregnating his/her master's daughter.

For questions of inheritance, legitimacy, paternity, succession to title and eligibility for certain professions to be determined, modern Anglo-Saxon legal systems require that newborns be registered as either male or female. In the U.S. today sex determination is governed by state laws. Illinois permits adults to change the sex recorded on their birth certificates should a physician attest to having performed the appropriate surgery. The New York Academy of Medicine, on the other hand, has taken an opposite view. In spite of surgical alterations of the external genitalia, the academy argued in 1966, the chromosomal sex remains the same. By that measure, a person's wish to conceal his or her original sex cannot outweigh the public interest in protection against fraud.

During this century the medical community has completed what the legal world began—the complete erasure of any form of embodied sex that does not conform to a male–female, heterosexual pattern. Ironically, a more sophisticated knowledge of the complexity of sexual systems has led to the repression of such intricacy.

In 1937 the urologist Hugh H. Young of Johns Hopkins University published a volume titled *Genital Abnormalities, Hermaphroditism and Related Adrenal Diseases.* The book is remarkable for its erudition, scientific insight and open-mindedness. In it Young drew together a wealth of carefully documented case histories to demonstrate and study the medical treatment of such "accidents of birth." Young did not pass judgment on the people he studied, nor did he attempt to coerce into treatment those intersexuals who rejected that option. And he showed unusual even-handedness in referring to those people who had had sexual experiences as both men and women as "practicing hermaphrodites."

One of Young's more interesting cases was a hermaphrodite named Emma who had grown up as a female. Emma had both a penis-size clitoris and a vagina, which made it possible for him/her to have "normal" heterosexual sex with both men and women. As a teenager Emma had had sex with a number of girls to whom s/he was deeply attracted; but at the age of nineteen s/he had married a man. Unfortunately, he had given Emma little sexual pleasure (though *he* had had no complaints), and so throughout that marriage and subsequent ones Emma had kept girlfriends on the side. With some frequency s/he had pleasurable sex with them. Young describes his subject as appearing "to be quite content and even happy." In conversation Emma occasionally told him of his/her wish to be a man, a circumstance Young said would be relatively easy to bring about. But Emma's reply strikes a heroic blow for self-interest:

> Would you have to remove that vagina? I don't know about that because that's my meal ticket. If you did that, I would have to quit my husband and go to work, so I think I'll keep it and stay as I am. My husband supports me well, and even though I

don't have any sexual pleasure with him, I do have lots with my girlfriends.

Yet even as Young was illuminating intersexuality with the light of scientific reason, he was beginning its suppression. For his book is also an extended treatise on the most modern surgical and hormonal methods of changing intersexuals into either males or females. Young may have differed from his successors in being less judgmental and controlling of the patients and their families, but he nonetheless supplied the foundation on which current intervention practices were built.

By 1969, when the English physicians Christopher J. Dewhurst and Ronald R. Gordon wrote *The Intersexual Disorders,* medical and surgical approaches to intersexuality had neared a state of rigid uniformity. It is hardly surprising that such a hardening of opinion took place in the era of the feminine mystique—of the post-Second World War flight to the suburbs and the strict division of family roles according to sex. That the medical consensus was not quite universal (or perhaps that it seemed poised to break apart again) can be gleaned from the near-hysterical tone of Dewhurst and Gordon's book, which contrasts markedly with the calm reason of Young's founding work. Consider their opening description of an intersexual newborn:

> One can only attempt to imagine the anguish of the parents. That a newborn should have a deformity . . . [affecting] so fundamental an issue as the very sex of the child . . . is a tragic event which immediately conjures up visions of a hopeless psychological misfit doomed to live always as a sexual freak in loneliness and frustration.

Dewhurst and Gordon warned that such a miserable fate would, indeed, be a baby's lot should the case be improperly managed; "but fortunately," they wrote, "with correct management the outlook is infinitely better than the poor parents—emotionally stunned by the event—or indeed anyone without special knowledge could ever imagine."

Scientific dogma has held fast to the assumption that without medical care hermaphrodites are doomed to a life of misery. Yet there are few empirical studies to back up that assumption, and some of the same research gathered to build a case for medical treatment contradicts it. Francies Benton, another of Young's practicing hermaphrodites, "had not worried over his condition, did not wish to be changed, and was enjoying life." The same could be said of Emma, the opportunistic hausfrau. Even Dewhurst and Gordon, adamant about the psychological importance of treating intersexuals at the infant stage, acknowledged great success in "changing the sex" of older patients. They reported on twenty cases of children reclassified into a different sex after the supposedly critical age of eighteen months. They asserted that all the reclassifications were "successful," and they wondered then whether reregistration could be "recommended more readily than [had] been suggested so far."

The treatment of intersexuality in this century provides a clear example of what the French historian Michel Foucault has called biopower. The knowledge developed in biochemistry, embryology, endocrinology, psychology and surgery has enabled physicians to control the very sex of the human body. The multiple contradictions in that kind of power call for some scrutiny. On the one hand, the medical "management" of intersexuality certainly developed as part of an attempt to free people from perceived psychological pain (though whether the pain was the patient's, the parents' or the physician's is unclear). And if one accepts the assumption that in a sex-divided culture people can realize their greatest potential for happiness and productivity only if they are sure they belong to one of only two acknowledged sexes, modern medicine has been extremely successful.

On the other hand, the same medical accomplishments can be read not as progress but as a mode of discipline. Hermaphrodites have unruly bodies. They do not fall naturally into a binary classification; only a surgical shoehorn can put them there. But why should we care if a "woman," defined as one who has breasts, a vagina, a uterus and ovaries and who menstruates, also has a clitoris large enough to penetrate the vagina of another woman? Why should we care if there are people whose biological equipment enables them to have sex "naturally" with both men and women? The answers seem to lie in a cultural need to maintain clear distinctions between the sexes. Society mandates the control of intersexual bodies because they blur and bridge the great divide. Inasmuch as hermaphrodites literally embody both sexes, they challenge traditional beliefs about sexual difference: they possess the irritating ability to live sometimes as one sex and sometimes the other, and they raise the specter of homosexuality.

But what if things were altogether different? Imagine a world in which the same knowledge that has enabled medicine to intervene in the management of intersexual patients has been placed at the service of multiple sexualities. Imagine that the sexes have multiplied beyond currently imaginable limits. It would have to be a world of shared powers. Patient and physician, parent and child, male and female, heterosexual and homosexual—all those oppositions and others would have to be dissolved as sources of division. A new ethic of medical treatment would arise, one that would permit ambiguity in a culture that had overcome sexual division. The central mission of medical treatment would be to preserve life. Thus hermaphrodites would be concerned primarily not about whether they can conform to society but about whether they might develop potentially life-threatening conditions—hernias, gonadal tumors, salt imbalance caused by adrenal malfunction—that sometimes accompany hermaphroditic development. In my ideal world medical intervention for intersexuals would take place only rarely before the age of reason; subsequent treatment would be a cooperative venture between physician, patient and other advisers trained in issues of gender multiplicity.

I do not pretend that the transition to my utopia would be smooth. Sex, even the supposedly "normal," heterosexual kind, continues to cause untold anxieties in Western society. And certainly a culture that has yet to come to grips—religiously and, in some states, legally—with the

ancient and relatively uncomplicated reality of homosexual love will not readily embrace intersexuality. No doubt the most troublesome arena by far would be the rearing of children. Parents, at least since the Victorian era, have fretted, sometimes to the point of outright denial, over the fact that their children are sexual beings.

All that and more amply explains why intersexual children are generally squeezed into one of the two prevailing sexual categories. But what would be the psychological consequences of taking the alternative road—raising children as unabashed intersexuals? On the surface that tack seems fraught with peril. What, for example, would happen to the intersexual child amid the unrelenting cruelty of the school yard? When the time came to shower in gym class, what horrors and humiliations would await the intersexual as his/her anatomy was displayed in all its nontraditional glory? In whose gym class would s/he register to begin with? What bathroom would s/he use? And how on earth would Mom and Dad help shepherd him/her through the mine field of puberty?

In the past thirty years those questions have been ignored, as the scientific community has, with remarkable unanimity, avoided contemplating the alternative route of unimpeded intersexuality. But modern investigators tend to overlook a substantial body of case histories, most of them compiled between 1930 and 1960, before surgical intervention became rampant. Almost without exception, those reports describe children who grew up knowing they were intersexual (though they did not advertise it) and adjusted to their unusual status. Some of the studies are richly detailed—described at the level of gym-class showering (which most intersexuals avoided without incident); in any event, there is not a psychotic or a suicide in the lot.

Still, the nuances of socialization among intersexuals cry out for more sophisticated analysis. Clearly, before my vision of sexual multiplicity can be realized, the first openly intersexual children and their parents will have to be brave pioneers who will bear the brunt of society's growing pains. But in the long view—though it could take generations to achieve—the prize might be a society in which sexuality is something to be celebrated for its subtleties and not something to be feared or ridiculed.

READING 6

The Berdache Tradition

Walter L. Williams

Because it is such a powerful force in the world today, the Western Judeo-Christian tradition is often accepted as the arbiter of "natural" behavior of humans. If Europeans and their descendant nations of North America accept something as normal, then anything different is seen as abnormal. Such a view ignores the great diversity of human existence.

This is the case for the study of gender. How many genders are there? To a modern Anglo-American, nothing might seem more definite than the answer that there are two: men and women. But not all societies around the world agree with Western culture's view that all humans are either women or men. The commonly accepted notion of "the opposite sex," based on anatomy, is itself an artifact of our society's rigid sex roles.

Among many cultures, there have existed different alternatives to "man" or "woman." An alternative role in many American Indian societies is referred to by anthropologists as *berdache*. . . . The role varied from one Native American culture to another, which is a reflection of the vast diversity of aboriginal New World societies. Small bands of hunter-gatherers existed in some areas, with advanced civilizations of farming peoples in other areas. With hundreds of different languages, economies, religions, and social patterns existing in North America alone, every generalization about a cultural tradition must acknowledge many exceptions.

This diversity is true for the berdache tradition as well, and must be kept in mind. My statements should be read as being specific to a particular culture, with generalizations being treated as loose patterns that might not apply to peoples even in nearby areas.

Briefly, a berdache can be defined as a morphological male who does not fill a society's standard man's role, who has a nonmasculine character. This type of person is often stereotyped as effeminate, but a more accurate characterization is androgyny. Such a person has a clearly recognized and accepted social status, often based on a secure place in the tribal mythology. Berdaches have special ceremonial roles in many Native American religions, and important economic roles in their families. They will do at least some women's work, and mix together much of the behavior, dress, and social roles of women and men. Berdaches gain social prestige by their spiritual, intellectual, or craftwork/artistic contributions, and by their reputation for hard work and generosity. They serve a mediating function between women and men, precisely because their character is seen as distinct from either sex. They are not seen as men, yet they are not seen as women either. They occupy an alternative gender role that is a mixture of diverse elements.

In their erotic behavior berdaches also generally (but not always) take a nonmasculine role, either being asexual or becoming the passive partner in sex with men. In some cultures the berdache might become a wife to a man. This male-male sexual behavior became the focus of an attack on berdaches as "sodomites" by the Europeans who, early on, came into contact with them. From the first Spanish conquistadors to the Western frontiersmen and the Christian missionaries and government officials, Western culture has had a considerable impact on the berdache tradition. In the last two decades, the most recent impact on the tradition is the adaptation of a modern Western gay identity.

To Western eyes berdachism is a compl puzzling phenomenon, mixing and rede very concepts of what is considere female. In a culture with only t genders, such individuals are formist, abnormal, deviant. Bu ans, the institution of another gender role means that berdaches are not deviant—indeed, they do conform to the requirements of a custom in which their culture tells them they fit. Berdachism is a way for society to recognize and assimilate some atypical individuals without imposing a change on them or stigmatizing them as deviant. This cultural institution confirms their legitimacy for what they are.

Societies often bestow power upon that which does not neatly fit into the usual. Since no cultural system can explain everything, a common way that many cultures deal with these inconsistencies is to imbue them with negative power, as taboo, pollution, witchcraft, or sin. That which is not understood is seen as a threat. But an alternative method of dealing with such things, or people, is to take them out of the realm of threat and to sanctify them.[1] The berdaches' role as mediator is thus not just between women and men, but also between the physical and the spiritual. American Indian cultures have taken what Western culture calls negative, and made it a positive; they have successfully utilized the different skills and insights of a class of people that Western culture has stigmatized and whose spiritual powers have been wasted.

Many Native Americans also understood that gender roles have to do with more than just biological sex. The standard Western view that one's sex is always a certainty, and that one's gender identity and sex role always conform to one's morphological sex is a view that dies hard. Western thought is typified by such dichotomies of groups perceived to be mutually exclusive: male and female, black and white, right and wrong, good and evil. Clearly, the world is not so simple; such clear divisions are not always realistic. Most American Indian worldviews generally are much more accepting of the ambiguities of life. Acceptance of gender variation in the berdache tradition is typical of many native cultures' approach to life in general.

Overall, these are generalizations based on those Native American societies that had an accepted role for berdaches. Not all cultures rec-

ognized such a respected status. Berdachism in aboriginal North America was most established among tribes in four areas: first, the Prairie and western Great Lakes, the northern and central Great Plains, and the lower Mississippi Valley; second, Florida and the Caribbean; third, the Southwest, the Great Basin, and California; and fourth, scattered areas of the Northwest, western Canada, and Alaska. For some reason it is not noticeable in eastern North America, with the exception of its southern rim. . . .

AMERICAN INDIAN RELIGIONS

Native American religions offered an explanation for human diversity by their creation stories. In some tribal religions, the Great Spiritual Being is conceived as neither male nor female but as a combination of both. Among the Kamia of the Southwest, for example, the bearer of plant seeds and the introducer of Kamia culture was a man-woman spirit named Warharmi.[2] A key episode of the Zuni creation story involves a battle between the kachina spirits of the agricultural Zunis and the enemy hunter spirits. Every four years an elaborate ceremony commemorates this myth. In the story a kachina spirit called *ko'lhamana* was captured by the enemy spirits and transformed in the process. This transformed spirit became a mediator between the two sides, using his peace-making skills to merge the differing lifestyles of hunters and farmers. In the ceremony, a dramatic reenactment of the myth, the part of the transformed *ko'lhamana* spirit, is performed by a berdache.[3] The Zuni word for berdache is *lhamana,* denoting its closeness to the spiritual mediator who brought hunting and farming together.[4] The moral of this story is that the berdache was created by the deities for a special purpose, and that this creation led to the improvement of society. The continual reenactment of this story provides a justification for the Zuni berdache in each generation.

In contrast to this, the lack of spiritual justification in a creation myth could denote a lack of tolerance for gender variation. The Pimas, unlike most of their Southwestern neighbors, did not respect a berdache status. *Wi-kovat,* their derogatory word, means "like a girl," but it does not signify a recognized social role. Pima mythology reflects this lack of acceptance, in a folk tale that explains male androgyny as due to Papago witchcraft. Knowing that the Papagos respected berdaches, the Pimas blamed such an occurrence on an alien influence.[5] While the Pimas' condemnatory attitude is unusual, it does point out the importance of spiritual explanations for the acceptance of gender variance in a culture.

Other Native American creation stories stand in sharp contrast to the Pima explanation. A good example is the account of the Navajos, which presents women and men as equals. The Navajo origin tale is told as a story of five worlds. The first people were First Man and First Woman, who were created equally and at the same time. The first two worlds that they lived in were bleak and unhappy, so they escaped to the third world. In the third world lived two twins, Turquoise Boy and White Shell Girl, who were the first berdaches. In the Navajo language the word for berdache is *nadle,* which means "changing one" or "one who is transformed." It is applied to hermaphrodites—those who are born with the genitals of both male and female—and also to "those who pretend to be *nadle,*" who take on a social role that is distinct from either men or women.[6]

In the third world, First Man and First Woman began farming, with the help of the changing twins. One of the twins noticed some clay and, holding it in the palm of his/her hand, shaped it into the first pottery bowl. Then he/she formed a plate, a water dipper, and a pipe. The second twin observed some reeds and began to weave them, making the first basket. Together they shaped axes and grinding stones from rocks, and hoes from bone. All these new inventions made the people very happy.[7]

The message of this story is that humans are dependent for many good things on the inventiveness of *nadle.* Such individuals were present from the earliest eras of human existence, and their presence was never questioned. They were part of

the natural order of the universe, with a special contribution to make.

Later on in the Navajo creation story, White Shell Girl entered the moon and became the Moon Bearer. Turquoise Boy, however, remained with the people. When First Man realized that Turquoise Boy could do all manner of women's work as well as women, all the men left the women and crossed a big river. The men hunted and planted crops. Turquoise Boy ground the corn, cooked the food, and weaved cloth for the men. Four years passed with the women and men separated, and the men were happy with the *nadle.* Later, however, the women wanted to learn how to grind corn from the *nadle,* and both the men and the women had decided that it was not good to continue living separately. So the women crossed the river and the people were reunited.[8]

They continued living happily in the third world, until one day a great flood began. The people ran to the highest mountaintop, but the water kept rising and they all feared they would be drowned. But just in time, the ever-inventive Turquoise Boy found a large reed. They climbed upward inside the tall hollow reed, and came out at the top into the fourth world. From there, White Shell Girl brought another reed, and they climbed again to the fifth world, which is the present world of the Navajos.[9]

These stories suggest that the very survival of humanity is dependent on the inventiveness of berdaches. With such a mythological belief system, it is no wonder that the Navajos held *nadle* in high regard. The concept of the *nadle* is well formulated in the creation story. As children were educated by these stories, and all Navajos believed in them, the high status accorded to gender variation was passed down from generation to generation. Such stories also provided instructions for *nadle* themselves to live by. A spiritual explanation guaranteed a special place for a person who was considered different but not deviant.

For American Indians, the important explanations of the world are spiritual ones. In their view, there is a deeper reality than the here-and-now. The real essence or wisdom occurs when one finally gives up trying to explain events in terms of "logic" and "reality." Many confusing aspects of existence can better be explained by actions of a multiplicity of spirits. Instead of a concept of a single god, there is an awareness of "that which we do not understand." In Lakota religion, for example, the term *Wakan Tanka* is often translated as "god." But a more proper translation, according to the medicine people who taught me, is "The Great Mystery."[10]

While rationality can explain much, there are limits to human capabilities of understanding. The English language is structured to account for cause and effect. For example, English speakers say, "It is raining," with the implication that there is a cause "it" that leads to rain. Many Indian languages, on the other hand, merely note what is most accurately translated as "raining" as an observable fact. Such an approach brings a freedom to stop worrying about causes of things, and merely to relax and accept that our human insights can go only so far. By not taking ourselves too seriously, or overinflating human importance, we can get beyond the logical world.

The emphasis of American Indian religions, then, is on the spiritual nature of all things. To understand the physical world, one must appreciate the underlying spiritual essence. Then one can begin to see that the physical is only a faint shadow, a partial reflection, of a supernatural and extrarational world. By the Indian view, everything that exists is spiritual. Every object—plants, rocks, water, air, the moon, animals, humans, the earth itself—has a spirit. The spirit of one thing (including a human) is not superior to the spirit of any other. Such a view promotes a sophisticated ecological awareness of the place that humans have in the larger environment. The function of religion is not to try to condemn or to change what exists, but to accept the realities of the world and to appreciate their contributions to life. Everything that exists has a purpose.[11]

One of the basic tenets of American Indian religion is the notion that everything in the universe is related. Nevertheless, things that exist are often seen as having a counterpart: sky and earth,

plant and animal, water and fire. In all of these polarities, there exist mediators. The role of the mediator is to hold the polarities together, to keep the world from disintegrating. Polarities exist within human society also. The most important category within Indian society is gender. The notions of Woman and Man underlie much of social interaction and are comparable to the other major polarities. Women, with their nurturant qualities, are associated with the earth, while men are associated with the sky. Women gatherers and farmers deal with plants (of the earth), while men hunters deal with animals.

The mediator between the polarities of woman and man, in the American Indian religious explanation, is a being that combines the elements of both genders. This might be a combination in a physical sense, as in the case of hermaphrodites. Many Native American religions accept this phenomenon in the same way that they accept other variations from the norm. But more important is their acceptance of the idea that gender can be combined in ways other than physical hermaphroditism. The physical aspects of a thing or a person, after all, are not nearly as important as its spirit. American Indians use the concept of a person's *spirit* in the way that other Americans use the concept of a person's *character*. Consequently, physical hermaphroditism is not necessary for the idea of gender mixing. A person's character, their spiritual essence, is the crucial thing.

THE BERDACHE'S SPIRIT

Individuals who are physically normal might have the spirit of the other sex, might range somewhere between the two sexes, or might have a spirit that is distinct from either women or men. Whatever category they fall into, they are seen as being different from men. They are accepted spiritually as "Not Man." Whichever option is chosen, Indian religions offer spiritual explanations. Among the Arapahos of the Plains, berdaches are called *haxu'xan* and are seen to be that way as a result of a supernatural gift from birds or animals. Arapaho mythology recounts the story of Nih'a'ca, the first *haxu'xan.* He pretended to be a woman and married the mountain lion, a symbol for masculinity. The myth, as recorded by ethnographer Alfred Kroeber about 1900, recounted that "These people had the natural desire to become women, and as they grew up gradually became women. They gave up the desires of men. They were married to men. They had miraculous power and could do supernatural things. For instance, it was one of them that first made an intoxicant from rainwater."[12] Besides the theme of inventiveness, similar to the Navajo creation story, the berdache role is seen as a product of a "natural desire." Berdaches "gradually became women," which underscores the notion of woman as a social category rather than as a fixed biological entity. Physical biological sex is less important in gender classification than a person's desire—one's spirit.

The myths contain no prescriptions for trying to change berdaches who are acting out their desires of the heart. Like many other cultures' myths, the Zuni origin myths simply sanction the idea that gender can be transformed independently of biological sex.[13] Indeed, myths warn of dire consequences when interference with such a transformation is attempted. Prince Alexander Maximilian of the German state of Wied, traveling in the northern Plains in the 1830s, heard a myth about a warrior who once tried to force a berdache to avoid women's clothing. The berdache resisted, and the warrior shot him with an arrow. Immediately the berdache disappeared, and the warrior saw only a pile of stones with his arrow in them. Since then, the story concluded, no intelligent person would try to coerce a berdache.[14] Making the point even more directly, a Mandan myth told of an Indian who tried to force *mihdacke* (berdaches) to give up their distinctive dress and status, which led the spirits to punish many people with death. After that, no Mandans interfered with berdaches.[15]

With this kind of attitude, reinforced by myth and history, the aboriginal view accepts human diversity. The creation story of the Mohave of the Colorado River Valley speaks of a time when people were not sexually differentiated. From this perspective, it is easy to accept that certain individuals might combine elements of masculinity and femininity.[16] A respected Mohave elder, speaking in the 1930s, stated this viewpoint simply: "From the very beginning of the world it was meant that there should be [berdaches], just as it was instituted that there should be shamans. They were intended for that purpose."[17]

This elder also explained that a child's tendencies to become a berdache are apparent early, by about age nine to twelve, before the child reaches puberty: "That is the time when young persons become initiated into the functions of their sex. . . . None but young people will become berdaches as a rule."[18] Many tribes have a public ceremony that acknowledges the acceptance of berdache status. A Mohave shaman related the ceremony for his tribe: "When the child was about ten years old his relatives would begin discussing his strange ways. Some of them disliked it, but the more intelligent began envisaging an initiation ceremony." The relatives prepare for the ceremony without letting the boy know of it. It is meant to take him by surprise, to be both an initiation and a test of his true inclinations. People from various settlements are invited to attend. The family wants the community to see it and become accustomed to accepting the boy as an *alyha.*

On the day of the ceremony, the shaman explained, the boy is led into a circle: "If the boy showed a willingness to remain standing in the circle, exposed to the public eye, it was almost certain that he would go through with the ceremony. The singer, hidden behind the crowd, began singing the songs. As soon as the sound reached the boy he began to dance as women do." If the boy is unwilling to assume *alyha* status, he would refuse to dance. But if his character—his spirit—is *alyha,* "the song goes right to his heart and he will dance with much intensity. He cannot help it. After the fourth song he is proclaimed." After the ceremony, the boy is carefully bathed and receives a woman's skirt. He is then led back to the dance ground, dressed as an *alyha,* and announces his new feminine name to the crowd. After that he would resent being called by his old male name.[19]

Among the Yuman tribes of the Southwest, the transformation is marked by a social gathering, in which the berdache prepares a meal for the friends of the family.[20] Ethnographer Ruth Underhill, doing fieldwork among the Papago Indians in the early 1930s, wrote that berdaches were common among the Papago Indians, and were usually publicly acknowledged in childhood. She recounted that a boy's parents would test him if they noticed that he preferred female pursuits. The regular pattern, mentioned by many of Underhill's Papago informants, was to build a small brush enclosure. Inside the enclosure they placed a man's bow and arrows, and also a woman's basket. At the appointed time the boy was brought to the enclosure as the adults watched from outside. The boy was told to go inside the circle of brush. Once he was inside, the adults "set fire to the enclosure. They watched what he took with him as he ran out and if it was the basketry materials, they reconciled themselves to his being a berdache."[21]

What is important to recognize in all of these practices is that the assumption of a berdache role was not forced on the boy by others. While adults might have their suspicions, it was only when the child made the proper move that he was considered a berdache. By doing woman's dancing, preparing a meal, or taking the woman's basket he was making an important symbolic gesture. Indian children were not stupid, and they knew the implications of these ceremonies beforehand. A boy in the enclosure could have left without taking anything, or could have taken both the man's and the woman's tools. With the community standing by watching, he was well aware that his choice would mark his assumption of berdache status. Rather than being seen as an involuntary test of his reflexes, this ceremony may be interpreted as a definite statement by the child to take on the berdache role.

Indians do not see the assumption of berdache status, however, as a free will choice on the part of the boy. People felt that the boy was acting out his basic character. The Lakota shaman Lame Deer explained:

> They were not like other men, but the Great Spirit made them *winktes* and we accepted them as such. . . . We think that if a woman has two little ones growing inside her, if she is going to have twins, sometimes instead of giving birth to two babies they have formed up in her womb into just one, into a half-man/half-woman kind of being. . . . To us a man is what nature, or his dreams, make him. We accept him for what he wants to be. That's up to him.[22]

While most of the sources indicate that once a person becomes a berdache it is a lifelong status, directions from the spirits determine everything. In at least one documented case, concerning a nineteenth-century Klamath berdache named Lele'ks, he later had a supernatural experience that led him to leave the berdache role. At that time Lele'ks began dressing and acting like a man, then married women, and eventually became one of the most famous Klamath chiefs.[23] What is important is that both in assuming berdache status and in leaving it, supernatural dictate is the determining factor.

DREAMS AND VISIONS

Many tribes see the berdache role as signifying an individual's proclivities as a dreamer and a visionary. . . .

Among the northern Plains and related Great Lakes tribes, the idea of supernatural dictate through dreaming—the vision quest—had its highest development. The goal of the vision quest is to try to get beyond the rational world by sensory deprivation and fasting. By depriving one's body of nourishment, the brain could escape from logical thought and connect with the higher reality of the supernatural. The person doing the quest simply sits and waits for a vision. But a vision might not come easily; the person might have to wait for days.

The best way that I can describe the process is to refer to my own vision quest, which I experienced when I was living on a Lakota reservation in 1982. After a long series of prayers and blessings, the shaman who had prepared me for the ceremony took me out to an isolated area where a sweat lodge had been set up for my quest. As I walked to the spot, I worried that I might not be able to stand it. Would I be overcome by hunger? Could I tolerate the thirst? What would I do if I had to go to the toilet? The shaman told me not to worry, that a whole group of holy people would be praying and singing for me while I was on my quest.

He had me remove my clothes, symbolizing my disconnection from the material world, and crawl into the sweat lodge. Before he left me I asked him, "What do I think about?" He said, "Do not think. Just pray for spiritual guidance." After a prayer he closed the flap tightly and I was left in total darkness. I still do not understand what happened to me during my vision quest, but during the day and a half that I was out there, I never once felt hungry or thirsty or the need to go to the toilet. What happened was an intensely personal experience that I cannot and do not wish to explain, a process of being that cannot be described in rational terms.

When the shaman came to get me at the end of my time, I actually resented having to end it. He did not need to ask if my vision quest were successful. He knew that it was even before seeing me, he explained, because he saw an eagle circling over me while I underwent the quest. He helped interpret the signs I had seen, then after more prayers and singing he led me back to the others. I felt relieved, cleansed, joyful, and serene. I had been through an experience that will be a part of my memories always.

If a vision quest could have such an effect on a person not even raised in Indian society, imagine its impact on a boy who from his earliest years had been waiting for the day when he could seek his vision. Gaining his spiritual power from his first vision, it would tell him what role to take in adult life. The vision might instruct him that he is going to be a great hunter, a craftsman, a warrior, or a shaman. Or it might tell him that he will be a berdache. Among the Lakotas, or Sioux,

there are several symbols for various types of visions. A person becomes *wakan* (a sacred person) if she or he dreams of a bear, a wolf, thunder, a buffalo, a white buffalo calf, or Double Woman. Each dream results in a different gift, whether it is the power to cure illness or wounds, a promise of good hunting, or the exalted role of a *heyoka* (doing things backward).

A white buffalo calf is believed to be a berdache. If a person has a dream of the sacred Double Woman, this means that she or he will have the power to seduce men. Males who have a vision of Double Woman are presented with female tools. Taking such tools means that the male will become a berdache. The Lakota word *winkte* is composed of *win,* "woman," and *kte,* "would become."[24] A contemporary Lakota berdache explains, "To become a *winkte,* you have a medicine man put you up on the hill, to search for your vision. You can become a *winkte* if you truly are by nature. You see a vision of the White Buffalo Calf Pipe. Sometimes it varies. A vision is like a scene in a movie."[25] Another way to become a *winkte* is to have a vision given by a *winkte* from the past.[26] . . .

By interpreting the result of the vision as being the work of a spirit, the vision quest frees the person from feeling responsible for his transformation. The person might even claim that the change was done against his will and without his control. Such a claim does not suggest a negative attitude about berdache status, because it is common for people to claim reluctance to fulfill their spiritual duty no matter what vision appears to them. Becoming any kind of sacred person involves taking on various social responsibilities and burdens.[27] . . .

A story was told among the Lakotas in the 1880s of a boy who tried to resist following his vision from Double Woman. But according to Lakota informants "few men succeed in this effort after having taken the strap in the dream." Having rebelled against the instructions given him by the Moon Being, he committed suicide.[28] The moral of that story is that one should not resist spiritual guidance, because it will lead only to grief. In another case, an Omaha young man told of being addressed by a spirit as "daughter," whereupon he discovered that he was unconsciously using feminine styles of speech. He tried to use male speech patterns, but could not. As a result of this vision, when he returned to his people he resolved himself to dress as a woman.[29] Such stories function to justify personal peculiarities as due to a fate over which the individual has no control.

Despite the usual pattern in Indian societies of using ridicule to enforce conformity, receiving instructions from a vision inhibits others from trying to change the berdache. Ritual explanation provides a way out. It also excuses the community from worrying about the cause of that person's difference, or the feeling that it is society's duty to try to change him.[30] Native American religions, above all else, encourage a basic respect for nature. If nature makes a person different, many Indians conclude, a mere human should not undertake to counter this spiritual dictate. Someone who is "unusual" can be accommodated without being stigmatized as "abnormal." Berdachism is thus not alien or threatening; it is a reflection of spirituality.

NOTES

1. Mary Douglas, *Purity and Danger* (Baltimore: Penguin, 1966), p. 52. I am grateful to Theda Perdue for convincing me that Douglas's ideas apply to berdachism. For an application of Douglas's thesis to berdaches, see James Thayer, "The Berdache of the Northern Plains: A Socioreligious Perspective," *Journal of Anthropological Research* 36 (1980): 292–93.
2. E. W. Gifford, "The Kamia of Imperial Valley," *Bureau of American Ethnology Bulletin 97* (1931): 12.
3. By using present tense verbs in this text, I am not implying that such activities are necessarily continuing today. I sometimes use the present tense in the "ethnographic present," unless I use the past tense when I am referring to something that has not continued. Past tense implies that all such practices have disappeared. In the absence of fieldwork to prove such disappearance, I am not pre-

pared to make that assumption, on the historic changes in the berdache tradition.
4. Elsie Clews Parsons, "The Zuni La' Mana," *American Anthropologist* 18 (1916): 521; Matilda Coxe Stevenson, "Zuni Indians," *Bureau of American Ethnology Annual Report 23* (1903): 37, Franklin Cushing, "Zuni Creation Myths," *Bureau of American Ethnology Annual Report* 13 (1894): 401–3. Will Roscoe clarified this origin story for me.
5. W. W. Hill, "Note on the Pima Berdache," *American Anthropologist 40* (1938): 339.
6. Aileen O'Bryan, "The Dine': Origin Myths of the Navaho Indians," *Bureau of American Ethnology Bulletin 163* (1956): 5; W. W. Hill, "The Status of the Hermaphrodite and Transvestite in Navaho Culture," *American Anthropologist 37* (1935): 273.
7. Martha S. Link, *The Pollen Path: A Collection of Navajo Myths* (Stanford: Stanford University Press, 1956).
8. O'Bryan, "Dine'," pp. 5, 7, 9–10.
9. Ibid.
10. Lakota informants, July 1982. See also William Powers, *Oglala Religion* (Lincoln: University of Nebraska Press, 1977).
11. For this admittedly generalized overview of American Indian religious values, I am indebted to traditionalist informants of many tribes, but especially those of the Lakotas. For a discussion of native religions see Dennis Tedlock, *Finding the Center* (New York: Dial Press, 1972); Ruth Underhill, *Red Man's Religion* (Chicago: University of Chicago Press, 1965); and Elsie Clews Parsons, *Pueblo Indian Religion* (Chicago: University of Chicago Press, 1939).
12. Alfred Kroeber, "The Arapaho," *Bulletin of the American Museum of Natural History 18* (1902–7): 19.
13. Parsons, "Zuni La' Mana," p. 525.
14. Alexander Maximilian, *Travels in the Interior of North America, 1832–1834*, vol. 22 of *Early Western Travels*, ed. Reuben Gold Thwaites, 32 vols. (Cleveland: A. H. Clark, 1906), pp. 283–84, 354. Maximilian was quoted in German in the early homosexual rights book by Ferdinand Karsch-Haack, *Das Gleichgeschlechtliche Leben der Naturvölker* (The same-sex life of nature peoples) (Munich: Verlag von Ernst Reinhardt, 1911; reprinted New York: Arno Press, 1975), pp. 314, 564.

15. Oscar Koch, *Der Indianishe Eros* (Berlin: Verlag Continent, 1925), p. 61.
16. George Devereux, "Institutionalized Homosexuality of the Mohave Indians," *Human Biology 9* (1937): 509.
17. Ibid., p. 501.
18. Ibid.
19. Ibid., pp. 508–9.
20. C. Daryll Forde, "Ethnography of the Yuma Indians," *University of California Publications in American Archaeology and Ethnology 28* (1931): 157.
21. Ruth Underhill, *Social Organization of the Papago Indians* (New York: Columbia University Press, 1938), p. 186. This story is also mentioned in Ruth Underhill, ed., *The Autobiography of a Papago Woman* (Menasha, Wisc.: American Anthropological Association, 1936), p. 39.
22. John Fire and Richard Erdoes, *Lame Deer, Seeker of Visions* (New York: Simon and Schuster, 1972), pp. 117, 149.
23. Theodore Stern, *The Klamath Tribe: A People and Their Reservation* (Seattle: University of Washington Press, 1965), pp. 20, 24. Theodore Stern, "Some Sources of Variability in Klamath Mythology," *Journal of American Folklore 69* (1956): 242ff. Leshe Spier, *Klamath Ethnography* (Berkeley: University of California Press, 1930), p. 52.
24. Clark Wissler, "Societies and Ceremonial Associations in the Oglala Division of the Teton Dakota," *Anthropological Papers of the American Museum of Natural History 11*, pt. 1 (1916): 92; Powers, *Oglala Religion,* pp. 57–59.
25. Ronnie Loud Hawk, Lakota informant 4, July 1982.
26. Terry Calling Eagle, Lakota informant 5, July 1982.
27. James S. Thayer, "The Berdache of the Northern Plains: A Socioreligious Perspective," *Journal of Anthropological Research 36* (1980): 289.
28. Fletcher, "Elk Mystery," p. 281.
29. Alice Fletcher and Francis La Flesche, "The Omaha Tribe," *Bureau of American Ethnology Annual Report 27* (1905–6): 132.
30. Harriet Whitehead offers a valuable discussion of this element of the vision quest in "The Bow and the Burden Strap: A New Look at Institutionalized Homosexuality in Native North America," in *Sexual Meanings,* ed. Sherry Ortner and Harriet Whitehead (Cambridge: Cambridge University Press, 1981), pp. 99–102. See also Erikson, "Childhood," p. 329.

READING 7

Gender Stereotypes and Roles

Susan Basow

ALL-OR-NONE CATEGORIZING

The all-or-none categorizing of gender traits is misleading. People just are not so simple that they either possess all of a trait or none of it. This is even more true when trait dispositions for groups of people are examined. Part a of Figure 1 illustrates what such an all-or-none distribution of the trait "strength" would look like: all males would be strong, all females weak. The fact is, most psychological and physical traits are distributed according to the pattern shown in Part b of Figure 1 with most people possessing an average amount of that trait and fewer people having either very much or very little of that trait.

To the extent that females and males may differ in the average amount of the trait they possess (which needs to be determined empirically), the distribution can be characterized by *overlapping normal curves,* as shown in Part c of Figure 1. Thus, although most men are stronger than most women, the shaded area indicates that some men are weaker than some women and vice versa. The amount of overlap of the curves generally is considerable. Another attribute related to overlapping normal curves is that differences within one group are usually greater than the differences between the two groups. Thus, more variation in strength occurs within a group of men than between the average male and the average female. . . . For example, although males on the average may be more aggressive than females on the average, greater differences may be found among males than between males and females. . . .

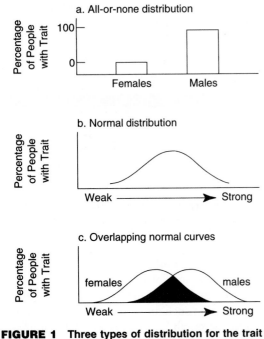

FIGURE 1 **Three types of distribution for the trait "strength."**

& Goldberg, 1985). People are simply not as consistent in their behavior across a variety of situations as one might like to believe. Mischel (1968) concludes that cross-situational consistencies rarely produce correlations greater than +.30; that is, a person does not usually exhibit the same trait to the same degree in every situation. Rather, human behavior is a function of both the person and the situation. The situation, in many cases, accounts for more than 90% of the variability in a person's behavior. For example, one's behavior during a church service or at a red light is almost entirely a function of the situation. As another example, how assertively a person acts depends not only on the person but on the situation itself. This can be readily verified from one's own experience. An individual can be very assertive in one situation (for example, in a class or group meeting) and markedly unassertive in another (for example, with a close friend).

Of course, some people may be more consistent than others in their behaviors in general and with respect to specific behaviors in particular (D. Bem & Allen, 1974). That is, some people may generally be more predictable than others across a wide range of situations. For example, people who strongly identify with a sex role are more predictable because they more often act according to sex role expectations than people who don't identify with such a role (S. L. Bem, 1975, 1985). And some people are more consistent than others with respect to a particular behavior (for example, "You can always count on Mary to be assertive"). On the whole, however, the trait approach to personality needs to be modified. Specific people interact with specific situations and produce specific behaviors; generalized traits rarely apply.

This concept of overlapping normal curves is critically important in understanding gender stereotypes because it undermines the basis of most discriminatory regulations and laws. Although most men are stronger than most women, denying women access to jobs requiring strength simply on the basis of sex is unjustified, because some women are stronger than some men (see shaded area in Part c of Figure 1). Thus, if most of the stereotypic traits are actually distributed in normal curves along a continuum (that is, people may be more or less dominant, more or less submissive) rather than distributed in an all-or-none fashion—dominant or submissive—then setting up two opposite and distinct lists of traits for females and males is entirely inappropriate and misleading. . . .

Strong debate exists over whether personality can be viewed in trait terms altogether. Despite their popularity, trait theories of personality have little empirical validity (see, for example, Chaplin

With reference to gender stereotypes, then, it can be concluded that (1) people cannot be viewed simply as collections of consistent traits, because situations also are important; (2) males and females specifically cannot be viewed as having unique traits that are opposite each other; and (3) whatever attributes are thought of as distinctly masculine or feminine are also possessed by at least some members of the other sex. . . .

SEX TYPING AND ANDROGYNY

Research in the mid-1970s on the degree to which individuals were sex-typed (that is, conformed to gender stereotypes) led to a redefinition of the older concept of androgyny. Since the two sets of personality traits viewed as stereotypically masculine (active-instrumental traits) and stereotypically feminine (nurturant-expressive traits) were statistically independent (that is, the way an individual scored on one set of traits was unrelated to the way she or he scored on the other set of traits), terms were needed to describe individuals who were high on both sets of traits and others who were low on both. Sandra Bem (1974, 1975, 1976) and others (for example, Spence & Helmreich, 1978) used the term *androgynous* to describe those individuals who scored high on both active-instrumental traits (such as assertiveness, self-reliance, and independence) and nurturant-expressive traits (such as understanding, compassion, and affection). These people were different from masculine-sex-typed individuals (high on instrumental-active traits, low on nurturant-expressive traits), feminine-sex-typed individuals (high on nurturant-expressive traits, low on instrumental-active traits), and *undifferentiated* individuals (those who scored low on both sets of traits) (Spence, Helmreich, & Stapp, 1974). Figure 2 presents this fourfold classification. One virtue of this fourfold typology is that it separates biological sex from psychological sex typing. Any person can be masculine-sex-typed, feminine-sex-typed, androgynous, or undifferentiated.

Being androgynous does not mean being neuter or imply anything about one's sexual orientation. Rather, it describes the degree of flexibility a person has regarding gender-stereotypic behaviors. The complex characteristics of androgynous individuals can be evidenced, depending on the situation, all in a single act or only in a number of different acts. Thus, a person may be an empathic listener when a friend has a problem, an assertive leader propelling a group to action, and an assertive and sensitive boss when an employee needs to be fired. . . .

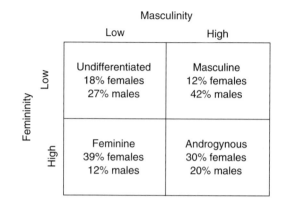

FIGURE 2 Fourfold classification of sex typing. Numbers are percentages of college students who typically fall into each cell. From S. L. Bem, 1981a.

The percentage of people who could be classified as androgynous varies as a function of many factors: the specific population studied, the measuring instrument and the scoring procedure used, and even the year in which a study is done. For example, males seem to have increased their level of androgyny during the 1970s compared to the 1960s, whereas females showed higher levels of androgyny in the 1960s (Heilbrun & Schwartz, 1982). One should note that there are no absolute cutoff points for the categories of androgynous and sex-typed individuals. Rather, the cutoffs typically are based on the median scores of a particular sample. The vast majority of studies have been conducted on college populations. In general, about 40% of all college students describe themselves as possessing traits viewed as more characteristic of their sex than of the other (that is, traditionally sex-typed). (See Figure 2.) About one-fourth of college populations are classified as androgynous (somewhat more females than males). Another 20% are characterized as undifferentiated (that is, low in both sets of traits). Finally, about 10% describe themselves as possessing traits viewed as more characteristic of the other sex than of their own (that is, cross-sex-typed). Thus, more than half of all college students are *not* traditionally sex-typed, although more males than females possess instrumental traits (masculine-sex-typed and androgynous) and more females than males possess expressive traits (feminine-sex-typed and androgynous).

Among other populations, degree of sex typing is unclear. There is evidence of increasing androgyny as people reach middle age. Racial differences in sex typing may also exist. One study of young adult women, most of whom had completed high school, found that the Black women had higher instrumentality scores than the White women (Binion, 1990). In terms of sex typing, more Black women (37%) than White women (16%) fell in the androgynous category, whereas more White women (38%) than Black women (28%) fell in the undifferentiated category. Again, we must be careful not to generalize from young, primarily White, well-educated individuals to the entire population.

More recently, Sandra Bem (1981b, 1985, 1987) has reconceptualized androgyny and sex typing to refer to cognitive schemata rather than personality types. Sex-typed individuals seem to be more aware than non-sex-typed individuals (both the androgynous and the undifferentiated) of gender and such gender-related issues as the number of men and women in a room, whether the topic discussed is masculine or feminine, and whether an occupation is gender-appropriate or not (Frable, 1989; Frable & Bem, 1985; J. B. Miller, 1984; C. J. Mills, 1983). Thus, sex typing may refer to the process of construing reality in terms of gender. Non-sex-typed individuals seem less ready to impose a gender-based classification system on reality.

The concept of androgyny, when first articulated, was hailed by some as a signpost leading the way toward gender equality and deplored by others as signifying the end of sex differentiation and thus the end of the world. Neither extreme view now seems justified. The concepts of sex typing and androgyny do have some utility in helping us understand how and why some males and females differ on some behaviors. For exam-ple, more behavioral differences exist between feminine-sex-typed and masculine-sex-typed people than between women and men as social groups, because most men and women are *not* traditionally sex-typed. This finding explains why there are so few strong gender differences in behavior at the same time that it suggests why we *think* there are (because we *expect* most men to be masculine-sex-typed and most women to be feminine-sex-typed). These concepts also emphasize the importance of looking for factors other than biology to account for gender differences.

For all its value, the concept of androgyny still has its limitations. Theoretically, androgyny may be a self-defeating concept in the sense that it depends on the existence of two separate sets of traits—masculine and feminine. Thus, it may serve to perpetuate the gender stereotypes themselves. One solution to this problem is to refer to masculine and feminine traits by their qualities—instrumental-agentic and expressive-nurturant—rather than by their stereotyped labels (Spence, 1983; Spence & Helmreich, 1980). Another solution is to go beyond the concept of androgyny altogether and speak in terms of sex role transcendence (Rebecca, Hefner, & Olenshansky, 1976).

A related problem is whether these two sets of traits adequately distinguish what is feminine from what is masculine (J. Archer, 1989; Deaux & Kite, 1987; Locksley & Colten, 1979). As we've already noted, gender refers to more than simply personality traits and indeed, to more personality traits than can be summarized by the terms *instrumental* and *expressive*. Gender and sex typing are multidimensional constructs, and bidimensional measures, such as the Bem Sex-Role Inventory (S. L. Bem, 1974, 1981a) or the Personal Attributes Questionnaire (Spence & Helmreich, 1978; Spence, Helmreich, & Stapp, 1974) are not sufficient. They tell us something but not everything we need to know about gender.

Another issue is whether androgyny is actually a unique type (an interaction between instrumental and expressive traits) or just the sum of its parts—that is, a linear combination of instrumental and expressive traits. Research suggests that androgyny does not have unique predictive power (J. A. Hall & Taylor, 1985; Lubinski, Tellegen, & Butcher, 1983). For example, with respect to self-esteem, creativity, and psychological adjustment, it is high scores on the instrumental-agentic trait scale that are beneficial (true of both masculine-sex-typed individuals and androgynous individuals), not high scores on both scales (Harrington & Andersen, 1981; Whitley, 1984, 1988a). Thus, the androgynous "ideal" may turn out to be a traditionally masculine one (Morawski, 1987). We need to understand why that is, and explanations in terms of personality traits alone will not help us.

Finally, a host of empirical problems have been raised with respect to measuring androgyny and sex typing. Different scales do not all seem to measure the same thing (A. C. Baldwin, Critelli, Stevens, & Russell, 1986; F. R. Wilson & Cook, 1984). Different scoring methods yield different results (for example, Handal & Salit, 1985). Sex-typing scales seem to measure more than two different factors (for example, Marsh et al., 1989; Pedhazur & Tetenbaum, 1979). Different researchers use different definitions of androgyny (for example, Heilbrun & Mulqueen, 1987). Sex-typing categories do not always predict stereotypic attitudes and beliefs (for example, J. Archer, 1989; Beauvais & Spence, 1987; Binion, 1990). And sex-typing categories do not always predict behavior (Lubinski et al., 1983; Myers & Gonda, 1982).

Many of these problems stem from inadequate understanding of the nature of androgyny and overly general use of the term (Morawski, 1987; Sedney, 1989). On the whole, however, if we view androgyny as a limited but valid construct whose parameters are still being explored, we will have a useful tool with which to understand some of the research on gender. We should not expect sex typing and androgyny, however, to be the only explanatory tools we will need. The concepts of power or status and the importance of situational determinants still play pivotal roles in any exploration of gender, since gender is not primarily a psychological variable but a socially constructed one. Psychologists have a tendency to overlook the latter variables, whereas sociologists have a tendency to overlook the former ones. Since gender is right at the intersection of the two fields, we need to keep as broad a perspective as possible. . . .

RESEARCH PROBLEMS

. . . Although research problems are liable to occur in any research area, the areas of sex comparisons and gender-related behaviors are particularly vulnerable to such problems, because these areas are very personal and in many ways, political. . . .

Problems can occur in one or more areas of any research project: the basic assumptions of the researchers, choice of subjects, experimental design and methodology, and interpretation of the results. We will look at each in turn.

Basic Assumptions

All experimenters bring certain assumptions to bear on their research, mainly because as human beings we cannot help but be influenced by our personal experiences and the sociohistorical contexts in which we live. Perhaps the most basic problem in examining the research on gender is the underlying assumption that *sex differences exist* and that *these differences are important* (see Hare-Mustin & Marecek, 1990, and Rhode, 1990, for theoretical explorations of this assumption). As A. Kaplan and Bean (1976) point out, because researchers study areas already thought to reflect male-female differences, such as hormonal cyclicity, the data reflecting these differences may be exaggerated. For example, much research has been done on the effect of female hormone cyclicity on moods; very little has been done on the effect of male hormones. The implication is that hormones play a larger role in female behavior than they do in male behavior. Similarly, Petersen (1983) observed that as research reveals fewer sex differences in cognitive abilities than previously had been thought, more and more research is done on the few remaining areas that do suggest a gender difference. Thus, we get an exaggerated picture of a male-female dichotomy and a limited understanding of the full range of human potential.

This emphasis on sex differences, as opposed to similarities, is further perpetuated by the policy of most journals to publish only statistically significant findings. The null hypothesis, meaning that there is no difference between groups, can never be proved. The strongest statement that can be made is that the null hypothesis cannot be rejected. Therefore, findings reflecting no difference usually do not get reported in the literature. Additionally, because journals have limited space, they have to reject a high percentage of submitted articles, and they naturally tend to accept those with positive findings. The number of studies testing for sex differences that were published in mainstream psychology journals increased during the 1970s, then decreased during the 1980s (Lykes & Stewart, 1986; Signorella, Vegega, & Mitchell, 1981). Whether this change is because the heyday of "sex difference" research has passed, or because fewer sex differences are found, or because editors of mainstream journals no longer find such research valuable or politically correct, is unclear. A debate has arisen recently regarding whether *every* study that uses people should test for sex differences (Baumeister, 1988; Eagly, 1987a, 1990; McHugh, Koeske, & Frieze, 1986). Doing so would give a more representative picture of how infrequently men and women differ, but it would also increase chance findings of difference.

Journals generally select articles on the basis of importance of the research topic. Although published research on topics related to gender has increased tremendously during the last 20 years, it is found mostly in feminist journals and books (M. Fine & Gordon, 1989; Lott, 1985; Lykes & Stewart, 1986). In mainstream psychology journals, the percentage of articles relating to gender still is small (10–17% in 1986) and only slowly increasing. In addition, most of this research is on gender differences or sex-typing differences, so the differences again are highlighted. And the emphasis is on individual factors rather than structural ones when behavior is explained or

changed. Thus, basic assumptions and theories operating in psychology are difficult to challenge and revise.

Another basic assumption in research on gender is that *sex differences can be attributed to either nature* (that is, biology—the essentialist position) *or nurture* (that is, the environment—the constructivist position). Even calling this topical area "*sex* differences" suggests that the underlying reason for any differences found is likely to be biological (related to sex) rather than cultural (related to gender). As many writers have noted, it is nearly impossible to separate the influences of biology and environment in humans because socialization begins at birth, and humans have such a tremendous capacity for learning. Gender identity is formed through a complex interaction of biological, psychological, and sociocultural factors. All these factors need to be taken into account when examining human behavior. The upsurge of interest in sociobiological theories since 1975 demonstrates that belief in pure biological determinism still has appeal (see Bleier, 1984, and Fausto-Sterling, 1985, for critiques). An interactionist perspective is needed, and we must determine the way this interaction operates for various behavior patterns in various contexts.

The third basic assumption influencing research is that *what males do is the norm;* what females do, if it is different from what males do, is deviant. Thus McClelland and colleagues (1953) based an entire theory of achievement motivation primarily on male subjects. The fact that this theory does not fit females as well as males should have made the validity and generalizability of the theory suspect but did not. Similarly, Kohlberg (1969) based a theory of moral development almost entirely on male subjects; females have been shown not to conform to his theory as well (Gilligan, 1982). Indeed, Grady (1981) reports that males appear as subjects in research nearly twice as often as do females. The important point here is that theories based solely or primarily on males have been generalized to all people even though the theories may not fit 51% of the human race. When women's behaviors and thoughts are included, the theories themselves frequently must be revised drastically. Such work already has begun.

Hare-Mustin and Marecek (1988) have analyzed the degree to which researchers have defined gender in terms of difference. They have noted two tendencies: the exaggeration of difference, which they call *alpha bias* (such as viewing men as instrumental, women as expressive); and the minimization of difference, which they call *beta bias* (such as ignoring women's greater child-care responsibilities in research on workplace productivity). Both biases support the existing gender hierarchy by making what is male normative and by focusing on individuals rather than on the power differential embedded within the organization of society (see also M. Fine & Gordon, 1989; A. S. Kahn & Yoder, 1989). This postmodern perspective is a result of two developments: the recognition on the part of social science researchers that science itself is socially constructed (K. J. Gergen, 1985; Harding, 1987; Unger, 1989a) and the application of post-modern theories, such as deconstruction, to psychology (Flax, 1987; Hare-Mustin & Marecek, 1988).

The assumptions that we have just reviewed all fit in with a positivist empiricist model of research in psychology, one that restricts analysis to a few clearly observable units of behavior. Such a model shapes research questions, findings, and interpretations. Yet this model ignores the inevitable effects of social constructs, such as status and power, on the research process itself. Mary Gergen (1988) and others (for example, M. Fine & Gordon, 1989; Unger, 1983, 1989; Wittig, 1989) suggest a more reflexive model of research, which requires an understanding of the reciprocal and interactive relationship that exists between the person and reality, and therefore between the experimenter and the "subject." The researcher, together with the persons being researched, exists within a specific cultural and historical setting. Such settings affect the entire research enterprise. For example, the assumption that men are the sexual aggressors and women are sexually passive has affected scientific research on the process of conception (E. Martin, 1991). The egg traditionally has been depicted as passively awaiting "pen-

etration" by active sperm (like Sleeping Beauty), whereas recent biological research finally has acknowledged that both the egg and the sperm play active roles in conception. . . .

Choice of Subjects

Research problems arise in choosing whom to study. Some researchers have used animals, because human experimentation in the biological area presents serious ethical and practical problems. The choice of which animals to study, however, is often a product of the experimenter's assumptions and biases. Donna Haraway (1989) forcefully demonstrates how the study of primates has reflected gender politics. For example, rhesus monkeys, who show different behaviors by sex, are studied more frequently than gibbons, who do not show such differences; yet gibbons are evolutionarily closer to humans than rhesus monkeys (Rosenberg, 1973). The generalizability of findings from animals is also questionable, because humans are unique in their development of the neocortex and in the plasticity of their behavior. Human behavior is extremely modifiable by experience. Although there may be similarities in behavior between humans and animals, the antecedents of behaviors may be quite different. It is curious, in this regard, to note the overwhelming number of studies on aggression that have used nonprimates, particularly rats and mice, and have generalized their findings to humans. (See Bleier, 1979, for an excellent discussion of this topic.)

Subjects may be selected to fit preexisting assumptions. For example, in examining the effect of menopause on women, one study simply excluded from the sample all women who worked outside the home, apparently on the grounds that such women were deviant (Van Hecke, Van Keep, & Kellerhals, 1975). Similarly, studies of attachment in infants nearly always look at mothers rather than fathers, on the assumption that infant-mother attachment is more important. Another example of bias in subject selection is the fact that 90% of all research on aggression has used male subjects, whereas females have been involved in only half the studies (McKenna & Kessler, 1977). As noted previously, males more often are used to represent all human beings, despite the frequent importance of gender as regards the topic studied. Indeed, significant self-selection may occur in some studies. Signorella and Vegega (1984) have found that women are most interested in signing up for experiments on "feminine" topics, such as revealing feelings and moods, whereas men are most interested in signing up for experiments on "masculine" topics, such as power and competition. Results from such studies may be biased and thus limited in generalizability.

Studying people with some abnormality or who need some form of treatment also is problematic, because by definition, these are individuals whose development differs from normal. Women who consult doctors for menstrual problems, for example, are a select group and cannot be assumed to represent women in general. People with inconsistent sex characteristics may be treated differently by their parents from other children, and research may be designed to specifically highlight their differences (for example, Stoller, 1968). Such problems limit the generalizability of findings.

Most research has used White, North American, middle-class, presumedly heterosexual subjects, which severely limits the generalizability of findings. For example, "women" have been found to be less assertive than "men," but this finding is not necessarily true for Black women and Black men (K. A. Adams, 1983; Reid, 1984). Who then is meant by the terms *women and men?* Elizabeth Spelman (1988) and others argue that we must become aware of our (usually hidden) assumptions about who represents the norm. As pointed out previously, each of us is embedded in a complex social matrix with respect to gender, race or ethnicity, class, sexual preference, able-bodiedness, and so on. Not only must researchers learn to stop privileging White, middle-class, heterosexual, Christian norms, but they must also actively seek out other groups to study (for example, Cannon, Higginbotham, & Leung, 1988; Scarr, 1988). The relative impossibility of speaking for all women or all men when the differences within each sex or gender group are enormous must constantly be borne in mind.

Some behaviors seem to be situation- or age-specific. Yet the vast majority of social psychological studies published in the mid-1980s were conducted on college students, especially within an experimental laboratory (Lykes & Stewart, 1986; Sears, 1986). We are left with a great deal of information about a select group of young men and women in atypical situations and very little information about the majority of men and women in natural situations. We therefore are likely to have an incomplete view regarding the great complexity of human behavior as it occurs outside the laboratory. Even the gender of the researcher/experimenter has been shown to be a very influential contextual variable, yet it is rarely even reported (Basow & Howe, 1987; Rumenik, Capasso, & Hendrick, 1977). Also not frequently reported is age of subject in topical areas where age may be influential. For example, menstrual problems appear to be age-related (Golub & Harrington, 1981). Clearly, such variables are important to control and need to be borne in mind when generalizations are made from research findings.

A major problem in many studies is the lack of an adequate control group. For example, female behavior during the menstrual cycle has been extensively studied but rarely compared to male behavior during a similar length of time. When men and women are compared (for example, on mood and behavioral variability over a four-week period), no differences are found (Dan, 1976; McFarlane, Martin, & Williams, 1988; J. S. Stein & Yaworsky, 1983). Thus, studies that focus on mood changes only in women distort the nature of the findings.

Design

As we have seen, feminist critiques of psychological research have emphasized the importance of getting outside the experimental laboratory and exploring issues of gender in more naturalistic contexts with a more diverse population than predominantly White middle-class college students. This is important because different methodologies will lead to different types of results. We now know that quantitatively oriented experimental research tends to minimize findings of gender differences (beta bias), whereas qualitatively oriented clinical research tends to maximize findings of gender differences (alpha bias) (M. Crawford, 1988). The point is not to determine which finding is "correct" but to understand how gender operates within different contexts. The increased use of different methodologies is apparent in feminist journals but, unfortunately, not in mainstream ones (M. Fine & Gordon, 1989; Lykes & Stewart, 1986). Thus the transformative potential of feminist methodology in the social sciences is not being realized (M. Crawford & Marecek, 1989).

Other problems afflict research design: lack of precise objective definitions of the behavior studied, selective perception of raters, and shifting anchor points. This last problem refers to the fact that we often evaluate male and female behavior differently. For example, what is seen as active for a boy may be different from what is seen as active for a girl. The use of different definitions of a behavior as a function of the sex of the ratee also may be a function of the sex of the rater. For example, men and women may use different definitions of "active behavior." Imprecise measures of behavior may also limit a study's findings. Besides the premenstrual syndrome having various definitions, actual physiological measures of cycle phase have varied enormously from study to study, some relying on self-reports, others relying on varying physiological measurements taken at varying intervals (Parlee, 1973).

Using an appropriate baseline, or standard, when measuring gender differences is imperative but not frequently found. For example, with respect to the menstrual cycle, it may be as accurate to posit a follicular phase (midcycle) syndrome of positive traits and behaviors as to posit a premenstrual syndrome of negative traits and behaviors (McFarlane et al., 1988; Parlee, 1973). Yet we hear far more of the latter than the former.

Three research designs used in studying sex differences should be examined particularly carefully since each has serious limitations:

1. *Correlation studies* do not demonstrate causation, although they are frequently interpreted that way by unsophisticated readers and, at times, by researchers themselves. Thus, a correlation between anxiety and the premenstrual phase has led many to assume that hormones determine mood in females, although such a relation may be caused by a third variable such as expectation of amount of flow (Paige, 1971). The causation also may occur in the opposite direction. For example, anxiety can bring on menstruation (see Parlee, 1973).

2. *Retrospective questionnaires* suffer from reliance on an individual's memory. For example, complaints of mood impairment during or before menstruation typically are found when mood is assessed retrospectively, but not when mood is assessed daily (for example, McFarlane et al., 1988). Questionnaires also may selectively lead the respondent to provide certain information—for example, by asking only about negative mood changes as a function of menstrual phase.

3. *Self-reports or observations* are affected by people's need to respond in a socially desirable way. As an example, men may be reluctant to admit mood changes because such changes contradict societal gender stereotypes. These methods also have a problem with selective perception or selective reporting by the respondent. For example, only negative mood changes may be observed in or admitted by women because that is the cultural and/or the reporter's expectation (McFarland, Ross, & DeCourville, 1989; D. N. Ruble, 1977).

An important problem in all psychological research, especially in this area, is the effect on the results of the experimenter's beliefs. Robert Rosenthal (1966; Rosenthal & Jacobson, 1968) has ingeniously demonstrated that in unconscious, nonverbal ways, experimenters can influence the outcome of an experiment to conform to the experimental hypotheses. Thus, in studies in which the experimenter expects to find moods varying with menstrual phase, she or he may indeed find them

(Moos et al., 1969). Because most researchers have been male, they unconsciously may have misperceived certain situations with humans and animals to put males in the better light. For example, Harry Harlow's (1962, 1965) research with monkeys has contributed a great deal to our understanding of attachment behavior. But reading some of Harlow's observations of the behavior of monkeys sometimes resembles viewing a soap opera with females "scheming" and acting "helpless" and males acting "intelligently" and "strongly." (See also Hrdy, 1986.) This brings us to the question of interpretation.

Interpretation

Statistical reporting and analysis are often a function of an experimenter's hypotheses and biases. To illustrate, although Dalton (1969) found that 27% of her female subjects got poorer grades before menstruation than at ovulation, she ignored the 56% who had no changes and the 17% who actually improved.

Another reporting problem arises in reviews such as that by Maccoby and Jacklin (1974). Although the reviewed studies varied greatly in quality, the results were simply tabulated without giving greater emphasis to the better research. Therefore, a finding of a high percentage of studies reporting no difference in an area may be due to there being no difference, or it may be due to a large number of inadequate experiments. . . .

Interpretation of scientific facts has sometimes determined the facts themselves. Recent feminist examinations of the history of science reveal numerous illustrations of gender, race, and class prejudices (Bleier, 1988; Hubbard, 1990; Katz, 1988; Russett, 1989; Sayers, 1987). For example, Shields (1975) found that when the frontal lobes of the brain were regarded as the main area of intellectual functioning, research studies found men had larger frontal lobes, relative to the parietal lobes, than women. When parietal lobes were regarded as more important, the findings themselves changed. Men now were found to have relatively larger parietal lobes, relative to their frontal lobes, than women. Today, there is no firm evidence of sex differences in brain structures or

proportions, so interest has turned to sex differences in brain organization, following a predictable pattern. When men were thought to be less lateralized than women, that was thought to be the superior organization. When men were thought to have more brain lateralization than women, then *that* was thought to be the superior organization. . . .

SUMMARY

. . . In examining the studies on female and male behaviors and characteristics, one must be aware of the many research problems that can invalidate the results. Science is constructed by people, and people are never value-free or impervious to social forces. As Sue Rosser (1988) notes, until our society is neutral with respect to gender, class, race, and sexual preference, it is impossible to assume that science will be. Therefore, it is incumbent upon all researchers to understand how the social context influences the research process. With this caution in mind, we will examine the current findings.

CURRENT FINDINGS

Aside from the physical area, few clear-cut differences between males and females have been found. Males, compared to females, tend to be more physically vulnerable, physically active, aggressive, power-oriented, and sexually active. Males have a slight edge in visual-spatial and quantitative skills after childhood, and they tend to dominate verbal and nonverbal communications. Females, compared to males, tend to mature faster and to be more people-oriented, more prosocial, and more emotionally expressive. Females have cyclic hormonal production after puberty and are capable of multiple orgasms. They may have a slight edge on some verbal tasks.

Far more numerous than the areas of gender difference are the areas in which no overall differences have been found or where differences are unclear because of the importance of situational factors. These areas include intelligence, memory, cognitive styles, creativity, temperament, empathy, nurturance, altruism, morality, assertiveness, achievement, and sexual responsiveness.

To give a clearer sense of how much the sexes differ, the magnitudes of the average gender differences can be compared. . . . Recall that *d* value is the size of the difference between male and female performance expressed in terms of a standard deviation. Gender differences can be divided into small, moderate, and large effects. Most of the small gender differences (*d* value equal to or less than .20, one-fifth of a standard deviation) are cognitive ones: overall verbal ability, SAT verbal scores, overall math ability, problem solving, computation skills, and spatial visualization. Small gender differences are also found in balance, social smiling (child), and noncompliance. Of small to moderate size (.20 < *d* < .40) are gender differences in spatial perception (before age 18), helping others, democratic leadership style, aggression (by adults), and approval of intercourse in serious relationships. Of moderate size (around one-half of a standard deviation, .40 < *d* < .60) are gender differences in activity level, grammar, SAT math scores, decoding skill, body expressiveness, and aggression (all ages). Of moderate to large size (.60 < *d* < .80) are gender differences in dash, spatial perception (after age 18), mental rotations, social smiling (adult), gaze, and speech errors. Large gender differences (over .80) are found for only a few comparisons: height, throwing distance, facial expressiveness, and approval of sexual intercourse without love.

From these comparisons, it's obvious that the gender differences we are examining are mostly of small to moderate size—large enough to be noticed but not large enough to provide a basis for statements (such as "all men are more aggressive than all women") or job applicant choice. As Eagly (1987b) notes, the meaning of the size of any particular gender difference is a function of the value attached to it. For example, if people value quantitative skills, then the slight edge males may have in these skills may seem very important. If people don't value facial expressiveness, then even the large advantage females have in this area will be viewed as unimportant.

Furthermore, situational and individual variability in most of these behaviors is enormous . . . Gender differences can be either magnified or minimized by situational factors, such as whether the person is observed by others or whether the research is conducted in the laboratory or in a natural setting. Individual factors, such as age, class, beliefs, and sex-typing category, also affect results. In general, masculine- and feminine-sex-typed individuals show stereotypical gender differences to a greater degree than androgynous or undifferentiated males and females. Another factor affecting results is the date of the research. Cognitive gender differences, in particular, have become smaller over time, probably due to changes in early childhood socialization and expectations.

In looking at explanations of the differences, social factors (roles, status, expectations, and learning history) seem to be the most powerful influences on gender differences, although biological predispositions may play a role in some cases (for example, aggression and nurturance). Even in these cases, however, nature and nurture interact, with environmental-social factors usually overpowering biological factors, shaping the behavior to conform to cultural expectations. We are all born with different physical, intellectual, and emotional potential, but these differences are not distributed by gender. The potentials that become actualized depend on the environment and the roles in which we are raised. And social factors and roles do differ on the basis of gender. Indeed, gender differences are maximized in situations in which gender roles are made salient, such as among strangers who are being observed, the traditional research design. Gender also serves as a stimulus cue for others; that is, people perceive and react to an individual depending upon that person's biological sex.

The question remains as to why the gender stereotypes remain and are so strongly believed when gender differences, to the extent that they exist, are relatively small and highly variable. To understand the tenacity of stereotypes, one needs to understand the nature of the stereotypes themselves. Once believed, stereotypes become confirmed and strengthened whenever someone behaves in the expected way. For example, whenever a female expresses fearfulness, an observer may remark, "That's just like a woman." The observer's belief in the stereotype then becomes stronger. On the other hand, when someone acts in a way contrary to the observer's expectation, instead of weakening the stereotype, the behavior in question is more likely to go unnoticed or to be classified as an exception. Thus, if a female does not act fearful, an observer might simply brush off the observation as unusual ("Oh, she's different"), if an observation is made at all. The stereotype itself remains inviolate and protected from refutation. Thus, we have the case where active athletic behavior on the part of girls is called atypical ("tomboyish") even though the majority of girls behave that way.

Another reason for the strength and persistence of stereotypes is that men and women tend to hold different roles, both in the home and in the workplace. The roles inhabited by women tend to be low-status and to involve nurturant-communal behaviors (mother, homemaker, nurse). Conversely, the roles inhabited by men tend to be high-status and to involve agentic-instrumental behaviors (paid employee, boss, political leader). Thus, in real life, women generally engage in more prosocial behaviors than men, and men generally engage in more power-related behaviors than women, but this apparent *sex* difference actually is a *role* difference. To the general observer, however, these different behaviors seem to confirm the stereotypes. The same is true with regard to sexual scripts and sexual behaviors. That is, males and females are given different scripts to follow, but when they follow the scripts, their behaviors are viewed as reflecting innate differences.

To challenge stereotypes, we need to get to the individual before he or she learns them; that is, we need to change the content of our gender socialization. In particular, we need to change the assignment of males and females to different social roles.

REFERENCES

Adams, K. A. (1983). Aspects of social context as determinants of black women's resistance to challenges. *Journal of Social Issues, 39,* 69–78.

Archer, J. (1989). The relationship between gender-role measures: A review. *British Journal of Social Psychology, 28,* 173–184.

Baldwin, A. C., Critelli, J. W., Stevens, L. C., & Russell, S. (1986). Androgyny and sex role measurement: A personal construct approach. *Journal of Personality and Social Psychology, 51,* 1081–1088.

Basow, S. A. & Howe, K. G. (1987). Evaluations of college professors: Effects of professors' sex-type and sex, and students' sex. *Psychological Reports, 60,* 671–678.

Baumeister, R. F. (1988). Should we stop studying sex differences altogether?[Letter to the editor]. *American Psychologist, 43,* 1092–1095.

Beauvais, C., & Spence, J. T. (1987). Gender, prejudice, and categorization. *Sex Roles, 16,* 89–100.

Bem, D., & Allen, A. (1974). On predicting some of the people some of the time: The search for cross-situational consistencies in behavior. *Psychological Review, 81,* 506–520.

Bem, S. L. (1974). The measurement of psychological androgyny. *Journal of Consulting and Clinical Psychology, 42,* 155–162.

Bem, S. L. (1975). Sex role adaptability: One consequence of psychological androgyny. *Journal of Personality and Social Psychology, 31,* 634–643.

Bem, S. L. (1976). Probing the promise of androgyny. In A. Kaplan & J. Bean (Eds.), *Beyond sex role stereotypes: Readings toward a psychology of androgyny* (pp. 47–62). Boston: Little, Brown.

Bem, S. L. (1981a). *Bem Sex-Role Inventory, professional manual.* Palo Alto, CA: Consulting Psychologists Press.

Bem, S. L. (1981b). Gender schema theory: A cognitive account of sex typing. *Psychological Review, 88,* 354–364.

Bem, S. L. (1985). Androgyny and gender schema theory: A conceptual and empirical integration. In T. B. Sonderegger (Ed.), *Nebraska Symposium on Motivation, 1984: Psychology and gender,* Vol. 32 (pp. 179–226). Lincoln, NE: University of Nebraska Press.

Bem, S. L. (1987). Gender schema theory and the romantic tradition. In P. Shaver & C. Hendrick (Eds.), *Sex and gender* (pp. 251–271). Newbury Park, CA: Sage.

Binion, V. J. (1990). Psychological androgyny: A Black female perspective. *Sex Roles, 22,* 487–507.

Bleier, R. (1979). Social and political bias in science: An examination of animal studies and their generalizations to human behaviors and evolution. In E. Tobach & B. Rosoff (Eds.), *Genes and gender II* (pp. 49–69). Staten Island: Gordian Press.

Bleier, R. (1984). *Science and gender: A critique of biology and its theories on women.* New York: Pergamon Press.

Bleier, R. (1988). A decade of feminist critiques in the natural sciences. *Signs: Journal of Women in Culture and Society, 14,* 186–195.

Cannon, L. W., Higginbotham, E., & Leung, M.L.A. (1988). Race and class bias in qualitative research on women. *Gender and Society, 2,* 449–462.

Chaplin, W. F., & Goldberg, L. R. (1985). A failure to replicate the Bem and Allen study of individual differences in cross-situational consistency. *Journal of Personality and Social Psychology, 47,* 1074–1090.

Crawford, M. (1988). Agreeing to differ: Feminist epistemologies and women's ways of knowing. In M. Crawford & M. Gentry (Eds.), *Gender and thought: Psychological perspectives* (pp. 128–145). New York: Springer-Verlag.

Crawford, M., & Marecek, J. (1989). Psychology reconstructs the female: 1968–1988. *Psychology of Women Quarterly, 13,* 147–165.

Dalton, K. (1969) *The menstrual cycle.* New York: Pantheon.

Dan, A. J. (1976). Patterns of behavioral and mood variation in men and women: Variability and the menstrual cycle. *Dissertation Abstracts International, 37,* 3145B–3146B.

Deaux, K., & Kite, M. E. (1987). Thinking about gender. In B. B. Hess & M. M. Ferree (Eds.), *Analyzing gender: A handbook of social science research* (pp. 92–117). Newbury Park, CA: Sage.

Eagly, A. H. (1987a). Reporting sex differences [Letter to the editor]. *American Psychologist, 42,* 756–757.

Eagly, A. H. (1987b). *Sex differences in social behavior: A social-role interpretation.* Hillsdale, NJ: Erlbaum.

Eagly, A. H. (1990). On the advantages of reporting sex comparisons [Letter to the editor]. *American Psychologist, 45,* 560–562.

Fausto-Sterling, A. (1985). *Myths of gender: Biological theories about women and men.* New York: Basic Books.

Fine, M., & Gordon, S. M. (1989). Feminist transformations of/despite psychology. In M. Crawford & M. Gentry (Eds.), *Gender and thought: Psychological perspectives* (pp. 146–174). New York: Springer-Verlag.

Flax, J. (1987). Postmodernism and gender relations in feminist theory. *Signs: Journal of Women in Culture and Society, 12,* 621–643.

Frable, D. E. S. (1989). Sex typing and gender ideology: Two facets of the individual's gender psychology that go together. *Journal of Personality and Social Psychology, 56,* 95–108.

Frable, D. E. S., & Bem, S. L. (1985). If you're gender-schematic, all members of the opposite sex look alike. *Journal of Personality and Social Psychology, 49,* 459–468.

Gergen, K. J. (1985). The social constructionist movement in modern psychology. *American Psychologist, 40,* 266–275.

Gergen, M. M. (1988). Building a feminist methodology. *Contemporary Social Psychology, 13*(2), 47–53.

Gilligan, C. (1982). *In a different voice: Psychological theory and women's development.* Cambridge, MA: Harvard University Press.

Golub, S., & Harrington, D. M. (1981). Premenstrual and menstrual mood changes in adolescent women. *Journal of Personality and Social Psychology, 41,* 961–965.

Grady, K. E. (1981). Sex bias in research design. *Psychology of Women Quarterly, 5,* 628–636.

Hall, J. A., & Taylor, M. C. (1985). Psychological androgyny and the masculinity × femininity interaction. *Journal of Personality and Social Psychology, 49,* 429–435.

Handal, P. J., & Salit, E. D. (1985). Gender-role classification and demographic relationships: A function of type of scoring procedures. *Sex Roles, 12,* 411–419.

Haraway, D. (1989). *Primate visions: Gender, race, and nature in the world of modern science.* New York: Routledge.

Harding, S. (Ed.). (1987). *Feminism and methodology: Social science issues.* Bloomington: Indiana University Press.

Hare-Mustin, R. T., & Marecek, J. (1988). The meaning of difference: Gender theory, postmodernism, and psychology. *American Psychologist, 43,* 455–464.

Hare-Mustin, R. T., & Marecek, J. (1990). *Making a difference: Psychology and the construction of gender.* New Haven: Yale University Press.

Harlow, H. F. (1962). The heterosexual affectional system in monkeys. *American Psychologist, 17,* 1–9.

Harlow, H. F. (1965). Sexual behavior in the rhesus monkeys. In F. A. Beach (Ed.), *Sex and behavior.* New York: Wiley.

Harrington, D. M., & Andersen, S. M. (1981). Creativity, masculinity, femininity, and three models of psychological androgyny. *Journal of Personality and Social Psychology, 41,* 744–757.

Heilbrun, A. B., Jr., & Mulqueen, C. M. (1987). The second androgyny: A proposed revision in adaptive priorities for college women. *Sex Roles, 17,* 187–207.

Heilbrun, A. B., Jr., & Schwartz, H. L. (1982). Sex-gender differences in level of androgyny. *Sex Roles, 8,* 201–214.

Hrdy, S. B. (1986). Empathy, polyandry, and the myth of the coy female. In R. Bleier (Ed.), *Feminist approaches to science* (pp. 119–146). New York: Pergamon Press.

Hubbard, R. (1990). *The politics of women's biology.* New Brunswick, NJ: Rutgers University Press.

Kahn, A. S., & Yoder, J. D. (1989). The psychology of women and conservatism: Rediscovering social change. *Psychology of Women Quarterly, 13,* 417–432.

Kaplan, A., & Bean, J. P. (1976). From sex stereotypes to androgyny: Considerations of societal and individual change. In A. Kaplan & J. Bean (Eds.), *Beyond sex-role stereotypes* (pp. 383–392). Boston: Little, Brown.

Katz, S. (1988). Sexualization and the lateralized brain: From craniometry to pornography. *Women's Studies International Forum, 11,* 29–41.

Kohlberg, L. (1969). Stage and sequence: The cognitive-developmental approach to socialization. In D. A. Goslin (Ed.), *Handbook of socialization and research* (pp. 347–480). Chicago: Rand McNally.

Locksley, A., & Colten, M. E. (1979). Psychological androgyny: A case of mistaken identity? *Journal of Personality and Social Psychology, 37,* 1017–1031.

Lott, B. (1985). The potential enrichment of social/personality psychology through feminist research, and vice versa. *American Psychologist, 40,* 155–164.

Lubinski, D., Tellegen, A., & Butcher, J. N. (1983). Masculinity, femininity, and androgyny viewed and assessed as distinct concepts. *Journal of Personality and Social Psychology, 44,* 428–439.

Lykes, M. B., & Stewart, A. J. (1986). Evaluating the feminist challenge to research in personality and social psychology: 1963–1983. *Psychology of Women Quarterly, 10,* 393–412.

Maccoby, E. E., & Jacklin, C. N. (1974). *The psychology of sex differences.* Stanford, CA: Stanford University Press.

Marsh, H. W., Antill, J. K., & Cunningham, J. D. (1989). Masculinity and femininity: A bipolar construct and independent constructs. *Journal of Personality, 57,* 625–663.

Martin, E. (1991). The egg and the sperm: How science has constructed a romance based on stereotypical male-female roles. *Signs: Journal of Women in Culture and Society, 16,* 485–501.

McClelland, D. C., Atkinson, J. W., Clark, R. A., & Lowell, E. G. (1953). *The achievement motive.* New York: Appleton-Century-Crofts.

McFarland, C., Ross, M., & DeCourville, N. (1989). Women's theories of menstruation and biases in recall of menstrual symptoms. *Journal of Personality and Social Psychology, 57,* 522–531.

McFarlane, J., Martin, C. L., & Williams, T. M. (1988). Mood fluctuations: Women versus men and menstrual versus other cycles. *Psychology of Women Quarterly, 12,* 201–223.

McHugh, M. C., Koeske, R. D., & Frieze, I. H. (1986). Issues to consider in conducting non-sexist psychological research: A guide for researchers. *American Psychologist, 41,* 879–890.

McKenna, W., & Kessler, S. (1977). Experimental design as a source of sex bias in social psychology. *Sex Roles, 3,* 117–128.

Miller, J. B. (1984). *The development of women's sense of self* (Work in Progress, No. 12). Wellesley, MA: Wellesley College, The Stone Center.

Mills, C. J. (1983). Sex-typing and self-schemata effects on memory and response latency. *Journal of Personality and Social Psychology, 45,* 163–172.

Mischel, W. (1968). *Personality and assessment.* New York: Wiley.

Moos, R., Kopell, B., Melges, F., Yalum, I., Lunde, D., Clayton, R., & Hamburg, D. (1969). Variations in symptoms and mood during the menstrual cycle. *Journal of Psychosomatic Research, 13,* 37–44.

Morawski, J. G. (1987). The troubled quest for masculinity, femininity, and androgyny. In P. Shaver & C. Hendrick (Eds.), *Sex and gender* (pp. 44–69). Newbury Park, CA: Sage.

Myers, A. M., & Gonda, G. (1982). Empirical validation of the Bem Sex-Role Inventory. *Journal of Personality and Social Psychology, 43,* 304–318.

Paige, K. E. (1971). The effects of oral contraceptives on affective fluctuations associated with the menstrual cycle. *Psychosomatic Medicine, 33,* 515–537.

Parlee, M. B. (1973). The premenstrual syndrome. *Psychological Bulletin, 80,* 454–465.

Pedhazur, E. J., & Tetenbaum, T. J. (1979). Bem Sex Role Inventory: A theoretical and methodological critique. *Journal of Personality and Social Psychology, 37,* 996–1016.

Petersen, A. C. (1983). *The development of sex-related differences in achievement.* Invited address at the meeting of the American Psychological Association, Anaheim.

Rebecca, M., Hefner, R., & Olenshansky, B. (1976). A model of sex role transcendence. *Journal of Social Issues, 32*(3), 197–206.

Reid, P. T. (1984). Feminism versus minority group identity: Not for Black women only. *Sex Roles, 10,* 247–255.

Rhode, D. L. (1990). Definitions of difference. In D. L. Rhode (Ed.), *Theoretical perspectives on sexual difference* (pp. 197–212). New Haven: Yale University Press.

Rosenberg, M. (1973). The biological basis for sex role stereotypes. *Contemporary Psychoanalysis, 9,* 374–391.

Rosenthal, R. (1966). *Experimenter effects in behavioral research.* New York: Appleton-Century-Crofts.

Rosenthal, R., & Jacobson, L. (1968). *Pygmalion in the classroom: Teacher expectations and pupils' intellectual development.* New York: Holt, Rinehart & Winston.

Rosser, S. V. (1988). Good science: Can it ever be gender-free? *Women's Studies International Forum, 11,* 13–19.

Ruble, D. N. (1977). Premenstrual symptoms: A reinterpretation. *Science, 197,* 291–292.

Rumenik, D. K., Capasso, D. R., & Hendrick, C. (1977). Experimenter sex effects in behavioral research. *Psychological Bulletin, 84,* 852–877.

Russett, C. E. (1989). *Sexual science: The Victorian construction of womanhood.* Cambridge, MA: Harvard University Press.

Sayers, J. (1987). Science, sexual difference, and feminism. In B. B. Hess & M. M. Ferree (Eds.), *Analyzing gender: A handbook of social science research* (pp. 68–91). Newbury Park, CA: Sage.

Scarr, S. (1988). Race and gender as psychological variables: Social and ethical issues. *American Psychologist, 43,* 56–59.

Sears, D. O. (1986). College sophomores in the laboratory: Influences of a narrow data base on social psychology's view of human nature. *Journal of Personality and Social Psychology, 51,* 515–530.

Sedney, M. A. (1989). Conceptual and methodological sources of controversies about androgyny. In R. Unger (Ed.), *Representations: Social constructions of gender* (pp. 126–144). Amityville, NY: Baywood.

Shields, S. (1975). Functionalism, Darwinism, and the psychology of women: A study in social myth. *American Psychologist, 30,* 739–754.

Signorella, M. L., & Vegega, M. E. (1984). A note on gender stereotyping of research topics. *Personality and Social Psychology Bulletin, 10,* 107–109.

Signorella, M. L., Vegega, M. E., & Mitchell, M. E. (1981). Subject selection and analyses for sex-related differences: 1968–1970 and 1975–1977. *American Psychologist, 36,* 988–990.

Spelman, E. V. (1988). *Inessential woman. Problems of exclusion in feminist thought.* Boston: Beacon Press.

Spence, J. T. (1983). Commenting on Lubinski, Tellegen, and Butcher's "Masculinity, femininity, and androgyny viewed and assessed as distinct concepts." *Journal of Personality and Social Psychology, 44,* 440–446.

Spence, J. T., & Helmreich, R. (1978) *Masculinity and femininity: The psychological dimensions, correlates, and antecedents.* Austin: University of Texas Press.

Spence, J. T., & Helmreich, R. L. (1980). Masculine instrumentality and feminine expressiveness: Their relationships with sex role attitudes and behavior. *Psychology of Women Quarterly, 5,* 147–163.

Spence, J. T., Helmreich, R., & Stapp, J. (1974). The Personal Attributes Questionnaire: A measure of sex role stereotyping and masculinity and femininity. *JSAS selected documents in psychology* (Ms. No. 617).

Stein, J. S., & Yaworsky, K. B. (1983, August). *Menstrual cycle and memory for affective and neutral words.* Paper presented at the meeting of the American Psychological Association, Anaheim.

Stoller, R. J. (1968). *Sex and gender: On the development of masculinity and femininity.* New York: Science House.

Unger, R. K. (1983). Through the looking glass: No wonderland yet! (The reciprocal relationship between methodology and models of reality.) *Psychology of Women Quarterly, 8,* 9–32.

Unger, R. K. (1989). Sex, gender, and epistemology. In M. Crawford & M. Gentry (Eds.), *Gender and thought: Psychological perspectives* (pp. 17–35). New York: Springer-Verlag.

Van Hecke, M. T., Van Keep, P. A., & Kellerhals, J. M. (1975). The aging women. *Acts Obstictrica et Gyne-*

cologia, 51, Scandinavica Supplement, 17–27.

Whitley, B. E., Jr. (1984). Sex-role orientation and psychological well-being: Two meta-analyses. *Sex Roles, 12,* 207–225.

Whitley, B. E., Jr. (1987). The relationship of sex role orientation to heterosexuals' attitudes toward homosexuals. *Sex Roles, 17,* 103–113.

Whitley, B. E., Jr. (1988a). Masculinity, femininity, and self-esteem: A multitrait-multimethod analysis.

Sex Roles, 18, 419–432.

Wilson, F. R., & Cook, E. P. (1984). Concurrent validity of four androgyny instruments. *Sex Roles, 11,* 813–837.

Wittig, M. A. (1989, August). *Frameworks for a feminist psychology of gender: Reconciling scientific and feminist values.* Paper presented at the meeting of the American Psychological Association, New Orleans.

PERSONAL ACCOUNT

He Hit Her

I was raised in Charleston, South Carolina, a city where racial and class lines are both evident and defined by street address. I had been taught all my life that black people were different than "us" and were to be feared, particularly in groups.

One summer afternoon when I was eighteen or nineteen, I was sitting in my car at a traffic light at the corner of Cannon and King streets, an area on the edge of the white part of the peninsular city, but progressively being inhabited by more and more blacks. It was hot, had been for weeks, and the sticky heat of South Carolina can be enraging by itself.

As I waited at the light, a young black couple turned the corner on the sidewalk and began to walk towards where I was sitting. The man was yelling and screaming and waving his arms about his head. The woman, a girl really, looked scared and was walking and trying to ignore his tirade. Perhaps it was her seeming indifference that finally did it, perhaps the heat, I don't know. As they drew right up next to my car though, he hit her. He hit her on the side of her head, open palmed, and her head bounced off the brick wall of the house on the corner and she sprawled to the ground, dazed and crying. The man stood over her, shaking his fist and yelling.

I looked around at the other people in cars around me, mostly whites, and at the other people on the sidewalks, mostly blacks, and I realized as everyone gaped that no one was going to do anything, no one was going to help, and neither was I. I don't think it was fear of the man involved that stopped me; rather, I think it was fear generated by what I had been told about the man that stopped me. Physically I was bigger than he was and I knew how to handle myself in a fight: I worked as a bouncer in a nightclub. What I was afraid of was what I had been told about blacks: that *en masse,* they hated

whites, and that given the opportunity they would harm me. I was afraid getting out of the car in that neighborhood would make me the focus of the fight and in a matter of time I would be pummeled by an angry black crowd. Also in my mind were thoughts of things I had heard voiced as a child: "They are different. Violence is a part of life for them. They beat, stab, and shoot each other all the time, and the women are just as bad as the men." So I sat and did nothing. The light changed and I pulled away.

The incident has haunted me over the last almost fifteen years. I have often thought about it and felt angry when I did. I believe that as I examined it over time the woman who had been hit, the victim, became less and less prominent, and the black man and myself more prominent. Then I had an epiphany about it.

What bothered me about the incident was not that a man had hit a woman and I had done nothing to intervene, not even to blow my horn, but that a man had hit a woman and I had done nothing to intervene and that this reflected on me as a man. "Men don't hit women, and other men don't let men hit women," was also part of my masculinity training as a boy. There was a whole list of things that "real" men did and things that "real" men didn't do, and somewhere on there was this idea that men didn't let other men hit women. I realized that the incident haunted me not because a man had hit a woman, but because my lack of response was an indictment of *my* masculinity. The horror had become that I was somehow less of a man because of my inaction. Part of the dichotomy that this set up was the notion that the black man had done something to *me,* not to the woman he hit, and it was here that my anger lay. I wonder how this influenced my perception of black men I encountered in the future.

Tim Norton

What Is Social Class?

Rewards and Opportunities:

The Politics and Economics of Class in the U.S.*

Gregory Mantsios

"[Class is] for European democracies or something else—it isn't for the United States of America. We are not going to be divided by class."
George Bush, 1988[1]

Strange words from a man presiding over a nation with more than 32 million people living in poverty and one of the largest income gaps between rich and poor in the industrialized world.** Politicians long before and long after George Bush have made and will continue to make statements proclaiming our egalitarian values and denying the existence of class in America. But they are not alone: most Americans dislike talking about class. We minimize the extent of inequality, pretend that class differences do not really matter, and erase the word "class" from our vocabulary and from our mind. In one survey, designed to solicit respondents' class identification, 35% of all those questioned told interviewers they had never thought about their class identification before that very moment.[2]

"We are all middle-class" or so it would seem. Our national consciousness, as shaped in large part by the media and our political leadership, provides us with a picture of ourselves as a nation

of prosperity and opportunity with an ever expanding middle class life style. As a result, our class differences are muted and our collective character is homogenized.

Yet class divisions are real and arguably the most significant factor in determining both our very being in the world and the nature of the society we live in.

THE EXTENT OF POVERTY IN THE U.S.

The official poverty line in 1990 was $12,675 for an urban family of four and $9,736 for a family of three. For years, critics have argued that the measurements used by the government woefully underestimate the extent of poverty in America.[3] Yet even by the government's conservative estimate, nearly one in eight Americans currently lives in poverty.

As deplorable as this is, the overall poverty rate for the nation effectively masks both the level of deprivation and the extent of the problem within geographic areas and within specific populations. Three short years prior to George Bush's speech, the Physicians Task Force on Hunger in America declared that "Hunger is a problem of epidemic proportion across the nation." Upon completing their national field investigation of hunger and malnutrition, the team of twenty-two prominent physicians estimated that there were up to 20 million citizens hungry at least some period of time each month.

. . . Appalling conditions of poverty are facts of life in the foothills of Appalachia, the reservations of Native America, the barrios of the Southwest, the abandoned towns of the industrial belt, and the ghettoes of the nation's urban centers. There are more than 2 million poor people in New York City alone, a figure than exceeds the entire population of some nations.

Today, the poor include the very young and the elderly, the rural poor and the urban homeless: increasingly, the poor also include men and women who work full time. When we examine

---

*The author wishes to thank Bill Clark for his assistance in preparing this selection.
**The income gap in the United States, measured as a percentage of total income held by the wealthiest 20% of the population vs. the poorest 20% is approximately 11 to 1. The ratio in Great Britain is 7 to 1, in Japan, it is 4 to 1. (see "U.N. National Accounts Statistics", Statistical Papers, Series M no. 79, N.Y., U.N. 1985 pp. 1–11.)

the incidence of poverty within particular segments of the population, the figures can be both shameful and sobering:

- more than one out of every five children in the U.S. (all races) lives below the poverty line[4]
- 39% of Hispanic children and 45% of Black children in the U.S. live below the poverty line[5]
- one in every four rural children is poor[6]
- if you are Black and 65 years of age or older, your chances of being poor are one in three[7]
- roughly 60% of all poor work at least part-time or in seasonal work[8]
- 2 million Americans worked full time throughout the year and were still poor[9]

Poverty statistics have either remained relatively constant over the years or have shown a marked increase in the incidence of poverty. The number of full-time workers below the poverty line, for example, increased by more than 50% from 1978 to 1986.[10]

THE LEVEL OF WEALTH

Business Week recently reported that the average salary for the CEO of the nation's top 1,000 companies was $841,000.[11] As high as this figure is, however, it fails to capture the level of compensation at the top of the corporate world. Short-term and long-term bonuses, stock options and stock awards can add significantly to annual compensation. Take the following examples:

- annual compensation in 1989, including short-term bonuses, for the Chief Executive Officer of UAL, came to $18.3 million; for the head of Reeboks, compensation came to $14.6 million (in what was not a particularly hot year in the sneaker business).[12]
- annual compensation, including short-term and long-term bonuses and stock awards, for the head of Time Warner Inc. totaled $78.2 million; for the CEO of LIN Broadcasting, it came to a whooping $186 million.[13]

The distribution of income in the United States is outlined in Table 1.

TABLE 1	
INCOME INEQUALITY IN THE U.S.[14]	
Income group (families)	**Percent of income received**
Lowest fifth	4.6
Second fifth	10.8
Middle fifth	16.8
Fourth fifth	24.0
Highest fifth	43.7
(Highest 5 percent)	(17.0)

By 1990, according to economist Robert Reich, the top fifth of the population took home more money than the other four-fifths put together.[15]

Wealth, rather than income, is a more accurate indicator of economic inequality. Accumulated wealth by individuals and families runs into the billions, with the U.S. now boasting at least 58 billionaires, many of them multi-billionaires. The distribution of wealth is far more skewed than the distribution of income. In 1986, the Joint Economic Committee of the U.S. Congress released a special report entitled "The Concentration of Wealth in the United States." Table 2 summarizes some of the findings.

It should be noted that because of the way the statistics were collected by the Congressional Committee, the figure for 90% of all other families includes half of the families who fall into the wealthiest quintile of the population. The "super rich," that is, the top one-half of one percent of the population, includes approximately 420,000 households with the average value of the wealth for each one of these households amounting to $8.9 million.[17]

TABLE 2	
DISTRIBUTION OF WEALTH IN THE U.S.[16]	
Families	**Percent of wealth owned**
The richest 10%	71.7
(The top 1/2%)	(35.1)
Everyone else, or 90% of all families	28.2

THE PLIGHT OF THE MIDDLE CLASS

The percentage of households with earnings at a middle-income level has been falling steadily.[18] The latest census figures show that the percentage of families with an annual income between $15,000 and $50,000 (approximately 50% and 200% of the median income) has fallen by nearly 10 percentage points since 1970.[19] While some of the households have moved upward and others have moved downward, what is clear is that the United States is experiencing a significant polarization in the distribution of income. The gap between rich and poor is wider and the share of income earned by middle-income Americans has fallen to the lowest level since the census bureau began keeping statistics in 1946. More and more individuals and families are finding themselves at one or the other end of the economic spectrum as the middle class steadily declines.

Furthermore, being in the middle class is no longer what it used to be. Once, middle class status carried the promise that one's standard of living would steadily improve over time. Yet 60% of Americans will have experienced virtually no income gain between 1980 and 1990. (Compare this to the income gains experienced by the wealthiest fifth of the population—up by 33%, and the wealthiest one percent of the population—up by 87%.)[20] One study showed that only one in five (males) will surpass the status, income, and prestige of their fathers.[21]

Nor does a middle class income any longer guarantee the comforts it once did. Home ownership, for example, has increasingly become out of reach for a growing number of citizens. During the last decade home ownership rates dropped from 44% to 36% among people in the 25–29 year old age group and from 61% to 53% among those in their thirties.[22]

THE REWARDS OF MONEY

The distribution of income and wealth in the U.S. is grossly unequal and becomes increasingly more so with time. The rewards of money, however, go well beyond those of consumption patterns and life style. It is not simply that the wealthy live such opulent life styles, it is that class position determines one's life chances. Life chances include such far-reaching factors as life expectancy, level of education, occupational status, exposure to industrial hazards, incidence of crime victimization, rate of incarceration, etc. In short, class position can play a critically important role in determining how long you live, whether you have a healthy life, if you fail in school, or if you succeed at work.

The link between economic status and health is perhaps the most revealing and most disheartening. Health professionals and social scientists have shown that income is closely correlated to such factors as infant mortality, cancer, chronic disease, and death due to surgical and medical complications and "misadventures."[23]

The infant mortality rate is an example that invites international as well as racial and economic comparisons. At 10.6 infant deaths per 1,000 live births, the U.S. places nineteenth in the world—behind such countries as Spain, Singapore, and Hong Kong; a statistic that is in and of itself shameful for the wealthiest nation in the world. When infant mortality only among Blacks in the U.S. is considered, the rate rises to 18.2 and places the U.S. 28th in rank—behind Bulgaria and equal to Costa Rica.[24] . . .

Analyses of the relationship between health and income are not always easy to come by. A recent study conducted in New York City, however, provided some important information. The study examined the difference in health status and delivery of health services among residents from different neighborhoods. The data provided allows for comparing incidents of health problems in neighborhoods where 40% or more of the population lives below the poverty line with those in other neighborhoods where less than 10% of the population lives below the poverty line. The study found that the incidence of health problems, in many categories, was several times as great in poorer neighborhoods. For example, death associated with vascular complications (from the heart or brain) occurred nearly twice as often in poor areas than in non-poor. Similarly, chances of being afflicted with bronchitis is 5 times as great in poor areas than in non-poor areas.[25] The study concluded, "The findings clearly indicate that certain segments of the population—poor, minority, and other disadvantaged groups—are especially vulnerable and bear a disproportionate share of preventable, and therefore unnecessary deaths and diseases."[26]*

The reasons for such a high correlation are many and varied: inadequate nutrition, exposure to occupational and environmental hazards, access to health-care facilities, quality of health services provided, ability to pay and therefore receive medical services, etc. Inadequate nutrition, for example, is associated with low birth weights and growth failure among low-income children and with chronic disease among the elderly poor. It has also been shown that the uninsured and those covered by Medicaid are far less likely to be given common hospital procedures than are patients with private medical coverage. . . .

DIFFERENCES IN OPPORTUNITY

The opportunity for social and economic success are the hallmarks of the American Dream. The dream is rooted to two factors: education and jobs.

Our nation prides itself on its ability to provide unprecedented educational opportunities to its citizens. As well it should. It sends more of its young people to college than any other nation in the world. There are nearly 13 million Americans currently enrolled in colleges and universities around the country, a result of the tremendous expansion of higher education since World War II. The establishment of financial assistance for veterans and for the needy, and the growth of

affordable public colleges all have had an important and positive effect on college enrollment. Most importantly from the point of view of a national consciousness, the swelling of college enrollments has affirmed our egalitarian values and convinced us that our educational system is just and democratic.

Our pride, however, is a false pride. For while we have made great strides in opening the doors of academe, the system of education in the United States leaves much to be desired and is anything but egalitarian.

More than a quarter of our adult population has not graduated from high school, nearly three quarters do not hold a college degree.[27] This is a record that does not bode well for the most industrialized and technologically advanced nation in the world. Perhaps more importantly, the level of educational achievement is largely class determined.

At least equal in importance to the amount of education received, is the quality of education. The quality of primary and secondary schools is largely dependent on geography and proximity to schools with adequate resources. Educational funding, and the tax base for it, are determined by residency and who can afford to live where. Schools in poorer districts are just not as likely to provide a high-quality education.

Student achievement in the classroom and on standardized tests is also class determined. Studies from the late 1970s showed a direct relation between SAT scores and family income. Grouping SAT scores into twelve categories from highest to lowest, researchers found that the mean family income decreased consistently from one group to the next as test scores declined. The study was done by examining the test results and family income of over 600,000 students![28] In other words, the higher the family income, the higher the test scores and vice versa. . . .

A STRUCTURAL PERSPECTIVE

. . . The distribution of income and wealth occurs because a society is structured and policies

---

*It should be noted that the study was conducted in a major metropolitan area where hospitals and health-care facilities are in close proximity to the population, rich and poor. One might expect the discrepancies to be even greater in poor, rural areas where access to health care and medical attention is more problematic.

are implemented in such a way to either produce or alleviate inequalities. A society can choose to minimize the gaps in wealth and power between its most privileged and its most disenfranchised. Government can serve as the equalizer by providing mechanisms to redistribute wealth from the top to the bottom. The promise of government as the great equalizer has clearly failed in the U.S. and rather than redoubling the efforts to redistribute wealth, traditional redistributive mechanisms, such as the progressive income tax, have declined in use in recent years. The tax rate for the wealthiest segment of the population, for example, steadily declined in spite of, or perhaps because of, the increasing concentration of wealth and power at the top. In 1944 the top tax rate was 94%, after World War II it was reduced to 91%, in 1964 to 72%, in 1981 to 50%, in 1990 to 28% (for those with an annual income over $155,000).*

Nor is it the case that conditions of wealth simply coexist side-by-side with conditions of poverty. The point is not that there are rich and poor, but that some are rich precisely because others are poor, and that one's privilege is predicated on the other's disenfranchisement. If it were not for the element of exploitation, we might celebrate inequality as reflective of our nation's great diversity.

The great anti-poverty crusader, Michael Harrington, tells of the debate in Congress over Richard Nixon's Family Assistance Plan during the 1970s. If the government provided a minimum income to everyone, "Who," asked a southern legislator, "will iron my shirts and rake the yard?"[29]

The legislator bluntly stated the more complex truth: the privileged in our society require a class-structured social order in order to maintain and enhance their economic and political well-being. Industrial profits depend on cheap labor and on a pool of unemployed to keep workers in check.

---

*Ironically those with an annual income between $75,000 and $150,000 pay a higher rate of 33%.

Real estate speculators and developers create and depend on slums for tax-evading investments. These are the injustices and irrationalities of our economic system.

What is worse is that inequalities perpetuate themselves. People with wealth are the ones who have the opportunity to accumulate more wealth.

It is this ability to generate additional resources that most distinguishes the nation's upper class from the rest of society. It is not simply bank interest that generates more money, but income producing property: buildings, factories, natural resources; those assets Karl Marx referred to as the means of production. Today, unlike the early days of capitalism, these are owned either directly or indirectly through stocks. Economists estimate that for the super rich, the rate of return on such investments is approximately 30%.[30] Economists have also designed a device, called Net Financial Assets (NFA), to measure the level and concentration of income-producing property. While Net Worth (NW), a figure that considers all assets and debts, provides a picture of what kind of life-style is being supported, the NFA figure specifically excludes in its calculation ownership of homes and motor vehicles. By doing so, the NFA figure provides a more reliable measure of an individual's life chances and ability to accumulate future resources. A home or a car are not ordinarily converted to purchase other resources, such as a prep school or college education for one's children. Neither are these assets likely to be used to buy medical care, support political candidates, pursue justice in the courts, pay lobbyists to protect special interests, or finance a business or make other investments. Net financial assets include only those financial assets normally available for and used to generate income and wealth.[31] Stock ownership, for example, is a financial asset and is highly concentrated at the top, with the wealthiest 10% of the population owning over 89% of the corporate stocks.[32] Since home ownership is the major source of wealth for those who own a house, removing home equity as well as car ownership from the calculations has a significant impact on how we view the question of equity.

- The median net household income in the U.S. is $21,744, net worth in the U.S. is $32,609, and the median Net Financial Assets is $2,599.
- While the top 20% of American households earn over 43% of all income, that same 20% holds 67% of Net Worth, and nearly 90% of Net Financial Assets.
- The median income of the top one percent of the population is 22 times greater than that of the remaining 99%. The median Net Financial Assets of the top one percent is 237 times greater than the median of the other 99% of the population.[33]

The ability to generate wealth on the part of this class of owners is truly staggering. It contrasts sharply with the ability of those who rely on selling their labor power. For those with income under $25,000, wage and salary income from labor comprised 90% of their total income.

There is also an entrepreneurial middle class in America that includes farmers, shopkeepers, and others. The small entrepreneurs, however, are becoming increasingly marginal in America and their income-producing property hardly exempts them from laboring.

The wealthy usually work too: their property income, however, is substantial enough to enable them to live without working if they chose to do so.

People with wealth and financial assets have disproportionate power in society. First, they have control of the workplace in enterprises they own. They determine what is produced and how it is produced. Second, they have enormous control over the media and other institutions that influence ideology and how we think about things, including class. Third, they have far greater influence over the nations' political institutions than their numbers warrant. They have the ability to influence not only decisions affecting their particular business ventures, but the general political climate of the nation.

SPHERES OF POWER AND OPPRESSION

. . . People do not choose to be poor or working class; instead they are limited and confined by the opportunities afforded or denied them by a social system. The class structure in the United States is a function of its economic system—capitalism, a system that is based on private rather than public ownership and control of commercial enterprises and on the class division between those who own and control and those who do not. Under capitalism, these enterprises are governed by the need to produce a profit for the owners, rather than to fulfill collective needs.

Racial and gender domination are other such forces that hold people down. Although there are significant differences in the way capitalism, racism and sexism affect our lives, there are also a multitude of parallels. And although race, class, and gender act independently of each other, they are at the same time very much interrelated.

On the one hand, issues of race and gender oppression cut across class lines. Women experience the effects of sexism whether they are well-paid professionals or poorly paid clerks. As women, they face discrimination and male domination, as well as catcalls and stereotyping. Similarly, a Black man faces racial oppression whether he is an executive, an auto worker, or a tenant farmer. As a Black, he will be subjected to racial slurs and be denied opportunities because of his color. Regardless of their class standing, women and members of minority races are confronted with oppressive forces precisely because of their gender, color, or both.

On the other hand, class oppression permeates other spheres of power and oppression, so that the oppression experienced by women and minorities is also differentiated along class lines. Although women and minorities find themselves in subordinate positions vis-à-vis white men, the particular issues they confront may be quite different depending on their position in the class structure. Inequalities in the class structure distinguish social functions and individual power, and these distinctions carry over to race and gender categories. . . .

. . . If you are Black and female, for example, you are much more likely to be poor and working class than you would be as a white male. Census

TABLE 3

CHANCES OF BEING POOR IN AMERICA[34]

	White male & female	White female head	Black male & female	Black female head
Poverty	1 in 9	1 in 4	1 in 3	1 in 2
Near Poverty	1 in 6	1 in 3	1 in 2	2 in 3

figures show that the incidence of poverty and near-poverty (calculated as 125% of the poverty line) varies greatly by race and gender.

In other words, being female and being non-white are attributes in our society that increase the chances of poverty and of lower-class standing. Racism and sexism compound the effects of classism in society.

NOTES

1. Quoted in George Will, "A Case for Dukakis," in *The Washington Post,* November 13, 1988, p. A27.
2. Marian Irish and James Prothro, *The Politics of American Democracy.* Engelwood Cliffs, N. J., Prentice-Hall, 1965, p. 2, 38.
3. See, for example, Patricia Ruggles, "The Poverty Line—Too Low for the 90's," in the *New York Times,* April 26, 1990, p. A31.
4. Bureau of Census, "Statistical Abstract of the U.S. 1990," Department of Commerce, Washington, D.C., 1990, p. 460.
5. Ibid.
6. Ibid.
7. Ibid.
8. *U.S. News and World Report,* January 1, 1988, pp. 18–24.
9. Ibid.
10. Ibid.
11. *Business Week,* October 19, 1990, p. 11.
12. Ibid, p. 12.
13. *Business Week,* May 6, 1991, p. 90.
14. U.S. Department of Commerce, "Statistical Abstract of the U.S. 1988," Washington, D.C., 1988, p. 428.
15. Robert Reich, "Secession of the Successful," *New York Times,* January 20, 1991, p. M42.
16. Joint Economic Committee of the U.S. Congress, "The Concentration of Wealth in the United States," Washington, D.C., 1986, p. 24.
17. Richard Roper, *Persistent Poverty: The American Dream Turned Nightmare,* Plenum Press, 1991, p. 60.
18. Chris Tilly, "U-Turn on Equality," *Dollars and Sense,* May 1986, p. 84.
19. Census, ibid, p. 450.
20. "And the Rich Get Richer," *Dollars and Sense,* October 1990, p. 5.
21. Richard DeLone, *Small Futures,* Harcourt Brace Jovanovich, 1978, pp. 14–19.
22. Roper, ibid, p. 32.
23. Melvin Krasner, *Poverty and Health in New York City,* United Hospital Fund of New York, 1989. See also, U.S. Dept of Health and Human Services, *Health Status of Minorities and Low Income Groups,* 1985; and Dana Hughes, Kay Johnson, Sara Rosenbaum, Elizabeth Butler, Janet Simons, *The Health of America's Children,* The Children's Defense Fund, 1988.
24. Physicians Task Force, ibid; Hughes, et al; ibid; and "World Development Report 1990," World Bank, Oxford University Press, 1990, pp. 232–233.
25. Krasner, ibid, p. 134.
26. Ibid, p. 166.
27. The Chronicle of Higher Education, *The Almanac of Higher Education, 1989–1990,* The University of Chicago Press, 1989.
28. Richard DeLone, ibid, p. 102.
29. Michael Harrington, *The New American Poverty,* Penguin, 1985, p. 3.
30. E. K. Hunt and Howard Sherman, *Economics,* Harper and Row, 1990, pp. 254–257.
31. Melvin Oliver and Thomas Shapiro, "Wealth of a Nation," *The American Journal of Economics and Sociology,* April 1990, p. 129.
32. The Joint Economic Committee, ibid.
33. Oliver, ibid, p. 129.
34. "Characteristics of the Population Below the Poverty Line: 1984," from Current Population Reports, Consumer Income Series P-60, No. 152, Washington, D.C., U.S. Department of Commerce, Bureau of the Census, June 1986, pp. 5–9.

I Am a Pakistani Woman

I am a Pakistani woman, raised in the U.S. and Canada, and often at odds with the western standard of beauty.

As a child in Nova Scotia and later growing up in New York and Indiana, I was proud of my uniqueness. On traditional Pakistani and Muslim holidays, I got to wear bright, fun clothes from my country and colorful jewelry. I had a whole rich tradition of my own to celebrate in addition to Christmas and Easter. However, as I started school, I somehow came to realize that being different wasn't so great—that in other people's viewpoint, I looked strange and acted funny. I learned the importance of fitting in and behaving like the other girls. This involved dressing well, giggling a lot, and having a superior, but flirtatious attitude toward boys. I was very outgoing and had very good grades, so outwardly I was able to "assimilate" with some success. But my sister, who was quiet and reticent often took the brunt of other children's cruelty. I realize how proud and ashamed I was of my heritage when I look at my relationship with my family.

A lesson I learned early on in the U.S. was that being beautiful took a lot of money. It is painful, as an adult, for me to consider the inexorable, never-ending pressure that my father was under to embody the dominant, middle-class cultural expressions of masculinity, as in success at one's job, making a big salary, and owning status symbols. I resented him so much then for being a poor, untenured professor and freelance writer. I wanted designer clothes, dining out at nice restaurants, and a big allowance. Instead, I had a deeply spiritual thinker, writer, and theologian for a dad. I love(d) him and am so very grateful for what he's taught me, but as a child I didn't think of him as a success.

The prettiest girls in school all had a seemingly endless array of outfits, lots of makeup and perfume, and everything by the "right" designers. I hated my mom for making many of my clothes and buying things on sale (and my mom was a great seamstress). I hungrily read about Brooke Shields's seemingly perfect life, with her excursions to expensive restaurants and appointments with personal trainers at exclusive spas. I felt a sense of hopelessness that I could never have the resources or opportunities necessary to compete, to be beautiful.

Instead I found safety in conformity. When I was in high school, the WASPy, preppy look was hot; it represented the epitome of success and privilege in America. I worked hard to purchase a wardrobe of clothes with a polo-horse insignia, by many hours at an after-school job. I tried to hide my exotic look behind Khakis, boat shoes, hair barrettes, and pearl studs. There was comfort in conformity. I saw the class "sex symbol" denigrated for wearing tight dresses and having a very well-developed body for a sixteen-year-old, and the more unique dressers dismissed as frivolous, trendy, and more than a little eccentric. You couldn't be too pretty, too ugly, too different—you had to just blend in.

Though I did it well, I perpetually felt like an imposter. This rigidly controlled, well-dressed preppy going through school with good grades in advanced placement classes in no way represented what I felt to be my true essence.

Hoorie I. Siddique

The Undeserving Poor

Michael B. Katz

By the mid-1980s, a new image dominated poverty discourse. Invoked unreflectively and automatically by commentators on poverty, the concept of the *underclass* captured the mixture of alarm and hostility that tinged the emotional response of more affluent Americans to the poverty of blacks increasingly clustered and isolated in postindustrial cities. What bothered observers most was not their suffering; rather, it was their sexuality, expressed in teenage pregnancy; family patterns, represented by female-headed households; alleged reluctance to work for low wages; welfare dependence, incorrectly believed to be a major drain on national resources; and propensity for drug use and violent crime, which had eroded the safety of the streets and the subways.

In fact, the very poor evoked two different images among affluent Americans. When they appeared pathetic, they were the homeless; when they seemed menacing, they became the underclass. Although membership among the homeless and underclass overlapped, public discourse implicity divided them by degree of personal responsibility for their situation. As long as they remained supplicants rather than militants, objects of charity rather than subjects of protest, the homeless became the new deserving poor.

THE HOMELESS

The homeless embody the contradictions of the postindustrial city. Huddled over steam vents, in doorways, on the benches of subway and train stations, they remind us daily that economic recovery has not lessened poverty or tempered inequality. They bear the most visible cost of the transformation of American cities by urban renewal, gentrification, and downtown revitalization; of the dismantling of the old industrial economy; and of government's war on welfare. They show that the richest and most powerful nation in the world cannot provide all its citizens with a decent and secure place in which to live. They tell us that the billions of dollars poured into urban reform have not rendered archaic "the other America." The growing number of families among them drive home the awful fact that among industrialized countries, only in America is childhood the age of greatest poverty.

Homelessness is both a condition and a category. The Stewart B. McKinney Homeless Assistance Act, passed by Congress in 1987, defines a homeless person as "one who lacks a fixed nighttime residence or whose nighttime residence is a temporary shelter, welfare hotel, transitional housing for the mentally ill, or any public and private place not designed as sleeping accommodations for human beings." This innocuous and seemingly objective definition begs questions: For how long does someone lack a nighttime residence before he or she becomes officially homeless? On what grounds do we exclude from the

homeless those driven to beg shelter from friends or relatives? However useful this definition is as a neutral description of a condition, homelessness remains an emotionally charged social category, a frame within which we gather, observe, study, count, think about, sometimes pity or despise numbers of poor people. Although we think of them as an undifferentiated group, the homeless are different from one another, varied in age, race, gender, family condition, and history.[1]

Nobody knows how many people are homeless in America, even by the McKinney Act's definition. Counting the homeless is extraordinarily difficult for several reasons, including their transience. Many people are homeless only for a short time, and the number of homeless in the course of a year far exceeds the number without shelter on any given night. The National Alliance to End Homelessness, for instance, estimated that 735,000 people were homeless every night; between 1.3 and 2 million would be homeless for at least one night in 1988; and 6 million Americans because of the disproportionately high cost of housing, are at "extreme risk of becoming homeless." In 1982, Hombs and Snyder, two homeless advocates, estimated the number as 2.2 million; in 1984, the U.S. Department of Housing and Urban Development reported the number as between 200,000 and 300,000. Hombs and Snyder were advocates for the homeless; HUD was an agent of the Reagan administration. In fact, these studies and others are flawed. All that can be said with confidence, and it is probably enough, is that shelter operators report large increases in the numbers of people who seek their services. Between January 1983 and December 1984 the number of families in New York City's shelters rose 67 percent; in 1987, most American cities reported annual increases between 15 and 50 percent in those identified as homeless.[2]

Although families with children comprise the fastest growing subgroup among the homeless population (according to the U.S. Conference of Mayors, in 1986 they were 28 percent of all homeless people in America's 25 largest cities), most homeless people still are individual adults, a majority men, though the number of women has increased notably in recent years. The age of the men averages between 34 and 37; the women generally are two to six years younger. Most homeless adults have never married and lack family to whom they can turn for help. Nearly half have graduated from high school, and the great majority have lived for a long time in the city that shelters them. Large numbers are Vietnam veterans; probably about 30 percent could be diagnosed as having some form of psychiatric disorder; and substantial numbers have alcohol and drug problems. Other notable subgroups among the homeless are adolescents who have run away from home or been turned out by their parents; elderly people, whose proportion among the homeless is much lower than among the whole population; and the rural homeless, who remain much less visible than their counterparts in cities.[3]

The reasons why so many more Americans are homeless reflect both structural change and government policy. Homeless people are casualties of the postindustrial city. The exit of manufacturing has removed many of the jobs at which they once might have worked. The new jobs for which they qualify within the service sector usually pay wages too low to meet escalating housing costs. Urban renewal has torn down low-cost housing, including the SRO (single room occupancy) hotels in which unattached poor people often lived. Indeed, as it has wiped out skid rows in cities across the country, urban redevelopment has obliterated housing for the poor. In only a little more than one decade, between 1970 and 1982, nearly half of all single-room units in America, some 1,116,000, vanished. Fueled by inflation and gentrification, rents rose rapidly in the 1970s. By 1980, 7 million households were paying more than half their income in rent.[4]

Demographic patterns worsened the housing problem. Increased migration of minorities into cities and growing numbers of single-parent families escalated the demand for more low-cost housing during the very years that urban redevelopment, inflation, and gentrification lessened the supply. Government policy exacerbated the problem in a number of ways. Its urban renewal and transportation policies financed the destruction of low-cost urban housing and accelerated the social and spatial transformation of cities, while its policies toward the mentally ill added to the number of people unable to support themselves and in need of housing.

For very good reasons, in the 1960s critics began to expose the flaws in public mental health systems that responded to mental illness by warehousing victims in massive and expensive institutions. In the same years, the advent of new drugs capable of controlling the behavior of the mentally ill made possible their discharge into communities. As a result, the population of mental hospitals dropped from a high of 559,000 in 1955 to a low of 130,000 in 1980. Its advocates promoted deinstitutionalization as part of a comprehensive policy that included community mental health clinics and appropriate aftercare. For the most part, it was not. Former patients, lacking work, struggled to find housing affordable on minimal incomes from disability insurance. Although the number of former patients did not grow after the great first wave of discharges, admissions declined, and many of the mentally ill who once would have been hospitalized were left on the streets, where they too joined the ranks of the homeless.[5]

Cuts in social welfare at both the federal and state levels compounded the difficulties poor people encountered finding housing. Between 1970 and 1985, the median value of AFDC benefits declined about one-third in constant dollars. At the same time, the value of General Assistance— that is, relief provided by state governments, dropped about 32 percent. In the early 1980s, the Reagan administration, as part of its war on welfare, successfully excised about 200,000 disabled people, many with psychiatric disorders, from the roles of Supplemental Social Security. It also radically reduced the role of the federal government in increasing the supply of low-cost housing. "The Reagan administration," claims Chester Hartman, wanted "to shut off the housing spigot altogether." As a result, new housing starts for all HUD lower-income housing programs dropped steadily from 183,000 in 1980 to 28,000 in 1985.

In the same years, the administration cut the Community Development Block Grant, of which about 30 percent was spent on housing rehabilitation; ended Neighborhood Self-Help Development grants, which helped communities resist housing displacement; reduced federal operating subsidies for public housing and funds for modernizing public housing; and raised the proportion of income to be paid by the poor for subsidized housing. In 1985, a HUD Deputy Assistant Secretary told the Urban League's convention: "We're basically backing out of the business of housing, period." The administration's answer to the problem was vouchers, a housing allowance poor people could spend as they wished. However, without incentives to build low-cost housing or subsidies, there was little likelihood that private developers would construct the massive number of low-cost units now needed; nor, without controls, was it likely that landlords would repair substandard buildings or refrain from charging excessive rents. The existing housing stock could not meet the demand for low-cost housing; neither through direct action nor incentives did the federal government increase the supply of new housing; income subsidies were too low to permit poor people to afford available housing without depriving themselves of other necessities. The result was a housing crisis of which the homeless were but the most visible tip.[6]

We know surprisingly little about how poor people throughout American history actually survived from day to day. Often, they have depended on incomes that seemed too low to sustain them and their families. The key to their survival, I suspect from what little research there is, has been a series of complex, intersecting networks. Some of these have centered on family. Kin have helped each other through crises. Others have linked neighbors in intricate chains of reciprocity, spontaneous and extraordinary acts of generosity between poor people themselves. Still others have

been more institutional: local labor markets that awarded jobs on the basis of friendship and patronage and, of critical importance, local sources of credit, mainly small merchants and landlords, who sustained people they knew through the times they lacked cash.

My sense, and I can offer it only as a hypothesis, is that homelessness, and indeed urban poverty, has become a different sort of problem than in the past because these networks either have been attenuated or have disappeared. Urban redevelopment has destroyed the basis of many neighborhood networks; retailing has almost disappeared from many inner-city neighborhoods, where national chains have replaced local merchants. Jobs have moved away from where people live, and few local labor markets of any significance still exist. Finally, there is the question of family. Family members may disperse to find work; pinched by the crisis in low-cost housing, they may often lack space in which to house their kin; with AFDC available, more young, single mothers seek their own housing, for which they are able to pay very little. All these factors may have weakened the network of supports within inner cities, transforming the experience of poverty and fueling the rise of homelessness.[7] . . .

Although some moral ambiguity hovers over the homeless today, their status among the very poor has improved. They are, as Mark Stern has argued, the new deserving poor. They represent a category as well as a condition. What accounts for its timing and appeal? (Sociologist Peter Rossi points out that the *Reader's Guide to Periodical Literature* listed no articles on homelessness in 1975, compared to 34 in 1984 and 48 in 1986. His own working bibliography in 1988 exceeded 60 single-spaced pages, with about three-quarters of the entries dating from 1980 or later.) The emergence of homelessness as a public problem reflects, first, its visibility. Homelessness does not take place in private, nor does it confine itself to ghetto areas where affluent persons rarely travel. On the contrary, it is defined by its public nature. Because homelessness manifests itself in public spaces, its spectacular increase has altered urban topography. As they appropriated spaces in railroad stations, subways, lobbies, and doorways, homeless people redefined urban space. They might not be helped, but they could not be ignored.

For Stern, it was the 1981 consent decree in New York City's Callahan case that initially turned homelessness into a public problem. "The decree committed the city to provide clean and safe shelter for every homeless man and woman who sought it and set standards against overcrowding in shelters." National political action reinforced events in New York City, as a coalition formed at the 1980 Democratic Convention organized demonstrations; two books, *Shopping Bag Ladies* by Ann Marie Rousseau and *Private Lives, Public Spaces* by Ellen Baxter and Kim Hopper, focused the attention of the public on the issue, and the harsh winter of 1981–82 finally forced it to the forefront of public consciousness.[8]

Stern locates the appeal of homelessness in its capacity to reestablish the "gift relationship" as the basis of public and private charity. Charity's historic role extended beyond the alleviation of poverty; it served to bind classes together and to reinforce social relations based on deference and obligation. In his great study of poverty in late nineteenth-century London, Gareth Stedman Jones wrote: "To give, from whatever motives, generally imposes an obligation upon the receiver. In order to receive one must behave in an acceptable manner, if only by expressing gratitude and humiliation." Responses to homelessness reflected the appeal of the gift relationship.[9] Plans for fighting homelessness, as Stern notes, tried to reestablish "the bond between giver and recipient" through voluntary rather than state action. Discourse on the homeless stressed "their almost saint-like spirits," and "docility and gratitude," rather than "anger and suspicion."[10]

The framing of homelessness as a problem for charity posed dilemmas for policy. First, it frustrated solutions to long-term problems because voluntarism cannot abolish homelessness. Not only does the appropriation of homelessness as a charity deflect attention away from its potential to energize a broader attack on poverty, it also inhibits direct, aggressive action by poor people on their own behalf, which is essential to the initiation of political reform. As the homeless organize unions, press their demands in demonstrations, and form coalitions with other poor people, their special appeal will fade. They will be warned that militance backfires; run into conflict with many of their liberal champions who, hurt, will retreat from their cause; and slip again into the ranks of the undeserving poor.[11]

The other problem is this: Homelessness illustrates Martha Minow's* dilemma of difference. For it is a social category, not a defining quality of persons. Those poor people with nowhere to live vary greatly in their characteristics. To collapse them into one category by abstracting one aspect of their lives is to subordinate their individuality; to mark them as different, and because they need help, as inferior to the rest of us; and to leave them with a label that can turn as quickly into a stigma as into a plea for help. Yet, without the creation of this category, public sympathy on behalf of those poor people included within it would not have swelled, many fewer volunteers would have responded, and poor people would have suffered even more.

Is there a way to energize public action that does not stigmatize and isolate? Is there in America a way to foster a discourse about poverty based on human dignity and community rather than on invidious categories and market-based models of public policy? The late 1980s provided little reason for optimism. For even more than homelessness, another new category began to dominate discussions of poverty. I refer, of course, to the underclass.

---

*Martha Minow, *Making All the Difference,* forthcoming, manuscript p. 5.

THE EMERGENCE OF THE UNDERCLASS AS A PUBLIC ISSUE

In 1987, *The New York Times* pointed to the recent discovery of an underclass by American social science:

> Social scientists have focused new energies on an "underclass" of Americans who live in near total isolation from mainstream society, and scholars are trying to learn more about the deteriorating inner-city areas where not working is the norm, crime is a commonplace and welfare is a way of life [italics in original].[12]

Two groups—black teenage mothers and black jobless youths—dominated the images of the underclass. The former received the most attention, and antipoverty policy, redefined as welfare reform, came to mean intervening in the alleged cycle of dependency in which young, unmarried black women and their children had become trapped. Black males became less a problem for social welfare and more of one for the police. Instead of training and employment, public policy responded by putting more of them in jail. Rates of incarceration in the United States soared above those in every other Western industrial democracy. Recidivism and prison overcrowding became the equivalent of welfare dependency and escalating AFDC rolls, and the privatization of prisons worked no better as a policy response than Ronald Reagan's early expectation of turning much of public welfare over to private charity.[13]

Not only did poverty discourse pay less attention to the joblessness of black males, it virtually ignored both the majority of the poor, who were not black and did not live in female-headed families, and the explosive growth of poverty among white adult males. . . .

Consider, as a prime example, the first major announcement of the underclass in the mass media, *Time* magazine's cover story, "The American Underclass," in its issue of August 19, 1977. "Behind [the ghetto's] crumbling walls lives a large group of people who are more intractable, more socially alien and more hostile than almost anyone had imagined. They are the unreachables: the American underclass." *Time* defined the underclass primarily by its values and behavior, which differed sharply from those of other Americans. "Their bleak environment nurtures values that are often at odds with those of the majority—even the majority of the poor. Thus the underclass produces a highly disproportionate number of the nation's juvenile delinquents, school dropouts, drug addicts and welfare mothers, and much of the adult crime, family disruption, urban decay and demand for social expenditures." As the description continued, the image became even more menacing. "Rampaging members of the underclass carried out much of the orgy of looting and burning that swept New York's ghettos during the July blackout. . . . They are responsible for most of the youth crime that has spread like an epidemic through the nation." Most persons in the underclass were "not looters or arsonists or violent criminals," admitted *Time,* but they remained "so totally disaffected from the system that many who would not themselves steal or burn only stand by while others do so, sometimes cheering them on."[14]

Like other commentators, the authors of the *Time* article failed to define the underclass clearly and consistently. For they described it not only by its behavioral pathology and deviant values, but by its relation to the process of social mobility as well. "Underclass" referred to people "stuck at the bottom, removed from the American dream," and therefore left unclear just who composed the underclass, whether its members represented a population disadvantaged by lack of mobility, in which case their numbers would include many poor people untainted by drugs, promiscuity, or criminality, or whether the term should be reserved as a label for behavior. *Time* stressed that the underclass differed from the rest of America. They were aliens, alarming strangers in our midst. Indeed, for *Time* the American underclass consisted of international outcasts: A confluence of factors—"the weakness of family structure, the presence of competing street values, and the lack of hope amidst affluence"—had created in America an "underclass unique among the world's poor people."[15]

During the next decade, mass media interpretations of the underclass changed very little. In 1986, *U.S. News and World Report*'s cover story, "A Nation Apart," reinforced the image of poor people of color in America's inner cities as strangers, aliens in their own country, defined primarily by their deviant values. A "second nation" had emerged within black America, "a nation outside the economic mainstream—a separate culture of have-nots drifting further apart from the basic values of the haves. Its growth is now the central issue in the country's urban centers." Little more than a year later, an article in *Fortune* reinforced the same interpretation. It defined "underclass communities" as "urban knots that threaten to become enclaves of permanent poverty and vice" and impose severe social and economic costs on the rest of American society, leaving business without a work force sufficiently skilled for jobs in the twenty-first century. Not so much their poverty or race as their "behavior—their chronic lawlessness, drug use, out-of-wedlock births, non-work, welfare dependency, and school failure," asserted the author, defined the underclass: "Underclass describes a state of mind and a way of life. It is at least as much a cultural as an economic condition."[16]

Social scientists did relatively little to modify the popular image of a menacing underclass defined by behavior rather than poverty. Indeed, when American social science discovered the underclass, it paid more attention to its behavior than to its origins in the transformations that intensified poverty within postindustrial cities. As early as 1969, Lee Rainwater criticized this constricted vision. Social scientists, he wrote, had neglected to analyze "the central fact about the American underclass—that it is created by, and its existence is maintained by, the operation of what is in other ways the most successful economic system known to man."[17]

Douglas Glasgow's *Black Underclass* (1980) tried to direct debate along the path urged by

Rainwater and later taken by William J. Wilson. Glasgow used the concept to frame his research on the young men who had participated in the great Watts riot of 1965. The emergence of an underclass as a "permanent fixture of our nation's social structure," he wrote, represented "one of the most significant class developments in the past two decades." By underclass, he meant "a permanently entrapped population of poor persons, unused and unwanted, accumulated in various parts of the country."[18] Blacks, disproportionately represented among the poor, remained particularly vulnerable to the magnetic force of the underclass. "Structural factors found in market dynamics and institutional practices, as well as the legacy of racism, produce and then reinforce the cycle of poverty and, in turn, work as a pressure exerting a downward pull toward underclass status."[19] Serious misconceptions, argued Glasgow, detracted attention from the obstacles confronting blacks. For example, references to statistics that pointed to improvements in blacks' economic status between 1959 and 1974 failed to note that white unemployment fell about twice as far as black, widening the unemployment gap between races, and that the proportion of blacks among the poor actually had increased. In both 1959 and 1974, blacks' poverty rate exceeded that of whites by about three times. The argument that significant numbers of blacks had moved into the middle class also misdirected interpretations of black experience. First, figures that showed increasing incomes for black families reflected the joint wages of employed husbands and wives. In fact, as individuals black men and women continued to earn less than their white counterparts, and the increasing number of single-headed black families offset the gains by those with two wage earners.[20]

Most serious were the unemployment problems of black youth. Their lack of work opportunity in the primary labor market locked many young blacks permanently into the underclass. Nor did all blacks who worked escape, because their low wages and occupational immobility trapped them in poverty despite their commitment to the work ethic. (Glasgow stressed that research has demonstrated the eagerness for work among black youths. He dismissed as a cruel myth the idea that they were unwilling to enter the labor market.) Blacks' detachment from the "standardized institutions" feeding the primary labor market reinforced their entrapment in the underclass. Indeed, this inability to escape poverty was, for Glasgow, the component that differentiated the underclass from a lower class, whose members realistically could expect mobility if not for themselves, then for their children.[21]

Therefore, "underclass" did not "connote moral or ethical unworthiness" or "any other pejorative meaning." Rather, it described a new population, "not necessarily culturally deprived, lacking in aspirations, or unmotivated to achieve," but the static poor, trapped in their situation by a variety of forces, primarily constricted opportunities and "limited alternatives provided by socialization patterns." Rejection by mainstream institutions, especially schools, fed the rage and desperation of ghetto youth. Rejection often maimed and broke them by denying their individuality and integrity. As a result, behavior considered destructive by many remained their "one great protection" against a system that assured them failure. Economic trends also trapped black youths in the underclass by eliminating entry-level jobs and reducing the need for unskilled labor. Of all the forces sustaining the underclass, however, racism remained the strongest. Despite the virtual disappearance of legal discrimination, computers now excluded people ostensibly "on the basis not of 'race' but of 'social profile.'" What, then, was the answer? What would help break up the underclass and move blacks out of poverty? The key was jobs, whose provision should be the prime goal of policies to alleviate the underclass crisis in America's cities.[22]

Glasgow's interpretation of the underclass excluded two themes that would dominate most subsequent discussion. First, he wrote only about men. Second, he scarcely mentioned black family structure. . . . Within a few years, however, writers on poverty associated with the conservative political revival had reestablished culture and family structure on the agenda of social science and public policy. This new legitimacy for old concerns—feminist attention to women's poverty—and demographic trends in the 1970s served to focus even moderate and liberal poverty discourse on family and culture. In the process, "underclass" assumed a connotation quite different than Glasgow had intended. One major example is Ken Auletta's book *The Underclass* (1982), which popularized the concept and pointed to its emerging meaning.[23]

Auletta based his book on observations of an experimental supported work program funded by the Manpower Demonstration Research Corporation in New York City. Despite his cautious conclusion that the program had succeeded, others, reading his account, could reach a less sanguine verdict.

Auletta defined the underclass as a relatively permanent minority of the poor with "four distinct categories": "(a) the *passive poor,* usually long-term welfare recipients; (b) the *hostile* street criminals who terrorize most cities, and who are often school dropouts and drug addicts; (c) the *hustlers,* who, like street criminals, may not be poor and who earn their livelihood in an underground economy, but rarely commit violent crimes; (d) the *traumatized* drunks, drifters, homeless shopping-bag ladies and released mental patients who frequently roam or collapse on city streets."[24] For Auletta as well as Glasgow, lack of mobility defined the underclass. However, Auletta remained more concerned with the behavior of the underclass than its origins and focused on strategies that taught its members how to enter the mainstream working world.

Although he intended his book to be nonideological, Auletta's account fit within the historic tradition of American poverty discourse. (This, certainly, is one explanation for the book's popularity and influence. Another is its resonance with a new consensus about the source of social problems.) Like those who wrote on poverty two centuries before him, Auletta began by separating poor people into two categories and identifying one of them primarily by its deviant behavior. Economic and occupational criteria did not determine class membership. In his definition, the source of stratification lay elsewhere. The underclass was a moral, not a sociological, category. Its members were the new undeserving poor. In the tradition of nineteenth-century social critics who fused crime, poverty, and ignorance into interchangeable eruptions of moral pathology, Auletta linked disparate groups into one class. His definition subsumed women on welfare, street criminals, hustlers, and homeless drunks, drifters, and bag ladies into one interchangeable unit identified not by income or dependence, but by behavior.[25]

Despite his narrative focus on a work training program, Auletta's discussion of poverty subordinated employment. It redirected discussion to family and behavior. "The struggle to overcome poverty," he wrote, "has entered a new phase, and one of the most significant problems that has emerged is family structure." Auletta traced the role of family structure in the work of E. Franklin Frazier, Kenneth Clark, and Daniel Patrick Moynihan and recounted the subsequent attack that drove it from the agendas of social science and public policy. Increasingly, though, he reported, the black family had reappeared as a major topic in discussions about poverty, and even "some leading black officials" had "become less inhibited on the subject." Therefore, when Auletta presented thirteen "facts about poverty and the underclass" which were "undebatable and unavoidable," women and family headed the list. His first fact was, "Poverty has become feminized," and his second, "Whether family dissolution is a cause or an effect of poverty, it unquestionably cannot be overlooked." None of his facts specified joblessness as a source of poverty.[26] . . .

JOBLESSNESS AND THE BLACK UNDERCLASS

The experience of young men underlines a paradox in recent black history. Affirmative action, equal opportunity programs, and other efforts by both the government and private sector have reduced discrimination and raised black youths' wages relative to whites. "Young blacks," report economists Richard Freeman and Harry Holzer, "have made advances in both occupation and education. Yet their *employment* problem has worsened, reaching levels that can only be described as catastrophic." As high as they are, unemployment statistics do not capture the full measure of the crisis because they are limited to active job seekers. More revealing are the statistics of labor force participation and ratios of employment to population. Between 1955 and 1984, the ratio of employment to the total population of 18- to 19-year-old black males dropped from 66 to 34; in the same period the ratio for employed white males remained nearly identical (64 and 60). In 1983, only 45 percent of black men aged 16 to 21 were employed compared to 73 percent of whites. "In many respects," Freeman and Holzer comment, "the urban unemployment characteristic of Third World countries appears to have taken root among black youths in the United States."[27]

No single, definitive explanation accounts for the employment crisis among young black men. Social scientists debate the relative influence of skills, work ethic, family background, job location and quality, and competition from women and immigrants. Sponsored by the National Bureau of Economic Research, several economists designed a survey to provide data with which to answer key questions about joblessness among young black males. They confined their survey to males because the problem is by far the most serious among them. In 1979, they interviewed 2,358 men in inner-city areas of Boston, Chicago, and Philadelphia. They also drew on the National Longitudinal Surveys of Labor Market Experience, also from 1979, for comparisons with black men living outside inner cities and with whites. The survey asked detailed questions about standard work activities, the hourly activities of these youths in a day, their desire to work, their use of drugs, their participation in illegal activities, and their perceptions of the labor market. *The Black Youth Employment Crisis* presents the major results.[28]

The findings are complex: No single factor is *the* cause of the unemployment problem. Nor do the studies based on the survey reveal patterns on which all the participating economists agree. Some findings, in fact, are much more robust than others. What unifies the studies is the finding that "black male youths are quite responsive to a number of economic incentives and to their social and family environment." In other words, "different incentives" should significantly improve the employment situation of black youths. Designing ways of changing these incentives remains the "major challenge" confronting public policy directed toward increasing employment among young black men.[29]

What do studies based on the surveys show about specific factors relating to black youth unemployment?

1. Young black men want jobs and wages comparable to whites', and their reluctance to take worse jobs lengthens their periods of unemployment. Nonetheless, they are more willing to take badly paying, dead-end jobs, although they do so only temporarily. Because young blacks model their expectations and aspirations on white society, their problem is means, not ends, and concerns about a "culture of poverty" defined by an absence of "middle-class aspirations" lack any foundation. Instead, the great problem young blacks face is "how to achieve their aspirations."[30]

2. The "dynamics of the transition to work" differ for inner-city black youths in four important and unfortunate ways. In contrast to white youths, their employment rate does not improve very much with age. As a consequence, joblessness will not disappear when they become older. Inner-city black youths remain unemployed or never employed far longer than whites. Black youths differ from white youths more in the ease with which they move into employment than in the rate at which they lose jobs. (This results primarily from the reluctance of employers to hire black youths.) Unlike whites and all black youths, however, the duration of their employment does not influence the chances that young black men from the inner city will leave work as a result of choice, layoff, or firing. The reason appears to be "the dead-end types of jobs inner-city blacks obtain."[31]

3. Black youths often do not live near the jobs for which they qualify. However, social scientists do not agree on the implications of this distance between home and potential work. The "spatial mismatch" hypothesis argues that "the outflow of people and firms has left those least able to find and commute to employment trapped far away from the areas where new jobs are opening." Research on the NBER data dispute this explanation, but as a critic points out, the issue—which has obvious and important consequences for policy—remains far from settled.[32]

4. Women substitute for black men in the "production process." Indeed, women's entry into the labor market could be the "most important" causal factor in the declining labor force participation rates of young black men in recent decades. By contrast, neither Hispanic nor non-Hispanic immigrants have harmed the employment prospects of black men.[33]

5. The difficulties black youths encounter finding jobs may be compounded by both employers' discrimination and an absence of references. Indeed, lack of references appears to be a neglected but important barrier to employment.[34]

6. Young black men respond to the quality of jobs. When jobs pay well and confer higher status, they do not want to lose them. As a result, they less often are absent, because a high rate of absence increases the chances of being fired.[35]

7. About one-quarter of the income earned by sample members derived from crime, but a

relatively small proportion of men earned most of it. These were predominantly the young men neither in work nor at school. As a group, these men were "very sensitive to economic incentives" and believed they could earn more money from crime. For this reason, between the carrot and the stick as policy responses, the carrot appears "more effective."[36]

8. Several factors influence the ability of young black men to escape from poverty. Among the most important is church-going. Young men who go to church often also attend school more regularly, work more frequently, and spend their leisure time more productively. The two next most important factors are "whether other members of the family work and whether the family is on welfare." The influence of the former is positive and of the latter, negative. The nature of the association between welfare and employment, however, remains cloudy. Is it causal? Does welfare dependence, that is, directly contribute to the low employment rate of young black men, or, as one commentator suggests, are welfare, dropping out of school, and poor employment "inextricably intertwined" in a complex and indeterminate manner?[37]

9. Black young men from homes with both parents present at age 14 succeed "only marginally better" than those from single-parent families. By itself, a female-headed home does not hamper "socioeconomic success."[38]

10. The relation of attitudes and aspirations to black youth employment remains uncertain. Two authors argue that attitudes and aspirations influenced the number of hours 20- to 24-year-old (but not 16- to 19-year-old) men worked in the past year and that their effect was independent of family background. The most important attitudes were the beliefs that "having a good education was very important" and that "the unemployed could find work if they wanted" and the perception that most of their friends were employed. The most important aspiration was a white collar

or crafts job by age 30. The question is how to interpret these findings. The authors cannot say whether attitudes result from or determine experience or how to encourage them. The commentator on their paper believes the findings support his theory "that the labor market behavior of black youths reflects a fear that they will be trapped for life in the menial jobs that are generally open to youth in the U.S. labor market but that whites have historically left behind as they matured and blacks have not." Those relatively few young men who somehow surmount this fear may remain more willing to accept the low-wage work available to young people because they believe it leads to better jobs in the future.[39]

Cultural theories of unemployment receive little support from the available data. The crisis in black youth unemployment relates more to the labor market and discrimination than to any unwillingness to work. Offered decent jobs, young black men by and large respond. Nor has the major change in black family structure—the increase in families headed by women—by itself eroded their willingness to work. What counts is whether the adults in the family work. That is the good news. The bad news is that the labor market trends show little sign of reducing the factors that retard the employment of black men. Most jobs available to them are dead-end jobs and do not offer enticing incentives; without work histories, they lack the references they need to convince potential employers of their reliability; the longer they lack work, the harder it is for them to find a job; tainted in employers' perception by discrimination, a reputation for low skills, and poor work habits, they remain at the end of the line for hiring; when they are hired, they usually work only for a short time. As welfare regulations, poor job prospects, inadequate day care, and the lack of health insurance trap single mothers in AFDC, black young men lack the critical assistance and example of a working adult. Even more ominously, as women enter the labor force, they take the low-wage jobs that otherwise would have been available to black men. . . .

Truly, the policy dilemmas are awesome. Nonetheless, by ignoring or subordinating the black youth employment crisis, poverty discourse has diverted attention from one of the most tragic and explosive problems of our time. The same cannot be said for the other group dominating images of the underclass, black teenage mothers. But is the rhetoric that surrounds them accurate and helpful? Or, in its own way, does it too distract attention from the major issues?

ADOLESCENT PREGNANCY AND FEMALE-HEADED FAMILIES

In 1986, an otherwise sympathetic radio talk show host told me, "I don't mind paying to help people in need, but I don't want my tax dollars to pay for the sexual pleasure of adolescents who won't use birth control." His outrage summed up popular stereotypes about the relation among adolescent pregnancy, welfare, and the underclass.

1. Adolescent pregnancy is an epidemic which shows no signs of abating.
2. The epidemic is spreading fastest among blacks.
3. Unmarried black mothers (especially adolescents) consume most of America's social welfare budget and drain public resources.
4. America's adolescents become pregnant so often for two primary reasons: They start to have sex earlier than their counterparts in other countries, and generous welfare benefits encourage them to become parents.
5. The easy availability of contraceptives and abortions along with sex education encourages adolescents to have sex and thereby increases the risk of pregnancy.
6. Adolescents lack the maturity to use contraceptives regularly.
7. Unmarried women with children comprise the core of a new, self-perpetuating underclass.[40]

All these common stereotypes are wrong. Indeed, discourse about adolescent pregnancy and female-headed families remains riddled with misconceptions and paradoxes that obscure the situations they are supposed to illuminate and intensify the problems they are intended to reform.

What, in fact, does the best available evidence show? Recall, first, that most poor people in America do not live in families headed by adolescent mothers or even by women. In 1980, 37 percent of poor people lived in female-headed families. Poverty is not synonymous with single parents. Nor does adolescent pregnancy consume a large share of the social welfare budget or gross national product. In 1980, the money spent on AFDC represented only about 4 percent of all the costs of major public assistance and social insurance programs for the elderly, totally disabled, and all others, and only a fraction of AFDC payments go to adolescent mothers. In 1984, all means-tested cash transfer payments by federal, state, and local governments used 0.8 percent of GNP or 2 percent of the share of GNP spent by governments.[41]

Consider, next, the question of birth rates. Among blacks, adolescent birth rates have fallen; among whites they have increased. Between 1970 and 1980, the birth rate of unmarried black women dropped 13 percent, in contrast to a 27 percent increase among unmarried white women. Nonetheless, black marital fertility fell even faster (38 percent), which means that the fraction of births occurring to unmarried women increased. Among just 15- to 19-year-old black women, the nonmarital fertility rate (births per 1,000 women) rose from 76.5 in 1960 to a peak of 90.8 in 1970 and has declined since then; by 1980 it had dropped to 83.0. Among whites, the rate, always lower than blacks', has risen steadily from 6.6 in 1960 to 10.9 in 1970 and 16.0 in 1980. In other words, between 1970 and 1980, the fertility of unmarried black 15- to 19-year-old women dropped almost 10 percent, while the rate for unmarried white women of the same age increased by 48 percent. Although the black rate remained more than five times as great as the white, adolescent pregnancy is not an issue just for blacks.[42] . . .

On one point public perceptions are correct: The proportion of all births that occur to unmarried adolescent black women has risen. One reason is that their fertility has fallen more slowly than fertility among older and married women. The other reason is the decline in the proportion who marry. Between 1960 and 1980, the proportion of never married black 14- to 24-year-olds increased from 65 to 82 percent. (Among whites, it rose only from 63 to 69 percent.) As a consequence, many more mothers had never married. The ratio of out-of-wedlock births (number of births to unmarried women per 1,000 births) for 15- to 19-year-old black women rose from 422 in 1960 to 852 in 1980; for 20- to 24-year-olds, the increase was from 200 to 561. Ratios also rose for white women of the same age, although they remained much lower: for 15- to 19-year-olds from 72 to 322, and for 20- to 24-year-olds, from 22 to 115.[43]

These trends, of course, have increased the proportion of families headed by women. Between 1960 and 1984, the proportion of households headed by women increased from 9.0 percent to 12.0 percent for whites and from 22.0 percent to 43.0 percent for blacks.[44] More than any others, these families are likely to be poor. (In 1982, women headed 71 percent of all poor black families.) The sources of the explosive growth in female-headed families differ by race. Two leading scholars, Garfinkle and McLanahan, argue that "the increase in women's labor force participation (and the economic dependence that accompanied it)" have been the major factor precipitating the growth in female-headed families among whites. For blacks, by contrast, declining employment opportunities for males have been most important.[45]

The relation between family structure and poverty also differs by race. Changes in family structure account for only a small proportion of the increased poverty among black families, according to Mary Jo Bane. "The poverty rate in 1979," she writes, "would have been about 16 percent lower than it was had family composition remained the same as it was in 1959. Family composition changes contributed almost nothing

to the increase in poverty between 1979 and 1983." Higher poverty rates "within household composition types," rather than family composition trends, account for most of the higher poverty rates among blacks. Had black and white household composition been identical in 1983, poverty rates among blacks still would have been much higher, because "55 percent of the difference between blacks and whites comes from higher poverty rates for blacks *within* household composition types."[46]

None of these trends, it is important to reiterate, result from generous welfare policies. After 1972, the number of children in female-headed households increased dramatically, while the number of children in households receiving AFDC declined. "If AFDC were pulling families apart and encouraging the formation of single-parent families," assert two researchers, "it is hard to understand why the number of children on the program would remain constant throughout a period in our history when family structures changed the most." (AFDC has permitted young women with children to move out of their parents' homes; whether or not this is a healthy development is, of course, a matter on which commentators disagree.) Nor does any relation exist between the fraction of children living in single-parent families and AFDC levels across states. Indeed, most women rely on AFDC for relatively short periods of time, although younger women seem least able to leave the rolls within a few years. "A majority of those who go on welfare will be off in less than two years," report Garfinkle and McLanahan, "but a substantial minority—and this minority accounts for the majority of the caseload at any point in time—will be dependent for a long time."[47]

Even the dynamics of the relation between household composition and poverty differ for black and white women, shows Bane. Black women usually do not become poor because of divorce or separation. More often, they already were poor. White women much more commonly become poor when their marriages break up. Black women's poverty, asserts Bane, results from "reshuffling"; white women's is more "event-driven." Of women in the Michigan Income Panel Dynamic Study: "Three-quarters of whites who were poor in the first year after moving into a female-headed or single-person household became poor simultaneously with the transition; in contrast, of the blacks who were poor after the transition, about two-thirds had also been poor before."[48]

Common stereotypes about the impact of pregnancy on the future of adolescent mothers withstand research no better than those that stress the role of welfare or the relations between household composition and poverty. In an important recent study, Frank Furstenberg and his colleagues asked what had happened to a group of adolescent mothers 17 years after the birth of their children. In 1984, 25 percent of these women did depend on welfare; another 25 percent earned less than $15,000 a year; 24 percent earned $15,000–24,999; and the remaining 26 percent more than $25,000. More than two-thirds of them had graduated from high school and nearly 30 percent had some post-high-school education. Work experience remained critical throughout these women's lives. Indeed, the women who had accumulated substantial work experience before they needed welfare remained by far the most likely to regain independence. Although their earnings undoubtedly would have been higher had they not become mothers at so young an age, the modest success enjoyed by many of them undercuts the easy equation between adolescent motherhood and a life of poverty.[49]

The real facts about adolescent pregnancy and female-headed households have important implications for debates about poverty. First, they qualify the panic about an "epidemic" of adolescent pregnancy. The issue is not the adolescent birth rate, but the response of pregnant adolescents and their marital status. Their increased resort to abortion, reluctance to marry the fathers of their children, and refusal to surrender their infants for adoption are the trends that have triggered the alarm about adolescent pregnancy and linked it to concerns about welfare policy and the emergence of an "underclass." Poverty, however, is not only a problem of adolescent pregnancy or female-headed families. Most poor people in America do not live in families headed by women. The absorption of poverty by family structure obscures the sources of poverty in the labor market, discrimination, and public policy. Conversely, American policies toward adolescent pregnancy remain perverse in a nation whose putative goals include reducing both it and abortion.

Adolescent pregnancy is not only a problem for blacks, and poverty among women of color does not result primarily from their household structure. Rather, it stems from the same structural forces that sustain joblessness among black men. Nor is their poverty the ironic result of a generous welfare system. On the contrary, an inadequate, punitive, perverse welfare system guarantees that most of them will remain poor. There is no inherent reason why women who head families should be poor. They are poor because they do not receive adequate public education, job training, or public support; because the jobs open to them pay so badly; and because of labor market trends and discrimination. . . .

NOTES

1. Committee on Health Care for Homeless People [hereafter referred to as CHCHP], Institute of Medicine, *Homelessness, Health, and Human Needs* (Washington, D.C.: National Academy Press, 1988), p. 137. Other useful sources include: Jon Erickson and Charles Wilhelm, eds., *Housing the Homeless* (New Brunswick, N.J.: Center for Urban Policy Research, 1986); Richard D. Bingham, Roy E. Green, Sammis B. White, *The Homeless in Contemporary Society* (Newbury Park, Cal: Sage Publications, 1987); Peter Marcuse, "Neutralizing Homelessness," *Socialist Review* 18 (January–March, 1988): 69–96; Peter H. Rossi, "First Out: Last In: Homelessness in America," unpublished lecture, August 1988; F. Stevens Redburn and Terry B. Buss, *Responding to America's Homeless: Public Policy Alternatives* (New York: Praeger, 1986); Robert A. Rosenthal, "Homeless in

Paradise: A Map of the Terrain," Ph.D. diss., University of California, Santa Barbara, 1987; Joel Blau, "The Homeless of New York: A Case Study," Ph.D. diss., Columbia University School of Social Work, 1987.

2. CHCHP, *Homelessness,* p. 4; Charles D. Cowan, William R. Breakey, and Pamela J. Fischer, "The Methodology of Counting the Homeless," in CHCHP, *Homelessness,* pp. 169–182; Jon Erickson and Charles Wilhelm, "Introduction," in Erickson and Wilhelm, eds., *Housing the Homeless,* p. xxvi.

3. CHCHP, *Homelessness,* pp. 5–18. An excellent recent overview of homelessness in one state is Phyllis Ryan, Ira Goldstein, and David Bartelt, *Homelessness in Pennsylvania: How Can This Be?* (Philadelphia: Coalition on Homelessness in Pennsylvania and The Institute for Public Policy Studies, Temple University, 1989).

4. Kim Hopper and Jill Hamberg, "The Making of America's Homeless: From Skid Row to New Poor, 1945–1984," in Rachel G. Bratt, Chester Hartman, Ann Meyerson, eds., *Critical Perspectives on Housing* (Philadelphia: Temple University Press, 1986), pp. 23, 21.

5. CHCHP, *Homelessness,* p. 28. On the political and economic factors contributing to deinstitutionalization, see Andrew T. Scull, *Decarceration* (Englewood Cliffs, N.J.: Prentice-Hall, 1977). Most of the authors who write about the homeless cite similar statistics and include policy toward the mentally ill as a contributing factor.

6. CHCHP, *Homelessness,* p. 28; Katz, *Shadow,* ch. 10; Chester Hartman, "Housing Policies Under the Reagan Administration," in Bratt, Hartman, and Meyerson, *Critical Perspectives on Housing,* pp. 362–374.

7. For examples of neighbor-based support networks early in the twentieth-century, see Michael B. Katz, *Poverty and Policy in American History* (New York: Academic Press, 1983), pp. 17–54, and "The History of an Impudent Poor Woman in New City from 1918 to 1923," unpublished manuscript. On an earlier period, see Christine Stansell, *City of Women: Sex and Class in New York 1789–1860* (New York: Knopf, 1986). For the more recent period, see Carol Stack, *All Our Kin: Strategies for Survival in a Black Community* (New York: Harper and Row, 1974).

8. Mark J. Stern, "The Emergence of Homelessness as a Public Problem," in Erickson and Wilhelm, *Housing the Homeless,* p. 113. Rossi, "First Out: Last In," p. 2.

9. Stern, "The Emergence of Homelessness," pp. 118–119; Gareth Stedman Jones, *Outcast London* (London: Oxford University Press, 1971), p. 253.

10. Stern, "The Emergence of Homelessness," p. 120.

11. Stern, "The Emergence of Homelessness," p. 121; on the necessity for poor people to take an active role in winning public policies that promote their interests, see Frances Fox Piven and Richard Cloward, *Poor People's Movements: Why they Succeed and How they Fail* (New York: Pantheon, 1977).

12. Isabel Wilkerson, "New Studies Zeroing In On Poorest of the Poor," *New York Times,* December 20, 1987, p. 26 [emphasis in original].

13. Elliot Currie, *Confronting Crime: An American Challenge* (New York: Pantheon, 1985). Comparative rates of prisoners per 100,000 population in the early 1980s were: Norway 45; Sweden 55; West Germany 60; Denmark 63; France 67; Great Britain 80; United States 217.

14. "The American Underclass," *Time,* August 29, 1977, pp. 14, 15.

15. "The American Underclass," pp. 14, 16.

16. David Whitman and Jeannye Thornton, "A Nation Apart," *U.S. News and World Report,* March 17, 1986, p. 18; Myron Magnet, "America's Underclass: What to Do?" *Fortune,* May 11, 1987, p. 130.

17. Lee Rainwater, "Looking Back and Looking Up," *Transaction 6* (February 1969): 9. A very good discussion of the origins of the underclass concept in American social science is in Robert Aponte, "Conceptualizing the Underclass: An Alternative Perspective," paper presented at the annual meeting of the American Sociological Association, August 26, 1988. The Aponte paper is also one of the two best criticisms of the concept I have read. The other is Nicky Gregson and Fred Robinson, "The Casualties of Thatcherism," paper presented at the annual meeting of the Association of American Geographers, March 20, 1989. For a summary of the most recent social science research on the underclass, see William J. Wilson, ed., "The Ghetto Underclass: Social Science Perspectives," special issue, *Annals of the American Academy of Political and Social Science* 501 (January 1989).

18. Douglas G. Glasgow, *The Black Underclass: Poverty, Unemployment, and Entrapment of Ghetto Youth* (New York: Random House, 1980),

p. 3. Glasgow is a former dean of the School of Social Work at Howard University and vice president of the National Urban League's Washington Operations Office. For his later formulation of the issue, see his "The Black Underclass in Perspective," in National Urban League, *The State of Black America 1987* (Washington: National Urban League, 1987), pp. 129–144.

19. Glasgow, *Black Underclass,* p. 4.
20. Glasgow, *Black Underclass,* pp. 5–6.
21. Glasgow, *Black Underclass,* pp. 7–8, 178.
22. Glasgow, *Black Underclass,* pp. 9–11, 173.
23. Some of the definitions of underclass current in late 1987 are listed in Wilkerson, "New Studies"; Ken Auletta, *The Underclass* (New York: Random House, 1982).
24. Auletta, *Underclass,* p. xvi.
25. For a similar example from the nineteenth century, see Michael B. Katz, *Poverty and Policy in American History* (New York: Academic Press, 1983), pp. 134–156.
26. Auletta, *Underclass,* pp. 260–268.
27. Richard B. Freeman and Harry J. Holzer, "The Black Youth Employment Crisis: Summary of Findings," in Richard B. Freeman and Harry J. Holzer, eds., *The Black Youth Employment Crisis* (Chicago and London: University of Chicago Press, 1986), pp. 3 and 7 (emphasis in original); Wilson, *Trurly Disadvantaged,* Table 2.88, p. 43.
28. Freeman and Holzer, "Employment Crisis," pp. 4–6.
29. Freeman and Holzer, "Employment Crisis," pp. 6–7.
30. Harry J. Holzer, "Black Youth Nonemployment: Duration and Job Search," in Freeman and Holzer, *Black Youth Employment Crisis,* p. 65.
31. John Ballen and Richard B. Freeman, "Transitions between Employment and Nonemployment," in Freeman and Holzer, *Black Youth Employment Crisis,* pp. 97–99.
32. David T. Ellwood, "The Spatial Mismatch Hypothesis: Are There Teenage Jobs Missing in the Ghetto," and Jonathan S. Leonard, "Comment," in Freeman and Holzer, *Black Youth Employment Crisis,* pp. 147–190.
33. George J. Borjas, "The Demographic Determinants of the Demand for Black Labor," in Freeman and Holzer, *Black Youth Employment Crisis,* p. 225. The finding that women substitute for black men in employment appears robust and supported by other research.
34. Jerome Culp and Bruce H. Dunson, "Brothers of a Different Color: A Preliminary Look at Employer Treatment of White and Black Youth," and Paul Osterman, "Comment," Freeman and Holzer, pp. 233–260. I phrased this conditionally because the findings, based on a very small sample, are very tentative.
35. Ronald Ferguson and Randall Filer, "Do Better Jobs Make Better Workers? Absenteeism from Work Among Inner-City Black Youths," in Freeman and Holzer, *Black Youth Employment Crisis,* pp. 291–293.
36. W. Kip Viscusi, "Market Incentives for Criminal Behavior," in Freeman and Holzer, *Black Youth Employment Crisis,* pp. 343–344. James W. Thompson and James Cataldo point out in their comment on this paper that Viscusi's is one of the first studies not based solely on an offender population (p. 347).
37. Richard B. Freeman, "Who Escapes? The Relation of Churchgoing and Other Background Factors to the Socioeconomic Performance of Black Male Youths from Inner-City Tracts"; Robert B. Lerman, "Do Welfare Programs Affect the Schooling and Work Patterns of Young Black Men?" and Samuel B. Myers, Jr., "Comment," in Freeman and Holzer, eds., *Black Youth Employment Crisis,* pp. 372–374 and 403–441.
38. Freeman, "Who Escapes?", p. 374.
39. Linda Datcher-Loury and Glenn Loury, "The Effects of Attitudes and Aspirations on the Labor Supply of Young Men," and Michael J. Piore, "Comment," in Freeman and Holzer, *Black Youth Employment Crisis,* pp. 377–401.
40. Some of the items in this list of misconceptions come from Elise F. Jones et al., *Adolescent Pregnancy in Industrialized Countries,* A Study Sponsored by the Alan Guttmacher Institute (New Haven and London: Yale University Press, 1986), pp. 298–299.
41. David T. Ellwood and Lawrence H. Summers, "Poverty in America: Is Welfare the Answer or the Problem?" in Sheldon H. Danziger and Daniel H. Weinberg, *Fighting Poverty: What Works and What Doesn't* (Cambridge: Harvard University Press, 1986), p. 85; Gary Burtless, "Public Spending for the Poor: Trends, Prospects, and Economic Limits," in Danziger and Weinberg, *Fighting Poverty,* pp. 23 and 40.
43. William Julius Wilson and Kathryn M. Neckerman, "Poverty and Family Structure: The Widen-

ing Gap between Evidence and Public Policy Issues," in Danziger and Weinberg, *Fighting Poverty,* pp. 236 and 238.

44. Harrell R. Rodgers, Jr., *Poor Women, Poor Families: The Economic Plight of America's Female-Headed Households* (Armonk, New York, and London, England: M.E. Sharp, Inc., 1986), p. 26.

45. Irwin Garfinkle and Sara S. McLanahan, *Single Mothers and Their Children: A New American Dilemma* (Washington, D.C.: The Urban Institute Press, 1986), p. 45.

46. Wilson and Neckerman, "Poverty and Family Structure," p. 240, Mary Jo Bane, "Household Composition and Poverty," in Danziger and Weinberg, *Fighting Poverty,* pp. 214–215 (emphasis in original).

47. Ellwood and Summers, "Is Welfare the Answer or the Problem," pp. 93–97; Robert Pear, "Young Mothers Said to Be on Welfare Longer," *New York Times,* September 10, 1986, p. A 28; Garfinkle and McLanahan, *Single Mothers,* p. 38.

48. Bane, "Household Composition and Poverty," p. 227.

49. Kathleen Mullan Harris, "Adolescent Childbearing and Welfare Experience: The Transition Out of Dependency," paper presented to Seminar on Race and City, PARSS Program, University of Pennsylvania, February 16, 1987, p. 27, and Table 3; Frank F. Furstenberg, Jr., J. Brooks-Gunn, S. Philip Morgan, *Adolescent Mothers in Later Life* (New York: Cambridge University Press, 1987), pp. 29, 40–43, 48–76

What Is Sexual Orientation?

READING 10

Homosexuality: A Social Phenomenon

Barbara Sherman Heyl

. . . This article focuses primarily on the theoretical debates over how best to explain the "condition" of homosexuality, once Western culture had conceptualized it that way. Is there something "essential" that makes homosexuals who they are, or has the identity grown out of social interaction? The sociological view tends to see homosexuality as a social construction, both at the macro level—where society defines what homosexual behavior means within its cultural boundaries, and at the micro level—where the individual, in interaction with others, acquires his or her own personal sense of a sexual identity.

VIEWING HOMOSEXUAL BEHAVIOR IN ITS SOCIETAL CONTEXT

Cross-Cultural Variations

If patterns of sexual behavior and the meanings given to them are products of the social, cultural, and historical context out of which they developed, then we can expect them to vary cross-culturally. Recently published research has documented homosexual behavior in different parts of the world and in different time periods; the behavior was found to be interconnected with the social relationships and cultural beliefs of the societies under study (Callender & Kochems, 1983; Dover, 1978; Herdt, 1981; Whitam & Mathy, 1986). These cross-cultural data allow us to compare different types of social organization and division of labor, and how they promote particular forms of homosexual behavior, as well as affect social responses to such behavior (Adam, 1985; Herdt, 1984).

. . . The kinship-structured society of Sambia in New Guinea included homosexual relations between older men and younger boys; the relations are ritualized and in a sense obligatory. This pattern was found in other societies on the eastern islands of Melanesia, as well as in southern New Guinea, and has been termed the "Melanesian" model by Barry Adam (1985). There are several characteristics of Melanesian-model societies that are influential in shaping the ritualized homosexuality that exists in those cultures. For example, these societies exhibit a high degree of gender separation and inequality (Herdt, 1984). Adam

(1985) notes that "men and women have separate residences, pathways, crops, foods and rites" (see Allen, 1967). Women are viewed as important for reproductive and labor purposes, but are considered by males to have a polluting influence on young males. As a result of this belief, males "develop a complex and extended system of magical practices to rescue boys from impure contact with their mothers and convert them into men. This conversion is not easy and typically involves the seclusion of youths during which time they are fed and 'grown' by older men" (Adam, 1985, pp. 25, 26).

Thus, in Melanesian societies the homosexual patterns are age-graded, with the older males contributing their semen to the younger males as a way of giving them "manhood," initiating them into warrior groups, and making them strong (Herdt, 1984, pp. 59–64, 181–183). Semen is highly valued as necessary not only in creating life but also as a way of "binding the male line" (Adam, 1985, p. 27). The young men are required to ingest semen from older males in order to become part of the lineage of their past male ancestors. A related but different method of masculinizing boys is practiced among the Sambia of New Guinea. These people segregate young boys from women by sending them to forest lodges for ten to fifteen years. During this seclusion the boys pass through a series of rites, including frequent fellatio practiced between the younger and older boys (Herdt, 1984). After the initiation procedures are completed the males are expected to marry women and to end homosexual behavior.

Separating the young males from any contact with women produces a stage of enforced bachelorhood that all Melanesian males must pass through in order to become adult males. Adam (1985) notes that this separation allows the adult males exclusive rights to "use women's productive and reproductive power for their own use" (p. 20). Thus, the bachelorhood status and its accompanying rituals facilitate the maintenance of social control by the older males over both the young men and the women. Since homosexual behavior in Melanesian societies is routine and

obligatory as part of the social organization of these societies, it is not perceived as deviant or abnormal behavior. Clearly, we cannot label this behavior according to our norms or view these men as "homosexuals"—a term that derives from our Western culture (see Herdt, 1984; Stoller, 1980).

Western Culture: Developing a Category of Homosexuality

Most Western cultures have not built overt homosexual behavior into their accepted and obligatory social roles; indeed homosexual behavior has long been discouraged and repressed. Not only has the Judeo-Christian religion taken a strong stand against homosexual behavior, but secular laws have prohibited acts of sodomy as well. There have been variations in this generally negative history; for example, the famous French Penal Code of 1791 did decriminalize homosexual acts between consenting adults (Greenberg & Bystryn, 1984). However, public opinion in nineteenth century Europe and the United States remained hostile to overt homosexual behavior.

In the late eighteenth and early nineteenth centuries the category of homosexuality emerged as a way of describing a condition and the homosexual as a type of person (Foucault, 1978; Richardson, 1984, p. 80). Until that time the moral and legal debates on homosexual behavior had centered on just that—behavior. The shift in focus defined homosexuality as a "state of being" that could exist prior to and without any overt homosexual act and, from somewhere inside the person, compelled a lifelong habitual preference for same-sex partners. Homosexuals became a highly stigmatized category of persons. (It should become clear now why it is inappropriate to use this term to describe the Melanesian males.)

Greenberg and Bystryn (1984) propose that one explanation for this conceptual development was the new capitalism of nineteenth century Europe and the United States which increased competition among men, sharpened the sexual division of labor, and strengthened the ideology of the family. Foucault (1978) and Weeks (1981) relate the conceptual development to the rise in the early nineteenth century of a "scientific" interest in sexual behavior. The medical profession, as part of the scientific community of this period, played a significant role in defining homosexuality by depicting it as a medical pathology or abnormality (Greenberg & Bystryn, 1984; Richardson, 1984).

EFFORTS SINCE THE NINETEENTH CENTURY TO EXPLAIN HOMOSEXUALITY

Shifts in the Major Theoretical Approaches to Homosexuality

The category of "homosexual," once it had been created, demanded an explanation. The first theoretical approach came from the biological/medical model, well established by the late nineteenth century and viewed as the key to understanding homosexuality as well as a wide variety of other perceived social problems, such as crime, alcoholism, retardation, and insanity. Physicians helped instill the idea that homosexuals were stricken by something beyond their control. The medicalization of homosexuality meant that homosexuals were subjected to efforts to cure them with such "therapeutic" interventions as castration, sterilization, and commitment to mental health facilities (Greenberg & Bystryn, 1984, p. 41). These developments launched the debates that continued into 1950s and 1960s over how one could define the biological or mental characteristic that placed "homosexuals" in a different category from the rest of the population; "was homosexuality congenital or acquired, ineradicable or susceptible to cure?" (Weeks, 1981, p. 86).

A second theoretical approach emerged in the early twentieth century that shifted attention to the psychological state of the individual and conceptualized homosexuality as a *sexual orientation* toward members of the same sex as sexual and love objects. Sigmund Freud's (1905; 1931) writings influenced this shift. His theory of homosexuality included the premise that humans came into the world with a capacity to be sexually attracted to both sexes. Richardson (1984) notes

that Freud's "concept of bisexuality was based on evidence that embryological remnants of the anatomical characteristics of the opposite sex, however rudimentary, are present in all individuals" (p. 81). Freud's theory of psychosexual development assumed that the normal process of libidinal development resulted in a heterosexual orientation. Homosexuality resulted from the development in the individual, beginning in early childhood, of a fixed and fundamental "sexual orientation" guiding the individual into later homosexual behavior. Thus, both the biological/medical model and the psychological/sexual orientation model posit that there is some "essential" trait about the person that explains his or her homosexuality.

An important turning point in these discussions came from the 1948 Kinsey studies of sexuality in the United States. This nationwide survey of self-reported sexual behavior revealed a much wider involvement in homosexual behavior in the male population than had been previously thought. The study also documented shifting patterns of such involvement over the life span of individual men. As Kinsey and his co-authors note (Kinsey, Pomeroy, & Martin, 1948), "The histories which have been available in the present study make it apparent that the heterosexuality or homosexuality of many individuals is not an all-or-none proposition" (p. 638). This conclusion supported Kinsey's decision to propose a continuum of categories to describe experience in a given age period in the individual's life, ranging from exclusively heterosexual experiences (category 0) to exclusively homosexual experiences (category 6), with five categories in between reflecting varying proportions of same-sex and opposite-sex sexual experiences.

The Kinsey continuum would allow researchers to more accurately describe the experiences of the population with respect to sexual partners than was allowed by the previous assumption that one could easily divide the population into two groups—the heterosexuals and the homosexuals. If behavior was to be an indicator of who could be considered "the homosexuals," then where on the continuum do we draw the line? Were the homosexuals only those who fit into category 6 (exclusively homosexual experiences), or did they include anyone from category 1 (had had only incidental homosexual contact, while having predominantly heterosexual experiences) through category 6? Additionally, Kinsey's data included reports by individuals of their psychic responses to members of the same and opposite sex, and these feelings varied across a continuum and across the life span of the respondents as well.

Kinsey's research posed a major challenge to both previous theoretical approaches. If either the biological or sexual orientation theories were true, how was one to explain changing patterns of homosexual behavior over the life span of one individual? By documenting diversity in lifestyles, sexual behavior patterns, and emotions, Kinsey promoted consideration by other researchers of the individual's own definition of self as relevant data in the debate on how to identify "the homosexual." This new consideration focuses attention again on homosexuality as a state of being—but this time, as Richardson (1984) states "It is, however, a different form of 'being' than previously conceived where the fundamental question was what caused a person to develop into a homosexual. The new question is: How does the state of being a person who *self-identifies as homosexual* come about?" (p. 83).

A third theoretical approach to homosexuality focused on this new question and was dominant in sociology in the United States and Britain from the 1960s to the present. It is known as the labeling interactionist perspective and derives from symbolic interactionism (Weeks, 1981, p. 94). It views the category of homosexuality as a product of the meanings we give the term in our Western culture (social process at the macro level), and sees the individuals who fit the category as those who have come to identify themselves as homosexuals (the result of social process at the micro level). This interactionist or social constructionist perspective allows for considering identity separate from behavior, which proved helpful in interpreting the Kinsey data. For example, since the Kinsey data documented gradations of heterosexual and homosexual experiences within the lives of individuals, then if sexual identity was a direct result of sexual behavior, we would expect all those who had engaged in both homosexual and heterosexual sexual activities to identify themselves as bisexual. Data indicate that such is not the case (Blumstein & Schwartz 1976, Humphreys, 1975, Paul, 1984). One explanation is that an identity as a bisexual is stigmatized by both the heterosexual and homosexual populations, so that many fewer people consider themselves "bisexual" than would be expected given their actual sexual behavior (Golden, 1987, pp. 30–31). Explaining homosexuality from the third perspective meant understanding how individuals arrived at a point where they identified themselves as homosexuals.

Research on the Causes of Homosexuality

Each of the three theoretical approaches discussed above has generated research designed to test the proposed explanation of homosexuality. Much of the resulting research was designed to reveal the ultimate causal explanation of homosexuality. Such a search is based on a belief that the category of "homosexual" consists of people who have some essential characteristic in common that differentiates them from "the heterosexuals" in the society. Just phrasing the problem in this way points to the difficulty a researcher would have locating such a characteristic. Both homosexual and heterosexual categories include people of very diverse backgrounds, personalities, and lifestyles. Even if researchers were able to divide the total population into two distinct and separate groups—homosexual and heterosexual—and discover a common characteristic of all homosexuals that was not characteristic of any heterosexual, the researcher still would have to be careful about announcing that this factor explained the "homosexuality" of the one group. The factor, depending on its nature, might well have developed as a *result* of living out a homosexual lifestyle. But in spite of the difficulties, such research has continued on the premise that something definite will emerge to explain why "homosexuals" are who they are.

Research from the biological or medical model has enjoyed particularly strong appeal since, if a particular gene or hormonal pattern could be found to explain homosexuality, then everyone could know definitively who the homosexuals were and why. The factor would solve issues of who or what is responsible for the condition, and the medical profession might even be able to "help" those found with this condition. Such is the seduction of the biological model. Indeed, biologists and geneticists have for decades searched for the biological key to homosexuality, but such an answer has been elusive.

First, the scientific basis of the research has changed. Biological research on homosexuality conducted during the 1940s or earlier has been thoroughly discredited now on grounds of incomplete understanding of genes and hormones, as well as faulty research designs (Richardson, 1981). Scientific understanding of human biology has developed significantly in recent decades, and technological developments have also facilitated more precise measurement of the sex hormones. However, in spite of these advances, a second set of methodological problems remain. For example, there continues to be a lack of data on the standards of biological characteristics that can appropriately be used as a basis for measurement of differences or deviations, repeated failure to find statistical differences between the "homosexuals" and the control groups, problems in identifying who belongs appropriately in what group (often the heterosexual sample is composed of men the researcher assumes to be heterosexual), failure to include any data on women, while still drawing conclusions about women, and the fact that hormones are influenced by many factors in the subject's world, including stress.

A third problem with the medical model is that it is based on the unwarranted assumption that biology can explain sexuality. Ricketts (1984) notes, that "explanations of a direct cause-and-effect relationship between biological factors and sexual orientation falter because they cannot embrace the complexity and variety of human sexual behavior" (p. 88). Given the diversity of ways in which humans can and do experience their sexuality, including changes in sexual behavior, attractions, and fantasies, it is not surprising that the careful assessment of the biological research results in the conclusion that this research has contributed little to our understanding of sexual identity (Hoult, 1984; Ricketts, 1984; Richardson, 1981). In spite of these research conclusions, the belief that there is a genetic or biochemical explanation for homosexuality still appears frequently in today's media and among the general population.

Research from the second theoretical approach views "sexual orientation" as "a relatively enduring psychological characteristic of the individual, largely determined in early life" (Richardson, 1984, p. 84). Researching the cause of a homosexual "sexual orientation" required documenting early learning experiences and the influences of family relationships on the young "pre-homosexual." Psychologists and psychoanalysts conducted such research by using their homosexual clients in psychotherapy as their source of data. Critics of such research have noted a number of methodological difficulties (see Browning, 1984; Richardson, 1981). First, when researchers draw samples solely from therapy clients, their data come from homosexuals who are likely different from other homosexuals who have not sought out psychotherapy. Second, research conclusions were reached without comparing the data on homosexuals with a control group of heterosexuals. Third, since the psychological researchers attempted to document the existence of a deep-seated, family-oriented sexual orientation, the data came from retrospective accounts. Not only is it difficult for adults to recall accurately events they experienced as children, but the retelling of those events, as well as descriptions of family relationships, can be influenced by their present circumstances and identity, the therapy process itself, and available knowledge about homosexuality. Fourth, most research was conducted with male clients only.

As the criticisms noted above gained recognition, research was conducted that included homosexuals not in therapy and compared their family backgrounds and personality data to heterosexuals, also not in therapy, who were interviewed and given the same questionnaires and standard personality tests as the homosexuals. One hypothesis had been that a homosexual orientation developed from a particular family structure involving a "dominant" mother and a "weak" or absent father. The use of the comparison group of heterosexuals was important in undermining this "explanation" of homosexuality, since there were heterosexuals whose family histories also revealed this pattern (e.g., see Marmor, 1965). Indeed, no single "family constellation" or other pattern, such as the child having identified more with one parent than the other, could be found to explain the adult lifestyle of homosexuality (Bell, Weinberg, & Hammersmith, 1981a; Hooker, 1969; Siegelman, 1974).

Gradually a body of research data accummulated, based on nonpatient and noninstitutionalized homosexual populations that showed that "most lesbians and gay men were remarkably similar to heterosexuals with the exception of their sexual preference" (Browning, 1984, p. 20). Researchers found that homosexuals did not constitute a clinical category. These conclusions led the American Psychiatric Association in 1973 to remove homosexuality from its manual that lists the known pathological clinical conditions. In 1974 the American Psychological Association took the same step.

Since the research from the first two theoretical perspectives failed to identify any biological or psychological factors that could differentiate homosexuals as a separate category from heterosexuals, then homosexuality could not be explained as a biological or psychological phenomenon. The third theoretical approach suggested that homosexuality was a social phenomenon—in that both the category and its contents, "the homosexuals," developed out of social process. The researcher from this approach acknowledges that the individual comes packaged with specific biological characteristics and, in the process of living through early childhood and adolescence, the individual has many experiences that contribute to his or her psychosexual development and individual personality. To develop a sexual identity, however, the individual picks out certain personal characteristics and past experiences as significant, while excluding others. The responses of other people to the individual are an integral part of the process. The individual takes these responses, as well as his or her own feelings about the experiences, into account when he or she assesses the experiences later for clues as to who he or she "really" is. Research from this approach to homosexuality focused on the social process of acquiring a sexual identity, and the next section is devoted to examining these efforts.

HOMOSEXUALITY AS A STATE OF IDENTITY

The question of how and when and under what conditions someone would or could acquire an identity as a homosexual was posed as a genuinely sociological question, and the research into this question benefited greatly from the interactionist perspective in sociology during the 1960s and 1970s. Proponents of this perspective assert that the development of one's personal identity (how an individual answers privately the question of "Who am I?") is an ongoing life process and takes place in a social context. The individual develops a sense of self in relation to major aspects of life, such as work and sex. For example, we develop an occupational or professional identity out of our experiences related to work and our interpretations, utilizing feedback from others, regarding who we are in our work roles. We develop a sexual identity out of all the experiences we have had involving sexuality and the meanings we attach to these experiences. Sexual identity summarizes our sense of self as sexual beings. Sexual orientation or sexual preference is one component of sexual identity that expresses our attraction to members of the same or opposite sex.

From this perspective sexual identity is a social construction. This is not the same as saying one's identity is freely chosen. We are, from this perspective, a product of all we have been through, including experiences which we may not have enjoyed or chosen, but experienced nonetheless. Out of these events and our feelings about them, we try to make sense out of what our life has been and who we are. The process may seem complicated but is remarkably ordinary. Gagnon (1977) notes "people become sexual in the same way they become everything else. Without much reflection, they pick up directions from their social environment" (p. 2). If this is descriptive of sexuality generally, then it also applies to homosexuality more specifically.

Given the premise of a gradual learning of sexual behavior patterns and identities, how does the social scientist conduct research on such a long drawn-out process involving interaction between the personal and the social? And how, if one perceives the culture as providing strong encouragement for heterosexuality (some view it as "compulsory heterosexuality"; see Adrienne Rich, 1980), can one gradually develop a homosexual identity?

One research strategy that derived from the labeling/interactionist tradition focuses on efforts to discover and document what stages of development an individual goes through in the process of acquiring a sexual identity. Beginning in the mid-1970s researchers used intensive interviews with self acknowledged gay males and lesbians to attempt to identify crucial stages or turning-point experiences in the process of reaching a homosexual identity. Following other developmental models, these models typically have an assumption of linear development. The process begins with no sexual identity or a presumption of heterosexuality and passes through experiences in a middle phase that could include some or all of the following: increasing awareness of attraction to members of the same sex, increasing knowledge about the category of "homosexual," sexual involvement with same-sex partners, and self-labeling as homosexual. The final stage of devel-

opment consists of the individual's acceptance of a strong lesbian or gay male identity. (See especially, Plummer, 1975; Troiden, 1979, 1988; Gramick, 1984; Sophie, 1986.)

One of the problems with a linear model is that it is assumed that those who reach the final stage have all passed through the same series of steps. Research designed to document "stage-sequential models," however, revealed diversity as well as patterns; the more specific the stages or steps were in a given model, the less likely the stages matched the experiences of the different individuals under study (Sophie, 1986, p. 50). . . .

Multiple Dimensions of a Homosexual Identity

The research on identity development documented not only that individuals followed different paths for reaching new identities, but also that identities, once formed, were not always as stable and permanent as people had thought they would be. Golden (1987) concludes "that the assumption that we inherently strive for congruence between our sexual feelings, activities, and identities may not be warranted, and that given the fluidity of sexual feelings, congruence may not be an achievable state" (p. 31). Thus, behavior, emotions, and identities do not necessarily develop into stable packages that can be easily labeled as heterosexual, gay or lesbian, or even bisexual, even though the individual or the society or the gay community might desire such consistency. Both researchers and therapists should be cautious about categorizing under familiar labels people who may in fact be growing and changing their identities. This is not to say that all identities are unstable; many individuals develop a strong and stable sense of self that serves as a guide and source of comfort to their behavior and life choices. But others continue to consider new information about themselves and may be more or less aware that where they are at any point in time is just one step in an ongoing developmental process. Thus, undergoing periods of questioning one's sexual identity may occur at various points in the life cycle. . . .

As researchers and therapists alike are acknowledging the different combinations of components of identity, they can watch for patterns. One pattern that was expected from Freudian theory and one which still shows up in views among the general population is not a pattern at all. The expected pattern was that gender identity—one's own sense of being male or female—would predict one's sexual preference. Freud's theory assumed that "gender inversion" helped explain homosexuality. Consequently, researchers have looked to see if homosexual males had acquired female gender identities, and if lesbians had male gender identities. Although the research has found that a small proportion of homosexual respondents indicate cross-gender identity, Luria (1979) notes, "Male homosexuals almost universally feel they are males, and female homosexuals virtually all feel they are women" (p. 179; see also Storms, 1980; Harry, 1982; Bell, Weinberg, & Hammersmith, 1981a, p. 188). . . .

Sexual Preference and Gender Role Behavior

Gender role behavior, or simply gender role, refers to patterns of behavior or activities routinely expected of a particular gender. Thus, males are expected to engage in masculine behavior patterns, thereby assuming a male gender role. However, individuals may develop a preference for the traditional activities of the opposite gender, and gender role preference may vary separately from either gender identity or sexual identity. Harry (1982) has diagrammed the various combinations, noting, for example, that a heterosexual male with a male gender identity could have a feminine gender role preference. He is, thus, biologically male, views himself as a male, but has a preference for activities routinely associated with women. Since this is behavior, it could be expressed in many different ways, such as through a pattern of effeminate behavior, cross-dressing, or by taking a job in a traditionally female occupation.

Cross-dressing and interest in cross-gender activities during childhood have been reported by adult homosexuals significantly more often than by adult heterosexuals. For example, in the Bell, Weinberg, and Hammersmith (1981b) study, 68 percent of the white homosexual males reported that they were "Not at all" or "Very little" interested in "boys' activities (e.g., baseball, football)" during grade school compared with 11 percent of the white heterosexual males. The matching statistics for black homosexual males were 37 percent compared with 4 percent for black heterosexual males. The homosexual males, more often than heterosexual males, reported that they had enjoyed stereotypical girls' activities, such as playing house, hopscotch, and jacks. Harry (1982) saw these results as replicating his own research findings. Similar differences were found for the female respondents. Seventy-one percent of the white homosexual women reported they "Very much" enjoyed playing typical boys' activities (e.g., baseball, football) compared with 28 percent of the white heterosexual women. The homosexual respondents also reported having cross-dressed and pretending to be the opposite gender more often than the heterosexual respondents did (Bell, Weinberg, & Hammersmith, 1981a). The Bell et al. (1981a) research concludes that "a child's display of gender nonconformity greatly increases the likelihood of that child's becoming homosexual regardless of his or her family background and regardless of how much the child identifies with either parent" (p. 189). The researchers note, however, that gender nonconformity was not characteristic of most of the homosexual respondents and was reported by a minority of heterosexuals (Bell et al., 1981a, p. 188).

. . . We are unable to draw a straight line from behavior patterns or even gender role preferences to sexual preference. . . . Clearly, the environment of prejudice and hostility towards homosexuality has an impact on the process of acquiring a sexual identity—be it homosexual or heterosexual. Herek (1985) notes that the influence may also flow the other way—that the process of developing an identity helps reinforce hostility; thus, "individuals also may gain a sense of who they are by clarifying what they are not" (p. 149).

Particularly as homosexuals have developed a stronger sense of themselves as a group, heterosexuals may have developed more of an identity as well. Indeed, as lesbian and gay communities have become more visible and organized, the opposition to them has also become more visible and organized. The in-group gets its identity by contrasting itself with the out-group, and the conflict promotes cohesion within both groups. This fundamental social process is one which sociology has documented as one of its earliest contributions to understanding society. In the case of homosexuality, however, we must recall that the negative label from society came long before persons so labeled organized themselves into a group. . . .

CONCLUSION

. . . I have argued here that the meanings given to behavior and to people who engage in that behavior derive from the culture and structure of the society involved. The major theoretical debate discussed in the chapter is whether or not those who fit our cultural category of "homosexuals" have something that defines their essence as homosexuals or are very much like everyone else except for their sexual preference, which was acquired over their lifespan in the same way as their other identities and in the same way as heterosexual identities. At least one theorist, Kenneth Plummer proposes that we consider both positions to be quite possibly correct. For example, a sexual orientation may be a kind of "essence," formed early in childhood and affecting later choices. Plummer (1981) notes,

> while some people develop restrictive and rigid orientations, others may be open and flexible, while still others may develop no "orientations" at all. . . . Likewise identities are—in all likelihood—highly variable throughout social encounters; but while for some people this may mean drastic restructuring of self conceptions at critical turning points in life, others may develop relatively stable identities at early moments in life and use these as foci to orientate most future contact. (p. 72)

Thus, diversity of experience is a key here; individuals have different ways of coping with life's experiences and different routes for arriving at a place where they feel comfortable with who they are and what they like best. But through it all, the learning and becoming take place within a social environment highly affected by the rules and guidelines of the culture at hand. And it should be remembered that cultural expectations can and do change. The process of forming and maintaining a positive homosexual identity can be especially complex and problematic in the face of conflicting pressures, definitions and attitudes, as the concerns and priorities of the gay community and the surrounding culture change over time.

REFERENCES

Adam, B.D. (1985). Age, structure, and sexuality: Reflections on the anthropological evidence on homosexual relations. *Journal of Homosexuality, 11* (3/4). 19–33.

Adam, B.D. (1987). *The rise of a gay and lesbian movement.* Boston: Twayne Publishers.

Allen, M.R. (1967). *Male cults and secret initiations in Melanesia.* Melbourne, Australia: Melbourne University Press.

Bell, A.P., Weinberg, M.S., & Hammersmith, S.K. (1981a). *Sexual preference: Its development in men and women.* Bloomington, IN: Indiana University Press.

Bell, A.P., Weinberg, M.S., & Hammersmith, S.K. (1981b). *Sexual preference: Statistical appendix.* Bloomington, IN: Indiana University Press.

Blumstein, P.W. & Schwartz, P. (1976). Bisexuality in women. *Archives of Sexual Behavior, 5,* 171–181.

Browning, C. (1984). Changing theories of lesbianism: Challenging the stereotypes. In T. Darty & S. Potter (Eds.), *Women-identified women* (pp. 11–30). Palo Alto, CA: Mayfield.

Callendar, C., & Kochems, L. (1983). The North American berdache. *Current Anthropology, 24,* 443–470.

Dover, K.J. (1978). *Greek homosexuality.* New York: Vintage Books.

Foucault, M. (1978). *The history of sexuality. Volume 1: An introduction.* New York: Random House.

Freud, S. (1905/1953). Three essays on the theory of sexuality. *Standard edition of the complete psychological works of Sigmund Freud, 7,* 136. London: Hogarth Press. (Originally published 1905).

Freud, S. (1931/1961). Female sexuality. *Standard edition of the complete psychological works of Sigmund Freud, 21,* 223. London: Hogarth Press. (Originally published 1931).

Gagnon, J.H. (1977). *Human sexualities.* Illinois: Scott, Foresman.

Golden, C. (1987). Diversity and variability in women's sexual identities. In Boston Lesbian Psychologies Collective (Eds.), *Lesbian psychologies: Explorations and Challenges* (pp. 18–34). Urbana, IL: University of Illinois Press.

Gramick, J. (1984). Developing a lesbian identity. In T. Darty & S. Potter (Eds.), *Women-identified women* (pp. 31–44). Palo Alto, CA: Mayfield.

Greenberg, D.F., & Bystryn, M.H. (1984). Capitalism, bureaucracy and male homosexuality. *Contemporary Crises, 8,* 33–56.

Harry, J. (1982). *Gay children grown up. Gender culture and gender deviance.* New York: Praeger.

Herdt, G.H. (1981). *Guardians of the flutes.* New York: McGraw-Hill.

Herdt, G.H. (Ed.). (1984). *Ritualized homosexuality in Melanesia.* Berkeley, CA: University of California Press.

Herek, G.M. (1985). On doing, being and not being: Prejudice and the social construction of sexuality. *Journal of Homosexuality, 12*(1), 135–151.

Hooker, E. (1969). Parental relations and male homosexuality in patient and nonpatient samples. *Journal of Consulting and Clinical Psychology, 33,* 140–142.

Hoult, T.F. (1984). Human sexuality in biological perspective: Theoretical and methodological considerations. *Journal of Homosexuality, 9*(2/3), 137–155.

Hudson, W.W., & Ricketts, W.A. (1980). A strategy for the measurement of homophobia. *Journal of Homosexuality, 5*(4), 357–372.

Humphreys, L. (1975). *Tearoom trade.* Chicago: Aldine.

King, D. (1981). Gender confusions: Psychological and psychiatric conceptions of transvestism and transsexualism. In K. Plummer (Ed.), *The making of the modern homosexual* (pp. 155–184). Totowa, NJ: Barnes and Noble.

Kinsey, A.C., Pomeroy, W.B., & Martin, C.E. (1948). *Sexual behavior in the human male.* Philadelphia: W.B. Saunders.

Luria, Z. (1979). Psychosocial determinants of gender identity, role, and orientation. In H.A. Katchadourian (Ed.), *Human sexuality: A comparative and developmental perspective* (pp. 163–193). Berkeley, CA: University of California Press.

Paul, J.P. (1984). The bisexual identity: An idea without social recognition. *Journal of Homosexuality, 9*(2/3), 45–63.

Plummer, K. (1975). *Sexual stigma: An interactionist account.* London: Routledge & Kegan Paul.

Plummer, K. (Ed). (1981). *The making of the modern homosexual.* Totowa, NJ: Barnes and Noble.

Rich, A. (1980). Compulsory heterosexuality and lesbian experience. *Signs, 5,* 631–660.

Richardson, D. (1981). Theoretical perspectives of homosexuality. In J. Hart & D. Richardson (Ed.), *The theory and practice of homosexuality.* London: Routledge & Kegan Paul.

Richardson, D. (1984). The dilemma of essentiality in homosexual theory. *Journal of Homosexuality. 9*(2/3), 79–90.

Richardson, D., & Hart, J. (1981). The development and maintenance of a homosexual identity. In J. Hart & D. Richardson (Eds.). *The theory & practice of homosexuality* (pp. 73–92). London: Routledge & Kegan Paul.

Ricketts, W. (1984). Biological research on homosexuality: Ansell's cow or Occam's razor? *Journal of Homosexuality, 9* (2/3),45–63.

Siegelman, M. (1974). Parental background of male homosexuals and heterosexuals. *Archives of Sexual Behavior, 3,* 3–18.

Sophie, J. (1986). A critical examination of stage theories of lesbian identity development. *Journal of Homosexuality, 12*(2), 39–51.

Stoller, R.J. (1980). Problems with the term "homosexuality." *The Hillside Journal of Clinical Psychiatry, 2,* 3–25.

Storms, M.D. (1980). Theories of sexual orientation. *Journal of Personality and Social Psychology, 38,* 783–792.

Troiden, R.R. (1988). *Gay and lesbian identity: A sociological analysis* Dix Hills, NY: General Hall.

Weeks, J. (1981). Discourse, desire and sexual deviance: Some problems in a history of homosexuality. In K. Plummer (Ed.), *The making of the modern homosexual* (pp. 76–111). London: Hutchinson.

Whitam, F.L., & Mathy, R.M. (1986). *Male homosexuality in four societies.* New York: Praeger.

READING 11

The Development of Gay, Lesbian, and Bisexual Identities

Heidi Levine
Nancy J. Evans

To understand the issues faced by gay, lesbian, and bisexual people on college campuses, we must first examine the life experiences of these individuals. What it means to be gay, lesbian, or bisexual is unique to each person; but some commonalities exist as individuals become aware of their attraction to others of the same sex and integrate these feelings into other aspects of their identity.

The research that considers timing and age factors in the gay and lesbian identity development process suggests that many developmental issues occur during the traditional undergraduate years (Bell, Weinberg, & Hammersmith, 1981; McDonald, 1982). As student development professionals, we know that this is a key time for identity development in general (Chickering, 1969; Erikson, 1986; Moore & Upcraft, 1990). College and university students are faced with many areas in which they need to reconsider their self-perceptions, develop new skills, and master developmental tasks. The possibility or certainty that one is gay, lesbian, or bisexual complicates these developmental challenges and adds an additional set of complicated issues that must be resolved. . . .

[Before we proceed,] a distinction must be made between the terms *homosexual identity* and *gay identity.* Homosexual identity is a narrower term, referring to sexual behavior only, whereas gay identity suggests the total experience of being gay (Warren, 1974). The use of the term *homosexual identity* is often viewed negatively by the gay and lesbian community because it has been used as a diagnostic label by many clinicians and is often associated with a negative self-image. *Gay identity,* however, has a positive connotation within the gay and lesbian communities and is seen as encompassing emotional, lifestyle, and political aspects of life rather than being exclusively sexual (Beane, 1981).

Jandt and Darsey (1981) noted that all definitions of homosexual or gay identity have in common a shift in perception of self as a member of the majority to self as a member of the minority. Along with this change in perception comes adoption of a new set of values and a redefinition of acceptable behavior. As such, development of a gay, lesbian, or bisexual identity is mainly an internal, psychological process. . . .

LESBIAN IDENTITY DEVELOPMENT

Differences in Identity Development Between Gay Men and Lesbians

Largely because of differences in the way men and women are socialized in Western society, a number of variations are evident in the patterns of identity development and lifestyles of gay men and lesbians (Cass, 1979).

The timing of events associated with the process of developing a gay or lesbian identity is different for men and women. Lesbians exhibit more variation than gay men in age at which awareness of attraction to individuals of the same sex occurs (Moses & Hawkins, 1986), and evidence suggests that gay men become aware of same-sex attractions, act on those attractions, and self-identify as gay at earlier ages than do lesbians. Men also disclose their homosexual identity earlier than women (DeMonteflores & Schultz, 1978; Sohier, 1985–1986; Troiden, 1988). Henderson (1984) proposed two hypotheses in reference to these timing variations: (1) women's sexual orientation may be more variable than men's and more tied to particular relationships, or (2) women are more likely to be influenced by societal norms that expect everyone to be heterosexual and so adhere longer to heterosexual behavior patterns and a heterosexual identity. Gramick (1984) concurred with the latter point of view.

Lesbians tend to establish ongoing love relationships earlier than gay men (Troiden, 1988) and are more likely to commit to a homosexual identity within the context of an intense emotional relationship, whereas gay men do so within the context of their sexual experiences (Groves & Ventura, 1983; Sohier, 1985–1986; Troiden, 1988). In general, emotional attachment is the most significant aspect of relationship for lesbians, but sexual activity is most important for gay men (DeMonteflores & Schultz, 1978; Gramick, 1984). As a result, lesbians tend to look for and maintain more stable, long-term relationships than do gay men (Gramick, 1984).

Although this pattern may be changing because of concern arising from the spread of AIDS, historically, gay men have been involved with many more one-time-only sexual partners than have lesbians (Kimmel, 1978; Marmor, 1980). This pattern, again, can be related to differences in the manner in which men and women are socialized; men are expected to be interested in sex before love, whereas women look for love before sex (Henderson, 1984; Westfall, 1988). Men are also encouraged to experiment sexually more than women (Coleman, 1981–1982). As one might expect given these socialization patterns, "tricking" (picking up unknown individuals for brief sexual liaisons) has been much more common among gay men than among lesbians who tend to meet others and interact in more intimate, private settings (Cronin, 1974; Gramick, 1984; Nuehring, Fein, & Tyler, 1974).

DeMonteflores and Schultz (1978) suggested that lesbians often use feelings to avoid thinking of themselves as homosexual whereas men use denial of feelings as a way to avoid self-labeling as gay. Women use the rationale that they merely love one particular woman, but men view their homosexual activity as insignificant because they are not emotionally involved with their partners.

Some researchers (Bell & Weinberg, 1978; Sohier, 1985–1986) have suggested that acceptance of homosexuality is easier for women than for men since sexual relationships between women are less stigmatized than those between men (DeMonteflores & Schultz, 1978; Marmor, 1980; Paul, 1984). The women's movement may have assisted lesbians to come out; there has been no comparable movement for men (DeMonteflores & Schultz, 1978). Also, since many lesbians become aware of their identity at later ages, they may have resolved other identity issues and be more adept at handling the coming out process than gay men who generally self-identity during their teens (Paul, 1984).

A number of writers have suggested that lesbians are more likely to view their sexuality as a choice, whereas gay men see it as a discovery (Henderson, 1984; Kimmel, 1978; Westfall, 1988). This distinction is particularly true for feminist lesbians. Feminist lesbians also identify more strongly with the political-philosophical aspects of their lifestyle, whereas gay men are more concerned with the physical-social aspects (Jandt & Darsey, 1981).

With regard to relationship development, lesbians more closely resemble other women than they do gay men (Marmor, 1980). Women, in general, are more concerned with the relational aspects of their attachments to other people and focus on establishing intimate, long-term relationships. Because they fear displeasing others, they may have difficulty breaking norms and acknowledging that they cannot accept the roles family, friends, and society have identified for them. Men, however, are taught to be independent, competitive, and autonomous. These factors appear to play an important role in the differences exhibited between lesbians and gay men.

Relational Versus Political Lesbians

Great variation exists in the way lesbians describe themselves and how they come to identify themselves as lesbian (Miller & Fowlkes, 1980). And as Golden (1987) noted, feelings, behaviors, and self-identification do not always agree nor do they always remain the same over time. Two major philosophical approaches to lesbianism can be identified in the literature, however; a traditional relational viewpoint that focuses on emotional and sexual attraction to other women (Moses, 1978; Ponse, 1980) and a radical feminist perspective that views the lesbian lifestyle as a political statement (Faraday, 1981; Lewis, 1979).

A number of theorists note that a distinction must be made between women who view their lesbianism as beyond their control and those who see it as a choice (Golden, 1987; Richardson, 1981b). Generally, lesbian feminists adhere to the latter viewpoint, but relational lesbians take the former position (Richardson, 1981b; Sophie, 1987).

In a small study of 20 self-identified lesbians, Henderson (1979) distinguished three groups: (1) *ideological lesbians,* women who can be viewed as radical feminists for whom a lesbian lifestyle is politically correct; (2) *personal lesbians,* women concerned with establishing an independent identity who find homosexuality supportive of this goal and who view lesbianism as a choice; and (3) *interpersonal lesbians,* women who find themselves involved with another woman, often to their chagrin, and who experience their involvement as a discovery rather than a choice.

Development of a Lesbian Identity

Although a number of writers believe that sexual activity between women has become more acceptable as a result of the women's movement and the freeing of sexual norms (Blumstein & Schwartz, 1974; Henderson, 1979), the developmental process of identifying oneself as a lesbian is still difficult.

Many lesbians recall being "tomboys" as youngsters: a preference for "masculine" rather than "feminine" activities as a child is often the first indication that they do not fit the heterosexual pattern (Lewis, 1979). This awareness intensifies during puberty when the adolescent finds herself attracted to women rather than men. This discovery can lead to intense feelings of loneliness. Because of the difficulty young lesbians experience in finding a support group of other lesbians or identifying positive role models, this period is particularly difficult in the person's life (Sophie, 1982).

Most lesbians have a history of sexual involvement with men and, contrary to popular belief, become involved with women not because of unsatisfactory relationships with men but rather because they experience greater emotional and sexual satisfaction from women (Groves & Ventura, 1983). Indeed, women frequently identify themselves as bisexual prior to adopting a lesbian identity.

It needs to be noted that most lesbians go through a period during which they reject their identity because they are unable to deal with the stigma associated with the label *lesbian* (Groves & Ventura, 1983). Often they seek security and an escape from their feelings of isolation and anxiety in heterosexual activity or marriage (Lewis, 1979; Sophie, 1982).

Usually involvement in an intense, all-encompassing love relationship with another woman is the decisive factor in embracing a lesbian identity (Groves & Ventura, 1983; Lewis, 1979). Such an involvement often develops slowly, starting out as a friendship.

Sophie (1982) noted that it is difficult for lesbians to feel good about themselves until they reconceptualize the term *lesbian* into positive terms. This process rarely occurs in isolation. Interaction with other lesbians and other sources of information about positive aspects of a lesbian lifestyle are helpful.

Coming out, both to other lesbians and to accepting heterosexuals, is also supportive of establishment of a lesbian identity (Richardson, 1981b; Sophie, 1982). Often the individual decides to come out because it takes too much energy to maintain a heterosexual image. Usually the individual comes out first to close friends who appear trustworthy (Lewis, 1979). As the woman becomes involved in the lesbian community, pressure is often applied to come out publicly (Lewis, 1979). Doing so can be viewed as the final step in the solidification of a lesbian identity.

Identity Development Models

A number of theorists have proposed models of identity development specific for lesbians. Ponse (1980) noted three steps in lesbian identity development: becoming aware of feeling different because of sexual-emotional attraction to other women, becoming involved in a lesbian relationship, and seeking out other lesbians. This model differs from many of the gay male models in that a serious relationship is formed *before* the individual becomes involved in the lesbian community.

Gramick (1984) pointed out that in attempting to make meaning of their experiences, many lesbians reinterpret past events, feelings, and behaviors as sexual that were not perceived as such at the time they occurred. She suggested that the process of developing a lesbian identity first involves strong emotional attachment to other women leading to a feeling of "differentness" within the context of the social environment but without a recognition that this difference might be labeled as lesbian. In adolescence, heterosexual socialization patterns strongly influence all young women and often delay development of homosexual identity. Meeting other lesbians and becoming emotionally and sexually involved with another woman are usually key events in confirming and accepting a lesbian identity. In Gramick's model, supportive others, as well as sexual involvements, play a crucial role in identity development.

Lewis (1979) identified five stages in the development of a lesbian identity and focused more on the political aspects of lesbianism. Her stages include (1) experience of discomfort with the heterosexual and patriarchal nature of socialization, (2) labeling self as different from other women, (3) becoming aware of lesbianism, (4) finding and becoming involved in a lesbian community, and (5) educating self about the lesbian lifestyle.

Also writing from a feminist perspective, Faderman (1984) suggested that . . . the first step for lesbian feminists, involves rejection of societal norms concerning the role of women and acceptance of a lesbian identity. This step is followed by experiences of prejudice and discrimination resulting in feelings of aloneness outside of the community of radical feminists and, finally, by sexual experiences with other women. Faderman suggested that because lesbian feminists are exposed to and accept the movement's political philosophy prior to their first homosexual experi-

ence they may not experience the guilt and shame felt by other lesbians and gay men. . . .

BISEXUAL IDENTITY

The gay rights movement has generally ignored bisexual men and women. Although Kinsey and his colleagues (Kinsey, Pomeroy, & Martin, 1948; Kinsey, Pomeroy, Martin, & Gebhard, 1953) discovered that more individuals are bisexual than strictly homosexual, later researchers and theorists have held to a rigid dichotomization of sexual behavior as either heterosexual or homosexual (Klein, Sepekoff, & Wolf, 1985). Acknowledging and attempting to understand the variation and fluidity of sexual attraction and behavior are important if we are to advance our knowledge of human sexuality and sexual identity development (Paul, 1985). . . .

Bisexuality comes in many forms. MacDonald (1982) identified four areas of variation: (1) individuals may have a preference for one gender over the other or may have no preference; (2) they may have partners of both sexes either simultaneously or sequentially; (3) they may be monogomous or have several partners; and (4) their bisexuality may be transitory, transitional, a basis for homosexual denial, or an enduring pattern. Zinik (1985) proposed the following criteria for assuming a bisexual identity: (1) being sexually aroused by both males and females, (2) desiring sexual activity with both, and (3) adopting bisexuality as a sexual identity label.

Two contrasting theories have been offered to account for bisexuality (Zinik, 1985): The conflict model suggests that bisexuality is associated with conflict, confusion, ambivalence, and an inability to determine one's sexual preference; the flexibility model hypothesizes that bisexuality is characterized by flexibility, personal growth, and fulfillment. The media tends to adhere to the former view, presenting bisexuality as a confused or conflicted lifestyle, as retarded sexual development, or as a denial of a true heterosexual or homosexual identity (Hansen & Evans, 1985).

Because the stigma attached to bisexuality is greater in many ways than that associated with homosexuality, many people who are bisexual in behavior do not identify themselves as such (Blumstein & Schwartz, 1974; Golden, 1987; Hansen & Evans, 1985; Paul, 1984; Zinik, 1985). Although some individuals are quite open about their identity, others hide it from both the heterosexual and the homosexual communities (Blumstein & Schwartz, 1977a). MacDonald (1981) suggested that bisexuals are less willing to disclose their identity than any other group because they believe that neither gays nor heterosexuals will accept them.

Bisexuals experience the same type of oppression as gay men and lesbians because society tends to group bisexuals with homosexuals. Heterosexuals assume that individuals are trying to excuse their homosexual inclinations by labeling themselves as bisexual (Blumstein & Schwartz, 1977a).

Because they do not conform to heterosexist culture, many bisexuals tend to align themselves with the gay and lesbian communities (Shuster, 1987). However, an individual's self-identification as bisexual is frequently met with skepticism in the homosexual community as well and viewed as an attempt to avoid the stigma of, or commitment to, a gay or lesbian lifestyle (Paul, 1984). The lesbian community, in particular, seems to have difficulty accepting bisexuality (Golden, 1987). Bisexuals are faced with considerable pressure to identify as homosexual and to behave in an exclusively homosexual manner (Blumstein & Schwartz, 1974; Hansen & Evans, 1985; Paul, 1985). Frequently, bisexuals respond to this pressure by pretending to be either exclusively homosexual or heterosexual depending on the social situation (Zinik, 1985).

Results of a study of 156 bisexuals conducted in the early 1970s (Blumstein & Schwartz, 1976, 1977a, 1977b) suggested that no identifiable bisexual life script exists and that identity and partner preferences change over the life course. Sexual experience and identity are not necessarily synonymous. The researchers identified several conditions that they saw as necessary for assumption of a bisexual identity: labeling, conflicting homosexual and heterosexual experiences, and contact with other bisexuals.

Zinik (1985) suggested that bisexual identity development may occur in stages similar to those proposed by Cass (1979) for homosexual identity formation. As with gay men and lesbians, the coming out process is one of both self-acknowledgment and disclosure to others (Shuster, 1987). Wide variation exists, however, in the timing and ordering of sexual experiences leading to a bisexual identification. In addition, because bisexuality lacks societal and scientific affirmation, acceptance of such an identity requires a high tolerance for ambiguity and is even harder than acceptance of a homosexual identity (MacDonald, 1981, Richardson & Hart, 1981). In most cases, bisexuals tend to identify in terms of particular relationships in which they are involved rather than with the abstract label bisexual (Shuster, 1987).

Although gay men and lesbians have formed support groups and political organizations, few such groups of bisexuals exist (Paul, 1985). As MacDonald (1981) noted, there is no "bisexual liberation movement" (p. 21). As a result, no clear bisexual identity exists, and little scientific research has examined the life experiences of bisexual men and women.

REFERENCES

Beane, J. (1981). "I'd rather be dead than gay": Counseling gay men who are coming out. *Personnel and Guidance Journal, 60,* 222–226.

Bell, A. P., & Weinberg, M. S. (1978). *Homosexualities: A study of diversity among men and women.* New York: Simon and Schuster.

Bell, A. P., Weinberg, M. S., & Hammersmith, S. K. (1981). *Sexual preference: Its development in men and women.* Bloomington: Indiana University.

Blumstein, P. W., & Schwartz, P. (1974). Lesbianism and bisexuality. In E. Goode & R. R. Troiden (Eds.), *Sexual deviance and sexual deviants* (pp. 278–295). New York: Morrow.

Blumstein, P. W., & Schwartz, P. (1976). Bisexuality in women. *Archives of Sexual Behavior, 5,* 171–181.

Blumstein, P. W., & Schwartz, P. (1977a). Bisexuality in men. In C. A. B. Warren (Ed.), *Sexuality: Encounters, identities, and relationships* (pp. 79–98). Beverly Hills, CA: Sage.

Blumstein, P. W., & Schwartz, P. (1977a). Bisexuality: Some social psychological issues. *Journal of Social Issues, 33,* 30–45.

Cass, V. C. (1979). Homosexual identity formation: A theoretical model. *Journal of Homosexuality, 4,* 219–235.

Chickering, A. W. (1969). *Education and identity.* San Francisco: Jossey-Bass.

Coleman, E. (1981–1982). Developmental stages of the coming out process. *Journal of Homosexuality, 7,* 31–43.

Cronin, D. M. (1974). Coming out among lesbians. In E. Goode & R. R. Troiden (Eds.), *Sexual deviance and sexual deviants* (pp. 268–277). New York: Morrow.

DeMonteflores, C., & Schultz, S. (1978). Coming out: Similarities and differences for lesbians and gay men. *Journal of Social Issues, 34*(3), 59–72.

Erikson, E. H. (1968). *Identity: Youth and crisis.* New York: Norton.

Faderman, L. (1984). The "new gay" lesbians. *Journal of Homosexuality, 10*(3/4), 85–95.

Faraday, A. (1981). Liberating lesbian research. In K. Plummer (Ed.), *The making of the modern homosexual* (pp. 112–129). Totowa, NJ: Barnes & Noble.

Golden, C. (1987). Diversity and variability in women's sexual identities. In Boston Lesbian Psychologies Collective (Eds.), *Lesbian psychologies: Explorations and challenges* (pp. 19–34). Urbana, IL: University of Illinois Press.

Gramick, J. (1984). Developing a lesbian identity. In T. Darty & S. Potter (Eds.), *Women-identified women.* (pp. 31–44). Palo Alto, CA: Mayfield.

Groves, P. A., & Ventura, L. A. (1983). The lesbian coming out process: Therapeutic considerations. *Personnel and Guidance Journal, 62,* 146–149.

Hansen, C. E., & Evans, A. (1985). Bisexuality reconsidered: An idea in pursuit of a definition. In F. Klein & T. J. Wolf (Eds.), *Bisexualities: Theory and research* (pp. 1–6). New York: Haworth.

Henderson, A. F. (1979). College age lesbianism as a developmental phenomenon. *Journal of American College Health, 28*(3), 176–178.

Henderson, A. F. (1984). Homosexuality in the college years: Development differences between men and women. *Journal of American College Health, 32,* 216–219.

Jandt, F. E., & Darsey, J. (1981). Coming out as a communicative process. In J. W. Chesebro (Ed.), *Gayspeak* (pp. 12–27). New York: Pilgrim.

Kimmel, D. C. (1978). Adult development and aging: A gay perspective. *Journal of Social Issues, 34,* 113–130.

Kinsey, A. C., Pomeroy, W. B., & Martin, C. E. (1948). *Sexual behavior in the human male.* Philadelphia: Saunders.

Kinsey, A. C., Pomeroy, W. B., Martin, C. E., & Gebhard, P. H. (1953). *Sexual behavior in the human female.* Philadelphia: Saunders.

Klein, F., Sepekoff, B., & Wolf, T. J. (1985). Sexual orientation: A multivariable dynamic process. In F. Klein & T. J. Wolf (Eds.), *Bisexualities: Theory and research* (pp. 35–49). New York: Haworth.

Lewis, S. G. (1979). *Sunday's women: A report on lesbian life today.* Boston: Beacon.

MacDonald, Jr., A. P. (1981). Bisexuality: Some comments on research and theory. *Journal of Homosexuality, 6*(3), 21–35.

MacDonald, Jr., A. P. (1982). Research on sexual orientation: A bridge that touches both shores but doesn't meet in the middle. *Journal of Sex Education and Therapy, 8,* 9–13.

Marmor, J. (1980). Overview: The multiple roots of homosexual behavior. In J. Marmor (Ed.), *Homosexual behavior: A modern reappraisal* (pp. 3–22). New York: Basic Books.

McDonald, G. J. (1982). Individual differences in the coming out process for gay men: Implications for theoretical models. *Journal of Homosexuality, 8*(1), 47–90.

Miller, P. Y., & Fowlkes, M. R. (1980). Social and behavior constructions of female sexuality. *Signs, 5,* 783–800.

Moore, L. V., & Upcraft, M. L. (1990). Theory in student affairs: Evolving perspectives. In L. V. Moore (Ed.), *Evolving theoretical perspectives on students.* (pp. 3–23). *New Directions for Student Services,* No. 51. San Francisco: Jossey-Bass.

Moses, A. E. (1978). *Identity management in lesbian women.* New York: Praeger.

Moses, A. E., & Hawkins, R. O. (1986). *Counseling lesbian women and gay men: A life issues approach.* Columbus, OH: Merrill.

Nuehring, E., Fein, S. B., & Tyler, M. (1974). The gay college student: Perspectives for mental health professionals. *The Counseling Psychologist, 4,* 64–72.

Paul, J. P. (1984). The bisexual identity: An idea without social recognition. In J. P. DeCecco & M. G. Shively (Eds.), *Bisexual and homosexual identities: Critical theoretical issues* (pp. 45–63). New York: Haworth.

Paul, J. (1985). Bisexuality: Reassessing our paradigms of sexuality. In F. Klein & T. J. Wolf (Eds.), *Bisexualities: Theory and research* (pp. 21–34). New York: Haworth.

Ponse, B. (1980). Lesbians and their worlds. In J. Marmor (Ed.), *Homosexual behavior: A modern reappraisal.* (pp. 157–175). New York: Basic Books.

Richardson, D. (1981b). Lesbian identities. In J. Hart & D. Richardson (Eds.), *The theory and practice of homosexuality* (pp. 111–124). London: Routledge & Kegan Paul.

Richardson, D., & Hart, J. (1981). The development and maintenance of a homosexual identity. In J. Hart & D. Richardson (Eds.), *The theory and practice of homosexuality* (pp. 73–92). London: Routledge & Kegan Paul.

Shuster, R. (1987). Sexuality as a continuum: The bisexual identity. In Boston Lesbian Psychologies Collective (Eds.), *Lesbian psychologies: Explorations and challenges* (pp. 56–71). Urbana, IL: University of Illinois Press.

Sohier, R. (1985–1986). Homosexual mutuality: Variation on a theme by E. Erikson. *Journal of Homosexuality, 12*(2), 25–38.

Sophie, J. (1982). Counseling lesbians. *Personnel and Guidance Journal, 60*(6), 341–344.

Sophie, J. (1987). Internalized homophobia and lesbian identity. *Journal of Homosexuality, 14,* 53–65.

Troiden, R. R. (1988). Homosexual identity development. *Journal of Adolescent Health Care, 9*(2), 105–113.

Warren, C. A. B. (1974). *Identity and community in the gay world.* New York: Wiley.

Westfall, S. B. (1988). Gay and lesbian college students: Identity issues and student affairs. *Journal of the Indiana University Student Personnel Association,* 1–6.

Zinik, G. (1985). Identity conflict or adaptive flexibility? Bisexuality reconsidered. In F. Klein & T. J. Wolf (Eds.), *Bisexualities: Theory and research* (pp. 7–19). New York: Haworth.

PERSONAL ACCOUNT

An Opportunity to Get Even

When I was a freshman in high school, my parents sent me to a private school. I got harassed a lot by a few of the sophomore guys there because I wore pants with the uniform (instead of the pleated miniskirts), I didn't wear makeup, and probably most important, I would not date any of them (and couldn't give a reason for that). Most of this harassment was anti-gay slurs with specific references to me on the bathroom walls. One of the guys often yelled comments such as "Hey Dyke, I got what you need right here" while grabbing his crotch. My name was written on many of the bathroom stalls (both male and female), with my sexual orientation, and a rhyme about a gang bang.

After about six weeks of this, I confided in my soccer coach. I told her about the harassment and came out to her. I don't know what I expected, but I did not expect any positive reaction. She told me she was glad I came out to her, and she promised to keep my confidentiality. She also offered me an opportunity to get back at the three guys who were harassing me the most. She told me that this was my battle and that I was going to have to learn how to fight.

She knew that the three guys were part of the boys soccer team, and made arrangements so that, as part of the homecoming festivities, our soccer team would play their's. By doing this she gave me the opportunity to "show them up" and make them look bad in front of the school. I did my best to accomplish that. For example, every time any of them came near me, I would run into them or trip them. My goal was to embarrass them in front of the school. It did not look good for the guys because a "dyke" challenged and defeated the "jocks."

What my soccer coach did for me meant a lot. First, she was literally the only person I was out to at that time, so she was a source of support. Further, she went out of her way to help me get even with the harassers. Because of what she did for me, the harassment stopped.

Carol A. Mabry

EXPERIENCING DIFFERENCE

FRAMEWORK ESSAY

In the first framework essay we defined race, sex, class, and sexual orientation as "master statuses" and described how these statuses have been named, aggregated, dichotomized, and stigmatized. In all of this, we were looking at the social construction of difference.

Now we turn to the *experience* of these statuses. Two examples illustrate what we mean. Some years ago, a friend suggested renting the video *Willow* to her children. The eldest, a seven-year-old, had seen the opening scenes on television and was horrified at the prospect: "They kill the mom and steal the baby. There's dead bodies and blood everywhere." When she asked about the movie, however, the man working in the video store, who had seen it several times, vouched that it was not violent.

If you have seen *Willow* you may recall that as the movie opens an evil queen rounds up all the pregnant women in the empire so as to slay the enchanted baby when she is born. The queen's soldiers kill the mother of the child but a midwife saves the baby and carries her into the forest. Then the midwife is attacked and killed by a pack of wild animals and the baby floats downstream in a basket.

This is a small lesson in the import of social status. What one notices in the world depends in large part on the statuses one occupies; in this way one may be said to experience one's social status. The seven-year-old noticed the violence both because of the unique person he is and because of his age, another master status. That the man in the video store did not see the movie as violent may be attributed, at least in part, to the same social status: age.

Although we are not specifically addressing age in this volume, it operates in some ways that are analogous to race, sex, class, and sexual orientation. There are innumerable ways that being young affects one's treatment: at a minimum, restric-

137

tions on driving, employment, military enlistment, marriage, abortion, admission to movies, and alcohol and cigarette consumption; insurance rates, mandatory school attendance, "status offenses" (acts that are only illegal for minors), exclusion from voting and other legal rights, and a general likelihood of being presumed untrustworthy and irresponsible.

In these ways, those defined as "young" are treated differently than those who are not so defined. Because of that treatment, the world looks different to them than to those who are older and no longer operating within these constraints. Those who are young notice things that older people need not notice, because they are not subject to the same rules. One's experience of the world is tied to the statuses one occupies.

A second example of experiencing one's status is offered by Lorene Cary in her autobiography, *Black Ice* (1991). Describing her life as one of the first black students in an exclusive and previously all-white prep school, Cary recalls what it was like to hear "one [white] girl after another say, 'It doesn't matter to me if somebody's white or black or green or purple. I mean people are just people'."

> Having castigated whites' widespread inability to see individuals [apart from] the skin in which they were wrapped, I could hardly argue with "its the person that counts." I didn't know why they always chose green and purple to dramatize their indifference, but my ethnicity seemed diminished when the talk turned to Muppets (1991:83–84).

While Cary notices that they are trying to express a commitment to fair treatment irrespective of race, she also hears her own *real* experiences being trivialized in a comparison to fictional green and purple creatures: Cary's status helps explain what she notices.

Because status affects how one is treated, status shapes one's perspective. In all, you experience your social statuses, you live through them, they are the filters through which you see and make sense of the world, in large measure they account for how you are treated and what you notice. In the sections that follow, we will focus on the experiences of privilege and stigma associated with master statuses.

THE EXPERIENCE OF PRIVILEGE

Just as Lorene Cary's status helps explain what she notices, status also explains what we *don't* notice. The following is an account of a classroom discussion between a black and a white woman. The white woman has argued that because she and the black woman share the status of being female, they should be allied. The black woman responds,

> "When you wake up in the morning and look in the mirror what do you see?"
> "I see a woman," replied the white woman.
> "That's precisely the issue," replied the black woman. "I see a black woman. For me, race is visible every day, because it is how I am *not* privileged in this culture. Race is invisible to you [because it is how you are privileged]" (Kimmel and Messner, 1989:3; emphasis added).

Thus, we are likely to be fairly unaware of the statuses we occupy that privilege us, i.e., provide us advantage, and acutely aware of those that are the source of trouble, i.e., that yield negative judgments and unfair treatment. The mirror metaphor used by the black woman in this conversation emerges frequently among those who are stigmatized: "I looked in the mirror and saw a gay man." These moments of suddenly realizing one's social position with all of its life-shaping ramifications are usually about recognizing how one is stigmatized and underprivileged—rarely about how one is privileged or advantaged by the statuses one occupies. But it is privilege that we will focus on in this section.

Examples of Privilege   This use of the term privilege was first developed by Peggy McIntosh (1988) from her experience teaching Women's Studies courses. In those courses she had noticed that while many men were willing to grant that women were disadvantaged (or "underprivileged") because of sexism, it was more difficult for them to acknowledge that they were themselves advantaged (or "overprivileged") because of it. Extending the analysis to race, McIntosh generated a list of the ways in which she, as a white woman, was overprivileged by virtue of racism. Her list of over forty white privileges included:

> I can turn on the television or open to the front page of the paper and see people of my race widely represented.
>
> When I am told about our national heritage or about "civilization," I am shown that people of my color made it what it is.
>
> I do not have to educate my children to be aware of systemic racism for their own daily protection.
>
> I can worry about racism without being seen as self-interested or self-seeking.
>
> I can think over many options, social, political, imaginative, or professional, without asking whether a person of my race would be accepted or allowed to do what I want to do (McIntosh, 1988:5–8).

When McIntosh later presented her analysis to public audiences, she learned about other white privileges: "A black woman said she was glad to hear me 'working on my own people,' because if she said these things about white privilege, she would be seen as a militant." Someone else noted that one of the privileges of being white was being able to be oblivious to those privileges. "Those in privileged groups are educated [to be oblivious] about what it is like for others, especially for others who have to be in their presence" (McIntosh, 1988).

One feature of privilege is that it makes life easier—it is easier to get around, to get what one wants, and to be treated in a way that is acceptable. Columnist Tony Kornheiser (1990) provides an example of this in his description of traveling with an African American colleague when both were using complimentary airline tickets. After Kornheiser, who is white, turned in his ticket and was assigned a seat, he watched the white ticket agent ask his black colleague for some identification:

> The black man handed over his ticket. The female agent glanced at it and asked, "Do you have some identification?" [Kornheiser had not been asked for any identification.]

"Yes, I do," the black man said, and he reached for his wallet. "But just out of curiosity, do you mind telling me why you want to see it?"

The agent grinned in embarrassment.

She said nothing in response.

"How about a credit card?" the black man said, and he pulled one out of his wallet.

"Do you have a work ID?" she asked, apparently hoping to see something with the black man's photo on it.

"No," he said, and whipped out another credit card.

"A driver's license would be fine," she said, sounding trapped.

"I don't have my driver's license with me," he said. "I'm taking the plane, not the car. . . ."

"That's fine sir, thank you," the agent finally said, shrinking a bit with each successive credit card. "Enjoy the flight."

The men rode the escalator up to the gate area in silence.

The white man shook his head. "I've probably watched that a hundred times in my life," he said. "But that's the first time I've ever *seen* it."

The black man nodded. He'd seen it more times than he cared to count. "You don't ever need to remind yourself that you're black," he said, "because every day there's somebody out there who'll remind you."

They walked on for a while, and the black man started to laugh to himself. Pirouetting, he modeled his outfit, an Italian-cut, double-breasted suit with a red rose in his lapel for Mother's Day. "I really can't look any better than this," he said sardonically. Then, he looked into his friend's eyes and said, "I had my driver's license. But if I show it, we may as well be in Soweto" (Kornheiser, 1990).

(In reading about Kornheiser's behavior during this exchange—he stands by and watches—one black student was particularly angered: "Whites will stand by and watch this happen, and either be oblivious to the slight or sympathize with you afterward, but they won't go to the mat and fight for you.")

Thus, Kornheiser noted for the first time a privilege that he has as a middle-class white: he is not assumed to be a thief. By contrast, his black colleague is presumed to have stolen the ticket no matter how upper-class or professional he may look. Similarly, many black and Latino students describe being closely monitored for shoplifting when they are in department stores—just as the students who work in security confirm that they are given explicit instructions to watch black and Latino customers for shoplifting. On hearing this, one black student realized why she had the habit of walking through stores with her hands out, palm open, in front of her: it was a way to prove she was not stealing.

Thus, one of the privileges of being white is that shoplifting is easier, since the security people in stores are busy watching the black and Latino customers. As Jeffrey Reiman discusses in selection 24, one explanation for the higher crime rates among blacks and the poor is that those who are white and middle- to upper-class are less likely to be arrested, charged, or convicted for their crimes.

Just as whites are not assumed to be thieves, they are not presumed to be violent (at least by other whites). By contrast, many whites presume blacks are violent. Even recent survey data show that 50 percent of whites believe this to be the case (National Opinion Research Center; 1990). Whites' fear of blacks—especially males—is fairly widespread. But, as law Professor Patricia Williams makes clear in selection 17, it is *blacks* whose lives are in danger as a consequence. When people are assumed to be criminal or potentially violent their life is at risk from preemptive violence directed against them; indeed, the violence directed at them is considered justified. One of the privileges experienced by those who are white and apparently middle-class is that they are not presumed to be potentially criminal or violent. Thus, they need not closely monitor their behavior in public for fear that others will perceive them as threatening. Few white women are likely to be surrounded by a SWAT team in a public restaurant because they have complained about spoiled milk—unlike the experience of the black woman described by Williams.[1]

In selection 15, David Mura describes a privilege likely to be invisible to those in single-race families, namely, the privilege of being recognized as a family. In the following account, the failure to perceive a family is linked to the expectation of black criminality.

> When my son was home visiting from college, we met in town one day for lunch. . . . On the way to the car, one of us thought of a game we'd often played when he was younger.
>
> "Race you to the car!"
>
> I passed my large handbag to him, thinking to more equalize the race since he was a twenty-year-old athlete. We raced the few blocks, my heart singing with delight to be talking and playing with my beloved son. As we neared the car, two young white men yelled something at us. I couldn't make it out and paid it no mind. When we arrived at the car, both of us laughing, they walked by and mumbled "Sorry" as they quickly passed, heads down.
>
> I suddenly understood. They hadn't seen a family. They had seen a young Black man with a pocketbook, fleeing a pursuing middle-aged white woman. My heart trembled as I thought of what could have happened if we'd been running by someone with a gun.
>
> Later I mentioned the incident in a three-day diversity seminar I was conducting at a Boston corporation. A participant related it that evening to his son, a police officer, and asked the son what he would have done if he'd observed the scene.
>
> The answer: "Shot out his kneecaps" (Lester, 1994:56–7).

Let us turn now from the privileges of race to the privileges of sexual orientation. The most obvious privilege enjoyed by heterosexuals is that they are free to talk to virtually anyone about their relationships and to display affection in almost any public setting. These displays are so commonplace that heterosexual couples who do not touch in public are sometimes assumed to be fighting. Those in same-sex relationships, however, can neither talk openly about their relationships nor display affection in public. Indeed, doing so puts them at risk of unemployment, ostracism, verbal abuse, loss of child custody, and potentially life-threatening physical assault.

---

[1]Despite whites' fear of violence at the hands of African Americans, crime is predominately *intra*-racial. In 1992, 66 percent of the perpetrators of violent crime against whites were white and 21 percent were black; in the same year, 86 percent of the perpetrators of violent crime against blacks were black and 7 percent were white. The remainder in each category include cases in which the race of the assailant was unknown, or there were multiple assailants of different races (Updegrave, 1994).

Even the ability to display a picture of one's partner on a desk at work stands as an invisible privilege of heterosexuality.

> Consider, for example, an employee who keeps a photograph on her desk in which she and her husband smile for the camera and embrace affectionately. . . . the photo implicitly conveys information about her private sexual behavior. [But] . . . most onlookers (if they even notice the photo) do not think of her partner primarily in sexual terms. . . .
>
> [But] if the photograph instead shows the woman in the same pose with a same-sex partner, everyone is likely to notice. As with the first example, the photograph conveys the information that she is in a relationship. But the fact that the partner is a woman overwhelms all other information about her. The *sexual* component of the relationship is not mundane and implicit as with the heterosexual spouse . . . (Herek, 1992:95–6; emphasis added).

Because heterosexual public affection is so commonplace, it rarely conjures up images of sexual activity. But that is exactly what we may think of when we see a same-sex couple embrace. This is why gay and lesbian people are often accused of "flaunting" their sexuality: *any* display of affection between them is understood by many heterosexuals as virtually a display of the sex act itself.

In the realm of class privilege, several readings in this text address the considerable differences in health, life-span, educational access, likelihood of arrest and imprisonment, and quality of life which accompany American class differences. But these are perhaps the more visible privileges of being middle- and upper-class. Less apparent is the privilege of being treated as a competent and generally valued member of the community. To get that treatment in his university, one working-class student described how he had to change out of his work clothes before going to class; another described sitting in the back of the classroom so that she could leave easily whenever her anxiety at not belonging there overwhelmed her.

Two privileges in particular appear common among non-stigmatized statuses: the sense of entitlement and the privilege of being "unmarked." The sense of entitlement—that one has the right to be respected, acknowledged, protected, and rewarded—is so much taken for granted by those in non-stigmatized statuses, that they are often shocked and angered when it is denied them.

> After a 1982 lecture by Barbara Smith at Yale's Afro-American Cultural Center, [whites in the audience] shot their hands up to express how excluded they felt because Smith's lecture, while broad in scope, clearly was addressed first and foremost to the women of color in the room. . . . What a remarkable sense of entitlement must drive their willingness to assert their experience of exclusion! If I wanted to raise my hand every time I felt excluded, I would have to glue my wrist to the top of my head (Ettinger, 1994:51).

Like entitlement, the privilege of occupying an "unmarked" status is shared by most of those in non-stigmatized categories. "Doctor" is an unmarked status; *woman* doctor is its marked variant. As Deborah Tannen writes in selection 14, an unmarked status is "what you think of when you are not thinking of anything special." Unmarked categories convey the usual and expected distribution of individuals; the distribution that does not require any special comment. Thus, the unmarked category tells us what a society takes for granted.

Theoretically the unmarked category "doctor" might include anyone, but in truth it refers to white males. How do we know that? Because other occupants of that status are usually marked: woman doctor, black doctor, etc. While the marking of a status signals infrequency, e.g., female astronaut or male nurse, it may also imply inferiority. A "woman doctor" may indicate that one is not considered a full-fledged member of the profession; a "black politician" is often presumed to represent only his black constituents.

Thus, a privilege of those who are not stigmatized is that their master statuses are not often used to discount their accomplishments or imply that they serve "special interests." Someone described as "a politician" is presumed to operate from a universality that someone described as "a white male politician" is not. Because white male politicians are rarely marked as that, their anchoring in the reality of their own master statuses is hidden. In this way, those in marked statuses appear always to be operating from an "agenda," or "special interest," while those in unmarked statuses can appear to be agenda-free: "women/black/gay/Hispanic politicians" are presumed to have special interests that "politicians" do not. Being white and male thus becomes invisible, since it is not regularly being identified as important. For this reason, some recommend marking *everyone's* race and sex as a way to recognize that we are all grounded in our master statuses.

This use of marked statuses also applies to classroom interactions. At white dominated universities, white students are unlikely to be asked to speak on behalf of all white people or to explain the "white experience." In this way, those who are white, male, heterosexual, and middle class look as if they have no race, sex, sexual orientation, or social class, and thus have the privilege of not having to often suffer through classroom discussions about the problems of "their people."

The Stigmatized and the Experience of Privilege; the Privileged and the Experience of Stigma We have described some of the privileges enjoyed by those in non-stigmatized statuses, but those with stigma also have some experience of privilege—it is just less frequent. For example, in 1991 the Urban Institute investigated racial discrimination in employment by sending pairs of black and white male college students (who had been coached to present virtually identical personal style, appearance, dialect, education, and job history) to apply for jobs in Washington D.C. and Chicago.

> In 20 percent [of the 576 job applications], the white applicant advanced farther in the hiring process [from obtaining a job application, to interview, to hiring] than his black counterpart, and in 15 percent the white applicant was offered a job while his equally qualified black partner was not. Blacks were favored over comparable white applicants in a much smaller share of cases; in 7 percent of the audits the black advanced farther in the hiring process, and in 5 percent only the black received the job offer (Turner, Fix, and Struyk, 1991:18).

Thus, black and white applicants both had some experience of preferential hiring, but the white applicant had about three times more of it. A similar study of job discrimination against Latino males conducted in Chicago and San Diego indicated an even larger gap between the amount of privilege experienced by Anglos and Latinos (Cross, Kenney, Mell, and Zimmermann, 1990).

Thus, concerns about "reverse discrimination" often miss the mark. While blacks, Latinos, Asian Americans, or white women are sometimes favored in hiring, they are not favored nearly as frequently as white males. Discrimination continues in its historic direction as evidenced as well in the constancy of race and sex differences in income. In 1975, black per-capita median annual income was 58.5 percent that of whites, by 1990 that figure had risen to only 59.0. In 1975, the same measure for Latinos was 56.1 percent of whites; by 1990 it had dropped to 55.1 percent (U.S. Department of Commerce; 1993:454).[2]

In 1975, the median earnings of women working full-time year-round were 58.8 percent of men's; in 1992, they were 70.6 percent (U.S. Department of Labor, 1993). In no occupational category do women earn as much as men (Bergmann, 1986; U.S. Department of Labor, 1991). For example, "on the average, men earned almost 30 percent more than women in information-systems management, almost 7 percent more in marketing, and almost 4 percent more in finance" (Benokraitis and Feagin, 1995:4). About half of the male/female wage gap can be attributed to discrimination (Treiman and Hartman, 1981).

Because the focus is so frequently on how stigma affects those who bear it, it is easy to assume that only the targets of racism, sexism, homophobia, or classism are affected by it. But that is not the case. For example,

> Think of white slaveowners and their wives: the meaning of the sexual difference between them was constructed in part by the alleged contrast between them as whites and other men and women who were Black; what was supposed to characterize their relationship was not supposed to characterize the relationship between white men and Black women, or white women and Black men. . . . So even though the white men and women were of the same race, and even though they were not the victims of racism, this does not mean that we can understand the relationship between them without reference to their race and to the racism that their lives enacted (Spelman, 1988:104–5).

Similarly, the interaction between men is affected by sexism, even though they are not themselves subject to it.

> For example, we can't understand the racism that fueled white men's lynching of Black men without understanding its connection to the sexism that shaped their protective and possessive attitudes toward white women. The ideology according to which whites are superior and ought to dominate Blacks is nested with the ideology according to which white men must protect their wives from attack by Black men. . . . That men aren't subject to sexism doesn't mean sexism has no effect on their relationships to each other, especially when the men are from different races in a racist society (Spelman, 1988:106).

These examples focus on race and sex, but the analysis can be easily extended to sexual orientation and social class, e.g., in the ways that homophobia shapes

---

[2]Income figures exclude "money income received before payments for personal income, taxes, Social Security, union dues, Medicare deductions, food stamps, health benefits, subsidized housing, or rent-free housing and goods produced and consumed on the farm" (U.S. Department of Commerce, 1993:425).

heterosexual relations or the ways that poverty affects interactions among those in the middle class. Thus, the most obvious privilege of those in non-stigmatized statuses—that they are not affected by stigma—proves questionable.

Those in privileged statuses may be unaware of the impact of stigma on their lives, as they may be unaware of the impact of privilege. Being unaware of one's own privilege, however, also bears on one's reaction to other's complaints of discrimination. Because privilege is usually invisible to those who possess it, those in privileged statuses may conclude that everyone is treated as they are. They are sometimes shocked to learn how others without the privilege are treated and may try to dismiss the experience by arguing that the event was exceptional rather than routine, that the victim was overreacting or misinterpreting, or that perhaps the victim even provoked the encounter. Such responses do not necessarily deny that the event took place as it was described; rather, they deny the meaning attributed to the event.

Hearing dismissals like these is usually frustrating because they reduce the teller to a child inadequate to judge the world. Often, such dismissals are framed in terms of the very stigma about which people are complaining, e.g. in the conviction that people complain too much about racism, sexism, or homophobia. In this way, what a stigmatized person says about their status is discounted precisely because they are stigmatized. The implication is that those who occupy a stigmatized status are the ones least able to assess its consequence. While such dismissals assume that those least involved have the most potential to be objective, their effect is to dismiss precisely those who have had the most experience with the topic.

This process, called "looping" or "re-reading," is described by many who have studied the lives of patients in psychiatric hospitals (Rosenhan, 1973; Schur, 1984; Goffman, 1961, 1963). If a patient says, "The staff here are being unfair to me," and they respond, "Of course he would think that—he's crazy" they have re-read, or looped, his words through his status. His words have been heard through his stigma and dismissed for exactly that reason.

Through such dismissals, those operating from positions of privilege can deny the experience of those without privilege. For example, college students who are in their late teens and early twenties often describe university staff as unresponsive to requests for tuition billing correction, residence change, or financial aid until they have had their parents call and complain. If the parents later said "I don't know why you had such a problem with those people. They were very nice to me. Did you do something to antagonize them?" that would indicate they were oblivious to their own privileged place in these university procedures as well as unaware of their child's underprivileged status in them.

There is a function served by these dismissals. Dismissing another's experience of status-based mistreatment masks the possibility that one has escaped such treatment precisely because of one's privilege. If we do not acknowledge that their status affects their treatment, we need not acknowledge that our status affects our treatment. Dismissing others' claims of status-based mistreatment allows us to believe that our treatment in the world is responsive to our individual merit but indifferent to our status. It allows us to avoid the larger truth that those who are treated well, those who are treated ill, and all the rest in between, are always evaluated both as individuals and as occupants of particular esteemed and disesteemed categories. Still, privilege does not inevitably yield this effect, and most are able to recognize their privilege when it is brought to their attention.

Hierarchies of Stigma and Privilege   While it may appear as if people can be easily separated into two categories—those in privileged statuses and those in stigmatized statuses—as Patricia Hill Collins makes clear in selection 19, every individual occupies several master statuses. The privilege or stigma that might be associated with one status emerges in the context of all one's other statuses. For example, a middle-class, male, heterosexual Mexican American may be privileged in terms of class, sex, and sexual orientation, but stigmatized by virtue of being Latino. Given the invisibility of privilege, he is more likely to notice the ways that his status as Latino stigmatize him than he is to notice the privileges that follow from his other statuses. Nonetheless, he is simultaneously all of his statuses; the privileges and disadvantages of each emerge in the context of all the others. An Anglo male and a Latino male may both be said to experience the privilege of sex, but they do not experience the same privilege.

While individuals may experience both privilege and the lack thereof in the mix of their various statuses, some stigmas are so strong as to cancel out the privileges that one's other statuses might have been expected to yield. For example, there is much evidence that the stigma of being black in America cancels out the privileges that might be expected to follow from being middle class.

> A black person who makes more than $50,000 a year will be virtually as [residentially] segregated as a black person who makes only $2500 a year. . . . A black person who makes more than $50,000 will be more segregated than a Hispanic person who makes $2500. [The reason for this is well-documented: whites move out of a neighborhood once the black population exceeds about 8 percent (Hacker, 1992:36).]
>
> Blacks earn 10 percent to 26 percent less than whites with similar educational backgrounds; regardless of age or education, they have higher levels of unemployment, and tend to stay unemployed longer than whites.
>
> Banks are more restrictive in providing commercial loans to black entrepreneurs and approve considerably less financing per dollar of equity than they would to white entrepreneurs. Black applicants are more likely to be rejected for home mortgages (Updegrave, 1989).

Research on the effect of other stigmatized racial statuses has not been as thorough, nor are its findings as consistent, but it is clear that for African Americans, middle-class standing provides little protection against racism.

Does the stigma of being an out-of-the-closet gay or lesbian cause one to lose the privileges that come from being middle-class, white, or both? Sexual orientation is not covered by the civil rights protections of federal legislation. There is no federal legislation barring discrimination in employment, housing, or health care against gays. This is why many imagine gay people to be all white and upper class: in the absence of employment protection this is the only group that can afford to publicly identify as gay (Lester, 1994). While some jurisdictions have enacted protections, many of those ordinances have later been challenged and repealed. At present, it appears that the stigma of being gay often overwhelms the privileges that one's other statuses might afford.

But which is more important: one's race, sex, sexual orientation, or social class? For the sizable population that occupies multiple stigmatized statuses, it makes little sense to argue which status presents the greater obstacle. Nonetheless, in much of the public discussion of racism, sexism, classism, and homophobia people are asked to make alliances on that basis; they are asked to pick a single status as the most significant one.

Philosopher Elizabeth Spelman (1988) suggests a way to assess how an individual or culture prioritizes these statuses. If each master status is imagined as a room we will enter, we can consider which sequential ordering of these rooms most accurately reflects the structure of a particular society or our own experience. If the first rooms we encounter are labeled black, white, or Asian, we will find ourselves in a room with those who share our "race," but are different in terms of sex, social class, ethnicity, and sexual orientation. If the second set of rooms is labeled male and female, we will find ourselves with people of the same race and sex. Other rooms might be labeled with sexual orientation or social class categorizations.

Many white feminists have presumed that the first set of rooms are sex categorizations, thus arguing that the statuses of female and male have priority over race or class designations; that one is discriminated against first by virtue of one's sex, and then by race. Latino, black, and other white feminists have countered that the first set of rooms are race classifications. In this case, it is argued that racism so powerfully affects people, that men and women within racial categories have more in common with one another than they do with those of the same sex but of a different race. Alliances of gay and lesbian people by implication assume that the first set of doors are marked gay and straight, with sex, race, and class following. In addition to the orderings that correspond to the historical experience of categories of people, each of us also likely maintains an ordering derived from our personal experience of these statuses.

THE EXPERIENCE OF STIGMA

The previous section considered the privileges conferred by some master statuses; now we turn to the consequences of occupying stigmatized master statuses.

In his classic analysis of stigma, sociologist Erving Goffman (1963) distinguished between the *discredited,* whose stigma is immediately apparent to an observer (e.g., race, sex, some physical disabilities), and the *discreditable,* whose stigma can be hidden (e.g., sexual orientation, social class). Since stigma plays out differently in the lives of the discredited and the discreditable, each will be examined separately.

The Discreditable: "Passing" The discreditable are those who are "passing," i.e., not publicly acknowledging the stigmatized statuses they occupy. (Were they to acknowledge that status, they would become discredited.) The term "passing" comes from "passing as white," which emerged as a phenomenon after 1875 when Southern states re-established racial segregation through hundreds of "Jim Crow"[3] laws. At that point, some African Americans passed as a way to get better jobs.

> [S]ome who passed as white on the job lived as black at home. Some lived in the North as white part of the year and as black in the South the rest of the time. More men passed than women . . . the vast majority who could have passed permanently did not do so, owing to the pain of family separation, condemnation by most blacks, their fear of whites, and the loss of the security of the black community. . . . Passing as white probably reached an all-time peak between 1880 and 1925 (Davis, 1991:56–57).

"Passing as white" is now quite rare and strongly condemned by African Americans, a reaction that "indicate[s] the resolute insistence that anyone with even the slightest trace of black ancestry is black, and a traitor to act like a white" (Davis, 1991:138). We will use the term "passing" here to refer to those who have not made their stigmatized status evident; it is similar to the phrase "being in the closet" which is usually applied to gays. Because it is among gays that passing is now most frequent—as well as most vehemently debated—many of our examples will focus on that stigmatized status.

One may come to be passing by happenstance as well as by choice. For example, the presumption that everyone is heterosexual can have the effect of putting gay people in the closet even when they had not intended to be. In the midst of a series of lectures on marriage and the family, one of our colleagues realized that he had been making assignments, lecturing, and encouraging discussion with the presumption that all of the students in the class had, or wanted to have, heterosexual relationships. Unless his gay and lesbian students wished to do something specific to counter his assumption, they were effectively passing. His actions forced them to choose between announcing or remaining silent about their status. Had he assumed that students in the class would only be involved with others of the same race, he would have created a similar situation for those in interracial relationships. Thus, assumptions about another's private life may have the effect of making them choose between silence or an announcement of something they may consider private.

Those who are gay especially face the problem of passing because others have mistaken their identity. Since most heterosexuals assume that everyone else is heterosexual, many social encounters either put a gay person in the closet or require they announce their status.

> Every encounter with a new classful of students, to say nothing of a new boss, social worker, loan officer, landlord, doctor, erects new closets [that] . . . exact from at least gay people new surveys, new calculations, new draughts and requisitions of secrecy or disclosure. Even an *out* gay person deals daily with interlocutors about whom she doesn't know whether they know or not [or whether they would care]. . . . The gay

---

[3]"Jim Crow" was "a blackface, singing-dancing-comedy characterization portraying black males as childlike, irresponsible, inefficient, lazy, ridiculous in speech, pleasure-seeking, and happy, [and was] a widespread stereotype of blacks during the last decades before emancipation. . . ." (Davis, 1991:51). "Jim Crow" laws were laws by which whites imposed segregation following the Civil War.

closet is not a feature only of the lives of gay people. But for many gay people it is still the fundamental feature of social life; there can be few gay people . . . in whose lives the closet is not a shaping presence (Sedgwick, 1990:68).

Inadvertent passing is also experienced by those whose racial status is not immediately apparent. An African American acquaintance who looks white is often in settings in which others do not know that she is African American—or in which she does not know if they know—and must regularly decide how and when to convey that information. This is important to her as a way to discourage racist remarks, since whites often assume it is acceptable to make racist remarks to one another (as men often assume it is acceptable to make sexist remarks to other men, or as straights presume it acceptable to make homophobic remarks to those they think are also straight). It is also important to her that others know she is black so that they understand the meaning of her words—so that they will hear her words through her status as an African American woman. In all, those whose stigma is not apparent must go to some lengths to avoid being in the closet by virtue of others' assumptions.

But passing may also be an intentional choice. For example, one of our students, who was in the process of deciding that he was gay, had worked for many years at a local library and became friends with several of his coworkers. Much of the banter at work, however, involved disparaging gay, or presumably gay, library patrons. As he grappled with a decision about his own sexual identity, his social environment reminded him that being gay is a stigmatized status in American society. The student did not so much face prejudice against himself (since he was not "out" to his work friends), but rather he faced an "unwilling acceptance of himself by individuals who are prejudiced against persons of the kind he can be revealed to be" (Goffman, 1963:42). Thus, he was not the person his friends took him to be. While survey research indicates that those who personally know a gay man hold consistently more positive feelings toward male homosexuals as a group (Herek and Glunt, 1993), the decision to reveal oneself as possessing a stigma that others have gone on record as opposed to is not lightly made.

The revelation of stigma changes one's interactions with "normals"—even those who are not particularly prejudiced against the group of which one is a member. The stigma itself, for a time, is there as something to be dealt with; the relationship is for a time changed. Revealing stigma risks permanently altering important relationships. Parents disown children who come out as gay, just as they do children involved in interracial relationships. Thus, the decision to pass or be "out" is not taken lightly. For the discreditable, what Goffman euphemistically described as "information management" is at the core of one's life. "To tell or not to tell; to let on or not to let on; to lie or not to lie; and in each case, to whom, how, when, and where" (Goffman, 1963:42). Such choices are faced daily by those who are discreditable, not just those who are gay and lesbian, but also those who are poor, have been imprisoned, attempted suicide, terminated a pregnancy through abortion, are HIV-positive, are drug or alcohol dependent, or have been the victims of incest or rape. Thinking back to the discussion of privilege, one item we might now add is that those who do not occupy stigmatized statuses needn't invest emotional energy in monitoring information about themselves; when they choose, they can talk openly about their personal history.

Still, there are both positive and negative aspects to passing. On the positive, passing lets the person with the stigma exert some power over the situation; they control the information, the flow of events, and their privacy. By withholding their identity until they choose to reveal it, they may create a situation in which others' prejudices are challenged. In some ways, passing is an effort to get one's "due"—to be judged as an individual rather than be discounted by virtue of one's stigma. Passing also limits one's exposure to verbal and physical abuse, allows for the development of relationships outside the constraints of stigma, and improves job and income security by reducing one's exposure to discrimination.

On the negative side, passing consumes a good deal of time, energy, and emotion in the management of personal information. It introduces a significant level of deception and secrecy into even close relationships. Passing also denies others the opportunity to prove themselves unprejudiced, and it makes one vulnerable to depredation from those who do know about one's stigma.

While the closet is a significant feature in the lives of all the discreditable, they do not all suffer similarly upon coming out. Literature professor Eve Kosofsky Sedgwick (1990) makes this clear in a comparison between coming out as a Jew and coming out as gay. Jews are unlikely to be told that it's a phase, that they are just angry at gentiles, that counseling might help them get over it, or that they aren't "really" Jewish—but responses such as these are the frequent reaction to those who come out as gay. In many ways, such reactions assume that those outside the stigmatized status are best able to judge the situation or that those who do not fit the stereotypes about the stigmatized group could not really be "full-fledged" members of it.

Continuing with Sedgwick's analogy, a person coming out as a Jew is unlikely to be told that they could control it if they wanted to, or that the hearer always knew that the person was Jewish and was just waiting for them to recognize it themselves (another claim that those without the stigma are best able to judge how it operates). Coming out as a Jew does not suggest that the one to whom this is revealed might also be Jewish or that it is their fault that you are Jewish, it is not likely to be construed as an invitation to an intimate relationship, nor is it likely to plunge the hearer into the closet as someone with a Jewish friend or relative. And at this point in history, one is unlikely to be beaten up or killed for revealing that one is Jewish.

The Discredited: Flaming   While the stigma experienced by the discreditable is complicated by invisibility, the experience of the discredited is complicated by visibility. As we shall see, those who are discredited suffer from being the subjects of a disproportionate share of attention and of being seen in terms of stereotypes. In the face of these difficulties it is not surprising that the discredited sometimes "flame."

Being discredited means that one's stigma is immediately apparent to others. As essayist bell hooks describes below, those who are discredited often have little patience for those who at least have the option of passing.

Many of us have been in discussions where a non-white person—a black person—struggles to explain to white folks that while we can acknowledge that gay people of all colors are harassed and suffer exploitation and domination, we also recognize that there is a significant difference that arises because of the visibility of dark skin. . . . While it in no way lessens the severity of such suffering for gay people, or the fear that it causes, it does mean that in a given situation the apparatus of protection and survival may be simply not identifying as gay. In contrast, most people of color have no choice. No one can hide, change, or mask dark skin color. White people, gay and straight, could show greater understanding of the impact of racial oppression on people of color by not attempting to make these oppressions synonymous, but rather by showing the ways they are linked and yet differ (hooks, 1989:125).

For the discredited, stigma is likely to be always shaping interaction with those who are not stigmatized, but its effect does not necessarily play out in ways one can easily determine. Those whose stigma is visible must daily decide whether the world is responding to them or their stigma. Florynce Kennedy, a black activist in the civil rights and women's movements once commented that the problem with being black in America was that you never knew whether what happened to you, good or bad, was because of your talents or because you were black (Kennedy, 1976). This was described in 1903 by sociologist W.E.B. Du Bois as the "double consciousness" of being black in America. The concept was key to Du Bois's classic, *The Souls of Black Folk,* for which he was rightfully judged "the father of serious black thought as we know it today" (Hare, 1982:xiii). Du Bois described double consciousness this way:

the Negro . . . [is] gifted with a second-sight in this American world—a world which yields him no true self-consciousness, but only lets him see himself through the revelation of the other world. It is a peculiar sensation, this double consciousness, this sense of always looking at one's self through the eyes of others, of measuring one's soul by the tape of a world that looks on in amused contempt and pity. One ever feels his twoness . . . (1982:45).

This sense of seeing oneself through the eyes of a critical other—one who does not at bottom value the category of which one is a member—of only with difficulty achieving a direct, unmediated vision of oneself (or the others with whom one shares stigma), ties back to our discussion of objectification in Framework Essay I. When those who are stigmatized view themselves from the perspective of the non-stigmatized, they have reduced themselves to objects. This theme of double or "fractured" consciousness can also be found in contemporary analyses of women's experience.

The greatest effect of being visibly stigmatized is on one's life chances—literally, one's chances for living. Thus, the readings in this text detail differences in income, employment, health, life span, education, targetting for violence, and the likelihood of arrest and imprisonment. In this essay, however, we will consider the more mundane difficulties created by stigmatization, particularly the sense of being "on stage."

The discredited often have the feeling of being watched or on display when they are in settings dominated by non-stigmatized people. For example, when women walk through male-dominated settings, they often feel on display in terms of their physical appearance. Asian, black, and Latino students in white/Anglo dominated settings often describe a feeling of being on display in campus dining facilities. In such cases, the discredited are likely to feel that others are evaluating them in terms of their stigmatized status.

As sociologist Rosabeth Moss Kanter (1980;1993) has shown, these feelings are likely to be accurate. When Kanter studied corporate settings in which there was one person visibly different from the others, she found that person likely to get a disproportionate share of attention. In fact, people in the setting were likely to closely monitor what the minority person did, which meant that their mistakes were more likely to be noticed—and that the mistakes of those in the rest of the group were more likely to be overlooked, since everyone was watching the minority person. Kanter focused on work settings, but found that this excessive attention to those who were visibly different persisted in after-work socializing as well. Thus, even at the time designated for relaxation among colleagues, the visibly different found themselves still on stage.

In addition to receiving a disproportionate share of attention, Kanter also found that the minority person's behavior was likely to be interpreted in terms of the prevailing stereotypes about the members of that category. For example, when there were only a few men in a setting in which women predominated, the men were likely to be subject to intense observation and their behavior was likely to be filtered through the stereotypes about men irrespective of their actual behavior. That is, perceptions were distorted to fit the pre-existing beliefs.

Prior to the entrance of a visibly different person, members of a setting are likely to see themselves as different from one another in various ways, as not necessarily constituting a coherent "us" in any special sense. Through contrast with the visibly different person, however, they notice their similarities. In this way, majority group members may construct dichotomies out of settings in which there are a few who are different. It is not surprising that those who are visibly different may sometimes isolate themselves in response.

Still, none of this is inevitable. Kanter argues strongly that as there is more diversity in a setting these processes abate but that the proportion of those who are visibly different must rise to about 15 percent before that change takes place. Until that point, however, those who are in the minority (or visibly stigmatized) are the subject of a good deal of attention. As a consequence they are often accused of "flaming." "Flaming" popularly refers to acting in an effeminate manner, with the intention of letting observers know that one is gay. Most likely, the term originated as a criticism of gay men but has since been appropriated more positively by that community. We use the term here to describe an unabashed display of one's stigmatized status.

Flaming is a charge those who are not stigmatized often level at those who are stigmatized. Although there are certainly occasions in which the discredited may deliberately make a show of their status, Kanter's work makes clear that when their representation is low, the discredited are likely to be charged with flaming no matter what they do. Subjected to a disproportionate amount of attention and viewed through the lens of stereotypes, almost anything the discredited do is likely to be noticed and attributed to the category of which they are a member. Thus, one of the frequent charges leveled at those in discredited groups is that they are "so" black, Latino, gay, etc., i.e., that they make too much of a show of their status.

There are various ways that this charge might affect those in discredited statuses. Many are careful to behave in ways deliberately contrary to expectations. At other times, however, flaming may be a deliberate goal. In the first session of one class, a student opened his remarks by saying "Well, you all know I am a gay man, and as a gay man I think . . .". The informal buzz of conversation stopped, other students stared at him, and one asked "How would we know you were gay?" The student pointed to a button showing a pink triangle he had pinned to his book bag and explained that he thought they knew that someone wearing it would be gay. (Pink triangles were assigned to gay men during the Nazi era, black triangles to lesbians and other "unwanted" women. Both have been adopted as badges of pride among gay activists. Still, his logic was weak: Anyone supportive of gay rights might wear the button.)

This announcement—which moved the student from a discreditable to a discredited status—may have been intended to keep his classmates from making overtly anti-gay comments in his presence. If they should make such comments, at least then all would know they were intended for his ears and his response. In a way, his was a strategy designed to counter the problem of passing described earlier: To avoid being mistakenly identified as straight and put into a position of inadvertent passing, he was in effect required to flame. In order to avoid misidentification, he had to find an opportunity to announce his status.

Similarly, light-skinned African Americans are encouraged to "flame" as black, lest they be accused of trying to pass. In adolescence, light-skinned black men are often derided by their black and white peers as not "really" black and so go to great lengths to counter that. As an instance of this, writer Itaberi Njeri offered a moving description of her cousin Jeffrey, who looked like singer Ricky Nelson, spent his brief life trying to demonstrate that he was black and tough, and died violently as a result (Njeri, 1991). While many light-skinned black men indicate that, when they are older, their skin color puts them at an advantage in both the black and white communities, in adolescence that is certainly not the case and thus they must "flame" their identity (Russell, Wilson, and Hall, 1992). However, light skin appears to be an advantage for black women throughout their lives.

But flaming does not only have this tragic side. For example, many bilingual Latino students talk about how much they enjoy a loud display of Spanish among Anglos; some Asian American students have described their pleasure in pursuing extended no-English-used card games in public spaces on campus. Black students and gay students sometimes entertain themselves by loudly affecting stereotypical behavior and then watching the disapproving looks that follow. Those who do not occupy stigmatized statuses may better appreciate these displays by remembering their experience of deliberating flaming as "obnoxious teenagers" in public settings—an experience many remember fondly. Thus, flaming may also be fun.

In all, those who are visibly stigmatized—who cannot or will not hide their identity—generate a variety of mechanisms to try to neutralize that stigma. Flaming is one of those mechanisms: It both announces one's stigmatized status and one's disregard for those who judge it negatively. Flaming neutralizes stigma by denying there is anything to be ashamed of. Thus, it functions as a statement of group pride.

European Ethnic Groups and Flaming   A variant on the theme of flaming emerges in an examination of ethnic group identification. In this case, it is possible that whites of European ancestry construe the ethnic identification of African Americans, Hispanics, and Asian Americans as a significant and perhaps enviable departure from their own experience.

Recent research documents that white Americans of European ancestry are undergoing both a loss and a transformation of ethnic identity. European immigrants who arrived in the peak 1880–1920 period (primarily Hungarians, Bohemians, Slovaks, Czechs, Poles, Russians [half of whom were Jews], and Italians), not only differed culturally and linguistically from one another, they differed as well from the Irish, German, Scandinavian, and English immigrants who preceded them. This distinctiveness has been replaced by a socioeconomic "convergence" among their descendants (Alba, 1990). While it was once the case that "to name an occupational group or class [was] very much the same thing as naming an ethnic group" (Glazer and Moynihan, 1970:vii), and that ethnic group, residential neighborhood, and political interest group once also coincided, this is no longer the case. Among most white Americans of European ancestry, ethnicity is no longer the criteria by which they are "channeled into locations in the social structure," nor is it the basis of "self-conscious communities whose members interact with each other to achieve common purposes" (Alba, 1990:17).

This convergence of ethnic groups has been accompanied by intermarriage. Because intermarriage is unlikely between those perceived as profoundly different and because intermarriage breaks down barriers between groups, it is generally understood as a sensitive barometer of inter-group relations. While European immigrants and their children tended to marry others from the same ethnic group, later generations freely intermarried. Further, children from those marriages now trace their own ethnicity across several lines, reducing their attachment to any one ethnic group.[4]

Thus, despite an apparent ethnic revival on college campuses (e.g., in ethnic studies programs or ethnic residential housing), those of European ancestry are in most ways experiencing a weakening of ethnic identity. They may enjoy special food and celebrations or have strong feelings attached to stories of immigration, but are unlikely to be involved in ethnic activities or organizations (Schaefer, 1990:145). Most important, this attachment to ethnic identity is likely to be in

---

[4]By contrast, marriages between blacks and non-Latino whites is the least common marital pattern. "Drawing on a number of sources, one can make the following estimates of intermarriage rates in the United States: Asian American rates are 10 percent to 25 percent (depending upon country of origin); black 2 percent; Native American 30 percent (not including Hispanics, many of whom have Indian ancestors)" (Yinger, 1985:167).

terms of the history of one's own family rather than to a particular culture or nationality (Alba, 1990).[5]

With such historical distance from the intensity of ethnic-group identification, the ethnic pride displayed by Chicanos, Puerto Ricans, Cuban Americans, African Americans, or any of those considered Asian American may seem inexplicable and even exclusionary. As one student said, "It makes me feel like I just don't have anything." Though he was himself a mix of Russian Jew, Italian Catholic, and Scotch-Irish Protestant ancestry, none of that seemed as compelling as the black, Asian, and Hispanic identities he saw around him.

The Expectations of Those Who Share One's Stigma   Stigma also affects interaction among those within the stigmatized category. It is others in the category from whom one learns a sense of group pride and lessons on how to behave, what to expect from those in and outside the category, and how to protect oneself. For those stigmatized by color, sex, or social class, such lessons likely come from family members. For those who are gay or lesbian, the lessons are usually provided later in life by members of the gay community.

Particularly for those with visible stigma, there are also likely to be frequent reminders that one will be seen by non-stigmatized others as representative of all those in the category. Thus, many in stigmatized categories must factor in virtually everyone's potential opinion: What will others in my category think? What will those who are not stigmatized think? Indeed, failing to deal with oneself as a stigmatized person may even be a criticism—"After all, who do you think you are?" In a sense, members of stigmatized categories may be said to police one another much as they are policed by those outside the category, with the difference that those within one's category can at least claim to be operating for one's defense.

This point is illustrated in a story from late tennis champion Arthur Ashe (1993). Ashe described watching his daughter play with a gift she had just received—a white doll—as they sat in the audience of a televised match in his honor. When the cameras panned his section of seats, he realized that he needed to get the doll away from his daughter or risk the anger of some black viewers who would argue that, by letting his child play with a white doll, he stood as a bad role model for the black community.

A different example is provided by a Mexican American acquaintance who worked in an office that employed only a few other Hispanics, most of whom felt that the routes to upward mobility were closed to them. Together they drafted a let-

---

[5]An exception to the process of convergence among European-originated groups may be white urban ethnics for whom Catholicism has played an important role. Throughout the nineteenth century, American Catholic churches were established as specifically ethnic churches (called "nationality churches"). These mostly urban churches were tailored to serve a particular ethnic group, which often included sending a priest from the home country who spoke the immigrants' native language. Thus, within a single urban area one might find separate Irish, Italian, and Polish Catholic churches, as well as effectively separate Catholic schools. The formation of ethnic churches meant that parishes also became ethnically segregated. On occasion, those parishes came to constitute stable, distinctive, working-class ethnic enclaves. In these cases ethnic identity continues as an active, viable reality.

ter to the firm's president detailing their concerns and seeking some corrective action. Although he had qualms about signing the letter, our acquaintance felt there was no alternative. Because he worked for management, he was then called in for an explanation of his behavior, which his supervisor saw as disloyal. Thus, he was put in the position of having to explain that, as a Chicano, he could not have refused to sign the letter.

Codes of conduct for those in stigmatized categories often require loyalty to the group, a fact of life that in this case the supervisor was unaware of. (Indeed, the operating rule for many in stigmatized statuses is to avoid public disagreement with one another or public airing of the group's "dirty laundry.") Such codes are not trivial since in their violation members of stigmatized categories risk ostracism from a critical support network. The reality of discrimination makes it foolhardy to reject those who share one's stigma. What would it have meant to Arthur Ashe to lose the support of fellow African Americans? To whom would our acquaintance have turned in that organization had he refused to sign the letter? When they are unaware of these pressures, those in privileged categories may make impossible demands of those who are stigmatized; when aware of these pressures, however, such requests are clear tests of loyalty.

POINTS OF CONTENTION, STAGES OF CONTENTIOUSNESS

This essay has focused on privilege and stigma and how they yield different treatment and different world views. In this final section we will focus on differing conceptions of exclusion and racism. Then we will consider the stages of identity development within which privilege and stigma are experienced.

As we said earlier, flaming sometimes leaves those who are not members of the stigmatized category feeling excluded. For example, when Latino students talked about their enjoyment of using Spanish, an Anglo friend immediately responded with a description of how excluded she felt on those occasions. While aware of this, the Latino students nonetheless made clear that they were not willing to forgo these opportunities. Non-Spanish-speaking friends would just have to understand that it wasn't anything personal against them. This may well mark the bottom line: Those not part of stigmatized categorizations will sometimes feel and be excluded by their friends.

But there is another question implied here: If the Hispanics exclude the Anglos, can the Anglos similarly exclude the Hispanics? As a way to approach this, consider the following two statements about gays and straights. In what ways are they similar, and in what ways different?

A heterosexual says, "I can't stand gays. I don't want to be anywhere around them."

A gay says, "I can't stand straights. I don't want to be anywhere around them."

While the statements are almost identical, they speak from very different positions of power. The heterosexual could likely structure his or her life so as to rarely interact with anyone gay, or at least anyone self-identified as gay. Most important, however, the heterosexual's attitude is consistent with major social, political, legal, and religious practices. Thus, the heterosexual in this example speaks from a position of some power, if only that derived from alignment with dominant cultural practices.

This is not the case for the gay person in this example, who is unlikely to be able to avoid contact with straights—and who would probably pay a considerable economic cost for self-segregation if that were attempted. There are no powerful institutional supports for hatred of straights. Analogously, the pleasure of exclusiveness enjoyed by bilingual Latino students exists against a backdrop of relative powerlessness, discrimination, stigmatization, and the general necessity of speaking English. The same might be said of men's disparagement of women compared to women's disparagement of men. As one student wrote, "As a male I have at times been on the receiving end of comments like, 'Oh, you're just like all men,' or 'Why can't men show more emotion?', but these comments or the sentiments behind them do not carry any power to affect my status. Even in the instance of a black who sees me as a representative of all whites, his vision of me does not change my privileged status."

Thus, the exclusiveness of those in non-stigmatized statuses has as its backdrop relative powerfulness, a sense of entitlement, infrequent discrimination based on master status, and a general ability to avoid those who might be prejudiced against people like oneself. The forms of exclusion available to minority group members are unlikely to tangibly affect the lives of those in privileged statuses. Being able to exclude someone from a dance or a club is not as significant as being able to exclude them from employment, residence, education, professional organizations, or financing.

This is what is meant when it is said that members of stigmatized categories may be prejudiced but cannot be racist or sexist, etc.; they do not have access to the institutional power by which to significantly affect the lives of those in non-stigmatized groups.

Apart even from this, however, the term *racist* carries different connotations for blacks and whites. As Robert Blauner describes in selection 13, among whites being a racist usually means being color conscious; those who are not color conscious are not racists. This understanding of what it means to be a racist has partly followed from the civil rights movement. If, as the civil rights movement taught, color should not make a difference in the way people are treated, whites who make a point of not noticing race argue that they are being polite and not racist (Frankenberg, 1993).

But given America's historical focus on race, it seems unrealistic for any of us to claim that we are oblivious to it. While many consider it impolite to mention race, differential treatment does not disappear as a consequence. Further, a refusal to notice race conveys that being black, Asian, or Latino is a "defect" it is indelicate (for whites) to mention. Thus, it can be argued that color-blindness is not really a strategy of politeness, it is a strategy of power-evasion. Since race clearly makes a difference in people's lives, pretending not to see it is a way to avoid noticing its effect, which has the consequence of maintaining racism. The alternative would be a strategy of race cognizance, i.e., of systematic attention to the impact of race on oneself and others (Frankenberg, 1993).

Differing conceptions of exclusiveness and racism can also be placed in the context of racial and ethnic identity development, which is the "understanding shared by members of ethnic groups, of what it means to be black, white, Chicano, Irish, Jewish, and so on" (White and Burke, 1987:311). Research on this topic indicates that the process of identity development is similar across race and ethnic groups, though the specific issues categories of people are concerned about vary. We offer here a brief composite sketch of what appear to be the stages of this development (Cross, 1971, 1978; Hazen, 1992, 1994; Helms, 1990; Morton and Atkinson, 1983; Thomas, 1970; Thomas and Thomas, 1971), suggesting that this framework might also apply to the sex, class, and sexual orientation identities we have focused on in this text. One important caution is necessary, however: Not everyone necessarily goes through each of these stages. For example, it is argued that African Americans are rarely found in the first stage (Hazen, 1992) we will detail below.

Among those in stigmatized categorizations, the first stage describes an internalization of the culture's negative image of oneself (though one may still criticize the dominant group). This stage may include the disparagement of others in one's stigma group and a strong desire to be accepted by dominant group members. For women, this might include being highly critical of other women. For those who are poor or gay, this stage might entail feelings of shame. For people of color, it might involve efforts to lighten one's skin, straighten hair, or have an eye tuck.

In the second stage, anger at the dominant culture emerges often as the result of specific encounters which bring to light the pervasiveness of racism, sexism, classism, and homophobia. Philosopher Sandra Bartky (1990), focusing on women's discovery of the extent of sexism, describes this as a period in which one sees sexism everywhere. Events and objects that had before been neutral are discovered to be suffused with sexist assumptions; it becomes impossible to get through the day without becoming enraged—and the injustices one discovers are communicated to everyone within earshot. One's own behavior is also subject to a new level of scrutiny. Things that used to be straightforward become moral tests.

The third stage is sometimes called an immersion stage, because it involves immersing oneself in the culture of one's own people. In the previous stage, the individual is in a sense focused on the dominant culture, because the dominant culture is the focus of anger. In this stage, however, the focus shifts to one's own group. Dominant group members and the dominant group culture become less relevant to one's pursuits. This is often a period of participation in segregated activities and organizations, as distance from dominant group members is sought. Anger is somewhat lessened here, but the process of re-evaluating one's old identity continues.

The final stage is described as a period of integration, as one's stigmatized categorization becomes integrated with the other aspects of one's life rather than taking precedence over them. Still, an opposition to stigmatization and discrimination continue. At this point, one can distinguish between supportive and unsupportive dominant group members and thus is more likely to establish satisfying relations with them.

For those who do not occupy stigmatized statuses, the first stage of race or ethnic identity development is identified as an unquestioning acceptance of dominant group values. This acceptance might take shape either as an obliviousness to discrimination or as the espousing of supremacist ideologies.

In the second stage, one becomes aware of stigmatization, often through an eye-opening encounter with discrimination. Such an encounter may produce a commitment to social change or a sense of powerlessness. As was the case for those in stigmatized categorizations, in this stage those in privileged statuses now also find themselves overwhelmed by all the forms of discrimination they see, often accompanied by a sense of personal guilt. In an attempt to affiliate and offer assistance, they are likely to seek alliances with those in stigmatized statuses. On college campuses the timing of this couldn't be worse since many of those in stigmatized statuses are likely to be at their peak level of anger at those in privileged groups.

In stage three, those in privileged statuses focus less on trying to win the approval of those in stigmatized groups and instead explore the history of privileged and stigmatized statuses. Learning how privilege has affected one's own life is often a central question in this period.

The final stage involves integrating one's privileged statuses with all the other aspects of one's life, recognizing those in stigmatized categorizations as distinctive individuals rather than romanticizing them as a category ("just because oppressors are bad, doesn't mean that the oppressed are good" [Spivak, 1994]), and understanding that many with privilege have worked effectively against discrimination.

It appears that this process is positively related to self-esteem for all American race and ethnic groups, but that the relationship is stronger for those who are Asian American, African American, and Latino than for those who are white (Hazen, 1994:55). Indeed, on various measures of self-esteem, African Americans score significantly higher than those in other race or ethnic groups, though this was not the case prior to the civil rights movement (Hazen, 1992).

We once observed an African American student explain to his white classmates that he and his sister both identified as black, even though their mother was white. At that point a white student asked why he didn't call himself white since he looked white and that status would yield him more privilege. In response, he detailed all the qualities he prized in the black community and said he would never give up that status to be white. Much of what he said was new to the white students; many had never thought there was anything positive about being black in America.

The student's question reflected the common assumption that those who are stigmatized wish they belonged to the privileged group. Yet the woman who asked the question was clear that she never wanted to be a male, and her response was equally surprising to the men in the class. Thus, many men presume there is nothing positive about being female, many straights assume there is nothing positive about being gay, and many in the middle and upper classes assume there is nothing positive in life for those who are poor. But most people value and appreciate the statuses they occupy. We may wish those statuses weren't stigmatized or over-privileged, but that does not mean we would want to be other than who we are.

The Readings in This Section

Our goal in this essay was to provide you with a framework by which to make sense of people's experience of privilege and stigma. Because there is a great deal of material that illustrates privilege and stigma, we have included readings here that raise issues or concepts generalizable to those in various stigmatized or privileged statuses.

REFERENCES

Alba, Richard D. 1990. *Ethnic Identity: The Transformation of White America.* New Haven, Connecticut: Yale University Press.

Ashe, Arthur. 1993. *Days of Grace.* New York: Ballantine.

Bartky, Sandra. 1990. *Femininity and Domination: Studies in the Phenomenology of Oppression.* New York: Routledge.

Benokraitis, Nijole, and Joe R. Feagin. 1995. *Modern Sexism: Blatant, Subtle, and Covert Discrimination.* 2d ed. Englewood Cliffs, New Jersey: Prentice Hall.

Bergmann, Barbara. 1986. *The Economic Emergence of Women.* New York: Basic Books.

Cary, Lorene. 1991. *Black Ice.* New York: Knopf.

Cross, H., G. Kenney, J. Mell, and W. Zimmerman. 1990. *Employer Practices: Differential Treatment of Hispanic and Anglo Job Seekers.* Washington, D.C.: The Urban Institute.

Cross, W.E. Jr. 1971. The Negro-to-black Conversion Experience: Toward a Psychology of Black Liberation. *Black World* 20 (9):13–17.

———. 1978. The Thomas and Cross Models of Psychological Nigresence: A Review. *The Journal of Black Psychology* 5 (1):13–31.

Davis, F. James. 1991. *Who is Black? One Nation's Definition.* University Park, Pennsylvania: Pennsylvania University Press.

Du Bois, W.E.B. 1982. *The Souls of Black Folk.* New York: Penguin (Originally published in 1903.)

Ettinger, Maia. 1994. The Pocahontas Paradigm, or Will the Subaltern Please Shut Up? *Tilting the Tower,* edited by Linda Garber, 51–55. New York: Routledge.

Frankenberg, Ruth. 1993. *White Women, Race Matters: The Social Construction of Whiteness.* Minneapolis, Minnesota: University of Minnesota Press.

Glazer, Nathan, and Daniel Patrick Moynihan. 1970. *Beyond the Melting Pot: The Negroes, Puerto Ricans, Jews, Italians, and Irish of New York City.* 2d ed. Cambridge, Massachusetts: MIT Press.

Goffman, Erving. 1961. *Asylums.* New York: Doubleday Anchor.

———. 1963. *Stigma: Notes on the Management of Spoiled Identity.* Englewood Cliffs, New Jersey: Prentice-Hall.

Hacker, Andrew. 1992. *Two Nations: Black and White, Separate, Hostile, Unequal.* New York: Ballantine.

Hare, Nathan. 1982. W.E. Burghart Du Bois: An Appreciation, pp. xiii–xxvii in *The Souls of Black Folk.* New York: Penguin (Originally published in 1969.)

Hazen, Sharlie Hogue. 1992. *The Relationship Between Ethnic/Racial Identity Development and Ego Identity Development.* Ph.D. proposal, Department of Psychology, George Mason University.

Hazen, Sharlie Hogue. 1994. *The Relationship Between Ethnic/Racial Identity Development and Ego Identity Development.* Ph.D. dissertation, Department of Psychology, George Mason University.

Helms, J.E. 1990. An Overview of Black Racial Identity Theory. *Black and White Racial Identity: Theory, Research, and Practice,* edited by J.E. Helms, 9–33. New York: Greenwood Press.

Herek, Gregory M. 1992. The Social Context of Hate Crimes. *Hate Crimes: Confronting Violence Against Lesbians and Gay Men,* edited by Gregory Herek and Kevin Berrill, 89–104. Newbury Park, California: Sage.

Herek, Gregory M., and Eric K. Glunt. 1993. Heterosexuals who Know Gays Personally Have More Favorable Attitudes. *The Journal of Sex Research,* 30:239-244.

hooks, bell. 1989. *Talking Back: Thinking Feminist, Thinking Black.* Boston: South End Press.

Kanter, Rosabeth Moss. 1993. *Men and Women of the Corporation.* New York: Basic Books, (Originally published in 1976.)

Kanter, Rosabeth Moss with Barry A. Stein. 1980. *A Tale of 'O': On Being Different in an Organization.* New York: Harper and Row.

Kennedy, Florynce. 1976. *Color Me Flo: My Hard Life and Good Times.* Englewood Cliffs, New Jersey: Prentice Hall.

Kimmel, Michael S. and Michael A. Messner, eds. 1989. *Men's Lives.* New York: Macmillan Publishing.

Kornheiser, Tony. 1990. The Ordinary Face of Racism. *Washington Post.* May 16, pp. F1, F9.

Lester, Joan. 1994. *The Future of White Men and Other Diversity Dilemmas.* Berkeley: Conari Press.

Morton, G., and Atkinson, D. R. 1983. Minority Identity Development and Preference for Counselor Race. *Journal of Negro Education* 52(2):156–161.

McIntosh, Peggy. 1988. White Privilege and Male Privilege: A Personal Account of Coming to See Correspondences Through Work in Women's Studies. Working Paper Number 189, Wellesley College, Center for Research on Women, Wellesley, Massachusetts.

National Opinion Research Center. 1990. *An American Profile: Opinions and Behavior 1972–1989.* Detroit: Gale Research.

Njeri, Itaberi. 1991. Who is Black? *Essence,* September, pp. 64–66, 114–16.

Rosenhan, D.L. 1973. On Being Sane in Insane Places. *Science* 179:250–258.

Russell, Kathy, Midge Wilson, and Ronald Hall. 1992. *The Color Complex: The Politics of Skin Color Among African Americans.* New York: Harcourt Brace Jovanovich.

Schaefer, Richard T. 1990. *Racial and Ethnic Groups.* 4th ed. Glenview, Illinois: Scott, Foresman/Little, Brown Higher Education.

Schur, Edwin. 1984. *Labeling Women Deviant: Gender, Stigma, and Social Control.* New York: Random House.

Sedgwick, Eve Kosofsky. 1990. *The Epistemology of the Closet.* Berkeley: University of California Press.

Spelman, Elizabeth. 1988. *Inessential Woman.* Boston: Beacon Press.

Spivak, Gayatre. 1994. George Mason University Cultural Studies presentation.

Thomas, C. 1970. Different Strokes for Different Folks. *Psychology Today* 4(4):48–53, 78–80.

Thomas, C., and Thomas, S. 1971. Something Borrowed, Something Black. In *Boys No More: A Black Psychologist's View of Community* edited by C. Thomas. Beverly Hills: Glencoe Press.

Treiman, Donald J. and Heidi I. Hartmann. 1981. *Women, Work, and Wages: Equal Pay for Jobs of Equal Value.* Washington, D.C.: National Academy Press.

Turner, Margery Austin, Michael Fix, and Raymond J. Struyk. 1991. *Opportunities Denied, Opportunities Diminished: Discrimination in Hiring.* Washington, D.C.: The Urban Institute.

Updegrave, Walter. 1989. Race and Money. *Money,* December, pp. 152–170.

Updegrave, Walter. 1994. You're Safer Than You Think. *Money,* June pp. 114–124.

U.S. Department of Commerce. 1993. *Statistical Abstract of the United States, 1992.* Washington, D.C.: U.S. Government Printing Office.

U.S. Department of Labor, Bureau of Labor Statistics. 1991, February 80. *Usual Weekly Earnings of Wage and Salary Workers: Fourth quarter, 1990.*

U.S. Department of Labor, Bureau of Labor Statistics. 1993. *Employment and Earnings.* Washington, D.C.: U.S. Government Printing Office

White, C.L., and Burke, P.J. 1987. Ethnic Role Identity Among Black and White College Students: An Interactionist Approach. *Sociological Perspectives* 30(3):310–331.

Yinger, Milton J. 1985. Ethnicity. *Annual Review of Sociology,* 11:151–180.

Oppression

Marilyn Frye

It is a fundamental claim of feminism that women are oppressed. The word 'oppression' is a strong word. It repels and attracts. It is dangerous and dangerously fashionable and endangered. It is much misused, and sometimes not innocently.

The statement that women are oppressed is frequently met with the claim that men are oppressed too. We hear that oppressing is oppressive to those who oppress as well as to those they oppress. Some men cite as evidence of their oppression their much-advertised inability to cry. It is tough, we are told, to be masculine. When the stresses and frustrations of being a man are cited as evidence that oppressors are oppressed by their oppressing, the word 'oppression' is being stretched to meaninglessness; it is treated as though its scope includes any and all human experience of limitation or suffering, no matter the cause, degree or consequence. Once such usage has been put over on us, then if ever we deny that any person or group is oppressed, we seem to imply that we think they never suffer and have no feelings. We are accused of insensitivity; even of bigotry. For women, such accusation is particularly intimidating, since sensitivity is one of the few virtues that has been assigned to us. If we are found insensitive, we may fear we have no redeeming traits at all and perhaps are not real women. Thus are we silenced before we begin: the name of our situation drained of meaning and our guilt mechanisms tripped.

But this is nonsense. Human beings can be miserable without being oppressed, and it is perfectly consistent to deny that a person or group is oppressed without denying that they have feelings or that they suffer.

We need to think clearly about oppression, and there is much that mitigates against this. I do not want to undertake to prove that women are oppressed (or that men are not), but I want to make clear what is being said when we say it. We need this word, this concept, and we need it to be sharp and sure.

The root of the word 'oppression' is the element 'press'. *The press of the crowd; pressed into military service; to press a pair of pants; printing press; press the button.* Presses are used to mold things or flatten them or reduce them in bulk, sometimes to reduce them by squeezing out the gasses or liquids in them. Something pressed is something caught between or among forces and barriers which are so related to each other that jointly they restrain, restrict or prevent the thing's motion or mobility. Mold. Immobilize. Reduce.

The mundane experience of the oppressed provides another clue. One of the most characteristic and ubiquitous features of the world as experienced by oppressed people is the double bind situations in which options are reduced to a very few and all of them expose one to penalty, censure or deprivation. For example, it is often a requirement upon oppressed people that we smile and be cheerful. If we comply, we signal our docility and our acquiescence in our situation. We need not, then, be taken note of. We acquiesce in being made invisible, in our occupying no space. We participate in our own erasure. On the other hand, anything but the sunniest countenance exposes us to being perceived as mean, bitter, angry or dangerous. This means, at the least, that we may be found "difficult" or unpleasant to work with, which is enough to cost one one's livelihood; at worst, being seen as mean, bitter, angry or dangerous has been known to result in rape, arrest, beating and murder. One can only choose to risk one's preferred form and rate of annihilation.

Another example: It is common in the United States that women, especially younger women, are in a bind where neither sexual activity nor sexual inactivity is all right. If she is heterosexually active, a woman is open to censure and punishment for being loose, unprincipled or a whore. The "punishment" comes in the form of criticism, snide and embarrassing remarks, being treated as an easy lay by men, scorn from her more restrained female friends. She may have to lie and hide her behavior from her parents. She must juggle the risks of unwanted pregnancy and dangerous contraceptives. On the other hand, if she refrains from heterosexual activity, she is fairly constantly harassed by men who try to persuade her into it and pressure her to "relax" and "let her hair down"; she is threatened with labels like "frigid," "uptight," "manhater," "bitch" and "cocktease." The same parents who would be disapproving of her sexual activity may be worried by her inactivity because it suggests she is not or will not be popular, or is not sexually normal. She may be charged with lesbianism. If a woman is raped, then if she has been heterosexually active she is subject to the presumption that she liked it (since her activity is presumed to show that she likes sex), and if she has not been heterosexually active, she is subject to the presumption that she liked it (since she is supposedly "repressed and frustrated"). Both heterosexual activity and heterosexual nonactivity are likely to be taken as proof that you wanted to be raped, and hence, of course, weren't *really* raped at all. You can't win. You are caught in a bind, caught between systematically related pressures.

Women are caught like this, too, by networks of forces and barriers that expose one to penalty, loss or contempt whether one works outside the home or not, is on welfare or not, bears children or not, raises children or not, marries or not, stays married or not, is heterosexual, lesbian, both or neither. Economic necessity; confinement to racial and/or sexual job ghettos; sexual harassment; sex discrimination; pressures of competing expectations and judgments about *women, wives* and *mothers* (in the society at large, in racial and ethnic subcultures and in one's own mind); dependence (full or partial) on husbands, parents or the state; commitment to political ideas; loyalties to racial or ethnic or other "minority" groups; the demands of self-respect and responsibilities to others. Each of these factors exists in complex tension with every other, penalizing or prohibiting all of the apparently available options. And

nipping at one's heels, always, is the endless pack of little things. If one dresses one way, one is subject to the assumption that one is advertising one's sexual availability; if one dresses another way, one appears to "not care about oneself" or to be "unfeminine." If one uses "strong language," one invites categorization as a whore or slut; if one does not, one invites categorization as a "lady" one too delicately constituted to cope with robust speech or the realities to which it presumably refers.

The experience of oppressed people is that the living of one's life is confined and shaped by forces and barriers which are not accidental or occasional and hence avoidable, but are systematically related to each other in such a way as to catch one between and among them and restrict or penalize motion in any direction. It is the experience of being caged in: all avenues, in every direction, are blocked or booby trapped.

Cages. Consider a birdcage. If you look very closely at just one wire in the cage, you cannot see the other wires. If your conception of what is before you is determined by this myopic focus, you could look at that one wire, up and down the length of it, and be unable to see why a bird would not just fly around the wire any time it wanted to go somewhere. Furthermore, even if, one day at a time, you myopically inspected each wire, you still could not see why a bird would have trouble going past the wires to get anywhere. There is no physical property of any one wire, *nothing* that the closest scrutiny could discover, that will reveal how a bird could be inhibited or harmed by it except in the most accidental way. It is only when you step back, stop looking at the wires one by one, microscopically, and take a macroscopic view of the whole cage, that you can see why the bird does not go anywhere; and then you will see it in a moment. It will require no great subtlety of mental powers. It is perfectly *obvious* that the bird is surrounded by a network of systematically related barriers, no one of which would be the least hindrance to its flight, but which, by their relations to each other, are as confining as the solid walls of a dungeon.

It is now possible to grasp one of the reasons why oppression can be hard to see and recognize: one can study the elements of an oppressive structure with great care and some good will without seeing the structure as a whole, and hence without seeing or being able to understand that one is looking at a cage and that there are people there who are caged, whose motion and mobility are restricted, whose lives are shaped and reduced.

The arresting of vision at a microscopic level yields such common confusion as that about the male door opening ritual. This ritual, which is remarkably widespread across classes and races, puzzles many people, some of whom do and some of whom do not find it offensive. Look at the scene of the two people approaching a door. The male steps slightly ahead and opens the door. The male holds the door open while the female glides through. Then the male goes through. The door closes after them. "Now how," one innocently asks, "can those crazy womenslibbers say that is oppressive? The guy *removed* a barrier to the lady's smooth and unruffled progress." But each repetition of this ritual has a place in a pattern, in fact in several patterns. One has to shift the level of one's perception in order to see the whole picture.

The door-opening pretends to be a helpful service, but the helpfulness is false. This can be seen by noting that it will be done whether or not it makes any practical sense. Infirm men and men burdened with packages will open doors for able bodied women who are free of physical burdens. Men will impose themselves awkwardly and jostle everyone in order to get to the door first. The act is not determined by convenience or grace. Furthermore, these very numerous acts of unneeded or even noisome "help" occur in counterpoint to a pattern of men not being helpful in many practical ways in which women might welcome help. What *women* experience is a world in which gallant princes charming commonly make a fuss about being helpful and providing small services when help and services are of little or no use, but in which there are rarely ingenious and

adroit princes at hand when substantial assistance is really wanted either in mundane affairs or in situations of threat, assault or terror. There is no help with the (his) laundry; no help typing a report at 4:00 a.m.; no help in mediating disputes among relatives or children. There is nothing but advice that women should stay indoors after dark, be chaperoned by a man, or when it comes down to it, "lie back and enjoy it."

The gallant gestures have no practical meaning. Their meaning is symbolic. The door-opening and similar services provided are services which really are needed by people who are for one reason or another incapacitated—unwell, burdened with parcels, etc. So the message is that women are incapable. The detachment of the acts from the concrete realities of what women need and do not need is a vehicle for the message that women's actual needs and interests are unimportant or irrelevant. Finally, these gestures imitate the behavior of servants toward masters and thus mock women, who are in most respects the servants and caretakers of men. The message of the false helpfulness of male gallantry is female dependence, the invisibility or insignificance of women, and contempt for women.

One cannot see the meanings of these rituals if one's focus is riveted upon the individual event in all its particularity, including the particularity of the individual man's present conscious intentions and motives and the individual woman's conscious perception of the event in the moment. It seems sometimes that people take a deliberately myopic view and fill their eyes with things seen microscopically in order not to see macroscopically. At any rate, whether it is deliberate or not, people can and do fail to see the oppression of women because they fail to see macroscopically and hence fail to see the various elements of the situation as systematically related in larger schemes.

As the cageness of the birdcage is a macroscopic phenomenon, the oppressiveness of the situations in which women live our various and different lives is a macroscopic phenomenon. Neither can be *seen* from a microscopic perspective. But when you look macroscopically you can see it a network of forces and barriers which are systematically related and which conspire to the immobilization, reduction and molding of women and the lives we live. . . .

It seems to be the human condition that in one degree or another we all suffer frustration and limitation, all encounter unwelcome barriers, and all are damaged and hurt in various ways. Since we are a social species, almost all of our behavior and activities are structured by more than individual inclination and the conditions of the planet and its atmosphere. No human is free of social structures, nor (perhaps) would happiness consist in such freedom. Structure consists of boundaries, limits and barriers; in a structured whole, some motions and changes are possible, and others are not. If one is looking for an excuse to dilute the word 'oppression', one can use the fact of social structure as an excuse and say that everyone is oppressed. But if one would rather get clear about what oppression is and is not, one needs to sort out the sufferings, harms and limitations and figure out which are elements of oppression and which are not.

From what I have already said here, it is clear that if one wants to determine whether a particular suffering, harm or limitation is part of someone's being oppressed, one has to look at it *in context* in order to tell whether it is an element in an oppressive structure: one has to see if it is part of an enclosing structure of forces and barriers which tends to the immobilization and reduction of a group or category of people. One has to look at how the barrier or force fits with others and to whose benefit or detriment it works. As soon as one looks at examples, it becomes obvious that not everything which frustrates or limits a person is oppressive, and not every harm or damage is due to or contributes to oppression.

If a rich white playboy who lives off income from his investments in South African diamond mines should break a leg in a skiing accident at Aspen and wait in pain in a blizzard for hours before he is rescued, we may assume that in that

period he suffers. But the suffering comes to an end; his leg is repaired by the best surgeon money can buy and he is soon recuperating in a lavish suite, sipping Chivas Regal. Nothing in this picture suggests a structure of barriers and forces. He is a member of several oppressor groups and does not suddenly become oppressed because he is injured and in pain. Even if the accident was caused by someone's malicious negligence, and hence someone can be blamed for it and morally faulted, that person still has not been an agent of oppression.

Consider also the restriction of having to drive one's vehicle on a certain side of the road. There is no doubt that this restriction is almost unbearably frustrating at times, when one's lane is not moving and the other lane is clear. There are surely times, even, when abiding by this regulation would have harmful consequences. But the restriction is obviously wholesome for most of us most of the time. The restraint is imposed for our benefit, and does benefit us; its operation tends to encourage our *continued* motion, not to immobilize us. The limits imposed by traffic regulations are limits most of us would cheerfully impose on ourselves given that we knew others would follow them too. They are part of a structure which shapes our behavior, not to our reduction and immobilization, but rather to the protection of our continued ability to move and act as we will.

Another example: The boundaries of a racial ghetto in an American city serve to some extent to keep white people from going in, as well as to keep ghetto dwellers from going out. A particular white citizen may be frustrated or feel deprived because s/he cannot stroll around there and enjoy the "exotic" aura of a "foreign" culture, or shop for bargains in the ghetto swap shops. In fact, the existence of the ghetto, of racial segregation, does deprive the white person of knowledge and harm her/his character by nurturing unwarranted feelings of superiority. But this does not make the white person in this situation a member of an oppressed race or a person oppressed because of her/his race. One must look at the barrier. It limits the activities and the access of those on both sides of it (though to different degrees). But it is a product of the intention, planning and action of whites for the benefit of whites, to secure and maintain privileges that are available to whites generally, as members of the dominant and privileged group. Though the existence of the barrier has some bad consequences for whites, the barrier does not exist in systematic relationship with other barriers and forces forming a structure oppressive to whites; quite the contrary. It is part of a structure which oppresses the ghetto dwellers and thereby (and by white intention) protects and furthers white interests as dominant white culture understands them. This barrier is not oppressive to whites, even though it is a barrier to whites.

Barriers have different meanings to those on opposite sides of them, even though they are barriers to both. The physical walls of a prison no more dissolve to let an outsider in than to let an insider out, but for the insider they are confining and limiting while to the outsider they may mean protection from what s/he takes to be threats posed by insiders—freedom from harm or anxiety. A set of social and economic barriers and forces separating two groups may be felt, even painfully, by members of both groups and yet may mean confinement to one and liberty and enlargement of opportunity to the other.

The service sector of the wives/mommas/assistants/girls is almost exclusively a woman-only sector; its boundaries not only enclose women but to a very great extent keep men out. Some men sometimes encounter this barrier and experience it as a restriction on their movements, their activities, their control or their choices of "lifestyle." Thinking they might like the simple nurturant life (which they may imagine to be quite free of stress, alienation and hard work), and feeling deprived since it seems closed to them, they thereupon announce the discovery that they are oppressed, too, by "sex roles." But that barrier is erected and maintained by men, for the benefit of men. It consists of cultural and economic forces and pressures in a culture and economy controlled by men in which, at every economic level and in all racial and ethnic subcultures, economy,

tradition—and even ideologies of liberation—work to keep at least local culture and economy in male control.*. . .

Talking Past Each Other
Black and White Languages of Race

Bob Blauner

For many African-Americans who came of age in the 1960s, the assassination of Martin Luther King, Jr. in 1968 was a defining moment in the development of their personal racial consciousness. For a slightly older group, the 1955 lynching of the fourteen-year-old Chicagoan Emmett Till in Mississippi had been a similar awakening. Now we have the protest and violence in Los Angeles and other cities in late April and early May of 1992, spurred by the jury acquittal of four policemen who beat motorist Rodney King.

The aftermath of the Rodney King verdict, unlike any other recent racial violence, will be seared into the memories of Americans of *all* colors, changing the way they see each other and their society. Spring 1992 marked the first time since the 1960s that incidents of racial injustice against an African-American—and by extension the black community—have seized the entire nation's imagination. Even highly publicized racial murders, such as those of African-American men in two New York City neighborhoods—Howard Beach (1986) and Bensonhurst (1989)—stirred the consciences of only a minority of whites. The response to the Rodney King verdict is thus a long-overdue reminder that whites still

---

*Of course this is complicated by race and class. Machismo and "Black manhood" politics seem to help keep Latin or Black men in control of more cash than Latin or Black women control; but these politics seem to me also to ultimately help keep the larger economy in *white* male control.

have the capacity to feel deeply about white racism—when they can see it in unambiguous terms.

The videotaped beating by four Los Angeles police officers provided this concreteness. To be sure, many whites focused their response on the subsequent black rioting, while the anger of blacks tended to remain fixed on the verdict itself. However, whites initially were almost as upset as blacks: An early poll reported that 86 percent of European-Americans disagreed with the jury's decision. The absence of any black from the jury and the trial's venue, Simi Valley, a lily-white suburban community, enabled mainstream whites to see the parallels with the Jim Crow justice of the old South. When we add to this mixture the widespread disaffection, especially of young people, with the nation's political and economic conditions, it is easier to explain the scale of white emotional involvement, unprecedented in a matter of racial protest since the 1960s.

In thirty years of teaching, I have never seen my students so overwrought, needing to talk, eager to do something. This response at the University of California at Berkeley cut across the usual fault lines of intergroup tension, as it did at high schools in Northern California. Assemblies, marches, and class discussions took place all over the nation in predominantly white as well as nonwhite and integrated high schools. Considering that there were also incidents where blacks assaulted white people, the scale of white involvement is even more impressive.

While many whites saw the precipitating events as expressions of racist conduct, they were much less likely than blacks to see them as part of some larger pattern of racism. Thus two separate polls found that only half as many whites as blacks believe that the legal system treats whites better than blacks. (In each poll, 43 percent of whites saw such a generalized double standard, in contrast to 84 percent of blacks in one survey, 89 percent in the other.)

This gap is not surprising. For twenty years European-Americans have tended to feel that systematic racial inequities marked an earlier era, not our own. Psychological denial and a kind of post-1960s exhaustion may both be factors in producing the sense among mainstream whites that civil rights laws and other changes resolved blacks' racial grievances, if not the economic basis of urban problems. But the gap in perceptions of racism also reflects a deeper difference. Whites and blacks see racial issues through different lenses and use different scales to weigh and assess injustice.

I am not saying that blacks and whites have totally disparate value systems and worldviews. I think we were more polarized in the late 1960s. It was then that I began a twenty-year interview study of racial consciousness published in 1989 as *Black Lives, White Lives.* By 1979 blacks and whites had come closer together on many issues than they had been in 1968. In the late 1970s and again in the mid-to-late 1980s, both groups were feeling quite pessimistic about the nation's direction. They agreed that America had become a more violent nation and that people were more individualistic and less bound by such traditional values as hard work, personal responsibility, and respect for age and authority. But with this and other convergences, there remained a striking gap in the way European-Americans and African-Americans evaluated *racial* change. Whites were impressed by the scale of integration, the size of the black middle class, and the extent of demonstrable progress. Blacks were disillusioned with integration, concerned about the people who had been left behind, and much more negative in their overall assessment of change.

In the 1990s this difference in general outlook led to different reactions to specific racial issues. That is what makes the shared revulsion over the Rodney King verdict a significant turning point, perhaps even an opportunity to begin bridging the gap between black and white definitions of the racial situation.

I want to advance the proposition that there are two languages of race in America. I am not talking about black English and standard English, which refer to different structures of grammar and dialect. "Language" here signifies a system of implicit understandings about social reality, and a racial language encompasses a worldview.

Blacks and whites differ on their interpretations of social change from the 1960s through the 1990s because their racial languages define the central terms, especially "racism," differently. Their racial languages incorporate different views of American society itself, especially the question of how central race and racism are to America's very existence, past and present. Blacks believe in this centrality, while most whites, except for the more race-conscious extremists, see race as a peripheral reality. Even successful, middle-class black professionals experience slights and humiliations—incidents when they are stopped by police, regarded suspiciously by clerks while shopping, or mistaken for messengers, drivers, or aides at work—that remind them they have not escaped racism's reach. For whites, race becomes central on exceptional occasions: collective, public moments such as the recent events, when the veil is lifted, and private ones, such as a family's decision to escape urban problems with a move to the suburbs. But most of the time European-Americans are able to view racial issues as aberrations in American life, much as Los Angeles Police Chief Daryl Gates used the term "aberration" to explain his officers' beating of Rodney King in March 1991.

Because of these differences in language and worldview, blacks and whites often talk past one another, just as men and women sometimes do. I first noticed this in my classes, particularly during discussions of racism. Whites locate racism in color consciousness and its absence in color blindness. They regard it as a kind of racism when students of color insistently underscore their sense of difference, their affirmation of ethnic and racial membership, which minority students have increasingly asserted. Many black, and increasingly also Latino and Asian, students cannot understand this reaction. It seems to them misinformed, even ignorant. They in turn sense a kind of racism in the whites' assumption that minorities must assimilate to mainstream values and styles. Then African-Americans will posit an idea that many whites find preposterous: Black people, they argue, cannot be racist, because racism is a system of power, and black people as a group do not have power.

In this and many other arenas, a contest rages over the meaning of racism. Racism has become the central term in the language of race. From the 1940s through the 1980s new and multiple meanings of racism have been added to the social science lexicon and public discourse. The 1960s were especially critical for what the English sociologist Robert Miles has called the "inflation" of the term "racism." Blacks tended to embrace the enlarged definitions, whites to resist them. This conflict, in my view, has been at the very center of the racial struggle during the past decade.

THE WIDENING CONCEPTION OF RACISM

The term "racism" was not commonly used in social science or American public life until the 1960s. "Racism" does not appear, for example, in the Swedish economist Gunnar Myrdal's classic 1944 study of American race relations, *An American Dilemma*. But even when the term was not directly used, it is still possible to determine the prevailing understandings of racial oppression.

In the 1940s racism referred to an ideology, an explicit system of beliefs postulating the superiority of whites based on the inherent, biological inferiority of the colored races. Ideological racism was particularly associated with the belief systems of the Deep South and was originally devised as a rationale for slavery. Theories of white supremacy, particularly in their biological versions, lost much of their legitimacy after the Second World War due to their association with Nazism. In recent years cultural explanations of "inferiority" are heard more commonly than biological ones, which today are associated with such extremist "hate groups" as the Ku Klux Klan and the White Aryan Brotherhood.

By the 1950s and early 1960s, with ideological racism discredited, the focus shifted to a more discrete approach to racially invidious attitudes *terms defined.*

and behavior, expressed in the model of prejudice and discrimination. "Prejudice" referred (and still does) to hostile feelings and beliefs about racial minorities and the web of stereotypes justifying such negative attitudes. "Discrimination" referred to actions meant to harm the members of a racial minority group. The logic of this model was that racism implied a double standard, that is, treating a person of color differently—in mind or action —than one would a member of the majority group.

By the mid-1960s the terms "prejudice" and "discrimination" and the implicit model of racial causation implied by them were seen as too weak to explain the sweep of racial conflict and change, too limited in their analytical power, and for some critics too individualistic in their assumptions. Their original meanings tended to be absorbed by a new, more encompassing idea of racism. During the 1960s the referents of racial oppression moved from individual actions and beliefs to group and institutional processes, from subjective ideas to "objective" structures or results. Instead of intent, there was now an emphasis on process: those more objective social processes of exclusion, exploitation, and discrimination that led to a racially stratified society.

The most notable of these new definitions was "institutional racism." In their 1967 book *Black Power,* Stokely Carmichael and Charles Hamilton stressed how institutional racism was different and more fundamental than individual racism. Racism, in this view, was built into society and scarcely required prejudicial attitudes to maintain racial oppression.

This understanding of racism as pervasive and institutionalized spread from relatively narrow "movement" and academic circles to the larger public with the appearance in 1968 of the report of the commission on the urban riots appointed by President Lyndon Johnson and chaired by Illinois Governor Otto Kerner. The Kerner Commission identified "white racism" as a prime reality of American society and the major underlying cause of ghetto unrest. America, in this view, was moving toward two societies, one white and one black (it is not clear where other racial minorities fit in). Although its recommendations were never acted upon politically, the report legitimated the term "white racism" among politicians and opinion leaders as a key to analyzing racial inequality in America.

Another definition of racism, which I would call "racism as atmosphere," also emerged in the 1960s and 1970s. This is the idea that an organization or an environment might be racist because its implicit, unconscious structures were devised for the use and comfort of white people, with the result that people of other races will not feel at home in such settings. Acting on this understanding of racism, many schools and universities, corporations, and other institutions have changed their teaching practices or work environments to encourage a greater diversity in their clientele, students, or work force.

Perhaps the most radical definition of all was the concept of "racism as result." In this sense, an institution or an occupation is racist simply because racial minorities are underrepresented in numbers or in positions of prestige and authority.

Seizing on different conceptions of racism, the blacks and whites I talked to in the late 1970s had come to different conclusions about how far America had moved toward racial justice. Whites tended to adhere to earlier, more limited notions of racism. Blacks for the most part saw the newer meanings as more basic. Thus African-Americans did not think racism had been put to rest by civil rights laws, even by the dramatic changes in the South. They felt that it still pervaded American life, indeed, had become more insidious because the subtle forms were harder to combat than old-fashioned exclusion and persecution.

Whites saw racism largely as a thing of the past. They defined it in terms of segregation and lynching, explicit white supremacist beliefs, or double standards in hiring, promotion, and admissions to colleges or other institutions. Except for affirmative action, which seemed the most blatant expression of such double standards, they were positively impressed by racial change. Many saw the relaxed and comfortable relations between whites and blacks as the heart of the matter. More crucial to blacks, on the other hand, were the underlying structures of power and position that continued to provide them with unequal portions of economic opportunity and other possibilities for the good life.

The newer, expanded definitions of racism just do not make much sense to most whites. I have experienced their frustrations directly when I try to explain the concept of institutional racism to white students and popular audiences. The idea of racism as an "impersonal force" loses all but the most theoretically inclined. Whites are more likely than blacks to view racism as a personal issue. Both sensitive to their own possible culpability (if only unconsciously) and angry at the use of the concept of racism by angry minorities, they do not differentiate well between the racism of social structures and the accusation that they as participants in that structure are personally racist.

The new meanings make sense to blacks, who live such experiences in their bones. But by 1979 many of the African-Americans in my study, particularly the older activists, were critical of the use of racism as a blanket explanation for all manifestations of racial inequality. Long before similar ideas were voiced by the black conservatives, many blacks sensed that too heavy an emphasis on racism led to the false conclusion that blacks could only progress through a conventional civil rights strategy of fighting prejudice and discrimination. (This strategy, while necessary, had proved very limited.) Overemphasizing racism, they feared, was interfering with the black community's ability to achieve greater self-determination through the politics of self-help. In addition, they told me that the prevailing rhetoric of the 1960s had affected many young blacks. Rather than taking responsibility for their own difficulties, they were now using racism as a "cop-out."

In public life today this analysis is seen as part of the conservative discourse on race. Yet I believe that this position originally was a progressive one, developed out of self-critical reflec-tions on the relative failure of 1960s movements. But perhaps because it did not seem to be "politically correct," the left-liberal community, black as well as white, academic as well as political, has been afraid of embracing such a critique. As a result, the neoconservatives had a clear field to pick up this grass-roots sentiment and to use it to further their view that racism is no longer significant in American life. This is the last thing that my informants and other savvy African-Americans close to the pulse of their communities believe.

By the late 1970s the main usage of racism in the mind of the white public had undoubtedly become that of "reverse racism." The primacy of "reverse racism" as "the really important racism" suggests that the conservatives and the liberal-center have, in effect, won the battle over the meaning of racism.

Perhaps this was inevitable because of the long period of backlash against all the progressive movements of the 1960s. But part of the problem may have been the inflation of the idea of racism. While institutional racism exists, such a concept loses practical utility if every thing and every place is racist. In that case, there is effectively nothing to be done about it. And without conceptual tools to distinguish what is important from what is not, we are lost in the confusion of multiple meanings.

BACK TO BASICS

While public discourse was discounting white racism as exaggerated or a thing of the past, the more traditional forms of bigotry, harassment, and violence were unfortunately making a comeback. (This upsurge actually began in the early 1980s but was not well noticed, due to some combination of media inattention and national mood.) What was striking about the Bernhard Goetz subway shootings in New York, the white on black racial violence in Howard Beach, the rise of organized hate groups, campus racism, and skinhead violence is that these are all examples of old-fashioned racism. They illustrate the power and persistence of racial prejudices and hate crimes in the tradition of classical lynchings. They are precisely the kind of phenomena that many social analysts expected to diminish as I did.

If there was one positive effect of this upsurge, it was to alert many whites to the destructive power of racial hatred and division in American life. At the same time, these events also repolarized racial attitudes in America. They have contributed to the anger and alienation of the black middle class and the rapid rise of Afrocentrism, particularly among college students.

As the gap in understanding has widened, several social scientists have proposed restricting the concept of racism to its original, more narrow meaning. However, the efforts of African-Americans to enlarge the meaning of racism is part of that group's project to make its view of the world and of American society competitive with the dominant white perspective. In addition, the "inflated" meanings of racism are already too rooted in common speech to be overturned by the advice of experts. And certainly some way is needed to convey the pervasive and systematic character of racial oppression. No other term does this as well as racism.

The question then becomes what to do about these multiple and confusing meanings of racism and their extraordinary personal and political charge. I would begin by honoring both the black and white readings of the term. Such an attitude might help facilitate the interracial dialogue so badly needed and yet so rare today.

Communication can only start from the understandings that people have. While the black understanding of racism is, in some sense, the deeper one, the white views of racism (ideology, double standard) refer to more specific and recognizable beliefs and practices. Since there is also a cross-racial consensus on the immorality of racist ideology and racial discrimination, it makes sense whenever possible to use such a concrete referent as discrimination, rather than the more global concept of racism. And reemphasizing discrimination may help remind the public that racial discrimination is not just a legacy of the past.

The intellectual power of the African-American understanding lies in its more critical and encompassing perspective. In the Rodney King events, we have an unparalleled opportunity to bridge the racial gap by pointing out that racism and racial division remain essential features of American life and that incidents such as police beatings of minority people and stacked juries are not aberrations but part of a larger pattern of racial abuse and harassment. Without resorting to the overheated rhetoric that proved counterproductive in the 1960s, it now may be possible to persuade white Americans that the most important patterns of discrimination and disadvantage are not to be found in the "reverse racism" of affirmative action but sadly still in the white racism of the dominant social system. And, when feasible, we need to try to bridge the gap by shifting from the language of race to that of ethnicity and class.

RACE OR ETHNICITY?

In the American consciousness the imagery of race—especially along the black-white dimension—tends to be more powerful than that of class or ethnicity. As a result, legitimate ethnic affiliations are often misunderstood to be racial and illegitimate.

Race itself is a confusing concept because of the variance between scientific and common sense definitions of the term. Physical anthropologists who study the distribution of those characteristics we use to classify "races" teach us that race is a fiction because all peoples are mixed to various degrees. Sociologists counter that this biological fiction unfortunately remains a sociological reality. People define one another racially, and thus divide society into racial groups. The "fiction" of race affects every aspect of peoples' lives, from living standards to landing in jail.

The consciousness of color differences, and the invidious distinctions based on them, have existed since antiquity and are not limited to any one corner of the world. And yet the peculiarly modern division of the world into a discrete number of hierarchically ranked races is a historic product of Western colonialism. In precolonial Africa the relevant group identities were national, tribal, or linguistic. There was no concept of an African or black people until this category was created by the combined effects of slavery, imperialism, and the anticolonial and Pan-African movements. The legal definitions of blackness and whiteness, which varied from one society to another in the Western hemisphere, were also crucial for the construction of modern-day races. Thus race is an essentially political construct, one that translates our tendency to see people in terms of their color or other physical attributes into structures that make it likely that people will act for or against them on such a basis.

The dynamic of ethnicity is different, even though the results at times may be similar. An ethnic group is a group that shares a belief in its common past. Members of an ethnic group hold a set of common memories that make them feel that their customs, culture, and outlook are distinctive. In short, they have a sense of peoplehood. Sharing critical experiences and sometimes a belief in their common fate, they feel an affinity for one another, a "comfort zone" that leads to congregating together, even when this is not forced by exclusionary barriers. Thus if race is associated with biology and nature, ethnicity is associated with culture. Like races, ethnic groups arise historically, transform themselves, and sometimes die out.

Much of the popular discourse about race in America today goes awry because ethnic realities get lost under the racial umbrella. The positive meanings and potential of ethnicity are overlooked, even overrun, by the more inflammatory meanings of race. Thus white students, disturbed when blacks associate with each other, justify their objections through their commitment to *racial* integration. They do not appreciate the ethnic affinities that bring this about, or see the parallels to Jewish students meeting at the campus Hillel Foundation or Italian-Americans eating lunch at the Italian house on the Berkeley campus.

When blacks are "being ethnic," whites see them as "being racial." Thus they view the iden-

tity politics of students who want to celebrate their blackness, their *chicanoismo,* their Asian heritages, and their American Indian roots as racially offensive. Part of this reaction comes from a sincere desire, almost a yearning, of white students for a color-blind society. But because the ethnicity of darker people so often gets lost in our overracialized perceptions, the white students misread the situation. When I point out to my class that whites are talking about race and its dynamics and the students of color are talking about ethnicity and its differing meaning, they can begin to appreciate each other's agendas.

Confounding race and ethnicity is not just limited to the young. The general public, including journalists and other opinion makers, does this regularly, with serious consequences for the clarity of public dialogue and sociological analysis. A clear example comes from the Chicago mayoral election of 1983. The establishment press, including leading liberal columnists, regularly chastised the black electorate for giving virtually all its votes to Harold Washington. Such racial voting was as "racist" as whites voting for the other candidate because they did not want a black mayor. Yet African-Americans were voting for ethnic representation just as Irish-Americans, Jews, and Italians have always done. Such ethnic politics is considered the American way. What is discriminatory is the double standard that does not confer the same rights on blacks, who were not voting primarily out of fear or hatred as were many whites.

Such confusions between race and ethnicity are exacerbated by the ambiguous sociological status of African-Americans. Black Americans are *both* a race and an ethnic group. Unfortunately, part of our heritage of racism has been to deny the ethnicity, the cultural heritage of black Americans. Liberal-minded whites have wanted to see blacks as essentially white people with black skins. Until the 1960s few believed that black culture was a real ethnic culture.

Because our racial language is so deepseated, the terminology of black and white just seems more "natural" and commonsensical than more ethnic labels like African-American or European-

American. But the shift to the term African-American has been a conscious attempt to move the discourse from a language of race to a language of ethnicity. "African-American," as Jesse Jackson and others have pointed out, connects the group to its history and culture in a way that the racial designation, black, does not. The new usage parallels terms for other ethnic groups. Many whites tend to dismiss this concern about language as mere sloganeering. But "African-American" fits better into the emerging multicultural view of American ethnic and racial arrangements, one more appropriate to our growing diversity. The old race relations model was essentially a view that generalized (often inappropriately) from black-white relations. It can no longer capture—if it ever could—the complexity of a multiracial and multicultural society.

The issue is further complicated by the fact that African-Americans are not a homogeneous group. They comprise a variety of distinct ethnicities. There are the West Indians with their long histories in the U.S., the darker Puerto Ricans (some of whom identify themselves as black), the more recently arrived Dominicans, Haitians, and immigrants from various African countries, as well as the native-born African-Americans, among whom regional distinctions can also take on a quasi-ethnic flavor.

Blacks from the Caribbean are especially likely to identify with their homeland rather than taking on a generic black or even African-American identity. While they may resist the dynamic of "racialization" and even feel superior to native blacks, the dynamic is relentless. Their children are likely to see themselves as part of the larger African-American population. And yet many native-born Americans of African descent also resist the term "African-American," feeling very little connection to the original homeland. Given the diversity in origin and outlook of America's largest minority, it is inevitable that no single concept can capture its full complexity or satisfy all who fall within its bounds.

For white Americans, race does not overwhelm ethnicity. Whites see the ethnicity of other whites; it is their own whiteness they tend to overlook. But even when race is recognized, it is not conflated with ethnicity. Jews, for example, clearly distinguish their Jewishness from their whiteness. Yet the long-term dynamic still favors the development of a dominant white racial identity. Except for recent immigrants, the various European ethnic identities have been rapidly weakening. Vital ethnic communities persist in some cities, particularly on the East Coast. But many whites, especially the young, have such diverse ethnic heritages that they have no meaningful ethnic affiliation. In my classes only the Jews among European-Americans retain a strong sense of communal origin.

Instead of dampening the ethnic enthusiasms of the racial minorities, perhaps it would be better to encourage the revitalization of whites' European heritages. But a problem with this approach is that the relationship between race and ethnicity is more ambiguous for whites than for people of color. Although for many white groups ethnicity has been a stigma, it also has been used to gain advantages that have marginalized blacks and other racial minorities. Particularly for working-class whites today, ethnic community loyalties are often the prism through which they view their whiteness, their superiority.

Thus the line between ethnocentrism and racism is a thin one, easily crossed—as it was by Irish-Americans who resisted the integration of South Boston's schools in the 1970s and by many of the Jews and Italians that sociologist Jonathan Rieder describes in his 1985 book *Canarsie.*

White students today complain of a double standard. Many feel that their college administrations sanction organization and identification for people of color, but not for them. If there can be an Asian business organization and a black student union, why can't there be a white business club or a white student alliance? I'd like to explain to them that students of color are organized ethnically, not racially, that whites have Hillel and the Italian theme house. But this makes little practical sense when such loyalties are just not that salient for the vast majority.

Out of this vacuum the emerging identity of "European-American" has come into vogue. I interpret the European-American idea as part of a yearning for a usable past. Europe is associated with history and culture. "America" and "American" can no longer be used to connote white people. "White" itself is a racial term and thereby inevitably associated with our nation's legacy of social injustice.

At various California colleges and high schools, European-American clubs have begun to form, provoking debate about whether it is inherently racist for whites to organize as whites—or as European-Americans. Opponents invoke the racial analogy and see such organizations as akin to exclusive white supremacist groups. Their defenders argue from an ethnic model, saying that they are simply looking for a place where they can feel at home and discuss their distinctive personal and career problems. The jury is still out on this new and, I suspect, burgeoning phenomenon. It will take time to discover its actual social impact.

If the European-Americans forming their clubs are truly organizing on an ethnic or panethnic rather than a racial model, I would have to support these efforts. Despite all the ambiguities, it seems to me a gain in social awareness when a specific group comes to be seen in ethnic rather than racial terms. During the period of the mass immigration of the late nineteenth century and continuing through the 1920s, Jews, Italians, and other white ethnics were viewed racially. We no longer hear of the "Hebrew race," and it is rare for Jewish distinctiveness to be attributed to biological rather than cultural roots. Of course, the shift from racial to ethnic thinking did not put an end to anti-Semitism in the United States—or to genocide in Germany, where racial imagery was obviously intensified.

It is unrealistic to expect that the racial groupings of American society can be totally "deconstructed," as a number of scholars now are advocating. After all, African-Americans and native Americans, who were not immigrants, can never be exactly like other ethnic groups. Yet a shift in this direction would begin to move our society from a divisive biracialism to a more inclusive multiculturalism.

To return to the events of spring 1992, I ask what was different about these civil disturbances. Considering the malign neglect of twelve Reagan-Bush years, the almost two decades of economic stagnation, and the retreat of the public from issues of race and poverty, the violent intensity should hardly be astonishing.

More striking was the multiracial character of the response. In the San Francisco Bay area, rioters were as likely to be white as nonwhite. In Los Angeles, Latinos were prominent among both the protesters and the victims. South Central Los Angeles is now more Hispanic than black, and this group suffered perhaps 60 percent of the property damage. The media have focused on the specific grievances of African-Americans toward Koreans. But I would guess that those who trashed Korean stores were protesting something larger than even the murder of a fifteen-year-old black girl. Koreans, along with other immigrants, continue to enter the country and in a relatively short time surpass the economic and social position of the black poor. The immigrant advantage is real and deeply resented by African-Americans, who see that the two most downtrodden minorities are those that did not enter the country voluntarily.

During the 1960s the police were able to contain riots within the African-American community. This time Los Angeles police were unable to do so. Even though the South Central district suffered most, there was also much destruction in other areas including Hollywood, downtown, and the San Fernando Valley. In the San Francisco Bay area the violence occurred primarily in the white business sections, not the black neighborhoods of Oakland, San Francisco, or Berkeley. The violence that has spilled out of the inner city is a distillation of all the human misery that a white middle-class society has been trying to contain—albeit unsuccessfully (consider the homeless). As in the case of an untreated infection, the toxic substances finally break out, threatening to contaminate the entire organism.

Will this widened conflict finally lead Americans toward a recognition of our common stake in the health of the inner cities and their citizens, or toward increased fear and division? The Emmett Till lynching in 1955 set the stage for the first mass mobilization of the civil rights movement, the Montgomery bus boycott later that year. Martin Luther King's assassination provided the impetus for the institution of affirmative action and other social programs. The Rodney King verdict and its aftermath must also become not just a psychologically defining moment but an impetus to a new mobilization of political resolve.

PERSONAL ACCOUNT

Where Are You From?

As a freshman at a predominantly white private college, I was confronted with a number of unusual situations. I was extremely young for a college freshman (I was sixteen), I was African American, and I was placed in upper-division courses, because of my academic background. So being accepted and fitting in were crucial to me.

I was enrolled in a course, Political Thought, with approximately thirty other students, mostly juniors and seniors who had taken courses with this professor before. I was the only African American in the class. During introductions for the first class, he never got around to letting me speak, even though he went alphabetically on the list (my last name begins with a "C"). Later, I began to be aware of his exclusion of me from class discussion. By the third class, I guess he felt there was no longer any way he could avoid speaking to me. He asked me a few questions about myself—where was I from, what high school had I attended, and what was my major. His questions began to seem like a personal attack, and then finally he asked, "Why are you here?" "Where are you from?" I was quite taken aback by his line of questioning, when one of the upperclassman (a white man) responded for me. "She's a freshman, Dr. B. Any more questions?" That guy became one of my closest friends. We have maintained contact ever since college. His response to Dr. B. totally changed the professor's way of treating me.

C.C.

READING 14

Wears Jump Suit. Sensible Shoes. Uses Husband's Last Name.

Deborah Tannen

Some years ago I was at a small working conference of four women and eight men. Instead of concentrating on the discussion I found myself looking at the three other women at the table, thinking how each had a different style and how each style was coherent.

One woman had dark brown hair in a classic style, a cross between Cleopatra and Plain Jane. The severity of her straight hair was softened by wavy bangs and ends that turned under. Because she was beautiful, the effect was more Cleopatra than plain.

The second woman was older, full of dignity and composure. Her hair was cut in a fashionable style that left her with only one eye, thanks to a side part that let a curtain of hair fall across half her face. As she looked down to read her prepared paper, the hair robbed her of bifocal vision and created a barrier between her and the listeners.

The third woman's hair was wild, a frosted blond avalanche falling over and beyond her shoulders. When she spoke she frequently tossed her head, calling attention to her hair and away from her lecture.

Then there was makeup. The first woman wore facial cover that made her skin smooth and pale, a black line under each eye and mascara that darkened already dark lashes. The second wore only a light gloss on her lips and a hint of shadow on her eyes. The third had blue bands under her eyes, dark blue shadow, mascara, bright red lipstick and rouge; her fingernails flashed red.

I considered the clothes each woman had worn during the three days of the conference: In the first case, man-tailored suits in primary colors with solid-color blouses. In the second, casual but stylish black T-shirts, a floppy collarless jacket and baggy slacks or a skirt in neutral colors. The third wore a sexy jump suit; tight sleeveless jersey and tight yellow slacks; a dress with gaping armholes and an indulged tendency to fall off one shoulder.

Shoes? No. 1 wore string sandals with medium heels; No. 2, sensible, comfortable walking shoes; No. 3, pumps with spike heels. You can fill in the jewelry, scarves, shawls, sweaters—or lack of them.

As I amused myself finding coherence in these styles, I suddenly wondered why I was scrutinizing only the women. I scanned the eight men at the table. And then I knew why I wasn't studying them. The men's styles were unmarked.

The term "marked" is a staple of linguistic theory. It refers to the way language alters the base meaning of a word by adding a linguistic particle that has no meaning on its own. The unmarked form of a word carries the meaning that goes without saying—what you think of when you're not thinking anything special.

The unmarked tense of verbs in English is the present—for example, *visit*. To indicate past, you mark the verb by adding *ed* to yield *visited*. For future, you add a word: *will visit*. Nouns are presumed to be singular until marked for plural, typically by adding *s* or *es,* so *visit* becomes *visits* and *dish* becomes *dishes.*

The unmarked forms of most English words also convey "male." Being male is the unmarked case. Endings like *ess* and *ette* mark words as "female." Unfortunately, they also tend to mark them for frivolousness. Would you feel safe entrusting your life to a doctorette? Alfre Woodard, who was an Oscar nominee for best supporting actress, says she identifies herself as an actor because "actresses worry about eyelashes and cellulite, and women who are actors worry about the characters we are playing." Gender markers pick up extra meanings that reflect common associations with the female gender: not quite serious, often sexual.

Each of the women at the conference had to make decisions about hair, clothing, makeup and accessories, and each decision carried meaning.

Every style available to us was marked. The men in our group had made decisions, too, but the range from which they chose was incomparably narrower. Men can choose styles that are marked, but they don't have to, and in this group none did. Unlike the women, they had the option of being unmarked.

Take the men's hair styles. There was no marine crew cut or oily longish hair falling into eyes, no asymmetrical, two-tiered construction to swirl over a bald top. One man was unabashedly bald; the others had hair of standard length, parted on one side, in natural shades of brown or gray or graying. Their hair obstructed no views, left little to toss or push back or run fingers through and, consequently, needed and attracted no attention. A few men had beards. In a business setting, beards might be marked. In this academic gathering, they weren't.

There could have been a cowboy shirt with string tie or a three-piece suit or a necklaced hippie in jeans. But there wasn't. All eight men wore brown or blue slacks and nondescript shirts of light colors. No man wore sandals or boots; their shoes were dark, closed, comfortable and flat. In short, unmarked.

Although no man wore makeup, you couldn't say the men didn't wear makeup in the sense that you could say a woman didn't wear makeup. For men, no makeup is unmarked.

I asked myself what style we women could have adopted that would have been unmarked, like the men's. The answer was none. There is no unmarked woman.

There is no woman's hair style that can be called standard, that says nothing about her. The range of women's hair styles is staggering, but a woman whose hair has no particular style is perceived as not caring about how she looks, which can disqualify her for many positions, and will subtly diminish her as a person in the eyes of some.

Women must choose between attractive shoes and comfortable shoes. When our group made an unexpected trek, the woman who wore flat, laced shoes arrived first. Last to arrive was the woman in spike heels, shoes in hand and a handful of men around her.

If a woman's clothing is tight or revealing (in other words, sexy), it sends a message—an intended one of wanting to be attractive, but also a possibly unintended one of availability. If her clothes are not sexy, that too sends a message, lent meaning by the knowledge that they could have been. There are thousands of cosmetic products from which women can choose and myriad ways of applying them. Yet no makeup at all is anything but unmarked. Some men see it as a hostile refusal to please them.

Women can't even fill out a form without telling stories about themselves. Most forms give four titles to choose from. "Mr." carries no meaning other than that the respondent is male. But a woman who checks "Mrs." or "Miss" communicates not only whether she has been married but also whether she has conservative tastes in forms of address—and probably other conservative values as well. Checking "Ms." declines to let on about marriage (checking "Mr." declines nothing since nothing was asked), but it also marks her as either liberated or rebellious, depending on the observer's attitudes and assumptions.

I sometimes try to duck these variously marked choices by giving my title as "Dr."—and in so doing risk marking myself as either uppity (hence sarcastic responses like "Excuse *me!*") or an overachiever (hence reactions of congratulatory surprise like "Good for you!").

All married women's surnames are marked. If a woman takes her husband's name, she announces to the world that she is married and has traditional values. To some it will indicate that she is less herself, more identified by her husband's identity. If she does not take her husband's name, this too is marked, seen as worthy of comment: she has *done* something; she has "kept her own name." A man is never said to have "kept his own name" because it never occurs to anyone that he might have given it up. For him using his own name is unmarked.

A married woman who wants to have her cake and eat it too may use her surname plus his, with or without a hyphen. But this too announces her marital status and often results in a tongue-tying string. In a list (Harvey O'Donovan, Jonathan Feldman, Stephanie Woodbury McGillicutty), the woman's multiple name stands out. It is marked.

I have never been inclined toward biological explanations of gender differences in language, but I was intrigued to see Ralph Fasold bring biological phenomena to bear on the question of linguistic marking in his book "The Sociolinguistics of Language." Fasold stresses that language and culture are particularly unfair in treating women as the marked case because biologically it is the male that is marked. While two X chromosomes make a female, two Y chromosomes make nothing. Like the linguistic markers *s, es* or *ess,* the Y chromosome doesn't "mean" anything unless it is attached to a root form—an X chromosome.

Developing this idea elsewhere, Fasold points out that girls are born with fully female bodies, while boys are born with modified female bodies. He invites men who doubt this to lift up their shirts and contemplate why they have nipples.

In his book, Fasold notes "a wide range of facts which demonstrates that female is the unmarked sex." For example, he observes that there are a few species that produce only females, like the whiptail lizard. Thanks to parthenogenesis, they have no trouble having as many daughters as they like. There are no species, however, that produce only males. This is no surprise, since any such species would become extinct in its first generation.

Fasold is also intrigued by species that produce individuals not involved in reproduction, like honeybees and leaf-cutter ants. Reproduction is handled by the queen and a relatively few males; the workers are sterile females. "Since they do not reproduce," Fasold says, "there is no reason for them to be one sex or the other, so they default, so to speak, to female."

Fasold ends his discussion of these matters by pointing out that if language reflected biology, grammar books would direct us to use "she" to include males and females and "he" only for specifically male referents. But they don't. They tell us that "he" means "he or she," and that "she" is used only if the referent is specifically female. This use of "he" as the sex-indefinite pronoun is an innovation introduced into English by grammarians in the 18th and 19th centuries, according to Peter Mühlhäusler and Rom Harré in "Pronouns and People." From at least about 1500, the correct sex-indefinite pronoun was "they," as it still is in casual spoken English. In other words, the female was declared by grammarians to be the marked case.

Writing this article may mark me not as a writer, not as a linguist, not as an analyst of human behavior, but as a feminist—which will have positive or negative, but in any case powerful, connotations for readers. Yet I doubt that anyone reading Ralph Fasold's book would put that label on him.

I discovered the markedness inherent in the very topic of gender after writing a book on differences in conversational style based on geographical region, ethnicity, class, age and gender. When I was interviewed, the vast majority of journalists wanted to talk about the differences between women and men. While I thought I was simply describing what I observed—something I had learned to do as a researcher—merely mentioning women and men marked me as a feminist for some.

When I wrote a book devoted to gender differences in ways of speaking, I sent the manuscript to five male colleagues, asking them to alert me to any interpretation, phrasing or wording that might seem unfairly negative toward men. Even so, when the book came out, I encountered responses like that of the television talk show host who, after interviewing me, turned to the audience and asked if they thought I was male-bashing.

Leaping upon a poor fellow who affably nodded in agreement, she made him stand and asked, "Did what she said accurately describe you?" "Oh, yes," he answered. "That's me exactly." "And what she said about women—does that sound like your wife?" "Oh yes," he responded. "That's her exactly." "Then why do you think she's male-bashing?" He answered, with disarm-

ing honesty, "Because she's a woman and she's saying things about men."

To say anything about women and men without marking oneself as either feminist or antifeminist, male-basher or apologist for men seems as impossible for a woman as trying to get dressed in the morning without inviting interpretations of her character.

Sitting at the conference table musing on these matters, I felt sad to think that we women didn't have the freedom to be unmarked that the men sitting next to us had. Some days you just want to get dressed and go about your business. But if you're a woman, you can't, because there is no unmarked woman.

Secrets and Anger?

David Mura

On the day our daughter was born, as my wife, Susie, and I waited for the doctor to do a cesarean section, we talked about names. Standing at the window, I looked out and said, "Samantha, the day you were born was a gray and blustery day." We decided on Samantha Lyn, after my sisters, Susan Lynn and Lynda. I felt to give the baby a Japanese name might mark her as too different, especially since we live in St. Paul, where Asian Americans are a small minority. I had insisted that her last name be hyphenated, Sencer-Mura. My wife had argued that such a name was unwieldy. "What happens when Samantha Sencer-Mura marries Bob Rodriguez-Stein?" she asked. "That's her generation's problem," I said, laughing.

I sometimes wish now we'd given her a Japanese middle name, as Susie had wanted. Perhaps it's because I sense that the world Samantha's inheriting won't be dominated by the melting-pot model, that multiculturalism is not a project but a reality, that in the next century there will no longer be a white majority in this country. Or perhaps I simply feel guilty about having given in to the dominant culture once again.

I am working on a poem about my daughter, about trying to take in her presence, her life, about trying to link her with my sense of the past—my father and mother, the internment camps, my grandparents. I picture myself serving her sukiyaki, a dish I shunned as a child and her shouting for more rice, brandishing her *hashi* (a word for chopsticks, which I never used as a child and only began to use after my trip to Japan). As I describe Samantha running through the garden, scattering petals, squashing tomatoes, I suddenly think of how someone someday will call her a "gook," that I know this with more certainty than I know she'll find happiness in love.

I speak to my wife about moving out to the West Coast or to Hawaii, where there would be more Asian Americans. In Hawaii, more than a third of the children are *happa* (mixed race). Samantha would be the norm, not the minority. I need to spend more time living in an Asian-American community. I can't tell its stories if I'm not a part of it. As I talk about moving one evening, Susie starts to feel uneasy. "I'm afraid you'll cross this bridge and take Sam with you, and leave me here," she says.

"But I've lived all my life on your side of the bridge. At most social gatherings, I'm the only person of color in the room. What's wrong with living awhile on my side of the bridge? What keeps you from crossing?"

Susie, a pediatric oncologist, works with families of all colors. Still, having a hybrid daughter is changing her experience. Often when she's in the grocery with Sam, someone will come up to her and say, "Oh, she's such a beautiful little girl. Where did you get her?" This has happened so often Susie swears she's going to teach Sam to say: "Fuck you. My genes came all the way over on the *Mayflower,* thank you."

These incidents mark ways Susie has experienced something negative over race that I have not. No one asks me where Sam came from: they assume I'm her father. For Susie, the encounters are a challenge to her position as Samantha's biological mother, the negation of an arduous pregnancy and the physical work of birth and motherhood. For me, they stir an old wound. The people who mistake Sam for an adopted child can't picture a white woman married to an Asian man.

Six ways of viewing identity: Identity is a social and historical construction. Identity is formed by political and economic and cultural exigencies. Identity is a fiction. Identity is a choice. Identity may appear unitary but is always fragmentary. Identity is deciding to acknowledge or not acknowledge political and economic and cultural exigencies.

When I address the question of raising my daughter, I address the question of her identity, which means I address the question of my identity, her mother's, our parents', and so on. But this multiplication of the self takes place along many lines. Who knows where it stops? At my grandparents? At the woman in the grocery store? At you, the imagined reader of this piece?

In the matrix of race and color in our society, there is the binary opposition of black and white. And then there are the various Others, determined by race or culture or gender or sexual preference—Native Americans, Hispanic Americans, Asian Americans, Japanese Americans, women, men, heterosexuals, homosexuals. None of these definitions stands alone; together they form an intricate, mazelike weave that's impossible to disentangle.

I wrote my memoir, *Turning Japanese,* to explore the cultural amnesia of Japanese Americans, particularly those of the third generation, like myself, who speak little or no Japanese. When I give readings, people often ask if I'm going to raise Samantha with a greater awareness of Japanese culture than I received as a child. The obvious answer is yes. I also acknowledge that the prospects of teaching her about Japanese culture feel to me rather daunting, and I now have more sympathy for my nisei parents, whom I used to criticize for forgetting the past.

And yet, near the end of my stay in Japan, I decided that I was not Japanese, that I was never going to be Japanese, and that I was not even going to be an expert on Japanese culture. My identity was as a Japanese American. That meant claiming the particularities of Japanese-American history; it meant coming to terms with how the dominant culture had formed me; it meant realizing my identity would always be partially occluded. Finally, it meant that the issues of race were central to me, that I would see myself as a person of color.

Can I teach these things to my daughter? My Japanese-American identity comes from my own experience. But I am still trying to understand that experience and still struggling to find language to talk about the issues of race. My failures are caused by more than a lack of knowledge; there's the powerful wish not to know. How, for instance, can I talk to my daughter about sexuality and race? My own life is so filled with shame and regret, so filled with experiences I would rather not discuss, that it seems much easier to opt for silence. It's simpler to pretend multiculturalism means teaching her *kanji* and how to conjugate Japanese verbs.

I know that every day Samantha will be exposed to images telling her that Asian bodies are marginalized, that the women are exotic or sensual or submissive, that the men are houseboys or Chinatown punks, kung fu warriors or Japanese businessmen—robotlike and powerful or robotlike and comic. I know that she will face constant pressure to forget that she is part Japanese American, to assume a basically white middle-class identity. When she reaches adolescence, there will be strong messages for her to dissociate herself from other people of color, perhaps from the children of recent Asian immigrants. She may find herself wanting to assume a privilege and status that come from not calling attention to her identity or from playing into the stereotype that makes Asian women seem so desirable to certain white men. And I know I will have no power over these forces.

Should I tell her of how, when I look at her mother, I know my desire for her cannot be separated from the way the culture has inculcated me with standards of white beauty? Should I tell her of my own desire for a "hallucinatory whiteness," of how in my twenties such a desire fueled a rampant promiscuity and addiction to pornography, to the "beautiful" bodies of white women? It's all too much to expect Samantha to take in. It should not even be written down. It should be kept hidden, unspoken. These forces should not exist.

Samantha's presence has made me more willing to speak out on issues of race, to challenge the status quo. I suppose I want her to inherit a different world than the one I grew up in.

One day last year, I was talking with two white friends about the landmark controversy over the Broadway production of *Miss Saigon.* Like many Asian Americans, I agreed with the protest by Actor's Equity against the producer's casting. I felt disturbed that again a white actor, the British Jonathan Pryce, was playing a Eurasian and that no Asian-American actor had been given a chance to audition for that role. Beyond that, I was upset by the Madame Butterfly plot of *Miss Saigon,* where an Asian woman pines for her white male lover.

Both my friends—Paula, a painter, and Mark, a writer—consider themselves liberals; Mark was active in the antiwar movement during the sixties. He was part of my wedding and, at the time, perhaps my closest male friend. But neither agreed with me about *Miss Saigon.* They argued that art represented freedom of the imagination, that it meant trying to get inside other people's skin. Isn't color-blind casting what we're striving for? they said.

"Why is it everyone gets so upset when a white actor may be denied a role?" I asked. "What about every time an Asian-American actor tries out for a part that says 'lawyer' or 'doctor' and is turned down?"

But reverse discrimination isn't the answer, they replied.

I don't recall exactly what happened after this. I think the argument trailed off into some safer topic, as such arguments often do. But afterward, I felt angrier and angrier and, at the same time, more despairing. I realized that for me the fact that Warner Oland, a Swede, played Charlie Chan was humiliating. It did not show me that art was a democracy of the imagination. But for Paula and Mark, my sense of shame was secondary to their belief in "freedom" in the arts.

When I talked to my wife about my anger and despair, she felt uncomfortable. These were her friends, too. She said I'd argued before with them about the role of politics in art. Mark had always looked ruefully at his political involvement in the sixties, when he felt he had gone overboard with his zealous self-righteousness. "He's threatened by your increasing political involvement," Susie said. She felt I should take our disagreement as just another incident in a long friendly dialogue.

But when I talked with a black friend, Garth, who's a writer, he replied: "Yeah, I was surprised too at the reaction of some of my white artist friends to *Miss Saigon.* It really told me where they were. It marked a dividing line."

For a while, I avoided talking about my feelings when Paula and Mark came by. Susie urged me to talk to them, to work it out. "You're trying to get me to have sympathy with how difficult this is for them or for you, how this creates tensions between you and them," I said. "But I have to have this conversation about *Miss Saigon* with every white friend I have. Each of you only has to have it with me." My wife said that I was taking my anger out on her—which, in part, I was.

Finally, in a series of telephone calls, I told Paula and Mark I not only felt that their views about *Miss Saigon* were wrong but that they were racially based. In the emotionally charged conversations, I don't think I used the word "racist," but I know my friends objected to my lumping them together with other whites. Paula said I was stereotyping them, that she wasn't like other whites. She told me of her friendships with a few blacks when she lived back East, of the history of her mother's involvement in supporting civil rights. "It's not like I don't know what discrimination is," she said. "Women get discriminated against, so do artists." Her tone moved back and forth between self-righteousness and resentment to distress and tears about losing our friendship.

Mark talked of his shame about being a WASP. "Do you know that I don't have a single male friend who is a WASP?" he said. I decided not to point out that, within the context of color, the difference between a WASP male and, say, an Irish Catholic, isn't much of a difference. And I also didn't remark that he had no friends of color other than myself. I suppose I felt such remarks would hurt him too much. I also didn't feel it was safe to say them.

A few months later, I had calmer talks with Mark, but they always ended with this distance between us. I needed some acknowledgment from him that, when we began talking about race, I knew more about it than he did, that our arguing about race was not the same as our arguing about free verse versus formal verse. That my experience gave me insights he didn't have.

"Of course, that's true," he said. "I know you've had different experiences." But for him, we had to meet on an equal basis, where his views on race were considered at the start as just as valid as mine. Otherwise, he felt he was compromising himself, giving away his soul. . . .

Inevitably I wonder if my daughter will understand my perspective as a person of color. Will she identify with white friends, and be fearful and suspicious of my anger and frustration? Or will she be working from some viewpoint I can't quite conceive, some line that marks her as a person of color and white and neither, all at the same time, as some new being whose experiences I will have to listen to and learn from? How can I prepare her for that new identity?

Will it be fair or accurate or helpful for me to tell her, "Unless the world is radically different, on some level, you will still have to choose: Are you a person of color or not?"

It took me many months to figure out what had gone down with Paula and Mark. Part of me wanted to let things go, but part of me knew that someday I'd have to talk to Samantha about race. If I avoided what was difficult in my own life, what would I be able to say to her? My black friend Alexs and I talked about how whites desperately want to do "the victim limbo," as he called it. Offered by many as a token of solidarity—"I'm just the same as you"—it's really a way of depoliticizing the racial question; it ignores the differences in power in this country that result from race.

When white people engage in conversation about racism, the first thing they often do, as Paula did with me, is the victim limbo: "I'm a woman, I know what prejudice is, I've experienced it." "I'm Jewish/working class/Italian in a WASP neighborhood, I know what prejudice is." The purpose of this is to show the person of color that he or she doesn't really experience anything the white person hasn't experienced, that the white person is a victim too. But Alexs and I both knew that the positions of a person of color and a white person in American society are not the same. "Whites don't want to give up their privilege and psychic comforts," said Alexs. "That's really why they're so angry. They have to choose whether they're going to give up power or fight for it."

Thinking this through, though, does not assuage the pain and bitterness I feel about losing white friendships over race, or the distance I have seen open up between me and my white friends. Nor does it help me explain to my daughter why we no longer see Paula or Mark. The compensation has been the numerous friendships that I've begun to have with people of color. My daughter will grow up in a household where the people who visit will be from a wider spectrum than were those Japanese Americans and whites who visited my parents' house in the suburbs of Chicago.

Not that teaching her about her Asian-American self has become any easier. My wife has been more conscious than I've been about telling Sam that she's Japanese. After playing with blond Shannon, the girl from next door, Sam said: "She's not Japanese, Mom. We're Japanese." "No," said Susie. "Daddy's Japanese, and you're part Japanese, but I'm not Japanese." Sam refused to believe this: "No, you're Japanese." After a few minutes, Susie finally sorted out the confusion. Sam thought being Japanese meant you had black hair.

For many liberal whites, what seems most important in any discussion of race is the need for hope, the need to find some link with people of color. They do not see how much that need serves as a tool of denial, how their claims of solidarity not only ignore real differences but also blot out the reality of people of color. How can we move forward, they ask, with all this rage you seem to feel? How can you stereotype me or group me in this category of whiteness?

I tell them they are still unwilling to examine what being white has meant to their existence. They think their rage at being classified as a white person is the same rage that people of color feel when they are being stereotyped. It is not. When whites feel anger about race, almost always they are feeling a threat to their comfort or power.

In the end, whites must exchange a hope based on naiveté and ignorance for one based on knowledge. For this naive hope denies connections, complexities. It is the drug of amnesia. It says there is no thread from one moment to the next, no cause and effect. It denies consequence and responsibility.

For my wife, this journey has been a difficult one. The arguments we have over race mirror our other arguments; at the same time, they exist in another realm, where I am a person of color and Susie is white. "I realize that in a way I've been passing too," she said a few months ago. "There's this comfort I've got to give up, this ease." At her clinic, she challenges the mainly white children's books in the waiting room, or a colleague's unconscious assumptions about Hmong families. More and more, she finds herself at gatherings where she as a white person is in the minority.

Breaking through denial, seeing how much needs to be changed, does not have to blunt the capacity for hope. For both of us, our daughter is proof of that capacity. And if I know that someday someone will call Samantha a gook, I know today she's a happy child. The love her mother and I share, the love we bear for her, cannot spare her from pain over race, and yet it can make her stronger. Sam will go further than we will, she will know more. She will be like nothing I can imagine, as I am like nothing my parents imagined.

Today my daughter told me she will grow up and work with her mother at the hospital. I'll be a grandpa and stay home and write poems and be with her children. Neither race nor ethnicity enters into her vision of the future. And yet they are already there, with our hopes, gathering shape.

A Question of Class

Dorothy Allison

. . . My people were not remarkable. We were ordinary, but even so we were mythical. We were the *they* everyone talks about, the ungrateful poor. I grew up trying to run away from the fate that destroyed so many of the people I loved, and having learned the habit of hiding, I found that I also had learned to hide from myself. I did not know who I was, only that I did not want to be *they,* the ones who are destroyed or dismissed to make the real people, the important people, feel safer. By the time I understood that I was queer, that habit of hiding was deeply set in me, so deeply that it was not a choice but an instinct. Hide, hide to survive, I thought, knowing that if I told the truth about my life, my family, my sexual desire, my real history, then I would move over into that unknown territory, the land of *they,* would never have the chance to name my own life, to understand it or claim it.

Why are you so afraid? my lovers and friends have asked me the many times when I have suddenly seemed to become a stranger, someone who would not speak to them, would not do the things they believed I should do, simple things like applying for a job, or a grant, or some award they were sure I could acquire easily. Entitlement, I have told them, is a matter of feeling like *we,* not *they.* But it has been hard for me to explain, to

make them understand. You think you have a right to things, a place in the world, I try to say. You have a sense of entitlement I don't have, a sense of your own importance. I have explained what I know over and over again, in every possible way I can, but I have never been able to make clear the degree of my fear, the extent to which I feel myself denied, not only that I am queer in a world that hates queers but that I was born poor into a world that despises the poor. The need to explain is part of why I write fiction. I know that some things must be felt to be understood, that despair can never be adequately analyzed; it must be lived. . . .

I have known I was a lesbian since I was a teenager, and I have spent a good twenty years making peace with the effects of incest and physical abuse. But what may be the central fact of my life is that I was born in 1949 in Greenville, South Carolina, the bastard daughter of a poor white woman from a desperately poor family, a girl who had left the seventh grade the year before, who worked as a waitress and was just a month past fifteen when she had me. That fact, the inescapable impact of being born in a condition of poverty that this society finds shameful, contemptible, and somehow deserved, has dominated me to such an extent that I have spent my life trying to overcome or deny it. I have learned with great difficulty that the vast majority of people pretend that poverty is a voluntary condition, that the poor are different, less than fully human, or at least less sensitive to hopelessness, despair, and suffering.

The first time I read Melanie Kaye Kantrowitz's poems, I experienced a frisson of recognition. It was not that my people had been "burned off the map" or murdered as hers had. No, we had been erased, encouraged to destroy ourselves, made invisible because we did not fit the myths of the middle class. Even now, past forty and stubbornly proud of my family, I feel the draw of that mythology, that romanticized, edited version of the poor. I find myself looking back and wondering what was real, what true. Within my family, so much was lied about, joked about, denied or told with deliberate indirection, an undercurrent of humiliation, or a brief pursed grimace that belies everything that has been said—everything, the very nature of truth and lies, reality and myth. What was real? The poverty depicted in books and movies was romantic, a kind of backdrop for the story of how it was escaped. The reality of self-hatred and violence was either absent or caricatured. The poverty I knew was dreary, deadening, shameful. My family was ashamed of being poor, of feeling hopeless. What was there to work for, to save money for, to fight for or struggle against? We had generations before us to teach us that nothing ever changed, and that those who did try to escape failed.

My mama had eleven brothers and sisters, of whom I can name only six. No one is left alive to tell me the names of the others. It was my grandmother who told me about my real daddy, a shiftless pretty man who was supposed to have married, had six children, and sold cut-rate life insurance to colored people out in the country. My mama married when I was a year old, but her husband died just after my little sister was born a year later. When I was five, Mama married the man she lived with until she died. Within the first year of their marriage Mama miscarried, and while we waited out in the hospital parking lot, my stepfather molested me for the first time, something he continued to do until I was past thirteen. When I was eight or so, Mama took us away to a motel after my stepfather beat me so badly it caused a family scandal, but we returned after two weeks. Mama told me that she really had no choice; she could not support us alone. When I was eleven I told one of my cousins that my stepfather was molesting me. Mama packed up my sisters and me and took us away for a few days, but again, my stepfather swore he would stop, and again we went back after a few weeks. I stopped talking for a while, and I have only vague memories of the next two years.

My stepfather worked as a route salesman, my mama as a waitress, laundry worker, cook, or fruit packer. I could never understand how, since

they both worked so hard and such long hours, we never had enough money, but it was a fact that was true also of my mama's brothers and sisters, who worked in the mills or the furnace industry. In fact, my parents did better than anyone else in the family, but eventually my stepfather was fired and we hit bottom—nightmarish months of marshals at the door, repossessed furniture, and rubber checks. My parents worked out a scheme so that it appeared my stepfather had abandoned us, but instead he went down to Florida, got a new job, and rented us a house. In the dead of night, he returned with a U-Haul trailer, packed us up, and moved us south.

The night we left South Carolina for Florida, my mama leaned over the back seat of her old Pontiac and promised us girls, "It'll be better there." I don't know if we believed her, but I remember crossing Georgia in the early morning, watching the red clay hills and swaying gray blankets of moss recede through the back window. I kept looking back at the trailer behind us, ridiculously small to contain everything we owned. Mama had, after all, packed nothing that wasn't fully paid off, which meant she had only two things of worth, her washing and sewing machines, both of them tied securely to the trailer walls. Through the whole trip, I fantasized an accident that would burst that trailer, scattering old clothes and cracked dishes on the tarmac.

I was only thirteen. I wanted us to start over completely, to begin again as new people with nothing of the past left over. I wanted to run away completely from who we had been seen to be, who we had been. That desire is one I have seen in other members of my family, to run away. It is the first thing I think of when trouble comes, the geographic solution. Change your name, leave town, disappear, and make yourself over. What hides behind that solution is the conviction that the life you have lived, the person you are, are valueless, better off abandoned, that running away is easier than trying to change anything, that change itself is not possible, that death is easier than this life. Sometimes I think it is that conviction—more seductive than alcoholism or violence and more subtle than sexual hatred or gender injustice—that has dominated my life, and made real change so painful and difficult.

Moving to central Florida did not fix our lives. It did not stop my stepfather's violence, heal my shame, or make my mother happy. Once there our lives became dominated by my mother's illness and medical bills. She had a hysterectomy when I was about eight and endured a series of hospitalizations for ulcers and a chronic back problem. Through most of my adolescence she superstitiously refused to allow anyone to mention the word cancer. (Years later when she called me to tell me that she was recovering from an emergency mastectomy, there was bitter fatalism in her voice. The second mastectomy followed five years after the first, and five years after that there was a brief bout with cancer of the lymph system which went into remission after prolonged chemotherapy. She died at the age of fifty-six with liver, lung, and brain cancer.) When she was not sick, Mama, and my stepfather, went on working, struggling to pay off what seemed an insurmountable load of debts.

By the time I was fourteen, my sisters and I had found ways to discourage most of our stepfather's sexual advances. We were not close but we united against our stepfather. Our efforts were helped along when he was referred to a psychotherapist after losing his temper at work, and was prescribed psychotropic drugs that made him sullen but less violent. We were growing up quickly, my sisters moving toward dropping out of school, while I got good grades and took every scholarship exam I could find. I was the first person in my family to graduate from high school, and the fact that I went on to college was nothing short of astonishing.

Everyone imagines her life is normal, and I did not know my life was not everyone's. It was not until I was an adolescent in central Florida that I began to realize just how different we were. The people we met there had not been shaped by the rigid class structure that dominated the South Carolina Piedmont. The first time I looked around my junior high classroom and realized that I did not know who those people were—not only as individuals but as categories, who their people were and how they saw themselves—I realized also that they did not know me. In Greenville, everyone knew my family, knew we were trash, and that meant we were supposed to be poor, supposed to have grim low-paid jobs, have babies in our teens, and never finish school. But central Florida in the 1960s was full of runaways and immigrants, and our mostly white working-class suburban school sorted us out, not by income and family background, but by intelligence and aptitude tests. Suddenly I was boosted into the college-bound track, and while there was plenty of contempt for my inept social skills, pitiful wardrobe, and slow drawling accent, there was also something I had never experienced before, a protective anonymity, and a kind of grudging respect and curiosity about who I might become. Because they did not see poverty and hopelessness as a foregone conclusion for my life, I could begin to imagine other futures for myself.

Moving into that new world and meeting those new people meant that I began to see my family from a new vantage point. I also experienced a new level of fear, a fear of losing what before had never been imaginable. My family's lives were not on television, not in books, not even comic books. There was a myth of the poor in this country, but it did not include us, no matter how hard I tried to squeeze us in. There was an idea of the good poor—hardworking, ragged but clean, and intrinsically noble. I understood that we were the bad poor, the ungrateful: men who drank and couldn't keep a job; women, invariably pregnant before marriage, who quickly became worn, fat, and old from working too many hours and bearing too many children; and children with runny noses, watery eyes, and bad attitudes. My cousins quit school, stole cars, used drugs, and took dead-end jobs pumping gas or waiting tables. We were not noble, not grateful, not even hopeful. We knew ourselves despised.

But in that new country, we were unknown. The myth settled over us and glamorized us. I saw it in the eyes of my teachers, the Lions' Club representative who paid for my new glasses, and the lady from the Junior League who told me about the scholarship I had won. Better, far better, to be one of the mythical poor than to be part of the *they* I had known before. *Don't let me lose this chance,* I prayed, and lived in fear that I might suddenly be seen again as what I knew I really was.

As an adolescent, I thought that the way my family escaped South Carolina was like a bad movie. We fled like runaway serfs and the sheriff who would have arrested my stepfather seemed like a border guard. Even now, I am certain that if we had remained in South Carolina, I would have been trapped by my family's heritage of poverty, jail, and illegitimate children—that even being smart, stubborn, and a lesbian would have made no difference. My grandmother died when I was twenty and after Mama went home for the funeral, I had a series of dreams in which we still lived up in Greenville, just down the road from where Granny had died. In the dreams I had two children and only one eye, lived in a trailer, and worked at the textile mill. Most of my time was taken up with deciding when I would finally kill my children and myself. The dreams were so vivid, I became convinced they were about the life I was meant to have had, and I began to work even harder to put as much distance as I could between my family and me. I copied the dress, mannerisms, attitudes, and ambitions of the girls I met in college, changing or hiding my own tastes, interests, and desires. I kept my lesbianism a secret, forming a relationship with an effeminate male friend that served to shelter and disguise us both. I explained to friends that I went home so rarely because my stepfather and I fought too much for me to be comfortable in his house. But that was only part of the reason I avoided home, the easiest reason. The truth was that I feared the person I might become in my mama's house.

It is hard to explain how deliberately and thoroughly I ran away from my own life. I did not forget where I came from, but I gritted my teeth and hid it. When I could not get enough scholarship money to pay for graduate school, I spent a year of blind rage working as a salad girl, substitute teacher, and maid. I finally managed to get a job by agreeing to take any city assignment where the Social Security Administration needed a clerk. Once I had a job and my own place far away from anyone in my family, I became sexually and politically active, joining the Women's Center support staff and falling in love with a series of middle-class women who thought my accent and stories thoroughly charming. The stories I told about my family, about South Carolina, about being poor itself, were all lies, carefully edited to seem droll or funny. I knew damn well that no one would want to hear the truth about poverty, the hopelessness and fear, the feeling that nothing you do will make any difference, and the raging resentment that burns beneath the jokes. Even when my lovers and I formed an alternative lesbian family, sharing all our resources, I kept the truth about my background and who I knew myself to be a carefully obscured mystery. I worked as hard as I could to make myself a new person, an emotionally healthy radical lesbian activist, and I believed completely that by remaking myself I was helping to remake the world.

For a decade, I did not go home for more than a few days at a time.

It is sometimes hard to make clear how much I have loved my family, that every impulse to hold them in contempt has sparked in me a counter-surge of stubborn pride. (What is equally hard to make clear is how much that impulse toward love and pride is complicated by an urge to fit us into the acceptable myths and theories of both mainstream society—Steven Spielberg movies or Taylor Caldwell novels, the one valorizing and the other caricaturing—and a lesbian feminist reinterpretation—the patriarchy as the villain and the trivialization of the choices the men and women of my family have made.) I have had to fight broad generalizations from every possible theoretical viewpoint. Traditional feminist theory has had a limited understanding of class differences or of how sexuality and self are shaped by both desire and denial. The ideology implies that we are all sisters who should turn our anger and suspicion only on the world outside the lesbian community. It is so simple to say the patriarchy did it, that poverty and social contempt are products of the world of the fathers. How often I felt a need to collapse my sexual history into what I was willing to share of my class background, to pretend that both my life as a lesbian and my life as a working-class escapee were constructed by the patriarchy. The difficulty is that I can't ascribe everything that has been problematic or difficult about my life simply and easily to the patriarchy, or even to the invisible and much-denied class structure of our society. . . .

One of the things I am trying to understand is how we internalize the myths of our society even as we hate and resist them. Perhaps this will be more understandable if I discuss specifically how some of these myths have shaped my life and how I have been able to talk about and change my own understanding of my family. I have felt a powerful temptation to write about my family as a kind of moral tale with us as the heroes and the middle and upper classes as the villains. It would be within the romantic myth, for example, to pretend that we were the kind of noble Southern whites portrayed in the movies, mill workers for generations until driven out of the mills by alcoholism and a family propensity to rebellion and union talk. But that would be a lie. The truth is that no one in my family ever joined a union. Taken as far as it can go, the myth of the poor would make my family over into union organizers or people broken by the failure of the unions. The reality of my family is far more complicated and lacks the cardboard nobility of the myth.

As far as my family was concerned, union organizers, like preachers, were of a different class, suspect and hated as much as they might be admired for what they were supposed to be trying to achieve. Serious belief in anything—any political ideology, any religious system, or any theory of life's meaning and purpose—was seen as unrealistic. It was an attitude that bothered me a lot when I started reading the socially conscious novels I found in the paperback racks when I was

eleven or so. I particularly loved Sinclair Lewis's novels and wanted to imagine my own family as part of the working man's struggle. But it didn't seem to be that simple.

"We were not joiners," my Aunt Dot told me with a grin when I asked her about the union. My cousin Butch laughed at that, told me the union charged dues and said, "Hell, we can't even be persuaded to toss money in the collection plate. An't gonna give it to no fat union man." It shamed me that the only thing my family wholeheartedly believed in was luck, and the waywardness of fate. They held the dogged conviction that the admirable and wise thing to do was to try and keep a sense of humor, not to whine or cower, and to trust that luck might someday turn as good as it had been bad—and with just as much reason. Becoming a political activist with an almost religious fervor was the thing I did that most outraged my family and the Southern working-class community they were part of.

Similarly, it was not my sexuality, my lesbianism, that was seen by my family as most rebellious; for most of my life, no one but my mama took my sexual preference very seriously. It was the way I thought about work, ambition, and self-respect that seemed incomprehensible to my aunts and cousins. They were waitresses, laundry workers, and counter girls. I was the one who went to work as a maid, something I never told any of them. They would have been angry if they had known, though the fact that some work was contemptible was itself a difficult notion. They believed that work was just work, necessary, that you did what you had to do to survive. They did not believe so much in taking pride in doing your job as they did in stubbornly enduring hard work and hard times when you really didn't have much choice about what work you did. But at the same time they did believe that there were some forms of work, including maid's work, that were only for black people, not white, and while I did not share that belief, I knew how intrinsic it was to how my family saw the world. Sometimes I felt as if I straddled cultures and belonged on neither side. I would grind my teeth at what I knew was my family's unquestioning racism but still take pride in their pragmatic endurance, but more and more as I grew older what I truly felt was a deep estrangement from the way they saw the world, and gradually a sense of shame that would have been completely incomprehensible to them.

"Long as there's lunch counters, you can always find work," I was told by both my mother and my aunts, and they'd add, "I can always get me a little extra with a smile." It was obvious that there was supposed to be nothing shameful about it, that needy smile across a lunch counter, that rueful grin when you didn't have rent, or the half-provocative, half-begging way my mama could cajole the man at the store to give her a little credit. But I hated it, hated the need for it and the shame that would follow every time I did it myself. It was begging as far as I was concerned, a quasi-prostitution that I despised even while I continued to use it (after all, I needed the money). But my mother, aunts, and cousins had not been ashamed, and my shame and resentment pushed me even further away from them.

"Just use that smile," my girl cousins used to joke, and I hated what I knew they meant. After college, when I began to support myself and study feminist theory, I did not become more understanding of the women of my family but more contemptuous. I told myself that prostitution is a skilled profession and my cousins were never more than amateurs. There was a certain truth in this, though like all cruel judgments made from the outside, it ignored the conditions that made it true. The women in my family, my mother included, had sugar daddies, not johns, men who slipped them money because they needed it so badly. From their point of view they were nice to those men because the men were nice to them, and it was never so direct or crass an arrangement that they would set a price on their favors. They would never have described what they did as prostitution, and nothing made them angrier than the suggestion that the men who helped them out did it just for their favors. They worked for a living, they swore, but this was different.

I always wondered if my mother had hated her sugar daddy, or if not *him* then her need for what he offered her, but it did not seem to me in memory that she had. Her sugar daddy had been an old man, half-crippled, hesitant and needy, and he treated my mama with enormous consideration and, yes, respect. The relationship between them was painful because it was based on the fact that she and my stepfather could not make enough money to support the family. Mama could not refuse her sugar daddy's money, but at the same time he made no assumptions about that money buying anything she was not already offering. The truth was, I think, that she genuinely liked him, and only partly because he treated her so well.

Even now, I am not sure whether or not there was a sexual exchange between them. Mama was a pretty woman and she was kind to him, a kindness he obviously did not get from anyone else in his life, and he took extreme care not to cause her any problems with my stepfather. As a teenager with an adolescent's contempt for moral failings and sexual complexity of any kind, I had been convinced that Mama's relationship with that old man was contemptible and also that I would never do such a thing. The first time a lover of mine gave me money, and I took it, everything in my head shifted. The amount she gave me was not much to her but it was a lot to me and I needed it. I could not refuse it, but I hated myself for taking it and I hated her for giving it to me. Worse, she had much less grace about my need than my mama's sugar daddy had displayed toward her. All that bitter contempt I had felt for my needy cousins and aunts raged through me and burned out the love I had felt. I ended the relationship quickly, unable to forgive myself for *selling* what I believed should only be offered freely—not sex but love itself.

When the women in my family talked about how hard they worked, the men would spit to the side and shake their heads. Men took real jobs—hard, dangerous, physically daunting work. They went to jail, not just the hard-eyed, careless boys who scared me with their brutal hands and cold eyes, but their gentler, softer brothers. It was another family thing, what people expected of my mama's family, my people. "His daddy's that one was sent off to jail in Georgia, and his uncle's another. Like as not, he's just the same," you'd hear people say of boys so young they still had their milk teeth. We were always driving down to the county farm to see somebody, some uncle, cousin, or nameless male relation. Shaven-headed, sullen and stunned, they wept on Mama's shoulder or begged my aunts to help. "I didn't do nothing, Mama," they'd say and it might have been true, but if even we didn't believe them, who would? No one told the truth, not even about how their lives were destroyed.

When I was eight years old, Butch, one of my favorite cousins, went to jail for breaking into pay phones with another boy. The other boy was returned to the custody of his parents. Butch was sent to the boys' facility at the county farm and after three months, my mama took us down there to visit, carrying a big basket of fried chicken, cold cornbread, and potato salad. Along with a hundred others we sat out on the lawn with Butch and watched him eat like he hadn't had a full meal in the whole three months. I stared at his head, which had been shaved near bald, and his ears, which were newly marked with fine blue scars from the carelessly handled razor. People were laughing, music was playing, and a tall lazy man in uniform walked past us chewing on tooth-picks and watching us all closely. Butch kept his head down, his face hard with hatred, only look-ing back at the guard when he turned away.

"Sons-a-bitches," he whispered, and my mama shushed him. We all sat still when the guard turned back to us. There was a long moment of quiet and then that man let his face relax into a big wide grin.

"Uh-huh," he said. That was all he said. Then he turned and walked away. None of us spoke. None of us ate any more. Butch went back inside soon after and we left. When we got back to the car, my mama sat there for a while crying quietly. The next week Butch was reported for fighting and had his stay extended by six months.

Butch was fifteen. He never went back to school and after jail he couldn't join the army. When he finally did come home we never talked, never had to talk. I knew without asking that the guard had had his little revenge, knew too that my cousin would break into another phone booth as soon as he could, but do it sober and not get caught. I knew without asking the source of his rage, the way he felt about clean, well-dressed, contemptuous people who looked at him like his life wasn't as important as a dog's. I knew because I felt it too. That guard had looked at me and Mama with the same expression he used on my cousin. We were trash. We were the ones they built the county farm to house and break. The boy who had been sent home had been the son of a deacon in the church, the man who managed the hardware store.

As much as I hated that man, and his boy, there was a way in which I also hated my cousin. He should have known better, I told myself, should have known the risk he ran. He should have been more careful. As I became older and started living on my own, it was a litany that I used against myself even more angrily than I used it against my cousin. I knew who I was, knew that the most important thing I had to do was protect myself and hide my despised identity, blend into the myth of both the "good" poor and the reasonable lesbian. Even when I became a feminist activist, that litany went on reverberating in my head, but by then it had become a ground-note, something so deep and omnipresent, I no longer heard it even when everything I did was set to the cadence that it established.

By 1975, I was earning a meager living as a photographer's assistant in Tallahassee, Florida, but the real work of my life was my lesbian fem-inist activism, the work I did with the local Women's Center and the committee to found a Feminist Studies Department at Florida State University. Part of my role as I saw it was to be a kind of evangelical lesbian feminist, and to help develop a political analysis of this woman-hating society. I did not talk about class, more than by giving lip service to how we all needed to think about it, the same way I thought we all needed to think about racism. I was a serious and determined person, living in a lesbian collective, studying each new book that purported to address feminist issues and completely driven by what I saw as a need to revolutionize the world. . . .

The idea of writing fiction or essays seemed frivolous when there was so much work to be done, but everything changed when I found myself confronting emotions and ideas that could not be explained away or postponed for a feminist holiday. The way it happened was simple and completely unexpected. One week I was asked to speak to two completely divergent groups: an Episcopalian Sunday School class and a juvenile detention center. The Episcopalians were all white, well-dressed, highly articulate, nominally polite, and obsessed with getting me to tell them (without their having to ask directly) just what it was that two women did together in bed. The delinquents were all women, eighty percent black and Hispanic, dressed in green uniform dresses or blue jeans and workshirts, profane, rude, fearless, witty, and just as determined to get me to talk about what it was that two women did together in bed.

I tried to have fun with the Episcopalians, teasing them about their fears and insecurities, and being as bluntly honest as I could about my sexual practices. The Sunday School teacher, a man who had assured me of his liberal inclinations, kept blushing and stammering as the questions about my growing up and coming out became more detailed. When the meeting was over, I stepped out into the sunshine angry at the contemptuous attitude implied by all their questions, and though I did not know why, also so deeply depressed that I couldn't even cry. The delinquents were different. Shameless, they had me blushing within the first few minutes, yelling out questions that were partly curious and partly a way of boasting about what they already knew.

"You butch or femme?" "You ever fuck boys?" "You ever want to?" "You want to have children?" "What's your girlfriend like?" I finally broke up when one very tall confident girl leaned

way over and called out, "Hey girlfriend! I'm getting out of here next weekend. What you doing that night?" I laughed so hard I almost choked. I laughed until we were all howling and giggling together. Even getting frisked as I left didn't ruin my mood. I was still grinning when I climbed into the waterbed with my lover that night, grinning right up to the moment when she wrapped her arms around me and I burst into tears.

It is hard to describe the way I felt that night, the shock of recognition and the painful way my thoughts turned. That night I understood suddenly everything that happened to my cousins and me, understood it from a wholly new and agonizing perspective, one that made clear how brutal I had been to both my family and myself. I understood all over again how we had been robbed and dismissed, and why I had worked so hard not to think about it. I had learned as a child that what could not be changed had to go unspoken, and worse, that those who cannot change their own lives have every reason to be ashamed of that fact and to hide it. I had accepted that shame and believed in it, but why? What had I or my cousins really done to deserve the contempt directed at us? Why had I always believed us contemptible by nature? I wanted to talk to someone about all the things I was thinking that night, but I could not. Among the women I knew there was no one who would have understood what I was thinking, no other working-class women in the women's collective where I was living. I began to suspect that we shared no common language to speak those bitter truths.

In the days after that I found myself remembering that afternoon long ago at the county farm, that feeling of being the animal in the zoo, the thing looked at and laughed at and used by the real people who watched us. For all his liberal convictions, that Sunday School teacher had looked at me with eyes that reminded me of Butch's long-ago guard. Suddenly I felt thrown back into my childhood, into all the fears and convictions I had tried to escape. Once again I felt myself at the mercy of the important people who knew how to dress and talk, and would always be given the benefit of the doubt while I and my family would not.

I felt as if I was at the mercy of an outrage so old I could not have traced all the ways it shaped my life. I understood again that some are given no quarter, no chance, that all their courage, humor, and love for each other is just a joke to the ones who make the rules, and I hated the rule makers. Finally I also realized that part of my grief came from the fact that I no longer knew who I was or where I belonged. I had run away from my family, refused to go home to visit, and tried in every way to make myself a new person. How could I be working-class with a college degree? As a lesbian activist? I thought about the guards at the detention center, and the way they had looked at me. They had not stared at me with the same picture-window emptiness they turned on the girls who came to hear me, girls who were closer to the life I had been meant to live than I could bear to examine. The contempt in their eyes was contempt for me as a lesbian, different and the same, but still contempt. . . .

In the late 1970s, the compartmentalized life I had created burst open. It began when I started to write and work out what I really thought about my family. . . . I went home again. I went home to my mother and my sisters, to visit, talk, argue, and begin to understand.

Once home I saw that, as far as my family was concerned, lesbians were lesbians whether they wore suitcoats or leather jackets. Moreover, in all that time when I had not made peace with myself, my family had managed to make a kind of peace with me. My girlfriends were treated like slightly odd versions of my sisters' husbands, while I was simply the daughter who had always been difficult but was still a part of their lives. The result was that I started trying to confront what had made me unable to really talk to my sisters for so many years. I discovered that they no longer knew who I was either, and it took time and lots of listening to each other to rediscover my sense of family, and my love for them.

It is only as the child of my class and my unique family background that I have been able to put together what is for me a meaningful politics, gained a sense of why I believe in activism, why self-revelation is so important for lesbians, reexamining the way we are seen and the way we see ourselves. There is no all-purpose feminist analysis that explains away all the complicated ways our sexuality and core identity are shaped, the way we see ourselves as parts of both our birth families and the extended family of friends and lovers we invariably create within the lesbian community. For me the bottom line has simply become the need to resist that omnipresent fear, that urge to hide and disappear, to disguise my life, my desires, and the truth about how little any of us understand—even as we try to make the world a more just and human place for us all. Most of all I have tried to understand the politics of *they*, why human beings fear and stigmatize the different while secretly dreading that they might be one of the different themselves. Class, race, sexuality, gender, all the categories by which we categorize and dismiss each other need to be examined from the inside.

The horror of class stratification, racism, and prejudice is that some people begin to believe that the security of their families and community depends on the oppression of others, that for some to have good lives others must have lives that are mean and horrible. It is a belief that dominates this culture; it is what made the poor whites of the South so determinedly racist and the middle class so contemptuous of the poor. It is a myth that allows some to imagine that they build their lives on the ruin of others, a secret core of shame for the middle class, a goad and a spur to the marginal working class, and cause enough for the homeless and poor to feel no constraints on hatred or violence. The power of the myth is made even more apparent when we examine how within the lesbian and feminist communities, where so much attention has been paid to the politics of marginalization, there is still so much exclusion and fear, so many of us who do not feel safe even within our chosen communities.

That Moment of Visibility

I never realized how much my working-class background and beliefs played a role in my education. My family, friends, and neighbors never placed much importance on college. Instead, we were strongly encouraged to find work immediately after high school so we could support ourselves financially. My sisters and I were encouraged to do secretarial work until we married. There was no particular positive status attached to obtaining a degree except maybe the chance of making a lot of money. In fact, friends who went to college were looked at somewhat suspiciously. Among my reference group, college was often seen as a way to get out of having to work.

No one in my family had ever gone to college. It was not financially feasible and a college environment was equal to the unknown. It really was scary terrain. When I decided to go to a local community college after having worked for five years in a secretarial position, family and friends could not understand my decision. Why would I choose college when I already had a job? I could pay bills, buy what I needed, and I had a savings account. So I started by taking a course a semester—and I barely got through the first course. Although I received a good grade, I felt incredibly isolated, like I was an impostor who did not belong in a classroom. I had no idea how someone in college was supposed to act. I stayed silent, scared, and consciously invisible most of the time. I was not even close to making a commitment to a college education when I signed up for a second course—but because my job paid for it (one of the benefits), I felt I had nothing to lose. I signed up for Introduction to Juvenile Delinquency and midway through, our class received an assignment to do a fifteen-page self-analysis applying some of the theories we were learning. The thought of consciously revealing myself when I was trying so hard not to look, act, or be different was not something I was willing (or, I think, able at the time) to do. When I discussed the assignment with the people close to me, they agreed that the assignment was too personal and revealing. I decided not to do it and I also decided that college was probably not for me.

I went to see my professor (who was the only woman in her department) to let her know that I was refusing to do the assignment and would not complete the course. We had spoken two or three times outside of class and she knew a little about me. I knew that she was also from a working-class background and had returned to school after working some years. I felt the least I could do was tell her I was quitting the class. When I said that I was unwilling to do the assignment, she stared at me for some time, and then asked me what I would prefer to write about. I was stunned that I was noticed and was being asked what I would like to do. When I had no reply, she asked if I would write a paper on the importance of dissent. All I could think to say was yes. I completed the course successfully and found an ally in my department. I can't overstate the importance of that moment of acknowledgement. It was the first time I felt listened to. It was the moment when you feel safe enough to reveal who you are, the deep breath you can finally take when you figure out that the person you're talking to understands, appreciates, and may even share your identity.

I think of this experience as a turning point for me—when I realized that despite all my conscious efforts to be invisible and to "pass," it was that moment of visibility and acknowledgement that kept me in school.

Rose B. Pascarell

I grew up poor, hated, the victim of physical, emotional, and sexual violence, and I know that suffering does not ennoble. It destroys. To resist destruction, self-hatred, or lifelong hopelessness, we have to throw off the conditioning of being despised, the fear of becoming that *they* that is talked about so dismissively, to refuse lying myths and easy moralities, to see ourselves as human, flawed and extraordinary. All of us—extraordinary.

Teleology on the Rocks
(or spirit-murdering the messenger)

Patricia J. Williams

My abiding recollection of being a student at Harvard Law School is the sense of being invisible. I spent three years wandering in a murk of unreality. I observed large, mostly male bodies assert themselves against one another like football players caught in the gauzy mist of intellectual slow motion. I stood my ground amid them, watching them deflect from me, unconsciously, politely, as if I were a pillar in a crowded corridor. Law school was for me like being on another planet, full of alienated creatures with whom I could make little connection. The school created a dense atmosphere that muted my voice to inaudibility. All I could do to communicate my existence was to posit carefully worded messages into hermetically sealed, vacuum-packed blue books, place them on the waves of that foreign sea, and pray that they would be plucked up by some curious seeker and understood.

Perhaps there were others who felt what I felt. Perhaps we were all aliens, all silenced by the dense atmosphere. Thinking that made me feel, ironically, less isolated. It was not merely that I was black and female, but a circumstance external to myself that I, and the collective, could not help internalizing.

When I became a law professor, I found myself on yet another planet: a planet with a sun as strong as a spotlight and an atmosphere so thin that my slightest murmur would travel for miles, skimming from ear to ear to ear, merrily distorting and retracting as it went. Again I comforted myself that my sense of alienation and now-heightened visibility were not inherent to my blackness and my femaleness, but an uncomfortable atmospheric condition afflicting everyone. But at the gyroscopic heart of me, there was and is a deep realization that I have never left the planet earth. I know that my feelings of exaggerated visibility and invisibility are the product of my not being part of the larger cultural picture. I know too that the larger cultural picture is an illusion, albeit a powerful one, concocted from a perceptual consensus to which I am not a party; and that while these perceptions operate as dictators of truth, they are after all merely perceptions.

My best friend from law school is a woman named C. For months now I have been sending her drafts of this book, filled with many shared

experiences, and she sends me back comments and her own associations. Occasionally we speak by telephone. One day, after reading the beginning of this chapter, she calls me up and tells me her abiding recollection of law school. "Actually it has nothing to do with law school," she says.

"I'll be the judge of that," I respond.

"Well," she continues, "it's about the time I was held at gunpoint by a SWAT team."

It turns out that during one Christmas vacation C. drove to Florida with two friends. Just outside Miami they stopped at a roadside diner. C. ordered a hamburger and a glass of milk. The milk was sour, and C. asked for another. The waitress ignored her. C. asked twice more and was ignored each time. When the waitress finally brought the bill, C. had been charged for the milk and refused to pay for it. The waitress started to shout at her, and a highway patrolman walked over from where he had been sitting and asked what was going on. C. explained that the milk was sour and that she didn't want to pay for it. The highway patrolman ordered her to pay and get out. When C. said he was out of his jurisdiction, the patrolman pulled out his gun and pointed it at her.

("Don't you think" asks C. when I show her this much of my telling of her story, "that it would help your readers to know that the restaurant was all white and that I'm black?" "Oh, yeah," I say. "And six feet tall.")

Now C. is not easily intimidated and, just to prove it, she put her hand on her hip and invited the police officer to go ahead and shoot her, but before he did so *he* should try to drink the damn glass of milk, and so forth and so on for a few more descriptive rounds. What cut her off was the realization that, suddenly and silently, she and her two friends had been surrounded by eight SWAT team officers, in full guerrilla gear, automatic weapons drawn. Into the pall of her ringed speechlessness, they sent a local black policeman, who offered her twenty dollars and begged her to pay and be gone. C. describes how desperately he was perspiring as he begged and, when she didn't move, how angry he got—how he accused her of being an outside agitator, that she could come from the North and go back to the North, but that there were those of "us" who had to live here and would pay for her activism.

C. says she doesn't remember how she got out of there alive or why they finally let her go; she supposes that the black man paid for her. But she does remember returning to the car with her two companions and the three of them crying, sobbing, all the way to Miami. "The damnedest thing about it," C. said, "was that no one was interested in whether or not I was telling the truth. The glass was sitting there in the middle of all this, with the curdle hanging on the sides, but nobody would taste it because a black woman's lips had touched it."

I think of C. a lot when I write, and of her truth-telling glass of sour, separated milk. The curd clinging to the sides; her words curdled in the air. The police with guns drawn, battlelines drawn, the contest over her contestation; the proof of the milk in the glass inadmissible, unaccounted for, unseen. The insolent fact of her words; defiant presumption as the subject for a war over the invisible. The thing I like best about C. is her insistence always to be exactly wherever she is in the universe. I am thankful she survives the messes she gets herself into.

In the early morning hours of December 20, 1986, three black men left their stalled car on Cross Bay Parkway, in Queens, New York, and went to look for help. They walked into the neighborhood of Howard Beach, entered a pizzeria, ordered pizzas, and sat down to eat. An anonymous caller to the police reported their presence as "black troublemakers"; a patrol car came, found no trouble, and left. After the men had eaten, they left the pizzeria and were immediately surrounded by a group of eight to ten white teenagers who taunted them with racial epithets. The white youths chased the black men a distance of approximately three miles, beating them severely along the way. One of the black men died, struck by a car as he tried to flee across a highway; another suffered permanent blindness in one eye.[1]

In the heated public controversy that ensued, as much of the attention centered on the community of Howard Beach, where the assault took place, as on the assaulters themselves. The chief cause of such attention was a veritable Greek chorus (composed of lawyers for the defendants as well as resident after resident of Howard Beach) repeating and repeating that the mere presence of three black men in that part of town at that time of night was reason enough to drive them out: "They had to be starting trouble"; "We're a strictly white neighborhood"; "What were they doing here in the first place?"[2] The pinnacle of legitimacy to which these particular questions rose is, to me, the most frightening aspect of this case. When Mayor Ed Koch was asked why he thought the young men were walking around Howard Beach, he dignified the question with the following answer: "I don't know . . . And neither did the 12 or so people who beat them. Because they didn't ask them. They didn't talk to them." One is left to speculate: if the attackers, those self-appointed gatekeepers, *had* asked and got an answer like "none of your business," would they then have been entitled to beat and attack out of public-spirited zeal? And, one wonders further, what explanation would have been sufficient to allow black males continued unmolested passage into the sanctified byways of Howard Beach?

Although the immensely segregationist instincts behind such statements may be evident, it is worth making explicit some of the presuppositions behind them:

> Everyone who lives here is white.
> No black could live here.
> No one here has a black friend.
> No white would employ a black here.
> No black is permitted to shop here.
> No black is ever up to any good.

Moreover, these presuppositions themselves are premised on certain lethal philosophies of life:

Better Safe Than Sorry "Are we supposed to stand around and do nothing, while these blacks come into our area and rob us?" asked one woman of a reporter, in the wake of the Howard

Beach attack. "'We ain't racial,' said 20-year old Michael Habe, who has lived in Howard Beach all his life. 'We just don't want to get robbed.'"[3] The hidden implication of such statements is that to be safe is not to be sorry; and to be safe is to be white and to be sorry is to be associated with blacks. Thus safety and sorrow, which are inherently alterable and random, are linked to inalterable essences. The expectation that uncertain conditions are immutable is a formula for frustration, a belief that feeds a sense of powerlessness. The rigid determinism of placing in the disjunctive things that are not in fact is a setup for betrayal by the very nature of reality.

The national repetition that white neighborhoods are safe and blacks bring sorrow is an incantation of powerlessness. And with the upsidedown logic of all irrational incantations, it imports a concept of white safety that necessarily endangers the lives as well as the rights of blacks.

It is also an incantation of innocence and guilt, related to the accusations that affirmative-action programs allow (presumably guilty?) blacks to displace innocent whites.[4] (Although even assuming that "innocent whites" are being displaced by blacks, does that make blacks less innocent in the pursuit of education and jobs?) In fact, in the wake of Howard Beach, police and the press rushed to service the public's interest in showing what unsavory dispositions the victims had. But the point that gets overlooked in all this is how racial slurs and attacks objectify people: "the incident could have happened to any black person who was there at that time and place. This is the crucial aspect of the Howard Beach affair that is now being muddied in the media. Bringing up Griffith's [the dead man] alleged involvement in a shooting incident a couple of years ago is another way of saying 'He was a criminal who deserved it.'"[5] It is thus that a pernicious game of Victim Responsibility was set in motion, itself slave to society's stereotypes of good and evil.

It does no one much good, however, to make race issues contests for some Holy Grail of innocence. In my own lifetime, segregation and antimiscegenation laws were still on the books in many states. During the lifetimes of my parents and grandparents, and for several hundred years before them, laws were used to prevent blacks from learning to read, write, own property, or vote; blacks were, by constitutional mandate, outlawed from the hopeful, loving expectations that come from being treated as a whole, rather than three-fifths of a person. When every resource of a wealthy nation is put to such destructive ends, it will take more than a few generations to mop up the mess.

We are all inheritors of that legacy, whether new to this world or new to this country, for it survives as powerful and invisibly reinforcing structures of thought, language, and law. Thus generalized notions of innocence and guilt have little place in the struggle for transcendence; there is no blame among the living for the dimensions of this historic crime, this national tragedy.[6] There is, however, responsibility for never forgetting another's history, for making real the psychic obliteration that does live on as a factor in shaping relations not just between blacks and whites (Mayor Koch asserted, during a trip to Howard Beach intended to promote racial harmony, that "most robberies were committed by blacks"), or between blacks and blacks (the mayor went on, moreover, to reassure his all-white audience that "most of the victims were black, too"[7]), but between whites and whites as well. Whites must take into account how much this history has projected onto blacks all criminality and all of society's ills. It has become the means for keeping white criminality invisible.

A Prejudiced Society Is Better than a Violent Society The attempt to split bias from violence has been this society's most enduring and fatal rationalization. Prejudice does hurt, however, just as absence of it can nourish and shelter. Discrimination can repel and vilify, ostracize and alienate. Any white person who doesn't believe it should spend a week telling everyone she meets that one of her parents or grandparents was black. I had a friend in college who discovered, having lived her life as a red-haired, gray-eyed white person, that she was one-sixteenth black (may-as-well-be-all-black, in other words). Before my eyes and despite herself, she began to externalize all the unconscious baggage that "black" bore for her, the self-hatred that racism is. She did not think of herself as a racist—nor had I—but she literally wanted to jump out of her skin, shed her flesh, start life over again. She confided that she felt fouled and betrayed. (She also asked me if I had ever felt this way. Her question dredged from some deep corner of my mind the recollection of feeling precisely that when, at the age of three or so, some white playmates explained that God had mixed mud with the pure clay of life in order to make me.)

In the Vietnamese language, "the word 'I' (*toi*) . . . means 'your servant'; there is no 'I' as such. When you talk to someone you establish a relationship."[8] Such a self-concept is a way of experiencing the other, of ritualistically sharing the other's essence and cherishing it. In our culture, seeing and feeling the dimension of harm done by separating self from other requires somewhat more work.[9] Very little in our language or culture encourages looking at others as parts of ourselves. With the imperviously divided symmetry of the marketplace, gains for whites are not felt as gains for blacks, and social costs to blacks are simply not seen as costs to whites. (One of the starkest examples of this has been the disastrous delay in responding to the AIDS epidemic: as long as it was seen to be an affliction of Haitians, Hispanics, Africans, and other marginalized groups such as drug users and homosexuals, its long-term implications were all but ignored.[10])

What complicates this structure of thought insofar as racism is concerned, however, is that the distancing does not stop with the separation of the white self from the black other. In addition, the cultural domination of blacks by whites means that the black self is placed at a distance even from itself, as in my example of blacks being asked to put themselves in the position of the white shopkeepers who scrutinize them. So blacks in a white society are conditioned from infancy to see in themselves only what others, who despise them, see.[11]

It is true that conforming to what others see in us is any child's—black or white—way of becoming socialized.[12] It is what makes children in our society appear so gullible, impressionable, "impolitely" honest, blindly loyal, and charming to the ones they imitate. Yet this conformity also describes a way of being that relinquishes the power of independent ethical choice. Although such a relinquishment can have desirable consequences, it presumes a fairly homogeneous social context in which values are collectively shared and enforced. (Is it any wonder that western anthropologists and ethnographers, for whom adulthood is manifested by the exercise of individual ethical judgment, are so quick to denounce tribal collective cultures as "childlike"?)

Our culture, in contrast, does not make all selves or I's the servants of others, but only some. Thus some I's are defined as "your servant," some as "your master." The struggle for the self becomes not a true mirroring of self-in-other, but a hierarchically inspired series of distortions, where some serve without ever being served; some master with no sense of what it is to be mastered; and almost everyone hides from the fact of this vernacular domination by clinging to the legally official definition of an I meaning "your equal."

In such an environment, relinquishing the power of individual ethical judgment to a collective ideal risks psychic violence, an obliteration of the self through domination by an all-powerful other. It is essential at some stage that the self be permitted to retreat into itself and make its own decisions with self-love and self-confidence. What links child abuse, the mistreatment of women, and racism is the massive external intrusion into psyche that dominating powers impose to keep the self from ever fully seeing itself.[13] Since the self's power resides in another, little faith is placed in the true self, in one's own experiential knowledge. It is thus that children's, women's, and blacks' power is actually reduced to the "intuitive" rather than to the real: social life is based primarily on the imaginary.[14] Furthermore, since it is difficult constantly to affirm the congruence of one's own self-imagining with what the other is thinking of the self—and since even that correlative effort is usually kept within limited family, neighborhood, or religious-racial boundaries—encounters cease even to be social and are merely presumptuous, random, and disconnected.

This peculiarly distancing standpoint allows dramas—particularly racial ones like Howard Beach—to unfold in scenarios weirdly unrelated to the incidents that generated them: at one end of the spectrum is a laissez-faire response that privatizes the self in order to remain unassailably justified in any and all activities. At the other is a pattern of generalizing particular others into terrifyingly uncontrollable "domains" of public wilderness against whom proscriptive barriers must be built.

The prototypical scenario of the privatized response to issues of racial accountability might be imagined as follows:

Cain: Abel's part of town is tough turf.

Abel: It upsets me when you say that; you have never been to my part of town. As a matter of fact, my part of town is a leading supplier of milk and honey.

Cain: The news that I'm upsetting you is too upsetting for me to handle. You were wrong to tell me of your upset because now I'm terribly upset.

Abel: I felt threatened first. Listen to me. Take your distress as a measure of my own and empathize with it. Don't ask me to recant and apologize in order to carry this conversation further.

What is problematic in this sort of discourse is that the issue of Cain's calling Abel's turf tough gets transformed into a discussion of how Abel challenges that statement. Though there is certainly an obligation to be careful in addressing others, the obligation to protect the feelings of the other gets put above the need to protect one's own; the self becomes subservient to the other, with no reciprocity; and the other becomes a whimsical master. Abel's feelings get deflected in

deference to Cain's; and Abel bears the double burden of raising his issue correctly and of being responsible for its impact on Cain should Cain take it wrong. Cain is rendered unaccountable, as long as the deflection continues, for both the care with which he expressed the initial statement and his own response to Abel, because in the end it is all Abel's fault.

Morality and responsiveness thus become split as Abel drowns in responsibility for valuative quality control; and Cain rests on the higher ground of a value-neutral zone. For example, here is more of the encounter between Mayor Koch and the black congregation in Queens: "In discussing the Howard Beach incident, Mr. Koch asked the people in Morning Star [Baptist Missionary Church] whether, if three white men were walking in Harlem after midnight, 'do you believe they would be absolutely safe?' 'Yes,' the congregation chorused. The Mayor did not think so, but said he was glad they did."[15] In reading this account, I had trouble figuring out what the mayor's motivation was in asking such a question. Was he implying that blacks would support racial violence if it occurred in reverse? And if he were implicitly asking for black understanding based on a presumed condoning of black-on-white violence, then wasn't he really asking blacks to understand that white-on-black violence isn't so hard to understand after all? That there is a sympathetic chord to be struck if only blacks would look deeply enough into themselves? If, as the story implies, Koch thought the congregation would say no, what he then would have "shown" (of himself, of institutional posture, if not of the teleological essence of things) is that racism is just human nature after all; that public absolution is simply a matter of pointing a finger and wailing "well, you did it too"; and that death in turf wars isn't racism but part of life.

Caught in conversations like this, blacks as well as whites will feel keenly circumscribed. Perhaps most people never intend to be racist or oppressive or insulting, but by describing zones of vulnerability, by setting up regions of conversational taboo and fences of rigidified politeness, the unintentional exile of individuals as well as races may be quietly accomplished and avoided indefinitely. A strong example of the degree to which racism may be transformed into issues of "courtesy" is the following: when Alan Hendrickse, the leader of the mixed-race chamber of the South African parliament, decided to go swimming at a "whites only" beach, President Botha demanded that he either apologize or resign, or else he would "have no choice but to dissolve the Parliament . . . When he started marching in on the beach, he embarrassed me and broke the rules of Parliament . . . It is a question of procedure."[16]

Another scenario of the distancing of the self from responsibility for racism is the inventing of some vast wilderness of others (composed, in the context of Howard Beach, of violent seventeen-year-old black males in running shoes and hooded sweatshirts) against which the self must barricade itself. It is this fear of the overwhelming other that animates many of the more vengefully racist comments from Howard Beach: "'We're a strictly white neighborhood,' Michelle Napolitano said. 'They had to be starting trouble.'"[17]

Not only do such attitudes set up angry, excluding boundaries, but they imply that the *failure* to protect and avenge is a bad policy, bad statesmanship, an embarrassment. They raise the stakes to a level beyond that of the unexpressed rage arising from the incident itself, as in the example of Cain and Abel. The need to avenge becomes a separate issue of protocol, of etiquette—not a loss of a piece of the self, which is the real cost of real tragedies, but a loss of self-regard. By "self-regard" I don't mean self-concept, as in self-esteem; I mean, again, that view of the self which is attained when the self steps outside to regard and evaluate the self; in which the self is watched by an imaginary other, a projection of the opinions of real others; in which "I" means "your master," not your servant; in which refusal of the designated other to be dominated is felt as a personal assault. Thus the failure to avenge is treated as a loss of self-regard; it is used

as a psychological metaphor for whatever trauma or original assault constituted the real loss to the self.[18] It is more abstract, more illusory, more constructed, more invented—and therefore potentially less powerful than real assault, in that it can with effort be unlearned as a source of vulnerability. This is the real message of the attempt to distinguish between prejudice and violence: names, as in the old sticks-and-stones ditty, or structures of thought, while undeniably influential, can be unlearned—or undone—as motivations for future destructive action. But as long as they are not unlearned, the exclusionary power of free-floating emotions make their way into the gestalt of prosecutorial and jury disposition and into what the law sees as a crime, sees as relevant, justified, provoked, or excusable.[19] Laws become described and enforced in the spirit of our prejudices.

The Evidentiary Rules of Legitimating Turf Wars
Here is a description of the arraignment of three of the white teenagers involved in the Howard Beach beatings:

> The three defense lawyers also tried to cast doubt on [the prosecutor's] account of the attack. The lawyers questioned why the victims walked all the way to the pizza parlor if, as they said, their mission was to summon help for their car, which broke down three miles away . . . At the arraignment, the lawyers said the victims passed two all-night gas stations and several other pizza shops before they reached the one they entered . . . A check yesterday of area restaurants, motels and gas stations listed in the Queens street directory found two eating establishments, a gas station and a motel that all said they were open and had working pay phones on Friday night . . . A spokesman for the New York Telephone Company, Jim Crosson, said there are six outdoor pay telephones along Cross Bay Boulevard on the way to the pizzeria.[20]

In the first place, lawyers must wonder about the relevance of all this. Does the answer to any of the issues raised by the defense team serve to prove that these black men assaulted, robbed, threatened, or molested these white men? Or even that the white men *reasonably* feared such a fate? The investigation into how many phone booths to a mile of the course establishes no reason why the white men would fear the black men's presence; its relevance is only to prove that there is no reason a black man should just walk, just wander, around Howard Beach. This is no mere semantic detail: it is central to understanding the real burdensomeness of proof in such cases. It is this unconscious restructuring of burdens of proof into burdens of white over black that permits people who believe they are not racist to condone and commit crimes of genocidal magnitude. It is easy to generalize all this away as linguistically technical or as society's sorrow ("I'm so tired of hearing blacks say that society's done them wrong," said a student of mine). But these gyrations kill with their razor-toothed presumption; it is we lawyers—who, with doctors, are the modern wizards and medicine people—who must define innocent murderousness as crime.

In addition, investigations into "closer" (really farther—from Howard Beach) alternatives eclipse the possibility of other explanations; they assume that the young black men were not headed for the subway, which in fact was not far from and in the same direction as the pizzeria; they assume that black people (and I have never heard the same public assumption about white people) need documented reasons for excursioning into neighborhoods where they do not live, for venturing beyond the bounds of the zones to which they are supposedly confined.

It is interesting to contrast this implicit requirement of documentation imposed on blacks walking down public streets in Howard Beach with the explicit lack of such a requirement in the contemporaneous public discussions of the murder of Eleanor Bumpurs. In that case, seven white officers burst into the private space of Mrs. Bumpurs' apartment and, while attempting an illegal eviction, shot and killed her. Here the availability of other, less intrusive options was consistently dismissed by lawmakers as presumption and idle hindsight; such rejection of other alternatives dismissed the burden that police officers have to use the least harmful method. In

the context of Howard Beach, however, such an analysis implicitly imposes a burden on non-residents of neighborhoods to stay out unless absolutely necessary; it implies that there is harm in the presence of those who do not "own" something specific there. Both analyses skirt the propriety and necessity of public-sector responsibility; both redefine public accountability in privatized terms. And whether those privatized terms operate to restrict or expand accountability is seemingly dichotomized according to the race of the actors.

Finally, this factualized hypothesizing was part of a news story, which means that the news—or what is purported to be fact—is in fact hypothesis, based on such silent premises as: they should have used the first phone they came to; they should have eaten at the first restaurant they found; they should have gone into a gas station and asked for help; surely they should have had the cash and credit cards to do any of the above or else not travel in strange neighborhoods. In elevating these to relevant issues, the *Times* only mirrored what was being done in the courtroom.

Privatized Innocence and Publicized Guilt   In his ill-fated trip to the town of Jamaica in Queens, purportedly to soothe tensions, Mayor Koch asked black churchgoers to understand the disgruntlement of residents of Howard Beach about the interracial march, by fourteen hundred protestors, through "their" streets. He asked them how they would feel if fourteen hundred white people took to the streets of Jamaica (a mostly black neighborhood) in such a march.[21] This question, from the chief executive of New York City's laws, accepts a remarkable degree of possessiveness about public streets—possessiveness, furthermore, that is racially and not geographically bounded. Koch was, in effect, pleading for acceptance of the privatization of public space. This is the de facto equivalent of segregation; it is exclusion in the guise of deep-moated property "interests" and "values." Lost is the fact that the object of discussion, the street, is public.

Furthermore, the structure of Koch's question implies that fourteen hundred black people took to the streets of Howard Beach: in fact it was a well-integrated crowd, blacks, browns, and whites, Howard Beach residents and others. Apparently crowds in New York are subject to the unwritten equivalent of Louisiana's race statutes (1/72 black blood renders the whole black) or of the Ku Klux Klan's "contamination by association" ("blacks and white-blacks" was how one resident of Forsythe County, the Georgia equivalent of Howard Beach, described an interracial crowd of protestors there). If, on the other hand, Koch were directing attention to the inconvenience, the noise, the pollution of that many people in those small streets, then I am sympathetic. At the same time, I have no problem moving past my sympathy as insignificant in proportion to the emotions that provoked such a spontaneous, peaceful outpouring of rage, sorrow, and pain.

If, however, Koch was simply appealing to the "gut," asking blacks to conjure up the vision of fourteen hundred angry white people descending on a black community, then I would have to say that yes, I would be frightened. It would also conjure up visions of fourteen hundred hooded white people burning crosses, or of fourteen hundred Nazis marching through Skokie, or of fourteen hundred cavalry men riding into an American Indian neighborhood—and yes, that vision would inspire great fear in me of their doing grave harm to the residents. But there is a clear difference. It is important to distinguish mass protests of violence from organized hate groups who openly threaten violence. By failing to distinguish at this level, Mayor Koch effectively manipulated into the hearts of many blacks and whites the specter of unspecified mobs, sweeping through one's home in pursuit of vague and diffusely dangerous ends: from this perspective, his was an appeal to thoughtlessness, to the pseudo-consolation of hunkering down and bunkering up against the approach of the hordes, to a view of the unneighborhooded "public" world as glacially overgeneralized.

Finally, the mayor's comments reveal his ignorance of the degree to which black people *have* welcomed, endured, and suffered white people

marching through their streets on one mission or another: white people have always felt free to cruise through black communities; most black neighborhoods have existed only as long as whites have permitted them to; blacks have been this society's perpetual tenants, sharecroppers, lessees. Blacks went from being owned by others to having everything around them owned by others. In a civilization that values private property above all else, this means a devaluation of person, a removal of blacks not just from the market but from the pseudo-spiritual circle of psychic and civic communion. . . . This limbo of disownedness keeps blacks beyond the pale of those who are entitled to receive the survival gifts of commerce, the life, liberty, and happiness whose fruits our culture locates in the marketplace. In this way blacks are analogically positioned exactly as they were during slavery or Jim Crow.[22]

There is also a subtler level to the enactment of this dispossession. Not long ago, when I first moved back to New York after some twenty years, I decided to go on a walking tour of Harlem. The tour, which took place on Easter Sunday, was sponsored by the New York Arts Society and was, with the exception of me, attended exclusively by young white urban-professional real-estate speculators. They were pleasant-faced, with babies strapped to their backs and balloons in their hands, and seemed like very nice people. Halfway through the tour, the guide asked the group if they wanted to "go inside some churches. It'll make the tour a little longer; but we'll probably get to see some services going on . . . Easter Sunday in Harlem is quite a show." A casual discussion ensued about the time it might take.

What astonished me was that no one had asked the churches if they wanted to be stared at like living museums. I wondered what would happen if a group of blue-jeaned blacks were to walk uninvited into a synagogue on Passover or St. Anthony's of Padua during high mass—just to peer, not pray. My feeling is that such activity would be seen as disrespectful, at the very least. Yet the aspect of disrespect, intrusion, seemed irrelevant to this well-educated, affable group of people. They deflected my observation with comments like "We just want to look," "No one will mind," and "There's no harm intended." As well-intentioned as they were, I was left with the impression that no one existed for them who could not be governed by their intentions.[23] While acknowledging the lack of apparent malice in this behavior,[24] I can't help thinking that it is a liability as much as a luxury to live without interaction. To live so completely impervious to one's own impact on others is a fragile privilege, which over time relies not simply on the willingness but on the inability of others—in this case blacks—to make their displeasure heard.

Reflecting on Howard Beach brought to mind a news story, from my fragmentary grammar-school recollections of the 1960s. A black man working for some civil-rights cause was killed by a white man for racially motivated reasons; the man was stabbed thirty-nine times, which prompted a radio commentator to observe that the point was not just murder but something beyond. I wondered for a long time what it was that would not die, what could not be killed by the fourth, fifth, or even tenth knife blow; what sort of thing would not die with the body but lived on in the mind of the murderer. Perhaps, as psychologists have argued, what the murderer was trying to kill was a part of his own mind's image, a part of himself and not a real other. After all, generally, statistically, and corporeally, blacks as a group are poor, powerless, and a minority. It is in the minds of whites that blacks become large, threatening, powerful, uncontrollable, ubiquitous, and supernatural.

There are societies in which the limits of life and death are defined very differently from our own. For example, in Buddhism and Hinduism, death may occur long before the body ceases to function, and life may, in the proper circumstances, continue for a time after the body is carried to its grave. These non-body-bound, uncompartmentalized ideas recognize the power of spirit, or what we in our secularized society might describe as the dynamism of self-as-reinterpreted-by-the-percep-

tions-of-others. These ideas comprehend the fact that a part of ourselves is beyond the control of pure physical will and resides in the sanctuary of those around us; a fundamental part of ourselves and of our dignity depends on the uncontrollable, powerful, external observers who make up a society. Surely a part of socialization ought to include a sense of caring responsibility for the images of others that are reposited within us.

Taking the example of the man who was stabbed thirty-nine times out of the context of our compartmentalized legal system, and considering it in the framework of a legal system that would recognize the moral, religious, or psychological, I am moved to see this act as not merely body murder but as spirit murder. Only one form of spirit murder is racism—cultural obliteration, prostitution, abandonment of the elderly and the homeless, and genocide are some of its other guises. One of the reasons I fear what I call spirit murder—disregard for others whose lives qualitatively depend on our regard—is that it produces a system of formalized distortions of thought. It produces social structures centered on fear and hate, a tumorous outlet for feelings elsewhere unexpressed.[25] When Bernhard Goetz shot four black teenagers in a New York subway, J., an acquaintance of mine, said she could "understand his fear because it's a fact that blacks commit most of the crimes." Actually U.S. Bureau of Justice Statistics for 1986 show that whites were arrested for 71.7 percent of all crimes; blacks and all others (including American Indian, Alaskan Native, Asian, and Pacific Islander) account for the remaining 28 percent. Furthermore, there is evidence that "whites commit more crimes, and that white offenders have consistently lower probabilities of arrest, than do either blacks or Mexican-Americans. This is particularly striking for armed robbery and burglary." But, "Controlling for the factors most likely to influence sentencing and parole decisions, the analysis still found that blacks and Hispanics are less likely to be given probation, more likely to receive prison sentences, more likely to receive longer sentences, and more likely to serve longer time."[26]

What impressed me, beyond the factual inaccuracy of J.'s statement, was the reduction of Goetz's crime to "his fear," which I translate to mean *her* fear; the four teenage victims became all blacks everywhere; and "most of the crimes" clearly meant, in order for the sentence to make sense, that most blacks commit crimes. (Some have taken issue with my interpretation of J.'s remarks. They point out that what she must have meant was that young black men are arrested and convicted for a disproportionate number of the muggings committed in the New York subway system. Looking past the fact that this is not what she said, and that it is precisely the unframed nature of what she *did* say that is the source of my concern, I am left wondering what the real point of such a criticism is: should the assumed specificity of reference therefore give white subway riders a license to kill based on the empiricism of "statistical fear"?)

What struck me, further, was that the general white population seems, in the process of devaluing its image of black people, to have blinded itself to the horrors inflicted by white people. One of the clearest examples of this socialized blindness is the degree to which Goetz's victims were relentlessly bestialized by the public and by the media in New York: images of the urban jungle, with young black men filling the role of "wild animals," were favorite journalistic constructions; young white urban professionals were mythologized, usually wrapped in the linguistic apparel of lambs or sheep, as the tender, toothsome prey. A typical example is the front-page story of the *New York Post* of June 15, 1987, two days before the jury's verdict clearing Goetz of all but illegal gun possession. The article, excoriating the prosecutor's office for even bringing the case, ran under an enormous headline referring to the victims as "predators." The corollary to such imagery is that it is the fate of domesticated white innocents to be slaughtered in meaningless and tragic sacrifice.[27] Locked into such a reification, the meaning of any act by the sheep against the wolves can never be seen as violent in its own right, for it is inherently uncharacteristic, brave, irresistibly and triumphantly parabolic. Thus, when prosecutor Gregory Waples cast Goetz as a "hunter" in his final summation, juror Michael Axelrod said that Waples "was insulting my intelligence. There was nothing to justify that sort of summation. Goetz wasn't a hunter."[28]

Nor do most white people seem to take as crime the dehumanizing cultural images of sterile, mindless white womanhood and expressionless, bored-but-righteous, assembly-line white manhood. (The short stories of Joyce Carol Oates and Raymond Carver often present characters who are prototypes of what I mean by this. They describe people of warmth, compassion, and variety trapped in flat sit-com lives. These people adjust to required expectations, but every now and then the repressed passion flares in sometimes wonderful but more often destructive ways.) I think, though this is hard to prove in any scientific way, that many whites do not expect whites (as compared to blacks) to rape, rob, or kill them (when in fact 54 percent of violent crimes are committed by friends, acquaintances, or relatives of the victims, according to 1987 Bureau of Justice Statistics.) They are surprised when it happens. Perhaps they blind themselves to the warning signals of approaching assault. Some do not even recognize white criminality when it does happen; they apologize for the assailant, think it must have been their fault; they misperceived the other's intent. A tragic example of this is the strangulation death in Central Park of college student Jennifer Levin, the "preppy murder case." If public response is a measure of anything at all, what fueled fascination was the fact that Robert Chambers, the wealthy WASP socialite who killed her, wasn't supposed to be the *type* of person who robbed, raped, or murdered.

To give another example, in the famous videotape Bernhard Goetz described to police in New Hampshire his intention to inflict as much harm as he could. He detailed his wish to see his victims dead; said if he had it to do over again, he'd do the same or worse; and expressed a retrospective desire to have gouged their eyes out. Yet in finding him not guilty of each of twelve counts of attempted murder, assault, and reckless endangerment, the jury discounted this confession entirely: "We felt he said a lot of things he was unsure about. He had nine days of thinking about what happened and reading newspapers, and combined with the guilt, we felt that he may have gotten confused. His own confusion coupled with his feelings of guilt might have forced him to make statements that were not accurate."[29]

This vignette may illustrate better what I mean:

> A lone black man was riding in an elevator in a busy downtown department store. The elevator stopped on the third floor, and a crowd of noisy white high school students got on. The black man took out a gun, shot as many of them as he could, before the doors opened on the first floor and the rest fled for their lives. The black man later explained to the police that he could tell from the "body language" of the students, from their "shiny eyes and big smiles," that they wanted to "play with him, like a cat plays with a mouse." Furthermore, the black man explained, one of the youths had tried to panhandle money from him and another asked him "how are you?"
>
> "That's a meaningless thing," he said in his confession, but "in certain circumstances, that can be a real threat." He added that a similar greeting had preceded the vicious beating of his father, a black civil rights lawyer in Mississippi, some time before. His intention, he confessed, was to murder the high school students.

My guess is that, in reading this tragic account, most white Americans would not hesitate to pronounce the severe contextual misapprehensions of the black gunman as a form of insanity. While degrees of sympathy might vary, I suspect that the consensus would be nearly unanimous that he presents a danger to himself and to others, that he should be institutionalized or imprisoned.

But the above story, with minor character alterations, is excerpted from Goetz's videotaped confession.[30] The public overwhelmingly presumed his innocence. Not only was it not proposed in most accounts that he be institutionalized—it was considered a failure of public institutions not to engage in more such punitive activities. This was reflected most blatantly in the fact that Goetz's defense was not that he was insane but that he acted *reasonably* in the circumstances.[31] It is reflected as well in the degree to which the public devoured, ex post facto, stories about the deviant behavior of the victims in this case. The victims' criminal propensities—allegations ranging from rape to robbery—were used not just to discuss whether deadly force should have been used defensively, but to show why the four young men deserved to be the objects of intent to kill. Imagine, moreover, again in the hypothetical case of the black gunman in the elevator, a public inquiry that focused attention on prior racist statements of the white high-schoolers, on their history of drinking and driving, on how they treated their girlfriends, on whether any of them had ever shoplifted and were only in the department store to do so again. Or imagine what might have happened if the black men in the Howard Beach case, even after the first few beatings, had decided to defend themselves by pulling guns and shooting repeatedly, to kill.

And it is reflected in the way in which Goetz became a cited authority and favorite interviewee on the subject of crime in New York: "Criminals," he declared, must realize that being shot is a "risk they are going to have to take."[32] I can think of no better example of the degree to which criminality has become lodged in a concept of the black "other."

If indeed Americans are subject to such emotional devastation, it is no wonder that the urge to act as victimizer is so irresistible, appears to be the only defensible thing to do—it is the defensive thing to do. It is no wonder that society has created in blacks a class (though not the only class, probably the most visible) of ready-made, prepackaged victims. To discount as much violence as we do must mean that we have a very angry population, suppressing explosive rage. Most white Americans, in urban areas at least, have seen the muttering "lunatic" black person who beats the air with his fists and curses aloud: most people cross the street; they don't choose him to satisfy their need to know the time of day.

Yet for generations, and particularly in the wake of the foaming public response to incidents like Howard Beach, the Goetz shooting, and Forsythe County, that is precisely how white America has looked to many a black American.

There is a doorway on East 13th Street in New York that for months had a huge piece of brown paper taped to it, with the legend "Goetz." It reminded me of the banners hung in windows for the parades of astronauts and other heros. In fact, a parade was all the Goetz hoopla lacked to make it into a proper festive event. After delivering their verdict, "defense attorney Nark Baker said the jurors asked for and received Bernhard Goetz' autograph on their jury certificates."[33] In describing the degree to which subway gunman Bernhard Goetz was made a folk hero, Kenneth Clark has written: "As a society adjusts to, or rewards, its accepted cruelties and continues to deny their consequences, it makes heroes of lawless 'respectables' and in so doing develops a selective form of moral indignation and outrage as a basis for the anomaly of a civilization without a conscience."[34]

For these reasons I think that we need to elevate spirit murder to the conceptual—if not punitive—level of a capital moral offense.[35] We need to see it for the cultural cancer it is, for the spiritual genocide it is wreaking on blacks, in whites, and to the abandoned and abused of all races and ages. We need to eradicate its numbing pathology before it wipes out what precious little humanity we have left. As Timothy Mitchell, pastor of Ebenezer Missionary Baptist Church, observed in 1986: "What happened to Michael Griffith [who was killed in the Howard Beach incident] can happen to any of us . . . The issue is whether we are free to walk around in our city and be seen and accepted and protected as God's children."

NOTES

1. Robert McFadden, "Police Seek New Witnesses to Howard Beach Attack," *New York Times,* January 6, 1987, p. B1.

2. Samuel Freedman, "In Howard Beach, Pride and Fear in a 'Paradise,'" *New York Times,* December 23, 1986, p. B4. Joyce Purnick, "Koch, Seeking Racial Talk, Gets Irate Reception at Queens Church," *New York Times,* December 29, 1986, p. B3.

3. Guy Trebay, "Howard Beach Memoirs," *Village Voice,* January 6, 1987, p. 16.

4. "A 'we-they' analysis . . . justifies a disadvantage that we (the majority) want to impose on ourselves to favor them (the minority). This type of thinking, however, leaves the choice of remedy and the time frame for that remedy in the hands of the majority; it converts affirmative action into a benefit, not a right. It neglects the possibility that the disadvantaged minority may have a moral claim to a particular remedy.

"The inner-circle commentators rarely deal with issues of guilt and reparation. When they do, it is often to attach responsibility in a scapegoat, someone of another time or place, and almost certainly of another social class than that of the writer. These writers tend to focus on intentional and determinable acts of discrimination inflicted on the victim by some perpetrator and ignore the more pervasive and invidious forms of discriminatory conditions inherent in our society. This 'perpetrator' perspective deflects attention from the victim-class, the Blacks, Native Americans, Chicanos, and Puerto Ricans who lead blighted lives for reasons directly traceable to social and institutional injustice." Richard Delgado, "The Imperial Scholar," *University of Pennsylvania Law Review,* 132 (1984), 570–571.

5. Vernon Reid, "Visible Man," *Village Voice,* January 6, 1987, p. 15.

6. "Emphasizing utility or distributive justice as the justification for affirmative action has a number of significant consequences. It enables the writer to concentrate on the present and the future and overlook the past . . . The past becomes irrelevant; one just asks where things are now and where we ought to go from here, a straightforward social-engineering inquiry . . . But . . . it robs affirmative action programs of their moral force in favor of a sterile theory of fairness or utility. No doubt there is a great social utility to affirmative action, but to base it solely on that ground ignores the right of minority communities to be made whole, and the obligation of the majority to render them whole." Delgado, "The Imperial Scholar," p. 570.

7. *New York Times,* December 29, 1986, p. B3.

8. Daniel Berrigan and Thich Nhat Hanh, *The Raft Is Not the Shore* (Boston: Beacon Press, 1975), p. 38.

9. "Who, if not us, will question once more the objective status of this 'I', which a historical evolution peculiar to our culture tends to confuse with the subject? This anomaly should be manifested in its particular effects on every level of language, and first and foremost in the grammatical subject of the first person in our languages, in the 'I love' that hypostatizes the tendency of a subject who denies it. An impossible mirage in linguistic forms among which the most ancient are to be found, and in which the subject appears fundamentally in the position of being determinant or instrumental of action.

"Let us leave aside the critique of all the abuses of the cogito ergo sum, and recall that, in my experience, the ego represents the centre of all the resistances to the treatment of symptoms.

"It was inevitable that analysis, after stressing the reintegration of the tendencies excluded by the ego, in so far as they are subjacent to the symptoms that it tackled in the first instance, and which were bound up for the most part with the failures of Oedipal identification, should eventually discover the 'moral' dimension of the problem." Jacques Lacan, "Agressivity in Psychoanalysis," in *Ecrits: A Selection,* trans. Alan Sheridan (New York: Norton, 1977), pp. 23–24.

10. See generally Phillip Boffey, "Health Experts Fault U.S. on Response to AIDS," *New York Times,* August 13, 1987, p. A20.

11. See generally Kenneth Clark, *Prejudice and Your Child* (Boston: Beacon Press, 1955), and *Dark Ghetto* (New York: Harper and Row, 1965); William Grier and Price Cobb, *Black Rage* (New York: Basic Books, 1968); James Comer and Alvin Poussaint, *Black Child Care* (New York: Simon and Schuster, 1975).

12. See generally Phillip Selznick, "Law, Society and Moral Evolution," in *Readings in Jurisprudence and Legal Philosophy,* ed. Phillip Shuchman (Boston: Little, Brown, 1979), pp. 947–949.

13. See generally Alice Miller, *The Drama of the Gifted Child,* trans. Ruth Ward (New York: Basic Books, 1984).

14. "An example relevant to the development of 'legal reification' can be found in any first grade classroom. It is 8:29 and children are playing, throwing food, and generally engaging in relatively undistorted communication. At 8:30 the teacher . . . calls the class to attention: it is time for the 'pledge of allegiance.' All face front, all suffer the same social rupture and privation, all fix their eyes on a striped piece of cloth. As they drone on, having not the slightest comprehension of the content of what they are saying, they are nonetheless learning the sort of distorted or reified communication that is expressed in the legal form. They are learning, in other words, that they are all abstract 'citizens' of an abstract 'United States of America,' that there exists 'liberty and justice for all,' and so forth—not from the content of the words but from the ritual which forbids any rebellion. Gradually, they will come to accept these abstractions as descriptive of a concrete truth because of the repressive and conspiratorial way that these ideas have been communicated (each senses that all the others 'believe in' the words and therefore they must be true), and once this acceptance occurs, any access to the paradoxically forgotten memory that these are mere abstractions is sealed off. And once the abstractions are reified, they can no longer be criticized because they signify a false concrete." Peter Gabel, "Reification in Legal Reasoning," *Research in Law and Society,* 3(1980), 26–27.

15. *New York Times,* December 29, 1986, p. B3.

16. "Apology on Beach Protest," *New York Times,* January 22, 1987, p. A3.

17. *New York Times,* December 23, 1986, p. B4, col. 6.

18. "Inner rage tends to burn out our connections to the real world. It tends to overwhelm reason and to destroy the faces and beings of others. In our anger we can only see ourselves. The inability to imagine the experience of the stranger, of the other, was exactly what made the Holocaust possible. The Nazi success in dehumanizing their victims has left us with such rage that we too can dehumanize, erase the individual faces of others. We must find a way to let our anger burn freely, openly without consuming or perverting . . . otherwise we remain victims forever." Ann Roiphe, "The Politics of Anger," *Tikkun,* 1(1987), 21–22.

19. "The judge in imposing a sentence normally takes for granted the role structure which might be analogized to the 'transmission' of the engine of justice. The judge's interpretive authorization of the 'proper' sentence can be carried out as a deed only because of these others; a bond between word

and deed abtains only because a system of social cooperation exists. That system guarantees the judge massive mounts of force—the conditions of effective domination—if necessary. It guarantees—or is supposed to—a relatively faithful adherence to the word of the judge in the deeds carried out against the prisoner. . . . If the institutional structure—the system of roles—gives the judge's understanding its effect, thereby transforming understanding into 'law,' so it confers meaning on the deeds which effect this transformation, thereby legitimating them as 'lawful.' A central task of the legal interpreter is to attend to the problematic aspects of the integration of role, deed, and word, not only where the violence (i.e., enforcement) is lacking for meaning, but also where meaning is lacking for violence." Robert Cover, "Violence and the Word," *Yale Law Journal,* 95(1986), 1619, 1629.

20. Robert McFadden, "3 Youths Charged in Racial Attack Ordered Held Without Bail," *New York Times,* December 24, 1986, p. B4.

21. *New York Times,* December 29, 1986, p. B3.

22. It is in understanding the degree to which black buying power is nevertheless a sustaining component in even the most parasitic white economies that reveals the logic behind the controversial boycott of white-owned businesses, called for by some black leaders in the wake of Howard Beach. "The Rev. Calvin O. Butts 3d of the Abyssinian Baptist Church said in one of the interviews: 'We're talking about getting the kind of respect that comes from the power of our vote and our buying power.'" Ronald Smothers, "Racial Violence Focus of Blacks in Day of Protest," *New York Times,* January 22, 1987, p. B3.

23. For an analysis that elevates precisely this thinking to normative principles of "good intentions" in the law, see Larry Simon, "Racially Prejudiced Governmental Actions," *San Diego Law Review,* 15 (1978), 1041.

24. "It is common for racial minorities, especially those who find themselves relatively isolated in predominantly white institutions, to have white colleagues express stereotyped or derogatory views either by way of direct statements or by unstated but implicit assumptions . . . It is obvious to the minority person that the speaker has not intended a racial slight—his tone is friendly and candid—and that he is unaware of the attitudinal source of the inadvertent derogation. And when other whites are present, they are unlikely to hear or be sensitive to the connotations of the demeaning remark." Charles Lawrence, "The Id, the Ego, and Equal Protection: Reckoning with Unconscious Racism," *Stanford Law Review,* 39 (1987), 341n100.

25. "Undoubtedly, something that is not expressed does not exist. But the repressed is always there—it insists, and it demands to come into being. The fundamental relation of man with this symbolic order is precisely the same one which founds this symbolic order itself—the relation of non-being to being." Jacques Lacan, "Sign, Symbol, Imaginary," in *On Signs,* ed. Marshall Blonsky (Baltimore: Johns Hopkins Press, 1985), p. 209.

26. Joan Petersilia, *Racial Disparities in the Criminal Justice System,* prepared for National Institute of Corrections, U.S. Department of Justice (Santa Monica: Rand, June 1983), pp. 44, xxiv.

27. Black attempts to invert this imagery have been logical but largely lost efforts. See generally Floyd Flake, "Blacks Are Fair Game," *New York Times,* June 19, 1987, p. A35.

28. *New York Newsday,* June 17, 1987, p. 5.

29. Ibid., p. 40.

30. "You Have To Think in a Cold-Blooded Way" *New York Times,* April 30, 1987, p. B6.

31. See generally Richard Restak, "The Law: The Fiction of the Reasonable Man," *Washington Post,* May 17, 1987, p. C3; George Fletcher, *Los Angeles Times,* May 17, 1987, part 5, p. 1.

32. "Jury Selection Begins in Trial of Bernhard Goetz," *Los Angeles Times,* March 24, 1987, part 1, p. 4.

33. *New York Newsday,* June 17, 1987, p. 40.

34. Kenneth Clark, "In Cities, Who Is the Real Mugger?" *New York Times,* January 14, 1987, p. 19.

35. See also Richard Delgado, "Words That Wound: A Tort Action for Racial Insults, Epithets and Name-Calling," *Harvard Civil Rights—Civil Liberties Law Review,* 17 (1982), 133.

Play Some Rolling Stones

I left my favorite tavern late on a Friday night. On my way home I stopped to listen to the acoustic reggae of a black street musician. I threw a few dollars into a jar and he asked me what I would like to hear. He spoke with a heavy Jamaican accent and said he could only play reggae. As he began to play my request, several other white males gathered around. As my song ended, a member of the group told the street musician to stop playing that "nigger music" and play some Rolling Stones. The musician replied that he only knew the words to reggae songs. With that, the white male kicked the musician's money jar from his stool, shattering it on the sidewalk. When I objected, the white guy turned on me. Luckily he had spent several hours in the tavern, because his first punch missed its mark. Unfortunately, the other five punches were on target.

At night in the hospital and twenty-two sutures later, I wondered if it was worth it. But when I went back down to the same area the following weekend, the musician thanked me graciously. Then he began to play a classic Rolling Stones song.

Mark Donald Stockenberg

Why Are Droves of Unqualified, Unprepared Kids Getting into Our Top Colleges? Because Their Dads Are Alumni.

John Larew

Growing up, she heard a hundred Harvard stories. In high school, she put the college squarely in her sights. But when judgment day came in the winter of 1988, the Harvard admissions guys were frankly unimpressed. Her academic record was solid—not special. Extracurriculars, interview, recommendations? Above average, but not by

much. "Nothing really stands out," one admissions officer scribbled on her application folder. Wrote another, "Harvard not really the right place."

At the hyperselective Harvard, where high school valedictorians, National Merit Scholarship finalists, musical prodigies—11,000 ambitious kids in all—are rejected annually, this young woman didn't seem to have much of a chance. Thanks to Harvard's largest affirmative action program, she got in anyway. No, she wasn't poor, black, disabled, Hispanic, native American, or even Aleutian. She got in because her mom went to Harvard.

Folk wisdom at Harvard holds that "Mother Harvard does not coddle her young." She sure treats her grandkids right, though. For more than 40 years, an astounding one-fifth of Harvard's students have received admissions preference because their parents attended the school. Today, these overwhelmingly affluent, white children of alumni—"legacies"—are three times more likely to be accepted to Harvard than high school kids who lack that handsome lineage.

Yalies, don't feel smug: Offspring of the Old Blue are two-and-a-half times more likely to be accepted than their unconnected peers. Dartmouth this year admitted 57 percent of its legacy applicants, compared to 27 percent of nonlegacies. At the University of Pennsylvania, 66 percent of legacies were admitted last year—thanks in part to an autonomous "office of alumni admissions" that actively lobbies for alumni children before the admissions committee. "One can argue that it's an accident, but it sure doesn't look like an accident," admits Yale Dean of Admissions Worth David.

If the legacies' big edge seems unfair to the tens of thousands who get turned away every year, Ivy League administrators have long defended the innocence of the legacy stat. Children of alumni are just smarter; they come from privileged backgrounds and tend to grow up in homes where parents encourage learning. That's what Harvard Dean of Admissions William Fitzsimmons told the campus newspaper, the

Harvard Crimson, when it first reported on the legacy preference last year. Departing Harvard President Derek Bok patiently explained that the legacy preference worked only as a "tie-breaking factor" between otherwise equally qualified candidates.

Since Ivy League admissions data is a notoriously classified commodity, when Harvard officials said in previous years that alumni kids were just better, you had to take them at their word. But then federal investigators came along and pried open those top-secret files. The Harvard guys were lying.

This past fall, after two years of study, the U.S. Department of Education's Office for Civil Rights (OCR) found that, far from being more qualified or even equally qualified, the average admitted legacy at Harvard between 1981 and 1988 was significantly *less* qualified than the average admitted nonlegacy. Examining admissions office ratings on academics, extracurriculars, personal qualities, recommendations, and other categories, the OCR concluded that "with the exception of the athletic rating, [admitted] nonlegacies scored better than legacies in *all* areas of comparison."

Exceptionally high admit rates, lowered academic standards, preferential treatment . . . hmmm. These sound like the cries heard in the growing fury over affirmative action for racial minorities in America's elite universities. Only no one is outraged about legacies.

- In his recent book, *Preferential Policies,* Thomas Sowell argues that doling out special treatment encourages lackluster performance by the favored and resentment from the spurned. His far-ranging study flits from Malaysia to South Africa to American college campuses. Legacies don't merit a word.
- Dinesh D'Souza, in his celebrated jeremiad *Illiberal Education,* blames affirmative action in college admissions for declining academic standards and increasing racial tensions. Lowered standards for minority applicants, he hints, may soon destroy the university as we know it.

Lowered standards for legacies? The subject doesn't come up.
- For all his polysyllabic complaints against preferential admissions, William F. Buckley Jr. (Yale '50) has never bothered to note that son Chris (Yale '75) got the benefit of a policy that more than doubled his chance of admission.

With so much silence on the subject, you'd be excused for thinking that in these enlightened times hereditary preferences are few and far between. But you'd be wrong. At most elite universities during the eighties, the legacy was by far the biggest piece of the preferential pie. At Harvard, a legacy is about twice as likely to be admitted as a black or Hispanic student. As sociologists Jerome Karabel and David Karen point out, if alumni children were admitted to Harvard at the same rate as other applicants, their numbers in the class of 1992 would have been reduced by about 200. Instead, those 200 marginally qualified legacies outnumbered all black, Mexican-American, native American, and Puerto Rican enrollees put together. If a few marginally qualified minorities are undermining Harvard's academic standards as much as conservatives charge, think about the damage all those legacies must be doing.

Mind you, colleges have the right to give the occasional preference—to bend the rules for the brilliant oboist or the world-class curler or the guy whose remarkable decency can't be measured by the SAT. (I happened to benefit from a geographical edge: It's easier to get into Harvard from West Virginia than from New England.) And until standardized tests and grade point average perfectly reflect the character, judgment, and drive of a student, tips like these aren't just nice, they're fair. Unfortunately, the extent of the legacy privilege in elite American colleges suggests something more than the occasional tie-breaking tip. Forget meritocracy. When 20 percent of Harvard's student body gets a legacy preference, aristocracy is the word that comes to mind.

A CASTE OF THOUSANDS

If complaining about minority preferences is fashionable in the world of competitive colleges, bitching about legacies is just plain gauche, suggesting an unhealthy resentment of the privileged. But the effects of the legacy trickle down. For every legacy that wins, someone—usually someone less privileged—loses. And higher education is a high-stakes game.

High school graduates earn 59 percent of the income of four-year college graduates. Between high school graduates and alumni of prestigious colleges, the disparity is far greater. A *Fortune* study of American CEOs shows the usual suspects—graduates of Yale, Princeton, and Harvard—leading the list. A recent survey of the Harvard Class of 1940 found that 43 percent were worth more than $1 million. With some understatement, the report concludes, "A picture of highly advantageous circumstances emerges here, does it not, compared with American society as a whole?"

An Ivy League diploma doesn't necessarily mean a fine education. Nor does it guarantee future success. What it *does* represent is a big head start in the rat race—a fact Harvard will be the first to tell you. When I was a freshman, a counselor at the Office of Career Services instructed a group of us to make the Harvard name stand out on our resumes: "Underline it, boldface it, put it in capital letters."

Of course, the existence of the legacy preference in this fierce career competition isn't exactly news. According to historians, it was a direct result of the influx of Jews into the Ivy League during the twenties. Until then, Harvard, Princeton, and Yale had admitted anyone who could pass their entrance exams, but suddenly Jewish kids were outscoring the WASPs. So the schools began to use nonacademic criteria—"character," "solidity," and, eventually, lineage—to justify accepting low-scoring blue bloods over their peers. Yale implemented its legacy preference first, in 1925—spelling it out in a memo four years later: The school would admit "Yale sons of

good character and reasonably good record . . . regardless of the number of applicants and the superiority of outside competitors." Harvard and Princeton followed shortly thereafter.

Despite its ignoble origins, the legacy preference has only sporadically come under fire, most notably in 1978's affirmative action decision, *University of California Board of Regents v. Bakke.* In his concurrence, Justice Harry Blackmun observed, "It is somewhat ironic to have us so deeply disturbed over a program where race is an element of consciousness, and yet to be aware of the fact, as we are, that institutions of higher learning . . . have given conceded preferences to the children of alumni."

If people are, in fact, aware of the legacy preference, why has it been spared the scrutiny given other preferential policies? One reason is public ignorance of the scope and scale of those preferences—an ignorance carefully cultivated by America's elite institutions. It's easy to maintain the fiction that your legacies get in strictly on merit as long as your admissions bureaucracy controls all access to student data. Information on Harvard's legacies became publicly available not because of any fit of disclosure by the university, but because a few civil rights types noted that the school had a suspiciously low rate of admission for Asian-Americans, who are statistically stronger than other racial groups in academics.

While the ensuing OCR inquiry found no evidence of illegal racial discrimination by Harvard, it did turn up some embarrassing information about how much weight the "legacy" label gives an otherwise flimsy file. Take these comments scrawled by admissions officers on applicant folders:

- "Double lineage who chose the right parents."
- "Dad's [deleted] connections signify lineage of more than usual weight. That counted into the equation makes this a case which (assuming positive TRs [teacher recommendations] and Alum IV [alumnus interview]) is well worth doing."
- "Lineage is main thing."

- "Not quite strong enough to get the clean tip."
- "Classical case that would be hard to explain to dad."
- "Double lineage but lots of problems."
- "Not a great profile, but just strong enough #'s and grades to get the tip from lineage."
- "Without lineage, there would be little case. With it, we'll keep looking."

In every one of these cases, the applicant was admitted.

Of course, Harvard's not doing anything other schools aren't. The practice of playing favorites with alumni children is nearly universal among private colleges and isn't unheard of at public institutions, either. The rate of admission for Stanford's alumni children is "almost twice the general population," according to a spokesman for the admissions office. Notre Dame reserves 25 percent of each freshman class for legacies. At the University of Virginia, where native Virginians make up two-thirds of each class, alumni children are automatically treated as Virginians even if they live out of state—giving them a whopping competitive edge. The same is true of the University of California at Berkeley. At many schools, Harvard included, all legacy applications are guaranteed a read by the dean of admissions himself—a privilege nonlegacies don't get.

LITTLE WHITE ELIS

Like the Harvard deans, officials at other universities dismiss the statistical disparities by pointing to the superior environmental influences found in the homes of their alums. "I bet that, statistically, [legacy qualifications are] a little above average, but not by much," says Paul Killebrew, associate director of admissions at Dartmouth. "The admitted group [of legacies] would look exactly like the profile of the class."

James Wickenden, a former dean of admissions at Princeton who now runs a college consulting firm, suspects otherwise. Wickenden wrote of "one Ivy League university" where the average combined SAT score of the freshman class was 1,350 out of a possible 1,600, compared to 1,280 for legacies. "At most selective schools, [legacy status] doubles, even trebles the chances of admission," he says. Many colleges even place admitted legacies in a special "Not in Profile" file (along with recruited athletes and some minority students), so that when the school's SAT scores are published, alumni kids won't pull down the average.

How do those kids fare once they're enrolled? No one's telling. Harvard, for one, refuses to keep any records of how alumni children stack up academically against their nonlegacy classmates—perhaps because the last such study, in 1956, showed Harvard sons hogging the bottom of the grade curve.

If the test scores of admitted legacies are a mystery, the reason colleges accept so many is not. They're afraid the alumni parents of rejected children will stop giving to the colleges' unending fundraising campaigns. "Our survival as an institution depends on having support from alumni," says Richard Steele, director of undergraduate admissions at Duke University, "so according advantages to alumni kids is just a given."

In fact, the OCR exonerated Harvard's legacy preference precisely because legacies bring in money. (OCR cited a federal district court ruling that a state university could favor the children of out-of-state alumni because "defendants showed that the alumni provide monetary support for the university.") And there's no question that alumni provide significant support to Harvard: Last year, they raised $20 million for the scholarship fund alone.

In a letter to OCR defending his legacies, Harvard's Fitzsimmons painted a grim picture of a school where the preference did not exist— a place peeved alumni turned their backs on when their kids failed to make the cut. "Without the fundraising activities of alumni," Fitzsimmons warned darkly, "Harvard could not maintain many of its programs, including needs-blind admissions."

Ignoring, for the moment, the question of how "needs-blind" a system is that admits one-fifth of each class on the assumption that, hey, their parents might give us money, Fitzsimmons's defense doesn't quite ring true. The "Save the Scholarship Fund" line is a variation on the principle of "Firemen First," whereby bureaucrats threatened with a budget cut insist that essential programs rather than executive perks and junkets will be the first to be slashed. Truth be told, there is just about nothing that Harvard, the richest university in the world, could do to jeopardize needs-blind admissions, provided that it placed a high enough priority on them.

But even more unclear is how closely alumni giving is related to the acceptance of alumni kids. "People whose children are denied admission are initially upset," says Wickenden, "and maybe for a year or two their interest in the university wanes. But typically they come back around when they see that what happened was best for the kids." Wickenden has put his money where his mouth is: He rejected two sons of a Princeton trustee involved in a $420 million fundraising project, not to mention the child of a board member who managed the school's $2 billion endowment, all with no apparent ill effect.

Most university administrators would be loathe to take such a chance, despite a surprising lack of evidence of the legacy/largess connection. Fitzsimmons admits Harvard knows of no empirical research to support the claim that diminishing legacies would decrease alumni contributions, relying instead on "hundreds, perhaps thousands of conversations with alumni whose sons and daughters applied."

No doubt some of Fitzsimmons's anxiety is founded: It's only natural for alumni to want their kids to have the same privileges they did. But the historical record suggests that alumni are far more tolerant than administrators realize. Admit women and blacks? *Well, we would,* said administrators earlier this century—*but the alumni just won't have it.* Fortunately for American universities, the bulk of those alumni turned out to be less craven than administrators thought they'd be. As more blacks and women enrolled over the past two decades, the funds kept pouring in, reaching an all-time high in the eighties.

Another significant historical lesson can be drawn from the late fifties, when Harvard's selectiveness increased dramatically. As the number of applications soared, the rate of admission for legacies began declining from about 90 percent to its current 43 percent. Administration anxiety rose inversely, but Harvard's fundraising machine has somehow survived. That doesn't mean there's *no* correlation between alumni giving and the legacy preference, obviously; rather, it means that the people who would withhold their money at the loss of the legacy privilege were far outnumbered by other givers. "It takes time to get the message out," explains Fitzsimmons, "but eventually people start responding. We've had to make the case [for democratization] to alumni, and I think that they generally feel good about that."

HEIR CUT

When justice dictates that ordinary kids should have as fair a shot as the children of America's elite, couldn't Harvard and its sister institutions trouble themselves to "get the message out" again? Of course they could. But virtually no one —liberal or conservative—is pushing them to do so.

"There must be no goals or quotas for any special group or category of applicants," reads an advertisement in the right-wing *Dartmouth Review.* "Equal opportunity must be the guiding policy. Males, females, blacks, whites, Native Americans, Hispanics . . . can all be given equal chance to matriculate, survive, and prosper based solely on individual performance."

Noble sentiments from the Ernest Martin Hopkins Institute, an organization of conservative Dartmouth alumni. Reading on, though, we find these "concerned alumni" aren't sacrificing *their* young to the cause. "Alumni sons and daughters," notes the ad further down, "should receive some special consideration."

Similarly, Harvard's conservative *Salient* has twice in recent years decried the treatment of Asian-Americans in admissions, but it attributes their misfortune to favoritism for blacks and Hispanics. What about legacy university favoritism—a much bigger factor? *Salient* writers have twice endorsed it.

What's most surprising is the indifference of minority activists. With the notable exception of a few vocal Asian-Americans, most have made peace with the preference for well-off whites.

Mecca Nelson, the president of Harvard's Black Students Association, leads rallies for the hiring of more minority faculty. She participated in an illegal sit-in at an administration building in support of Afro-American studies. But when it comes to the policy that Asian-American activist Arthur Hu calls "a 20-percent-white quota," Nelson says, "I don't have any really strong opinions about it. I'm not very clear on the whole legacy issue at all."

Joshua Li, former co-chair of Harvard's Asian-American Association, explains his complacency differently: "We understand that in the future Asian-American students will receive these tips as well."

At America's elite universities, you'd expect a somewhat higher standard of fairness than that—especially when money is the driving force behind the concept. And many Ivy League types *do* advocate for more just and lofty ideals. One of them, as it happens, is Derek Bok. In one of Harvard's annual reports, he warned that the modern university is slowly turning from a truth-seeking enterprise into a money-grubbing corporation—at the expense of the loyalty of its alums. "Such an institution may still evoke pride and respect because of its intellectual achievements," he said rightly. "But the feelings it engenders will not be quite the same as those produced by an institution that is prepared to forgo income, if need be, to preserve values of a nobler kind."

Forgo income to preserve values of a nobler kind—it's an excellent idea. Embrace the preferences for the poor and disadvantaged. Wean alumni from the idea of the legacy edge. And

above all, stop the hypocrisy that begrudges the great unwashed a place at Harvard while happily making room for the less qualified sons and daughters of alums.

After 70 years, it won't be easy to wrest the legacy preference away from the alums. But the long-term payoff is as much a matter of message as money. When the sons and daughters of today's college kids fill out *their* applications, the legacy preference should seem not a birthright, but a long-gone relic from the Ivy League's inequitable past.

READING 19

Toward a New Vision: Race, Class, and Gender as Categories of Analysis and Connection

Patricia Hill Collins

The true focus of revolutionary change is never merely the oppressive situations which we seek to escape, but that piece of the oppressor which is planted deep within each of us.
—*Audre Lorde,* Sister Outsider, *123*

Audre Lorde's statement raises a troublesome issue for scholars and activists working for social change. While many of us have little difficulty assessing our own victimization within some major system of oppression, whether it be by race, social class, religion, sexual orientation, ethnicity, age or gender, we typically fail to see how our thoughts and actions uphold someone else's subordination. Thus, white feminists routinely point with confidence to their oppression as women but resist seeing how much their white skin privileges them. African-Americans who possess eloquent analyses of racism often persist in viewing poor White women as symbols of white power. The radical left fares little better. "If only people of color and women could see their true class interests," they argue, "class solidarity would eliminate racism and sexism." In essence, each group identifies the type of oppression with which it feels most comfortable as being fundamental and classifies all other types as being of lesser importance.

Oppression is full of such contradictions. Errors in political judgment that we make concerning how we teach our courses, what we tell our children, and which organizations are worthy of our time, talents and financial support flow smoothly from errors in theoretical analysis about the nature of oppression and activism. Once we realize that there are few pure victims or oppressors, and that each one of us derives varying amounts of penalty and privilege from the multiple systems of oppression that frame our lives, then we will be in a position to see the need for new ways of thought and action.

To get at that "piece of the oppressor which is planted deep within each of us," we need at least two things. First, we need new visions of what oppression is, new categories of analysis that are inclusive of race, class, and gender as distinctive yet interlocking structures of oppression. Adhering to a stance of comparing and ranking oppressions—the proverbial, "I'm more oppressed than you"—locks us all into a dangerous dance of competing for attention, resources, and theoretical supremacy. Instead, I suggest that we examine our different experiences within the more fundamental relationship of damnation and subordination. To focus on the particular arrangements that race or class or gender take in our time and place without seeing these structures as sometimes parallel and sometimes interlocking dimensions of the more fundamental relationship of domination and subordination may temporarily ease our consciences. But while such thinking may lead to short term social reforms, it is simply inadequate for the task of bringing about long term social transformation.

While race, class and gender as categories of analysis are essential in helping us understand the structural bases of domination and subordination,

new ways of thinking that are not accompanied by new ways of acting offer incomplete prospects for change. To get at that "piece of the oppressor which is planted deep within each of us," we also need to change our daily behavior. Currently, we are all enmeshed in a complex web of problematic relationships that grant our mirror images full human subjectivity while stereotyping and objectifying those most different than ourselves. We often assume that the people we work with, teach, send our children to school with, and sit next to . . . will act and feel in prescribed ways because they belong to given race, social class or gender categories. These judgments by category must be replaced with fully human relationships that transcend the legitimate differences created by race, class and gender as categories of analysis. We require new categories of connection, new visions of what our relationships with one another can be. . . .

[This discussion] addresses this need for new patterns of thought and action. I focus on two basic questions. First, how can we reconceptualize race, class and gender as categories of analysis? Second, how can we transcend the barriers created by our experiences with race, class and gender oppression in order to build the types of coalitions essential for social exchange? To address these question I contend that we must acquire both new theories of how race, class and gender have shaped the experiences not just of women of color, but of all groups. Moreover, we must see the connections between these categories of analysis and the personal issues in our everyday lives, particularly our scholarship, our teaching and our relationships with our colleagues and students. As Audre Lorde points out, change starts with self, and relationships that we have with those around us must always be the primary site for social change.

How Can We Reconceptualize Race, Class and Gender as Categories of *Analysis*?

To me, we must shift our discourse away from additive analyses of oppression (Spelman 1982;

Collins 1989). Such approaches are typically based on two key premises. First, they depend on either/or, dichotomous thinking. Persons, things and ideas are conceptualized in terms of their opposites. For example, Black/White, man/woman, thought/feeling, and fact/opinion are defined in oppositional terms. Thought and feeling are not seen as two different and interconnected ways of approaching truth that can coexist in scholarship and teaching. Instead, feeling is defined as antithetical to reason, as its opposite. In spite of the fact that we all have "both/and" identities, (I am both a college professor and a mother—I don't stop being a mother when I drop my child off at school, or forget everything I learned while scrubbing the toilet), we persist in trying to classify each other in either/or categories. I live each day as an African-American woman—a race/gender specific experience. And I am not alone. Everyone has a race/gender/class specific identity. Either/or, dichotomous thinking is especially troublesome when applied to theories of oppression because every individual must be classified as being either oppressed or not oppressed. The both/and position of simultaneously being oppressed and oppressor becomes conceptually impossible.

A second premise of additive analyses of oppression is that these dichotomous differences must be ranked. One side of the dichotomy is typically labeled dominant and the other subordinate. Thus, Whites rule Blacks, men are deemed superior to women, and reason is seen as being preferable to emotion. Applying this premise to discussions of oppression leads to the assumption that oppression can be quantified, and that some groups are oppressed more than others. I am frequently asked, "Which has been most oppressive to you, your status as a Black person or your status as a woman?" What I am really being asked to do is divide myself into little boxes and rank my various statuses. If I experience oppression as a both/and phenomenon, why should I analyze it any differently?

Additive analyses of oppression rest squarely on the twin pillars of either/or thinking and the necessity to quantify and rank all relationships in order to know where one stands. Such approaches typically see African-American women as being more oppressed than everyone else because the majority of Black women experience the negative effects of race, class and gender oppression simultaneously. In essence, if you add together separate oppressions, you are left with a grand oppression greater than the sum of its parts.

I am not denying that specific groups experience oppression more harshly than others—lynching is certainly objectively worse than being held up as a sex object. But we must be careful not to confuse this issue of the saliency of one type of oppression in people's lives with a theoretical stance positing the interlocking nature of oppression. Race, class and gender may all structure a situation but may not be equally visible and/or important in people's self-definitions. In certain contexts, such as the antebellum American South and contemporary South America, racial oppression is more visibly salient, while in other contexts, such as Haiti, El Salvador and Nicaragua, social class oppression may be more apparent. For middle class White women, gender may assume experiential primacy unavailable to poor Hispanic women struggling with the ongoing issues of low paid jobs and the frustrations of the welfare bureaucracy. This recognition that one category may have salience over another for a given time and place does not minimize the theoretical importance of assuming that race, class and gender as categories of analysis structure all relationships.

In order to move toward new visions of what oppression is, I think that we need to ask new questions. How are relationships of domination and subordination structured and maintained in the American political economy? How do race, class and gender function as parallel and interlocking systems that shape this basic relationship of domination and subordination? Questions such as these promise to move us away from futile theoretical struggles concerned with ranking oppressions and towards analyses that assume race, class and gender are all present in any given setting, even if one appears more visible and salient than the others. Our task becomes redefined as one of reconceptualizing oppression by uncovering the connections among race, class and gender as categories of analysis.

1. INSTITUTIONAL DIMENSION OF OPPRESSION

Sandra Harding's contention that gender oppression is structured along three main dimensions —the institutional, the symbolic, and the individual—offers a useful model for a more comprehensive analysis encompassing race, class and gender oppression (Harding 1989). Systemic relationships of domination and subordination structured through social institutions such as schools, businesses, hospitals, the work place, and government agencies represent the institutional dimension of oppression. Racism, sexism and elitism all have concrete institutional locations. Even though the workings of the institutional dimension of oppression are often obscured with ideologies claiming equality of opportunity, in actuality, race, class and gender place Asian-American women, Native American men, White men, African-American women, and other groups in distinct institutional niches with varying degrees of penalty and privilege.

Even though I realize that many . . . would not share this assumption, let us assume that the institutions of American society discriminate, whether by design or by accident. While many of us are familiar with how race, gender and class operate separately to structure inequality, I want to focus on how these three systems interlock in structuring the institutional dimension of oppression. To get at the interlocking nature of race, class and gender, I want you to think about the antebellum plantation as a guiding metaphor for a variety of American social institutions. Even though slavery is typically analyzed as a racist institution, and occasionally as a class institution, I suggest that slavery was a race, class, gender specific institution. Removing any one piece from our analysis diminishes our understanding of the true nature of relations of domination and subordination under slavery.

Slavery was a profoundly patriarchal institution. It rested on the dual tenets of White male authority and White male property, a joining of the political and the economic within the institution of the family. Heterosexism was assumed and all Whites were expected to marry. Control over affluent White women's sexuality remained key to slavery's survival because property was to be passed on to the legitimate heirs of the slave owner. Ensuring affluent White women's virginity and chastity was deeply intertwined with maintenance of property relations.

Under slavery, we see varying levels of institutional protection given to affluent White women, working class and poor White women, and enslaved African women. Poor White women enjoyed few of the protections held out to their upper class sisters. Moreover, the devalued status of Black women was key in keeping all White women in their assigned places. Controlling Black women's fertility was also key to the continuation of slavery, for children born to slave mothers themselves were slaves.

African-American women shared the devalued status of chattel with their husbands, fathers and sons. Racism stripped Blacks as a group of legal rights, education, and control over their own persons. African-Americans could be whipped, branded, sold, or killed, not because they were poor, or because they were women, but because they were Black. Racism ensured that Blacks would continue to serve Whites and suffer economic exploitation at the hands of all Whites.

So we have a very interesting chain of command on the plantation—the affluent White master as the reigning patriarch, his White wife helpmate to serve him, help him manage his property and bring up his heirs, his faithful servants whose production and reproduction were tied to the requirements of the capitalist political economy, and largely propertyless, working class White men and women watching from afar. In essence, the foundations for the contemporary roles of elite White women, poor Black women, working class White men, and a series of other groups can be seen in stark relief in this fundamental American social institution. While Blacks experienced the most harsh treatment under slavery, and thus made slavery clearly visible as a racist institution, race, class and gender interlocked in structuring slavery's systemic organization of domination and subordination.

Even today, the plantation remains a compelling metaphor for institutional oppression. Certainly the actual conditions of oppression are not as severe now as they were then. To argue, as some do, that things have not changed all that much denigrates the achievements of those who struggled for social change before us. But the basic relationships among Black men, Black women, elite White women, elite White men, working class White men and working class White women as groups remain essentially intact.

A brief analysis of key American social institutions most controlled by elite White men should convince us of the interlocking nature of race, class and gender in structuring the institutional dimension of oppression. For example, if you are from an American college or university, is your campus a modern plantation? Who controls your university's political economy? Are elite White men over represented among the upper administrators and trustees controlling your university's finances and policies? Are elite White men being joined by growing numbers of elite White women helpmates? What kinds of people are in your classrooms grooming the next generation who will occupy these and other decision-making positions? Who are the support staff that produce the mass mailings, order the supplies, fix the leaky pipes? Do African-Americans, Hispanics or other people of color form the majority of the invisible workers who feed you, wash your dishes, and clean up your offices and libraries after everyone else has gone home?

If your college is anything like mine, you know the answers to these questions. You may be affiliated with an institution that has Hispanic women as vice-presidents for finance, or substantial numbers of Black men among the faculty. If so, you are fortunate. Much more typical are colleges where a modified version of the plantation as a metaphor for the institutional dimension of oppression survives.

2. THE SYMBOLIC DIMENSION OF OPPRESSION

Widespread, societally-sanctioned ideologies used to justify relations of domination and subordination comprise the symbolic dimension of oppression. Central to this process is the use of stereotypical or controlling images of diverse race, class and gender groups. In order to assess the power of this dimension of oppression, I want you to make a list, either on paper or in your head, of "masculine" and "feminine" characteristics. If your list is anything like that compiled by most people, it reflects some variation of the following:

Masculine	Feminine
aggressive	passive
leader	follower
rational	emotional
strong	weak
intellectual	physical

Not only does this list reflect either/or dichotomous thinking and the need to rank both sides of the dichotomy, but ask yourself exactly which men and women you had in mind when compiling these characteristics. This list applies almost exclusively to middle class White men and women. The allegedly "masculine" qualities that you probably listed are only acceptable when exhibited by elite White men, or when used by Black and Hispanic men against each other or against women of color. Aggressive Black and Hispanic men are seen as dangerous, not powerful, and are often penalized when they exhibit any of the allegedly "masculine" characteristics. Working class and poor White men fare slightly better and are also denied the allegedly "masculine" symbols of leadership, intellectual competence, and human rationality. Women of color and working class and poor White women are also not represented on this list, for they have never had the luxury of being "ladies." What appear to be universal categories representing all men and women instead are unmasked as being applicable to only a small group.

It is important to see how the symbolic images applied to different race, class and gender groups interact in maintaining systems of domination and subordination. If I were to ask you to repeat the same assignment, only this time, by making separate lists for Black men, Black women, Hispanic women and Hispanic men, I suspect that your gender symbolism would be quite different. In comparing all of the lists, you might begin to see the interdependence of symbols applied to all groups. For example, the elevated images of White womanhood need devalued images of Black womanhood in order to maintain credibility.

While the above exercise reveals the interlocking nature of race, class and gender in structuring the symbolic dimension of oppression, part of its importance lies in demonstrating how race, class and gender pervade a wide range of what appears to be universal language. Attending to diversity in our scholarship, in our teaching, and in our daily lives provides a new angle of vision on interpretations of reality thought to be natural, normal and "true." Moreover, viewing images of masculinity and femininity as universal gender symbolism, rather than as symbolic images that are race, class and gender specific, renders the experiences of people of color and of non-privileged White women and men invisible. One way to dehumanize an individual or a group is to deny the reality of their experiences. So when we refuse to deal with race or class because they do not appear to be directly relevant to gender, we are actually becoming part of some one else's problem.

Assuming that everyone is affected differently by the same interlocking set of symbolic images allows us to move forward toward new analyses. Women of color and White women have different relationships to White male authority and this difference explains the distinct gender symbolism

applied to both groups. Black women encounter controlling images such as the mammy, the matriarch, the mule and the whore, that encourage others to reject us as fully human people. Ironically, the negative nature of these images simultaneously encourages us to reject them. In contrast, White women are offered seductive images, those that promise to reward them for supporting the status quo. And yet seductive images can be equally controlling. Consider, for example, the views of Nancy White, a 73-year old Black woman, concerning images of rejection and seduction:

> My mother used to say that the black woman is the white man's mule and the white woman is his dog. Now, she said that to say this: we do the heavy work and get beat whether we do it well or not. But the white woman is closer to the master and he pats them on the head and lets them sleep in the house, but he ain't gon' treat neither one like he was dealing with a person. (Gwaltney, 148)

Both sets of images stimulate particular political stances. By broadening the analysis beyond the confines of race, we can see the varying levels of rejection and seduction available to each of us due to our race, class and gender identity. Each of us lives with an allotted portion of institutional privilege and penalty, and with varying levels of rejection and seduction inherent in the symbolic images applied to us. This is the context in which we make our choices. Taken together, the institutional and symbolic dimensions of oppression create a structural backdrop against which all of us live our lives.

3. THE INDIVIDUAL DIMENSION OF OPPRESSION

Whether we benefit or not, we all live within institutions that reproduce race, class and gender oppression. Even if we never have any contact with members of other race, class and gender groups, we all encounter images of these groups and are exposed to the symbolic meanings attached to those images. On this dimension of oppression, our individual biographies vary tremendously. As a result of our institutional and symbolic statuses, all of our choices become political acts.

Each of us must come to terms with the multiple ways in which race, class and gender as categories of analysis frame our individual biographies. I have lived my entire life as an African-American woman from a working class family and this basic fact has had a profound impact on my personal biography. Imagine how different your life might be if you had been born Black, or White, or poor, or of a different race/class/gender group than the one with which you are most familiar. The institutional treatment you would have received and the symbolic meanings attached to your very existence might differ dramatically from what you now consider to be natural, normal and part of everyday life. You might be the same, but your personal biography might have been quite different.

I believe that each of us carries around the cumulative effect of our lives within multiple structures of oppression. If you want to see how much you have been affected by this whole thing, I ask you one simple question—who are your close friends? Who are the people with whom you can share your hopes, dreams, vulnerabilities, fears and victories? Do they look like you? If they are all the same, circumstance may be the cause. For the first seven years of my life I saw only low income Black people. My friends from those years reflected the composition of my community. But now that I am an adult, can the defense of circumstance explain the patterns of people that I trust as my friends and colleagues? When given other alternatives, if my friends and colleagues reflect the homogeneity of one race, class and gender group, then these categories of analysis have indeed become barriers to connection.

I am not suggesting that people are doomed to follow the paths laid out for them by race, class and gender as categories of analysis. While these three structures certainly frame my opportunity structure, I as an individual always have the choice of accepting things as they are, or trying to change them. As Nikki Giovanni points out, "we've got to live in the real world. If we don't

like the world we're living in, change it. And if we can't change it, we change ourselves. We can do something" (Tate 1983, 68). While a piece of the oppressor may be planted deep within each of us, we each have the choice of accepting that piece or challenging it as part of the "true focus of revolutionary change."

How can we transcend the barriers created by our experiences with race, class and gender oppression in order to build the types of coalitions essential for social change?

Reconceptualizing oppression and seeing the barriers created by race, class and gender as interlocking categories of analysis is a vital first step. But we must transcend these barriers by moving toward race, class and gender as categories of connection, by building relationships and coalitions that will bring about social change. What are some of the issues involved in doing this?

1. DIFFERENCES IN POWER AND PRIVILEGE

First, we must recognize that our differing experiences with oppression create problems in the relationships among us. Each of us lives within a system that vests us with varying levels of power and privilege. These differences in power, whether structured along axes of race, class, gender, age or sexual orientation, frame our relationships. African-American writer June Jordan describes her discomfort on a Caribbean vacation with Olive, the Black woman who cleaned her room:

> . . . even though both "Olive" and "I" live inside a conflict neither one of us created, and even though both of us therefore hurt inside that conflict, I may be one of the monsters she needs to eliminate from her universe and, in a sense, she may be one of the monsters in mine (1985, 47).

Differences in power constrain our ability to connect with one another even when we think we are engaged in dialogue across differences. Let me give you an example. One year, the students in my course "Sociology of the Black Community" got into a heated discussion about the reasons for the upsurge of racial incidents on college campuses. Black students complained vehemently about the apathy and resistance they felt most White students expressed about examining their own racism. Mark, a White male student, found their comments particularly unsettling. After claiming that all the Black people he had ever known had expressed no such beliefs to him, he questioned how representative the view points of his fellow students actually were. When pushed further, Mark revealed that he had participated in conversations over the years with the Black domestic worker employed by his family. Since she had never expressed such strong feelings about White racism, Mark was genuinely shocked by class discussions. Ask yourselves whether that domestic worker was in a position to speak freely. Would it have been wise for her to do so in a situation where the power between the two parties was so unequal?

In extreme cases, members of privileged groups can erase the very presence of the less privileged. When I first moved to Cincinnati, my family and I went on a picnic at a local park. Picnicking next to us was a family of White Appalachians. When I went to push my daughter on the swings, several of the children came over. They had missing, yellowed and broken teeth, they wore old clothing and their poverty was evident. I was shocked. Growing up in a large eastern city, I had never seen such awful poverty among Whites. The segregated neighborhoods in which I grew up made White poverty all but invisible. More importantly, the privileges attached to my newly acquired social class position allowed me to ignore and minimize the poverty among Whites that I did encounter. My reactions to those children made me realize how confining phrases such as "well, at least they're not Black," had become for me. In learning to grant human subjectivity to the Black victims of poverty, I had simultaneously learned to demand White victims of poverty. By applying categories of race to the objective conditions confronting me, I was quantifying and ranking oppressions and

missing the very real suffering which, in fact, is the real issue.

One common pattern of relationships across differences in power is one that I label "voyeurism." From the perspective of the privileged, the lives of people of color, of the poor, and of women are interesting for their entertainment value. The privileged become voyeurs, passive onlookers who do not relate to the less powerful, but who are interested in seeing how the "different" live. Over the years, I have heard numerous African-American students complain about professors who never call on them except when a so-called Black issue is being discussed. The students' interest in discussing race or qualifications for doing so appear unimportant to the professor's efforts to use Black students' experiences as stories to make the material come alive for the White student audience. Asking Black students to perform on cue and provide a Black experience for their White classmates can be seen as voyeurism at its worst.

Members of subordinate groups do not willingly participate in such exchanges but often do so because members of dominant groups control the institutional and symbolic apparatuses of oppression. Racial/ethnic groups, women, and the poor have never had the luxury of being voyeurs of the lives of the privileged. Our ability to survive in hostile settings has hinged on our ability to learn intricate details about the behavior and world view of the powerful and adjust our behavior accordingly. I need only point to the difference in perception of those men and women in abusive relationships. Where men can view their girlfriends and wives as sex objects, helpmates and a collection of stereotypes categories of voyeurism—women must be attuned to every nuance of their partners' behavior. Are women "naturally" better in relating to people with more power than themselves, or have circumstances mandated that men and women develop different skills? . . .

Coming from a tradition where most relationships across difference are squarely rooted in relations of domination and subordination, we have much less experience relating to people as different but equal. The classroom is potentially one powerful and safe space where dialogues among individuals of unequal power relationships can occur. The relationship between Mark, the student in my class, and the domestic worker is typical of a whole series of relationships that people have when they relate across differences in power and privilege. The relationship among Mark and his classmates represents the power of the classroom to minimize those differences so that people of different levels of power can use race, class and gender as categories of analysis in order to generate meaningful dialogues. In this case, the classroom equalized racial difference so that Black students who normally felt silenced spoke out. White students like Mark, generally unaware of how they had been privileged by their whiteness, lost that privilege in the classroom and thus became open to genuine dialogue. . . .

2. COALITIONS AROUND COMMON CAUSES

A second issue in building relationships and coalitions essential for social change concerns knowing the real reasons for coalition. Just what brings people together? One powerful catalyst fostering group solidarity is the presence of a common enemy. African-American, Hispanic, Asian-American, and women's studies all share the common intellectual heritage of challenging what passes for certified knowledge in the academy. But politically expedient relationships and coalitions like these are fragile because, as June Jordan points out:

> It occurs to me that much organizational grief could be avoided if people understood that partnership in misery does not necessarily provide for partnership for change: When we get the monsters off our backs all of us may want to run in very different directions (1985, 47).

Sharing a common cause assists individuals and groups in maintaining relationships that transcend their differences. Building effective coalitions involves struggling to hear one another and developing empathy for each other's points of view. The coalitions that I have been involved in that lasted and that worked have been those where commitment to a specific issue mandated collaboration as the best strategy for addressing the issue at hand.

Several years ago, masters degree in hand, I chose to teach in an inner city, parochial school in danger of closing. The money was awful, the conditions were poor, but the need was great. In my job, I had to work with a range of individuals who, on the surface, had very little in common. We had White nuns, Black middle class graduate students, Blacks from the "community," some of whom had been incarcerated and/or were affiliated with a range of federal anti-poverty programs. Parents formed another part of this community, Harvard faculty another, and a few well-meaning White liberals from Colorado were sprinkled in for good measure.

As you might imagine, tension was high. Initially, our differences seemed insurmountable. But as time passed, we found a common bond that we each brought to the school. In spite of profound differences in our personal biographies, differences that in other settings would have hampered our ability to relate to one another, we found that we were all deeply committed to the education of Black children. By learning to value each other's commitment and by recognizing that we each had different skills that were essential to actualizing that commitment, we built an effective coalition around a common cause. Our school was successful, and the children we taught benefitted from the diversity we offered them.

. . . None of us alone has a comprehensive vision of how race, class and gender operate as categories of analysis or how they might be used as categories of connection. Our personal biographies offer us partial views. Few of us can manage to study race, class and gender simultaneously. Instead, we each know more about some dimensions of this larger story and less about others. . . . Just as the members of the school had special skills to offer to the task of building the school, we have areas of specialization and expertise, whether scholarly, theoretical, pedagogical or within areas of race, class or gender. We do not all have to do the same thing in the same way. Instead, we must support each other's efforts, realizing that they are all part of the larger enterprise of bringing about social change.

3. BUILDING EMPATHY

A third issue involved in building the types of relationships and coalitions essential for social change concerns the issue of individual accountability. Race, class and gender oppression form the structural backdrop against which we frame our relationship—these are the forces that encourage us to substitute voyeurism . . . for fully human relationships. But while we may not have created this situation, we are each responsible for making individual, personal choices concerning which elements of race, class and gender oppression we will accept and which we will work to change.

One essential component of this accountability involves developing empathy for the experiences of individuals and groups different than ourselves. Empathy begins with taking an interest in the facts of other people lives, both as individuals and as groups. If you care about me, you should want to know not only the details of my personal biography but a sense of how race, class and gender as categories of analysis created the institutional and symbolic backdrop for my personal biography. How can you hope to assess my character without knowing the details of the circumstances I face?

Moreover, by taking a theoretical stance that we have all been affected by race, class and gender as categories of analysis that have structured our treatment, we open up possibilities for using those same constructs as categories of connection in building empathy. For example, I have a good White woman friend with whom I share common interests and beliefs. But we know that our racial differences have provided us with different experiences. So we talk about them. We do not assume that because I am Black, race has only affected me and not her or that because I am a Black woman, race neutralizes the effect of gender in my life while accenting it in hers. We take those same categories of analysis that have created cleavages in our lives, in this case, categories of race and gen-

der, and use them as categories of connection in building empathy for each other's experiences.

Finding common causes and building empathy is difficult, no matter which side of privilege we inhabit. Building empathy from the dominant side of privilege is difficult, simply because individuals from privileged backgrounds are not encouraged to do so. For example, in order for those of you who are White to develop empathy for the experiences of people of color, you must grapple with how your white skin has privileged you. This is difficult to do, because it not only entails the intellectual process of seeing how whiteness is elevated in institutions and symbols, but it also involves the often painful process of seeing how your whiteness has shaped your personal biography. Intellectual stances against the institutional and symbolic dimensions of racism are generally easier to maintain than sustained self-reflection about how racism has shaped all of our individual biographies. Were and are your fathers, uncles, and grandfathers really more capable than mine, or can their accomplishments be explained in part by the racism members of my family experienced? Did your mothers stand silently by and watch all this happen? More importantly, how have they passed on the benefits of their whiteness to you?

These are difficult questions, and I have tremendous respect for my colleagues and students who are trying to answer them. Since there is no compelling reason to examine the source and meaning of one's own privilege, I know that those who do so have freely chosen this stance. They are making conscious efforts to root out the piece of the oppressor planted within them. To me, they are entitled to the support of people of color in their efforts. Men who declare themselves feminists, members of the middle class who ally themselves with anti-poverty struggles, heterosexuals who support gays and lesbians, are all trying to grow, and their efforts place them far ahead of the majority who never think of engaging in such important struggles.

Building empathy from the subordinate side of privilege is also difficult, but for different reasons. Members of subordinate groups are understandably reluctant to abandon a basic mistrust of members of powerful groups because this basic mistrust has traditionally been central to their survival. As a Black woman, it would be foolish for me to assume that White women, or Black men, or White men or any other group with a history of exploiting African-American women have my best interests at heart. These groups enjoy varying amounts of privilege over me and therefore I must carefully watch them and be prepared for a relation of domination and subordination.

Like the privileged, members of subordinate groups must also work toward replacing judgments by category with new ways of thinking and acting. Refusing to do so stifles prospects for effective coalition and social change. Let me use another example from my own experiences. When I was an undergraduate, I had little time or patience for the theorizing of the privileged. My initial years at a private, elite institution were difficult, not because the coursework was challenging (it was, but that wasn't what distracted me) or because I had to work while my classmates lived on family allowances (I was used to work). The adjustment was difficult because I was surrounded by so many people who took their privilege for granted. Most of them felt entitled to their wealth. That astounded me.

I remember one incident of watching a White woman down the hall in my dormitory try to pick out which sweater to wear. The sweaters were piled up on her bed in all the colors of the rainbow, sweater after sweater. She asked my advice in a way that let me know that choosing a sweater was one of the most important decisions she had to make on a daily basis. Standing knee-deep in her sweaters, I realized how different our lives were. She did not have to worry about maintaining a solid academic average so that she could receive financial aid. Because she was in the majority, she was not treated as a representative of her race. She did not have to consider how her classroom comments or basic existence on campus contributed to the treatment her group would receive. Her allowance protected her from having to work, so she was free to spend her time studying, partying, or in her case, worrying about which sweater to wear. The degree of inequality in our lives and her unquestioned sense of entitlement concerning that inequality offended me. For a while, I categorized all affluent White women as being superficial, arrogant, overly concerned with material possessions, and part of my problem. But had I continued to classify people in this way, I would have missed out on making some very good friends whose discomfort with their inherited or acquired social class privileges pushed them to examine their position.

Since I opened with the words of Audre Lorde, it seems appropriate to close with another of her ideas. . . .

> Each of us is called upon to take a stand. So in these days ahead, as we examine ourselves and each other, our works, our fears, our differences, our sisterhood and survivals, I urge you to tackle what is most difficult for us all, self-scrutiny of our complacencies, the idea that since each of us believes she is on the side of right, she need not examine her position (1985).

I urge you to examine your position.

REFERENCES

Butler, Johnnella. 1989. "Difficult Dialogues." *The Women's Review of Books* 6, no. 5.

Collins, Patricia Hill. 1989. "The Social Construction of Black Feminist Thought." *Signs.* Summer 1989.

Harding, Sandra. 1986. *The Science Question in Feminism.* Ithaca, New York: Cornell University Press.

Gwaltney, John Langston. 1980. *Drylongso: A Self-Portrait of Black America.* New York: Vintage.

Lorde, Audre. 1984. *Sister Outsider.* Trumansberg, New York: The Crossing Press,

———. 1985 "Sisterhood and Survival." Keynote address, conference on the Black Woman Writer and the Diaspora, Michigan State University.

Jordan, June. 1985. *On Call: Political Essays.* Boston: South End Press.

Spelman, Elizabeth. 1982. "Theories of Race and Gender: The Erasure of Black Women." *Quest* 5: 36-32.

Tate, Claudia, ed. 1983. *Black Women Writers at Work.* New York: Continuum.

I Am Legally Blind

Like approximately 1.1 million people in the United States, I am legally blind, which means that I have some remaining vision. Therefore, I have the option to "come out" as a blind person or "pass" as someone who is fully sighted.

When I am passing, I avoid using my magnifier or my reading glasses, which have an obviously protruded lens and require me to hold items close to my face. By not asking for assistance, I avoid having to tell anyone I am blind. In restaurants, I order without consulting the menu. If I go out walking, I leave my white cane at home. I get on buses and subway trains without asking anyone to identify which line I'm boarding. I purchase items in stores without using my pocket magnifier to read labels or prices. On elevators that have not been adapted to meet ADA (Americans with Disabilities Act of 1990) guidelines of "reasonable accommodation," I take my best shot at hitting the right button. Therefore, I am never quite sure if I am exiting on the floor that I want. I wander through unfamiliar neighborhoods and buildings that are invariably marked with small print signs that are placed above doorways.

There is a price I pay for passing as a sighted person. I give away ten-dollar bills when I mean to pay one dollar. I come home from grocery stores with brands or flavors of items that I don't like or that cost too much. But, the highest cost is freedom: I relinquish my rights to life, liberty and the pursuit of happiness. Here's what happens when I don't ask for help.

When I don't solicit information about buses, trains, and elevators, I waste a lot of time trying to find specific destinations and end up feeling frustrated, angry, and exhausted. When I leave my white cane at home, I give up my right to travel freely because I can't navigate in unfamiliar places or go anywhere at all after dark: I jeopardize my own safety because I trip and fall on curbs, stairs, bumps, and potholes. I surrender my freedom of choice when, in fast food restaurants where the menus are inaccessible to me, I order the same food time and time again. I limit my choice of products when I don't use my visual aids because I have to choose by label color rather than to read the print, and I don't learn about new products, either. If I hadn't identified myself as a blind person at the University, I would have relinquished my right to pursue an education because I would have had no adaptive equipment nor would I have made use of the university's Disability Support Services. I would have

failed in school, which is exactly what I did, both in high school and the first time I attended college.

So, why in the world would I ever choose to pass? Because sometimes, I get sick of people's stares, whispers, ignorant comments, and nosy questions. When I ask for directions or for someone to read something to me, I am often responded to as if I am stupid or a child. People often answer my questions in irritated or condescending tones. More times than not, they don't answer verbally, but point at the object instead, which forces me to have to ask again or to explain why I am asking. This happens a lot at checkout stands.

I have had people grab my arm and try to pull me where I don't want to go. Recently, at a concert, my companion and I, with my white cane in hand, were easing our way through the aisle to our seats when a woman jumped up, grabbed my arm, knocking me off balance, then pushed me toward my seat. She didn't even ask if I wanted help. It really was an assault. Indeed, to a mugger or rapist, my white cane identifies me as a potential victim.

When I go shopping, I behave differently than fully sighted people do. I must juggle my list, purse, magnifier, reading glasses as well as the product and shopping basket or cart. I hold items very close to my face to read product labels, tags, and prices. A surprising number of people have asked "What are you looking for?" Sometimes, I reply, "Why do you ask?" I don't like having to explain my methods of adaptation. I have been followed by security guards and even stopped once in a drug store. The guard said that I was "acting suspiciously." He felt pretty bad when I told him that I was trying to see the prices. After that, whenever I went into that store, he was right there asking me if I needed any help finding things. Even though he meant well, the end result was that he still was following me. Ever since that experience, I stay alert to the possibility that I might look suspicious and I stand in open areas when I go into my purse for my glasses. I don't like having to be concerned about this, but I like the idea of being nabbed for shoplifting even less.

These are the paradoxical consequences of passing or coming out. Both cause me trouble, although I have learned the hard way that the more I use adaptive techniques and aids, and the more often I ask for help, the more efficient and independent I become. Thus, when I am "out," I am true to my own needs and desires.

Beth Gordon

Black Sexuality
The Taboo Subject

Cornel West

"Here," she said, "in this here place, we flesh; flesh that weeps, laughs; flesh that dances on bare feet in grass. Love it. Love it hard. Yonder they do not love your flesh. They despise it. They don't love your eyes; they'd just as soon pick em out. No more do they love the skin on your back. Yonder they flay it. And O my people they do not love your hands. Those they only use, tie, bind, chop off and leave empty. Love your hands! Love them. Raise them up and kiss them. Touch others with them, pat them together, stroke them on your face 'cause they don't love that either. *You* got to love it, *You!* . . . This is flesh I'm talking about here. Flesh that needs to be loved."
Toni Morrison, *Beloved* (1987)

Americans are obsessed with sex and fearful of black sexuality. The obsession has to do with a search for stimulation and meaning in a fast-paced, market-driven culture; the fear is rooted in visceral feelings about black bodies and fueled by sexual myths of black women and men. The dominant myths draw black women and men either as threatening creatures who have the potential for sexual power over whites, or as harmless, desexed underlings of a white culture. There is Jezebel (the seductive temptress), Sapphire (the evil, manipulative bitch), or Aunt Jemima (the sexless, long-suffering nurturer). There is Bigger Thomas (the mad and mean predatory craver of white women), Jack Johnson, the super performer—be it in athletics, entertainment, or sex—who excels others naturally and prefers women of a lighter hue), or Uncle Tom (the spineless, sexless—or is it impotent?—sidekick of whites). The myths offer distorted, dehumanized creatures whose bodies—color of skin, shape of nose and lips, type of hair, size of hips—are already distinguished from the white norm of beauty and

whose fearful sexual activities are deemed disgusting, dirty, or funky and considered less acceptable.

Yet the paradox of the sexual politics of race in America is that, behind closed doors, the dirty, disgusting, and funky sex associated with black people is often perceived to be more intriguing and interesting, while in public spaces talk about black sexuality is virtually taboo. Everyone knows it is virtually impossible to talk candidly about race without talking about sex. Yet most social scientists who examine race relations do so with little or no reference to how sexual perceptions influence racial matters. My thesis is that black sexuality is a taboo subject in white and black America and that a candid dialogue about black sexuality between and within these communities is requisite for healthy race relations in America.

The major cultural impact of the 1960s was not to demystify black sexuality but rather to make black bodies more accessible to white bodies *on an equal basis.* The history of such access up to that time was primarily one of brutal white rape and ugly white abuse. The Afro-Americanization of white youth—given the disproportionate black role in popular music and athletics—has put white kids in closer contact with their own bodies and facilitated more human interaction with black people. Listening to Motown records in the sixties or dancing to hip hop music in the nineties may not lead one to question the sexual myths of black women and men, but when white and black kids buy the same billboard hits and laud the same athletic heroes the result is often a shared cultural space where some humane interaction takes place.

This subterranean cultural current of interracial interaction increased during the 1970s and 1980s, even as racial polarization deepened on the political front. We miss much of what goes on in the complex development of race relations in America if we focus solely on the racial card played by the Republican Party and overlook the profound multicultural mix of popular culture that has occurred in the past two decades. In fact, one of the reasons Nixon, Reagan, and Bush had to play a racial card, that is, had to code their language about race, rather than simply call a spade a spade, is due to the changed *cultural* climate of race and sex in America. The classic scene of Senator Strom Thurmond—staunch segregationist and longtime opponent of interracial sex and marriage—strongly defending Judge Clarence Thomas—married to a white woman and an alleged avid consumer of white pornography—shows how this change in climate affects even reactionary politicians in America.

Needless to say, many white Americans still view black sexuality with disgust. And some continue to view their own sexuality with disgust. Victorian morality and racist perceptions die hard. But more and more white Americans are willing to interact sexually with black Americans *on an equal basis*—even if the myths still persist. I view this as neither cause for celebration nor reason for lament. Anytime two human beings find genuine pleasure, joy, and love, the stars smile and the universe is enriched. Yet as long as that pleasure, joy, and love is still predicated on myths of black sexuality, the more fundamental challenge of humane interaction remains unmet. Instead, what we have is white access to black bodies on an equal basis—but not yet the demythologizing of black sexuality.

This demythologizing of black sexuality is crucial for black America because much of black self-hatred and self-contempt has to do with the refusal of many black Americans to love their own black bodies—especially their black noses, hips, lips, and hair. Just as many white Americans view black sexuality with disgust, so do many black Americans—but for very different reasons and with very different results. White supremacist ideology is based first and foremost on the degradation of black bodies in order to control them. One of the best ways to instill fear in people is to terrorize them. Yet this fear is best sustained by convincing them that their bodies are ugly, their intellect is inherently underdeveloped, their culture is less civilized, and their future warrants less concern than that of other peoples. Two hundred and forty-four years of slavery and nearly a century of institutionalized terrorism in the form of segregation, lynchings, and second-class citizenship in America were aimed at precisely this devaluation of black people. This white supremacist venture was, in the end, a relative failure—thanks to the courage and creativity of millions of black people and hundreds of exceptional white folk like John Brown, Elijah Lovejoy, Myles Horton, Russell Banks, Anne Braden, and others. Yet this white dehumanizing endeavor has left its toll in the psychic scars and personal wounds now inscribed in the souls of black folk. These scars and wounds are clearly etched on the canvas of black sexuality.

How does one come to accept and affirm a body so despised by one's fellow citizens? What are the ways in which one can rejoice in the intimate moments of black sexuality in a culture that questions the aesthetic beauty of one's body? Can genuine human relationships flourish for black people in a society that assaults black intelligence, black moral character, and black possibility?

These crucial questions were addressed in those black social spaces that affirmed black humanity and warded off white contempt—especially in black families, churches, mosques, schools, fraternities, and sororities. These precious black institutions forged a mighty struggle against the white supremacist bombardment of black people. They empowered black children to learn against the odds and supported damaged black egos so they could keep fighting; they preserved black sanity in an absurd society in which racism ruled unabated; and they provided opportunities for black love to stay alive. But these grand yet flawed black institutions refused to engage one fundamental issue: *black sexuality.* Instead, they ran from it like the plague. And they obsessively condemned those places where black sexuality was flaunted: the streets, the clubs, and the dance halls.

Why was this so? Primarily because these black institutions put a premium on black survival in America. And black survival required accommodation with and acceptance from white America. Accommodation avoids any sustained association with the subversive and transgressive—be it communism or miscegenation. Did not the courageous yet tragic lives of Paul Robeson and Jack Johnson bear witness to this truth? And acceptance meant that only "good" negroes would thrive—especially those who left black sexuality at the door when they "entered" and "arrived." In short, struggling black institutions made a Faustian pact with white America: avoid any substantive engagement with black sexuality and your survival on the margins of American society is, at least, possible.

White fear of black sexuality is a basic ingredient of white racism. And for whites to admit this deep fear even as they try to instill and sustain fear in blacks is to acknowledge a weakness—a weakness that goes down to the bone. Social scientists have long acknowledged that interracial sex and marriage is the most *perceived* source of white fear of black people—just as the repeated castrations of lynched black men cries out for serious psychocultural explanation.

Black sexuality is a taboo subject in America principally because it is a form of black power over which whites have little control—yet its visible manifestations evoke the most visceral of white responses, be it one of seductive obsession or downright disgust. On the one hand, black sexuality among blacks simply does not include whites, nor does it make them a central point of reference. It proceeds as if whites do not exist, as if whites are invisible and simply don't matter. This form of black sexuality puts black agency center stage with no white presence at all. This can be uncomfortable for white people accustomed to being the custodians of power.

On the other hand, black sexuality between blacks and whites proceeds based on underground desires that Americans deny or ignore in public and over which laws have no effective control. In fact, the dominant sexual myths of black women and men portray whites as being "out of control"—seduced, tempted, overcome, overpowered by black bodies. This form of black

sexuality makes white passivity the norm— hardly an acceptable self-image for a white-run society.

Of course, neither scenario fully accounts for the complex elements that determine how any particular relationship involving black sexuality *actually* takes place. Yet they do accent the crucial link between black sexuality and black power in America. In this way, to make black sexuality a taboo subject is to silence talk about a particular kind of power black people are perceived to have over whites. On the surface, this "golden" side is one in which black people simply have an upper hand sexually over whites, given the dominant myths in our society.

Yet there is a "brazen" side—a side perceived long ago by black people. If black sexuality is a form of black power in which black agency and white passivity are interlinked, then are not black people simply acting out the very roles to which the racist myths of black sexuality confine them? For example, most black churches shunned the streets, clubs, and dance halls in part because these black spaces seemed to confirm the very racist myths of black sexuality to be rejected. Only by being "respectable" black folk, they reasoned, would white America see their good works and shed its racist skin. For many black church folk, black agency and white passivity in sexual affairs was neither desirable nor tolerable. It simply permitted black people to play the role of the exotic "other"—closer to nature (removed from intelligence and control) and more prone to be guided by base pleasures and biological impulses.

Is there a way out of this Catch-22 situation in which black sexuality either liberates black people from white control in order to imprison them in racist myths or confines blacks to white "respectability" while they make their own sexuality a taboo subject? There indeed are ways out, but there is no one way out for all black people. Or, to put it another way, the ways out for black men differ vastly from those for black women. Yet, neither black men nor black women can make it out unless both get out, since the degradation of both are inseparable though not identical.

Black male sexuality differs from black female sexuality because black men have different self-images and strategies of acquiring power in the patriarchal structures of white America and black communities. Similarly, black male heterosexuality differs from black male homosexuality, owing to the self-perceptions and means of gaining power in the homophobic institutions of white America and black communities. The dominant myth of black male sexual prowess makes black men desirable sexual partners in a culture obsessed with sex. In addition, the Afro-Americanization of white youth has been more a male than a female affair, given the prominence of male athletes and the cultural weight of male pop artists. This process results in white youth—male and female—imitating and emulating black male styles of walking, talking, dressing, and gesticulating in relation to others. One irony of our present moment is that just as young black men are murdered, maimed, and imprisoned in record numbers, their styles have become disproportionately influential in shaping popular culture. For most young black men, power is acquired by stylizing their bodies over space and time in such a way that their bodies reflect their uniqueness and provoke fear in others. To be "bad" is good not simply because it subverts the language of the dominant white culture but also because it imposes a unique kind of order for young black men on their own distinctive chaos and solicits an attention that makes others pull back with some trepidation. This young black male style is a form of self-identification and resistance in a hostile culture; it also is an instance of machismo identity ready for violent encounters. Yet in a patriarchal society, machismo identity is expected and even exalted—as with Rambo and Reagan. Yet a black machismo style solicits primarily sexual encounters with women and violent encounters with other black men or aggressive police. In this way, the black male search for power often reinforces the myth of black male sexual prowess—a myth that tends to subordinate black and white

women as objects of sexual pleasure. This search for power also usually results in a direct confrontation with the order-imposing authorities of the status quo, that is, the police or criminal justice system. The prevailing cultural crisis of many black men is the limited stylistic options of self-image and resistance in a culture obsessed with sex yet fearful of black sexuality.

This situation is even bleaker for most black gay men who reject the major stylistic option of black machismo identity, yet who are marginalized in white America and penalized in black America for doing so. In their efforts to be themselves, they are told they are not really "black men," not machismo-identified. Black gay men are often the brunt of talented black comics like Arsenio Hall and Damon Wayans. Yet behind the laugh lurks a black tragedy of major proportions: the refusal of white and black America to entertain seriously new stylistic options for black men caught in the deadly endeavor of rejecting black machismo identities.

The case of black women is quite different, partly because the dynamics of white and black patriarchy affect them differently and partly because the degradation of black female heterosexuality in America makes black female lesbian sexuality a less frightful jump to make. This does not mean that black lesbians suffer less than black gays—in fact, they suffer more, principally owing to their lower economic status. But this does mean that the subculture of black lesbians is fluid and the boundaries are less policed precisely because black female sexuality in general is more devalued, hence more marginal in white and black America.

The dominant myth of black female sexual prowess constitutes black women as desirable sexual partners—yet the central role of the ideology of white female beauty attenuates the expected conclusion. Instead of black women being the most sought after "objects of sexual pleasure"—as in the case of black men—white women tend to occupy this "upgraded," that is, degraded, position primarily because white beauty plays a weightier role in sexual desirability for women in racist patriarchal America. The ideal of female beauty in this country puts a premium on lightness and softness mythically associated with white women and downplays the rich stylistic manners associated with black women. This operation is not simply more racist to black women than that at work in relation to black men; it also is more devaluing of women in general than that at work in relation to men in general. This means that black women are subject to more multilayered bombardments of racist assaults than black men, in addition to the sexist assaults they receive from black men. Needless to say, most black men—especially professional ones— simply recycle this vulgar operation along the axis of lighter hues that results in darker black women bearing more of the brunt than their already devalued lighter sisters. The psychic bouts with self-confidence, the existential agony over genuine desirability, and the social burden of bearing and usually nurturing black children under these circumstances breeds a spiritual strength of black women unbeknownst to most black men and nearly all other Americans.

As long as black sexuality remains a taboo subject, we cannot acknowledge, examine, or engage these tragic psychocultural facts of American life. Furthermore, our refusal to do so limits our ability to confront the overwhelming realities of the AIDS epidemic in America in general and in black America in particular. Although the dynamics of black male sexuality differ from those of black female sexuality, new stylistic options of self-image and resistance can be forged only when black women and men do so together. This is so not because all black people should be heterosexual or with black partners, but rather because all black people—including black children of so-called "mixed" couples—are affected deeply by the prevailing myths of black sexuality. These myths are part of a wider network of white supremacist lies whose authority and legitimacy must be undermined. In the long run, there is simply no way out for all of us other than living out the truths we proclaim about genuine humane interaction in our psychic and sexual lives. Only by living against the grain can we keep alive the possibility that the visceral feelings about black bodies fed by racist myths and promoted by market-driven quests for stimulation do not forever render us obsessed with sexuality and fearful of each other's humanity.

THE MEANING OF DIFFERENCE

FRAMEWORK ESSAY

The first framework essay in this text considered how contemporary American master statuses are named, aggregated, dichotomized, and stigmatized. The second essay focused on the experience of privilege and stigma that accompanies those master statuses. In this final section we will look at the *meaning* that is attributed to difference. What significance are differences of race, sex, class, and sexual orientation presumed to have? What difference does difference make?

The conferral of meaning on master-status differences is not accomplished simply by individual action. Neither individual prejudice nor interpersonal interactions explain pervasive societal practices. Rather, these meanings are constructed and conferred in the functioning of social institutions. Thus, the readings in this section have been organized around law and politics, the economy, science, and popular culture. Many of these readings are generalizable to the variety of stigmatized and privileged master statuses.

In this framework essay we will focus on the concept of ideology. Social hierarchies are not built on ideologies alone—as is clear in the readings on law, the economy, and science—but being able to see and understand the operation of ideology goes a long way toward breaking out of constructions of difference. In the section that follows we will define ideology and consider how it is conveyed through stereotypes and "natural-law" language. We will then consider the ideologies about difference which have been conveyed by science and popular culture.

Ideology

The concept of ideology has its contemporary origins in the work of Marx and Engels, particularly *The German Ideology* (1846), and is now a well-elaborated concept in both the social sciences and the humanities. In general, an ideology can be defined as a widely-shared belief or idea, which has been constructed and disseminated by the powerful, is primarily reflective of their experience, and ulti-mately functions to their benefit.

Since ideologies are anchored in the experience of their creators, they offer only a partial view of the world. "Ideologies are not simply false, they can be 'partly true,' and yet also incomplete [or] distorted. . . . [They are not] consciously crafted by the ruling class and then injected into the minds of the majority; [they are] instead *produced* by specifiable, complex, social conditions" (Brantlinger, 1990:80). While ideologies primarily reflect the experience of their creators, they nonetheless become the pervasive ideas of a society. Thus, ideologies have the power to supplant, distort, or silence the experience of those outside their produc-tion.

Although a variety of beliefs may be found in the different segments of any society, those beliefs do not all have an equal chance of becoming socially domi-nant since no belief can become pervasive without a means for its dissemination. Those who control the means of disseminating ideas have a better chance of hav-ing their ideas become the ones that prevail. Thus, in *The German Ideology,* Marx and Engels concluded that "the ideas of the ruling class are in every epoch the rul-ing ideas."

For example, the idea that people are rewarded on the basis of their merit would appear to be an ideology. It is a specific idea promoted by those with power—for example, teachers in the schools and employers in the workplace—and there are many occasions when they explicitly articulate this idea. Report cards, award ban-quets, and merit raises are all occasions for the expression of the belief that peo-ple are rewarded on the basis of their merit.

But certainly, most of us know that this idea is not really true: people are not only or even primarily rewarded on the basis of their merit. The idea that merit is rewarded reflects the views of our teachers and bosses more than our own experi-ence, and their statuses provide them with the opportunity to disseminate that belief. Their reiteration of this idea has the possibility of overwhelming our own real and contrary experience. Even though our own experience has not generally been that people are rewarded based on their merit, we are still likely to subscribe to this general philosophy because we hear it reproduced so often. In any event, we have few safe opportunities to describe our contrary belief and little chance of getting it widely disseminated.

In this way, the idea that people are rewarded on the basis of merit displays the characteristics of an ideology. It is a belief that primarily reflects the experi-ence of those with power, but is presented as universally valid. The idea over-whelms and silences the voices of those who are outside its production. In effect, ideologies ask us to discount our own experience: "Well, even though I haven't often found that those with merit were the ones rewarded, I still believe this is generally true."

This conflict between one's own experience and the ideas conveyed by an ide-ology is implied in W.E.B. Du Bois's description of the "double consciousness" experienced by African Americans discussed in Framework Essay II. It is also what many feminist analyses refer to as the double or fractured consciousness experienced by women. In both cases, the dominant ideas fail to reflect the lived experience of people in these categories. For example, the actual experience of poverty, discrimination, motherhood, sexual assault, life in a black neighborhood, or in a gay relationship rarely coincides with the public discourse on those topics. Because those in stigmatized categories do not control the production or distribution of the prevailing ideas (though some may be allowed to participate in the processes), their experience is not likely to be reflected in them. Thus, the ideology not only silences their experience, it may invalidate it even in their own minds: "I must be the one who's crazy!" In this way, the dominant discourse can invade and overwhelm our own experience, since what we know doesn't fit (Kasper, 1986; Smith, 1978 and 1990).

The ideas which so dominate a culture as to become the prevailing and unquestioned beliefs, were described in the 1920s by Italian political theorist Antonio Gramsci as the *hegemonic,* or ruling, ideology. Gramsci argued that social control depended more on consent than coercion, and that "in order to consolidate their hegemony [or domination], ruling groups must elaborate and maintain a popular system of ideas and practices—through education, the media, religion, folk wisdom, etc.—which he called 'common sense'" (Omi and Winant, 1994:67). Thus, common sense beliefs are likely to embody widely shared ideas primarily reflective of the interests and experience of those who are powerful. We are all encouraged to express such notions even when that requires discounting our own experience.

Mechanisms for Conveying Ideologies

Hegemonic ideologies often take the form of common sense beliefs and are especially embodied in stereotypes and what has been called "natural-law" language.

Natural-law Language   When people use the world *natural* they usually mean that something is inevitable, predetermined, or outside human control (Pierce, 1971). *Human nature* and *instinct* (in reference to humans) are used in much the same way. For example, "It's only natural to care about what others think," "It's human nature to want to get ahead," or "It's just instinctive to be afraid of someone different," all convey the sense that something is inevitable, automatic, and independent of one's will.

Thus, it is not surprising when, in discussions about discrimination, someone says, "It's only natural for people to be prejudiced," or "It's human nature to want to be with your own kind." Such phrasings convey a belief in the inevitability of discrimination and prejudice, as if such processes emerge independent of anyone's will.

Even on an issue of which we disapprove, the word *natural* can convey this sense of inevitability. For example, "I abhor racism, but it's only natural," puts nature on the side of prejudice. Arguing that something is natural because it happens frequently, yields the same result. "All societies have discriminated against women, so there is little we can do about it," implies (illogically) that something that happens frequently must therefore be inevitable. (Something that happens frequently as likely argues for the presence of an extensive set of social controls ensuring the outcome.) In all, such language treats human behavior as if it were bound by "natural law" (Pierce, 1971).

There are at least three consequences that follow from natural-law language. First, it closes off discussion, as if having described something as natural makes any further exploration of the topic unnecessary. This makes sense given that the word *natural* is equated with inevitability: If something is inevitable then there is little sense in questioning it.

Second, because natural-law language treats behavior as predetermined, it over-looks the actual cultural and historical variability in human societies—it denies the reality of social variability and change. If something is natural, it should happen everywhere and always. Yet there is virtually no human behavior that emerges everywhere and always; all social life is susceptible to change. Thus, natural-law language masks the variability of social life.

Third, natural-law language treats individuals as passive, lacking an interest in or control over social life. If it is natural to dislike those who are different, then there is really nothing we can do about that feeling. It is no one's responsibility; it is just natural. If there is nothing I can do about my own behavior, there is little I could expect to do about the behavior of others. Human nature is, thus, depicted as a limitation beyond which people cannot expect to move (Gould, 1981). Describing certain behavior as "only natural" implies that personal and social change is impossible.

In all these ways—by closing off discussion, masking variability and change, and treating humans as passive—natural-law language tells us not to question the world that surrounds us. Natural-law language has this effect no matter what context it emerges in: "It's only natural to discriminate," "It's only natural to want to have children," "It's only natural to marry and settle down," "Inequality is only natural; the poor will always be with us," "Aggression and war are just human nature," "Greed is instinctive." In each case, natural-law language not only discourages questions, it carries a covert recommendation about what one *ought* to do. Natural-law language is prescriptive, not descriptive: If something is "just natural" you cannot prevent others from doing it, and you are well-advised to do it yourself. Thus, natural-law language serves as a forceful mechanism of social control (Pierce, 1971).

Over all, natural-law language can be used to convey hegemonic ideologies: it reduces the complexity and historic variability of the social world to a claim for universal and ahistoric processes, offering a partial and distorted truth that silences those with contrary experience. To extend Patricia Hill Collins's analysis in selection 19, natural-law language can make "racism, sexism, [homophobia,] and poverty appear to be natural, normal, and an inevitable part of everyday life." Thus, natural-law language itself contributes to the creation of difference.

Stereotypes   Natural-law language and stereotypes function similarly. In stereotyping, all the individuals in a category are assumed to possess the same set of characteristics. Thus, a stereotype is a prediction that "members of a group will behave in certain ways" (Andre, 1988:259)—that black men will have athletic ability, that Asian American students will excel in the sciences. As philosopher Judith Andre argues (1988), stereotypes persist despite evidence to the contrary because they are not formulated in a way that is testable or falsifiable. Thus, stereotypes can be distinguished from descriptions. Descriptions offer no prediction; they can be tested for accuracy and rejected when they are wrong; they encourage explanation and a consideration of historical variability.

For example, "Most great American athletes today are African American" is a description. First, there is no prediction involved: there is no implication that a particular African American can be expected to be a good athlete, or that someone who is white will be a poor one. Second, the claim is falsifiable, i.e., it can be tested for accuracy and proven wrong (e.g., by asking what proportion of the last two decades' Olympic medal-winners were African American). Third, the statement turns our attention to explanation and historical variation: Why might this be the case? Has this always been the case?

By contrast, "African Americans are good athletes" is a stereotype. It attempts to characterize a whole population, thus denying the inevitable variation among the people in the category. It predicts that members of a group will behave in a particular way. It cannot be falsified since there is no direct way to test the claim. Further, the stereotype denies the reality of historical and cultural variation by suggesting that something has always been the case. Thus, stereotypes essentialize: they assume that if you know something about the physical package someone comes in, you can predict their behavior.

Stereotypes resemble natural-law language in that both offer broad-based predictions about behavior. Stereotypes predict that members of a particular category will possess particular attributes; natural-law language predicts that certain behavior is inevitable. Neither is anchored in any social or historical context and, for that reason, both are frequently wrong. Basketball-great Bill Russell's reaction when asked if he thought African Americans were "natural" athletes makes clear the similarity of natural-law language and stereotyping. As Russell said, this was a stereotypic image of African American athletes that deprecated the skill and effort he brought to his craft—as if he were great because he was black, rather than because of the talent he cultivated in hours of work.

Stereotyping and Asian Americans   As we have indicated, stereotypes explain differential life outcomes by attributing essentialistic qualities to all those in a particular category. The current depiction of Asian Americans as a "model minority" is a prime example of this. As the U.S. Commission on Civil Rights makes clear, this stereotype masks the considerable economic, educational, and occupational heterogeneity among Asian Americans. The model-minority stereotype is itself a fairly recent invention: Among those now called "model minority" are categories of people previously barred as unworthy to immigrate, denied citizenship through naturalization, and placed in internment camps as potential traitors.

In American culture, the production of stereotypes is often driven by the necessity of explaining why some categories of people succeed more than others (Steinberg, 1989). Thus, behind the model minority stereotype is the claim that if racism has not been an impediment to the success of Asian Americans, it could not have been an impediment to African Americans. Just as Asian immigrants at the turn of the century were seen through the lens of the American black/white dichotomy, the status of Asian Americans is invoked in the contemporary debate about whether racism is an adequate explanation for the economic problems faced by African Americans.

> The myth of the Asian-American "model minority" has been challenged, yet it contin-ues to be widely believed. One reason for this is its instructional value. For whom are Asian Americans supposed to be a "model"? Shortly after the Civil War, southern planters recruited Chinese immigrants in order to pit them against the newly freed blacks as "examples" of laborers willing to work hard for low wages. Today, Asian Americans are again being used to discipline blacks. . . . Our society needs an Asian-American "model minority" in an era anxious about a growing black underclass (Takaki, 1993:416).

A brief review of American immigration policy explains the misguided nature of the comparison between African and Asian Americans. From 1921 until 1965, U.S. immigration was restricted by national-origin quotas that set limits on the number of immigrants from each nation based on the percentage of people from that country residing in the U.S. at the time of the *1890,* then later 1920, census. This had the obvious and intended effect of severely restricting immigration from Asia, as well as from southern and eastern Europe and Africa. The civil rights movement of the 1960s raised national embarrassment about this quota system such that in 1965 Congress passed the Hart-Celler Act which replaced national-origin quotas with an annual 20,000 person limit for every nation regardless of its size. Within that quota, preference went first to those who were relatives of Amer-ican citizens and then to those with occupational skills needed in America.

The result was an increase in the total volume of immigration as well as a change in its national composition. While fewer immigrated from Europe than could have, quotas were easily filled from countries that had before 1965 been effectively barred from immigration. Because few from non-European countries could immigrate on the grounds of having family in America—previous restric-tions would have made that almost impossible—the quotas were filled with peo-ple meeting designated *occupational* needs. Thus, those immigrating to the U.S. since 1965 have had high educational and occupational profiles. Noting only examples from Asian nations, while 16.2 percent of Americans have completed four or more years of college, as of 1980 66.2 percent of immigrants from India and 59.8 percent of those from Taiwan had completed four or more years of col-lege. While 12.3 percent of Americans are located in "professional speciality occupations," as of 1980 42.8 percent of immigrants from India, 30.4 percent of those from Taiwan, and 19.1 percent of those from Hong Kong are in such occu-pations (Portes and Rimbaut, 1990:60 and 70). These high occupational and edu-cational profiles have characterized immigrants from African as well as Asian countries.[1]

---

[1]Those with high educational profiles do not always realize high incomes, however. For example, while Nigerian and Iranian immigrants have high educational profiles, their household incomes have been low, a situation most likely explained by the recency of their arrival in the U.S. Similarly, although Asian immigrants may have a high household income [as a result of income pooling] their average individual income is lower than that for European immigrants and U.S. natives (Portes and Rimbaut, 1990). Note that the figures above are lower if U.S. born Asian, Indians, and Taiwanese are included.

In all, selective immigration goes a long way toward explaining the success of some of those who are recent immigrants from Asian countries. The middle and upper-class professionals and entrepreneurs who have immigrated to the United States did not suddenly become successful in the U.S. Rather, they continued their home-country success here.

However, it is important not to confuse the situation of people who are immigrants with those who are refugees. (U.S. policy has traditionally restricted refugee status to those who seek asylum from Communist countries.) The circumstances of arrival and resettlement for those who have fled their home countries make the refugee population exceedingly heterogeneous and quite different from those who have immigrated to the United States (Haines, 1989). Thus, Vietnamese, Laotian, Cambodian, and Hmong refugees are unlikely to have the high occupational or educational profiles of Asian immigrants.

Ironically, the misguided contemporary formulation—if Asian Americans can make it, why can't African Americans?—is an echo of an earlier question: If European immigrants could make it, why can't African Americans? The answer to that question is summarized below:

> Conditions within the cities to which they had migrated [beginning in the 1920s], not slavery, strained blacks' ability to retain two-parent families. Within those cities, blacks faced circumstances that differed fundamentally from those found earlier by European immigrants. They entered cities in large numbers as unskilled and semiskilled manufacturing jobs were leaving, not growing. The discrimination they encountered kept them out of the manufacturing jobs into which earlier immigrants had been recruited. One important goal of public schools had been the assimilation and "Americanization" of immigrant children; by contrast, they excluded and segregated blacks. Racism enforced housing segregation, and residential concentration among blacks increased at the same time it lessened among immigrants and their children. Political machines had embraced earlier immigrants and incorporated them into the system of "city trenches" by which American cities were governed; they excluded blacks from effective political power until cities had been so abandoned by industry and deserted by whites that resistance to black political participation no longer mattered. All the processes that had opened opportunities for immigrants and their children broke down for blacks. . . . (Katz, 1989:51).

Stereotyping and African Americans While there have been some fundamental changes in white Americans' attitudes towards African Americans, it can also be argued that there has been little change. Before the civil rights movement of the 1960s, only a minority of whites supported the principle of equal treatment of blacks and whites; now that position is the dominant one. Still, whether informally or in response to opinion surveys, whites continue to feel free to comment negatively about blacks. "If one goes out into American society and talks with [white] taxi drivers or nurses or transportation executives or schoolteachers or a host of others about problems of race in American life, one would have to put blinders on one's eyes and cotton [batting] in one's ears not to see and hear the negative characterizations routinely expressed about blacks" (Sniderman and Piazza, 1993:36).

As political scientists Paul Sniderman and Thomas Piazza's (1993) ground-breaking survey research makes clear, negative stereotypes about African Americans prevail across all educational levels among whites. "With the exception of citizens who are uncommonly well educated and uncommonly liberal, what is striking is the sheer pervasiveness throughout contemporary American society of negative characterizations of blacks" (Sniderman and Piazza, 1993:50). Still, the proportion of whites who subscribe to the full range of stereotypes is relatively small—"39 percent accept only one or two [of the stereotypes they were presented with], 22 percent don't accept any at all, whereas only 2 percent accept all of them" (Sniderman and Piazza, 1993:46). As their research demonstrates, whites who hold the most consistently negative opinion of blacks also hold negative opinions about Jews and generally accept an authoritarian value system. While neither age nor income affect the white rate of stereotyping, education does have an effect: As the years of schooling increase, acceptance of stereotypes diminishes.

Apart from the acceptance of stereotypes, whites also appear to practice a double standard. Making use of an innovative questionnaire design, Sniderman and Piazza compared whites' responses to the situation of *individual* African Americans with their response to public policy issues affecting African Americans as a *group*. They found that while whites were generally non-discriminatory in their response to individual African Americans, even those the survey question characterized negatively, whites still discriminated against African Americans as a group when the questions related to public policy.

> Claims for government assistance made on behalf of blacks as *individuals* are treated [by white survey respondents] as those made on behalf of individual whites, and indeed, insofar as race makes a difference, a black who has lost his or her job meets with a more sympathetic and generous response [in the survey] than a white who has lost his or her job. On the other hand, when it comes to judgments about what blacks as a group are entitled to, a racial double standard manifestly persists. . . .
>
> The evenhandedness characteristic of reactions to blacks as individuals is not characteristic of reactions to blacks as a group. We found significantly more support for government guarantees of equal opportunity for women than for blacks (Sniderman and Piazza, 1993:13 and 169).

Whites who were well-educated did not operate from this double standard, but other whites—irrespective of their political orientation—did. "Thus, conservatives with a high school education or less are almost three times as likely to approve of government assurances of equal opportunity for women as for blacks—plainly a double standard. But the same is true on the left" (Sniderman and Piazza, 1993:83). (Sniderman and Piazza argue that education lessens this double standard because it encourages consistency in thinking.) "Given this duality of response, it is easier to understand why whites see themselves as living in a world where the meaning of race has changed, while blacks see themselves as living in a world where its meaning has remained much the same" (Sniderman and Piazza, 1993:68).

Social Institutions and the Support of Ideologies

The specific messages carried by natural-law language and stereotypes are often echoed in and validated by the workings of social institutions. In the sections that follow we will consider how science and popular culture historically constructed the meaning of difference, especially focusing on the meaning late nineteenth- and early twentieth-century scientists attributed to race, class, sex, and sexual orientation differences. Throughout, the congruence between scientific pronouncements, popular culture messages, and the prejudices of the day is striking. Whether the example is historic or contemporary, the risk is that social institutions are shaped by hegemonic ideologies more than they themselves change those ideologies.

Science   The need to explain the meaning of human difference forcefully emerged with Europeans' fifteenth-century discovery and conquest of previously unknown regions and peoples. "Three centuries of exploration brought home as never before the tremendous diversity of human behavior and life patterns within environments and under circumstances dramatically different from those of Europe. . . . Out of that large laboratory of human experience was born the [idea of the] conflict between nature and nurture" (Degler, 1991:4–5).

The "nature-nurture conflict" generally provided two ways to explain human variation. Explanations from the nature side stressed that the diversity of human societies—and the ability of some to conquer and dominate others—reflected significant biological differences between populations. Explanations from the nurture side argued that human diversity resulted from historical, environmental, and cultural difference (although the word *culture* would not have been used this way until the late nineteenth century). From the nature side, humans were understood to act out behaviors that were biologically driven. From the nurture side, humans were something of a *tabula rasa,* a blank slate, on which particular cultural expectations were inscribed.

Whether nature or nurture was understood to dominate, however, the discussion of the meaning of human difference always assumed that differences could be ranked as to their worth (Gould, 1981). Thus, the real question was whether the rankings that were reflected in social hierarchies were the result of nature and thus inevitable and fixed, or could be affected by human action and were thus subject to social change.

The question was not theoretical. In the 1800s in America, its backdrop was the appropriation of Native American territories and the forced relocation of vast numbers of people beginning with the Indian Removal Act of 1830; the 1848 signing of the Treaty of Guadalupe Hidalgo ending the Mexican-American War and ceding what is now Texas, New Mexico, California, Utah, Nevada, and Arizona to the United States with the 75,000 Mexican nationals residing in those territories becoming U.S. citizens; passage of the Chinese Exclusion Act; a prolonged national debate about slavery and women's suffrage; the unprecedented immigration of poor and working-class people from southern and eastern Europe; and at the close of the century the internationally publicized trial of English playwright Oscar Wilde and his sentencing to two years hard labor for homosexuality.

Thus, to ask whether social hierarchy reflected natural, permanent, and inherent differences in capability (the nature side) or was the product of specific social and historical circumstances and was therefore susceptible to change (the nurture side), posed a profound question. Because Africans were held by whites in slavery, did that mean that Africans were by their nature inferior to whites? Were Native Americans literally "savages" occupying some middle ground between animals and civilized humans, and did they therefore benefit from domination by those who were supposedly more advanced? Did the dissimilarity of Chinese immigrants from American whites mean they were not "human" in the way whites were? If homosexuality was congenital, did that mean that homosexuals were profoundly different from heterosexuals? Were women closer to plants and animals than to civilized men, as some social scientists asserted (Degler, 1991:28)? Were the poor and working classes comprised of those who not only lacked the talents by which to rise in society but who also passed their defects on to their progeny? In all, were individuals and categories of people located in the statuses for which they were best suited? If one believed that the existent social order simply reflected immutable biological differences, the answer to the question would likely be affirmative. That would not have been the case, however, for those who believed that these differences were the outcome of specific social and historical processes overlaying a shared humanity. In all, the question behind the nature-nurture debate was about the *meaning* of what appeared to be *natural* difference.

In this debate, Charles Darwin's publication of *The Origin of the Species* (1859) and *The Descent of Man* (1871) shifted the weight of popular and scholarly opinion toward the nature side of the equation (Degler, 1991). In its broadest terms, Darwin's conclusions challenged head on the two central beliefs of the time (Darwin was himself quite distressed to have arrived at these conclusions [Shipman, 1994]). First, in its argument for evolutionary change his work challenged "traditional, Christian belief in a single episode of creation of a static, perfect, and unchanging world." The significance of evolutionary change was clear: "If the world were not created perfect, then there was no implicit justification for the way things were . . ." (Shipman, 1994:18).

Second, his work implied that all humans shared a common ancestry. If the differentiation among birds were the result of adaptation to distinctive environments, then their differences existed within an overall framework of similarity and common ancestry. By analogy, the distinctiveness of human populations might also be understood as "variability within overall similarity" (Shipman, 1994:22)—a shocking possibility at the time. "It was the age of imperialism and most non-Europeans were regarded, even by Darwin, as 'barbarians'; he was astonished and taken aback by their wildness and animality. The differences among humans seemed so extreme that the humanity . . . of some living groups was scarcely credible" (Shipman, 1994:19).

While these two features of Darwin's work buttressed the nurture side of the equation, the idea that change in the physical environment resulted in the success of some species and demise of others (the idea of natural selection) bolstered the pre-existent concept of "survival of the fittest." This phrase had been authored by English sociologist Herbert Spencer, who had been applying evolutionary principles to human societies several years before Darwin published *The Origin of the Species.*

Spencer's position, eventually called *social Darwinism,* was extremely popular in America. Spencer strongly believed that modern societies were inevitably improvements over earlier forms of social organization and that progress would necessarily follow from unimpeded competition for social resources. In all, social Darwinism argued that those more advanced naturally rose to the top of any stratification ladder.

Through social Darwinism, the prevailing hierarchies—slave owner over people held in slavery, white over Mexican and Native American, native-born over immigrant, upper-class over poor, male over female—could be attributed to natural processes, and justified as a reflection of inherent differences among categories of people. As a sociologist at the turn of the century framed it, "under the tutelage of Darwinism the world returns again to the idea that *might* as evidence of fitness has something to do with *right*" (Degler, 1991:13).

Social Darwinism has since been discredited, largely on the ground that it "falsely equates history with evolution" (Sayers, 1982:38); in effect, it attributes the supremacy of certain groups to biology and evolution rather than to the exercise of power within specific historical and economic contexts. Social Darwinism lacked a socially or historically grounded explanation for social stratification. Instead, it treated those hierarchies as a reflection of the intrinsic merit of categories of people. Thus, social Darwinism was brought to the defense of slavery, colonialism, immigration quotas, the criminalization of homosexuality, the forced relocation of Native Americans, and the legal subordination of women.

For example, social Darwinism was used to justify keeping women subordinate. Spencer argued that the specialization of tasks, also called the division of labor, was the outcome of a biologically mandated evolution. The sexual division of labor "was a product of the organic law of progress," thus making equal treatment of men and women hopeless and even potentially dangerous.

This argument emerged explicitly in the battle against equal education for women. As American institutions of higher education yielded to the logic of the women's movement that women should have access to the same level of education as men—Vassar College was founded in 1865, Smith and Wellesley ten years later, and by 1870 many state universities had become coeducational— biologist Edward Clarke published a book (1873) that argued that the physical energy that education required would endanger women's reproductive abilities (an idea first put forward by Spencer). Clarke's case was based on meager and questionable empirical evidence, citing seven clinical cases, only one of which actually supported his position (Sayers, 1982:14). His work was a response to social rather than scientific developments, since it was prompted by no new discoveries in the field of biology. Nonetheless, the book was an immediate and enduring success. For the next thirty years it was used to argue against women's education despite the accumulation of evidence refuting its claims. While Clarke's research should have been suspect, it instead became influential in policy making. In part, "the reason why Clarke's argument seemed so serviceable to those opposed to women's higher education was that it was couched in biological terms and thus appeared to offer a legitimate scientific basis for conservative opposition to equal education" (Sayers, 1982:11).

In a similar fashion, scientific ideas shaped the emerging ideologies about the meaning of same-sex relationships. While there was no gay rights movement in the United States until after the Second World War, by the turn of the century in Europe a tradition of literary reflection on homosexuality had developed in France, and a gay rights movement had emerged in Germany (Adam, 1987). At the same time, however, an international move to criminalize sexual relations between men gathered momentum: a revision of the German criminal code increased the penalties for male homosexuality, the British prosecuted Oscar Wilde, and Europe and the United States experienced a social reform movement directed against prostitution and male homosexuality. (The possibility of sexual relations between women was not considered until later.)

As sociologists Peter Conrad and Joseph Schneider describe in selection 30, criminalization was countered by physicians arguing, from a social Darwinist position, that homosexuality was the product of "hereditary weakness" and was thus beyond individual control. Though their hope was for increased tolerance, scientists who took this position offered the idea of "homosexuality as a medical entity and the homosexual as a distinctive kind of person" (Conrad and Schneider, 1980:184). Thus they contributed to the idea that heterosexual and homosexual people were profoundly different from each other.

Science also supported the argument that people of different skin colors were different in significant, immutable ways. Certainly Spencer's idea of the survival of the fittest was understood to support the belief that whites were superior to all people of color: "The most prevalent form of social Darwinism at the turn of the century was actually racism, that is, the idea that one people might be superior to another because of differences in their biological nature" (Degler, 1991:15).

The scientific defense of American slavery first emerged with the work of Swiss naturalist Louis Agassiz and Philadelphia physician, Samuel Morton. Both were emminent scientists of their time. Agassiz immigrated to America in 1840, became a professor at Harvard, and garnered immense popularity by countering the biblically-based theory of the unity of all people (which attributed race differences to "degeneration" from that shared origin), with a "scientific" theory that different races had descended from different moments of creation, "different Adams" (Gould, 1981:39).

Physician and researcher Samuel Morton tested Agassiz's notions about the ranking of different races by measuring the cranial capacity of human skulls on the assumption that intelligence and skull size were positively related. His results "matched every good Yankee's prejudices—whites on top, Indians in the middle, and blacks on the bottom; and, among whites, Teutons and Anglo-Saxons on top, Jews in the middle, and Hindus on the bottom" (Gould, 1981:53).

As we now know, Morton's findings were simply wrong: there were *"no significant differences among races for Morton's own data"* (Gould, 1981:67). The way that Morton erred points to the embedding of science in prevailing ideologies. It was not that he lacked the skills and standards of our contemporary science, rather it was that he failed to correctly use even the scientific principles of his own era. There is no evidence that Morton intended to deceive. Rather, his assumption of white superiority was so firm that he was oblivious to his own errors and illogic, errors that yielded the conclusion of white superiority only because of his miscalculations.

The use of questionable research in the service of prevailing beliefs (Gould, 1981) was reflected as well in the American application and development of intelligence testing, which affirmed social distinctions based on class and color. In 1904, Alfred Binet, director of the psychology lab at the Sorbonne, was commissioned by the French minister of public education to develop a test to identify children whose poor performance in school might indicate a need for special education. The test Binet developed aimed to separate intelligence from education, and comprised a series of tasks that children of "normal" intelligence were expected to have mastered. Binet's own claims for the test were fairly limited; he did not equate intelligence with the number produced by his test, arguing that intelligence was too complex a factor to be reduced to a simple number. Nor did he construe his test as measuring inborn, permanent, or inherited limitations (Gould, 1981).

Binet's hesitations regarding use of the test, however, were quickly discarded by the emerging field of American psychology which embraced the idea of testing intelligence. Intelligence, or the lack thereof, was not only used to justify American race and ethnic divisions, it was also treated as the primary explanation of social class divisions. "The people who are doing the drudgery are, as a rule, in their proper places," wrote H. H. Goddard, who introduced the Binet test to America. Stanford psychologist Lewis M. Termin (author of the Stanford-Binet IQ test), argued that "the children of successful and cultured parents test higher than children from wretched and ignorant homes for the simple reason that their heredity is better" (Degler, 1991:50). Indeed, "Terman believed that class boundaries had been set by innate intelligence" (Gould, 1981:183). In all, systems of stratification were defended by social science as simply reflecting the distribution of ability.

Such conclusions were used to shape decisions about the distribution of educational resources. For example, intelligence was described as a capacity that could be equated with the capacity of a jug for a certain amount of milk. A pint jug could not be expected to hold a quart of milk; it was pointless to waste "too much" education on someone whose capacity was supposedly limited. The findings of intelligence testers were thus used to advocate particular social policies, as for example in the control of immigration. While it is not clear that the work of intelligence testers directly affected the Immigration Restriction Act of 1924 (Degler, 1991), the ultimate shape of the legislation restricted immigration from southern and eastern Europe, which was consistent with intelligence testers' claims about the relative intelligence of the "races" in Europe. Throughout the 1930s, these quotas prevented the admission of Jews from southern and eastern Europe as they attempted to flee the impending holocaust (Gould, 1981).

Still, by about 1930 there was a considerable body of research showing that social environment more than biology accounted for differing IQ scores and that the tests themselves did not measure innate intelligence but rather familiarity with the culture of those who wrote the tests. In the end, the psychologists who had promoted intelligence testing were forced to repudiate the idea that intelligence was inherited or that it could be separated from cultural knowledge.[2]

Whether measuring cranial capacity, developing paper-and-pencil intelligence tests, positing the effect of education on women, or arguing for hereditary weakness as an explanation of homosexuality, the work of these scientists supported the prevailing ideologies about the merit and appropriate social location of people of different sexes, races, ethnic groups, sexual orientations, and social classes. Most of these scientists do not appear to have been ideologically motivated; indeed they were sometimes troubled by their own findings. Still, their research was riddled with technical errors as well as questionable results and interpretation. In all, their research revealed "the surprising malleability of 'objective,' quantitative data in the interest of a preconceived idea" (Gould, 1981:147). Precisely because their research confirmed prevailing beliefs, it was more likely to be celebrated than scrutinized.

Why were these findings eventually repudiated? Since they offered a defense of the status quo and confirmed the prevailing ideology, who would have successfully criticized them?

First, the scientific defense of immutable hierarchy was eroded by the steady accumulation of evidence of the "intellectual equality and therefore the equal cultural capacity of all peoples" (Degler, 1991:61). A good deal of that research was produced by the many "prominent or soon to be prominent" male and female scholars of African American, Chinese, and European immigrant ancestry who— after finally being admitted to institutions of higher education—were pursuing scientific research and publishing systematic critiques of the existent literature. Black scholars such as W.E.B. Du Bois and E. Franklin Frazier, and those of European immigrant ancestry such as anthropologists Franz Boas, Alfred Kroeber, and Edward Sapir, trenchantly criticized the social science of the day and by their very presence challenged prevailing expectations (Degler, 1991).

The presumptions about the meaning of race were also especially challenged by increased inter-racial contact. The 1920s began the Great Migration (which continued through the 1960s) in which hundreds of thousands of African Americans from the rural south moved to northern cities. The movement to northern and coastal urban centers continued in the following two World Wars as black, Latino, Asian, and Native American men joined the armed forces and women followed war-time employment opportunities. The 1920s also brought the Harlem Renaissance, an outpouring of creativity from black writers, scholars, and artists in celebration of African and African American culture. "During the twenties, American

---

[2]While "it is hard to find any broad aspect of human performance or anatomy that has no heritable component at all," it is misguided to equate heritable with inevitable. "Genes do not make specific bits and pieces of a body; they code for a range of forms under an array of environmental conditions." A second common fallacy "consists in assuming that if heredity explains a certain percentage of variation among individuals within a group, it must also explain a similar percentage of the difference in [averages] between groups—whites and blacks, for example. But variation among individuals within a group and differences in mean values between groups are entirely separate phenomena. One item provides no license for speculation about the other" (Gould, 1981:156).

[white] social scientists of all kinds . . . gained an unprecedented opportunity to observe blacks in a fresh and often transforming way" (Degler, 1991:197). In short, their attitudes and expectations changed as a result of increased contact.

Generally, the scientific argument for the presence of inherent difference in the capability of categories of people was advanced by upper-class, native-born, white males on the faculty of prestigious universities. Few others would have had the means by which to disseminate their ideas or the prestige by which make those ideas influential. These theories of essential difference were not written by Native Americans, Mexicans, women, gays, African Americans, or immigrants from Asia or southern and eastern Europe. Most of these people lacked access to the public forums by which to make their experience known until the rise of the antislavery, suffrage, labor, and gay rights movements. Insofar as the people in these categories could be silenced, it was somewhat easier to depict them as essentially and profoundly different.

Popular Culture   Like the sciences, popular culture (i.e., the forms of entertainment available for mass consumption such as popular music, theater, film, literature, and television) may convey ideologies about difference and social hierarchy. At virtually the same time as social Darwinism gained popularity in America— indeed within two years of Louis Agassiz's arrival in the States in 1840—America's first minstrel show was organized. Both minstrel shows and the scientific use of social Darwinism offered a defense of slavery.

Minstrel shows, which became an enormously popular form of entertainment, were musical variety shows in which white males in "blackface" ridiculed blacks, abolitionism, and women's suffrage. Indeed, "women's rights was, together with abolition, one of the white minstrel shows' most consistently lampooned targets" (Garber, 1992:277). Minstrel show images had a lasting impact; they can be seen in the movies and cartoons of the 1930s and 1940s and in current American stereotypes.

Minstrel shows repeated and elaborated into stock themes certain images of blacks. As these shows traveled the country, their images were impressed upon whites who themselves had no direct contact with blacks and thus no information by which to counter the minstrel images.

The three primary characters of the minstrel show—the happy slave, Zip Coon, and the mammy—each functioned to legitimate slavery (Riggs, 1987). The image of the happy slave—singing and dancing, naive and childlike, taken care of through old age by the master, a virtual member of the family—asserted that blacks held in slavery were both contented and cared for. Zip Coon was a depiction of a northern, free black man characterized by a ridiculous use of language and laughable attempts to emulate whites; its point was that blacks lacked the intelligence to handle freedom. The mammy was depicted as a large and presumably unattractive black woman fully devoted to the white family she served. Like the happy slave, the mammy was unthreatening and content—no sexual competition to the white mistress of the house, no children of her own demanding attention, committed to and fulfilled by her work with her white family. Thus, the characters of the minstrel show hid the reality of slavery. The happy slave and mammy denied the brutality of the slave system. Zip Coon denied the reality of blacks' organization of the underground railroad, their production of slave narratives in books and lectures, and their organization of slave rebellions and escapes.

In all, minstrel shows offered an ideology about slavery constructed by and in the interests of those with power. They functioned to ridicule antislavery activists and to legitimate the status quo. Minstrel shows asserted that blacks did not mind being held as slaves and that they did not suffer loss and pain in the same way that whites did. The minstrel show was not the only source of this ideology, but as a form of popular entertainment it was a very effective means of disseminating such beliefs. The shows traveled to all parts of the country, their message masked as mere entertainment. The fact that they were part of popular culture made it easier to ignore their serious message—after all, they were "just" entertainment.

But within popular culture, an effective counter to the ideology of the minstrel show emerged in the speakers of the antislavery lecture circuit and in the publication of numerous slave narratives. Appearing as early as 1760, these narratives achieved an enormous and enduring popularity among Northern white readers. Frederick Douglass, the renowned anti-slavery activist, was both the most famous public lecturer in the history of the movement and wrote its best selling slave narrative. Whether as book or lecture, slave narratives provided an image of blacks as human beings. Access to the life histories of people who had been held as slaves provided the first opportunity for most whites to see a shared humanity between themselves and those held in slavery (Bodziock, 1990). Thus, slave narratives directly countered the images of the minstrel show. While popular culture offers a variety of sometimes mutually inconsistent messages, all parties do not meet equally on its terrain. Those with power have better access and more legitimacy, but popular culture cannot be so tightly controlled as to entirely exclude the voice of the less powerful.

Contemporary Popular Culture   Our discussion of the ideologies embedded in popular culture closes with a brief look at contemporary television images and how they have contributed to the belief that American society is now essentially open to people of all races and sexes.

Television probably stands as the most pervasive and influential form of popular culture today; it is also one of the most examined. What is immediately apparent in the world of television is the homogeneity of its population—a homogeneity which greatly contrasts with the realities of American life. For example, less than 1 percent of television's characters are Latino, less than 1 percent are Asian, less than 1 percent Native American, and slightly more than 1 percent are poor or lower income. African Americans are represented on television at rates from about 8 to 11 percent (Gerbner, 1993).

American demographics, however, are not only more heterogeneous than these figures, they are increasingly heterogeneous. As of 1990, 9 percent of the U.S. population was of Hispanic origin (an increase of 53 percent over the previous decade), 2.9 percent were classified as Asian or Pacific Islander (an increase of 107.8 percent), 0.8 percent were classified as American Indian, Eskimo, or Aleut (an increase of 37.9 percent), and 12.1 percent were African American (an increase of 13.2 percent) (U.S. Department of Commerce, 1993). In all, Latinos, Asian Americans, African Americans, Native Americans, and those classified by the census as "other races" comprise almost 29 percent of the American population, but they are only about 13 percent of television characters. While those who could be classified as poor or lower income constitute only about 1 percent of television characters, in 1990 13.5 percent of the U.S. population fell below the federally defined poverty line, an increase from a level of 11.7 percent in 1979. In all, the world of television is much more uniformly white and middle class than the nation. Difference itself is not visible on television.

But more than quantitative representation is important here. Television also offers us stories about the nature of our world. As communication professors Sut Jhally and Justin Lewis note in their study of *The Bill Cosby Show,* media images occupy an ambivalent space in our heads.

> Many of us know that most television is fiction, yet we see television as a key source of information about the world we live in. It is simultaneously real *and* unreal. We may know, for example, that television exaggerates the scale of violent crime for dramatic purposes; nevertheless, studies show that the more television we watch, the more violent we assume the world to be. Our awareness of exaggeration, in other words, is only momentary. . . . Television provides us with pictures of the world, of *our world,* and the knowledge that most of these pictures are fictional does not immunize us from believing in them (Jhally and Lewis, 1992:17).

Jhally and Lewis's analysis of audience reaction to *The Bill Cosby Show* indicates that one lesson whites take from television is that racism no longer hinders the advancement of African Americans. This notion comes from the status African Americans are depicted as having on television—like most other television characters, they are now also middle class. "Thirty percent of the working class characters on television between 1971 and 1976 were black; between 1984 and 1989 none of them were. The black working class seems to have disappeared from our screens" (Jhally and Lewis, 1992:58–59, 60).

While the proportion of the population that is middle class is generally overstated by television, the upward mobility that television would lead us to think African Americans have experienced is a particularly dramatic misrepresentation of reality, as many of the readings in this text make clear. Indeed, the case that Jhally and Lewis make is that even if you knew the actual situation of African Americans, the images you gathered from television would still seem more real. Even news reporting contributes to the belief that discrimination no longer limits the upward mobility of minorities, since the presence of minority news anchors is often construed to mean that prestigious and well-paid positions are now open to all (Entman, 1990).

Thus, the ideology is conveyed that American society is now open, that the civil rights movement of the past corrected racial discrimination, and that those who have not succeeded have only themselves to blame.

> During our analysis of the content of three major networks' programming, we came across only one program, *Quantum Leap,* that offered a glimpse of these racial divi-

sions. What was significant about this program, however, was that the story took place not in the present but in the past, during the early days of the Civil Rights movement. *Quantum Leap* was only able to show us racial divisions in the United States by traveling back in time to the "bad old days." All black characters in stories set in the present seemed blissfully free of racial impediments. Recent attempts by Hollywood to deal with racial inequality adopt the same strategy. Racism, whether in *Mississippi Burning, Driving Miss Daisy,* or *The Long Walk Home,* is safely confined to history. There are, of course, some exceptions (notably the work of Spike Lee), but the general impression is clear; racial inequality is behind us; we now live in Bill Cosby's brave new world, where anyone can make it (Jhally and Lewis, 1992:136).

This treatment of racism and discrimination as in the past is an analysis consistent with that put forward by policy makers over the last two decades. Thus, popular culture conveys the prevailing political opinion. It is, therefore, not surprising that white Americans think affirmative action programs are no longer necessary—popular culture tells them that this is the case. "White people are not prepared to deal with the problem of racial inequality because they no longer see that there *is* a problem" (Jhally and Lewis, 1992:136). Like all ideologies, the belief that discrimination no longer exists reflects the experience and interest of those with power and silences the experience of those outside its production. It can prevail over much empirical evidence—and even our own direct experience—by virtue of standing as the accepted and unquestioned way of thinking.

Many of the same themes that contemporary television has produced about African Americans can be found as well in the depiction of women's status. First, women on television are notable by their absence. While women comprise 51 percent of the population, they are one-third or less of all the characters on prime-time, news, and children's programming (Gerbner, 1993). Only on game shows and the soaps does the representation of women increase beyond that number. As advertisers have discovered that boys avoid programming that features female characters (but that girls will watch shows that feature boys), even Saturday morning children's television has become dominated by male characters with only occasional, minor roles played by females (Carter, 1991). Indeed—except for Miss Piggy—even the Muppets appear to be all male (Basow, 1992:158).

Women of all colors are not only underrepresented on television, their depiction on it significantly misrepresents their real-world situation. For example, consistent with the middle-class bias of television, "not only are more women on TV now shown as employed (75%) than is the case in real life (56%), but [*Roseanne* notwithstanding] most of these women have professional careers (for example, lawyers or managers), whereas most real women work in low-paying, low-status jobs" (Basow, 1992:159). Insofar as people confuse the real world with television, they are likely to conclude that discrimination against women is a thing of the past; they are even likely to think that women have privileged access to employment.

In selection 32, Susan Faludi details journalism's contribution to such misrepresentations in her analysis of "trend" stories. Trend stories are ones for which there is no empirical evidence. Indeed, trend stories often run counter to the evidence since they are concocted on the basis of anecdote and the general impressions of editors and reporters. As Faludi describes it, trend stories suggest that women's access to the workplace is now unaffected by sexism; that women are happy with their current status; and that if they are unhappy the cause is their own overcommitment to work not the discrimination they might experience there. Thus women are presented as the recipients of equal treatment, as no longer suffering from discrimination, and as bearing the responsibility for their own unhappiness or lack of achievement.

This image stands in considerable contrast to reality. While women's circumstances have unquestionably improved, differential treatment has not been eliminated, as selection 25 from the National Committee on Pay Equity makes clear. The gap between the median income of full-time working women and men persists, with discrimination explaining about half of the difference (Cherry, 1989).

Thus, it would be mistaken to conclude that women no longer experience discrimination in the labor force, or that they are generally satisfied with their circumstances. "Repeatedly in national surveys, majorities of women say they are still far from equality. . . . In poll after poll in the decade, overwhelming majorities of women said they needed equal pay and equal job opportunities, they needed an Equal Rights Amendment, they needed the right to an abortion without government interference, they needed a federal law guaranteeing maternity leave, they needed decent child care services" (Faludi, 1991:xv).

In all, television conveys the ideology that sex and race no longer bear on one's rank in the system of stratification.

Conclusion

As Karl Marx first considered it, ideology was "the mechanism whereby there can occur a difference between how things really are in the economy and the wider society and how people think they are" (Marshall, 1994:234). In this framework essay we have examined how science and popular culture can support the pervasive ideologies about the meaning of color, class, sexual orientation, and sex. The readings that follow focus on law and politics, the economy, science, and popular culture as social institutions that interpret and construct what difference means.

REFERENCES

Adam, Barry D. 1987. *The Rise of a Gay and Lesbian Movement.* Boston: G. K. Hall & Co.

Andre, Judith. 1988. Stereotypes: Conceptual and Normative Considerations. *Racism and Sexism: An Integrated Study.* Ed. Paula S. Rothenberg, 257–262. New York: St. Martin's Press.

Basow, Susan A. 1992. *Gender Stereotypes and Roles.* Pacific Grove, California: Brooks/Cole Publishing.

Bodziock, Joseph. 1990. The Weight of Sambo's Woes. *Perspectives on Black Popular Culture.* Ed. Harry B. Shaw, 166–79. Bowling Green, Ohio: Bowling Green State University Popular Press.

Brantlinger, Patrick. 1990. *Crusoe's Footprints: Cultural Studies in Britain and America.* New York: Routledge.

Carter, B. 1991. Children's TV: Where Boys Are King. *The New York Times,* pp. A1, C18, May 1.

Conrad, Peter, and Joseph W. Schneider. 1980. *Deviance and Medicalization.* Philadelphia: Temple University Press.

Cherry, Robert. 1989. *Discrimination: Its Economic Impact on Blacks, Women, and Jews.* Lexington, Massachusetts: Lexington Books.

Degler, Carl N. 1991. *In Search of Human Nature: The Decline and Revival of Darwinism in American Social Thought.* New York: Oxford University Press.

Entman, Robert M. 1990. Modern Racism and the Images of Blacks in Local Television News. *Critical Studies in Mass Communication* 7:332–345.

Faludi, Susan 1991. *Backlash: The Undeclared War Against American Women.* New York: Crown Publishers.

Garber, Marjorie. 1992. *Vested Interests: Cross Dressing and Cultural Anxiety.* New York: Harper.

Gerbner, George. 1993. Women and Minorities on Television: A Study in Casting and Fate. The Cultural Indicators Project, Annenberg School for Communication, University of Pennsylvania.

Gould, Stephen Jay. 1981. *The Mismeasure of Man.* New York: W. W. Norton.

Haines, David W. 1989. *Refugees as Immigrants.* Totowa, New Jersey: Rowman and Littlefield.

Jhally, Sut, and Justin Lewis. 1992. *Enlightened Racism: The Cosby Show and the Myth of the American Dream.* Boulder, Colorado: Westview Press.

Kasper, Anne 1986. Consciousness Re-evaluated: Interpretive Theory and Feminist Scholarship. *Sociological Inquiry* 56(1).

Katz, Michael B. 1989. *The Undeserving Poor.* New York: Pantheon Books.

Marshall, Gordon. 1994. *The Concise Oxford Dictionary of Sociology.* Oxford: Oxford University Press.

Omi, Michael, and Howard Winant. 1994. *Racial Formation in the United States.* New York: Routledge.

Pierce, Christine. 1971. Natural Law Language and Women. *Woman in Sexist Society.* Ed. Vivian Gornick and Barbara K. Moran, 242–258. New York: New American Library.

Portes, Alejandro, and Ruben G. Rumbaut. 1990. *Immigrant America: A Portrait.* Berkeley: University of California Press.

Riggs, Marlon. 1987. *Ethnic Notions.* California Newsreel (video).

Sayers, Janet. 1982. *Biological Politics: Feminist and Anti-feminist Perspectives.* London: Tavistock Publications.

Shipman, Pat. 1994. *The Evolution of Racism: Human Differences and the Use and Abuse of Science.* New York: Simon and Schuster.

Smith, Dorothy. 1978. A Peculiar Eclipsing: Women's Exclusion from Men's Culture. *Women's Studies International Quarterly* 1:281–295.

Smith, Dorothy. 1990. *The Conceptual Practices of Power: A Feminist Sociology of Knowledge.* Boston: Northeastern University Press.

Sniderman, Paul M., and Thomas Piazza. 1993. *The Scar of Race.* Cambridge, Mass. Harvard University Press.

Steinberg, Steven. 1989. *The Ethnic Myth: Race, Ethnicity, and Class in America.* Boston: Beacon Press.

Takaki, Ronald. 1993. *A Different Mirror: A History of Multicultural America.* Boston, Massachusetts: Little, Brown.

United States Department of Commerce. 1993. *Statistical Abstract of the United States, 1992.* Washington, D.C.: U.S. Government Printing Office.

Law and Politics

Ten Key Supreme Court Cases

Individuals' lives are affected not only by social practices but also by law as interpreted in the courts. Under U.S. federalism Congress makes laws, the president swears to uphold the law, and the Supreme Court interprets the law. When state laws appear to be in conflict with the United States Constitution or when the terminology of the Constitution is vague, the Supreme Court interprets such laws. We will focus here on Supreme Court rulings that have defined the roles individuals are allowed to assume in American society.

As the supreme law above laws enacted by Congress, the U.S. Constitution determines individual and group status. A brief document, the Constitution describes the division of power between the federal and state governments, as well as the rights of individuals. Only sixteen amendments to the Constitution have been added since the ratification of the Bill of Rights (the first ten amendments). Although the Constitution appears to be sweeping in scope—relying on the principle that all men are created equal—in reality the Constitution is an exclusionary document. It omitted women, Native Americans, and African Americans except for the purpose of determining a population count. In instances where the Constitution was vague on the rights of each of these groups, clarification was later sought through court cases.

Federalism provides four primary methods by which citizens may influence the political process. First, the Constitution grants citizens the right to petition the government, that is, the right to lobby. Second, as a civic duty citizens are expected to vote and seek office. Once in office citizens can change conditions by writing new legislation, known as *statutory law*. Third, changes can be achieved through the lengthy procedure of passing constitutional amendments, which affect all citizens. Controversial amendments have often become law after social movement activists advocated passage for several years or after a major national upheaval, such as the Civil War.

Last, the Constitution provides that citizens can sue to settle disputes. Through this method, sweeping social changes can take place when Supreme Court decisions affect all the individuals in a class. Thus, the assertion of individual rights has become a key tool of those who were not privileged by the Constitution to clarify their status in American society.

An examination of landmark cases reveals the continuous difficulties some groups have had in securing their rights through legal remedy. The Court has often taken a narrow perspective on what classes of people were to receive equal protection of the law, or were covered under the privileges and immunities clause.[1] Each group had to bring suit in every area where barriers existed. For example, white women who were citizens had to sue to establish that they had the right to inherit property, to serve on juries, to enter various professions, and in general to be treated as a class apart from their husband and family. Blacks sued to attend southern state universities and law schools, to participate in the all-white Democratic Party primary election,[2] to attend public schools which had been ordered to desegregate by the Supreme Court, and to vote without having to pay a poll tax. When these landmark cases were decided, they were perceived to herald sweeping changes in policy. Yet they proved to be only a guide to determining the rights of individuals.

I. *DRED SCOTT V. SANFORD* (1857)

Prior to the Civil War the Constitution was not precise on whether one was simultaneously a citizen of a given state and of the entire United States. Slavery further complicated the matter because the status of slaves and free persons of color was not specified in the Constitution nor were members of either group considered citizens. Each state had the option of determining the status and rights of these non-whites.

A federal form of government permitted flexibility by allowing states to differ on matters such as rights for its citizens. Yet as a newly invented form of government, a number of issues that were clear under British law were not settled until the Thirteenth, Fourteenth, and Fifteenth Amendments were added to the United States Constitution. Federalism raised questions about rights and privileges because a citizen was simultaneously living under the laws of a state and of the United States. Who had rights and privileges guaranteed by the Constitution? Did all citizens have all rights and privileges?

For example, what was the status of women? The Constitution provided for citizenship, but did not specify which rights and privileges were granted to female citizens. State laws considered white men and white women citizens, yet white women were often not allowed to own property, sue in court, or vote. Under federalism, each state enacted laws determining the rights and status of free blacks, slaves, white men, and white women so long as the laws did not conflict with the United States Constitution.

The *Dred Scott* case of 1846 considered the issues of slavery, property, citizenship, and the supremacy of the United States over individual states when a slave was taken to a free territory. The Court's holding primarily affected blacks, now called African Americans,[3] who sought the benefits of citizenship. Broadly, the case addressed American citizenship, a matter not clearly defined until passage of the Fourteenth Amendment in 1868.

Dred Scott was an enslaved man owned by Dr. John Emerson, a U.S. Army surgeon stationed in Missouri. When Emerson was transferred to Rock Island, Illinois, where slavery was forbidden, he took Dred Scott with him. Emerson was subsequently transferred to Fort Snelling, a territory (now Minnesota) where slavery was forbidden by the Missouri Compromise of 1820. In 1838, he returned to Missouri with Dred Scott.

In 1846 Scott brought suit in a Missouri circuit court to obtain his freedom on the grounds he had resided in free territory for periods of time. Scott won the case and his freedom. However, the judgment was reversed by the Missouri Supreme Court. Later when John Sanford, a citizen of New York and the brother of Mrs. Emerson arranged for the sale of Scott, the grounds were established for Scott to take his case to the federal circuit court in Missouri. The federal court ruled that Scott and his family were slaves and therefore the "lawful property" of Sanford. With the financial assistance of abolitionists, Scott appealed his case to the Supreme Court.

The Court's decision addressed these key questions:

1. Are blacks citizens?
2. Are blacks entitled to sue in court?
3. Can one have all the privileges and immunities of citizenship in a state, but not the United States?
4. Can one be a citizen of the United States and not be qualified to vote or hold office?

Excerpts from the Supreme Court Decision in *Dred Scott v. Sanford*[4]

Mr. Chief Justice Taney delivered the opinion of the Court:

. . . The question is simply this: Can a Negro, whose ancestors were imported into this country and sold as slaves, become a member of the political community formed and brought into existence by the Constitution of the United States, and as such become entitled to all the rights, and privileges and immunities, guaranteed by that instrument to the citizen? One of which rights is the privilege of suing in a court of the United States. . . .

The question before us is whether the class of persons described are constituent members of this sovereignty? We think they are not, and that they are not included, and were not intended to be included, under the word "citizens" in the Constitution, and can therefore claim none of the rights and privileges which that instrument provides for and secures to citizens of the United States.

In discussing this question, we must not confound the rights of citizenship which a State confer within its own limits and the rights of citizenship as a member of the Union. It does not by any means follow, because he has all the rights and privileges of a citizen of a State, that he must be a citizen of the United States. He may have all of the rights and privileges of a citizen of a State, and yet not be entitled to the rights and privileges of a citizen in any other State. . . .

Undoubtedly a person may be a citizen . . . although he exercises no share of the political power, and is incapacitated from holding particular office. Those who have not the necessary qualifications cannot vote or hold the office, yet they are citizens.

The court is of the opinion, that . . . Dred Scott was not a citizen of Missouri within the meaning of the Constitution of the United States, and not entitled as such to sue in its courts: and, consequently, that the Circuit Court had no jurisdiction. . . .

II. THE CIVIL WAR AMENDMENTS

The Civil War (1861–1865) was fought over slavery, as well as the issue of supremacy of the national government over the individual states.

After the Civil War members of Congress known as the Radical Republicans sought to protect the freedom of the former slaves by passing the Thirteenth, Fourteenth, and Fifteenth Amendments. These amendments, especially the Fourteenth, have provided the foundation for African Americans, as well as women, gays, Native Americans, immigrants, and those who are disabled to bring suit for equal treatment under the law.

Amendment XIII, 1865

(Slavery)

This amendment prohibited slavery and involuntary servitude in the United States. The entire amendment follows:

Section 1. Neither slavery nor involuntary servitude, except as a punishment whereof the party shall have been duly convicted, shall exist within the United States, or any place subject to their jurisdiction.

Section 2. Congress shall have power to enforce this article by appropriate legislation.

Amendment XIV, 1868

(Citizenship, Due Process, and Equal Protection of the Laws)

This amendment defined citizenship; prohibited the states from making or enforcing laws which abridged the privileges or immunities of citizenship; forbade states to deprive persons of life, liberty, or property without due process of law; and forbade states to deny equal protection of the law to any person. Over time the Fourteenth Amendment became the most important of the Reconstruction amendments. Key phrases such as "privileges and immunities," "deprive any person of life, liberty, or the pursuit of justice," and "deny to any person within its jurisdiction equal protection of the law" have caused this amendment to be the subject of more Supreme Court cases than any other provision of the Constitution. The entire amendment follows:

Section 1. All persons born or naturalized in the United States, and subject to the jurisdiction thereof, are citizens of the United States and of the State wherein they reside. No State shall make or enforce any law which shall abridge the privileges or immunities of citizens of the United States; nor shall any State deprive any person of life, liberty, or property, without due process of law; nor deny to any person within its jurisdiction the equal protection of the laws.

Section 2. Representatives shall be apportioned among the several States according to their respective numbers, counting the whole number of persons in each State, excluding Indians not taxed. But when the right to vote at any election for the choice of electors for President and Vice President of the United States, Representatives in Congress, the Executive and Judicial officers of a State, or the members of the Legislature thereof, is denied to any of the male inhabitants of such State, being twenty-one years of age, and citizens of the United States, or in any way abridged, except for participation in rebellion, or other crime, the basis of representation therein shall be reduced in proportion which the number of such male citizens shall bear to the whole number of male citizens twenty-one years of age in such State.

Section 3. No person shall be a Senator or Representative in Congress, or elector or President and

Vice President, or hold any office, civil or military, under the United States, or under any State, who, having previously taken an oath, as a member of Congress, or as an officer of the United States, or as a member of any State legislature, or as an executive or judicial officer of any State, to support the Constitution of the United States, shall have engaged in insurrection or rebellion against the same, or given aid or comfort to the enemies thereof. But Congress may by a vote of two-thirds of each House, remove such disability.

Section 4. The validity of the public debt of the United States, authorized by law, including debts incurred for payments of pensions and bounties for services in suppressing insurrection or rebellion, shall not be questioned. But neither the United States nor any State shall assume or pay any debt or obligation incurred in aid of insurrection or rebellion against the United States, or any claim for the loss or emancipation of any slave, but all such debts, obligations and claims shall be held illegal and void.

Section 5. The Congress shall have power to enforce, by appropriate legislation, the provisions of this article.

Amendment XV, 1870

(The Right to Vote)

The entire amendment follows:

Section 1. The right of citizens of the United States to vote shall not be denied or abridged by the United States or by any State on account of race, color, or previous condition of servitude.

Section 2. The Congress shall have power to enforce this article by appropriate legislation.

As we have seen, the Thirteenth, Fourteenth, and Fifteenth Amendments were added to the Constitution expressly with former slaves in mind. In Section 1 of the Fourteenth Amendment, the definition of citizenship was clarified and granted to blacks. In the Fifteenth Amendment black males, former slaves, were granted the right to vote. For women, however, the situation was different.

During the nineteenth century there was no doubt that white females were U.S. citizens, but their rights as citizens were unclear. For example, although they were citizens, women were not automatically enfranchised. Depending on state laws, they were barred from owning property, holding office, or voting. The 1872 case of *Bradwell v. The State of Illinois* specifically tested whether women as United States citizens had the right to become members of the bar. More generally it addressed whether the rights of female citizens included the right to pursue any employment.

III. *BRADWELL V. THE STATE OF ILLINOIS* (1872)

Mrs. Myra Bradwell applied to the Supreme Court of Illinois for a license to practice law. Her petition included certification that she was of good character and met other qualifications through examination. She also filed an affidavit stating that she was a U.S. citizen who was born in Vermont although she was currently residing in Chicago, Illinois. She petitioned the court for a license under the Fourteenth Amendment.

The Court's decision addressed these key questions:

1. Is Bradwell a citizen?
2. Is the right to practice law a privilege or immunity of a U.S. citizen?
3. Can a married woman practice law?
4. Did the legislators of Illinois intend to exclude females from the practice of law?
5. What is the proper role and status of women?

This case hinges on an interpretation of the "privileges and immunities" clause (Section 1) of the Fourteenth Amendment, which was defined over time through cases that came to the Supreme Court. (Specific privileges and immunities are not enumerated in the Constitution.) Justice Bradley's opinion is of particular importance because it goes beyond a review of the scope of the Fourteenth Amendment, analyzing which privileges and immunities Bradwell possessed or lacked as a woman.

Excerpts From the Supreme Court Decision in *Bradwell v. The State of Illinois*[5]

Mr. Justice Miller delivered the opinion of the Court:

We agree with him [Bradwell's counsel] that there are privileges and immunities belonging to citizens of the United States. . . . But the right to admission to practice in the courts of a State is not one of them. This right in no sense depends on citizenship of the United States. . . .

The right to control and regulate the granting of a license to practice law in the courts of a State is one of those powers which are not transferred for its protection to the Federal government, or controlled by citizenship of the United States. . . .

Mr. Justice Bradley:

. . . The civil law, as well as nature herself, has always recognized a wide difference in the respective spheres and destinies of man and woman. Man is, or should be, woman's protector and defender. The natural and proper timidity and delicacy which belongs to the female sex is evidently unfit for many of the occupations of civil life. The constitution of the family organization, which is founded in the divine ordinance, as well as in the nature of things, indicates the domestic sphere as that which properly belongs to the domain and functions of womanhood. The harmony, not to say identity, of interests and views which belong, should belong, to the family institution is repugnant to the idea of a woman adopting a distinct and independent career from that of her husband. So firmly fixed was this sentiment in the founders of the common law that it became a maxim of that system of jurisprudence that a woman had no legal existence separate from her husband, who was regarded as her head and representative in the social state. . . . Many of the special rules of law flowing from and dependent upon this cardinal principle still exist in full force in most States. One of these is, that a married woman is incapable, without her husband's consent, of making contracts which shall be binding on her or him. This very incapacity was one circumstance which the Supreme Court of Illinois deemed important in rendering a married woman incompetent fully to perform the duties and trusts that belong to the office of attorney and counsellor.

. . . The paramount destiny and mission of women are to fulfill the noble and benign offices of wife and mother. This is the law of the Creator.

. . . I am not prepared to say that it is one of her fundamental rights and privileges to be admitted into every office and position, including those which require highly special qualifications and demanding special responsibilities. In the nature of things it is not every citizen of every age, sex, and condition that is qualified for every calling and position. It is the prerogative of the legislator to prescribe regulations founded on nature, reason, and experience for the due admission of qualified persons to professions and callings demanding special skill and confidence. This fairly belongs to the police power of the State. . . . It is within the province of the legislature to ordain what offices, positions, and callings shall be filled and discharged by men. . . .

IV. *MINOR V. HAPPERSETT* (1875)

The Fifteenth Amendment was not viewed as a triumph for women because it specifically denied them the vote. Section 2 of the Fourteenth Amendment for the first time made reference to males as citizens. Since black men were included but women of all races were omitted, women were left to continue to seek changes through the courts. This was a difficult route because in subsequent cases judges often held a narrow view that the legislators wrote the amendment only with black males in mind. Thus, a pattern was soon established in which white women followed black men and women in asserting their rights as citizens as seen in the 1875 case of *Minor v. Happersett*. In *Dred Scott* the question was whether Scott was a citizen; in *Minor* the question was whether *Minor* as a citizen had the right to vote. In both cases the Supreme Court said no.

Virginia Minor, a native born, free, white citizen of the United States and the state of Missouri, over the age of twenty-one wished to vote for President, Vice-President, and members of Congress in the election of November 1872. She applied to the registrar of voters but was not allowed to vote because she was not a "male citizen of the United States." As a citizen of the United States, Minor sued under the privileges and immunities clause of the Fourteenth Amendment.

The Court's decision addressed these key questions:

1. Who is covered under the term *citizen?*
2. Is suffrage one of the privileges and immunities of citizenship?
3. Did the Constitution, as originally written, make all citizens voters?
4. Did the Fifteenth Amendment make all citizens voters?
5. Can a state confine voting to only male citizens without violating the Constitution?

While women were citizens of the United States and the state where they resided they did not automatically possess all the privileges granted to male citizens, such as suffrage. This landmark case was not overturned until the passage of the Nineteenth Amendment, which enfranchised women in 1920.[6]

Excerpts from the Supreme Court Decision in *Minor v. Happersett*[7]

Mr. Chief Justice Waite delivered the opinion of the Court:

. . . It is contended [by Minor's counsel] that the provisions of the Constitution and laws of the State of Missouri which confine the right of suffrage and registration therefore to men, are in violation of the Constitution of the United States, and therefore void. The argument is, that as a woman, born or naturalized in the United States is a citizen of the United States and of the State in which she resides, she has the right of suffrage as one of the privileges and immunities of her citizenship, which the State cannot by its laws or Constitution abridge.

There is no doubt that women may be citizens. . . .

. . . From this it is apparent that from the commencement of the legislation upon this subject alien women and alien minors could be made citizens by naturalization, and we think it will not be contended that native women and native minors were already citizens by birth.

. . . More cannot be necessary to establish the fact that sex has never been made one of the elements of citizenship in the United States. In this respect men have never had an advantage over women. The same laws precisely apply to both. The Fourteenth amendment did not affect the citizenship of women any more than it did of men . . . therefore, the rights of Mrs. Minor do not depend upon the amendment. She has always been a citizen from her birth, and entitled to all the privileges and immunities of citizenship. The amendment prohibited the State, of which she is a citizen, from abridging any of her privileges and immunities as a citizen of the United States.

. . . The direct question is, therefore, presented whether all citizens are necessarily voters.

The Constitution does not define the privileges and immunities of citizens. For that definition we must look elsewhere.

. . . The [Fourteenth] amendment did not add to the privileges and immunities of a citizen. It simply furnished an additional guarantee for the protection of such as he already had. No new voters were necessarily made by it.

. . . No new State has ever been admitted to the Union which has conferred the right of suffrage upon women, and this has never been considered a valid objection to her admission.

. . . Certainly, if the courts can consider any question settled, this is one. For nearly ninety years the people have acted upon the idea that the Constitution, when it conferred citizenship, did not necessarily confer the right of suffrage. . . . Our province is to decide what the law is, not to declare what it should be.

The *Dred Scott, Bradwell,* and *Minor* cases point to the similarity in the status of black men and women of all races in nineteenth century America. As one judicial scholar noted, race and sex were comparable classes, distinct from all others. Historically, these "natural classes" were considered permanent and unchangeable.[8] Thus, both slavery and the subjugation of women have been described as a caste system where one's status is fixed from birth and not alterable based on wealth or talent.[9]

Indeed, the connection between the enslavement of black people and the legal and social standing of women was often traced to the Old Testament. Historically slavery was justified on the grounds that one should look to Abraham; the Bible refers to Abraham's wives, children, men servants, maid servants, camels, and cattle as his property. A man's wife and children were considered his slaves. By the logic of the nineteenth century if women were slaves why shouldn't blacks be also?

Thus, the concepts of race and sex have been historically linked. Since "the doctrines were developed by the same people for the same purpose it is not surprising to find anti-feminism to be an echo of racism, and vice versa."[10]

Additional constitutional amendments were necessary for women and African Americans to exercise the privileges of citizenship which were automatically granted to white males. Nonetheless, even after amendments were enacted African Americans still had to fight for enforcement of the law.

V. *PLESSY V. FERGUSON* (1896)

After the Civil War the northern victors imposed military rule on the South.[11] White landowners and former slave holders often found themselves with unproductive farmland and no free laborers. Aside from the economic loss of power, white males were in a totally new political environment: Black men had been elevated to citizens; former slaves were now eligible to vote, run for office, and hold seats in the state or national legislature. To ensure the rights of former slaves, the U.S. Congress passed the Civil War Amendments and provided federal troops to oversee federal elections.

However, when federal troops were withdrawn from the southern states in 1877, enfranchised black men became vulnerable to former masters who immediately seized political control of the state legislatures. In order to solidify political power, whites rewrote state constitutions to disenfranchise black men. To ensure that all blacks were restricted to a subordinate status, southern states systematically enacted "Jim Crow" laws,

rigidly segregating society into black and white communities. These laws barred blacks from using the same public facilities as whites, including schools, hospitals, restaurants, hotels, and recreation areas. With the cooperation of southern elected officials, the Ku Klux Klan, a white supremacist, terrorist organization, grew in membership. The return of political power to whites without any federal presence to protect the black community, set the stage for "separate but equal" legislation to become a constitutionally valid racial doctrine.

Under slavery interracial sexual contact was forbidden but white masters nonetheless had the power to sexually exploit the black women who worked for them. The children of these relationships, especially if they looked white, posed potential inheritance problems because whites feared that such children might seek to exercise the privileges accorded to their white father. In order to keep all children of such relationships subordinate in the two-tiered racial system, descent was based on the race of the mother. Consequently, regardless of color all the children of black women were defined as black.

This resulted in a rigid biracial structure where all persons with "one drop" of black blood were labeled black. Consequently, the "black" community consisted of a wide range of skin color based on this one-drop rule. Therefore, at times individuals with known black ancestry might look phenotypically white. This situation created a group of African Americans who had one-eighth or less African ancestry.

Louisiana was one of the few states to modify the one-drop rule of racial categorization because it considered mulattoes a valid racial category. A term derived from Spanish, *mulatto* refers to the offspring of a "pure African Negro" and a "pure white." Over time, *mulatto* came to encompass children of whites and "mixed Negroes."

These were the social conditions in 1896, when Homer Adolph Plessy, a mulatto, sought to test Louisiana laws which imposed racial segregation. Plessy and other mulattoes decided to test the applicability of the law requiring racial separation on railroad cars traveling in interstate transportation.

In 1890, Louisiana had followed other southern states in enacting Jim Crow laws which were written in compliance with the Equal Protection Clause of Section 1 of the Fourteenth Amendment. These laws required separate accommodations for white and black railroad passengers. In this case, Plessy, a U.S. citizen and a resident of Louisiana, who was $\frac{1}{8}$ black, paid for a first-class ticket on the East Louisiana Railway traveling from New Orleans to Covington, Louisiana. When he entered the passenger train Plessy took a vacant seat in a coach designated for white passengers. He claimed that he was entitled to every "recognition, right, privilege, and immunity" granted to white citizens of the United States by the Constitution. Under Louisiana law, the conductor, who knew Plessy, was required to ask him to sit in a coach specifically assigned to non-white persons. By law, passengers who sat in the inappropriate coach were fined or imprisoned. When Plessy refused to comply with the order, he was removed from the train and imprisoned.

Plessy v. Ferguson is the one case that solidified the power of whites over blacks in southern states. Through state laws, and with the additional federal weight in the *Plessy* decision, whites began to enforce rigid separation of the races in every aspect of life.

In *Plessy,* Justice John Marshall Harlan wrote the only dissenting opinion. Usually in Supreme Court cases attention is focused on the majority, rather than the dissenting opinion. However, in this case Justice Harlan's dissent is noteworthy because his views on race and citizenship pointed out a line of reasoning which eventually broke down segregation and second-class citizenship for blacks.

Justice Harlan's background as a Kentucky slaveholder who later joined the Union side during the Civil War is cited as an explanation of his views. Some scholars speculate that his shift from slaveholder to a defender of the rights of blacks was caused by his observation of beatings, lynchings, and the use of intimidation tactics against blacks in Kentucky after the Civil War. In a quirk of history, when *Plessy v. Ferguson* was overturned in 1954 by a unanimous opinion in *Brown v. Board of Education,* Justice Harlan's grandson was a member of the Supreme Court.

The Court's decision addressed these key questions:

1. How is a black person defined?
2. Who determines when an individual is black or white?
3. Does providing separate but equal facilities violate the Thirteenth Amendment?
4. Does providing separate but equal facilities violate the Fourteenth Amendment?
5. Does a separate-but-equal doctrine imply inferiority of either race?
6. Can state laws require the separation of the two races in schools, theaters, and railway cars?
7. Does the separation of the races when applied to commerce within the state of Louisiana abridge the privileges and immunities of the "colored man,"[12] deprive him of equal protection of the law, or deprive him of his property without due process of law under the Fourteenth Amendment?

Excerpts from the Supreme Court Decision in *Plessy v. Ferguson*[13]

Mr. Justice Brown delivered the opinion of the Court:

. . . An [1890] act of the General Assembly of the State of Louisiana, provid[ed] for separate railway carriages for the white and colored races.

. . . No person or persons, shall be admitted to occupy seats in coaches, other than the ones assigned to them on account of the race they belong to.

. . . The constitutionality of this act is attacked upon the ground that it conflicts both with the Thirteenth Amendment of the Constitution, abolishing slavery, and the Fourteenth Amendment, which prohibits certain restrictive legislation.

. . . A statute which implied merely a legal distinction between the white and colored races . . . has no tendency to destroy the legal equality of the two races, or reestablish a state of servitude.

. . . The object of the amendment [the Fourteenth Amendment] was undoubtedly to enforce the absolute equality of the two races before the law, but in the nature of things it could not have been intended to abolish distinctions based upon color, or a commingling of the two races upon terms unsatisfactory to either.

Laws permitting and even requiring their separation in places where they are liable to be brought into contact do not necessarily imply the inferiority of either race to the other, and have been generally, if not universally recognized as within the competency of the state legislatures in the exercise of their police power. The most common instance of this is connected with the establishment of separate schools for white and colored children, which has been held to be a valid exercise of the legislative power even by courts of States where the political rights of the colored race have been longest and most earnestly enforced. One of the earliest of these cases is that of *Roberts v. City of Boston,* 5 Cush. 198, in which the Supreme Judicial Court of Massachusetts held that the general school committee of Boston had power to make provision for the instruction of colored children in separate schools established exclusively for them, and to prohibit their attendance upon the other schools.

. . . We are not prepared to say that the conductor, in assigning passengers to the coaches according to their race, does not act at his peril. . . . The power to assign to a particular coach obviously implies the power to determine to which race the passenger belongs, as well as the power to determine who, under the laws of the particular State, is to be deemed a white, and who is a colored person.

. . . We consider the underlying fallacy of the plaintiff's argument to consist in the assumption that the enforced separation of the two races stamps the colored race with a badge of inferiority. If this be so, it is not by reason of anything found in the act, but solely because the colored race chooses to put that construction upon it. . . . The argument also assumes that social prejudices may be overcome by legislation, and that equal rights cannot be secured to the negro except by an enforced commingling of the two races. We cannot accept this proposition. If the two races are to meet upon terms of social equality, it must be the result of natural affinities, a mutual appreciation of each other's merits and a voluntary consent of individuals.

. . . If the civil and political rights of both races be equal one cannot be inferior to the other civilly or politically. If one race be inferior to the other socially, the Constitution of the United States cannot put them upon the same plane.

It is true that the question for the proportion of colored blood necessary to constitute a colored person, as distinguished from a white person, is one upon which there is a difference of opinion in the different States, some holding that any visible admixture of black blood stamps the persons as belonging to the colored races, others that it depends upon the preponderance of blood . . . still others that the predominance of white blood must only be in the proportion of three fourths. . . . But these are questions to be determined under the laws of each State. . . .

Mr. Justice Harlan in the dissenting opinion:

. . . It was said in argument that the statute of Louisiana does not discriminate against either race, but prescribes a rule applicable alike to white and colored citizens. . . . [But] everyone knows that the statute in question had its origin in the purpose, not so much to exclude white persons from railroad cars occupied by blacks, as to exclude colored people from coaches occupied by or assigned to white persons.

. . . It is one thing for railroad carriers to furnish, or to be required by law to furnish, equal accommodations for all whom they are under a legal duty to carry. It is quite another thing for government to forbid citizens of the white and black races from travelling in the same public conveyance, and to punish officers of railroad companies for permitting persons of the two races to occupy the same passenger coach. If a State can prescribe, as a rule of civil conduct, that whites and blacks shall not travel as passengers in the same railroad coach, why may it not so regulate the use of the streets of its cities and towns as to compel white citizens to keep on one side of a street and black citizens to keep on the other? Why may it not, upon like grounds, punish whites and blacks who ride together in street cars or in open vehicles on a public road or street? Why may it not require sheriffs to assign whites to one side of a court-room and blacks to the other? And why may it not also prohibit the commingling of the two races in the galleries of legislative halls or in public assemblages convened for the consideration of the political questions of the day? Further, if this statute of Louisiana is consistent with the personal liberty of citizens, why may not the State require the separation in railroad coaches of native and naturalized citizens of the United States, or of Protestants and Roman Catholics?

. . . In my opinion, the judgment this day rendered will, in time, prove to be quite pernicious as the decision made by this tribunal in the Dred Scott case.

. . . The thin disguise of "equal" accommodations for passengers in railroad coaches will not mislead anyone, nor atone for the wrong this day done.

Thus, the *Plessy v. Ferguson* decision firmly established the separate but equal doctrine in the South until the National Association for the Advancement of Colored Persons (NAACP) began to systematically attack Jim Crow laws. It is ironic that in *Plessy* the systematic social, political, and economic suppression of blacks in the South through Jim Crow laws was justified in terms of a case decided in the northern city of Boston, where the segregation of schools occurred in practice *(de facto),* but not by force of law *(de jure).* In that 1849 case *(Roberts v. City of Boston,* 5 Cush. 198) a parent had unsuccessfully sued on behalf of his daughter to attend a public school. Thus, educational access became both the first and last chapter—in the 1954 case of *Brown v. Board of Education*—of the doctrine of separate but equal.

VI. *BROWN V. BOARD OF EDUCATION* (1954)

Unlike many of the earlier cases brought by individual women, blacks, or Native Americans, *Brown v. Board of Education* was the result of a concerted campaign against racial segregation led by Howard University School of Law graduates and the NAACP. In the 1930s, the NAACP Legal Defense Fund began to systematically fight for fair employment, fair housing, and desegregation of public education. Key lawyers in the campaign against segregation were Charles Houston, Thur-

good Marshall, James Nabrit, and William Hastie. Marshall later became a Supreme Court justice, Nabrit became president of Howard University, and Hastie became a federal judge.

By using the Fourteenth Amendment, *Brown* became the key case in an attempt to topple the 1896 separate but equal doctrine. Legal strategists knew that educational opportunity and better housing conditions were essential if black Americans were to achieve upward mobility. While one group of lawyers focused on restrictive covenant cases[14] which prevented blacks from buying housing in white neighborhoods, another spearheaded the drive for blacks to enter state-run professional schools.

In 1954, suits were brought in Kansas, South Carolina, Virginia, and Delaware on behalf of black Americans seeking to attend nonsegregated public schools. However, the case is commonly referred to as *Brown v. Board of Education.* The plaintiffs in the suit contended that segregation in the public schools denied them equal protection of the laws under the Fourteenth Amendment. The contention was that since segregated public schools were not and could not be made equal, black American children were deprived of equal protection of the laws.

The Court's unanimous decision addressed these key questions:

1. Are public schools segregated by race detrimental to black children?
2. Does segregation result in an inferior education for black children?
3. Does the maintenance of segregated public schools violate the Equal Protection Clause of the Fourteenth Amendment?
4. Is the maintenance of segregated public school facilities *inherently* unequal?
5. What was the intent of the framers of the Fourteenth Amendment regarding distinctions between whites and blacks?
6. Is the holding in *Plessy v. Ferguson* applicable to public education?
7. Does segregation of children in public schools *solely on the basis of race,* even though the

physical facilities and other "tangible" factors may be equal, deprive the children of the minority group of equal educational opportunities?

Excerpts from the Supreme Court Decision in *Brown v. Board of Education*[15]

Mr. Chief Justice Warren delivered the opinion of the Court:

. . . In each of these cases [NAACP suits in Kansas, South Carolina, Virginia, and Delaware] minors of the Negro race, through their legal representatives, seek the aid of the courts in obtaining admission to the public schools of their community on a nonsegregated basis. . . . This segregation was alleged to deprive the plaintiffs of the equal protection of the laws under the Fourteenth Amendment. In each of the cases other than the Delaware case, a three-judge federal district court denied relief to the plaintiffs on the so-called "separate but equal" doctrine announced by this Court in *Plessy v. Ferguson,* 163 U.S. 537. Under that doctrine, equality of treatment is accorded when the races are provided substantially equal facilities, even though these facilities be separated. . . .

The plaintiffs contend that segregated schools are not "equal" and cannot be made "equal," and that hence they are deprived of the equal protection of the laws.

. . . The most avid proponents of the post-[Civil] War amendments undoubtedly intended them to remove all legal distinctions among "all persons born or naturalized in the United States."

In the first cases in this Court construing the Fourteenth Amendment, decided shortly after its adoption, the Court interpreted it as prescribing all state imposed discriminations against the Negro race. The doctrine of "separate but equal" did not make its appearance in this Court until 1896 in *Plessy v. Ferguson, supra,* involving not education but transportation.

In these days, it is doubtful that any child may reasonably be expected to succeed in life if he is denied the opportunity of an education. Such an opportunity where the state has undertaken to provide it, is a right which must be made available to all on equal terms.

We come then to the question presented: Does segregation of children in public schools solely on the basis of race, even though the physical facilities and other "tangible" factors may be equal, deprive the children of the minority group of equal educational opportunities? We believe that it does.

To separate them [the children] from others of similar age and qualifications solely because of their race generates a feeling of inferiority as to their status in the community that may affect their hearts and minds in a way unlikely ever to be undone.

We conclude that in the field of public education the doctrine of "separate but equal" has no place. Separate educational facilities are inherently unequal. Therefore, we hold that the plaintiffs and others similarly situated for whom the actions have been brought are, by reason of the segregation complained of, deprived of the equal protection of the laws guaranteed by the Fourteenth Amendment.

. . . We have now announced that such segregation is a denial of the equal protection of the laws.

VII. *YICK WO V. HOPKINS* (1886)

In the 1880s the questions of citizenship and the rights of citizens were raised again by Native Americans and Asian immigrants. While the status of citizenship for African Americans was settled by the Thirteenth and Fourteenth Amendments, the extent of the privileges and immunities clause still needed clarification. Yick Wo, a Chinese immigrant living in San Francisco brought suit under the Fourteenth Amendment to see if it covered all persons in the territorial United States regardless of race, color, or nationality.

The Chinese were different than European immigrants because they came to the United States under contract to work as laborers building the transcontinental railroad. When Chinese workers remained, primarily in California, after the completion of the railroad in 1869, Congress became anxious about this "foreign element" that was non-Christian and non-European. Chinese immigrants were seen as an economic threat because they would work for less than white males. To address the issue of economic competition the Chinese Exclusion Act was passed in 1882 in order to prohibit further immigration to the United States. This gave the Chinese the unique status among immigrants of being the only group barred from entry into the United States and barred from becoming naturalized U.S. citizens.

Yick Wo, a subject of the Emperor of China, went to San Francisco in 1861 where he operated a laundry at the same premise for twenty-two years with consent from the Board of Fire Wardens. When the consent decree expired on October 1, 1885, Yick Wo routinely reapplied to continue to operate a laundry. He was, however, denied a license. Of the over 300 laundries in the city and county of San Francisco, about 240 were owned by Chinese immigrants. Most of these laundries were wooden, the most common construction material used at that time, although it posed a fire hazard. Yick Wo and more than 150 of his countrymen were arrested and charged with carrying on business without having special consent, while those who were not subjects of China and were operating some 80 laundries under similar conditions, were allowed to conduct business.

Yick Wo stated that he and 200 of his countrymen with similar situations petitioned the Board of Supervisors for permission to continue to conduct business in the same buildings they had occupied for more than 20 years. The petitions of all the Chinese were denied, while all petitions of those who were not Chinese were granted (with one exception).

Did this prohibition of the occupation and destruction of the business and property of the Chinese laundrymen in San Francisco constitute the proper regulation of business or was it discrimination and a violation of important rights secured by the Fourteenth Amendment?

The Court's decision addressed these key questions:

1. Does this municipal ordinance regulating public laundries within the municipality of San Francisco violate the United States Constitution?
2. Does carrying out this municipal ordinance violate the Fourteenth Amendment?
3. Does the guarantee of protection of the Fourteenth Amendment extend to all persons within the territorial jurisdiction of the United States regardless of race, color, or nationality?
4. Are the subjects of the Emperor of China who, temporarily or permanently, reside in the United States entitled to enjoy the protection guaranteed by the Fourteenth Amendment?

Excerpts from the Supreme Court Decision in *Yick Wo v. Hopkins*[16]

Mr. Justice Matthews delivered the opinion of the Court:

. . . In both of these cases [*Yick Wo v. Hopkins* and *Wo Lee v. Hopkins*] the ordinance involved was simply a prohibition to carry on the washing and ironing of clothes in public laundries and washhouses, within the city and county of San Francisco, from ten o'clock p.m. until six o'clock a.m. of the following day. This provision was held to be purely a police regulation, within the competency of any municipality.

. . . The rights of the petitioners are not less because they are aliens and subjects of the Emperor of China.

The Fourteenth amendment to the Constitution is not confined to the protection of citizens. It says: "Nor shall any State deprive any person of life, liberty, or property without due process of law; nor deny to any person within its jurisdiction the equal protection of the laws." These provisions are universal in their application, to all persons within the territorial jurisdiction, without regard to any differences of race, or color, or of nationality; and the equal protection from the laws is a pledge of the protection of equal laws. . . .

Though the law itself be fair on its face and impartial in appearance, yet, it is applied and administered by public authority with an evil eye and unequal hand, so as practically to make unjust and illegal discriminations between persons in similar circumstances. . . .

. . . No reason whatever, except the will of the supervisors, is assigned why they should not be permitted to carry on, in the accustomed manner, their harmless and useful occupation, on which they depend for a livelihood. And while this consent of the supervisors is withheld from them and from two hundred others who have also petitioned, all of whom happened to be Chinese subjects, eighty others, not Chinese subjects, are permitted to carry on similar business under similar conditions. The fact of this discrimination is admitted. No reason for it is shown, . . . no reason for it exists except hostility to the race and nationality to which the petitioners belong, and which in the eye of the law is not justified. The discrimination is, therefore, illegal, and the public administration which enforces it is a denial of the equal protection of the laws and a violation of the Fourteenth amendment of the Constitution. The imprisonment of the petitioners is, therefore illegal, and they must be discharged.

The decision in *Yick Wo* demonstrated the Court's perspective that the Fourteenth Amendment applied to all persons, citizens and non-citizens.

VIII. *ELK V. WILKINS* (1884)

In the late nineteenth century, Native Americans constituted a problematic class when the Supreme Court considered citizenship. Although Native Americans were the original inhabitants of the territory which became the United States they were considered outside the concept of citizenship. They were viewed as a separate nation, and described as uncivilized, alien people who were not worthy of citizenship in the political community. As Native Americans were driven from their homeland and pushed farther west, the United States government developed a policy of containment by establishing reservations. Native Americans who lived with their tribe on such reservations were presumed to be members of "not strictly speaking, foreign states, but alien nations." The Constitution made no provisions for naturalizing Native Americans or defining the status of those who chose to live in the territorial United States, rather than be assigned to reservations. It was presumed that Native Americans would remain on the reservations. The framers of the Constitution had not given any thought as to when or how a Native American might become a U.S. citizen. When the Naturalization Law of 1790 was written, only Europeans were antici-

pated as future citizens. The citizenship of Native Americans was not settled until 1924, when a statutory law, not a constitutional amendment, granted citizenship.

Elk v. Wilkins raised the question of citizenship and voting behavior as a privilege of citizenship. In 1857, the Court had easily dismissed Dred Scott's suit on the grounds that he was not a citizen. Since he did not hold citizenship he could not sue. *Minor v. Happersett* in 1872 considered the citizenship and voting issue with a female plaintiff. In that case, citizenship was not in doubt but the court stated that citizenship did not automatically confer the right to suffrage. In *Elk,* a Native American claimed citizenship and the right to vote. Before considering the right to vote the Court first examined whether Elk was a citizen and the process by which one becomes a citizen.

As midwest cities emerged from westward expansion in the 1880s, a few Native Americans left their reservations to live and work in those cities. John Elk left his tribe and moved to Omaha, Nebraska under the jurisdiction of the United States. In April 1880, he attempted to vote for members of the city council. Elk met the residency requirements in Nebraska and Douglas County for voting. Claiming that he complied with all of the statutory provisions, Elk asserted that under the Fourteenth and Fifteenth Amendments he was a citizen of the United States, who was entitled to exercise the franchise, regardless of race or color. He further claimed that Wilkins, the voter registrar "designedly, corruptly, willfully, and maliciously" refused to register him for the sole reason that he was a Native American.

The Court's decision addressed these key questions:

1. Is a Native American still a member of an Indian tribe when he voluntarily separates himself from his tribe and seeks residence among the white citizens of the state?
2. What was the intent of the Fourteenth Amendment regarding who could become a citizen?

3. Can Native Americans become naturalized citizens?
4. Can Native Americans become citizens of the United States without the consent of the U.S. government?
5. Must Native Americans adopt the habits of a "civilized" life before they become U.S. citizens?
6. Is a Native American who is taxed a citizen?

Excerpts from the Supreme Court Decision in *Elk v. Wilkins*[17]

Mr. Justice Gray delivered the opinion of the Court.

. . . The plaintiff . . . relies on the first clause of the first section of the Fourteenth amendment of the Constitution of the United States, by which "all persons born or naturalized in the United States, and subject to the jurisdiction thereof, are citizens of the United States and of the State wherein they reside"; and on the Fifteenth amendment, which provides that "the right of citizens of the United States to vote shall not be denied or abridged by the United States or by any State on account of race, color, or previous condition of servitude."

. . . The question then is, whether an Indian, born a member of the Indian tribes within the United States, is, merely by reason of his birth within the United States, and of his afterwards voluntarily separating himself from his tribe and taking up his residence among white citizens, a citizen of the United States, within the meaning of the first section of the Fourteenth amendment of the Constitution.

. . . The Indian tribes, being within the territorial limits of the United States, were not, strictly speaking, foreign States; but they were alien nations, distinct political communities, with whom the United States might and habitually did deal, as they thought fit, either through treaties made by the President and Senate, or through acts of Congress in the ordinary forms of legislation. The members of those tribes owed immediate allegiance to their several tribes, and were not a part of the United States. They were in a dependent condition, a state of pupilage, resembling that of a ward to his guardian.

. . . They were never deemed citizens of the United States, except under explicit provisions of treaty or statute to that effect, either declaring a certain tribe, or such members of it as chose to remain behind on the removal of the tribe westward, to be citizens, or authorizing individuals of particular tribes to become citizens. . . .

This [opening] section of the Fourteenth amendment contemplates two sources of citizenship, and two sources only: birth and naturalization.

. . . Slavery having been abolished, and the persons formerly held as slaves made citizens. . . . But Indians not taxed are still excluded from the count [U.S. Census count for apportioning seats in the U.S. House of Representatives],[18] for the reason that they are not citizens. Their absolute exclusion from the basis of representation, in which all other persons are now included, is wholly inconsistent with their being considered citizens.

. . . Such Indians, then, not being citizens by birth, can only become in the second way mentioned in the Fourteenth Amendment, by being "naturalized in the United States," by or under some treaty or statute.

. . . The treaty of 1867 with the Kansas Indians strikingly illustrates the principle that no one can become a citizen of a nation without its consent, and directly contradicts the supposition that a member of an Indian tribe can at will be alternately a citizen of the United States and a member of the tribe.

. . . But the question whether any Indian tribes, or any members thereof, have become so far advanced in civilization, that they should be let out of the state of pupilage, and admitted to the privileges and responsibilities of citizenship, is a question to be decided by the nation whose wards they are and whose citizens they seek to become, and not by each Indian for himself.

. . . And in a later case [Judge Deady in the District Court of the United States for the District of Oregon] said: "But an Indian cannot make himself a citizen of the United States without the consent and co-operation of the government. The fact that he has abandoned his nomadic life or tribal relations, and adopted the habits and manners of civilized people, may be a good reason why he should be made a citizen of the United States, but does not of itself make him one. To be a citizen of the United States is a political privilege which no one, not born to, can assume without its consent in some form.

Mr. Justice Harlan in the dissenting opinion:

. . . We submit that the petition does sufficiently show that the plaintiff is taxed, that is, belongs to the class which, by the laws of Nebraska, are subject to taxation.

. . . The plaintiff is a citizen and *bona fide* resident of Nebraska. . . . He is subject to taxation, and is taxed, in that State. Further: The plaintiff has become so far incorporated with the mass of the people of Nebraska that . . . he constitutes a part of her militia.

By the act of April 9, 1866, entitled "An Act to protect all persons in the United States in their civil rights, and furnish means for their vindication" (14 Stat. 27), it is provided that "all persons born in the United States and not subject to any foreign power, excluding Indians not taxed, are hereby declared to be citizens of the United States". . . . Beyond question, by that act, national citizenship was conferred directly upon all persons in this country, of whatever race (excluding only "Indians not taxed"), who were born within the territorial limits of the United States, and were not subject to any foreign power. Surely every one must admit that an Indian, residing in one of the States, and subject to taxation there, became by force alone of the act of 1866, a citizen of the United States, although he may have been, when born, a member of a tribe.

. . . If he did not acquire national citizenship on abandoning his tribe [moving from the reservation] and . . . by residence in one of the States, subject to the complete jurisdiction of the United States, then the Fourteenth amendment has wholly failed to accomplish, in respect of the Indian race, what, we think, was intended by it, and there is still in this country a despised and rejected class of persons, with no nationality; who born in our territory, owing no allegiance to foreign power, and subject, as residents of the States, to all the burdens of government, are yet not members of any political community nor entitled to any of the rights, privileges, or immunities of citizens of the United States.

In all, the Court never addressed Elk's right to vote because the primary question involved Elk's citizenship. By excluding him from citizenship because he had not been naturalized and because

there was no provision for naturalization, John Elk was left outside of the political community as was Dred Scott.

IX. *LAU V. NICHOLS* (1974)

In the nineteenth century, Native Americans and Asian immigrants sought to exercise rights under the Fourteenth Amendment although it had been designed explicitly to protect blacks. In the twentieth century again issues first raised by African Americans, such as equality in public education, presented other minority groups with an opportunity to test their rights under the Constitution.

Brown v. Board of Education forced the Court to consider the narrow question of the distribution of resources between black and white school systems. The *Brown* decision addressed only education. It did not extend to the other areas of segregation in American society, such as the segregation of public transportation (e.g., buses) or public accommodations (e.g., restaurants and hotels). Indeed, *Brown* had not even specified how the integration of the school system was to take place. All of these questions were taken up by the Civil Rights movement which followed the *Brown* decision.

Once the separate but equal doctrine was nullified in education immigrants raised other issues of equality. In the 1970s, suits were brought on behalf of the children of illegal immigrants, non-English speaking children of Chinese ancestry, and children of low-income parents.

In *Lau v. Nichols,* a non-English-speaking minority group questioned equality in public education. The case was similar to *Brown* because it concerned public education, the Equal Protection Clause of the Fourteenth Amendment, and the suit was brought on behalf of minors; but the two cases also differed in many respects. The 1954 decision in *Brown* was part of a series of court cases attacking segregated facilities primarily in southern states. It addressed only the issues of black/white interaction.

In *Lau v. Nichols* a suit was brought on behalf of children of Chinese ancestry who attended public schools in San Francisco. Although the children did not speak English, their classes in school were taught entirely in that language. (Some of the children received special instruction in the English language and others did not.) The suit did not specifically ask for bilingual education nor did the Court require it, but *Lau* led to the development of such programs. In bilingual education, the curriculum is taught in children's native language, but they are also given separate instruction in the English language and over time they are moved into English throughout their courses.

The *Lau* decision hinged in part on Department of Health, Education, and Welfare guidelines that prohibited discrimination in federally assisted programs. The decision was narrow because it only instructed the lower court to provide appropriate relief. The Court's ruling did not guarantee minority language rights, nor did it require bilingual education.

The Court's decision addressed these key questions:

1. Does a public school system that provides for instruction only in English violate the equal protection clause of the Fourteenth Amendment?
2. Does a public school system that provides for instruction only in English violate section 601 of the Civil Rights Act of 1964?
3. Do Chinese-speaking students who are in the minority receive fewer benefits from the school system than the English-speaking majority?
4. Must a school system which has a minority of students who do not speak English provide bilingual instruction?

Excerpts from the Supreme Court Decision in *Lau v. Nichols*[19]

Mr. Justice Douglas delivered the opinion of the Court:

> The San Francisco, California, school system was integrated in 1971 as a result of a federal court decree. The District Court found that there are 2,856 students of Chinese ancestry in the school system who do not speak English. Of those who have that language deficiency, about 1,000 are given supplemental courses in the English language. About 1,800 however, do not receive that instruction.
>
> This class suit brought by non-English-speaking Chinese students against officials responsible for the operation of the San Francisco Unified School District seeks relief against the unequal educational opportunities, which are alleged to violate, *inter alia,* the Fourteenth Amendment. No specific remedy is urged upon us. . . .
>
> The Court of Appeals [holding that there was no violation of the Equal Protection Clause of the Fourteenth Amendment or of section 601 of the Civil Rights Act of 1964] reasoned that "[e]very student brings to the starting line of his educational career different advantages and disadvantages caused in part by social, economic and cultural background, created and continued completely apart from any contribution by the school system." . . . Section 71 of the California Education Code states that "English shall be the basic language of instruction in all schools." That section permits a school district to determine "when and under what circumstances instruction may be given bilingually". . . .
>
> Under these state-imposed standards there is no equality of treatment merely by providing students with the same facilities, textbooks, teachers, and curriculum; for students who do not understand English are effectively foreclosed from any meaningful education.
>
> . . . We know that those who do not understand English are certain to find their classroom experiences wholly incomprehensible and in no way meaningful.
>
> We do not reach the Equal Protection Clause argument which has been advanced but rely solely on section 601 of the Civil Rights Act of 1964, 42 U.S.C. section 2000d. to reverse the Court of Appeals.
>
> That section bans discrimination based "on the ground of race, color, or national origin, in any program or activity receiving Federal financial assistance." The school district involved in this litigation receives large amounts of federal financial assistance. The Department of Health, Education, and Welfare (HEW), which has authority to promulgate

regulations prohibiting discrimination in federally assisted school systems, in 1968 issued one guideline that "[s]chool systems are responsible for assuring that students of a particular race, color, or national origin are not denied the opportunity to obtain the education generally obtained by other students in the system." In 1970 HEW made the guidelines more specific, requiring school districts that were federally funded "to rectify the language deficiency in order to open" the instruction to students who had "linguistic deficiencies". . . .

It seems obvious that the Chinese-speaking minority receive fewer benefits than the English-speaking majority from respondents' school system which denies them a meaningful opportunity to participate in the educational program—all earmarks of the discrimination banned by the regulations. . . .

Lau differed from *Brown* because it was not decided on the basis of the Fourteenth Amendment but on the Civil Rights Act of 1964. In reference to *Brown* the justices noted that equality of treatment was not achieved by providing students with the same facilities, textbooks, teachers, or curriculum. *Lau* underscores the idea that equality may not be achieved by treating different categories of people in the same way.

X. SAN ANTONIO SCHOOL DISTRICT V. RODRIGUEZ (1973)

The 1973 case of *San Antonio School District v. Rodriguez* raised the question of equality in public education from another perspective. As was the case in *Brown* and *Lau,* the Fourteenth Amendment required interpretation. However, unlike the earlier cases the issue was the financing of local public schools.

Education is not a right specified in the Constitution. Under a federal system, education is a local matter in each state. This allows for the possibility of vast differences between states and even within states on the quality of instruction, methods of financing, and treatment of non-white students. Whereas the *Brown* decision examined inequality between races, *San Antonio* considered inequality based on financial resources through local property taxes. *San Antonio* raised the ques-

tion of the consequence of the unequal distribution of wealth among Texas school districts. As with *Brown* and *Lau,* minors were involved; however the issue was not race or language instruction, but social class. Did the Texas school system discriminate against the poor?

Traditionally, the states have financed schools based on property tax assessments. Since wealth is not evenly distributed, some communities are able to spend more on education and provide greater resources to children. This is the basis of the *San Antonio* case where the charge was that children in less affluent communities necessarily received an inferior education because those communities had fewer resources to draw upon. The Rodriguez family contended that the Texas school system of financing public schools through local property taxes denied them equal protection of the laws in violation of the Fourteenth Amendment.

Financing public schools in Texas entailed state and local contributions. About half of the revenues were derived from a state-funded program which provided a minimal educational base; each district then supplemented state aid with a property tax. The Rodriguez family brought a class action suit on behalf of school children who claimed to be members of poor families who resided in school districts with a low property tax base. The contention was that the Texas system's reliance on local property taxation favored the more affluent and violated equal protection requirements because of disparities between districts in per-pupil expenditures.

The Court's decision addressed these key questions:

1. Does Texas' system of financing public school education by use of a property tax violate the Equal Protection Clause (Section 1) of the Fourteenth Amendment?
2. Does the Equal Protection Clause apply to wealth?
3. Is education a fundamental right?
4. Does this state law impinge on a fundamental right?

5. Is a state system for financing public education by a property tax which results in interdistrict disparities in per-pupil expenditures unconstitutionally arbitrary under the Equal Protection Clause?

Excerpts from the Supreme Court Decision in *San Antonio School District v. Rodriguez*[20]

Mr. Justice Powell delivered the opinion of the Court:

. . . The District Court held that the Texas system [of financing public education] discriminates on the basis of wealth in the manner in which education is provided for its people. Finding that wealth is a "suspect" classification and that education is a "fundamental" interest, the District Court held that the Texas system could be sustained only if the State could show that it was premised upon some compelling state interest.

. . . We must decide, first, whether the Texas system of financing public education operates to the disadvantage of some suspect class or impinges upon a fundamental right explicitly or implicitly protected by the Constitution, thereby requiring strict judicial scrutiny. If so, the Texas scheme must still be examined to determine whether it rationally furthers some legitimate, articulated state purpose and therefore does not constitute an invidious discrimination in violation of the Equal Protection Clause of the Fourteenth Amendment.

. . . In concluding that strict judicial scrutiny was required, the [District] court relied on decisions dealing with the rights of indigents to equal treatment in the criminal trial and appellate processes, and on cases disapproving wealth restrictions on the right to vote. Those cases, the District Court concluded, established wealth as a suspect classification. Finding that a local property tax system discriminated on the basis of wealth, it regarded those precedents as controlling. It then reasoned, based on decisions of this Court affirming the undeniable importance of education, that there is a fundamental right to education and that, absent some compelling state justification, the Texas system could not stand.

We are unable to agree that this case, which in significant aspects is *sui generis,* may be so neatly fitted under the Equal Protection Clause. Indeed, we find neither the suspect-classification nor the fundamental-interest analysis persuasive.

The wealth discrimination discovered by the District Court in this case, and by several other courts that have recently struck down school financing in other States, is quite unlike any of the forms of wealth discrimination heretofore reviewed by this Court.

. . . First, in support of their charge that the system discriminates against the "poor," appellees have made no effort to demonstrate that it operates to the peculiar disadvantage of any class fairly definable as indigent, or as composed of persons whose incomes are beneath any designated poverty level. Indeed, there is reason to believe that the poorest families are not necessarily clustered in the poorest property districts. . . .

Second, neither appellees nor the District Court addressed the fact that . . . lack of personal resources has not occasioned an absolute deprivation of the desired benefit. The argument here is not that the children in districts having relatively low assessable property values are receiving no public education; rather, it is that they are receiving a poorer quality education than that available to children in districts having more assessable wealth. Apart from the unsettled and disputed question whether the quality of education may be determined by the amount of money expended for it, a sufficient answer to appellee's argument is that, at least where wealth is involved, the Equal Protection Clause does not require absolute equality or precisely equal advantages. . . .

For these two reasons . . . the disadvantaged class is not susceptible of identification in traditional terms. . . .

. . . [I]t is clear that appellee's suit asks this Court to extend its most exacting scrutiny to review a system that allegedly discriminates against a large, diverse, and amorphous class, unified only by the common factor of residence in districts that happen to have less taxable wealth than other districts. The system of alleged discrimination and the class it defines have none of the traditional indicia of suspectness: the class is not saddled with such disabilities, or subjected to such a history of purposeful unequal treatment, or relegated to such a position of political powerlessness as to command extraordinary protection from the majoritarian political process.

We thus conclude that the Texas system does not operate to the peculiar disadvantage of any suspect class. . . .

Education, of course, is not among the rights afforded explicit protection under our Federal Constitution. Nor do we find any basis for saying it is implicitly so protected. . . .

In sum, to the extent that the Texas system of school financing results in unequal expenditures between children who happen to reside in different districts, we cannot say that such disparities are the product of a system that is so irrational as to be invidiously discriminatory. . . .

Mr. Justice White, with whom Mr. Justice Douglas and Mr. Justice Brennan join, dissenting:

. . . In my view, the parents and children in Edgewood, and in like districts, suffer from an invidious discrimination violative of the Equal Protection Clause. . . .

There is no difficulty in identifying the class that is subject to the alleged discrimination and that is entitled to the benefits of the Equal Protection Clause. I need go no further than the parents and children in the Edgewood district, who are plaintiffs here and who assert that they are entitled to the same choice as Alamo Heights to augment local expenditures for schools but are denied that choice by state law. This group constitutes a class sufficiently definite to invoke the protection of the Constitution. . . .

In San Antonio v. Rodriguez the Court did not find that the differences between school districts constituted invidious discrimination. A majority of the justices felt that Texas satisfied constitutional standards under the Equal Protection Clause. On the other hand, four justices in dissenting opinions saw a class (the poor) that was subject to discrimination and which lacked the protection of the Constitution.

XI. *BOWERS V. HARDWICK* (1986)

In most of the cases we have considered, plaintiffs have sued on the basis that their rights under the Fourteenth Amendment were violated. However, cases can reach the Supreme Court by several routes, one of which is a *writ of certiorari* which is directed at an inferior court to bring the record of a case into a superior court for re-examination and review. This was the case in *Bowers v. Hardwick* in which the constitutionality of a Georgia sodomy statute was challenged. This became a key case in the battle for constitutional rights for gay women and men.

The case of *Bowers v. Hardwick* began on the issue of privacy because the behavior in question took place in Michael Hardwick's home. In deciding the case, however, the justices shifted from the issue of privacy to question whether gays have a fundamental right to engage in consensual sex.

Michael Hardwick's suit was based on the following facts. On August 3, 1982, a police officer went to Hardwick's home to serve Hardwick a warrant for failure to pay a fine. Hardwick's roommate answered the door, but was not sure if Hardwick was at home. The roommate allowed the officer to enter and approach Hardwick's bedroom. The officer found the bedroom door partly open and observed Hardwick engaged in oral sex with another man. The officer arrested both men, charged them with sodomy, and held them in the local jail for ten hours.

The Georgia sodomy statute under which the men were charged made "any sexual act involving the sex organs of one person and the mouth or anus of another" a felony punishable by imprisonment for up to twenty years. When the district attorney decided not to submit the case to a grand jury, Hardwick brought suit attacking the constitutionality of the Georgia statute. Later, a divided court of appeals held that the Georgia statute violated Hardwick's fundamental rights. The Attorney General of Georgia appealed that judgment to the Supreme Court.

The Court's decision on the case was split. Five justices ruled that the constitutional right of privacy did not apply to Hardwick's case; four argued that it did. While the Georgia statute did not specify that only homosexual sodomy was prohibited, the Court's majority opinion was framed in those terms. (Most legal prohibitions are directed at nonprocreative acts irrespective of the sex of the participants.) The majority opinion also equated consensual sex within the home to criminal conduct within the home, an equation criticized by both gay rights activists and the dissenting justices.

> [The majority opinion] emphasized that the home does not confer immunity for criminal conduct, comparing gay sex first to drugs, firearms, and stolen goods and then to adultery, incest, and bigamy. In so doing, the Court evoked images of dissolution, fear, seizure, and instability. . . . [and] the stereotypical fear of gay men as predators and child molesters. . . . The majority [opinion] advances, mostly by implication, its view of gay sexuality as unrelated to recognized forms of sexual activity or intimate relationships, and as exploitative, predatory, threatening to personal and social stability. [Writing for the dissent] Justice Blackmun excoriates the majority's choice of analogies and its failure to explain why it did not use nonthreatening analogies such as private, consensual heterosexual activity or even sodomy within marriage for comparison[21]

While the majority argued that the past criminalization of sodomy argued for its continued criminalization, critics responded that "Whereas the task of the Court was to decide whether the criminalization of sodomy is consistent with the Constitution, the majority treated the fact of past criminalization as determinative. . . . It had no answer to Justice Blackmun's contention 'that by such lights, the Court should have no authority to invalidate miscegenation laws'."[22]

The Court's decision addressed these key questions:

1. Does Georgia's sodomy law violate the fundamental rights of gays?
2. Does the Constitution confer the fundamental right to engage in homosexual sodomy?
3. Is Georgia's sodomy law selectively being enforced against gays?

Excerpts from the Supreme Court Decision in *Bowers v. Hardwick*[23]

Mr. Justice White delivered the opinion of the Court:

> This case does not require a judgment on whether laws against sodomy between consenting adults in general, or between homosexuals in particular, are wise or desirable. . . . The issue presented is whether the Federal Constitution confers a fundamental right upon homosexuals to engage in sodomy and hence invalidates the laws of the many States that still makes such contact illegal and have done so for a very long time.
>
> We first register our disagreement with the Court of Appeals and with respondent that the Court's prior cases have construed the Constitution to confer a right of privacy that extends to homosexual sodomy. . . .
>
> Precedent aside, however, respondent would have us announce, as the Court of Appeals did, a fundamental right to engage in homosexual sodomy. This we are quite unwilling to do. . . .
>
> It is obvious to us that neither of these formulations [*Palko v. Connecticut*, 302 U.S. 319 (1937) and *Moore v. East Cleveland*, 431 U.S. 494 (1977)] would extend a fundamental right to homosexuals to engage in acts of consensual sodomy. Proscriptions against that conduct have ancient roots. . . . Sodomy was a criminal offense at common law and was forbidden by the laws of the original thirteen States when they ratified the Bill of Rights. In 1868, when the Fourteenth Amendment was ratified, all but 5 of the 37 States in the Union had criminal sodomy laws. In fact, until 1961, all 50 States outlawed sodomy, and today 24 States and the District of Columbia continue to provide criminal penalties for sodomy performed in private and between consenting adults. . . . Against this background, to claim that a right to engage in such conduct is "deeply rooted in this Nation's history and tradition" or "implicit in the concept of ordered liberty" is, at best, facetious. . . .
>
> Respondent . . . asserts that the result should be different where the homosexual conduct occurs in the privacy of the home. He relies on *Stanley v. Georgia*, 394 U.S. 557, (1969) . . . where the Court held that the First Amendment prevents conviction for possessing and reading obscene material in the privacy of one's home: "If the First Amendment means anything, it means that a State has no business telling a man, sitting alone in his house, what books he may read or what films he may watch . . .".
>
> *Stanley* did protect conduct that would not have been protected outside the home, and it partially prevented the enforcement of state obscenity laws;

but the decision was firmly grounded in the First Amendment. The right pressed upon us here has no similar support in the text of the Constitution, and it does not qualify for recognition under the prevailing principles for construing the Fourteenth Amendment. Its limits are also difficult to discern. Plainly enough, otherwise illegal conduct is not always immunized whenever it occurs in the home. Victimless crimes, such as the possession and use of illegal drugs, do not escape the law where they are committed at home. *Stanley* itself recognized that its holding offered no protection for the possession in the home of drugs, firearms, or stolen goods. . . . And if respondent's submission is limited to the voluntary sexual conduct between consenting adults, it would be difficult, except by fiat, to limit the claimed right to homosexual conduct while leaving exposed to prosecution adultery, incest, and other sexual crimes even though they are committed in the home. We are unwilling to start down that road. . . .

Justice Blackmun, with whom Justice Brennan, Justice Marshall, and Justice Stevens join dissenting:

This case is no more about "a fundamental right to engage in homosexual sodomy," as the Court purports to declare, . . . than *Stanley v. Georgia,* 394 U.S. 557 (1969), . . . was about a fundamental right to watch obscene movies. . . . Rather, this case is about "the most comprehensive of rights and the right most valued by civilized men," namely, "the right to be let alone." *Olmstead v. United States,* 277 U.S. 438, (1928) (Brandeis, J., dissenting).

The statute at issue, Ga. Code Ann. section 16-6-2 (1984), denies individuals the right to decide for themselves whether to engage in particular forms of private, consensual sexual activity. The Court concludes that section 16-6-2 is valid essentially because "the laws of . . . many States . . . still make such conduct illegal and have done so for a very long time . . ." (Holmes, J., dissenting). Like Justice Holmes [dissenting in *Lochner v. New York,* 198 U.S. 45 (1905)], I believe that "[i]t is revolting to have no better reason for a rule of law than that it was laid down in the time of Henry IV. It is still more revolting if the grounds upon which it was laid down have vanished long since, and the rule simply persists from blind imitation of the past."

Holmes, The Path of Law, 10 *Harvard Law Review* 457, 469 (1897). I believe we must analyze Hardwick's claim in the light of the values that underlie the constitutional right to privacy. If that right means anything, it means that, before Georgia can prosecute its citizens for making choices about the most intimate aspects of their lives, it must do more than assert that the choice they have made is an "'abominable crime not fit to be named among Christians'."

Like the statute that is challenged in this case, the rationale of the Court's opinion applies equally to the prohibited conduct regardless of whether the parties who engage in it are married or unmarried, or are of the same or different sexes. Sodomy was condemned as an odious and sinful type of behavior during the formative period of the common law. That condemnation was equally damning for heterosexual and homosexual sodomy. Moreover, it provided no special exemption for married couples. The license to cohabit and to produce legitimate offspring simply did not include any permission to engage in sexual conduct that was considered a "crime against nature."

The Court's decision did not uphold Michael Hardwick's contention that his sexual conduct in the privacy of his own home was constitutionally protected. While the decision was seen as a blow to the assertion of gay rights, the majority's narrow one-vote margin also indicated the Court's shifting opinion on this issue.

Notes

1. Privileges and immunities refer to the ability of one state to discriminate against the citizens of another state. A resident of one state cannot be denied legal protection, access to the courts, or property rights in another state.
2. In *Smith v. Allwright,* 321 U.S. 649 (1944) the Supreme Court held that a 1927 Texas law that authorized political parties to establish criteria for membership in the state Democratic party violated the Fifteenth Amendment. In effect, the criteria excluded non-whites from the Democratic party. Since only party members could vote in the primary election, the result was a whites-only primary. The Democratic party so dominated politics

in the southern states after the Civil War that winning the primary was equivalent to winning the general election.

3. Americans of African descent have been called blacks, Negroes, colored, or African Americans depending on the historical period.

4. 19 Howard 393 (1857).

5. 16 Wallace 130 (1872).

6. The Nineteenth Amendment that was ratified on August 18, 1920, stated, "The right of citizens of the United States to vote shall not be denied or abridged by the United States or by any state on account of sex. Congress shall have the power to enforce this article by appropriate legislation."

7. 21 Wallace 162 (1875).

8. Crozier, "Constitutionality of Discrimination Based on Sex," 15 *B.U.L. Review,* 723, 727–28 (1935) as quoted in William Hodes, "Women and the Constitution: Some Legal History and a New Approach to the Nineteenth Amendment" *Rutgers Law Review,* Vol. 25, 1970, p. 27.

9. Hodes, p. 45.

10. Gunnar Myrdal, *An American Dilemma: The Negro Problem and Modern Democracy.* New York: Harper and Row (2nd ed. 1962 [1944]), p. 1073–1074 as quoted in Hode, p. 29. This same biblical ground has yielded the idea that women are extensions of their husbands and his status.

11. The states under military rule were Virginia, North Carolina, South Carolina, Georgia, Florida, Tennessee, Alabama, Mississippi, Texas, Louisiana, and Arkansas.

12. The term *colored* was used in Louisiana to describe persons of mixed race who had some African ancestry.

13. 163 U.S. 537 (1896).

14. Restrictive covenants were written in deeds restricting the use of the land. Covenants could prohibit the sale of land to non-white or non-Christians.

15. 347 U.S. 483 (1954).

16. 118 U.S. 356 (1886).

17. 112 U.S. 94 (1884).

18. Native Americans and slaves posed a problem when taking the census count which was the basis for apportioning seats in the U.S. House of Representatives. Some states stood to lose representation if some of their slave or Native American population was not counted. Blacks were counted as 3/5 of a white man and only those Native Americans who were taxed were counted.

19. 414 U.S. 563 (1974).

20. 411 U.S. 1 (1973).

21. Rhonda Copelon, "A Crime Not Fit to be Named: Sex, Lies, and the Constitution," p. 182. In David Kairys (ed.), *The Politics of Law,* pp. 177–194, New York: Pantheon.

22. Copelon, p. 184.

23. 478 U.S. 186 (1986).

READING 22

The Rise and Fall of Affirmative Action

James E. Jones, Jr.

INTRODUCTION

Twenty years ago as a novice in the academic arena I wrote an article entitled "The Bugaboo of Employment Quotas."[1] It began: "It is a tribute to the power of persuasive public relations that new terms or slogans can be created, or old terms imbued with new meanings which become code words triggering mindless support of, or opposition to, the concept symbolized by the magic slogan. . . . The term 'quota' [seems to] stimulate lurid fantasies in the minds of otherwise sober and conservative citizens. . . . Undefined, laden with old prejudices, one need only label the opposed activity to evoke the desired opposition. In the current flap over the Government's halting efforts to require affirmative action to ensure equality of employment opportunity in government assisted construction, we can see a classic example of the 'lurid fantasies' reaction to a program."[2]

There followed an article exploring the development, theory, design, and argument for the legality and constitutionality of the revised Philadelphia Plan. That plan, as we shall see below, was pivotal to the modern affirmative action concept. Little did I realize that 20 years later I would still be writing and speaking on the same issues addressed in that publication.

I am bitterly disappointed that affirmative action is still a current events topic in the 1990s. However, the Supreme Court's decision in *City of Richmond v. J. A. Croson Co.,*[3] a case invalidating the city of Richmond's program requiring a percentage of city contracts or subcontracts set aside for minorities or women, enunciated such stringent standards for approval of such programs as to put their continued legality in grave jeopardy. The lack of clarity which has typified recent Supreme Court cases ensures that the debates on affirmative action, both in and out of the Court, will continue for some time to come. . . .

Although the title I have used here is "The Rise and Fall of Affirmative Action," I shall endeavor to convey my conviction that, like the mythical Phoenix, affirmative action shall rise again.

AFFIRMATIVE ACTION DEFINED

The modern debate over affirmative action has occupied us for over 20 years without achieving resolution of the underlying issues or contributing to clarification of what divides the nation. . . .

As a working definition of affirmative action I have adopted the following formulation: "Public or private actions or programs which provide or seek to provide opportunities or other benefits to persons on the basis of, among other things, their membership in a specified group or groups."[4] This definition permits us to direct attention to earlier efforts of the country to deal with the nagging problem of racism before the modern emergence, in 1961, of the presidential effort to utilize the affirmative action concept to secure equality of *employment opportunity* in government service and in government contracting.

Most of the cases today which directly address the issue of affirmative action have involved one of the following: (1) programs or plans for the enrollment of minorities or women in schools, primarily professional schools; (2) the set-aside of a percentage of subcontracts for minority or female subcontractors; or (3) the imposition of targets or goals for minority or female participation in employment.

It is worth noting that in the school desegregation cases involving busing to ensure desegregation, percentages of black or white students were required to be transferred between schools to achieve some semblance of proportionate representation. Busing has incurred inordinate attention and resistance over time; however, the cases were rarely if ever identified as involving affirmative action as the terminology has been used in modern debate. The Supreme Court has finally begun to recognize that the underlying principles are the same.[5]

SOME HISTORICAL BACKGROUND

In 1987 we celebrated the bicentennial of the American Constitution. I am certain that countless schoolchildren from grades K through 6 and beyond were treated to the glorious phrases which we celebrate in that memorable document. I am equally sure, however, that few if any were told that the Constitution was never conceived of as a color-blind document. Whatever "original intent" may mean, on this point the intent of the founding fathers is certainly clear. From the Declaration of Independence to the signing of the Articles of Confederation they did not intend that the brave statement "All men are created equal" include blacks. Moreover, blacks, slave or free, were not included in the word "citizens." The Supreme Court in *Dred Scott v. Sanford*[6] in 1857, concluding that at the time of the adoption of the Constitution, blacks were considered a "subordinate and inferior class of beings" who had no rights except those which whites might choose to grant them, made these limitations in our fundamental documents clear. I believe all students should be required to read that case as a peek into our dim, dark past. It is a well-documented statement of the status of black people in America. Moreover, it is irrefutable constitutional history that the Constitution of the United States was not color-blind.[7]

It took the Civil War and two constitutional amendments to affect the conditions described in the *Dred Scott* case as a matter of law. However, even with the Thirteenth and Fourteenth amendments on the books, the translation of the new *freedmen* from the condition of servitude to the condition of freedom and socioeconomic independence required more than brave words on yellowing parchment. While the Thirteenth Amendment abolished slavery, it did nothing to provide protection for the ex-slaves in their efforts to use the newly won freedom.

Whatever else the Fourteenth Amendment was intended to accomplish, there is compelling documentation to indicate that it was designed to place beyond constitutional doubt the early efforts of the federal government to aid the former slaves. Congress had adopted a series of social welfare laws expressly delineating the racial groups entitled to participate in the benefits of each program. These race-specific measures were adopted over the objections of critics who opposed giving special assistance to a single racial group. The most far-reaching of these programs was the 1866 Freedmen's Bureau Act, which was passed less than a month after Congress approved the Fourteenth Amendment. The evidence is overwhelming that one reason for the adoption of the amendment was to provide a clear constitutional basis for such race-conscious programs.[8]

What was striking about the Reconstruction Era legislation was the range and diversity of the measures designed to provide race-related relief. Included were programs providing land, education, special monies for colored military personnel, charters to organizations to support the aged or indigent and destitute colored women and children, federal charters for banks, and even the establishment of a special hospital in the District of Columbia for freedmen. Few if any of these programs were restricted to identified victims of specific acts of discrimination. All were race-specific. "Affirmative action" (i.e., racial preference) was the law and policy of the United States. Yet, more than 120 years later we are still litigating the legality and constitutionality of the principle.

One might question why Congress was concerned with the enactment of the Fourteenth Amendment to authorize the Freedmen's Bureau acts and related legislation. The language of the amendment makes it clear that it applies only to states. However, much of the legislation of that era (such as the Civil Rights Act of 1866, 42 U.S.C. 1983) was directed specifically at states, and it seems that Congress merely failed to recognize that there was anything in the Constitution which might have barred its actions at the federal level. It was not until much later in the development of our constitutional law that the loophole was closed, when the Fifth Amendment's due process clause was interpreted to prohibit conduct of the federal government which, if engaged in by a state, would violate the Fourteenth Amendment's equal protection clause. This incorporation of the Fourteenth Amendment equal protection standards into the Fifth was not fully accomplished until the 1950s.[9]

In the balance of my discussion in this essay I have adopted a perverse approach. Usually, one declares a proposition in the affirmative. Instead, I purport to declare a series of negatives. Why? Most people have learned whatever they know about affirmative action from the media. Most media presentations have been unsympathetic to affirmative action and frequently contain misconceptions and misinformation. In an effort to respond, I shall concentrate on what affirmative action is not.

NOT A NOVEL CONCEPT

The legal and conceptual underpinnings of the term "affirmative action" are rooted in ancient history of Anglo-American law. The basic concept comes from equity, which was originally a separate body of law administered in England by the court of chancery. Legal rules were unduly rigid and legal remedies were often inadequate. To do equity was to attempt to make things right, an attempt at fundamental fairness, if you will. When we became a separate country we retained the English system of common law, including the concept of equity.

More modern adaptations of the flexibility and equitable responses to novel problems where the law has proved inadequate are most readily illustrated by the New Deal's proliferation of administrative agencies during the Depression of the

1930s. Much of the social legislation of that era empowered the courts or the agencies to require such affirmative action as would effectuate the purposes of the law.

The "preferential treatment" or "reverse discrimination" aspects of modern affirmative action are also not novel. As noted earlier, as far back as 1866 in the congressional debates over the enactment of the Freedmen's Bureau acts, Congress explored both the constitutionality and the desirability of race-conscious remedies for the freedmen and other refugees of war. The reading of those debates impresses me with two things: (1) except for differences in terminology the concepts discussed were the same as modern debates over affirmative action; (2) it was clear that one of the purposes of that Congress was to resolve any doubt that such race-conscious programs were legal.

NOT ONE CONCEPT BUT TWO

The first and older notion of affirmative action is as remedy postadjudication, or as part of the adjudication process. It was called into being only after parties had adjudicated the issue before the court; the court had determined that a wrong had been done by the defendant to the plaintiff and exercised its power to fashion relief. This remedial power involves two aspects: (1) the power of the court to grant *make-whole relief* to the identified victims of the defendant's misconduct, *and* (2) the power, and the duty, of the court to issue such orders as would ensure compliance with the law in the future. The second aspect is *prospective* relief that focuses on the bad deeds of the defendant and not upon entitlement of identified victims of discrimination.

The second concept is affirmative action as legislative or executive program. Both approaches are directed to remedying a situation considered to be socially undesirable. In the first instance it has been determined by a court to be a violation of existing law. In the second instance, a legislative or administrative agency determines that some problem needs specific attention. A private entity, without benefit of adjudication or pressure by a public body, may also decide that a situation in which it has responsibility or authority needs attention. It could establish a program to deal with such a problem. Charitable institutions abound that are devoted to addressing particular problems.

Since at least 1969, beginning with the first case arising under Title VII of the Civil Rights Act of 1964 to reach the court of appeals, federal courts in designing remedies to deal with employment discrimination have imposed affirmative action plans upon defendants as part of their prospective relief after adjudication. This practice has tended to blur the distinction in modern debates between the two contexts in which affirmative action arises.

The principal modern application of the second concept was first embodied in an executive order issued by President Kennedy in 1961 and carried forward to the present day by an executive order issued by Lyndon Johnson in 1965.[10]

It should be noted that those executive orders required government contractors to refrain from discrimination *and* to take affirmative action to ensure equality of employment opportunity. They were not concerned with either the guilt of any defendants or the entitlements of any victims. They were concerned with addressing an existing social problem that had been unresponsive to other efforts.[11]

NOT A RESULT BUT A PROCESS

The federal government's affirmative action programs in employment require every good-faith effort to reach objectives or goals. They do not require that any particular goal be reached. Failure to reach the goal does not require the employer to lose his status as a contractor but may result in an investigation to determine what good-faith efforts he made to achieve the objectives. The federal government first embarked upon this approach in 1969 when the Department of Labor issued the revised Philadelphia Plan. After analyzing the relevant labor market and determining the availability of both qualified minorities and jobs subject to the federal government's contracting program, the Secretary of

Labor mandated that contractors participating in such programs make every good-faith effort to achieve a range of minority participation. The goals were well within the availability of minorities in the *qualified* labor pool. The requirement was to make every good-faith effort to reach the targets; it did not call for the impossible. Legal challenges to the program were successfully met.[12]

What we learn from Supreme Court cases is that a quota is a system which restricts or requires participation of a fixed and inflexible number or ratio of minorities, which includes sanctions to enforce compliance with the requirements, and in which the relevance of the requirements to the class affected and to the evil perceived is questionable or unestablished.[13] These "quota" elements are *not* those which are present in plans and programs which have met with approval in the courts.

NOT A MANDATE TO HIRE THE UNQUALIFIED

I have been unable to discover any affirmative action program, or any case imposing affirmative action as remedy, or after a consent decree, that requires the hiring of the unqualified. Affirmative action *methodology* excludes from the goals those people in the protected class in the labor market who are unqualified. The assertions of people who would mislead us regarding affirmative action when faced with these legal points are, "Well, you know how people behave. The employers will hire anybody just so they reach their quotas."

The logic of that argument would seem to be that since some people will continue to violate the law we ought to repeal the laws.

NOT CONCEIVED BY "LIBERALS"

. . . The modern affirmative action obligation which we have traced to John F. Kennedy's 1961 executive order had *its* "roots" in the prior administration.

In 1959, then Vice President Nixon was in charge of the president's executive order program prohibiting discrimination by government contractors. In his final report to President Eisenhower, Nixon identified the problem. It was not that evil people, with bad motives, intentionally harmed victims, but rather that *systems* operated in a business-as-usual fashion and kept re-creating the patterns of the past. I have paraphrased it here, but this is a "textbook" formulation of what we now call institutional racism or institutional sexism.

In 1961, John F. Kennedy responded by issuing an executive order which required federal contractors, and subcontractors, to take affirmative action to ensure equality of opportunity. He also *separately* prohibited intentional discrimination on the basis of race, color, religion, national origin, and so forth.

The implementation of goals and timetables occurred under the Nixon-Ford administration. The revised Philadelphia Plan was issued when George Schultz, the secretary of state under President Reagan, was secretary of labor serving under President Nixon. As indicated above, the Philadelphia Plan was unsuccessfully challenged in court, was unsuccessfully challenged in Congress, and ultimately the Department of Labor issued general rules and regulations requiring affirmative action for all government contractors.[14]

Every president since Roosevelt . . . has either issued his own executive order or continued the order in effect when he was elected. While there was much "sound and fury" from the Reagan administration regarding the demise of the affirmative action rules, and even a proposal that the executive order be revised, the fact is that these rules stand on the books as the existing requirements. Documentation of failure to enforce them would subject the government to legal action in the court.[15] Reagan signed into law bills requiring affirmative action. It would be difficult to sustain a charge that Eisenhower, Nixon, and Reagan were "liberals."

We heard little from the Bush administration regarding its intentions except first vetoing legislative efforts to address civil rights cases which threatened affirmative action and other equal employment gains. Bush finally signed the Civil Rights Act of 1991 which Congress passed with some minor compromise language addressing the quota issue. Efforts by some in his administration to water down the affirmative action requirements under the existing executive order were quickly rejected by the president.

NOT REJECTED BY MAJOR PRIVATE EMPLOYERS

Under the Reagan administration the United States Department of Justice aggressively attacked affirmative action, appearing in the Supreme Court in opposition to existing programs and counseling cities and other local entities to revoke or modify their affirmative action requirements. During that era representatives of large employers particularly indicated that they not only considered goals and timetables good business but believed them to be right as well. More significantly, both they and their lawyers concluded that it was legally prudent to maintain affirmative action programs. So long as programs are not declared illegal, and all efforts of the Justice Department during the earlier period failed to establish that the programs violated Title VII, then employers are able to use them defensively when they are accused of individual or class-action discrimination in Title VII cases.

The burden of the so-called reverse-discrimination plaintiff who would challenge the employer's affirmative action plan requires proof of intent to discriminate. The official rules and regulations of the Equal Employment Opportunity Commission accord to an employer operating under a bona fide affirmative action plan a good-faith defense against litigation. Although that defense might not be considered operative against the unconsenting plaintiff, it would certainly seem reasonable that the Supreme Court would conclude that the employer's good-faith compliance with such an affirmative action plan is a legitimate business justification for his action. Answers to these questions await future litigation.

NOT ABANDONED BY PUBLIC EMPLOYERS

In the last several years the number of states with programs requiring affirmative action has increased appreciably. In 1989 there were at least 36, including the District of Columbia. At the University of Wisconsin we recently completed a survey of equal employment and affirmative action in local governments, and at its most conservative projection our data suggest that 958 local governments have affirmative action in contracting programs. A less conservative but still plausible projection would put that estimate at more than 2,000 such programs.[16]

The National Association of Counties, representing more than 2,100 of the nation's 3,106 counties, adopted a resolution committed to maintaining affirmative action goals and timetables to increase minority hiring. State and local government organizations had earlier opposed changes in the president's executive order with regard to goals and timetables.[17] In an earlier case the Supreme Court indicated that the making of choices among allocation of resources for competing legitimate ends lies more properly with elected officials than with the Court.[18] . . .

NOT INEFFECTIVE

For those who could possibly benefit from affirmative action-those who are already qualified, able, and available—affirmative action programs have been both effective and efficient. Although there were some older studies that questioned the effectiveness of the government's executive order program, they are based on earlier data, much of it collected before the government established goals and timetables. More recent, comprehensive studies of the impact of affirmative action make it clear that there has been increased minority participation in jobs subject to the federal executive order.[19]

The *efficiency* aspect of the program relates to the requirement of an undertaking by the employer on his own to improve the participation rate of the qualified affected groups without the necessity of additional enforcement mechanisms. Since there is no claim that anybody is guilty of anything illegal, immoral, or unethical, targeting accomplishes participation of the underutilized groups with a minimum of animosity and divisiveness. That which persists is generated by representatives of those who have had the advantages of the past and want to continue those prerogatives in the future.

We do not *yet* have sufficient economic data to evaluate the effectiveness of affirmative action as remedy. It would seem self-evident that court-ordered affirmative action would also be effective *if monitored.*

NOT A BOON TO THE UNDERCLASS

It is not likely that any of the affirmative action programs have measurably helped the underclass of America, which seems to be growing. I should limit this assertion to affirmative action in employment, since training and educational programs certainly would and should target members of our society who lack the education and skills to be beneficiaries of other affirmative action programs.

This is not a minority problem alone. Most of the unemployed poor, most of the people in this country who are below the poverty level, are not minorities. Minorities are disproportionately represented in this group, to be sure, but it is mostly white. Women, single heads of households, are disproportionately represented in the group, and a disproportionate number of those are also black.

It is obvious on its face that affirmative action goals and timetables in employment, which focus upon qualified protected-class members, could have no appreciable impact on the plight of the people who are unqualified. The reason is clear. For persons without education or skills, without some qualification that is in demand, affirmative action in employment is of little benefit.

If anti-affirmative action forces are victorious in attacks on contract setasides, then efforts in employment, in education and training, in housing and health and all other social activities wherein special efforts have been undertaken to include minorities, will also cease.

NEITHER UNCONSTITUTIONAL NOR ILLEGAL

In the last 20 years, the Supreme Court has addressed the constitutionality and the legality of affirmative action in a multiplicity of settings. It has been confronted with the programs of private parties, of states, and of Congress itself. It has looked at admission to educational institutions, at government subcontracting, and at employment in hiring and in layoffs. Most of these cases have been decided by a divided Court, often with a plurality opinion not supported by a majority of the Court, and with "opinion salad" of three or four concurrences and dissents. What often gets lost in all this confusion is the basic posture of affirmative action programs. The Supreme Court has never held that the principle of affirmative action is impermissible. Even when the Justices have found a particular program to be over the line, they have stuck to the position that the Constitution of the United States and the civil rights laws do allow for some affirmative action programs. The Court has articulated factors that should be considered and conditions that must be met for a particular plan to be upheld, but the basic concept is still considered constitutional and legal. As a practical matter, however, it may well be that what the Court has given with one hand it has taken away with the other.

Except to deny review of numerous employment cases, the United States Supreme Court did not enter the affirmative action debate until *DeFunis v. Odegaard,*[20] a law school admissions case that the Supreme Court accepted for review and then dismissed as moot. Then Justice Douglas in dissent spawned a host of commentary and the debate raged on until the Court addressed the issue again in *Regents of the University of*

California v. Bakke.[21] In these two cases, at issue were affirmative action programs established for minority students by a law school in the first instance and a medical school in the second. In both cases the universities had sought to reserve a set number of seats in the entering classes for minorities. Due to the limited number of places in the entering class, and the differential performance rates of minorities generally as compared to majority candidates on admissions examinations, it was unlikely that sufficient minorities would be admitted into those classes if acceptance for admission were determined by rank-ordering applicants by grade point and test scores.

Both these cases involved two American myths: (1) "distinctions between citizens solely because of their ancestry are by their nature odious to a free people whose institutions are founded upon the doctrine of equality",[22] (2) the myth of merit.

As far as the first myth—classification by race or ancestry being odious to a free people—is concerned, we might well contemplate the lessons learned from a brief examination of the status of America circa 1857 as illustrated by the Supreme Court's decision in *Dred Scott v. Sanford.*

Even more paradoxical, at the moment when the Supreme Court in 1943 intoned this principle of equality, racial segregation was the law of the land and constitutionally valid. Indeed, how can racial separation exist without classification by race in the first instance? In 1943 we were engaged with our allies in World War II, a war to make the world free for democracy. The military forces of the United States were segregated by race. Merit was irrelevant to the classification. Blacks who scored above the 90th percentile on the navy's exams were still ineligible for officers' training. In the army and air force, they were relegated to segregated units. The war effort was color-coded.

Granted, since this country's inception we have been chasing something called a meritocracy. Divorced from England, where positions of aristocracy were determined primarily by birthright, a

principle we rejected, the new America believed that positions of leadership were to be determined on the basis of merit. Somewhere along the line we got the notion that we could discover superior intellectual ability by a series of tests, could rank people in order of their performance thereon, and could thus determine comparative merit. A score of 100 demonstrated merit superior to 99, 99 to 98, 98 to 97, and so on. In our pursuit of meritocracy, we have imbued test performance with the halo of superior merit, at least in theory. Those who achieve high test scores perceive themselves as having a right to the best opportunities. The fact of the matter is that virtually no system operates in such a stilted fashion. I suspect the use of tests in jobs has its roots in educational testing. The first affirmative action cases to reach the Supreme Court were school admission cases.[23] Schools that claim that merit controls admission have always had a multiplicity of exceptions, ranging from the size of the contribution of alumni and the relationship of the applicants to such benefactors, to the determination that no matter what the merit of the applicants, certain ones would not be admissible. Even when the exclusions were modified, frequently a quota limiting the number of applicants from certain classes of people was imposed.*

Similarly, in almost all civil service systems where merit allegedly controls, actual practice deviates from the principle. What usually happens is that the top three candidates or the top five (or some other number) on the eligibility list are referred to the selecting officer, who may, without explanation, choose anyone from that group. Moreover, in most instances veterans are given points to add to their scores, not because of any test performance but as entitlement for service to the country.

---

*An interesting aside on the myth of merit from the past: No matter how bright and agile a woman was, prior to affirmative action, she would not be acceptable as an appointment to West Point, to the naval academy, or to other military schools. After affirmative action, however, a woman cadet was chosen to lead the entire corps at West Point in 1989. The football teams of all the academies were disproportionately black.

It is important to note also that in neither *DeFunis* nor *Bakke* was there an assertion that the minority applicants were unqualified. The issues were that the majority plaintiff scored higher on the tests and had better grades than some minority candidates accepted and therefore was entitled to a position, which but for the affirmative action program he would have received, or so the argument goes.

The pivotal opinion in the *Bakke* case was that of Justice Powell. He and four of his colleagues found that it was not *per se* unconstitutional to use race in affirmative action programs when the programs were appropriately crafted. However, Powell concluded that the particular program offended the law. Four other colleagues of his agreed that it offended the law and thought that the discussion of the constitutionality of the programs was inappropriate. In that case, with the welter of opinions, everybody won and everybody lost.

The next significant case on affirmative action in the Supreme Court was *United Steelworkers of America v. Weber.*[24] The Court there approved an affirmative action program over the protests of a white male employee who alleged reverse discrimination. The company and its union voluntarily entered into a program to deal with what they perceived to be a problem of minority workers' entry into skilled crafts. Noting the widespread exclusion of blacks by construction industry unions, the Court approved a voluntary program which provided in-house training for the skilled jobs, with participation in the program divided equally between black and white employees on the basis of seniority. The narrow issue the Court decided in the *Weber* case was that voluntary adoption of such a program under the circumstances did not violate Title VII of the Civil Rights Act of 1964, which prohibited employment discrimination. Again, the Court was divided, with dissenting opinions contending that the majority misread the statute.

In *Fullilove v. Klutznick*[25] the Court examined a program in which Congress had established a 10 percent set-aside of certain federal contracts for minority contractors. By a 6-3 vote the Court sustained the constitutionality of the program, although several opinions were written taking different approaches. Thus, the theory upon which the Court sustained the program is somewhat uncertain. Significantly, then Chief Justice Warren Burger determined that the judiciary was not the exclusive branch to address the effects of past discrimination; rather, elected officials, such as chief executives and appropriate legislative bodies, are the more appropriate governmental entities to establish affirmative action programs to deal with the legacy of our past.[26] A major issue dividing the Supreme Court in these affirmative action cases was by what standard courts should evaluate programs which admittedly used race classification as a significant ingredient. . . .

In 1987, the Supreme Court decided two affirmative action cases—one involving affirmative action as program, the other as remedy.

In *Johnson v. Transportation Agency, Santa Clara County, California,*[27] a male employee of the county brought an employment discrimination action alleging that he was denied a promotion because of his sex. In the rankings on the eligibility list a woman ranked below the man, just barely, and was chosen over him. The lower court granted retroactive promotion and pay and enjoined the county agency from further discrimination. On appeal, the Ninth Circuit reversed, holding that the county agency's affirmative action plan, which had been adopted to obtain a balance between the sexes in the workforce, was valid. The plan contained neither an express statement fixing its duration nor a statement that it was intended to be permanent, nor did the agency show that it had a history of purposeful discrimination. The agency did demonstrate conspicuous imbalance in its workforce. The plaintiff had failed to show that the plan prevented or would preclude men from obtaining promotions. The plan did not set quotas in any job classification but established a long-range goal to attain a workforce whose composition in all major job classifications approximated the distribution of women, minorities, and handicapped persons in the county labor market. At the time no woman had ever held any of the agency's 238 skilled craft positions.

The Supreme Court upheld the county's action, again with a multiplicity of opinions. Justice O'Connor concurred in the results. The majority stated that it applied to the county the standard enunciated in *Weber.* Thus at the very least, the case establishes that a governmental entity can voluntarily adopt an affirmative action plan, at least dealing with sex, where it was reasonable for it to consider sex as one factor in making its decision. The case did not litigate the constitutional issue, as the plaintiff did not raise it.

In *United States v. Paradise,*[28] a case which had been in litigation in one form or another since 1971, the federal district court finally ordered the state of Alabama to hire one black for every white state trooper and to adopt a promotion plan based on numerical goals as well as on the availability of qualified applicants from the pool of black state troopers eligible for promotion. The Court again debated its fundamental differences. However, a plurality suggested that "In determining whether race conscious remedies are appropriate we look to several factors, including the necessity for the relief and the efficacy of alternative remedies, the flexibility and duration of the relief, including the availability of waiver provisions; the relationship of the numerical goals to the relevant labor markets; and the impact of the relief on the rights of third parties."[29] . . .

In *City of Richmond v. J. A. Croson,* there is finally a majority on the issue of which standard shall be applicable to race-based remedial programs. The Supreme Court struck down a provision enacted by the Richmond city council whereby prime contractors awarded city construction contracts were required to subcontract at least 30 percent of the dollar amount to one or more minority-owned business enterprises. The Court cleared up the confusion which had been spawned by the plurality in [a previous case] regarding whether the state actor must itself be implicated in prior discrimination as a predicate for establishing an affirmative action program. If

a local subdivision of a state has the delegated authority to do so, the Supreme Court concluded it may act to eradicate the effects of private discrimination within its own jurisdiction. It was not necessary to implicate the state or local entity in the discrimination. It would be enough if the city demonstrated that it was a passive participant in a system of racial exclusion practiced by other elements of the industry.

Significantly, the majority of the Court concluded that strict scrutiny was the required standard of analysis. To institute a program requiring classification based on race (1) any racial classification must be justified by a compelling government interest; (2) the means chosen by the state to effectuate its purpose must be narrowly tailored to the achievement of that goal. The Court found neither prong of the strict-scrutiny test satisfied in the *Croson* case. The case directs our attention to the *details* upon which these programs rest as well as the *details* upon which the plans themselves, in a remedial sense, rest. It seems that the factor analysis set forth in the plurality opinion in *Paradise* is endorsed by a majority. The difficulty is that one is unable to conclude with certainty the specificity to which compliance with these programs will be held.

One of the intriguing and vexing issues is the concentration by Justice O'Connor on the extent to which the city would be required to explore available alternatives prior to instituting any "quotas." She has shown preoccupation with the utilization of alternatives in previous cases involving the imposition of an affirmative action remedy (*Local 28 of Sheetmetal Workers International Association v. EEOC* and *U.S. v. Paradise,* 480 U.S. 149 (1987)). If a state or local entity, in order to receive Supreme Court approval, must have actually attempted to utilize race-neutral alternatives and failed before instituting race-specific programs, few existing affirmative action programs would meet the standard. Again, clarification must await future litigation.

It should be emphasized that the Supreme Court has given significantly more deference to the programs imposed by Congress. At least in the first case in which a congressional program was implicated, *Fullilove v. Klutznick,* the Court recognized the distinction between the power of Congress to act under the Fourteenth Amendment, Section 5, and the powers of states or other entities to act. The Court nods in the direction of those distinctions in the *Croson* case. However it should be remembered that the strict-scrutiny standard was not applied to the congressional program in *Fullilove,* as a majority of the Court could not agree that it was the applicable constitutional measure. There exist a myriad of federal programs with one or another degree of specificity in the factual predicate established in the record. Many of these programs involve funds which are made available to state and local entities, which then must craft an acceptable affirmative action program to meet the federal requirements. These and other affirmative action efforts are in a state of confusion following the *Croson* case.[30] The Ninth Circuit applied strict scrutiny in a San Francisco set-aside case and found it unconstitutional as it applied to set-aside for minorities, but used a midlevel standard of review to the set-aside program for women and found that aspect of the program constitutional.[31]

In *Milwaukee County Pavers Ass'n v. Fiedler*[32] the Seventh Circuit affirmed a decision of the district court approving a state program under which federal highway grants required minority contract set-asides as a condition of the grants.[33] That court held: ". . . The joint lesson of *Fullilove* and *Croson* is that the federal government can, by virtue of the enforcement clause of the Fourteenth Amendment, engage in affirmative action with a freer hand than states and municipalities can do. And one way it can do that is by authorizing states to do things that they could not do without federal authorization."[34]

The Supreme Court in *Metro Broadcasting, Inc. v. F.C.C.,*[35] in a 5-4 decision, affirmed FCC programs awarding enhancement for minority ownership in comparative proceedings for new licenses, and giving preference in "distress sales" to minority-controlled firms, over challenges that

such programs were unconstitutional. The majority of the Court concluded that such policies had been specifically mandated by Congress and were constitutionally permissible as they served the important governmental objectives of enhancing broadcast diversity within the power of Congress and were substantially related to those objectives.

The dissents sharply attacked the new standard, contending, instead, that the strict-scrutiny standard should apply to this act of Congress. The dissent distinguished *Fullilove* on the basis that Congress there was acting under the residual powers of the Fourteenth Amendment, Section 5, and may provide a basis for reconsidering the latitude for race-based classifications approved in *Fullilove.*[36] The Supreme Court, however, declined to revisit *Fullilove* in denying review of the *Milwaukee Pavers Ass'n* case.[37] . . .

NO PARTICULAR LEVEL OF SCRUTINY CONSTITUTIONALLY REQUIRED

The Supreme Court debate over the applicability of the strict-scrutiny standard versus some intermediate level of review is an internal debate between competing "academic" theories of analysis neither of which is compelled by the Constitution. I hasten to add that neither is prohibited by the Constitution, nor is there any apparent reason why both might not operate, as indeed they do. By a 5-4 majority in *Croson,* the strict-scrutiny standard is applied to state classifications by race even where affirmative action programs are involved and the action of the state is "benign" with regard to the race so classified. Where the classification is based on sex, on the other hand, the Supreme Court has utilized a different, so-called sliding, scale of scrutiny.

The strict-scrutiny standard did not come etched in articles of the Constitution in its original or its amended form. It is a doctrine of rather recent vintage, suggested in a footnote in *United States v. Carolene Products Co.* in 1938.[38] It has been said that Justice Harlan Stone, a former law professor at Columbia University, was probably using the footnote to spark debate over ideas he had not fully developed.[39] As nearly as I can tell, this "strict-scrutiny analysis" was not again referred to until Stone's concurring opinion in 1942 in *Skinner v. State of Oklahoma.*[40] . . .

It should be noted that the issue of the applicability of the strict-scrutiny standard to efforts by a state, or the federal government, to classify by race in order to do something beneficial to the group so classified did not arise until the affirmative action cases. The earliest one of which I am aware is the *Regents of the University of California v. Bakke,* which we have examined above.[41]

To summarize the commentary on the choice of level of scrutiny which the Court adopted, I submit that there is no compelling rationale for using the strict-scrutiny standard to evaluate affirmative action programs designed to address the persistent national problem of underutilization. Lack of equitable participation by minorities in the largess of a democratic system is an adequate basis for concluding that those programs deserve a treatment different from classification by race that serves to perpetuate the disadvantaged position of minority persons. Making the distinction between the level of scrutiny applied when classification by sex is at issue and that utilized when race or other ethnicity is at issue is not particularly persuasive. Just as the Court decided in the forties that strict scrutiny was necessary to protect discrete and insular minorities from deprivation, it could as easily have decided that the intermediate level of scrutiny was appropriate when the purpose of the program was to benefit the race so classified.[42] . . .

NEITHER MORAL ISSUE NOR MATTER OF REPARATIONS

The survival of affirmative action programs for the future is not a moral issue, nor a matter of reparations; it is a matter of the survival of this nation. In 1987 the Hudson Institute compiled *Workforce 2000, Work and Workers for the 21st Century.* Subsidized by a grant from the Labor Department, this study contains a host of scenarios, assumptions, and projections for the year 2000. . . .

Workforce 2000, chapter 3, suggests that *demographics* are *destiny.* I think that probably is a safe assertion. The conclusions the report draws are the following:

1. The average age of the population of the workforce will rise and the pool of young workers entering the labor market will shrink;
2. More women will enter the workforce, although the rate of increase will taper off;
3. Minorities will be a larger share of new entrants into the labor force;
4. Immigrants will represent the largest share of the increase in the population in the workforce since World War I.[43]

The only fact enunciated above that would be subject to manipulation by external forces, it seems to me, is the fourth one, regarding the size of the immigrant pool.

By the year 2000 it is projected that approximately 47 percent of the workforce will be women, with 61 percent of the women in the country at work. Additionally, women will constitute about three-fifths of the new entrants into the labor force between 1985 and the year 2000.[44] Minorities—blacks, Hispanics, and others—will constitute 29 percent of the net additions to the workforce between 1985 and the year 2000 and will account for more than 15 percent of the workforce in the year 2000.[45]

The report projects that by the year 2000 white males, thought a generation ago to be the mainstays of the economy, will constitute only 15 percent of the net additions to the labor force.[46]

If minorities and women continue to join the workforce at such disproportionate rates, it will not be too long before they are the majority.

If we assume a work life of 30 years, by the time the 18–24-year-old entries into the workforce in 1990 get to retirement age, the workforce upon which the health of their retirement fund and of our America will depend will be overwhelmingly minority and female. Those people are the targets of today's affirmative action programs which are threatened with discontinuance.

Let me suggest that while in my generation the argument for affirmative action was based on a moral imperative—an argument not too persuasive in some sectors of our society—the issue now is a matter of the national economic health. Indeed, health and happiness in the "golden years" of today's "me" generation may well depend upon the vigor of affirmative action.

Prognosticators assure us, and point to evidence readily available, that the jobs of the future will be predominantly high-tech ones requiring a greater degree of skill and education. Moreover, as our world of work becomes more complicated, frequent training and retraining are likely to be necessary. If there is not a sufficient educational base to begin with, keeping up with changing technical needs and absorbing new training will be impossible. We cannot afford to have minorities and women excluded from mainstream education and job activities. We cannot risk increasing percentages of dropouts of minority males, black males in particular, from the labor market. We cannot afford the increasing rate of incarceration of larger and larger proportions of the minority population, particularly the males.

It costs from a low figure of $20,000 to a high one of $40,000 a year to keep an inmate in prison. That is more money than the cost of maintaining a student for one year in our most expensive private colleges. There certainly must be some other way we can utilize our resources.

If these projections, which have come principally from government-subsidized research, are close to accurate, we must stop thinking, if we do, of affirmative action as a program that shows a preference for minorities or women or grants them a privilege. We must consider it an obligation to reach out and include them in the mainstream of our society, and an obligation on their part to participate to the fullest of their potential.

Now one might argue, as some of the optimistic prognostications do, that a combination of an ageing workforce, a declining percentage of young people going into that workforce, and an increase in high-tech jobs equals tight labor markets, and therefore the job demand will take care of the utilization of all of our human capital. That rosy view ignores history. The modern push of blacks for antidiscrimination measures occurred in 1941 when Asa Philip Randolph threatened President Roosevelt with a March on Washington if the president didn't do something about discrimination by war contractors. At the point of implementation of Executive Order 8802 there was a *tight labor market,* at least for skilled craftsmen. And yet, fully qualified black craftsmen, graduates from the industrial arts departments of a myriad of segregated colleges, were denied employment on the basis of race.

It was only as the job market tightened during the war that women were heavily recruited for light assembly work in the war industries. Despite the glamorization of the role of women workers in the war effort—epitomized in the popular song "Rosie the Riveter"—even into the midfifties women were still considered the "secondary workforce."

We must maintain the momentum which has been achieved in the last 15 or 20 years in opening up employment opportunities. Even more imperative is the mounting of new initiatives to ensure that women, minorities, and all of our society referred to by the sociologists as the "underclass" be drawn into the educational process.

We should realize that it takes at least a generation—that is, 20 years—to develop a potentially competent worker. For various high-tech activities it will take somewhat longer than that. If we let affirmative action fall by the wayside now, and if old patterns of underutilization of women and minorities reassert themselves—as I believe they would—by the time the cumulative impact of the neglect manifested itself we would have lost an entire generation of progress.

Although the leadership cohorts of today—that is, persons aged 45 to 65—may have less reason to feel threatened by these projections, for those who are on the threshold of their careers, *the crisis is now.*

CONCLUSION

All of us in this country are the ultimate victims of invidious discrimination. The fraud of racism, which has infected our society since its inception, has tarnished our Constitution, our laws, our education, our science, our morals, and our religions. It has been the most persistent and devisive element in this society and one that has limited our growth and happiness as a nation. The only way to put racism behind us is to be race conscious in our remedies. Affirmative action alone cannot solve all of our problems, but it can continue to make a contribution. If sustained sufficiently over time it could help to cleanse our country of the effects of its sordid history.

If we do not continue to address this issue, racism will continue to be a strain and a drain upon our corporate resources. If there is such a thing as human capital, our society cannot afford to continue to underutilize what is likely to become an ever-increasing share of its human resources.[47]

NOTES

An earlier version of this paper was delivered as a Distinguished Lecture at Northeastern University, Boston, Massachusetts, October 18, 1989.

1. *Wisconsin Law Review* (1970): 341–403.
2. Ibid., p. 341.
3. 488 U.S. 469 (1989).
4. James E. Jones, Jr., "The Origins of Affirmative Action," *University of California-Davis Law Review* 21 (1988): 383–419; quotation, p. 389.
5. See *United States v. Paradise,* 480 U.S. 149 (1987), concurring opinion of Justice Stevens at 189–90; *City of Richmond v. J. A. Croson Co.,* 488 U.S. 469 (1989), concurring opinion of Justice Scalia at 521–23, 525–26; dissenting opinion of Justice Marshall at 535–40.
6. 60 U.S. 393 (1857).
7. The Chief Justice of the Court wrote that "[T]here are two clauses in the Constitution which point directly and specifically to the negro race as a separate class of persons, and show clearly that they were not regarded as a portion of the people or citizens of the government then formed." Ibid. at 411. . . . ."[T]he language of the Declaration of Independence and of the Articles of Confederation, in addition to the plain words of the Constitution itself; the legislation of the different states, before, about the time, and since the Constitution was adopted; . . . the legislation of the Congress from the time of its adoption to a recent period; and we have the constant and uniform action of the Executive Department, all concurring together and leading to the same result [that is, that blacks were not a portion of the people or citizens of the government]." Ibid. at 426.
8. See Eric Schnapper, "Affirmative Action and the Legislative History of the Fourteenth Amendment," *Virginia Law Review* 71 (1985): 753–98, esp. pp. 780–85; see also Judith Baer, *Equality Under the Constitution: Reclaiming the Fourteenth Amendment* (Ithaca, N.Y.: Cornell University Press, 1983) (particularly ch. 4 and the references cited therein).
9. See *Bolling v. Sharpe,* 347 U.S. 497 (1954); see also Kenneth L. Karst, "The Fifth Amendment's Guarantee of Equal Protection," *North Carolina Law Review* 55 (1977): 541–62; and Schnapper, "Affirmative Action," p. 787.
10. Executive Order 11246, *Code of Federal Regulations* (1964–65 comp.): 339.
11. The best judicial discussion of the two contexts in which affirmative action arises is found in *Associated Contractors of Massachusetts v. Altshuler,* 490 F.2d 9 (1st Cir. 1973), *cert. denied,* 416 U.S. 957 (1974).
12. *Contractors Association of Eastern Pennsylvania v. Secretary of Labor,* 442 F.2d 159 (3d Cir. 1971), *cert denied,* 404 U.S. 854 (1971).
13. See Jones, "The Bugaboo of Employment Quotas," pp. 373–78.
14. Affirmative Action Rules are in *Code of Federal Regulations* 41 (rev. 1991): part 60–2.
15. See, e.g., *Legal Aid Society of Almeda County v. Brennan,* 608 F.2d 1319 (9th Cir. 1979), *cert. denied,* 447 U.S. 921 (1980).
16. Leslie A. Nay and James E. Jones, Jr., "Equal Employment and Affirmative Action in Local Governments: A Profile," *Law and Inequality* 8.1 (1989): 103–49.
17. See *New York Times,* March 6, 1986.

18. See *Fullilove v. Klutznick,* 448 U.S. 448 (1980); see also Jones, "Origins of Affirmative Action," p. 383.

19. For citation of the authorities, see James E. Jones, Jr., "The Genesis and Present Status of Affirmative Action: Economic, Legal, and Political Realities," *Iowa Law Review* 70 (1985): 901–44, esp. pp. 932–39.

20. 416 U.S. 312 (1974).

21. 438 U.S. 265 (1978).

22. *Hirabayshi v. United States,* 320 U.S. 81, 100 (1943); *Loving v. Commonwealth of Virginia,* 388 U.S. 1, 11 (1967).

23. *DeFunis v. Odegaard,* 416 U.S. 312 (1974), and *Regents of the University of California v. Bakke,* 438 U.S. 265 (1978).

24. 443 U.S. 193 (1979).

25. 448 U.S. 448 (1980).

26. Ibid. at 483.

27. 480 U.S. 616 (1987).

28. 480 U.S. 149 (1987).

29. Ibid. at 171.

30. See *H. K. Porter Company, Inc. v. Metropolitan Dade County,* 825 F.2d 324 (11th Cir. 1987), *cert. granted and judgment vacated,* 489 U.S. 1062 (1989); see also *Michigan Road Builders Association, Inc. v. Milliken,* 834 F.2d 583 (6th Cir. 1987), *judgment affirmed,* 489 U.S. 1061 (1989).

31. *Associated General Contractors of California, Inc. v. City and County of San Francisco,* 813 F.2d 922 (9th Cir. 1987), cited with approval it seems by O'Connor in her *Croson* opinion, 488 U.S. 469 (1989) at 489–90.

32. 922 F.2d 419 (7th Cir. 1991).

33. 731 F. Supp. 1395 (W.D. Wis. 1990).

34. 922 F.2d at 423–24.

35. 110 S. Ct. 2997 (1990).

36. 110 S. Ct. 3030–32, 3044–45.

37. 111 S. Ct. 2261 (*cert. denied,* June 3, 1991), 731 F. Supp. 1395.

38. 304 U.S. 144, 152 n. 4 (1938); see also Lewis F. Powell, Jr., "*Carolene Products* Revisited," *Columbia Law Review* 82 (1982): 1087–92.

39. See Alpheus Thomas Mason, *Harlan Fisk Stone: Pillar of the Law* (New York: Viking Press, 1956), p. 513.

40. 316 U.S. 535 (1942).

41. The substantive issue was not joined in *DeFunis v. Odegaard,* 416 U.S. 312 (1974).

42. See, e.g., Herman Schwartz, "The 1986 and 1987 Affirmative Action Cases: It's All Over but the Shouting," *Michigan Law Review* 86 (1987): 524–76, esp. pp. 524, 545–76; see also Mary C. Daly, "Some Runs, Some Hits, Some Errors— Keeping Score in the Affirmative Action Ball-park from Weber to Johnson," *Boston College Law Review* 30 (1988): 1–97; George Rutherglen and Daniel R. Ortiz, "Affirmative Action under the Constitution and Title VII: From Confusion to Convergence," *UCLA Law Review* 35 (1988): 467–518.

43. William B. Johnston and Arnold E. Packer, *Work-force 2000: Work and Workers for the 21st Century* (Indianapolis: Hudson Institute, and Washington, D.C.: U.S. Department of Labor, 1987), pp. 15–16.

44. Ibid., p. 85.

45. Ibid., p. 89.

46. Ibid., p. 95.

47. Jones, "Origins of Affirmative Action," p. 418.

READING 23

English in a Multicultural America

Dennis Baron

The protection of the Constitution extends to all,—to those who speak other languages as well as to those born with English on the tongue. Perhaps it would be highly advantageous if all had ready understanding of our ordinary speech, but this cannot be coerced by methods which conflict with the Constitution,—a desirable end cannot be promoted by prohibited means.
—*Associate Supreme Court Justice
James Clark McReynolds
Meyer v. Nebraska, 1923*

In the United States today there is a growing fear that the English language may be on its way out as the American lingua franca, that English is losing ground to Spanish, Chinese, Vietnamese, Korean, and the other languages used by newcomers to our shores.

However, while the United States has always been a multilingual as well as a multicultural nation, English has always been its unofficial official language. Today, a greater percentage of Americans speak English than ever before, and the descendants of nonanglophones or bilingual speakers still tend to learn English—and become monolingual English speakers—as quickly as their German, Jewish, Irish, or Italian predecessors did in the past.

Assimilated immigrants, those who after several generations no longer consider themselves "hyphenated Americans," look upon more recent waves of newcomers with suspicion. Similarly, each generation tends to see the language crisis as new in its time. But reactions to language and ethnicity are cyclical, and the new immigrants from Asia and Latin America have had essentially the same experience as their European predecessors, with similar results.

ENGLISH VS. GERMAN

As early as the 18th century, British colonists in Pennsylvania, remarking that as many as one-third of the area's residents spoke German, attacked Germans in terms strikingly similar to those heard nowadays against newer immigrants. Benjamin Franklin considered the Pennsylvania Germans to be a "swarthy" racial group distinct from the English majority in the colony. In 1751 he complained,

> Why should the Palatine Boors be suffered to swarm into our Settlements, and by herding together establish their Language and Manners to the exclusion of ours? Why should Pennsylvania, founded by the English, become a Colony of Aliens, who will shortly be so numerous as to Germanize us instead of our Anglifying them, and will never adopt our Language or Customs, any more than they can acquire our Complexion?

The Germans were accused by other 18th-century Anglos of laziness, illiteracy, clannishness, a reluctance to assimilate, excessive fertility, and Catholicism (although a significant number of them were Protestant). In some instances they were even blamed for the severe Pennsylvania winters.

Resistance to German, long the major minority language in the country, continued throughout the 19th century, although it was long since clear that, despite community efforts to preserve their language, young Germans were adopting English and abandoning German at a rate that should have impressed the rest of the English-speaking population.

After the US entered World War I, most states quickly banned German—and, in some extreme cases, all foreign languages—from school curricula in a wave of jingoistic patriotism. In 1918, for example, Iowa Gov. William Harding forbade the use of foreign languages in schools, on trains, in public places, and over the telephone (a more public instrument then than it is now), even going so far as to recommend that those who insisted on conducting religious services in a language other than English do so not in churches or synagogues but in the privacy of their own homes.

Similarly, in 1919 the state of Nebraska passed a broad English-only law prohibiting the use of foreign languages at public meetings and proscribing the teaching of foreign languages to any student below the ninth grade. Robert T. Meyer, a teacher in the Lutheran-run Zion Parochial School, was fined twenty-five dollars because, as the complaint read, "between the hour of 1 and 1:30 on May 25, 1920," he taught German to ten-year-old Raymond Papart, who had not yet passed the eighth grade.

Upholding Meyer's conviction, the Nebraska Supreme Court found that most parents "have never deemed it of importance to teach their children foreign languages." It agreed as well that the teaching of a foreign language was harmful to the health of the young child, whose "daily capacity for learning is comparatively small." Such an argument was consistent with the educational theory of the day, which held as late as the 1950s that bilingualism led to confusion and academic failure, and was harmful to the psychological well-being of the child. Indeed, one psychologist claimed in 1926 that the use of a foreign language in the home was a leading cause of mental retardation. . . .

The US Supreme Court reversed Meyer's conviction in a landmark decision in 1923. But the decision in *Meyer v. Nebraska* was to some extent an empty victory for language teachers: while their calling could no longer be restricted, the ranks of German classes had been devastated by the instant linguistic assimilation that World War I forced on German Americans. In 1915 close to 25 percent of the student population studied German in American high schools. Seven years later only 0.6 percent—fewer than 14,000 high school students—were taking German.

ENGLISH VS. SPANISH

Like German in the Midwest, Spanish was the object of vilification in the American Southwest. This negative attitude toward Spanish delayed statehood for New Mexico for over 60 years. In 1902, in one of New Mexico's many tries for statehood, a congressional subcommittee held hearings in the territory, led by Indiana Senator Albert Jeremiah Beveridge, a "progressive" Republican who believed in "America first! Not only America first, but America only." Witness after witness before the Beveridge subcommittee was forced to admit that in New Mexico, ballots and political speeches were either bilingual or entirely in Spanish; that census takers conducted their surveys in Spanish; that justices of the peace kept records in Spanish; that the courts required translators so that judges and lawyers could understand the many Hispanic witnesses; that juries deliberated in Spanish as much as in English; and that children, who might or might not learn English in schools, as required by law, "relapsed" into Spanish on the playground, at home, and after graduation.

One committee witness suggested that the minority language situation in New Mexico resembled that in Senator Beveridge's home state of Indiana: "Spanish is taught as a side issue, as German would be in any State in the Union. . . .

This younger generation understands English as well as I do." And a sympathetic senator reminded his audience, "These people who speak the Spanish language are not foreigners; they are natives, are they not?"

As Franklin did the Germans in Pennsylvania, Senator Beveridge categorized the "Mexicans" of the American Southwest as non-natives, "unlike us in race, language, and social customs," and concluded that statehood must be contingent on assimilation. He recommended that admission to the Union be delayed until a time "when the mass of the people, or even a majority of them, shall, in the usages and employment of their daily life, have become identical in language and customs with the great body of the American people; when the immigration of English-speaking people who have been citizens of other States does its modifying work with the 'Mexican' element." Although New Mexico finally achieved its goal of statehood, and managed to write protection of Spanish into its constitution, schools throughout the Southwest forbade the use of Spanish among students. Well into the present century, children were routinely ridiculed and punished for using Spanish both in class and on the playground.

LANGUAGE AND POWER

As the New Mexican experience suggests, the insistence on English has never been benign. The notion of a national language sometimes wears the guise of inclusion: we must all speak English to participate meaningfully in the democratic process. Sometimes it argues unity: we must speak one language to understand one another and share both culture and country. Those who insist on English often equate bilingualism with lack of patriotism. Their intention to legislate official English often masks racism and certainly fails to appreciate cultural difference: it is a thinly-veiled measure to disenfranchise anyone not like "us" (with notions of "us," the real Americans, changing over the years from those of English ancestry to northwestern European to "white" monolingual English speakers).

American culture assumes monolingual competence in English. The ability to speak another language is more generally regarded as a liability than a refinement, a curse of ethnicity and a bar to advancement rather than an economic or educational advantage.

In another response to non-English speaking American citizens, during the nineteenth century, states began instituting English literacy requirements for voting to replace older property requirements. These literacy laws generally pretended to democratize the voting process, though their hidden goal was often to prevent specific groups from voting. The first such statutes in Connecticut and Massachusetts were aimed at the Irish population of those states. Southern literacy tests instituted after the Civil War were anti-Black. California's test (1892) was aimed at Hispanics and Asians. Alaska's, in 1926, sought to disenfranchise its Native Americans. Wyoming's (1897) was anti-Finn and Washington state's (1889), anti-Chinese.

The literacy law proposed for New York State in 1915, whose surface aim was to ensure a well-informed electorate, targeted a number of the state's minorities. It was seen both as a calculated attempt to prevent New York's one million Yiddish speakers from voting and as a means of stopping the state's German Americans from furthering their nefarious war aims. When it was finally enacted in 1921, supporters of the literacy test saw it as a tool to enforce Americanization, while opponents charged the test would keep large numbers of the state's newly enfranchised immigrant women from voting. Later, the law, which was not repealed until the Voting Rights Act of 1965, effectively disenfranchised New York's Puerto Rican community.

AN OFFICIAL LANGUAGE?

Although many Americans simply assume English is the official language of the United States, it is not. Nowhere in the US Constitution is English privileged over other languages, and while a few subsequent federal laws require the use of English for special, limited purposes—air traffic control, product labels, service on federal juries—no law establishes English as the language of the land.

In the xenophobic period following World War I, several moves were made to establish English at the federal level, but none succeeded. On the other hand, many states at that time adopted some form of English-only legislation. This included regulations designating English the language of state legislatures, courts, and schools, making English a requirement for entrance into such professions as attorney, barber, physician, private detective, or undertaker, and in some states even preventing nonanglophones from obtaining hunting and fishing licenses.

More recently, official language questions have been the subject of state and local debate once again. An English Language Amendment to the US Constitution (the ELA) has been before the Congress every year since 1981. In 1987, the year in which more than 74 percent of California's voters indicated their support for English as the state's official language, thirty-seven states discussed the official English issue. The next year, official language laws were passed in Colorado, Florida, and Arizona. New Mexico and Michigan have taken a stand in favor of English Plus, recommending that everyone have a knowledge of English plus another language. . . .

Official American policy has swung wildly between toleration of languages other than English and their complete eradication. But neither legal protection nor community-based efforts has been able to prevent the decline of minority languages or to slow the adoption of English, particularly among the young. Conversely, neither legislation making English the official language of a state nor the efforts of the schools has done much to enforce the use of English: Americans exhibit a high degree of linguistic anxiety but continue to resist interference with their language use on the part of legislators or teachers.

A number of states have adopted official English. Illinois, for example, in the rush of postwar isolationism and anti-British sentiment, made

American its official language in 1923; this was quietly changed to English in 1969. Official English in Illinois has been purely symbolic; it is a statute with no teeth and no discernible range or effect. In contrast, Arizona's law, which became part of the state constitution, was the most detailed and the most restrictive of any of the sixteen state official language laws currently on the books. It required all government officials and employees—from the governor down to the municipal dog catcher—to use English and only English during the performance of government business.

[In 1990] Arizona's law was ruled unconstitutional by the US District Court for the District of Arizona. Arizona's law was challenged by Maria-Kelley Yniguez, a state insurance claims administrator fluent in Spanish and English, who had often used Spanish with clients. Yniguez feared that, since she was sworn to uphold the state constitution, speaking Spanish to clients of her agency who knew no other language might put her in legal jeopardy.

Judge Paul G. Rosenblatt, of the US District Court for the District of Arizona, found that the English-only article 28 of the Arizona constitution violated the First Amendment of the US Constitution protecting free speech. The ruling voiding the Arizona law will not affect the status of other state official English laws. However, it is clear that other courts may take the Arizona decision into consideration.

TEACHING OUR CHILDREN

Perhaps the most sensitive area of minority-language use in the US has been in the schools. Minority-language schools have existed in North America since the 18th century. In the 19th century bilingual education was common in the Midwest—St. Louis and a number of Ohio cities had active English-German public schools—as well as in parochial schools in other areas with large nonanglophone populations. More commonly, though, the schools ignored non-English speaking children altogether, making no curricular or pedagogical concessions to their presence in class. Indeed, newly instituted classroom speech requirements in the early part of this century ensured that anglophone students with foreign accents would be sent to pathologists for corrective action. And professional licensing requirements that included speech certification tests were used to keep Chinese in California and Jews in New York out of the teaching corps.

The great American school myth has us believe that the schools Americanized generations of immigrants, giving them English and, in consequence, the ability to succeed. In fact, in allowing nonanglophone children to sink or swim, the schools ensured that most of them would fail: dropout rates for non-English speakers were extraordinarily high and English was more commonly acquired on the streets and playgrounds or on the job than in the classroom.

We tend to think past generations of immigrants succeeded at assimilation while the present generation has (for reasons liberals are willing to explain away) failed. In fact, today's Hispanics are acquiring English and assimilating in much the same way and at the same pace as Germans or Jews or Italians of earlier generations did.

California presented an extreme model for excluding children with no English: it segregated Chinese students into separate "oriental" English-only schools until well into the 20th century. The ending of segregation did little to improve the linguistic fortunes of California's Chinese-speakers, who continued to be ignored by the schools. They were eventually forced to appeal to the Supreme Court to force state authorities to provide for their educational needs. The decision that resulted in the landmark case of *Lau v. Nichols* (1974) did not, however, guarantee minority-language rights, nor did it require bilingual education, as many opponents of bilingual education commonly argue. Instead the Supreme Court ordered schools to provide education for all students whether or not they spoke English, a task our schools are still struggling to carry out.

Confusion over language in the schools seems a major factor behind official language concerns.

Bilingual education is a prime target of English-only lobbying groups, who fear it is a device for minority language maintenance rather than for an orderly transition to English. Troubling to teachers as well is the fact that bilingual programs are often poorly defined, underfunded, and inadequately staffed, while parents and students frequently regard bilingual as a euphemism for remedial. In its defense, we can say that second language education did not come into its own in this country until after World War II. Bilingual education, along with other programs designed to teach English as a second language, are really the first attempts by American schools in more than two centuries to deal directly with the problem of non-English speaking children. They represent the first attempts to revise language education in an effort to keep children in school; to keep them from repeating the depressing and wasteful pattern of failure experienced by earlier generations of immigrants and nonanglophone natives; to get them to respect rather than revile both English, frequently perceived as the language of oppression, and their native tongue, all too often rejected as the language of poverty and failure.

Despite resistance to bilingual education and problems with its implementation, the theory behind it remains sound. Children who learn reading, arithmetic, and other subjects in their native language while they are being taught English will not be as likely to fall behind their anglophone peers, and will have little difficulty transferring their subject-matter knowledge to English as their English proficiency increases. On the other hand, when nonanglophone children or those with very limited English are immersed in English-only classrooms and left to sink or swim, as they were for generations, they will continue to fail at unacceptable rates.

ENGLISH IS HERE TO STAY

Those Americans who fear that unless English is made the official language of the United States by means of federal and state constitutional amendments they are about to be swamped by new waves of non-English-speakers should realize that even without restrictive legislation, minority languages in the US have always been marginal. Research shows that Hispanics, who now constitute the nation's largest minority-language group, are adopting English in the second and third generation in the same way that speakers of German, Italian, Yiddish, Russian, Polish, Chinese or Japanese have done in the past. However, as the experience of Hispanics in southern California suggests, simply acquiring English is not bringing the educational and economic successes promised by the melting-pot myth. Linguistic assimilation may simply not be enough to overcome more deep-seated prejudices against Hispanics.

Nonetheless, there are many minority-language speakers in the US, and with continued immigration they will continue to make their presence felt. The 1980 Census showed that one in seven Americans speaks a language other than English, or lives with someone who does. Even if the courts do not strike down English-only laws, it would be difficult to legislate minority languages out of existence because we simply have no mechanisms in this country to carry out language policy of any kind (schools, which are under local and state control, have been remarkably erratic in the area of language education). On the other hand, even in the absence of restrictive language legislation, American society enforces its own irresistible pressure to keep the United States an English-speaking nation. The Census also reports that 97 percent of Americans identify themselves as speaking English well or very well. English may not be official, but it is definitely here to stay.

. . . The issue of minority languages will not soon go away, and a constitutional amendment cannot force people to adopt English if they are unwilling or unable to do so. Nor will English cease to function as the nation's official language even if it does not have a constitutional amendment to establish it.

English-only legislation, past and present, no matter how idealistic or patriotic its claims, is supported by a long history of nativism, racism, and religious bigotry. While an English Language Amendment to the US Constitution might ultimately prove no more symbolic than the selection of an official bird or flower or fossil, it is possible that the ELA could become a tool for linguistic repression. Those who point to Canada or Belgium or India or the Soviet Union as instances where multilingualism produces civil strife would do well to remember that such strife invariably occurs when minority-language rights are suppressed. In any case, such examples have little in common with the situation in the United States.

The main danger of an ELA, as I see it, would be to alienate minority-language speakers, sabotaging their chances for education and distancing them further from the American mainstream, at the same time hindering rather than facilitating the linguistic assimilation that has occurred so efficiently up to now in the absence of legal prodding.

READING 24

The Rich Get Richer and the Poor Get Prison

Jeffrey H. Reiman

A CRIME BY ANY OTHER NAME . . .

Think of a crime, any crime. Picture the first "crime" that comes into your mind. What do you see? The odds are you are not imagining a mining company executive sitting at his desk, calculating the costs of proper safety precautions, and deciding not to invest in them. Probably what you do see with your mind's eye is one person physically attacking another or robbing something from another on the threat of physical attack. Look more closely. What does the attacker look like? It's a safe bet he (and it is a *he,* of course) is not wearing a suit and tie. In fact, my hunch is that

you—like me, like almost anyone in America—picture a young, tough, lower-class male when the thought of crime first pops into your head. You (we) picture someone like the Typical Criminal described above. And the crime itself is one in which the Typical Criminal sets out to attack or rob some specific person.

This last point is important. What it indicates is that we have a mental image not only of the Typical Criminal, but also of the Typical Crime. If the Typical Criminal is a young lower-class male, the Typical Crime is *one-on-one harm*—where harm means either physical injury or loss of something valuable or both. If you have any doubts that this is the Typical Crime, look at any random sample of police or private eye shows on television . . . A study of TV crime shows by The Media Institute in Washington, D.C., indicates that, while the fictional criminals portrayed on television are on the average both older and wealthier than the real criminals who figure in the FBI Uniform Crime Reports, "TV crimes are almost 12 times as likely to be violent as crimes committed in the real world."[1] In short, TV crime shows broadcast the double-edged message that the "one-on-one" crimes of the poor are the typical crimes of all and thus not uniquely caused by the pressures of poverty; *and* that the criminal justice system pursues rich and poor alike—thus when the criminal justice system happens mainly to pounce on the poor in real life, it is not out of any class bias.

It is important to identify this model of the Typical Crime because it functions like a set of blinders. It keeps us from calling a mine disaster a mass murder even if 26 men are killed, even if someone is responsible for the unsafe conditions in which they worked and died. In fact, I argue that this particular piece of mental furniture so blocks our view that it keeps us from using the criminal justice system to protect ourselves from the greatest threats to our persons and possessions.

What keeps a mine disaster from being a mass murder in our eyes is the fact that it is not one-on-one harm. What is important here is not the numbers but the *intent to harm someone.* An attack by a gang on one or more persons or an attack by one individual on several fits the model of one-on-one harm. That is, for each person harmed there is at least one individual who wanted to harm that person. Once he selects his victim, the rapist, the mugger, the murderer, all want this person they have selected to suffer. A mine executive, on the other hand, does not want his employees to be harmed. He would truly prefer that there be no accident, no injured or dead miners. What he does want is something legitimate. It is what he has been hired to get: maximum profits at minimum costs. If he cuts corners to save a buck, he is just doing his job. If 26 men die because he cut corners on safety, we may think him crude or callous but not a killer. He is, at most, responsible for an *indirect harm,* not a one-on-one harm. For this, he may even be criminally indictable for violating safety regulations—but not for murder. The 26 men are dead as an unwanted consequence of his (perhaps overzealous or undercautious) pursuit of a legitimate goal. And so, unlike the Typical Criminal, he has not committed the Typical Crime. Or so we generally believe. As a result, 26 men are dead who might be alive now if cutting corners of the kind that leads to loss of life, whether suffering is specifically intended or not, were treated as murder.

This is my point. Because we accept the belief—encouraged by our politician's statements about crime and by the media's portrayal of crime—that the model for crime is one person specifically intending to harm another, we accept a legal system that leaves us unprotected against much greater dangers to our lives and well-being than those threatened by the Typical Criminal . . . .

WEEDING OUT THE WEALTHY

The offender at the end of the road in prison is likely to be a member of the lowest social and economic groups in the country.[2]

This statement in the *Report of the President's Commission on Law Enforcement and Administration of Justice* is as true today as it was nearly [three] decades ago when it was written. Our pris-

ons are indeed, as Ronald Goldfarb has called them, the National Poorhouse.[3] To most citizens this comes as no surprise—recall the Typical Criminal and the Typical Crime. Dangerous crimes, they think, are mainly committed by poor people. And seeing that prison populations are made up primarily of the poor only makes them surer of this. They think, in other words, that the criminal justice system gives a true reflection of the dangers that threaten them.

In my view, it also comes as no surprise that our prisons and jails predominantly confine the poor. But this is not because these are the individuals who most threaten us. Instead, it is because the criminal justice system effectively weeds out the well-to-do, so that *at the end of the road in prison,* the vast majority of those we find there come from the lower classes. This "weeding out" process starts before the agents of law enforcement go into action. Our very definition of crime *excludes* a wide variety of actions at least as dangerous as those included and often worse. Is it any accident that the kinds of dangerous actions excluded are the kinds most likely to be performed by the affluent in America? Even before we mobilize our troops in the war on crime, we have already guaranteed that large numbers of upper-class individuals will never come within their sights.

But this process does not stop at the definition of crime. It continues throughout each level of the criminal justice system. At each step, from arrest to sentencing, the likelihood of being ignored or released or lightly treated by the system is greater the better off one is economically. As the late U.S. Senator Philip Hart has written:

> Justice has two transmission belts, one for the rich and one for the poor. The low-income transmission belt is easier to ride without falling off and it gets to prison in shorter order.
>
> The transmission belt for the affluent is a little slower and it passes innumerable stations where exits are temptingly convenient.[4]

This means that the criminal justice system functions from start to finish in a way that makes certain that "the offender at the end of the road in prison is likely to be a member of the lowest social and economic groups in the country."

For the same criminal behavior, the poor are more likely to be arrested; if arrested, they are more likely to be charged; if charged, more likely to be convicted; if convicted, more likely to be sentenced to prison; and if sentenced, more likely to be given longer prison terms than members of the middle and upper classes.[5] In other words, the image of the criminal population one sees in our nation's jails and prisons is distorted by the shape of the criminal justice system itself. It is the face of evil reflected in a carnival mirror, but it is no laughing matter.

The face in the criminal justice carnival mirror is also very frequently a black face. Although blacks do not comprise the majority of the inmates in our jails and prisons, they make up a proportion that far outstrips their proportion in the population.[6] But here, too, the image we see is distorted by the processes of the criminal justice system itself. Edwin Sutherland and Donald Cressey write, in their widely used textbook, *Criminology,* that

> numerous studies have shown that African-Americans are more likely to be arrested, indicted, convicted, and committed to an institution than are whites who commit the same offenses, and many other studies have shown that blacks have a poorer chance than whites to receive probation, a suspended sentence, parole, commutation of a death sentence, or pardon.[7]

There can be little doubt that the criminal justice process is distorted by racism as well as by economic bias.[8] Nevertheless, it does not pay to look at these as two independent forms of bias. It is my view that, at least as far as criminal justice is concerned, racism is simply one powerful form of economic bias. . . . Thus racism will be treated here as either a form of economic bias or a tool that achieves the same end.

In the remainder of this discussion, I show how the criminal justice system functions to *weed out the wealthy* (meaning both middle- and upper-class offenders) at each stage of the process

and thus produces a distorted image of the crime problem. Before entering into this discussion, two provisos should be noted. First, it is not my view that the poor are all innocent victims persecuted by the evil rich. The poor do commit crimes, and my own assumption is that the vast majority of the poor who are confined in our prisons are guilty of the crimes for which they were sentenced. In addition, there is good evidence that the poor do commit a greater portion of the crimes against person and property listed in the FBI Index than the middle and upper classes do, relative to their numbers in the national population. [But] crimes in the FBI Index are not the acts that threaten us most. What I will try to prove in what follows is that the poor are arrested and punished by the criminal justice system much more frequently than their contribution to the crime problem would warrant—thus the criminals who populate our prisons as well as the public's imagination are disproportionately poor.

The second proviso is this. The following discussion has been divided into three sections that correspond to the major criminal justice decision points. . . . As always, such classifications are a bit neater than reality, and so they should not be taken as rigid compartments. Many of the distorting processes operate at all criminal justice decision points. So, for example, while I will primarily discuss the light-handed treatment of white-collar criminals in the section on sentencing, it is also true that white-collar criminals are less likely to be arrested, or charged, or convicted than are blue-collar criminals. The section in which a given issue will be treated is a reflection of the point in the criminal justice process at which the disparities are most striking. Suffice it to say, however, that the disparities between the treatment of the poor and the non-poor are to be found at all points of the process.

Arrest

The problem with most official records of who commits crime is that they are really statistics on who gets arrested and convicted. If, as I will show, the police are more likely to arrest some people than others, these official statistics may tell us more about police than about criminals. In any event, they give us little reliable data about those who commit crime and do not get caught. Some social scientists, suspicious of the bias built into official records, have tried to devise other methods of determining who has committed a crime. Most often, these methods involve an interview or questionnaire in which the respondent is assured of anonymity and asked to reveal whether or not he has committed any offenses for which he could be arrested and convicted. Techniques to check reliability of these self-reports have also been devised; however, if their reliability is still in doubt, common sense would dictate that they would understate rather than overstate the number of individuals who have committed crimes and never come to official notice. In light of this, the conclusions of these studies are rather astounding. It would seem that crime is the national pastime.

The President's Crime Commission conducted a survey of 10,000 households and discovered that "91 percent of all Americans have violated laws that could have subjected them to a term of imprisonment at one time in their lives."[9] They also report the findings of a study of 1690 persons (1020 males, 670 females) mostly from the state of New York. Asked which of 49 felonies and misdemeanors (excluding traffic offenses) they had committed:

> Ninety-one percent of the respondents admitted they had committed one or more offenses for which they might have received jail or prison sentences. Thirteen percent of the males admitted to grand larceny, 26 percent to auto theft, and 17 percent to burglary. Sixty-four percent of the males and 27 percent of the females committed at least one felony for which they had not been apprehended.[10]

Keep in mind that a felony is a crime for which an individual can serve one or more years in prison and that many of the individuals now in jail are there only for misdemeanors.

A number of other studies support the conclusion that serious criminal behavior is widespread among middle- and upper-class individuals, although these individuals are rarely, if ever, arrested. Some of the studies show that there are

no significant differences between economic classes in the incidence of criminal behavior.[11] Others conclude that while lower-class individuals do commit more than their share of crime, arrest records overstate their share and understate that of the middle and upper classes.[12]

Still other studies suggest that some forms of serious crime—forms usually associated with lower-class youth—show up *more frequently* among higher-class persons than among lower.[13] For instance, Empey and Erikson interviewed 180 white males aged 15 to 17 who were drawn from different economic strata. They found that "virtually all respondents reported having committed not one but a variety of different offenses." Although youngsters from the middle classes constituted 55 percent of the group interviewed, they admitted to 67 percent of the instances of breaking and entering, 70 percent of the instances of property destruction, and an astounding 87 percent of all the armed robberies admitted to by the entire sample.[14] Williams and Gold studied a national sample of 847 males and females between the ages of 13 and 16.[15] Of these, 88 percent admitted to at least one delinquent offense. . . .

The simple fact is that for the same offense, *a poor person is more likely to be arrested, and if arrested charged, than a middle- or upper-class person.*[16]

This means, first of all, that poor people are more likely to come to the attention of the police. Furthermore, even when apprehended, the police are more likely to formally charge a poor person and release a higher-class person *for the same offense.* Gold writes that

> boys who live in poorer parts of town and are apprehended by police for delinquency are four to five times more likely to appear in some official record than boys from wealthier sections who commit the same kinds of offenses. These same data show that, at each stage in the legal process from charging a boy with an offense to some sort of disposition in court, boys from different socioeconomic backgrounds are treated differently, so that those eventually incarcerated in public institutions, that site of most of the research on delinquency, are selectively poorer boys.[17]

Based on a study of self-reported delinquent behavior, Gold finds that when individuals were apprehended, "if the offender came from a higher status family, police were more likely to handle the matter themselves without referring it to the court."[18]

Terence Thornberry reaches a similar conclusion in a more recent study of 3475 delinquent boys in Philadelphia. Thornberry found that among boys arrested *for equally serious offenses* and who had *similar prior offense records,* police were more likely to refer the lower-class youths than the more affluent ones to juvenile court. The police were more likely to deal with the wealthier youngsters informally, for example, by holding them in the station house until their parents came rather than instituting formal procedures. Of those referred to juvenile court, Thornberry found further that for *equally serious offenses* and with *similar prior records,* the poorer youngsters were more likely to be institutionalized than were the affluent ones. The wealthier youths were more likely to receive probation than the poorer ones. As might be expected, Thornberry found the same relationships when comparing the treatment of black and white youths apprehended for equally serious offenses.[19] . . .

A study of drunken driving "demonstrated that minority group members, the lower class, males, and youth are consistently more likely to be convicted of driving while intoxicated than are whites, the upper class, and older persons."[20] A study of the treatment of employee theft found that *for the same amount stolen* "more lower status employees (cleaners, servicemen, stock personnel) than higher status ones (executives, salespersons, white collar workers) were prosecuted. A significantly larger proportion of the former (73 percent) than of the latter (50 percent) were prosecuted."[21]

Any number of reasons can be offered to account for these differences in treatment. Some argue that they reflect the fact that the poor have less privacy.[22] What others can do in their living rooms or backyards, the poor do on the street. Others argue that a police officer's decision to book a poor youth and release a middle-class youth reflects either the officer's judgment that the higher-class youngster's family will be more likely and more able to discipline him or her than the lower-class youngster's, or differences in the degree to which poor and middle-class complainants demand arrest. Others argue that police training and police work condition police officers to be suspicious of certain kinds of people, such as lower-class youth, blacks, Mexicans, and so on,[23] and thus more likely to detect their criminality. Still others hold that police mainly arrest those with the least political clout,[24] those who are least able to focus public attention on police practices or bring political influence to bear, and these happen to be the members of the lowest social and economic classes.

Regardless of which view one takes, and probably all have some truth in them, one conclusion is inescapable: One of the reasons that the offender "at the end of the road in prison is likely to be a member of the lowest social and economic groups in the country" is that the police officers who guard the access to the road to prison make sure that more poor people will make the trip than well-to-do people.

The *weeding out of the wealthy* starts at the very entrance to the criminal justice system: The decision about whom to investigate, arrest, or charge is not made simply on the basis of the offense committed or the danger posed. It is a decision that is distorted by a systematic economic bias that works to the disadvantage of the poor.

This economic bias is a two-edged sword. Not only are the poor arrested and charged out of proportion to their numbers for the kinds of crimes poor people generally commit—burglary, robbery, assault, and so forth—but when we reach the kinds of crimes poor people almost never have the opportunity to commit, such as antitrust violations, industrial safety violations, embezzlement, serious tax evasion, the criminal justice system shows an increasingly benign and merciful face. The more likely that a crime is the type committed by middle- and upper-class people, the less likely that it will be treated as a criminal offense. When it comes to crime in the streets, where the perpetrator is apt to be poor, he or she is even more likely to be arrested, formally charged, and so on. When it comes to crime in the suites, where the offender is apt to be affluent, the system is most likely to deal with the crime non-criminally, that is, by civil litigation or informal settlement. . . . Not only is the main entry to the road to prison held wide open to the poor, but the access routes for the wealthy are largely sealed off. Once again, we should not be surprised at who we find in our prisons.

Many writers have commented on the extent and seriousness of "white-collar crime," so I will keep my remarks to a minimum. Nevertheless, for those of us trying to understand how the image of crime is created, four points should be noted.

1. White-collar crime is costly; it takes far more dollars from our pockets than all the FBI Index Crimes combined.
2. White-collar crime is widespread, probably much more so than the crimes of the poor.
3. White-collar criminals are rarely arrested or charged; the system has developed kindlier ways of dealing with the more delicate sensibilities of its higher-class clientele.
4. When the white-collar criminals are prosecuted and convicted, their sentences are either suspended or very light when judged by the cost their crimes have imposed on society. . . .

Concerning item 4 above, there are many reasons for this. Perhaps most important is the fact that with many of these law violations, the government has the choice to proceed criminally or civilly and usually chooses the latter. That is, with upper-class lawbreakers, the authorities prefer to sue in civil court for damages or for an injunction rather than treat the wealthy as common criminals. Judges have on occasion stated in open court that they "would not make criminals of reputable businessmen."[25] One would think that it would be up to the businessmen to make criminals of themselves by their actions, but alas, *this* right is reserved for the lower classes.

Another tool that the government uses to spare the corporate executive the trials of criminality is the consent decree. Senator Philip Hart said of the

consent decree that it "is a negotiated instrument whereby a firm, in effect, says it has done nothing wrong and promises never to do it again. The agreement is filed in court and that's the end of it, unless the firm is caught doing it again."[26] Imagine if this were available to burglars. Instead of arresting them and giving them a criminal record, the police would ask them to sign a statement promising never to do it again and file it in court. This alternative, however, is reserved for a higher class of thief.

Examples of reluctance to use the full force of the criminal process for crimes not generally committed by the poor can be multiplied ad infinitum. Let me close with one final example that typifies this particular distortion of criminal justice policy.

Embezzlement is the crime of misappropriating money or property entrusted to one's care, custody, or control. Since the poor are rarely entrusted with tempting sums of money or valuable property, this is predominantly a crime of the middle and upper classes. The U.S. Chamber of Commerce estimates the annual economic cost of embezzlement (adjusted for 1980) at $5.4 billion, nearly two-thirds the total value of all the property and money stolen in all FBI Index property crimes in 1980. Thus it is fair to conclude that embezzlement imposes a cost on society comparable to that imposed by the Index property crimes. Nevertheless, the FBI reports that in 1980, when there were 1,863,300 arrests for Index property crimes, there were 8500 arrests for embezzlement nationwide.[27] Although their cost to society is comparable, the number of arrests for property crimes was *219 times greater* than the number of arrests for embezzlement. Roughly, this means that there was one property crime arrest for every $4600 stolen, and one embezzlement arrest for every $635,000 "misappropriated." Note that even the language becomes more delicate as we deal with a "better class" of crook.

The clientele of the criminal justice system form an exclusive club. Entry is largely a privilege of the poor. The crimes they commit are the crimes that qualify one for admission—and they are admitted in greater proportion than their share of those crimes. Curiously enough, the crimes the affluent commit are not the kind that easily qualify one for membership in the club.

Conviction

Between arrest and imprisonment lies the crucial process that determines guilt or innocence. Studies of individuals accused of similar offenses and with similar prior records show that the poor defendant is more likely to be adjudicated guilty than is the wealthier defendant.[28] In the adjudication process the only thing that *should* count is whether the accused is guilty and whether the prosecution can prove it beyond a reasonable doubt. Unfortunately, at least two other factors that are irrelevant to the question of guilt or innocence significantly affect the outcome: One is the ability of the accused to be free on bail prior to trial, and the second is access to legal counsel able to devote adequate time and energy to the case. Since both bail and high-quality legal counsel cost money, it should come as no surprise that here as elsewhere the poor do poorly. "A defendant in a criminal court," writes Abraham Blumberg, "is really beaten by the deprivations and limitations imposed by his social class, race and ethnicity. These in turn preclude such services as bail, legal counsel, psychiatric services, expert witnesses, and investigatory assistance. In essence the concomitants of poverty are responsible for the fact that due process sometimes produces greatly disparate results in an illmatched struggle."[29]

Being released on bail is important in several respects. First and foremost, of course, is the fact that those who are not released on bail are kept in jail like individuals who have been found guilty. They are thus punished while they are still legally innocent. . . . Beyond the obvious ugliness of punishing people before they are found guilty, confined defendants suffer from other disabilities. Specifically, they cannot actively aid in their own defense by seeking out witnesses and evidence. Several studies have shown that among defendants accused of the same offenses, those who

make bail are more likely to be acquitted than those who do not.[30]

Furthermore, since the time spent in jail prior to adjudication of guilt may count as part of the sentence if one is found guilty, the accused are often placed in a ticklish position. Let us say the accused believes that he or she is innocent or at least that the state cannot prove guilt, and let us say also that he or she has been in the slammer for two months awaiting trial. Along comes the prosecutor to offer a deal: If you plead guilty to such-and-such (usually a lesser offense than has been charged, e.g., possession of burglar's tools instead of burglary), the prosecutor promises to ask the judge to sentence you to two months. In other words, plead guilty and walk out of jail today—or maintain your innocence, stay in jail until trial, and then be tried for the full charge instead of the lesser offense! Plea-bargaining is an everyday occurrence in the criminal justice system. Contrary to the Perry Mason image, the vast majority of criminal convictions in the United States are reached without a trial. It is estimated that between 70 and 95 percent of convictions are the result of a negotiated plea,[31] that is, a bargain in which the accused agrees to plead guilty (usually to a lesser offense than he or she is charged with or to one offense out of many he or she is charged with) in return for an informal promise of leniency from the prosecutor with the tacit consent of the judge. If you were the jailed defendant offered a deal like this, how would you choose? . . .

The advantages of access to adequate legal counsel during the adjudicative process are obvious but still worthy of mention. In 1963, the U.S. Supreme Court handed down the landmark *Gideon v. Wainwright* decision, holding that the states must provide legal counsel to the indigent in all felony cases. As a result, no person accused of a serious crime need face their accusers without a lawyer. However, the Supreme Court has not held that the Constitution requires that individuals are entitled to lawyers able to devote equal time and resources to their cases. Even though *Gideon* represents significant progress in making good on the constitutional promise of equal treatment before the law, we still are left with two transmission belts of justice: one for the poor and one for the affluent. There is, to be sure, an emerging body of case law on the right to effective assistance of counsel,[32] however, this is yet to have any serious impact on the assembly-line legal aid handed out to the poor.

Indigent defendants, those who cannot afford to retain their own lawyers, will be defended either by a public defender or by a private attorney assigned by the court. Since the public defender is a salaried attorney with a case load much larger than that of a private criminal lawyer,[33] and since court-assigned private attorneys are paid a fixed fee that is much lower than they charge their regular clients, neither is able or motivated to devote much time to the indigent defendant's defense. Both are strongly motivated to bring their cases to a close quickly by negotiating a plea of guilty. Since the public defender works in day-to-day contact with the prosecutor and the judge, the pressures on him or her to negotiate a plea as quickly as possible, instead of rocking the boat by threatening to go to trial,[34] are even greater than those that work on court-assigned counsel. . . .

Needless to say, the distinct legal advantages that money can buy become even more salient when we enter the realm of corporate and other white-collar crime. Indeed, it is often precisely the time and cost involved in bringing to court a large corporation with its army of legal eagles that is offered as an excuse for the less formal and more genteel treatment accorded to corporate crooks. This excuse is, of course, not equitably distributed to all economic classes, anymore than quality legal service is. What this means in simple terms is that regardless of actual innocence or guilt, one's chances of beating the rap increase as one's income increases. Regardless of what fraction of crimes are committed by the poor, the criminal justice system is distorted so that an even greater fraction of those convicted will be poor. And with conviction comes sentencing.

Sentencing

. . . The system is doubly biased against the poor. First, there is the class bias *between* crimes. . . . The crimes that poor people are likely to commit carry harsher sentences than the "crimes in the suites" committed by well-to-do people. Second, for *all* crimes, the poor receive less probation and more years of confinement than well-off defendants *convicted of the same offense,* assuring us once again that the vast majority of those who are put behind bars are from the lowest social and economic classes in the nation.

[A] *New York Times* article . . . reports the results of a study done by the *New York Times* on sentencing in state and federal courts. The *Times* states that "crimes that tend to be committed by the poor get tougher sentences than those committed by the well-to-do," that federal "defendants who could not afford private counsel were sentenced nearly twice as severely as defendants with private or no counsel," and that a "study by the Vera Institute of Justice of courts in the Bronx indicates a similar pattern in the state courts."[35]

Looking at federal and state courts, Stuart Nagel concludes that

> not only are the indigent found guilty more often, but they are much less likely to be recommended for probation by the probation officer, or to be granted probation or suspended sentences by the judge.

And, further, that

> the federal data show that this is true also of those with no prior record: 27 percent of the indigent with no prior record were not recommended for probation against 16 percent of the non-indigent; 23 percent indigent did not receive suspended sentences or probation against 15 percent non-indigent. Among those of both groups with "some" prior record the spread is even greater.[36]

. . . As usual, data on racial discrimination in sentencing exist in much greater abundance than data on class discrimination, but they tell the same story of the treatment of those who cannot afford the going price of justice. Most striking perhaps is the fact that over 44 percent of the inmates of all correctional facilities in the United States—state and federal prisons as well as local jails—are black, while blacks account for a little under one-quarter of all arrests in the nation. Even when we compare the percentage of blacks arrested for serious (i.e., FBI Index) crimes with the percentage of blacks in federal and state prisons (where presumably those convicted of such offenses would be sent), blacks still make up over 46 percent of the inmates but only about 33 percent of the arrestees, which is still a considerable disparity. Furthermore, when we look at federal prisons, where there is reason to believe racial and economic discrimination is less prevalent than in state institutions, we find that the average sentence for a white inmate in 1979 was 98.9 months, as compared to 130.2 months (over $2\frac{1}{2}$ years more!) for nonwhite inmates. The nonwhite inmate serves, on the average, 20 more months for a drug law violation than the white inmate, and almost twice as long for income tax evasion.[37]

Studies have confirmed that black burglars receive longer sentences than do white burglars. And blacks who plead guilty receive harsher sentences than whites who do, although by an act of dubious mercy of which Americans ought hardly be proud, blacks often receive lighter sentences for murder and rape than whites as long as the victim was black as well.[38] . . . This dubious mercy extends to the death penalty. In Florida, for example, blacks "who kill whites are nearly forty times more likely to be sentenced to death than those who kill blacks." Moreover, among "killers of whites, blacks are five times more likely than whites to be sentenced to death."[39] . . .

The criminal justice system is sometimes thought of as a kind of sieve in which the innocent are progressively sifted out from the guilty, who end up behind bars. I have tried to show that the sieve works another way as well. It sifts the affluent out from the poor, so it is not merely the guilty who end up behind bars, but the guilty poor.

. . . The criminal justice system does not simply weed the peace-loving from the dangerous, the law-abiding from the criminal. At every stage, starting with the very definitions of crime and progressing through the stages of investigation, arrest, charging, conviction, and sentencing, the system *weeds out the wealthy*. It refuses to define as "crimes" or as serious crimes the dangerous and predatory acts of the well-to-do—acts that, as we have seen, result in the loss of hundreds of thousands of lives and billions of dollars. Instead, the system focuses its attention on those crimes likely to be committed by members of the lower classes. Among those acts defined as "crimes," the system is more likely to investigate and detect, arrest and charge, convict and sentence a lower-class individual than a middle- or upper-class individual who has committed *the same offense, if not a worse one!*

The people we see in jails and prisons may well be dangerous to society. But they are not *the* danger to society, not *the gravest* danger to society. Individuals who pose equal or greater threats to our well-being walk the streets with impunity. The criminal justice system is a mirror that hides as much as it reveals. It is a carnival mirror that throws back a distorted image of the dangers that lurk in our midst—and conveys the impression that those dangers are the work of the poor. . . .

Notes

1. *The Washington Post,* January 11, 1983, p. C10.
2. *The Challenge of Crime in a Free Society: A Report by the President's Commission on Law Enforcement and Administration of Justice* [Washington, D.C.: U.S. Government Printing Office, February 1967].
3. Ronald Goldfarb, "Prisons: The National Poorhouse," *The New Republic,* November 1, 1969, pp. 15–17.
4. Philip A. Hart, "Swindling and Knavery, Inc.," *Playboy,* August 1972, p. 158.
5. Compare the statement of Professor Edwin H. Sutherland, one of the major luminaries of twentieth-century criminology: "First, the administrative processes are more favorable to persons in economic comfort than to those in poverty, so that if two persons on different economic levels are

equally guilty of the same offense, the one on the lower level is more likely to be arrested, convicted, and committed to an institution. Second, the laws are written, administered and implemented primarily with reference to the types of crimes committed by people of lower economic levels." E. H. Sutherland, *Principles of Criminology* (Philadelphia: Lippincott, 1939), p. 179.

6. For example, in 1972 when blacks made up 11.3 percent of the national population, they accounted for 42.5 percent of the population of the nation's jails. U.S. Bureau of the Census, Current Population Reports, Special Studies, Series P-23, No. 54, *The Social and Economic Status of the Black Population in the United States, 1974* (Washington, D.C.: U.S. Government Printing Office, 1975), pp. 11 and 173.

7. Edwin H. Sutherland and Donald R. Cressey, *Criminology,* 9th edition (Philadelphia: Lippincott, 1974), p. 133. The following studies are cited (p. 133, note 4) in support of this point: Edwin M. Lemert and Judy Rosberg, "The Administration of Justice to Minority Groups in Los Angeles County," *University of California Publications in Culture and Society,* 2, No. 1 (1948), pp. 1–28; Thorsten Sellin, "Race Prejudice in the Administration of Justice," *American Journal of Sociology,* 41 (September, 1935), pp. 212-217; Sidney Alexrad, "Negro and White Male Institutionalized Delinquents," *American Journal of Sociology* 57 (May, 1952) pp. 569–574; Marvin E. Wolfgang, Arlene Kelly, and Hans C. Nolde, "Comparison of the Executed and the Commuted Among Admissions to Death Row," *Journal of Criminal Law, Criminology, and Police Science,* 53 (September, 1962), pp. 301-311; Nathan Goldman, *The Differential Selection of Juvenile Offenders for Court Appearance* (New York: National Council on Crime and Delinquency, 1963); Irving Piliavin and Scott Briar, "Police Encounters with Juveniles," *American Journal of Sociology,* 70 (September, 1964) pp. 206-214; Robert M. Terry, "The Screening of Juvenile Offenders," *Journal of Criminal Law, Criminology, and Police Science,* 58 (June 1967), pp. 173-181. See also Ramsey Clark, *Crime in America* (New York: Simon and Schuster, 1970), p. 51: "Negroes are arrested more frequently and on less evidence than whites and are more often victims of mass or sweep arrests"; and Donald Taft, *Criminology,* 3rd edition (New York: Macmillan, 1956), p. 134: "Negroes are more likely to be suspected of crime than are whites. They are also more likely to be arrested. If the perpetrator of a crime is known to be a Negro the police may arrest all Negroes who were near the scene—a procedure they would rarely dare to follow with whites. After arrest Negroes are less likely to secure bail, and so are more liable to be counted in jail statistics. They are more liable than whites to be indicted and less likely to have their cases nol prossed or otherwise dismissed. If tried, Negroes are more likely to be convicted. If convicted they are less likely to be given probation. For this reason they are more likely to be included in the count of prisoners. Negroes are also more liable than whites to be kept in prison for the full terms of their commitments and correspondingly less likely to be paroled."

8. For an overview of this double distortion, see Thomas J. Dolan, "The Case for Double Jeopardy: Black and Poor," *International Journal of Criminology and Penology,* 1 (1973), pp. 129–150.

9. Isidore Silver, "Introduction" to the Avon edition of *The Challenge of Crime in a Free Society* (New York: Avon Books, 1968), p. 31.

10. *Challenge,* p. 43. (Emphasis added.) The study referred to is James S. Wallerstein and C. J. Wyle, "Our Law-abiding Lawbreakers," *Probation,* XXV (April, 1947), pp. 107-112.

11. This is the conclusion of Austin L. Porterfield, *Youth in Trouble* (Fort Worth: Leo Potishman Foundation, 1946); Fred J. Murphy, M. Shirley, and H. L. Witmer, "The Incidence of Hidden Delinquency," *American Journal of Orthopsychiatry,* XVI (October, 1946), pp. 686–96; James F. Short, Jr., "A Report on the Incidence of Criminal Behavior, Arrests, and Convictions in Selected Groups," *Proceedings of the Pacific Sociological Society,* 1954, pp. 110–18 (published as Vol. XXII, No. 2, of *Research Studies of the State College of Washington* (Pullman, Washington, 1954)]; F. Ivan Nye, James F. Short, Jr. and Virgil J. Olson, "Socioeconomic Status and Delinquent Behavior," *American Journal of Sociology,* 63 (January, 1958), pp. 381-389; Maynard L. Erikson and Lamar T. Empey, "Class Position, Peers and Delinquency," *Sociology and Social Research,* 49 (April, 1965), pp. 268-282; William J. Chambliss and Richard H. Nagasawa, "On the Validity of Official Statistics—a Comparative Study of White, Black, and Japanese High-School Boys," *Journal of Research in Crime and Delinquency,* 6 (January,

1969), pp. 71-77; Eugene Doleschal, "Hidden Crime," *Crime and Delinquency Literature,* 2, No. 5 (October, 1970), pp. 546-572; Nanci Koser Wilson, *Risk Ratios in Juvenile Delinquency* (Ann Arbor, Michigan: University Microfilms, 1972); and Maynard L. Erikson, "Group Violations, Socioeconomic Status and Official Delinquency," *Social Forces,* 52, No. 1 (September, 1973), pp. 41-52.

12. This is the conclusion of Martin Gold, "Undetected Delinquent Behavior," *Journal of Research in Crime and Delinquency,* 3, No. 1 (1966), pp. 27-46; and of Sutherland and Cressey, *Criminology,* 9th edition (Philadelphia: Lippincott, 1974), pp. 137 and 220.

13. Cf. Larry Karacki and Jackson Toby, "The Uncommitted Adolescent: Candidate for Gang Socialization," *Sociological Inquiry,* 32 (1962), pp. 203-215; William R. Arnold, "Continuities in Research—Scaling Delinquent Behavior," *Social Problems,* 13, No. 1 (1965), pp. 59-66; Harwin L. Voss, "Socio-economic Status and Reported Delinquent Behavior," *Social Problems,* 13, No. 3 (1966), pp. 314-324; LaMar Empey and Maynard L. Erikson, "Hidden Delinquency and Social Status," *Social Forces,* 44, No. 4 (1966), pp. 546-554; Fred J. Shanley, "Middle-class Delinquency as a Social Problem," *Sociology and Social Research,* 51 (1967), pp. 185-198; Jay R. Williams and Martin Gold, "From Delinquent Behavior to Official Delinquency," *Social Problems,* 20, No. 2 (1972), pp. 209-229.

14. Empey and Erikson, "Hidden Delinquency and Social Status," pp. 549, 551. Nye, Short, and Olson also found destruction of property to be committed most frequently by upper-class boys and girls. "Socioeconomic Status and Delinquent Behavior," p. 385.

15. Op. cit., footnote 13, above.

16. Comparing socioeconomic status categories "scant evidence is found that would support the contention that group delinquency is more characteristic of the lower-status levels than other socioeconomic status levels. . . . In fact, *only arrests seem to be more characteristic of the low-status category* than the other categories." Erikson, "Group Violations, Socioeconomic Status and Official Delinquency," p. 15. (Emphasis added.)

17. Gold, "Undetected Delinquent Behavior," p. 28. (Emphasis added.)

18. Ibid., p. 38.

19. Terence P. Thornberry, "Race, Socioeconomic Status and Sentencing in the Juvenile Justice System," *The Journal of Criminal Law and Criminology,* 64, No. 1 (1973), pp. 90-98.

20. Doleschal and Klapmuts, "Toward a New Criminology," p. 614, reporting the conclusions of Ross L. Purdy, *Factors in the Conviction of Law Violators: The Drinking Driver* (Ann Arbor, Michigan: University Microfilms, 1971).

21. Gerald Robin, "The Corporate and Judicial Disposition of Employee Thieves," *Wisconsin Law Review,* No. 3 (Summer, 1967), p. 693.

22. See for example D. Chapman, "The Stereotype of the Criminal and the Social Consequences," *International Journal of Criminology and Penology,* 1, (1973), p. 24.

23. This view is widely held, although the degree to which it functions as a self-fulfilling prophecy is less widely recognized. Versions of this view can be seen in *Challenge,* p. 79; Jerome Skolnick, *Justice Without Trial* (New York: John Wiley, 1966), pp. 45-48, 217-218; and Jessica Mitford, *Kind and Usual Punishment,* p. 53. Piliavin and Briar write in "Police Encounters with Juveniles":

    Compared to other youths, Negroes and boys whose appearance matched the delinquent stereotype were more frequently stopped and interrogated by patrolmen—often even in the absence of evidence that an offense had been committed—usually were given more severe dispositions for the same violations. Our data suggest, however, that these selective apprehension and disposition practices resulted not only from the intrusion of long-held prejudices of individual police officers but also from certain job-related experiences of law-enforcement personnel. First, the tendency of police to give more severe dispositions to Negroes and to youths whose appearance correspond to that which police associated with delinquents partly reflected the fact, observed in this study, that these youths also were much more likely than were other types of boys to exhibit the sort of recalcitrant demeanor which police construed as a sign of the confirmed delinquent. Further, officers assumed, partly on the basis of departmental statistics, that Negroes and juveniles who "look tough" (e.g. who wear chinos, leather jackets, boots, etc.) commit crimes more frequently than do other types of youths. (p. 212)

Cf. Albert Reiss, *The Police and the Public* (New Haven: Yale University Press, 1971). Reiss attributes the differences to the differences in the actions of complainants.

24. Richard J. Lundman, for example, found higher arrest rates to be associated with "offender powerlessness." "Routine Police Arrest Practices: A Commonweal Perspective," *Social Problems,* 22, No. 1 (October, 1974), pp. 127-141.
25. *Task Force Report: Crime and Its Impact,* p. 107.
26. Hart, "Swindling and Knavery, Inc.," p. 158.
27. UCR-1980, p. 191.
28. See, for example, Theodore G. Chiricos, Phillip D. Jackson, and Gordon P. Waldo, "Inequality in the Imposition of a Criminal Label," *Social Problems,* 19, No. 4 (Spring, 1972), pp. 553-572.
29. Abraham S. Blumberg, *Criminal Justice* (Chicago: Quadrangle, 1967), p. 33. Even for the middle-class defendant, the state with its greater financial, investigatory, and legal personnel resources, holds the advantage over the accused—so the poor person is doubly disadvantaged. Cf. Abraham S. Goldstein, "The State and the Accused: Balance of Advantage in Criminal Procedure," in *Crime, Law and Society,* eds., Goldstein and Goldstein, pp. 173-206.
30. See, for example, C. E. Ares, A. Rankin, and J. H. Sturz, "The Manhattan Bail Project: An Interim Report on the Use of Pre-Trial Parole," *NYU Law Review,* 38 (1963), p. 67; C. Foote, "Compelling Appearances in Court-Administration of Bail in Philadelphia," *University of Pennsylvania Law Review,* 102 (1954), pp. 1031-79; and C. Foote, "A Study of the Administration of Bail in New York City," *University of Pennsylvania Law Review,* 106 (1958), p. 693. For statistics on persons held in jail awaiting trial, see *Black Population in the U.S.,* (see note 5, above) p. 171; and U.S.L.E.A.A., *Survey of Inmates of Local Jails 1972—Advance Report* (Washington, D.C.: U.S. Government Printing Office, 1974), pp. 5 and 8.
31. Blumberg, *Criminal Justice,* pp. 28-29; *Challenge,* p. 134; and Donald J. Newman, *Conviction: The Determination of Guilt or Innocence Without Trial* (Boston: Little, Brown, 1966), p. 3.
32. A good summary of these developments can be found in Joel Jay Finer, "Ineffective Assistance of Counsel," *Cornell Law Review,* 58, No. 6 (July, 1973), pp. 1077-1120.
33. See, for example, Dallin H. Oaks and Warren Lehman, "Lawyers for the Poor," in *Law and Order: The Scales of Justice,* ed., A. Blumberg, pp. 92-93; also Jerome H. Skolnick, "Social Control in the Adversary System," in *Criminal Justice: Law and Politics,* ed., Cole (Belmont, Calif.: Duxbury, 1972), p. 266. "The National Legal Aid and Defender Association has suggested that experienced attorneys handle no more than 150 felony cases per year, rather than . . . the case load of over 500 felony cases per attorney with which some public defender offices in major cities are burdened." Finer, "Ineffective Assistance of Counsel," p. 1120.
34. In several essays, Abraham S. Blumberg has described the role of the public defender as an officer of the court bureaucracy rather than as a defender of the accused. See his "Lawyers with Convictions," in *Law and Order: The Scales of Justice,* pp. 51-67; "The Practice of Law as Confidence Game: Organizational Cooptation of a Profession," in *Criminal Law in Action,* ed., William J. Chambliss (Santa Barbara, Calif.: Hamilton Publishing Co., 1975), pp. 262-275; and his book *Criminal Justice* (Chicago: Quadrange, 1967), esp. pp. 13-115.
35. Lesley Oelsner, "Wide Disparities Mark Sentences Here," *The New York Times,* September 27, 1972, p. 1. Stuart Nagel writes, "The reasons for the economic class sentencing disparities, holding crime and prior record constant, are due possibly to the quality of legal representation that the indigent receive and probably to the appearance that an indigent defendant presents before a middle-class judge or probation officer." "Disparities in Sentencing Procedure," *UCLA Law Review,* 14 (August, 1967), p. 1.
36. Nagel, "The Tipped Scales of American Justice," p. 39.
37. *Sourcebook-1981,* pp. 463, 477, 490.
38. Henry Allen Bullock, "Significance of the Racial Factor in the Length of Prison Sentences," in *Crime and Justice in Society,* ed., R. Quinney (Boston: Little, Brown, 1969), p. 425; also, Marvin E. Wolfgang and Marc Riedel, "Race, Judicial Discretion and the Death Penalty," in *Criminal Law in Action,* ed., Chambliss, p. 375.
39. William J. Bowers and Glenn L. Pierce, "Racial Discrimination and Criminal Homicide Under Post-*Furman* Capital Statutes," in H. A. Bedau, ed., *The Death Penalty in America* [New York: Oxford University Press, 1982], pp. 206-224.

The Economy

The Wage Gap:

Myths and Facts

National Committee on Pay Equity

1. THE UNITED STATES LABOR FORCE IS OCCUPATIONALLY SEGREGATED BY RACE AND SEX.

- In 1992, women constituted 45.7 percent of all workers in the civilian labor force (over 57 million women).[1]
- People of color constituted 14.5 percent of all workers.[2]
- Labor force participation is almost equal among white women, Black women, and women of Hispanic origin. In 1992, 57.2 percent (7.1 million) of Black women, 61.3 percent (52.7 million) of white women, and 52.8 percent (4.2 million) of Hispanic women were in the paid labor force.[3]

- In 1992, women were:
  99.0 percent of all secretaries
  93.5 percent of all registered nurses
  98.8 percent of all pre-school and kindergarten teachers
  89.0 percent of all telephone operators
  73.2 percent of all teachers (excluding colleges and universities)
  86.6 percent of all data entry keyers
  Women were only:
  8.7 percent of all engineers
  30.3 percent of all lawyers and judges
  15.1 percent of all police and detectives
  8.2 percent of all precision, production, craft, and repair workers
  26.2 percent of all physicians[4]

The U.S. labor force is segregated by sex and race.

OCCUPATIONS WITH THE HIGHEST CONCENTRATION BY RACE/ETHNICITY/SEX[5]

Black women:	Social workers; postal clerks; dieticians; child-care workers and teacher's aides; private household cooks and cleaners; nursing aides, orderlies, and attendants
Black men:	Vehicle washers and equipment cleaners; bus drivers; concrete and terrazzo workers; guards; sheriffs, bailiffs, and other law enforcement
Hispanic women:	Private household cleaners and servants; child-care workers; janitors and cleaners; health service occupations; sewing machine operators; graders and sorters
Hispanic men:	Janitors and cleaners; construction trades; machine operators and tenders; cooks; drivers-sales workers; handlers, laborers, and helpers; roofers; groundskeepers, gardeners, farm and agricultural workers
White women:	Physical therapists; dental hygienists; secretaries and stenographers; bookkeepers, accounting and auditing clerks
White men:	Marketing, advertising, and public relations managers; engineers, architects, and surveyors; dentists; firefighters; construction supervisors; tool and die makers
Asian women:	Marine life workers; electrical assemblers; dressmakers; launderers
Asian men:	Physicians; engineers; professors; technicians; baggage porters; cooks; launderers; long shore equipment operators
Native American women:	Welfare aides; child-care workers; teacher's aides; forestry (except logging)
Native American men:	Marine life workers; hunters; forestry (except logging); fishers

2. ECONOMIC STATUS.

- In 1992, 58 percent of all women were either the sole supporter of their families or their husbands earned less than $15,000.[6]
- Over 8.8 million women work full time in jobs that pay wages below the poverty line (in 1992 for a family of three the poverty line was $11,186 per year). They work in jobs such as day care, food counter, and many service jobs. Many more women than men are part of the working poor (125 percent of the poverty level) and work in jobs such as clerical, blue collar, and sales.[7]
- In 1992, married couple families with two children present had a median income of $43,818 while female headed households with two children present had a median income of only $11,591.[8]
- Women of color are in the lowest paid jobs.
- The majority of women, just as the majority of men, work out of economic necessity to support their families. Women do not work for "pin money."

OCCUPATIONS AND AVERAGE SALARIES OF OCCUPATIONS WITH A HIGH PERCENTAGE OF WOMEN OF COLOR[9]

Occupation	Annual Weekly Salary	Percentage of Women of Color
Social workers	$489	16
Health aides	309	22
Nursing aides	266	31
Food preparation workers	236	10
Sewing machine operators	217	28
Cleaners and servants	191	26
Child-care workers	154	14

In 1992 median weekly salaries for all men were $505 and $381 for all women. Women of color represented approximately 7 percent of all workers.

3. THE WAGE GAP IS ONE OF THE MAJOR CAUSES OF ECONOMIC INEQUALITY IN THE UNITED STATES TODAY.

- In 1992, all men, working year-round full-time, were paid a median salary of $30,358.
- All women, working year-round full-time, were paid a median salary of $21,440.
- Therefore, women were paid 70.6 cents compared to each dollar paid to men.

The breakdown by race shows the double burden that women of color face because of race and sex discrimination.

YEAR-ROUND FULL-TIME EARNINGS FOR 1992[10]

Race/Sex	Earnings	Earnings as a Percentage of White Men's
White men	$31,012	100.0
Black men	22,369	72.1
Hispanic men	20,049	64.6
White women	21,659	69.8
Black women	19,819	63.9
Hispanic women	17,138	55.3

Data for Asian/Pacific Islanders and Native Americans is not available.

4. THE WAGE GAP HAS FLUCTUATED, BUT HAS NOT DISAPPEARED IN THE LAST SEVERAL DECADES.

Over the last decade, the wage gap has narrowed by about ten cents, from 60.2 percent in 1980 to 70.6 percent in 1992. However, a significant portion of the change is due to the fact that men's real earnings have fallen over the last several years. 38 percent of the change in the wage ratio can be attributed to the drop in men's earnings, while 62 percent is due to the increase in women's earnings over the decade.

COMPARISON OF MEDIAN EARNINGS OF YEAR-ROUND FULL-TIME WORKERS, BY SEX, SELECTED YEARS

Year	Median Earnings		Women's Earnings as a Percent of Men's	Year	Median Earnings		Women's Earnings as a Percent of Men's
	Women	Men			Women	Men	
1992	$21,440	$30,358	70.6	1973	$6,335	$11,186	56.6
1991	20,553	29,421	69.8	1972	5,903	10,202	57.9
1990	20,656	28,843	71.6	1971	5,593	9,399	59.5
1989	18,780	27,430	68.5	1970	5,323	8,966	59.4
1988	17,606	26,656	66.0	1969	4,977	8,227	60.5
1987	16,909	26,008	65.0	1966	3,973	6,848	58.0
1986	16,232	25,256	64.3	1965	3,823	6,375	60.0
1985	15,624	24,195	64.5	1964	3,690	6,195	59.6
1984	14,780	23,218	63.7	1963	3,561	5,978	59.6
1983	13,915	21,881	63.6	1962	3,446	5,974	59.5
1982	13,014	21,077	61.7	1961	3,351	5,644	59.4
1981	12,001	20,260	59.2	1960	3,293	5,317	60.8
1980	11,197	18,612	60.2	1959	3,193	5,209	61.3
1979	10,151	17,014	59.7	1958	3,102	4,927	63.0
1978	9,350	15,730	59.4	1957	3,008	4,713	63.8
1977	8,618	14,626	58.9	1956	2,827	4,466	63.3
1976	8,099	13,455	60.2	1955	2,719	4,252	63.9
1975	7,504	12,758	58.8	1946	1,710	2,588	66.1
1974	6,772	11,835	57.2				

5. THE CAUSE OF THE WAGE GAP IS DISCRIMINATION.

Differences in education, labor force experience, and commitment (years in the labor force) do not account for the entire wage gap.

- In 1992, women with college degrees earned $11,721 less per year than their white male colleagues, and only $1,916 more per year than white men with only a high-school diploma.
- College educated Hispanic women actually earned less than white men who had never taken a college course.[12]
- The National Academy of Sciences (NAS) found in 1981 that usually less than a quarter (25 percent) of the wage gap is due to differences in education, labor force experience, and commitment.
- According to the 1986 NAS study, *Women's Work, Men's Work,* "each additional percentage point female in an occupation was associated with $42 less in median annual earnings."
- According to the 1987 National Committee on Pay Equity (NCPE) study, in New York State, for every 5 to 6 percent increase in Black and Hispanic representation in a job there is one salary grade decrease. (One salary grade decrease amounts to a 5 percent salary decrease.)
- A 1985 U.S. Census Bureau study reported that differences in education, labor force experience, and commitment account for only 14.6 percent of the wage gap between men and women.

6. EMPLOYERS ARE ALWAYS COMPARING DIFFERENT JOBS IN ORDER TO SET WAGES.

- Two-thirds of employees are paid according to a formal job evaluation system.

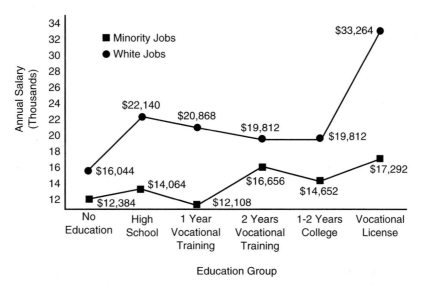

White vs. Minority Wage Inequity by Education for Entry-Level Jobs

7. THE COST OF IMPLEMENTING PAY EQUITY.

• Achieving pay equity usually costs about 2 to 5 percent of an employer's payroll budget.

For example, in the State of Minnesota, after conducting a job evaluation study, it was determined that there was a 20 percent gap between comparable male-dominated and female-dominated jobs. It cost the state 3.7 percent of the payroll budget to eliminate this inequity. The adjustments were phased-in over a four-year period and have resulted in a narrowing of the wage gap by nine percentage points, without affecting overall employment for women in the state.

8. PAY EQUITY IS BEING ADDRESSED ALL OVER THE COUNTRY.

• All but five states (Alaska, Arkansas, Delaware, Georgia, and Idaho) have addressed the issue of pay equity.
• Twenty-four states and the District of Columbia have conducted job evaluation studies to deter-

mine if their wage setting systems are discriminatory.
• Twenty states have actually adjusted wages for women in jobs that have been found to be underpaid because of wage bias.
• Four states (New York, New Jersey, Florida, and Wisconsin) and Washington, D.C., have addressed race in addition to sex discrimination.[13]

9. EVERYONE IN SOCIETY BENEFITS FROM PAY EQUITY.

A. Men's wages will not be lowered. Employers cannot remedy discrimination by penalizing another group. Men who are working in predominantly female jobs will also be paid more if pay equity adjustments are made. Everyone benefits from women and people of color being paid fairly. Whether it is your mother, sister, wife, or daughter, wage discrimination hurts the entire family. Men of color will benefit in additional ways to those listed for all men: elimination of race from the wage setting system will boost their wages and men of color are more likely to be found in undervalued "women's" occupations.

B. Employers benefit because the employees' productivity will increase if there is a sense of fairness in how wages are set. Also, pay equity helps employers recruit and retain the best workers.

C. Society benefits because if wage discrimination is eliminated, the need for government subsidies for food stamps, health care, etc., will not be as great. In addition, when workers whose wages were lowered by discrimination are paid fairly, their pensions will be greater upon retirement and they will need less government assistance in their senior years.

WHERE WE GET THE STATISTICS

The U.S. Department of Commerce, Census Bureau, collects wage data every ten years. This data provides in-depth information for Blacks, whites, Hispanics, Asian/Pacific Islanders, and Native Americans. The 1990 decennial census figures of the national work force and occupational data sorted by gender and race had not been released as of January 1994.

The Census Bureau also provides annual salary data for Blacks, whites, and Hispanics. They gather this information in March of the following year and release it in September. Therefore, the annual salary data for 1993 will not have been released until September of 1994.

The U.S. Department of Labor, Bureau of Labor Statistics (BLS), provides quarterly reports each year on weekly salaries for Blacks, whites, and Hispanics. They also provide an annual average of weekly wages.

Notes

1. U.S. Department of Labor, Bureau of Labor Statistics, 1992 Annual Average Tables from *Employment and Earnings,* Jan., 1993.
2. Ibid.

3. U.S. Department of Commerce, Census Bureau, Current Population Reports, Consumer Income. Series P-60, No. 184, Table No. 31.
4. U.S. Department of Labor, Bureau of Labor Statistics, 1992 Annual Average Tables, Table 5.
5. Data for Black, Hispanic, and white men and women from the U.S. Department of Labor Bureau of Labor Statistics, 1992 Annual Averages, unpublished tables. Data for Asian and Native American men and women from U.S. Department of Commerce, 1980 Decennial Census.
6. U.S. Department of Commerce, Census Bureau, Current Population Reports, Consumer Income, Series P-60, No. 184, Table No. 28.
7. U.S. Department of Commerce, Census Bureau, Current Population Reports, Consumer Income, Series P-60, No. 185, Table A.
8. U.S. Department of Commerce, Census Bureau, Current Population Reports, Consumer Income, Series P-60, No. 184, Table No. 18.
9. U.S. Department of Labor, Bureau of Labor Statistics, 1992 Annual Averages, unpublished data.
10. U.S. Department of Commerce, Census Bureau, Current Population Reports, Consumer Income, Series P-60, No. 184, Table No. 31.
11. *Background on the Wage Gap,* National Committee on Pay Equity, 1126 Sixteenth Street, NW, Suite 411, Washington, D.C., 20036.
12. U.S. Department of Commerce, Census Bureau, Current Population Reports, Consumer Income, Series P-60, No. 184, Table No. 30.
13. *Pay Equity in the Public Sector,* 1993 Addendum, National Committee on Pay Equity, 1126 Sixteenth Street, NW, Suite 411, Washington, D.C., 20036.

READING 26

The Racial Income Gap

Andrew Hacker

Since their first arrival, and continuing after they started receiving wages, black Americans have figured disproportionately among the nation's poor. Of course, differences in incomes can have explanations apart from race. After all, a lot of white people are poor, and a number of blacks are very visibly rich. Even so, after other factors have been accounted for, race still seems to play a role in how people fare financially. A recurrent theme of this [discussion] will be how being black or white affects economic opportunities and outcomes.

Any discussion of incomes and earnings will depend strongly on statistics. While we cannot measure equity with precision, numerical disparities represent real facts about the races. Each year, the census asks a national sample of Americans to estimate their total incomes during the previous year. The table [below] gives some of the results from the 1990 survey, reported first as median incomes and then by how much blacks received for every $1,000 that went to whites.

The listings for families and for all men and women include every sort of income, ranging from pensions and welfare payments to disability benefits and capital gains. The figures for employed men and women reflect only the earnings of individuals who held full-time jobs throughout the year. The relative incomes for black families as a group and for black men are embarrassingly low, in particular when compared with those for the earnings of black women.

In 1990, the most recent figures available at this writing, personal income received by everyone living within the country added up to a grand total of $3.6 trillion. While black Americans made up 12.1 percent of the tabulated population, they ended up with only 7.8 percent of the mone-

tary pie. Earnings by some 134 million gainfully employed persons accounted for $2.8 trillion of the income total. Black workers comprised 10.1 percent of that employment force, but received only 8.0 percent of all earnings.

White households are more apt to have both a husband and wife present, which raises the likelihood of multiple incomes. In fact, 59 percent of white families have two or more earners, while only 47 percent of black families do. As it happens, among married couples, a smaller percentage of white wives work: 61 percent have jobs, compared with 68 percent of black married women. Since the earnings of black men tend to be lower, fewer of their families can afford the luxury of full-time housewives. When white wives work, they are more likely to take part-time jobs and their paychecks tend to be supplemental; whereas among black families, the husbands' and wives' earnings are often of equal value. And since more black families are headed by single women, a higher proportion of their households must make do with only one income. Moreover, when black single mothers work—and the majority do—it is generally at a job paying relatively low wages.

So the question arises whether income ratios would change if black families had the same mixture of single parents and married couples as white households now do. If this became the case, then many more black homes would have someone bringing in a man's earnings. Were this change to occur, the income ratio for black families would only rise from $580 to $732, not exactly an impressive improvement. The reason is that while having more men's incomes would help, it would not accomplish very much since black men still make considerably less than white men. Moreover, even if more black households had a man in residence, some of the men would be unemployed or removed from the labor force for other reasons. So emulating the white family structure would close only about half of the income gap.

On the whole, increased education tends to bring in higher incomes. While we can always find exceptions, for most people most of the time,

INCOMES AND EARNINGS[1]
(1990 Medians)

	White	Black	Ratio*
Families	$36,915	$21,423	$580
All Men	$21,170	$12,868	$608
All Women	$10,317	$ 8,328	$807
Employed Men	$30,598	$22,167	$725
Employed Women	$20,759	$18,838	$907

*Incomes of blacks per $1,000 for whites. Earnings for Year-Round Fulltime workers.

EDUCATION AND EARNINGS[2]

(Earnings of Blacks per $1,000 for Whites)

	Men	Women
High School Not Finished	$797	$974
4 Years of High School	$764	$942
1 to 3 Years of College	$825	$925
4 Years of College	$798	$1,002
5+ Years of College	$771	$973

staying in school does pay off. The figures in the table above show how the rule works along a racial continuum. To make the comparisons as firm as possible, the table covers only individuals who worked full time throughout the entire year.

A steady economic progression is evident for all four groups: among black and white men and women, incomes ascend with added years of school. The catch is that even when black men reach the same academic level as white men, their incomes stay several steps behind. Thus among men with four years of college, blacks still earn only $798 for each $1,000 going to whites in that educational stratum. Even worse, black college men end up just a few dollars ahead of whites who went no further than high school. When black men persevere to graduate school, they still receive only $771 compared with their white counterparts, even less than for black men who never finished college. Hence the advice so often offered to blacks, that they should stay in school, seems valid only insofar as it informs them that with additional education they will move ahead of others of their own race. There is little evidence that spending more years in school will improve their positions in relation to whites.

Of course, the table also shows that black women come much closer to parity, with their white counterparts making between $925 and $1,002 for each $1,000 earned by white women at their level. The greater equity among women results largely from the fact that few women of either race rise far in the earnings hierarchy. The comparative status of black women warrants only a muted cheer: achieving equality is easier within an underpaid cohort. Yet there remains the question of why black men are denied even the limited equity that black women enjoy.

If we want to find out how much income disparities result from racial bias, then we must do our best to compare similar groups, since additional elements like age and experience can distort comparisons. A census study that examined the earnings of male attorneys between the ages of thirty-five and forty-five found that black lawyers averaged $790 for every $1,000 made by their white counterparts.[3] Given that these men are in the same age range and have the same level of education, it could be argued that race accounts for at least part of the $210 earnings gap. Of course, we would have to know a lot more about the individuals in question. Factors like talent, intelligence, and temperament could affect the equation. Or the variance in earnings might reflect different law schools the men attended and how well they did there. After all, it hardly needs mentioning that not all educations are comparable. If more of the white lawyers in the cohort went to Harvard, while the black lawyers were apt to have studied at Howard, then some people might use this fact to justify some part of the $210 difference.

As it happens, black *women* lawyers in the same age group make $930 for every $1,000 going to their white colleagues. Moreover, this similarity holds even though black women attend the same spectrum of law schools as black men. So a question must arise: if black women in the legal profession are paid nearly as much as white women, then why don't black men make almost as much as white men? A suspicion cannot help but arise that some of the racial earnings spread among men stems from the fact that black men are given fewer opportunities to rise to better-paid positions.

Measured in economic terms, the last two decades have not been auspicious ones for Americans of any race. Between 1970 and 1990, the median income for white families, computed in constant dollars, rose from $34,481 to $36,915, an increase of 8.7 percent. During these decades, black family income barely changed at all going from $21,151 to $21,423. In relative terms, black incomes dropped from $613 to $580 for each $1,000 received by whites. As it happened, the incomes of white men also dropped during this period, so if white families recorded a modest rise, it was because more of them had wives who could go to work.

However, medians—like averages—can conceal important variations. The four configurations that follow show how incomes were distributed among black and white families in 1970 and 1990. The shapes for both races changed in revealing ways. In 1970, the black incomes depicted at the bottom left took the form of a classical pyramid, beginning with a fairly broad base and tapering at each subsequent level. Twenty years later, the base had become much wider, and families were arrayed more evenly among the higher brackets. This change reflects not only the much-heralded growth of a black middle class, but also a significant shift in black America's social structure, signaling a separation of better-off blacks from those at the lowest level.

In 1970, the white distribution had the shape of a chunky column, with a heavy girth in the middle ranges. By 1990, aggregate income had moved toward the top. The figure had become an inverted pyramid, with more than half of the homes in the two top tiers. The rise in better-off households came in part from a growth in highly paid positions during the 1980s; but the principal

reason was that by 1990 many more white homes had two earners. At the same time, between 1970 and 1990, the size of the two bottom tiers had barely changed. However, there had been a shift in the composition of the white poor. In 1970, it consisted largely of the elderly, or employed persons working for very low wages. By 1990, low-income white households were more apt to be those headed by women.

During the two decades, the proportion of black households with incomes over $50,000 expanded by 46 percent, while the share of white homes at that level rose by only 35 percent. Even if whites were not advancing as fast, they were not falling behind; so it cannot be argued that blacks were replacing whites in better-paid positions.

Nor does the fact that more black families enjoy incomes of over $50,000 mean that many black men and women have jobs paying at that level. Indeed, only 3.4 percent of all black men make $50,000 or more; most $50,000 homes result from two or more sets of earnings. In contrast, 12.1 percent of white men receive over $50,000, and many more of them are the sole or dominant earners in their households. So while there is now a much larger black middle class, more typically, the husband is likely to be a bus driver earning $32,000, while his wife brings home $28,000 as a teacher or a nurse. A white middle-class family is three to four times more likely to contain a husband earning $75,000 in a managerial position, which allows him to support a nonworking wife. It is not easy to visualize these two couples living on the same block, let alone becoming acquainted with one another.

Some thirty years ago, federal officials devised a formula to designate which Americans could be considered poor. The poverty threshold is adjusted every year, to keep pace with the cost of living. In 1990, an older woman living by herself would fall in the poverty cohort if her income fell below $6,268. A single mother with two children was counted as poor if their income was lower than $10,530. In most parts of the United States, $6,268 spells not simply poverty, but a good

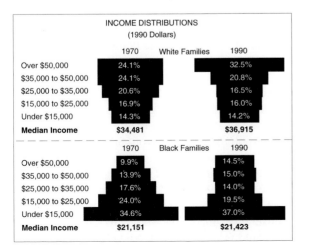

INCOME DISTRIBUTIONS
(1990 Dollars)

	1970	White Families	1990
Over $50,000	24.1%		32.5%
$35,000 to $50,000	24.1%		20.8%
$25,000 to $35,000	20.6%		16.5%
$15,000 to $25,000	16.9%		16.0%
Under $15,000	14.3%		14.2%
Median Income	**$34,481**		**$36,915**

	1970	Black Families	1990
Over $50,000	9.9%		14.5%
$35,000 to $50,000	13.9%		15.0%
$25,000 to $35,000	17.6%		14.0%
$15,000 to $25,000	24.0%		19.5%
Under $15,000	34.6%		37.0%
Median Income	**$21,151**		**$21,423**

chance of malnutrition. Nor is it possible to bring up, say, two teenagers on $10,530 a year. Even adding in the dollar value of school lunches, food stamps, and medical benefits, the formula understates the number of Americans who are truly poor. Another problem is that the figures ignore variations in living costs. A widow might manage on $6,268 in rural Arkansas, but that would barely pay her rent in Boston or Brooklyn. Still, if we make appropriate adjustments, the official poverty percentage can tell us a lot about who is poor and why.

As the next table shows, 44.8 percent of black children live below the poverty line, compared with 15.9 percent of white youngsters. So black children are almost three times as likely as whites to grow up in poor surroundings. The ratio runs higher for all black families, and is somewhat similar for black people as a whole. However, the poverty figures have a much closer ratio (1.48) among households headed by women. Indeed, the proportion in poverty among white single mothers (37.9 percent) exceeds that for the black population as a whole. For women who must raise children on their own, being white loses much of its advantage.

The poverty figures also show that some two thirds of poor white Americans live in suburbs or rural areas. Anyone who has traveled along the back roads of outlying America has seen the homes of people who are white and poor. How-ever, their homes are less likely to be clustered together in slum neighborhoods, unless one applies that description to decaying trailer parks. Among the poor white families who do live in urban areas, less than a quarter of them reside in low-income tracts. This suggests that there are relatively few white ghettos. Urban black families below the poverty line are more visibly segregated: no less than 70 percent of such households are concentrated in low-income neighborhoods.

Of course, there is a white underclass.[5] Its members can be found among the addicted and the homeless, among men who have never held steady jobs, and women who have spent many years on welfare. The nation's prisons still have plenty of white criminals, some of whom are quite vicious and others who have made careers in small-time larcenies. Even so, neither sociologists nor journalists have shown much interest in depicting poor whites as a "class." In large measure, the reason is racial. For whites, poverty tends to be viewed as atypical or accidental. Among blacks, it comes close to being seen as a natural outgrowth of their history and culture. At times, it almost appears as if white poverty must be covered up, lest it blemish the reputation of the dominant race. This was not always the case. In the past, sociology textbooks dilated at length about families like the Jukes and the Kallikaks, who remained mired in squalor from generation to generation. In earlier days, too, white people could be "trash," whether along the tobacco roads or in pellagra-infested pine barrens. While class bias prompted these discursions, at least they granted that white people could occupy the lowest stratum of society.

Apart from people who are independently wealthy and those with generous pensions, enjoying the modest comforts of life requires having a decent job. Altogether, about 80 percent of Americans' personal income comes from wages and salaries or other gainful earnings.

Between 1939 and 1959, the earnings of black men relative to whites improved by over a third. Those who made the move to Northern cities relocated in search of employment. They were

POVERTY PERCENTAGES[4]

	White	Black	Multiple
All Persons	8.8%	31.9%	3.63
All Children	15.9%	44.8%	2.82
All Families	8.1%	29.3%	3.62
Female Headed Households	37.9%	56.1%	1.48

WHERE POOR AMERICANS LIVE

	White	Black
Central Cities	32.7%	60.3%
Suburbs	35.2%	17.5%
Nonmetropolitan	32.1%	22.2%
	100.0%	100.0%

willing to take blue-collar positions once reserved for immigrants, but which newer generations of whites were beginning to spurn. This period saw the emergence of a stable black working class, underpinned by two-parent families and orderly neighborhoods. If many saw themselves as "poor," that status did not have the connotations conveyed by "poverty" today. The earnings of black women also grew during this period, as they turned from domestic employment to better-paid occupations.

However, during the past twenty years, as the accompanying table shows, the relative earnings of black men has tapered off. Between 1970 and 1990, their earnings relative to white workers' improved by only $27; in fact, black men lost ground during this period's second decade. (And this was a period when affirmative action supposedly gave blacks preferences in hirings and promotions.) The decline in blue-collar employment hit black men especially hard. Each year found the economy offering fewer factory jobs, while more were being created in the white-collar sector.

If black women have fared better, it is because more of them have been seen as suitable for office positions. Professional and clerical occupations generally call for attitudes and aptitudes associated with the white world. . . . Black women apparently satisfy employers on these counts more readily than black men. Even so, by 1980, it became clear that black women would still fall short of parity with their white female colleagues. While white women were later in entering the labor force in large numbers, their arrival on the scene brought pressures to move them into professional and supervisory positions,

which has in turn increased the pay gap between white and black women.

Black men, women, and children were brought to this country for a singular purpose: to work. Indeed, the demand for their labor was so great that slaves continued to be smuggled in even after that traffic had been banned by the Constitution. In the years following emancipation, former slaves found that their services would not necessarily be needed. Their labor, like that of other Americans, would be subject to the vagaries of a market economy. The capitalist system has been frank in admitting that it cannot always create jobs for everyone who wants to work. This economic reality has certainly been a pervasive fact of black life. For as long as records have been kept, in good times and bad, white America has ensured that the unemployment imposed on blacks will be approximately double that experienced by whites. Stated very simply, if you are black in America, you will find it at least twice as hard to find or keep a job.

The ratios in the [next] table make it clear that black Americans get jobs only after white applicants have been accommodated. In periods of prosperity, when the economy requires more workers, blacks who had been unemployed are offered vacant positions. But as last hired, they can expect to be the first fired. In bleak times, the jobless rate among blacks can approach 20 percent, as it did in 1983. Since 1974, unemployment rates for blacks have remained at double-digit levels, and they have not fallen below twice the white rate since 1976. Even more depressing, the gap between the black and white figures grew during the 1980s, suggesting that the economy has little interest in enlisting black contributions.

It is frequently remarked that many black men and women lack the kinds of skills that modern employment requires. However, these charges are hardly new. They were also common in the past, when blacks were shunted to the end of the line even for laboring jobs. And today, whites who barely make it through high school continue to get the first openings in the building trades. Moreover, blacks who do stay in school soon

EARNINGS OF BLACK WORKERS[6]

(per $1,000 for Whites)

	Men	Women
1939	$450	$379
1950	$613	$369
1960	$669	$696
1970	$704	$851
1980	$751	$917
1990	$731	$900

UNEMPLOYMENT RATES[7]

Year	White	Black	Multiple
1960	4.9	10.2	2.08
1961	6.0	12.4	2.07
1962	4.9	10.9	2.22
1963	5.0	10.8	2.16
1964	4.6	9.6	2.09
1965	4.1	8.1	1.98
1966	3.3	7.3	2.21
1967	3.4	7.4	2.18
1968	3.2	6.7	2.09
1969	3.1	6.4	2.06
1960s Average			**2.11**
1970	4.4	8.2	1.86
1971	5.4	9.9	1.83
1972	5.0	10.0	2.00
1973	4.3	8.9	2.07
1974	5.0	9.9	1.98
1975	7.8	14.8	1.90
1976	7.0	13.1	1.87
1977	6.2	13.1	2.11
1978	5.2	11.9	2.29
1979	5.1	11.3	2.22
1970s Average			**2.01**
1980	6.3	14.3	2.27
1981	6.7	14.2	2.12
1982	8.6	18.9	2.20
1983	8.4	19.5	2.32
1984	6.5	15.9	2.45
1985	6.2	15.1	2.44
1986	6.0	14.5	2.42
1987	5.3	13.0	2.45
1988	4.7	11.7	2.49
1989	4.5	11.4	2.53
1980s Average			**2.37**
1990	4.1	11.3	2.76

skills, so the question arises as to why these places haven't been offered to native-born black Americans. This issue is not new, since it has long been argued that immigrant labor takes bread from the mouths of citizens. In most cases, though, aliens and immigrants acquiesce to wages and working conditions that black and white Americans are unwilling to accept. Indeed, newcomers often put up with what are essentially Third World terms of employment to gain a foothold in the American economy. And if these workers are exploited, it is often by employers or supervisors of their own origins who arrived here not much earlier. Nor is it likely that the pay for such jobs can be raised appreciably.

What black Americans want is no more nor less than what white Americans want: a fair chance for steady employment at decent pay. But this opportunity has been one that the nation's economy continues to withhold. To be black in America is to know that you remain last in line for so basic a requisite as the means for supporting yourself and your family. More than that, you have much less choice among jobs than workers who are white. . . .

learn there is no assured payoff. Those who finish college have a jobless rate 2.24 times that for whites with diplomas, an even greater gap than that separating black and white high school graduates.

Exacerbating the situation today is the fact that millions of jobs are being filled by legal and illegal aliens, largely from Latin America and Asia. Few of the positions they take call for special

Notes

1. Table on Incomes and Earnings: *Money Income of Households, Families, and Persons in the United States,* Series P-60, No. 174 (Bureau of the Census, 1991). Unless otherwise noted, all the figures cited in [this discussion] have been derived from this census study.
2. Table on Education and Earnings: *Money Income of Households, Families, and Persons in the United States.* Series P-60, No. 174 (Bureau of the Census, 1991).
3. *Earnings by Occupation and Education.* Subject Report PC80-2-8B (Bureau of the Census, 1984).
4. Table on Poverty. *Poverty in the United States: 1990,* Series P-60, No. 175 (Bureau of the Census, 1991).
5. See, for example, James Howard Kunstler, "Schuylerville Stands Still," *New York Times Magazine* (April 25, 1990). For some urban counter-

parts, see Jay MacLeod, *Ain't No Making It* (Westview Press, 1987).

6. Table on Earnings Ratios: for 1940 through 1970, *Historical Statistics of the United States;* for 1980 and 1990, *Current Population Reports,* Series P-60, No. 174 (Bureau of the Census, 1991).

7. Table on Unemployment: For 1960 through 1988, *Statistical Abstract of the United States.* For 1989 and 1990, *Employment and Earnings* (Bureau of Labor Statistics, 1991).

Civil Rights Issues Facing Asian Americans in the 1990s

United States Commission on Civil Rights

In the spring of 1991 the *Wall Street Journal* and NBC News conducted a national poll of voters' opinions about a variety of social and economic issues. The poll revealed that the majority of American voters believe that Asian Americans[1] are not discriminated against in the United States. Some even believe that Asian Americans receive "too many special advantages."[2] The poll shows plainly that the general public is largely unaware of the problems Asian Americans confront. Considering the widely held image of Asian Americans as the "model minority," this is hardly surprising. Yet participants at the Civil Rights Commission's Roundtable Conferences in Houston, San Francisco, and New York[3] recounted numerous incidents of anti-Asian prejudice and discrimination. Their statements made evident that, contrary to the widespread belief captured in the *Wall Street Journal*/NBC News poll, Asian Americans encounter many discriminatory barriers to equal opportunity and full participation in our society.

This report seeks to focus attention on the civil rights issues that confront Asian Americans in the 1990s.[4] The report compiles evidence confirming that Asian Americans do face widespread prejudice, discrimination, and barriers to equal oppor-

tunity. Asian Americans are frequently victims of racially motivated bigotry and violence; they face significant barriers to equal opportunity in education and employment; and they do not have equal access to a number of public services, including police protection, health care, and the court system. . . .

ASIANS IN THE UNITED STATES: A BRIEF HISTORY

The first Asians to arrive in the United States in large numbers were the Chinese, who came to work on Hawaiian plantations by the 1840s and to the West Coast of the mainland starting in the early 1850s to work in gold mines and later to help build the cross-country railroads. The Chinese were followed in the late 19th and early 20th centuries by Japanese and Filipinos and, in smaller numbers, by Koreans and Asian Indians. Restrictive immigration laws produced a 40-year hiatus in Asian immigration starting in the 1920s, but in 1965, when anti-Asian immigration restrictions were liberalized, a new wave of immigration began bringing people from Southeast Asia, China, Korea, the Philippines, and other Asian countries to the United States.

The history of Asian Americans in this country is replete with incidents of discrimination against them. Asian Americans experienced, at one time or another, discriminatory immigration and naturalization policies; discriminatory Federal, State, and local laws; discriminatory governmental treatment; considerable prejudice on the part of the general public; and outright violence. Not only was today's Asian American community shaped by historical forces, but today's civil rights issues need to be viewed in the context of past discrimination against Asian Americans.

NATURALIZATION AND IMMIGRATION LAWS

Throughout most of their history in this country Asians have been victimized by discriminatory naturalization and immigration laws. These laws have had the legacy of making Asian American newcomers feel unwelcome in their adopted country and have also been important in shaping the Asian American community as it exists today.

As this country became a nation, its founders sought to restrict eligibility for citizenship. In 1790 Congress passed a law limiting naturalization to "free white persons."[5] The law was modified in 1870, after the adoption of the 14th amendment, to include "aliens of African nativity and persons of African descent." At that time Congress considered and rejected extending naturalization rights to Asians,[6] thus making Asian immigrants the only racial group barred from naturalization.[7] Because the 14th amendment granted citizenship to all persons born in the United States, however, the American-born children of Asian immigrants were citizens. Filipinos and Asian Indians were granted eligibility for naturalization in 1946,[8] but it was not until 1952, with the McCarran-Walter Act,[9] that naturalization eligibility was extended to all races.[10] Thus, through most of this country's history, immigrant Asians were ineligible to become citizens.

Despite these anti-Asian naturalization laws, immigrants came to the United States from several Asian countries starting in the mid-19th century. As each successive Asian group arrived in this country, increasingly harsh immigration laws restricting the group's immigration were imposed. The first immigration ban was against the Chinese. In the 1850s Chinese immigrants began coming to the United States mainland to work in California's gold mines and quickly spread to mining in other Western States as well. Later, they played an essential role in building this country's transcontinental railroads. After the railroads were completed in 1869, jobs became scarcer on the West Coast, and worker resentment of the low wage rates accepted by Chinese workers intensified. Pressure built to limit the immigration of Chinese, culminating with the passage of the Chinese Exclusion Act in 1882,[11] which suspended the immigration of Chinese laborers for 10 years.[12] In 1892 the Geary Act[13] extended the immigration ban for another 10 years and required Chinese living in the United States to

obtain "certificates of residence" to prove that they were legal residents.[14] In 1904 the Chinese immigration ban was extended indefinitely.[15] Since the Chinese living in this country were predominately male, the result of these immigration restrictions was that the Chinese population in the United States declined from 105,465 in 1880 to 61,639 by 1920.[16]

Shortly after Chinese immigration was halted by the Chinese Exclusion Act, a new wave of Asian immigration began, this time from Japan. Although a few Japanese had immigrated to Hawaii in the 1870s and 1880s, Japanese did not come to the mainland in noticeable numbers until the 1890s.[17] At first largely urban, the Japanese soon became engaged predominantly in agricultural pursuits and related trade.[18]

Although the number of Japanese in this country was not large (fewer than 25,000 in the 1900 census),[19] pressure soon developed on the West Coast to restrict Japanese immigration. In response to this pressure, the Japanese Government, fearing a loss of international prestige if U.S. immigration laws banned Japanese immigration, negotiated the Gentleman's Agreement[20] with President Theodore Roosevelt in 1907.[21] According to this agreement, the Japanese Government would voluntarily restrict the emigration of unskilled Japanese to the United States. In return, the parents, wives, and children of Japanese already in the United States would be allowed entrance. Unlike the Chinese Exclusion Act, the Gentleman's Agreement permitted the entrance of large numbers of Japanese "picture brides."[22] As a result, the Japanese population in the United States, initially much smaller than the Chinese population, grew from roughly 25,000 in 1900 to almost 127,000 in 1940, far exceeding the 1940 Chinese population of roughly 78,000.[23]

Asian immigration was further limited by the Immigration Act of 1917,[24] which banned immigration from all countries in the Asia-Pacific Triangle except for the Philippines, a U.S. territory, and Japan.[25] Japanese immigration was subsequently limited by the Immigration Act of 1924.[26] This act restricted annual immigration from all countries to 2 percent of the countries' national origin populations living in the United States in 1890, with an overall cap of 150,000, and also specifically banned immigration of persons who were ineligible for citizenship, i.e., Asians.[27] Since immigration from all other Asian countries had already been halted, this provision appeared to be targeted at the Japanese.

The immigration to the U.S. mainland by Filipinos, largely laborers, which had begun just after 1900, increased substantially in the 1920s as demand for their labor increased, at least in part as a result of the exclusion of the Japanese.[28] Filipinos spread across the country quickly, most of them working in agriculture and in domestic service.[29] Immigration from the Philippines, a U.S. territory, continued apace until a few years before the Tydings-McDuffie Act of 1934,[30] which gave the Philippines Commonwealth status and defined Filipinos not born in the United States as aliens. The Tydings-McDuffie Act placed a quota of 50 immigrants per year on immigration from the Philippines[31] and did not allow the families of resident Filipinos to immigrate.[32] One year later, the Repatriation Act[33] authorized funds to pay for one-way tickets back to the Philippines for resident Filipinos, provided that they agreed not to return to the United States. Only 2,000 Filipinos took advantage of this offer, however.[34]

The discriminatory immigration laws were relaxed slowly starting in 1943, when the Chinese Exclusion Act was repealed[35] and an annual quota of 105 Chinese immigrants was set.[36] The Filipino and Indian quotas were increased by presidential proclamation in 1946.[37] The 1945 War Brides Act[38] permitted the immigration of Asian (and other national origin) spouses and children of American servicemen.[39] It was only in 1952 that the McCarran-Walter Act ended the ban on Asian immigration and for the first time in American history granted Asian immigrants naturalization rights. The act, however, retained the national origins system established in the Immigration Act of 1924.[40] Since very few Asians (apart from Chinese) resided in the United States in 1890, this provision effectively continued discrimination against Asian immigration.[41] It was not until 1965 that amendments to the McCarran-

Walter Act[42] replaced the national origins system with a fixed annual quota of 20,000 per country, permitting a sizable Asian immigration.[43] The 1965 amendments retained a preference for highly skilled workers first introduced in the 1952 act.[44]

Beginning in the late 1960s, the opening of the doors to Asian immigrants produced a second major wave of Asian immigration. Many of these new immigrants were highly educated professionals as a result of the preference system for skilled workers. In the 1970s and early 1980s immigration from Asia intensified, as Southeast Asian refugees came to this country as a result of upheavals in Southeast Asia brought on by the Vietnam War. Over 400,000 Asians came to the United States during the 1960s, and Asians constituted roughly 13 percent of all immigrants during the decade. During the 1970s Asian immigration increased to roughly 1.6 million, constituting 36 percent of all immigration.[45] Asian immigration continued apace into the 1980s. The second wave of Asian immigration was heavily Filipino, Korean, and Southeast Asian, and to a lesser extent Chinese and Indian. Japanese immigrants continued to come, but in much smaller numbers than the other groups.

The net effect of the changing immigration and naturalization policies towards Asians is that some Asian Americans, predominantly Japanese Americans and to a lesser extent, Chinese Americans,[46] have been here for generations, while a great number of Asian Americans are immigrants (many of whom entered the United States after 1965) or their children.

ANTI-ASIAN BIGOTRY AND VIOLENCE

Bigotry and violence against Asians began almost as soon as Asians arrived in this country, making Asian Americans feel that they were unwelcome outsiders in the United States. As early as the late 1840s, the Know-Nothing Party, which was largely anti-Catholic in the Eastern United States, promoted anti-Asian sentiments in the Western United States.[47] In the 1860s and 1870s, before the Chinese Exclusion Act, many unions and political parties in the West adopted anti-Chinese platforms. In 1862 anti-Coolie clubs formed in San Francisco and spread to other cities in California.[48] In 1870 a large-scale "anti-Oriental" mass meeting took place in San Francisco,[49] and several California unions, including the Knights of St. Crispin, "organized on an anti-Chinese basis."[50] By 1871 both the Democratic and Republican parties in California had adopted platforms opposing Chinese immigration,[51] and both national parties had anti-Chinese resolutions in their platforms in the years 1876, 1880, 1888, and 1904.[52]

Anti-Chinese sentiments were propagated by the Western media, joined occasionally by the eastern press. For example, the *New York Times* warned:

> We have four millions of degraded negroes in the South. We have political passion and religious prejudice everywhere. The strain upon the constitution is about as great as it can bear. And if, in addition, to all the adverse elements we now have, there were to be a flood-tide of Chinese population—a population befouled with all the social vices, with no knowledge or appreciation of free institutions or constitutional liberty, with heathenish souls and heathenish propensities, whose character, and habits, and modes of thought are firmly fixed by the consolidating influence of ages upon ages—we should be prepared to bid farewell to republicanism and democracy.[53]

The anti-Chinese sentiments of western workers erupted into violence in the 1870s. In October 1871 roughly 20 Chinese were massacred in Los Angeles by a white mob who also burned and looted their homes and stores.[54] In 1877 a similar incident occurred in San Francisco's Chinatown, and in Chico, California, five Chinese farmers were murdered.[55] The violence spread to other Western States in the 1880s. There were anti-Chinese riots in Denver and Rock Springs, Wyoming, and the cities of Seattle and Tacoma chased their Chinese residents out of town. In 1887, 31 Chinese miners were "robbed, murdered, and mutilated" in the Snake River (Oregon) Massacre.[56]

After the Chinese Exclusion Act of 1882, anti-Asian sentiments were directed against the Japanese, and later, at the Filipinos. In the early 1900s, many white workers began to resent competition from Japanese workers, and in 1905 delegates from more than 67 labor organizations formed the Asiatic Exclusion League in San Francisco.[57] The Asiatic Exclusion League spoke of the "yellow peril" and the "Asiatic horde" threatening to invade the United Sates.[58] Like the Chinese before them, the Japanese and the Filipinos were shunned. Anti-Filipino race riots broke out in 1928 and 1930 in Washington and California. In California, the rioting that took place in Watsonville was prompted by press coverage of the arrest of a Filipino man for walking with a white girl to whom he was engaged.[59]

STATE AND LOCAL ANTI-ASIAN LAWS

Although United States immigrants of many ethnic groups (for instance, Irish, Jews, and Italians) have experienced bigotry and violence akin to that experienced by Asian Americans, Asian Americans share with American blacks the distinction of having been the targets of widespread legal discrimination that hindered their ability to participate fully in the American dream.

The strong anti-Asian sentiments in the Western States led to the adoption of many discriminatory laws at the State and local levels, similar to those aimed at blacks in the South. Many of these laws took advantage of the discriminatory aspect of naturalization laws by restricting the rights of persons "ineligible to become citizens," i.e., Asians.[60] In addition, segregation in public facilities, including schools, was quite common until after the Second World War.

As early as the 1850s laws discriminatory against the Chinese were enacted by the State of California. In 1852 California imposed a "foreign miner's tax" of $3 for any miner who was not an intending citizen.[61] In 1855 California imposed a tax on ships landing at California ports amounting to $50 per disembarking passenger ineligible to become a citizen, and in 1858 California temporarily prohibited Chinese from landing in California altogether.[62] In 1862 California passed a head tax of $2.50 per month on most Chinese living in the State.[63]

In 1880 California enacted a miscegenation law prohibiting whites from marrying "negro, mulatto, or Mongolian."[64] After a Filipino successfully argued his right to marry a white woman in court on the basis that Filipinos are Malay and not Mongolian, the legislature extended the marriage prohibitions to Filipinos in 1933.[65] Laws prohibiting intermarriage between Asians and whites were widespread in other States as well.[66]

Whereas the earlier California anti-Asian laws were targeted at the Chinese, the 1913 Alien Land Law was targeted at Japanese farmers. This law prohibited persons ineligible to become citizens from purchasing land in the State of California and limited lease terms to 3 years or less. Many Japanese got around this law by leasing or purchasing land in the name of their American-born children.[67] To close the loopholes in the 1913 law, a stricter law was passed in 1920 preventing Japanese immigrants from acting as guardians for minors in matters pertaining to land ownership and also prohibiting them from leasing land.[68] Other States also had similar laws preventing Asian immigrants from owning land.[69]

Local laws were also discriminatory. For example, the city and county of San Francisco passed ordinances that were apparently race neutral but that had adverse impacts on Chinese residents. As a case in point, in 1873 the city of San Francisco passed the Laundry Ordinance, which imposed a tax on laundries of $1.25 on a laundry employing one horse-drawn vehicle, $4 on a laundry employing two horse-drawn vehicles, and $15 on laundries employing more than two horse-drawn vehicles. The ordinance also imposed a $15 tax on a laundry that had no horse-drawn vehicles at all.[70] This law was clearly targeted at the Chinese, since virtually no Chinese laundries operated horse-drawn vehicles.[71] In a similar vein, San Francisco passed the Cubic Air Ordinance, requiring that living spaces have at least 500 cubic feet of space per person, and this law was only enforced in Chinatown.[72]

Asians often fought both State and local laws in the courts. Sometimes they were successful, but the courts were also discriminatory. For example, in 1854 the California Supreme Court decided in the case of *People v. Hall*[73] that Chinese could not testify against whites in court. Hall, a white man, had been convicted of murdering a Chinese man on the basis of testimony by one white and three Chinese witnesses. The supreme court overthrew his conviction, ruling that the Chinese witnesses should not have testified based on a State law that did not allow blacks, mulattos, or Indians to testify in favor of or against whites in court.[74] The wording of the decision illustrates the degree of racial bigotry against Asians even among those in the judiciary:

> Indian as commonly used refers only to the North American Indian, yet in the days of Columbus all shores washed by Chinese waters were called the Indies. In the second place the word "white" necessarily excludes all other races than Caucasian; and in the third place, even if this were not so, I would decide against the testimony of Chinese on grounds of public policy.[75]

Despite the discriminatory tendencies of the courts, Chinese residents of San Francisco successfully fought the discriminatory enforcement of San Francisco's Laundry Ordinance, passed in 1880, which governed the sites and manner of laundry operations. Their fight led to the United States Supreme Court landmark decision, *Yick Wo v. Hopkins*. . . .[76]

The public school systems of California and other Western States were generally segregated. In 1860 California barred Asians, blacks, and Native Americans from attending its public schools. In 1884 the California Supreme Court held that the 1860 law was unconstitutional. As a result of this decision, the State set up a system of "oriental" (usually, Chinese) schools starting in 1885. In a 1902 decision, the U.S. Supreme Court upheld the constitutionality of separate but equal schools for Asian students.[77]

In 1906 the city of San Francisco decided that Japanese and Korean students could not attend white schools and instead had to attend Chinese schools, setting off an international incident. The Japanese Government protested the decision vigorously, and as a result, President Theodore Roosevelt persuaded San Francisco to back down with respect to Japanese students. It was this incident that heightened Japanese awareness of anti-Japanese sentiments in the U.S. and prompted the negotiations that ultimately led to the Gentleman's Agreement of 1907.[78]

INTERNMENT OF JAPANESE AMERICANS DURING WORLD WAR II

Perhaps the most disgraceful incident in this country's history of discrimination against Asian Americans is the wartime evacuation and internment of Japanese Americans during the 1940s. On February 19, 1942, 2½ months after Japan attacked Pearl Harbor, President Roosevelt signed Executive Order 9066 authorizing the Army to evacuate any persons from sensitive areas for reasons of national defense,[79] and on March 2, 1942, General DeWitt announced the evacuation of persons of Japanese descent from an area bordering the Pacific Ocean.[80] Initially, evacuated persons were merely relocated to other areas of the country, but the decision was made quickly to intern them in relocation camps.[81] In evacuating the Japanese, the Army generally gave less than 7 days notice, thus forcing families to sell their properties and possessions at a fraction of their true value.[82] Persons were allowed to bring to the camps only what they could carry. Eventually over 100,000 Japanese Americans were moved to internment camps in the Midwest, and many remained there for the duration of the war. They were officially released on January 2, 1945.[83]

Executive Order 9066 and General DeWitt's evacuation order were made despite the fact that government intelligence reports did not support the notion that resident Japanese posed a threat to national security.[84] No similar evacuation was ordered for persons of German or Italian descent. The Commission on Wartime Relocation and Internment of Civilians (CWRIC), established by Congress in 1980 to investigate the wartime internment, concluded that:

> The promulgation of Executive Order 9066 was not justified by military necessity, and the decisions which followed from it—detention, ending detention and ending exclusion—were not driven by analysis of military conditions. The broad historical causes which shaped these decisions were race prejudice, war hysteria and a failure of political leadership. Widespread ignorance of Japanese Americans contributed to a policy conceived in haste and executed in an atmosphere of fear and anger at Japan. A grave injustice was done to American citizens and resident aliens of Japanese ancestry who, without individual review or any probative evidence against them, were excluded, removed and detained by the United States during World War II. . . .[85]

Executive Order 9066 was upheld by the Supreme Court in two famous wartime cases, *Korematsu v. United States*[86] and *Hirabayashi v. United States*,[87] which upheld the criminal convictions of Korematsu and Hirabayashi for challenging the evacuation and internment orders. It was not until the mid-1980s that their convictions were overturned when it was discovered that the U.S. Government had "'deliberately omitted relevant information and provided misleading information' to the Supreme Court on the crucial 'military necessity' issue."[88]

Redress for the Japanese Americans interned during the war was slow in coming. In 1948 Congress passed the Japanese American Evacuation Claims Act, which appropriated $38 million to reimburse Japanese Americans who had been interned for their losses. This amounted to only 10 cents on the dollar of actual losses.[89] In 1976 President Ford issued Presidential Proclamation 4417, which rescinded Executive Order 9066 and apologized to those who had been interned.[90] Finally, in 1988, prompted by the conclusions of the CWRIC report, Congress passed the Civil

Liberties Act of 1988,[91] authorizing compensation of $20,000 for living survivors of the internment camps. This money has only just begun to be paid, however.[92]

Nearly 50 years later, the issues surrounding Japanese internment remain emotional. In 1989 the State of California legislature passed a resolution "requiring schools to teach that the internment stemmed from racism, hysteria over the war and poor decisions by the country's political leaders."[93] In response to the passage, Assemblyman Gil Ferguson introduced a new resolution in 1990 that would have required schools to teach that there was some justification for the internment.[94] Although the measure was overwhelmingly defeated, its introduction demonstrates that the issue is not yet resolved in the minds of all Americans. . . .

ASIAN AMERICANS IN THE 1990S: A DEMOGRAPHIC AND SOCIOECONOMIC PORTRAIT

The demographic and socioeconomic portrait of Asian Americans contained in this section reveals that today's Asian American community is extremely heterogeneous—comprised of many ethnicities, new immigrants and persons whose families have been here for generations, and persons of all socioeconomic statuses. This diversity means that the civil rights issues facing Asian Americans are themselves diverse, ranging from issues facing those who are not proficient in English, such as inadequate bilingual and English as a Second Language programs in our public schools, to issues affecting highly educated professionals, such as the existence of an invisible "glass ceiling" that limits opportunities for Asian Americans at the top of their professions.

DEMOGRAPHY OF ASIAN AMERICANS

With a population of roughly 7.3 million, Asian Americans today make up slightly less than 3 percent of the United States population. . . . Over the past decade, their population share has risen dramatically, from 1.5 percent to 2.9 percent of the total population. The Asian American population more than doubled, growing by 108 percent, twice as fast as the Hispanic population, which grew by 53 percent, 8 times as fast as the black population, which grew by 13 percent, and 15 times as fast as the white population, which grew by 6 percent. The Asian American population is expected to continue to grow rapidly.

The principal reason for the growth in the Asian American population is the post-1965 influx of immigrants and refugees from Asia and the Pacific Islands.[95] After 40 years of being virtually banned from the United States by immigration laws, people from Asia began to come here in greater numbers starting in 1965, when the United States abandoned the "national origins" system of immigration. The Vietnam War and its aftermath caused Asian immigration to accelerate starting in the mid-1970s. In every year since 1974 (except for 1977), immigrants from Asia made up over 40 percent of all immigrants to this country.[96] Not only do Asian immigrants make up a large percentage of all new immigrants, but new Asian immigrants make up a large percentage of the total Asian American population. Asian immigrants arriving in 1980, for instance, constituted 6.4 percent of the total Asian American population that year. The percentage of the Asian American population who were new immigrants declined gradually over the 1980s, but was still as high as 2.8 percent in 1988.[97]

Because of these high recent rates of immigration, a large proportion of Asian Americans are foreign born. . . . As of 1980, 62.1 percent of Asian Americans were foreign born, compared with 6.2 percent of the general U.S. population. Because of the high rates of immigration since 1980, the current proportion of Asian Americans who are foreign born is likely to be substantially higher.[98] On the other hand, because of the restrictive immigration laws of the past, Asian American adults who are native born are likely to belong to families that have been here for several generations.

Although the overall proportion of foreign born among Asian Americans is high, this proportion differs substantially across subgroups. . . . In 1980 over 90 percent of Southeast Asians (Vietnamese, Laotians, Cambodians, and Hmong) but only 28 percent of Japanese Americans were born abroad. Recent Japanese immigration has been slight and largely temporary, and most Japanese Americans are descendants of Japanese immigrants who came here before 1924. The two other groups that came to this country in large numbers before Asian immigration was restricted, Chinese and Filipinos, both had percentages of foreign born of around 64 percent in 1980.[99]

The large number of recent immigrants among Asian Americans translates into a large percentage of Asian Americans with limited English proficiency. As of 1980, 15 percent of Asian Americans did not speak English well, or did not speak it at all. Consistent with the immigration patterns discussed above, the extent of limited English proficiency was least prevalent among Japanese Americans (9 percent) and among Asians whose countries of origin use English (Indians and Filipinos) and most common among Southeast Asian groups (60 percent or more).[100]

Asian Americans are heavily concentrated in certain geographic areas. Coming to the United States across the Pacific Ocean, most Asian groups initially settled in the Western United States. Although only 19 percent of the general U.S. population lived in the West in 1980, 56 percent of the Asian American population did. Three non-Western States also have sizable Asian American populations: New York, Illinois, and Texas.[101] The percentage living in the West varies considerably across Asian groups, however. Japanese Americans, 80 percent of whom lived in the West in 1980, are the most concentrated in the Western United States. Around half of Chinese Americans and less than half of Americans from Southeast Asia lived in Western States in 1980. Asian Indians and Pakistanis were the least con-

centrated in the West, with 19 and 24 percent, respectively, living in the West in 1980.[102]

SOCIOECONOMIC STATUS OF ASIAN AMERICANS

Summary statistics show that Asian Americans as a group are more educated, more likely to be in high-paying occupations, less likely to be unemployed, and have higher family incomes than the general population. It may be tempting to conclude from these statistics that Asian Americans do not face discrimination or encounter barriers to equal opportunity, that they have fully overcome them, or that they have not suffered the adverse consequences of racial prejudice. However, such a conclusion would be totally unwarranted and misleading. For one thing, focusing on the average experience of Asian Americans masks large socioeconomic differences among Asian American subgroups, as well as differences within groups. Many Asian Americans have not achieved the high socioeconomic status enjoyed by the fictional "average" Asian American. More important, socioeconomic status is at best a poor indicator of the discrimination experienced by Asian Americans or any other group. Even those Asians who appear to be doing well by "outcome" measures of socioeconomic status may experience barriers to equal opportunity that keep them from achieving the full measure of their potential. Furthermore, they may have to bear significant costs along the road to socioeconomic success, and their experiences with discrimination may leave scars that are not discernible in statistics that measure socioeconomic status.

The Asian American population is extremely heterogeneous in terms of socioeconomic status. Many Asian Americans do not share in the relatively favorable socioeconomic outcomes attributed to the "average" Asian American. In particular, the newer immigrant groups from Southeast Asia have sharply lower socioeconomic status than other Asian Americans. Table 1 shows that, whereas 34 percent of all Asian Americans were college graduates in 1980, the proportion of col-

TABLE 1

CHARACTERISTICS OF ASIAN AMERICANS BY COUNTRY OF ORIGIN: 1980

	Percent college graduates[a]	Percent managers or professionals[b]	Unemploy- ment rate[c]	Relative median family income[d]	Poverty rate[e]
Chinese	36.6	32.6	3.6	1.13	10.5
Filipino	37.0	25.1	4.8	1.19	6.2
Japanese	26.4	28.5	3.0	1.37	4.2
Asian Indian	51.9	48.5	5.8	1.25	10.6
Korean	33.7	24.9	5.7	1.03	12.5
Vietnamese	12.9	13.4	8.2	.65	33.5
Laotian	5.6	7.6	15.3	.26	67.2
Thai	32.3	23.4	5.5	.97	13.4
Cambodian	7.7	10.8	10.6	.45	46.9
Hmong	2.9	9.4	20.0	.26	65.5
Pakistani	58.4	45.2	5.7	1.08	10.5
Indonesian	33.3	24.2	6.1	1.06	15.2
All Asian Americans	34.3	29.7	4.6	1.19	10.3
Hawaiian	9.6	15.9	7.0	.96	14.3
All Pacific Islander Americans	9.3	15.6	7.3	.90	16.1
All Americans	16.2	22.7	6.5	1.00	9.6

Source: U.S. Bureau of the Census, *We, the Asian and Pacific Islander Americans*, pp. 12–13, Table 7.
[a]Percentage of all persons age 25 and over who have completed 4 or more years of college.
[b]Percentage of employed persons age 16 and over whose occupation is in a managerial or professional specialty.
[c]Unemployment rate for persons age 16 and over.
[d]Median family income as a fraction of the median family income for the entire U.S. population.
[e]Percentage of families with income below the poverty level.

lege graduates among Southeast Asians ranged from 13 percent for the Vietnamese, to 3 percent for the Hmong. Similarly, whereas Asian Americans as a group had a median family income almost 20 percent higher than that of the general population, Southeast Asian family incomes ranged from 35 percent lower than the national average for the Vietnamese to 74 percent lower for the Hmong. Southeast Asian unemployment rates and poverty rates were also substantially higher than those of Asian Americans as a group.

There is also considerable variation in socioeconomic status even among the more established Asian American groups. Even though Chinese, Asian Indians, and Koreans all had higher median family incomes than the general population, these groups also had poverty rates as high or higher than that of the general population, indicating that not all members of these groups are doing as well.[103]

Asian Americans' high average levels of family income, educational attainment, and occupational prestige do not necessarily mean that Asian Americans do not face significant barriers to equal economic opportunity or other forms of discrimination and prejudice. Barriers to equal opportunity may force Asian Americans to expend extra efforts as they strive to reach socioeconomic success, and they may retard or ultimately prevent Asian Americans from reaching the full measure of their potential. Discrimination and prejudice may also exact a toll of pain and suffering that cannot be compensated for by mere socioeconomic success.

There are indications that high levels of family income may be an artifact created by Asian Americans' concentration in high cost of living areas, the larger average number of workers in many Asian American families, or the high education levels of many Asian Americans. Further-

more, if Asian Americans have larger than average families, high levels of total family income
may not necessarily translate into high levels of
per capita income. The Commission's recent
study on the economic status of Asian Americans
showed that it is important to look beyond total
family income when examining the socioeconomic status of population groups. For example,
the study found that:

1. Taking the different regional distributions of
   Asian Americans and non-Hispanic whites
   into account lowers the average family
   incomes of most Asian American groups relative to the average family income of non-Hispanic whites; this effect is greater for foreign-
   born Asian Americans than for those born in
   the United States.[104]
2. The percentage of family income coming
   from the earnings of family members other
   than the husband is larger for Asian American
   families than for non-Hispanic white families.[105]
3. Although most foreign-born Asian American
   groups have total family incomes that are
   as high or higher than those of U.S.-born
   non-Hispanic whites, the reverse is true for
   per capita income: for most foreign-born
   Asian American groups, per capita income is
   less than that of U.S.-born non-Hispanic
   whites.[106]
4. When differences in education and other skills
   are taken into account along with region of
   residence, Asian American men earn about the
   same as or less than white men.[107]

. . . Even Asian Americans with comparatively high levels of family income and occupational prestige may still suffer from discrimination that impedes their success.[108] For instance,
the Commission study found that highly educated
Asian Americans earned less relative to their
white counterparts than Asian Americans with
less education, suggesting that Asian Americans
may have difficulty translating their greater educational attainment into increased income.[109]

Moreover, Asian Americans were much less
likely to be in managerial jobs than comparable
non-Hispanic whites, suggesting the existence of
a "glass ceiling" that blocks Asian Americans
from achieving managerial positions.[110] Finally,
racial prejudice and resulting bigotry and violence know no socioeconomic barriers: Asian
Americans with high socioeconomic status are
just as likely as those with low socioeconomic
status to be targets of hatred.

DISCRIMINATION AND BARRIERS TO EQUAL OPPORTUNITY FOR ASIAN AMERICANS: SOME CONTRIBUTORY FACTORS

Knowledge of the history of Asian Americans in
the United States and of the nature and diversity
of today's Asian American population are essential to a full understanding of the civil rights
problems confronting Asian Americans in the
1990s. It is equally important to have an appreciation of some basic underlying factors that contribute to discrimination against Asian Americans
and create barriers to equal opportunity for Asian
Americans.

Some of these factors arise out of the tendency
of the general public and the media to stereotype
Asian Americans. Most Americans have very little knowledge of the history and cultures of Asian
Americans and very little awareness of the diversity among them. This ignorance leads many to
lump together Asian Americans in a single group
and to perceive them through stereotypes. Other
factors that underlie discrimination against Asian
Americans include the linguistic, cultural, and
religious differences that exist between many
Asian Americans, particularly recent immigrants,
and the general public. These differences foster
misunderstandings between Asian and non-Asian
Americans and among different Asian ethnic
groups themselves, impede Asian Americans'
access to public services, and serve as serious
barriers to the equal opportunity of Asians in the
United States. Seven contributory factors are discussed below.

1) Viewing Asian Americans as a Model Minority Whereas, in the past, Asians were often stereotyped as sneaky, obsequious, or inscrutable, perhaps foremost among today's stereotypes of Asian Americans is the "model minority" stereotype. According to this stereotype, which is based partly on uncritical reliance on statistics revealing the high average family incomes, educational attainment, and occupational status of Asian Americans, Asian Americans are hardworking, intelligent, and successful.[111] As complimentary as it might sound, this stereotype has damaging consequences. First, it leads people to ignore the very real social and economic problems faced by many segments of the Asian American population and may result in the needs of poorer, less successful Asian Americans being overlooked. Second, emphasis on the model minority stereotype may also divert public attention from the existence of discrimination even against more successful Asian Americans (e.g., "glass ceiling" in employment and discriminatory admissions policies in institutions of higher learning). Third, the model minority stereotype may result in undue pressure being put on young Asian Americans to succeed in school, particularly in mathematics and science classes, and in their careers. Too much pressure to succeed on young Asian Americans has been linked to mental health problems and even teen suicide.[112] Finally, the origin of this stereotype was an effort to discredit other minorities by arguing that if Asian Americans can succeed, so can blacks and Hispanics, and many Asian Americans resent being used in this fashion.[113]

This model minority stereotype is not a recent phenomenon. More than a decade ago, the misleading nature and damaging consequences of the stereotype had already been clearly pointed out. For instance, in 1978 the President's Commission on Mental Health noted:

> There is widespread belief that Asian and Pacific Americans do not suffer the discrimination and disadvantages associated with other minority groups. The fact is that in spite of recent efforts to promote civil rights and equal opportunities for ethnic minorities in the United States, Asian and Pacific Americans have been largely neglected and ignored. . . .[114]

In 1980, based on the analysis of all available evidence, the U.S. Commission on Civil Rights concluded:

> The belief is widely held that Asian Americans are a successful minority who no longer suffer from disadvantage. This belief, however, is not supported by the facts. Many Asian Americans take issue with the "model minority" perspective. . . .[115]

and

> Asian Americans as a group are not the successful minority that the prevailing stereotype suggests. Individual cases of success should not imply that the diverse peoples who make up the Asian American communities are uniformly successful. . . . Despite the problems Asian Americans encounter, the success stereotype appears to have led policy makers to ignore those truly in need.[116]

2) Perceiving Asian Americans as Foreigners A second contributing factor is the perception that all Asians in this country are foreigners. It is perhaps this perception that led to American acceptance of the internment of Japanese Americans during World War II. The perception that all Asians are foreigners may also explain why Asian Americans whose families have been in the United States for generations or many Asian American youths who were born here are frequently the objects of such queries and comments as: "Where did you learn English?" and "You speak such good English."

More seriously, Asian Americans of all groups tend to suffer adverse consequences when international events cause tensions between the United States and Asian countries. For instance, many Americans take out their frustrations about Japan's economic success on Asian Americans of all national origins. The 1982 killing of Vincent Chin was prompted by his killers' resentment of the Japanese for their automobile exports to the United States.[117] The perception of Asian Americans as foreigners may also impede their acceptance in all areas of their lives and contribute to subtle as well as overt forms of discrimination against them in education, employment, and other arenas.[118]

3) Stereotyping Asian Americans as Unaggressive and Lacking in Communications Skills Asian Americans, while viewed as intelligent and talented at mathematics and science, are considered unaggressive and lacking in good communication skills. This stereotype may blind employers to the qualifications of individual Asian Americans and hence contribute to the glass ceiling that impedes Asian Americans' success in managerial careers. It may also lead teachers and counselors to discourage Asian American students from even pursuing nontechnical careers.

4) Limited English Proficiency Many Asian Americans, recent immigrants in particular, have limited English proficiency, and some do not speak or understand English at all. Persons with limited English proficiency face a serious barrier to full participation in American society and our economy. A person's ability to learn about and gain access to public services (such as education, police services, and health care), employment, and the larger American society are often severely hampered by limited English proficiency. Thus, providing Asian Americans with truly equal opportunity requires substantial efforts to bridge the gap in communication (e.g., providing interpretive services) and to facilitate the learning of English. However, partly as a result of the practical difficulty of servicing the diverse language needs of Asian Americans (i.e., several dialects of Chinese, Japanese, Tagalog, Vietnamese, Lao, Khmer, Thai, and others), limited-English-proficient Asian Americans are drastically underserved in the areas of interpretation and English instruction.

5) Cultural Differences Asian immigrants come from societies that have very different cultures from the mainstream cultures in the United States. Cultural differences often lead to misunderstandings, which in turn can lead to discriminatory treatment or to intergroup tensions, as in the case of Korean American store owners and their customers who are members of minority groups. These tensions can erupt into full scale racial conflict. Bridging cultural gaps requires not only that new immigrants be given a real opportunity to acculturate, but also that all Americans acquire a greater awareness of other cultures.

6) Religious Diversity Many Asian Americans adhere to religions that are not widely practiced in the United States, such as Buddhism, Hinduism, Islam, and Sikhism, to name a few. These religions are unfamiliar to most Americans educated in the Judeo-Christian tradition, and, despite the long tradition of religious tolerance, these religious differences generate hostility against Asian Americans. Not only do the religious differences between Asian Americans and the general public contribute to anti-Asian bigotry and violence, but they can at times cause other conflicts when the practices and requirements of non-Western religions are incompatible with long-established mainstream traditions.

7) Preimmigration Trauma Another factor hampering some Asian Americans' access to equal opportunity arises out of the wartime ordeals they have endured, as well as negative experiences they have had with governmental officials in their home countries. The problems faced by many Asian Americans in acculturating to this country are exacerbated by their preimmigration experiences: many recent Asian immigrants, particularly the Vietnamese, Cambodians, Hmong, and Laotians, are refugees, who come from war-torn countries and have survived ordeals in their own countries and on their journeys to the United States. Many lost loved ones during the war and live in incomplete families in this country. Refugees often carry scars from psychological trauma and many suffer from post-traumatic stress disorder, which make it difficult for them to cope with day-to-day life, let alone face the challenge of adjusting to a new society. In addition, they may bring to this country an ingrained distrust of authority arising out of negative experiences they had with governmental officials in their countries of origin. This distrust may deter many from interactions with governmental agencies in the United States, such as the police, welfare offices, and so on. As a result, a gulf may arise between the police and the Asian American community, adversely affecting police-community relations. Because of their unwillingness to convey their needs forcefully, many Asian Americans may not receive many basic public services.

REFERENCES

1. The term Asian Americans is used in this report to refer to persons of Asian descent who are either citizens or intending citizens of the United States, or who plan to spend the rest of their lives in the United States.
2. Michel McQueen, "Voters' Responses to Poll Disclose Huge Chasm Between Social Attitudes of Blacks and Whites," *Wall Street Journal,* May 17, 1991, p. A16.
3. The Commission's Roundtable Conferences on Asian American Civil Rights Issues for the 1990s were held in Houston, TX, on May 27, 1989; in New York, NY, on June 23, 1989; and in San Francisco, CA, on July 29, 1989.
4. Asian American groups considered in this report are persons having origins in the Far East, Southeast Asia, and the Indian subcontinent. At times, the report also includes information about Pacific Islanders, but limited resources precluded a systematic investigation of the civil rights issues facing Pacific Islanders.
5. U.S. Commission on Civil Rights, *The Tarnished Golden Door: Civil Rights Issues in Immigration* (September 1980), p. 10 (hereafter cited as *The Tarnished Golden Door*).
6. Roger Daniels, *Asian America: Chinese and Japanese in the United States Since 1850* (Seattle, WA: University of Washington Press, 1988), p. 43 (hereafter cited as *Asian America*).
7. These laws were widely held to bar the naturalization of the Chinese. In 1922 the Supreme Court held that the naturalization bar applied to Japanese (Ozawa v. United States, 260 U.S. 178 (1922)). The following year, the Supreme Court held that East Indians were also barred from naturalization, because the term "white" did not include all Caucasians (United States v. Thind, 261 U.S. 204 (1923)).
8. *The Tarnished Golden Door,* p. 10.
9. Pub 1. No 82-414.66 Stat. 163 (1952).
10. Don Teruo Hata, Jr., and Nadine Ishitani Hata, "Run Out and Ripped Off: A Legacy of Discrimination," *Civil Rights Digest,* vol 9, no 1 (Fall 1976), p. 10 (hereafter cited as "Run Out and Ripped Off").
11. Ch. 126, 22 Stat. 58 (1882).
12. *The Tarnished Golden Door,* p. 8. In 1888 the Scott Act widened the immigration ban to all Chinese except for officials, merchants, teachers, students, and tourists. The Scott Act also denied reentry to any Chinese who had left the United States, even though the Chinese Exclusion Act had allowed reentry of all Chinese who had been in this country in 1880. Ibid. and *Asian America,* p. 57.
13. Ch. 60, 27 Stat. 25 (1892).
14. *Asian America,* p. 58.
15. Ch. 1630, 33 Stat. 428 (1904); *The Tarnished Golden Door,* p. 8. As noted below, the ban was eventually lifted in 1943.
16. Ronald Takaki, *Strangers from a Different Shore: A History of Asian Americans* (Boston: Little Brown, 1989), pp. 111–12 (hereafter cited as *Strangers from a Different Shore*).
17. *Asian America,* pp. 101–02.
18. Ibid., p. 107.
19. Ibid., p. 115.
20. Exec. Order No. 589.
21. *Asian America,* p. 125.
22. Ibid., pp. 125–27.
23. Ibid., p. 90 and p. 115.
24. Pub. L. No. 301, 39 Stat. 874 (1917).
25. *Asian America,* p. 150.
26. Pub. L. No. 139, 43 Stat. 153 (1924).
27. Except for Filipinos, who, as residents of a U.S. territory, were United States nationals.
28. *Strangers From a Different Shore,* pp. 57–58.
29. Ibid., pp. 316–19.
30. Ch. 84, 48 Stat. 459 (1934).

31. State of California, Attorney General's Asian/Pacific Advisory Committee, *Final Report* (December 1988), p. 38 (hereafter cited as Attorney General's Report).
32. *Strangers From a Different Shore,* p. 337.
33. Pub. L. No. 202, 49 Stat. 478 (1935). The time in which Filipinos could "benefit" from the statute was extended in Congress' next session. Pub. L. No. 645, 49 Stat. 1462 (1936).
34. *Strangers From a Different Shore,* pp. 332–33.
35. Pub. L. No. 199, 57 Stat. 600 (1943).
36. *The Tarnished Golden Door,* p. 10.
37. Proc. 2696, 3 C.F.R. 86 (1946).
38. Pub. L. No. 271, 59 Stat. 659 (1945).
39. *The Tarnished Golden Door,* p. 10.
40. Ibid., p. 11.
41. Ibid., p. 11. Another provision of the McCarran-Walter Act counted persons of half-Asian descent against the quotas for their Asian country of origin.
42. Pub. L. No. 89–236, 79 Stat. 911 (1965).
43. E. P. Hutchinson, *Legislative History of American Immigration Policy: 1798–1965* (Philadelphia: University of Pennsylvania Press, 1981), pp. 369–78.
44. Ibid., pp. 308–09, 377–78.
45. U.S. Commission on Civil Rights, *The Economic Status of Americans of Asian Descent: An Exploratory Investigation* (Clearinghouse Publication 95, October 1988), p. 19 (hereafter cited as *The Economic Status of Americans of Asian Descent*).
46. As noted above, because the 19th century Chinese immigrants were heavily male, the Chinese American population fell precipitously after the Chinese Exclusion Act of 1882, and only a small proportion of today's Chinese Americans are descendants of the early Chinese immigrants.
47. *The Tarnished Golden Door,* p. 7.
48. *Asian America,* p. 36.
49. "Run Out and Ripped Off," p. 5.
50. *Asian America,* p. 38.
51. Ibid., p. 37.
52. Ibid., p. 45.
53. "Growth of the United States Through Emigration—The Chinese," *New York Times,* Sept. 3, 1865, p. 4.
54. "Run Out and Ripped Off," p. 5.
55. Attorney General's Report, p. 34.
56. *Asian America,* pp. 60–64.
57. "Run Out and Ripped Off," p. 7.
58. Attorney General's Report, pp. 34–35.
59. *Strangers From a Different Shore,* pp. 326–30.
60. See above discussion of naturalization laws that made Asians ineligible to become citizens.
61. "Run Out and Ripped Off," p. 4. Price levels have increased by a factor of 10 since the mid-19th century, so a tax of $3 in 1850 would be equivalent to a tax today of $30.
62. Ibid., pp. 4–5.
63. *Strangers from a Different Shore,* p. 82.
64. Ibid., pp. 101–02.
65. Ibid., p. 330.
66. Ibid.
67. *Asian America,* pp. 139–44.
68. Ibid., pp. 145–47.
69. For example, the State of Washington also had such a law. Ibid., pp. 146–47.
70. A $15 tax is the equivalent of roughly $150 in today's dollars.
71. "Run Out and Ripped Off," p. 5.
72. *Asian America,* p. 39.
73. 4 Cal. 309 (1854).
74. "Run Out and Ripped Off," p. 4.
75. *Asian America,* p. 54.
76. 118 U.S. 356 (1886). The case was a landmark decision for several reasons: 1) it brought heightened scrutiny to cases involving improperly motivated classifications; 2) it is a clear example of how discriminatory impact alone can be used to unmask invidious classifications; and 3) it extended Federal equal protection guarantees under the 14th amendment beyond United States citizens to temporary or permanent residents. (Philip T. Nash, "Asian Americans and the Supreme Court: Employment and Education Issues," 1991, pp. 6–7.)
77. Connie Young Yu, "The Others: Asian Americans and Education," *Civil Rights Digest,* vol. 9, no. 1 (Fall 1976), p. 45.
78. *Strangers From a Distant Shore,* pp. 201–03.
79. "Run Out and Ripped Off," p. 8.
80. *Asian America,* p. 214.
81. Commission on Wartime Relocation and Internment of Civilians, *Personal Justice Denied* (Washington, DC: Government Printing Office, 1982), pp. 101–07 (hereafter cited as *Personal Justice Denied*).
82. Ibid., p. 217, and Attorney General's Report, p. 38.
83. "Run Out and Ripped Off," p. 8.
84. *Personal Justice Denied,* pp. 51–60.

85. Ibid., p. 18.

86. 323 U.S. 214 (1944).

87. 320 U.S. 81 (1943).

88. Peter Irons, "Justice Long Overdue," *New Perspectives,* vol. 18, no. 1 (Winter/Spring 1986), p. 6, quoting Judge Patel's decision vacating Korematsu's conviction.

89. "Run Out and Ripped Off," p. 8.

90. *Asian America,* p. 331.

91. 28 C.F.R. 74.

92. In October 1990 the first Japanese internment camp survivors—those who were the oldest—received their reparation checks. (Michael Isikoff, "Delayed Reparations and an Apology: Japanese Americans Held During War Get First Checks," *Washington Post,* Oct. 10, 1990.) The second round of checks began in October, 1991. (Japanese American National Library, *Bulletin,* vol. 2, no. 4 (Summer 1991), p. 1.)

93. Steven A. Capps, "Assembly Kills 'Justification' for Internment." *San Francisco Examiner,* Aug. 29, 1990.

94. Ibid.

95. During the decade of the 1980s immigration has been responsible for roughly two-thirds of the population growth of Asian Americans. See U.S. Bureau of the Census, *United States Population Estimates, by Age, Sex, Race, and Hispanic Origin: 1980 to 1988,* Current Population Reports, Series P-25, No. 1045 (January 1990), p. 82, table 7.

96. Ibid., p. 27, table X.

97. Ibid., p. 83, table 7.

98. As of November 1991, the 1990 census detail had not been released.

99. The percentage foreign born is higher for both of these groups than for the Japanese for two reasons. First, there has been a substantial post-1965 immigration from both the Philippines and China. Second, when Asian immigration was cut off by restrictive immigration laws in the 1920s, the majority of Chinese and Filipinos in this country were men, and thus early Chinese and Filipino immigrants had fewer children than the Japanese, among whom women numbered almost as many as men.

100. See table 1.2.

101. U.S. Bureau of the Census, *We, the Asian and Pacific Islander Americans,* p. 3, table 1.

102. It should be noted that the census does not distinguish between Asian Americans—i.e., Asians who are either citizens or intending citizens or who plan to remain in the United States for their entire lives—and Asian nationals temporarily living in the United States. To the extent that the income of Asian nationals (often highly paid Japanese executives) are reflected in the summary statistics of Asian Americans' incomes, the average income of Asian Americans may be overstated.

103. See table 1.3.

104. *The Economic Status of Americans of Asian Descent,* p. 31.

105. Ibid., pp. 35–36.

106. Ibid., p. 42.

107. Ibid., pp. 68–69 and 78–79.

108. For instance, chap. 5 [of the report] looks at the possibility that admissions quotas in highly selective colleges and universities might limit Asian Americans' educational opportunities, and chap. 6 discusses the "glass ceiling" that appears to place limits on the career advancement of Asian Americans.

109. *The Economic Status of Americans of Asian Descent,* pp. 70–71.

110. Ibid., pp. 72–76.

111. For general discussions of the model minority stereotype, its validity, and its implications, see Ki-Taek Chun, "The Myth of Asian American Success and Its Educational Ramifications," *IRCD Bulletin,* vol. 15, no. 1–2 (Winter/Spring 1980), pp. 1–12, and Won Moo Hurh and Kwang Chung Kim, "The 'Success' Image of Asian Americans: Its Validity, and Its Practical and Theoretical Implications," *Ethnic and Racial Studies,* vol. 12, no. 4 (October 1989), pp. 512–38.

112. Joan E. Rigdon, "Exploding Myth—Asian-American Youth Suffer a Rising Toll from Heavy Pressures: Suicides and Distress Increase As They Face Stereotypes and Parents' Expectations," *Wall Street Journal,* July 10, 1991.

113. See *Asian America,* pp. 317–19, for a discussion of the origin of the term, "model minority."

114. President's Commission on Mental Health, Report of the Special Populations Subpanel on the Mental Health of Asian/Pacific Americans, *Task Force Panel Reports,* vol. 3 (1978), p. 785.

115. U.S. Commission on Civil Rights, *Success of Asian Americans: Fact or Fiction?* (Washington, DC: Government Printing Office, 1980), p. 19.

116. Ibid., p. 24.

117. See chap. 2 [of the report] for an account of Vincent Chin's killing.
118. For a discussion of how the perception that Asian Americans are foreigners affects Japanese Americans, see Bill Hosokawa, "Accentuating the American in Japanese American," *Perspectives (The Civil Rights Quarterly),* vol. 14, no. 3 (Fall 1982), pp. 40–44.

Making Sense of Diversity: Recent Research on Hispanic Minorities in the United States

Alejandro Portes and Cynthia Truelove

. . . A good part of the literature on [Hispanic minorities] focuses on comparisons of its labor market performance and general socioeconomic condition with those of other ethnic groups and the US population at large. The sociological literature on these issues has sought to answer three questions: First, are there significant differences in the condition of Hispanic groups both in comparison with the US population and among themselves? Second, are there significant differences in the *process* by which education, occupation, and income are achieved? And third, if there are differences in this process, what are their principal causes?

Table 1 presents a summary of descriptive statistics, drawn from the 1980 census. Aside from age and nativity, included as background information, the rest of the figures indicate that the socioeconomic performance of Hispanics is generally inferior to that of the US population as a whole and, by extension, that of the white non-Hispanic majority. This is true of education, occupation, income, and entrepreneurship (measured by rates of self-employment), although less so of labor force participation especially among females.

The same figures also indicate major disparities among Spanish-origin groups. In general, mainland Puerto Ricans are in the worst socioeconomic situation, a fact manifested by high levels of unemployment, female-headed families, and poverty, and correspondingly low levels of education, occupation, and income. Mexicans occupy an intermediate position, although one consistently below the US population. To be noted is that the size of this group, which represents the majority of all Hispanics, has a disproportionate weight in aggregate figures that purport to describe the Spanish-origin population as a whole.

A more favorable situation is that of Cubans—whose occupation, family income, and self-employment rates come close to US averages—and of the "Other Spanish" group, which behaves in a similar manner. This last category is a sum of immigrant groups too small to be counted individually, plus those who declared their ancestry as Spanish-origin without further specification. Because of this heterogeneity, it is difficult to provide a meaningful interpretation either of the absolute condition of this category or of the processes that have led to it.

This basic picture of the situation and heterogeneity of the Spanish-origin population is familiar to sociologists working in this field (Nelson & Tienda 1984, Pérez 1986, Pedraza-Bailey 1985b). More interesting is the question of the causal factors that produce the above differences. Here the basic question is whether the condition of a specific minority is explainable entirely on the basis of its background characteristics or whether it is due to other factors. If members of a given group are found to attain socioeconomic positions comparable to native-born Americans with similar human capital endowments, then the observed differences can be imputed to the group's current average levels of education, work experience, and other significant causal variables. If, on the other hand, differences persist after equalizing statistically the minority's background, then other factors must come into play. If the gap is one of disadvantage, discrimination is generally assumed to play a role; if the gap is advantageous to the minority, then collective characteristics of the

TABLE 1

SELECTED CHARACTERISTICS OF SPANISH-ORIGIN GROUPS, 1980. (SOURCE: U.S. BUREAU OF THE CENSUS 1983A: TABLES 39, 48, 70; 1983B: TABLES 141, 166–171.)

Variable	Mexicans	Puerto Ricans	Cubans	Other Spanish	Total US
Number—millions	8.7	2.0	0.8	3.1	226.5
Median age	21.9	22.3	37.7	25.5	30.0
Percent native born	74.0	96.9	22.1	60.5	93.8
Percent female headed families	16.4	35.3	14.9	20.5	14.3
Median years of school completed[a]	9.6	10.5	12.2	12.3	12.5
Percent high school graduates[a]	37.6	40.1	55.3	57.4	66.5
Percent with 4+ years of college[a]	4.9	5.6	16.2	12.4	16.2
Percent in labor force[b]	64.6	54.9	66.0	64.6	62.0
Percent females in labor force[b]	49.0	40.1	55.4	53.4	49.9
Percent married women in labor force[c]	42.5	38.9	50.5	45.7	43.9
Percent self-employed[d]	3.5	2.2	5.8	4.5	6.8
Percent unemployed	9.1	11.7	6.0	8.0	6.5
Percent professional specialty, executive, and managerial occupations—males	11.4	14.1	22.0	19.0	25.8
females[d]	12.6	15.5	17.9	17.2	24.7
Percent operators and laborers—males	30.4	30.9	23.1	23.8	18.3
females[d]	22.0	25.5	24.2	19.9	11.7
Median family income	14,765	10,734	18,245	16,230	19,917
Median income of married couples with own children	14,855	13,428	20,334	16,708	19,630
Percent of families with incomes of $50,000+	1.8	1.0	5.2	3.6	5.6
Percent of all families below poverty level	20.6	34.9	11.7	16.7	9.6

[a]Persons 25 years of age or older.
[b]Persons 16 years of age or older.
[c]Women 16 years of age or older; husband present and own children under 6 years of age.
[d]Employed persons 16 years of age or older.

group are explored in search of a possible explanation.

Several analyses, especially those of educational attainment, tend to support the "no difference, no discrimination" hypothesis. This is the conclusion reached, for example, by Hirschman & Falcón (1985) after a broad-gauged study of educational levels among religio-ethnic groups in the United States. However, these authors also report that, after controlling for all possible relevant predictors, the Mexican educational attainment still falls 1.4 years below the norm.

Similarly, in a study of occupational attainment based on the 1976 Survey of Income and Education (SEI) . . . significant ethnic effects on occupational attainment are found in the Mexican and Cuban groups. The Mexican coefficient is negative, indicating lower occupational levels than those expected on the basis of the group's average characteristics; the Cuban effect is, however, positive, indicating above-average attainment. . . . A subsequent and more carefully specified analysis of SEI wage data by Reimers (1985) yields similar conclusions. After controlling for selection bias and human capital predictors, Reimers finds that male Puerto Rican wage levels fall 18% below the average for white non-Hispanic men; those of Mexicans and other Hispanics are 6% and 12% below, respectively. These sizable differences are interpreted as evidence of labor market discrimination. Cuban men, however, receive wages 6% *above* white non-Hispanics of similar human capital endowment. These differences lead the author to conclude: "The major Hispanic-American groups differ so much among themselves . . . that it makes little sense to lump them under a single "Hispanic" or "minority" rubric for either analysis or policy treatment" (Reimers 1985:55).

This basic conclusion is supported by studies based on different and more recent data sets which also tend to replicate the finding of significant disadvantages in occupational and earnings attainment for Mexicans and, in particular, Puerto Ricans and a small but consistent advantage for Cubans, relative to their human capital levels (Nelson & Tienda 1985, Pérez 1986, Jasso & Rosenzweig 1985: Table 4).

These differences lead naturally to the more sociologically intriguing question of their possible cause. The argument that there is discrimination in the labor market will not do because such explanation does not clarify why discrimination operates differentially among presumably similar groups and not at all in certain cases. Thus, there is no alternative but to dig into the particular characteristics and history of each group in search of suitable answers. To do this, we must abandon not only the general label "Hispanic," but also leave behind the residual category "Other Spanish." This is necessary not because of lack of substantive importance of the groups that form it, but because the category is itself too heterogeneous to permit a valid summary explanation. Left are the three major Spanish-origin groups—Mexicans, Puerto Ricans, and Cubans.

When comparing the socioeconomic performance of these groups, two major riddles emerge: First, why is it that Mexicans and Puerto Ricans differ so significantly in such characteristics as labor force participation, family structure, and poverty as well as in levels of wage discrimination. Second, why it is that Cubans register above-average occupations and family incomes relative to their levels of human capital. The below-average socioeconomic condition of the first two groups is *not* itself a riddle since the historical literature above has fully clarified the roots of exploitation and labor market discrimination in both cases. What historical accounts do not explain is why the present condition of these groups should be so markedly different. Similarly, the absolute advantage of Cubans relative to other Spanish-origin groups is not mysterious since it is well known that this minority was formed, to a large extent, by the arrival of upper and middle-class persons who left Cuba after the advent of the Castro Revolution. The riddle in this case is why the collective attainment of Cubans should exceed, at times, what can be expected on the basis of their average human capital endowment.

A fairly common explanation of the latter result is that Cubans were welcomed in the United States as refugees from a communist regime and thus received significant government aid denied to other groups. This explanation is mentioned in passing by Jasso & Rosenzweig (1985:18), among other authors, and is vigorously defended by Pedraza-Bailey (1985b) in her comparative study of Cuban and Mexican immigrants. However, this interpretation runs immediately against evidence from other refugee groups who have received equal or more generous federal benefits than Cubans, but whose socioeconomic condition is more precarious. Southeast Asian refugees, for example, benefited from the extensive aid provisions mandated by the 1980 Refugee Act, more comprehensive and generous than those made available to Cubans during the sixties; however, levels of unemployment, poverty, and welfare dependence among most Southeast Asian groups continue to exceed those of almost every other ethnic minority (Tienda & Jensen 1985, Bach et al 1984).

The favorable governmental reception of Cubans in the United States is certainly a factor contributing to their adaptation, but it must be seen as part of a complex which may be labeled the distinct *mode of incorporation* of each immigrant minority. This alternative interpretation says that the condition of each group is a function both of average individual characteristics and of the social and economic context in which its successive cohorts are received. A sociological explanation to the above riddles is found in the distinct modes of incorporation of the three major Spanish-origin groups.

Mexican immigrants and new Mexican-American entrants into the labor force tend to come from modest socioeconomic origins and have low average levels of education. In addition, however, they enter labor markets in the Southwest and Midwest where Mexican laborers have traditionally supplied the bulk of unskilled labor. Social networks within the ethnic community tend to direct new workers toward jobs similar to their co-ethnics, a pattern reinforced by the orientation of employers. Lacking a coherent entrepreneurial community of their own or effective political representation, Mexican wage workers are thus thrown back onto their own individual resources, "discounted" by past history and present discrimination against their group (Barrera 1980, Nelson & Tienda 1985). Because many Mexican workers are immigrants and a substantial proportion are undocumented (Passel 1985; Bean et al 1983, 1986; Browning & Rodríguez 1985), they continue to be seen by many employers as a valuable source of low-wage pliable labor. This employer "preference," which may account for the relatively low average rates of Mexican unemployment, creates simultaneous barriers for those with upward mobility aspirations.

Puerto Ricans migrants fulfilled a similar function for industry and agriculture in the Northeast during an earlier period, but with two significant differences. First, they entered labor markets which, unlike those of the Southwest, were highly unionized. Second, they were US citizens by birth and thus entitled to legal protection and not subject to ready deportation as were many Mexicans. These two factors com-

bined over time to make Puerto Rican workers a less pliable, more costly, and better organized source of labor. Employer preferences in the Northeast thus shifted gradually toward other immigrant groups—West Indian contract workers in agriculture (DeWind et al 1977, Wood 1984) and Dominican, Colombian, and other mostly undocumented immigrants in urban industry and services (Sassen-Koob 1979, 1980; Glaessel-Brown 1985; Waldinger 1985). Lacking an entrepreneurial community to generate their own jobs and shunted aside by new pools of "preferred" immigrant labor in the open market, Puerto Ricans in the mainland confronted a difficult economic situation. Record numbers have migrated back to the Island during the last two decades, while those remaining in the Northeast continue to experience levels of unemployment and poverty comparable only to those of the black population (Bean & Tienda 1987: Ch. 1, Centro de Estudios Puertorriqueños 1979).

The Cuban pattern of adaptation is different because the first immigrant cohorts created an economically favorable context of reception for subsequent arrivals. This was due to the fact that the bulk of early Cuban migration was composed of displaced numbers of the native bourgeoisie rather than laborers (Pérez 1986). These refugees brought the capital and entrepreneurial skills with which to start new businesses after an early period of adaptation. Ensuing middle-class waves followed a similar course, leading eventually to the consolidation of an enclave economy in South Florida. The characteristics of the Cuban enclave have been described at length in the sociological literature (Wilson & Portes 1980, Portes & Manning 1986, Wilson & Martin 1982). . . .

In 1977, black- and Mexican-owned businesses were the most numerous in absolute terms, reflecting the size of the respective populations. In per capita terms, however, Cuban-owned firms were by far the most numerous and the largest both in terms of receipts and number of employees. . . . By 1984, five of the ten largest Hispanic-owned firms in the country and four of the ten largest banks were part of the Cuban enclave, at a time when this group represented barely 5% of the Spanish-origin population.

For our purposes, the significance of an enclave mode of incorporation is that it helps to explain how successive cohorts of Cuban immigrants have been able to make use of past human capital endowment and to exceed at times their expected level of attainment. Employment in enclave firms has two principal advantages for new arrivals: First, it allows many to put to use their occupational skills and experience without having to wait for a long period of cultural adaptation. Second, it creates opportunities for upward mobility either within existing firms or through self-employment. The bond between co-ethnic employers and employees helps fledgling immigrant enterprises survive by taking advantage of the cheap and generally disciplined labor of the new arrivals. The latter benefit over the long term, however, by availing themselves within the enclave of mobility chances that are generally absent in outside employment.

A longitudinal study of Cuban and Mexican immigrants conducted during the 1970s provides an illustration of different patterns of adaptation, conditioned by the presence or absence of an enclave mode of incorporation. By the early 1970s, the middle-class emigration from Cuba had ceased, and new arrivals came from more modest socioeconomic origins, comparable to those of Mexican legal immigrants. The study interviewed samples of Cuban refugees and Mexican legal immigrants at the time of their arrival during 1973–1974. The study followed both samples for six years, interviewing respondents twice during that interval. Results of the study have been reported at length elsewhere (Portes & Bach 1985). Table 2 presents data from the last follow-up survey which took place in 1979–1980. The first finding of note is the degree of concentration of Cuban respondents, 97% of whom remained in the Miami metropolitan area. By comparison, the Mexican sample dispersed throughout the Southwest and Midwest, with the largest concentration—24%—settling in the border city of El Paso.

Otherwise, samples were similar in their knowledge of English—low for both groups after six years—and their rates of home ownership. They differed sharply, however, in variables relating to their labor market position. More than a third of 1973 Cuban arrivals were employed by co-ethnic firms in 1979, and one fifth had become self-employed by that time; these figures double and quadruple the respective percentages in the Mexican sample. Despite their concentration in a low-wage region of the United States, the Cuban average monthly income after six years was significantly greater than that among Mexicans.

However, a closer look at the data shows that there were no major differences in income among those employed in large Anglo-owned firms, commonly identified as part of the "primary" labor market. Nor were there significant income differences among those employed in the smaller firms identified with the "secondary" sector; in

TABLE 2		

THE SOCIOECONOMIC POSITION OF CUBAN AND MEXICAN IMMIGRANTS AFTER SIX YEARS IN THE UNITED STATES. SOURCE: PORTES & BACH (1985): CHS. 6–7.

Variable	Mexicans (N = 455)	Cubans (N = 413)
Percent in city of principal concentration	23.7	97.2
Percent who speak English well	27.4	23.7
Percent home owners	40.2	40.0
Percent self-employed	5.4	21.2
Percent employed by other Mexicans/Cubans	14.6	36.3
Average monthly income[a]	$ 912	$1057
Average monthly income of employees in large Anglo-owned firms[a]	$1003	$1016
Average monthly income in small nonenclave firms[a]	$ 880	$ 952
Average monthly income in enclave firms[a]	NA	$1111
Average monthly income of the self-employed, Cubans[a]	NA	$1495

[a]1979 dollars

both samples, these incomes were much lower than among primary sector employees. The significant difference between Cuban and Mexican immigrants in the study lies with the large proportion of the former employed in enclave firms where their average income was actually the highest of those in both samples. In addition, Cuban immigrants who had become self-employed exceeded the combined monthly income of both samples by approximately $500 or one half of the total average.

No comparable empirical evidence at present supports the mode-of-incorporation hypothesis as an explanation of the observed occupational and income differences among Mexicans and Puerto Ricans. This is due to the scarcity of comparative studies between Puerto Rican patterns of attainment and those of other minorities. (For a recent exception, see Tienda & Lee 1986). The available information points, however, to the gradual displacement of Puerto Ricans by newer immigrant groups as sources of low-wage labor for agricultural and urban employers in the Northeast (DeWind 1977, Glaessel-Brown 1985). This evidence is congruent with the interpretation of the current situation of one group—Mexicans—as an outcome of its continued incorporation as a preferred source of low-wage labor in the Southwest and Midwest and with that of the other—Puerto Ricans—as a consequence of its increasing redundancy for the same labor market in its principal area of concentration. . . .

Notes

Bach, R. L., Gordon, L. W., Haines, D. W., Howell, D. R. 1984. The economic adjustment of Southeast Asian refugees in the U.S. In *U.N. Commission for Refugees, World Refugee Survey 1983,* pp. 51–56. Geneva: United Nations

Barrera, M. 1980. *Race and Class in the Southwest: A Theory of Racial Inequality.* Notre Dame, Ind: Notre Dame Univ. Press

Bean, F. D., King, A. G., Passel, J. S. 1983. The number of illegal migrants of Mexican origin in the United States: Sex ratio based estimates for 1980. *Demography* 20:99–109

Bean, F. D., Tienda, M. 1987. *The Hispanic Population of the United States.* New York: Russell Sage Found

Browning, H. L., Rodríguez, N. 1985. The migration of Mexican indocumentados as a settlement process: Implications for work. See Borjas & Tienda, 1985, pp. 277–97

DeWind, J., Seidl, T., Shenk, J. 1977. Contract labor in U.S. agriculture. *NACLA Rep. Americas* 11 (Nov.–Dec):4–37

Glaessel-Brown, E. 1985. *Colombian Immigrants in the Industries of the Northeast.* Ph.D. thesis. Dep. Polit. Sci., MIT

Hirschman, C., Falcón, L. M. 1985. The educational attainment of religio-ethnic groups in the United States. *Res. Sociol. Educ. Social.* 5:83–120

Jasso, G., Rosenzweig, M. R. 1985. *What's in a name? Country-of-origin influences on the earnings of immigrants in the United States.* Bull. #85–4, Econ. Dev. Ctr., Univ. Minn. (Mimeo)

Nelson, C., Tienda, M. 1985. The structuring of Hispanic ethnicity: Historical and contemporary perspectives. *Ethnic Racial Stud.* 8(Jan) 49–74

Passel, J. S. 1985. *Undocumented immigrants: How many?* Presented at Ann. Meet. Am. Statist. Assoc., Las Vegas

Pedraza-Bailey, S. 1985a. *Political and Economic Migrants in America: Cubans and Mexicans.* Austin: Univ. Tex. Press

Pedraza-Bailey, S. 1985b. Cuba's exiles: Portrait of a refugee migration. *Int. Migration Rev.* 19 (Spring): 4–34

Pérez, L. 1986. Immigrant economic adjustment and family organization: The Cuban success story reexamined. *Int. Migration Rev.* 20 (Spring):4–20

Portes, A., Bach, R. L. 1985. *Latin Journey, Cuban and Mexican Immigrants in the United States.* Berkeley: Univ. Calif. Press

Portes, A., Manning, R. D. 1986. The immigrant enclave: Theory and empirical examples. In *Competitive Ethnic Relations,* pp. 47–64. ed. J. Nagel, S. Olzak, Orlando, Fla: Academic Press

Reimers, C. W. 1985. A comparative analysis of the wages of Hispanics, blacks, and non-Hispanic whites. See Borjas & Tienda 1985, pp. 27–75

Sassen-Koob, S. 1980. Immigrant and minority workers in the organization of the labor process. *J. Ethnic Stud.* 1 (Spring):1–34

Sassen-Koob, S. 1979. Formal and informal associations: Dominicans and Colombians in New York. *Int. Migration Rev.* 13 (Summer) 314–32

Tienda, M., Jensen, L. 1985. *Immigration and public assistance participation: Dispelling the myth of dependency. Discuss. Pap.* #777–85. Inst. Res. Poverty, Univ. Wisc.-Madison, Mimeo

Tienda, M., Lee, D. T. 1986. *Migration, market insertion, and earnings determination of Mexicans, Puerto Ricans, and Cubans.* Pres. Ann. Meet. Am. Sociol. Assoc. New York

U.S. Bureau of the Census. 1983a. *General Population Characteristics, United States Summary.* Washington, DC: USGPO

U.S. Bureau of the Census. 1983b. General Social and Economic Characteristics, United States Summary. Washington, DC. USGPO

Waldinger, R. 1985. Immigration and industrial change in the New York City apparel industry. See Borjas & Tienda 1985, pp. 323–49

Wilson, K. L., Martin, W. A. 1982. Ethnic enclaves: A comparison of the Cuban and black economies in Miami. *Am. J. Sociol.* 88(July):135–60

Wilson, K. L., Portes, A. 1980. Immigrant enclaves: An analysis of the labor market experiences of Cubans in Miami. *Am. J. Sociol.* 86(Sept):295–319

Wood, C. H. 1984. *Caribbean cane cutters in Florida: A study of the relative cost of foreign and domestic labor.* Presented at Ann. Meet. Am. Sociol. Assoc. San Antonio

Science

READING 29

The Mismeasure of Woman

Carol Tavris

Brain: Dissecting the Differences

It must be stated boldly that conceptual thought is exclusive to the masculine intellect . . . [but] it is no deprecation of a woman to state that she is more sensitive in her emotions and less ruled by her intellect. We are merely stating a difference, a difference which equips her for the special part for which she was cast . . . Her skull is also smaller than man's; and so, of course, is her brain.[1]
—*T. Lang,* The Difference Between a Man and a Woman

In recent years the sexiest body part, far and away, has become the brain. Magazines with cover stories on the brain fly off the newsstands, and countless seminars, tapes, books, and classes teach people how to use "all" of their brains. New technologies, such as PET scans, produce gorgeous photographs of the brain at work and play. Weekly we hear new discoveries about this miraculous organ, and it seems that scientists will soon be able to pinpoint the very neuron,

the very neurotransmitter, responsible for joy, sadness, rage, and suffering. At last we will know the reasons for all the differences between women and men that fascinate and infuriate, such as why men won't stop to ask directions and why women won't stop asking men what they are feeling.

In all this excitement, it seems curmudgeonly to sound words of caution, but the history of brain research does not exactly reveal a noble and impartial quest for truth, particularly on sensitive matters such as sex and race differences. Typically, when scientists haven't found the differences they were seeking, they haven't abandoned the goal or their belief that such differences exist; they just moved to another part of the anatomy or a different corner of the brain.

A century ago, for example, scientists tried to prove that women had smaller brains than men did, which accounted for women's alleged intellectual failings and emotional weaknesses. Dozens of studies purported to show that men had larger brains, making them smarter than women. When scientists realized that men's greater height and weight offset their brain-size advantage, however, they dropped this line of research like a shot. The scientists next tried to argue that women had smaller frontal lobes and larger parietal lobes than men did, another brain pattern thought to account for women's intellectual inferiority. Then it was reported that the parietal lobes might be associated with intellect. Panic in the labs—until anatomists suddenly found that women's parietal lobes were *smaller* than they had originally believed. Wherever they looked, scientists conveniently found evidence of female inferiority, as Gustave Le Bon, a Parisian, wrote in 1879:

> In the most intelligent races, as among the Parisians, there are a large number of women whose brains are closer in size to those of gorillas than to the most developed male brains. This inferiority is so obvious that no one can contest it for a moment; only its degree is worth discussion.[2]

We look back with amusement at the obvious biases of research a century ago, research designed to prove the obvious inferiority of women and minorities (and non-Parisians). Today, many researchers are splitting brains instead of weighing them, but they are no less determined to find sex differences. Nevertheless, skeptical neuroscientists are showing that biases and values are just as embedded in current research—old prejudices in new technologies.

The brain, like a walnut, consists of two hemispheres of equal size, connected by a bundle of fibers called the corpus callosum. The left hemisphere has been associated with verbal and reasoning ability, whereas the right hemisphere is associated with spatial reasoning and artistic ability. Yet by the time these findings reached the public, they had been vastly oversimplified and diluted. Even the great neuroscientist Roger Sperry, the grandfather of hemispheric research, felt obliged to warn that the "left-right dichotomy . . . is an idea with which it is very easy to run wild."[3] And many people have run wild with it: Stores are filled with manuals, cassettes, and handbooks that promise to help people become fluent in "whole-brain thinking," to beef up the unused part of their right brain, and to learn to use the intuitive right brain for business, painting, and inventing.

The fact that the brain consists of two hemispheres, each characterized by different specialties, provides a neat analogy to the fact that human beings consist of two genders, each characterized by different specialties. The analogy is so tempting that scientists keep trying to show that it is grounded in physical reality. Modern theories of gender and the brain are based on the idea that the left and right hemispheres develop differently in boys and girls, as does the corpus callosum that links the halves of the brain.

According to one major theory, the male brain is more "lateralized," that is, its hemispheres are specialized in their abilities, whereas females use both hemispheres more symmetrically because their corpus callosum is allegedly larger and contains more fibers. Two eminent scientists, Norman Geschwind and Peter Behan, maintained that this sex difference begins in the womb, when the male fetus begins to secrete testosterone—the hormone that will further its physical development as a male. Geschwind and Behan argued that testosterone in male fetuses washes over the brain, selectively attacking parts of the left hemisphere, briefly slowing its development, and producing right-hemisphere dominance in men. Geschwind speculated that the effects of testosterone on the prenatal brain produce "superior right hemisphere talents, such as artistic, musical, or mathematical talent."[4]

Right-hemisphere dominance is also thought to explain men's excellence in some tests of "visual-spatial ability"—the ability to imagine objects in three-dimensional space (the skill you need for mastering geometry, concocting football formations, and reading maps). This is apparently the reason that some men won't stop and ask directions when they are lost; they prefer to rely on their right brains, whereas women prefer to rely on a local informant. It is also supposed to be the reason that men can't talk about their feelings and would rather watch television or wax the car. Women have interconnected hemispheres, which explains why they excel in talk, feelings, intuition, and quick judgments. Geschwind and Behan's theory had tremendous scientific appeal, and it is cited frequently in research papers and textbooks. *Science* hailed it with the headline "Math Genius May Have Hormonal Basis."[5]

The theory also has had enormous popular appeal. It fits snugly, for example, with the Christian fundamentalist belief that men and women are innately different and thus innately designed for different roles. . . .

. . . In a book by two Christian fundamentalists, *The Language of Love,* the authors, Gary Smalley and John Trent, write:

> most women spend the majority of their days and nights camped out on the right side of the brain [which] harbors the center for feelings, as well as the primary relational, language, and communication skills . . . and makes an afternoon devoted to art and fine music actually enjoyable.[6]

You can hear the chuckling from men who regard art museums and concert halls as something akin to medieval torture chambers, but I'm sure that the many men who enjoy art and fine music, indeed who create art and fine music, would not find that last remark so funny. Geschwind and Behan, of course, had argued that male specialization of the right hemisphere explained why men *excel* in art and fine music. But since Smalley and Trent apparently do not share these prissy female interests, they relegate them to women—to women's brains.

The two hemispheres of the brain do have different specialties, but it is far too simple-minded (so to speak) to assume that human abilities clump up in opposing bunches. Most brain researchers today believe that the two hemispheres complement one another, to the extent that one side can sometimes take over the functions of a side that has been damaged. Moreover, specific skills often involve components from both hemispheres: one side has the ability to tell a joke, and the other has the ability to laugh at one. Math abilities include both visual-spatial skills and reasoning skills. The right hemisphere is involved in creating art, but the left hemisphere is involved in appreciating and analyzing art. As neuropsychologist Jerre Levy once said, "Could the eons of human evolution have left half of the brain witless? Could a bird

whose existence is dependent on flying have evolved only a single wing?"[7]

These qualifications about the interdependence of brain hemispheres have not, however, deterred those who believe that there are basic psychological differences between the sexes that can be accounted for in the brain. So let's consider their argument more closely.

The neuroscientist Ruth Bleier, who at her untimely death was Professor of Neurophysiology at the University of Wisconsin, carefully examined Geschwind and Behan's data, going back to many of their original references.[8] In one such study of 507 fetal brains of 10 to 44 weeks gestation, the researchers had actually stated that they found *no significant sex differences* in these brains. If testosterone had an effect on the developing brain, it would surely have been apparent in this large sample. Yet Geschwind and Behan cited this study for other purposes and utterly ignored its findings of no sex differences.

Instead, Geschwind and Behan cited as evidence for their hypothesis a study of *rats'* brains. The authors of the rat study reported that in male rats, two areas of the cortex that are believed to be involved in processing visual information were 3 percent thicker on the right side than on the left. In one of the better examples of academic gobbledygook yet to reach the printed page, the researchers interpreted their findings to mean that "in the male rat it is necessary to have greater spatial orientation to interact with a female rat during estrus and to integrate that input into a meaningful output." Translation: When having sex with a female, the male needs to be able to look around in case a dangerous predator, such as her husband, walks in on them.

Bleier found more holes in this argument than in a screen door. No one knows, she said, what the slightly greater thickness in the male rat's cortex means for the rat, let alone what it means for human beings. There is at present no evidence that spatial orientation is related to asymmetry of the cortex, or that female rats have a lesser or deficient ability in this regard. And although Geschwind and Behan unabashedly used their limited findings to account for male "superiority" in math and art, they did not specifically study the incidence of genius, talent, or even modest giftedness in their sample, nor did they demonstrate a difference between the brains of geniuses and the brains of average people.

Bleier wrote to *Science,* offering a scholarly paper detailing these criticisms. *Science* did not publish it, on the grounds, as one reviewer put it, that Bleier "tends to err in the opposite direction from the researchers whose results and conclusions she criticizes" and because "she argues very strongly for the predominant role of environmental influences."[9] Apparently, said Bleier, one is allowed to err in only one direction if one wants to be published in *Science*. The journal did not even publish her critical Letter to the Editor.

At about the same time, however, *Science* saw fit to publish a study by two researchers who claimed to have found solid evidence of gender differences in the splenium (posterior end) of the corpus callosum.[10] In particular, they said, the splenium was larger and more bulbous in the five female brains than in the nine male brains they examined, which had been obtained at autopsy. The researchers speculated that "the female brain is less well lateralized—that is, manifests less hemispheric specialization—than the male brain for visuospatial functions." Notice the language: The female brain is *less specialized* than, and by implication inferior to, the male brain. They did not say, as they might have, that the female brain was *more integrated* than the male's. The male brain is the norm, and specialization, in the brain as in academia, is considered a good thing. Generalists in any business are out of favor these days.

This article, which also met professional acclaim, had a number of major flaws that, had they been part of any other research paper, would have been fatal to its publication. The study was based on a small sample of only fourteen brains. The researchers did not describe their methods of selecting the brains in that sample, so it is possible that some of the brains were diseased or otherwise abnormal. The article contained numerous unsupported assumptions and leaps of faith. For example, there is at present absolutely no evidence that the number of fibers in the corpus callosum is even related to hemispheric specialization. Indeed, no one knows what role, if any, the callosum plays in determining a person's mental abilities. Most damaging of all, the sex differences that the researchers claimed to have found in the size of the corpus callosum were not statistically significant, according to the scientific conventions for accepting an article for publication.

Bleier again wrote to *Science,* delineating these criticisms and also citing four subsequent studies, by her and by others, that independently failed to find gender differences of any kind in the corpus callosum. *Science* failed to publish this criticism, as it has failed to publish all studies that find no gender differences in the brain.

Ultimately, the most damning blow to all of these brain-hemisphere theories is that the formerly significant sex differences that brain theories are attempting to account for—in verbal, spatial, and math abilities—are fading rapidly. Let's start with the famed female superiority in verbal ability. Janet Hyde, a professor of psychology at the University of Wisconsin, and her colleague Marcia Linn reviewed 165 studies of verbal ability (including skills in vocabulary, writing, anagrams, and reading comprehension), which represented tests of 1,418,899 people. Hyde and Linn reported that at present in America, there simply are no gender differences in these verbal skills. They noted: "Thus our research pulls out one of the two wobbly legs on which the brain lateralization theories have rested."[11]

Hyde recently went on to kick the other leg, the assumption of overall male superiority in mathematics and spatial ability. No one disputes that males do surpass females at the highly gifted end of the math spectrum. But when Hyde and her colleagues analyzed 100 studies of mathematics performance, representing the testing of 3,985,682 students, they found that gender differences were smallest and favored *females* in samples of the general population, and grew larger, favoring males, only in selected samples of precocious individuals.[12]

What about spatial abilities, another area thought to reveal a continuing male superiority? When psychologists put the dozens of existing studies on spatial ability into a giant hopper and looked at the overall results, this was what they reported: Many studies show no sex differences. Of the studies that do report sex differences, the magnitude of the difference is often small. And finally, there is greater variation *within* each sex than *between* them. As one psychologist who reviewed these studies summarized: "The observed differences are very small, the overlap [between men and women] large, and abundant biological theories are supported with very slender or no evidence."[13] . . .

It is sobering to read, over and over and over again in scholarly papers, the conclusions of eminent scientists who have cautioned their colleagues against generalizing about sex differences from poor data. One leader in brain-hemisphere research, Marcel Kinsbourne, observing that the evidence for sex differences "fails to convince on logical, methodological, and empirical grounds," then asked:

> Why then do reputable investigators persist in ignoring [this evidence]? Because the study of sex differences is not like the rest of psychology. Under pressure from the gathering momentum of feminism, and perhaps in backlash to it, many investigators seem determined to discover that men and women "really" are different. It seems that if sex differences (e.g., in lateralization) do not exist, then they have to be invented.[14]

These warnings have, for the most part, gone unheeded. Poor research continues to be published in reputable journals, and from there it is disseminated to the public. Many scientists and science writers continue to rely on weak data to support their speculations, like using pebbles as foundation for a castle. Because these speculations fit the dominant beliefs about gender, however, they receive far more attention and credibility than they warrant. Worse, the far better evidence that fails to conform to the dominant beliefs about gender is overlooked, disparaged,

or, as in Bleier's experience, remains unpublished.

As a result, ideas enter the common vocabulary as proven facts when they should be encumbered with "maybes," "sometimes," and "we-don't-know-yets." Scientist Hugh Fairweather, reviewing the history of sex differences research in cognition, concluded: "What had before been a possibility at best slenderly evidenced, was widely taken for a fact; and 'fact' hardened into a 'biological' dogma."[15]

Now, it is possible that reliable sex differences in the brain will eventually be discovered. Will it then be all right . . . to go on the air to celebrate how delightfully but innately different men and women are? Should we then all make sure we have a male brain and a female brain in every household? Should we then worry about the abnormality of households like mine, in which the male is better at intuitive judgments and the female has the adding-machine mentality?

The answers are no, for three reasons. First, theories of sex differences in the brain cannot account for the complexities of people's everyday behavior. They cannot explain, for instance, why, if women are better than men in verbal ability, so few women are auctioneers or diplomats, or why, if women have the advantage in making rapid judgments, so few women are air-traffic controllers or umpires. Nor can brain theories explain why abilities and ambitions change when people are given opportunities previously denied to them. Two decades ago, theorists postulated biological limitations that were keeping women out of men's work like medicine and bartending. When the external barriers to these professions fell, the speed with which women entered them was dizzying. Did everybody's brain change? Today we would be amused to think that women have a brain-lateralization deficiency that is keeping them out of law school. But we continue to hear about the biological reasons that keep women out of science, math, and politics. For sex differences in cognitive abilities to wax and wane so rapidly, they must be largely a result of education, motivation, and opportunity, not of innate differences between male and female brains.

Second, the meanings of terms like "verbal ability" and "spatial reasoning" keep changing too, depending on who is using them and for what purpose. For example, when [people] . . . speak of women's verbal abilities, they usually mean women's interest in and willingness to talk about relationships and feelings. But in studies of total talking time in the workplace, men far exceed women in the talk department. In everyday life, men interrupt women more than vice versa, dominate the conversation, and are more successful at introducing new topics and having their comments remembered in group discussions.[16] What does this mean for judgments of which sex has the better "verbal ability"?

Third, the major key problem with biological theories of sex differences is that they deflect attention from the far more substantial evidence for sex similarity. The finding that men and women are more alike in their abilities and brains than different almost never makes the news. Researchers and the public commit the error of focusing on the small differences—usually of the magnitude of a few percentage points—rather than on the fact that the majority of women and men overlap. For example, this is what the author of a scientific paper that has been widely quoted as *supporting* sex differences in brain hemispheres actually concluded:

> Thus, one must not overlook perhaps the most obvious conclusion, which is that basic patterns of male and female brain asymmetry seem to be more similar than they are different.[17]

Everyone, nevertheless, promptly overlooked it. . . .

The 70-Kilogram Man and the Pregnant Person

Why women are not the same as men

What do these stories have in common?

- In the spring of 1990, the Board of Directors of the all-women Mills College, in Oakland, California, voted to admit men for the sake of the school's financial survival. The ensuing protest by the female students, photographed weeping and desolate, outraged the public—especially, judging from phone calls to talk shows and letters to the editor of various newspapers, the male public. The reaction was angry and unsympathetic to the women students' unhappiness: Quit sniveling and join the twentieth century. You women can't have it both ways. If you demand access to all-male schools, you don't get to turn around and demand the right to have all-female schools. A priest, writing to the *Los Angeles Times,* said the students' reaction was a dangerous sign of man-hating.

- "Myra" and "Jim" married as law students and planned to have an egalitarian marriage and independent careers.[18] After a few years, they had a baby—an event that changed Myra's life, but not Jim's. They couldn't find reliable live-in help; the baby was, Myra said, more "absorbing and exhausting" than she had anticipated; Jim's law firm would not permit him to spend less time at work so he could help with the baby, and he was not prepared to give up his high salary for another position. As a result, Myra quit her job to care for the baby. When Myra and Jim divorced, the judge was unsympathetic to Myra's situation. He awarded her no spousal support and minimum child care, because, he said, a professional woman should be able to take care of herself.

  Myra now works full-time to support herself and her child, but not at a career that is remotely comparable to her former husband's (or to her own). She had to take a job that would allow her time off when her son was sick, that would never require late hours or trial appearances, and that would finish at 5:00 so she could pick her son up from the day-care center on time. Many people today have no sympathy for women like Myra. "You wanted to be equal with men under the law," runs their attitude, "and the law is treating you equally. You can't cry now for special protection."

- A few years ago, the results of a massive study of 22,071 volunteer physicians made headlines across the country: taking small doses of aspirin can reduce the chances of having a heart attack. There were no women in the study. A compilation of studies of the effects of drug treatments on the likelihood of having subsequent heart attacks involved 13,385 patients; there were no women in any of these studies. And in still another research project, a study used a sample only of men to examine the effects of diet on . . . breast cancer. An editor of the *New England Journal of Medicine,* Marcia Angell, replying to charges of gender bias in medicine, said, "Gender bias is not serious in a way that distorts research. It doesn't serve women well to see sexism where it doesn't exist."[19]

What all of these stories share, I believe, is a confusion between gender equality and gender sameness: the idea that to be equal in life and law, the sexes must be the same. But to deny that men and women differ in their basic natures, personality traits, and abilities, is not to deny that men and women differ at all. Of course they do. They differ in the life experiences that befall them. They differ in the work they do, at home and at "work." They differ in reproductive processes. They differ, most of all, in power, income, and other resources. By ignoring these real differences in men's and women's lives and bodies, people who take the normalcy of men for granted have fallen prey to a third error: Generalizing from the experiences and even the physiology of men to all humanity on the grounds that everyone is like men—and usually a narrow band of middle-class white men, at that.

The assumption that "there are no differences that matter" is the guiding principle of egalitarians who believe that *equality of opportunity and result* rests on *treating men and women as if they were the same.* Because the emphasis on sex differences has, for centuries, been a flimsy disguise for the belief in female deficiencies, the modern women's movement at first downplayed or rejected any discussion of differences, demanding that women be treated like men, no better, no worse. I still share these concerns, but I don't cling to them as fer-

vently or apply them as universally as I once did, and I will try to explain why.

The confusion between equality and sameness must be untangled, because it has now become abundantly clear that in many domains the assumption of sameness has led to unfair and unequal results. Here is an illustration that affects everyone, which we might call "The Exasperating Ladies-Room Problem." Most public restrooms in airports, theaters, movie houses, or restaurants are equal in terms of the size and number of stalls they allot to men and women. But everyone who has ever used a busy public restroom knows that they are not equal in result: Women are always waiting in line. A Cornell engineering student, Anh Tran, discovered why this is so. She and a male assistant monitored "toilet time" for each person at high-use rest stops in Washington, D.C. The men took an average of forty-five seconds each, while the women spent an average of seventy-nine seconds each. Because men and women differ in dress, anatomy, and personal needs, the researchers concluded that restroom allocation, to be *fair,* should be *different:* a fairer allocation of toilets would be 60-40, favoring women.[20] (California was the first to pass such legislation in 1987; in 1990 a "potty parity" law went into effect in New York, requiring all public facilities to have as many stalls in women's restrooms as there are stalls and urinals in men's; and in 1989, Virginia revised its plumbing code to require twice as many stalls in women's restrooms as in men's—except in restaurants and nightclubs.)

Unfortunately, in several arenas the assumption of sameness has produced rather more disastrous consequences for women than having to wait longer than men in restroom lines. Two of those arenas, which together affect so much of our lives, are medicine and the law.

THE 70-KILOGRAM MAN

. . . though they of different sexes be,
Yet on the whole they are the same as we,
For those that have the strictest searchers been,
Find women are but men turned outside in.[21]

Modern medicine seems to agree with this bit of nineteenth-century doggerel—women, on the whole, are the same as "we" men. In the field of medicine, both in research and clinical practice, the male body can therefore be used as the medical norm.

In anatomy textbooks, for example, the illustrations that show a full body typically show a male body, except for the illustrations of the female reproductive system. A group of psychologists examined eight major anatomy textbooks now in use in medical schools, documenting the sex ratio for all illustrations of bodies and body parts. In general anatomy chapters, males made up 64 percent of the illustrations, females 11 percent (in the remaining illustrations gender was not apparent). Only in the sections on reproductive anatomy were female and male bodies represented in equal numbers. The drastic omission of women from the realm of "human" anatomy, the authors concluded, "creates the impression that female bodies are somehow uncommon or abnormal" except for their sexual and reproductive functions.[22] The message, they suggest, is that women's bodies are most suited to reproduction, whereas men's bodies are capable of all activities. . . .

Medical students are trained on the male model—literally. The paradigm patient in medical school is "the 70-kilogram man" (or, in older schools not on the metric system, the "154-pound man"). According to Perri Klass, who is a pediatrician and writer, and Lila Wallis, an internist and former president of the American Medical Women's Association, medical students learn what the average man's heart weighs and what his minimum urine output should be; they treat him for allergies, appendicitis, diarrhea, and prostate problems. They compute dosages of medication based on his weight. And the 70-kilogram man is definitely a macho guy; he never gets ovarian cysts, fibroids, or any other female disorder.[23]

Medical research, too, is overwhelmingly based on men and a male standard of normalcy. A 1990 report released by the Government Accounting Office sharply criticized the National Institutes of Health for continuing to exclude women from most studies of drug effects, diseases, and treatments (a violation of NIH's own 1986 policy of including more women) and for devoting only 13 percent of its research funds to research on women. For years, congresswomen and female physicians have been observing that the bulk of money for medical research in America is directed to the problems that male members of Congress have, apparently on the principle that "we fund what we fear." So there has been ample funding for, say, large-scale studies of heart disease in men, but not for comparably large-scale studies of the causes of breast cancer or the effects of high cholesterol on women.

Psychologist Margrit Eichler, at the Ontario Institute for Studies in Education, and two psychiatrists at the Toronto Western Hospital, Anna Lisa Reisman and Elaine Borins, examined all issues of four professional journals in the year 1988: *The New England Journal of Medicine, The American Journal of Psychiatry, The American Journal of Trauma,* and *The Canadian Journal of Surgery.* They found evidence of gender bias in all stages of the research process: in the very titles of the articles, in research design, methods, data collection and interpretation, and in treatment recommendations. This bias turned up in American and Canadian journals and cut across all medical specialties.[24] . . .

Of course, experimenters often exclude females from research—even female rats in rat studies—because it is simpler and cheaper to use male animals. The female's estrous cycle disrupts responses in certain behavioral and biological tests, and increases variation among animals. The goal in research is to minimize this variation, the better to determine the precise effects of the drug or treatment in question. So researchers often plead that it would be too costly to add women to their studies. But of course males and females *do* vary physiologically, and eliminating this variation means that the results of many experiments cannot be applied to females in any simple or direct way. If you want to know the effects of

Drug X and you throw women out of your study because the menstrual cycle affects their responses to medication, you cannot then extrapolate from your study of men to women, precisely *because* the menstrual cycle affects their responses to medication. . . .

The traditional reliance on the male body as a medical norm has two serious consequences for women's health. First, many physicians regard conditions that are normal or at least medically safe for women as if they were abnormal or dangerous, and treat them inappropriately. The most blatant example of this error is the treatment of pregnant women. Perri Klass, who was pregnant while a medical student, writes that medical school conveys the attitude "that pregnancy is a deeply dangerous medical condition, that one walks a fine line, avoiding one serious problem after another, to reach the statistically unlikely outcome of a healthy baby and a healthy mother."[25]

Second, many physicians ignore conditions that *are* problems for women, for example mistakenly believing, as Ramey says, that "women don't die of heart disease." The results of two recent studies of sex bias in the decision to recommend coronary-bypass surgery are cause for alarm. In a group of patients who had taken specialized tests that showed evidence of heart disease, 40 percent of the men but only *4 percent* of the women were referred by their physicians for the next medical test to see if bypass surgery was warranted. The women had the same symptoms, the same abnormal test results, but apparently the doctors did not take their symptoms seriously. Because many cardiologists tend to neglect heart disease symptoms (such as chest pain) in women, by the time women are referred for coronary artery surgery, they are older and sicker than men would be with comparable symptoms. As a result, women are nearly twice as likely as men to die from this surgical procedure.[26]

There are signs of improvement on the horizon, however. Government institutions and many physicians have become aware of gender bias in research and practice, which is the first step toward correcting it. A few large-scale studies have begun, including a ten-year, $500-million women's health study to be conducted (at last) by the National Institutes of Health. Research on women and heart disease is increasing. For example, it was known that men who quit smoking reduce their smoking-related risk of heart attack within two years; but no one knew if the same would be true for women. Now physician Lynn Rosenberg and her colleagues have found that for women, no matter how long they have smoked or how much, the elevated risk of heart attack due to smoking disappears within a few years of quitting.[27] Lung cancer is an equal-opportunity disease for smokers of both sexes, and it is good to know that both sexes benefit by quitting.

Until research programs are more evenly balanced, women would do well to be prudent yet cautious in following medical advice that has been based exclusively on men—for example, struggling feverishly to get their cholesterol levels down to a fictitious ideal number. (Eating sensibly and nutritiously, of course, has its own benefits.) A friend of mine, a healthy sixty-five-year-old woman, discovered at a routine medical exam that her cholesterol level was 260. Her male physician said to her: "If you were a man, I would know how to advise you, and I might even consider recommending medication. But we just don't know what a level of 260 means for a woman of your age, considering that you have no other risk factors, and I don't want to risk subjecting you to the side effects of medication." At least he was candid; many physicians confidently treat their female patients as they would treat males. . . .

CAN WOMEN BE "DIFFERENT" AND "EQUAL"?

Equality is a platitudinous concept that practically everybody supports because it can be given any meaning we like. . . . Formal agreement on equality as a value masks the fact that we haven't a clue as to what is supposed to be equal to what, and in what way, or to what degree.[28]

—*Phillip E. Johnson,* Stanford Law Review

During a recent dinner party, a friend of mine got himself into a charming verbal muddle. In his desire to use the encompassing "he or she" instead of the generic male "he," my friend found himself referring to the "pregnant person"—"he or she. . . ." Surely, we all agreed, this was carrying equality too far! But my friend's gaffe goes right to the heart of the legal dilemma of sexual equality. As in medicine, the law regards the male as the legal standard of a human being. Therefore, women may be treated like men, in which case they are equal to them, or not like men, in which case they are deficient or special. But they are never treated specifically *as women.* There is no concept in the law of what is normal for women.

Robin West, Professor of Law at the University of Maryland, argues that modern jurisprudence (like medicine) is masculine rather than human: the values, dangers, fears, and other real-life experiences of women's lives are not, she says, "reflected at any level whatsoever in contracts, torts, constitutional law, or any other field of legal doctrine." The Rule of Law does not value intimacy, for example, but autonomy: "Nurturant, intimate labor is neither valued by liberal legalism nor compensated by the market economy. It is not compensated in the home and it is not compensated in the workplace—wherever intimacy is, there is no compensation. Similarly, separation of the individual from his or her family, community, or children is not understood to be a harm, and we are not protected against it."[29] The law, she argues, simply does not reflect the female experience: "Women are absent from jurisprudence because women *as human beings* are absent from the law's protection" (emphasis in original).[30]

Christine Littleton, Professor of Law at UCLA, argues that women's inequality in society results from devaluing women's real-life biological and cultural differences from men. Efforts to achieve equality through precisely equal treatment, therefore, are doomed to fail, because men and women are not starting from the same place. "As a concept," she says, "equality suffers from a 'mathematical fallacy'—that is, the view that only things that are the same can ever be equal."[31] Equality has been the rallying cry of every subjugated group in American society, she maintains, but the time has come to examine its inherent dangers and fallacies.

The ideology of equality evolved from legitimate attacks on the "separate spheres" theory of blacks and women—i.e., that blacks and women "naturally" inhabit separate arenas of life (for blacks, their own race; for women, the home and family). The separate-spheres ideology historically put both blacks and women at a disadvantage; it kept black people out of white railway cars and white law schools, for example, and kept women at home. It is no wonder, then, that women and minorities are rightly wary of any legislation or legal ruling based on arguments about natural differences or separate spheres, for such regulations have invariably served to exclude them from many areas of social, political, and economic life.

For example, special protection laws—such as those forbidding women to work at night in some jobs or to lift heavy objects—were used to restrict women's opportunities and relegate them to lower status and poorer-paying occupations. There were no special laws, however, protecting women from long and excruciating labor in sweatshops. So the modern women's movement has understandably opposed any laws or policies that would essentially be female-specific, fearing these would be used against women's best interests. Their attitude reflects Mae West's observation: "Men are always trying to protect me," she said. "Can't imagine what from."

For these reasons, the initial response of legal scholars to the traditionally asymmetrical treatment of women and men under the law was to argue in favor of perfect symmetry: because there are no natural differences and no inevitably separate spheres, both sexes must be treated alike. Women cannot be given any special considerations *and* be considered equal. Wendy Williams, an articulate spokesperson for this view, has warned that "we can't have it both ways [and] we need to think carefully about which way we want to have it."[32] . . .

Christine Littleton calls the model of legal symmetry the "assimilation" ideal, for it is based, she says, on the "notion that women, given the chance, really are or could be just like men."[33] Thus, institutions should be required to treat women as they already treat men, admitting those who are "qualified," and demanding that once admitted, women behave like men. If a law firm requires that its partners put in long hours and sacrifice their family relationships and child-care obligations, then that's what a woman must do if she wants to be a successful attorney. If a gadget manufacturer requires workers to be at least 5′9″ tall, because of the height of the conveyor belt on the assembly line, then only women who are at least 5′9″ can be hired. It is a "woman's gotta do what a man's gotta do" model of equality.

The symmetrical model has great appeal for the legal system, for liberals, and for many people who see in this vision a way to eradicate rigid sex roles that constrain men as well as women. It seems to be fair and logical, and applying it universally is certainly easier than trying to grapple with slippery exceptions. Nevertheless, notice that at the core of this vision is our now-familiar male standard of normalcy: The goal is to treat women *as men already are treated.* "To the extent that women cannot or will not conform to socially male forms of behavior, they are left out in the cold," observes Littleton. "To the extent they do or can conform, they do not achieve equality *as women,* but as social males" (emphasis in original).[34]

Now many scholars of legal issues are questioning the wisdom and the consequences of the symmetrical vision of legal equality, and focusing on the male bias at its heart. One of their most powerful arguments against symmetry is the accumulating evidence that treating women like men often produces disastrously unequal outcomes. In 1986 a New York State Task Force on Women and the Law found that on virtually all issues of specific concern to women—notably domestic violence, rape, child support, day care,

and pregnancy—being treated equally under the law leads to unequal results. So did a major review in 1990 of gender bias in the courts conducted by the Judicial Council of California.[35]

The simmering ideas of equality versus sameness come to a boil on the one great indisputable sex difference where law and medicine combine forces: The male body doesn't become pregnant; the female body does. Efforts to combat the illogical belief that the female body is not a deficient male body, however, have led to the equally illogical conclusion that the female body is just like the male body—even the pregnant female body.

Certainly the law itself goes around in circles. Sometimes it has regarded pregnant women as being different from men, and, as many legal experts fear, it has used that difference to justify inequality. For example, the law has, in various times and places, required pregnant teenagers to leave school (but not penalized teenage fathers); allowed pregnant women to be fired from their jobs; or required nonpregnant women to be sterilized in order to keep their jobs. Sometimes the law has regarded pregnant women as being the same as men, thereby denying them special considerations. And sometimes the law has granted pregnant women, but not men, those benefits.

In the famous case of the *California Federal Savings and Loan Association v. Guerra* (hereafter *Cal Fed*), a woman named Lillian Garland took an *unpaid* pregnancy leave from her job at the Savings and Loan. Under a 1978 law, she was entitled to get her job back after four months, but *Cal Fed* challenged the law on the grounds that it discriminated against men. This case polarized many women's groups. Some supported Garland, but others, including the National Organization for Women and the National Woman's Political Caucus, supported *Cal Fed*'s reasoning. The case made its way to the Supreme Court, which had to resolve the conflict in this situation between equal treatment and preferential treatment. They ruled, six to three, that preferential treatment of pregnant women is not unconstitutional. California and other states may pass laws to permit maternity leaves.

According to equal-rights advocates, pregnancy should be treated like any disability that might cause workers of either sex to lose a few days' or a few months' work. Women's-rights advocates disagree. Sociologist Barbara Rothman puts the matter this way:

> A woman lawyer is exactly the same as a man lawyer. A woman cop is just the same as a man cop. And a pregnant woman is just the same as . . . well, as, uh . . . It's like disability, right? Or like serving in the army?

"Pregnancy is just exactly like pregnancy," she concludes. "There is nothing else quite like it. That statement is not a glorification or a mystification. It is a statement of fact. Having a baby grow in your belly is not like anything else one can do. It is unique. How can uniqueness be made to fit into an equality model?"[36] To Rothman, pregnant women are not in need of protection, and they are certainly not weaker or stupider than men or nonpregnant women; but it is ridiculous, demeaning, and antiwoman to ignore the special condition of pregnancy.

In *The Female Body and the Law*, political scientist Zillah Eisenstein illuminates the male bias in the law by showing what would happen if the model of the basic human being were not the male body, but the pregnant female body. (There's an imaginative idea for you!) The law, she shows, would immediately have to become more complex and sensitive to human diversity than it is, because pregnancies range from being uncomplicated and uneventful to being seriously disabling to the mother-to-be, and because some women, like all men, will not become pregnant.

Thus, the law would recognize that the pregnant worker may have needs that are different from those of the nonpregnant worker: to avoid nausea, she may need to eat several small snacks throughout the day rather than have one break at lunchtime. Further, the needs of individual pregnant women will differ: some will require considerable time off, and others will be able to work right up to the delivery (and return two hours later). Some pregnant workers may not differ at all from their nonpregnant coworkers, female or male, and will neither need nor want special considerations. These are all *equal* ways of being, Eisenstein points out, if we remove the male standard of normalcy.

But if pregnancy occurs with so many variations, why not regard it as something comparable to illness and disability, which affect both sexes and which also occur in degrees of seriousness and incapacity? For many, the answer is that once again, it is the male norm that construes pregnancy as a *dis*ability rather than, say, as an additional ability. "Normal pregnancy may make a woman unable to 'work' for days, weeks, or months, but it also makes her able to reproduce," says Littleton. "From whose viewpoint is the work that she cannot do 'work,' and the work that she is doing *not* work? Certainly not from hers."[37]

In addition, medicine and law, based as they are on the male experience, fail to recognize the female viewpoint of what is distinctive about the experience of reproduction. The male perception of pregnancy, as Rothman points out, consists of two steps: In goes a seed, out comes the result. It is a "mother as flowerpot" view of pregnancy.[38] In contrast, the woman's experience is continuous from conception to baby. By making the male experience the norm, Rothman argues, we deny that continuity, the nine-month relationship a mother has with the fetus—calming it down when it's fussy, trying to sleep when it is too big, feeling it grow and change. By regarding pregnancy from the male perspective, and by celebrating high-tech prenatal technology over the continuous maternal relationship, law and medicine have created the impression that women are merely containers for the fetus, and untrustworthy, inefficient containers at that.

Rothman, who has been studying the social consequences of changes in reproductive technology, fears that pregnant women are fast becoming viewed as "the unskilled workers on a reproductive assembly line." They are blamed for producing "flawed products"— i.e., damaged newborns or fetuses with defects. "America is developing a legal and medical system to monitor pregnant women, control them, keep them in line with 'fetal-abuse' statutes," she argues.[39] In the meantime, people conveniently overlook the more likely causes of "flawed fetuses," such as the appalling lack of prenatal services and care for poor women, the growing evidence of the *male* contribution to birth defects, and the exposure to leads and other toxins in the workplace that are hazardous to men's *and* women's reproductive ability. . . .

Let's start by stipulating what a woman-centered standard of pregnancy does *not* mean. It does not mean a return to concepts of "maternal instinct," the "sanctity of motherhood," and other saccharine ideas that historically have relegated women to their roles as mothers. It does not mean that men should concentrate on business and women on babies, or that women are superior to men in the ability and desire to love and nurture children. It does not mean a return to the protective legislation that treats women differently in the name of protecting their "special" reproductive processes, but has the effect of confining them to lesser-paying, lower-status jobs. It does not mean that employers would be able to fire female employees because of possible risks to their possible fetuses, while ignoring the risks to male fertility of the same hazardous job conditions.

But law and social policy can accommodate the ways in which the female and male experiences of procreation differ. According to Barbara Rothman's guidelines, for the entire duration of pregnancy, women would have full rights of personal privacy, bodily autonomy, and individual decision making. The fetus would not be regarded as a separate person or have rights that supersede those of its mother. The fetus would be part of its mother's body as long as it is in her body. The state may not force her to undergo a pregnancy that she does not want, just as it may not force her to abort a pregnancy that she does want.

The point, says Rothman, is that pregnancy, like abortion, "takes its meaning from the woman in whose body the pregnancy is unfolding."[40]

That is why for one woman, pregnancy is a mystical and special experience; for another, an experience no different from having a bad back or swollen ankles. That is why for one woman, an abortion (or a miscarriage) is a minor inconvenience or a major relief; for another, or even for the same woman on another occasion, it is the death of a baby. That is why for one surrogate mother, a fetus is a chick she is merely incubating; for another, or even for the same woman on another occasion, a fetus is an anticipated baby-to-be.

What woman-centered policies share is the premise that it must be the pregnant woman, not the state, who decides what pregnancy means to her. Without such policies, society will continue down its current path, moving toward a chilling invasion of privacy into women's bodies, a severe restriction of women's freedom, and a relegation of women's rights to third place—after men and fetuses.

WOMEN'S RIGHTS VERSUS EQUAL RIGHTS

Perhaps if difference were not so costly, we, as feminists, could think about it more clearly. Perhaps if equality did not require uniformity, we, as women, could demand it less ambivalently.[41]
—*Christine Littleton,* California Law Review

Equality under the law would be an excellent goal for women if it weren't that it always seems to travel a one-way street of making women equal to men. Sometimes, women do not fit the male norm in medicine and law, and the problem with the dream of equality is that it excludes such real-life sex differences. Theories of equality can operate only if those differences can be smoothed over, if women's lives and experiences can be made comparable to experiences that men can have too. Equality theories are inherently prejudiced against women, because they focus on the "differences" that are in women (it is women who do the differing from the norm), and because they mistakenly assume that social institutions, such as banks and schools, are already egalitarian and gender-neutral—it's just a matter of fitting women into them.

This is why many legal scholars, men and women, are now arguing that the right to be treated as an equal doesn't always entail identical treatment. Ronald Dworkin writes, "If I have two children and one is dying of a disease that is making the other uncomfortable, I do not show equal concern if I flip a coin to decide which should have the remaining dose of the drug."[42]

It's a good metaphor, for most parents realize that loving their children equally does not necessarily require treating them identically. One child may need more help with homework. One may have a gift for athletics or music that warrants special favors. One may have a disability that requires attention. But parents can hope to treat their children in ways to assure equal *outcomes* for them: people who know they are loved, who can earn a living at work they enjoy, who are valued for the individuals they are. Most parents intuitively operate on a notion of equality that encompasses the real differences among their children. "I was fortunate enough to have a mother who believed her four very different children should be equals," says Littleton. "I now want the same for all of us."[43]

Many alternative ideas to equality-as-sameness are blooming today, and they are sources of exciting possibilities as well as passionate debates over which policies will enhance the status of women and produce the most equitable results all around. Mary Ann Mason urges a return to "the flexible, pragmatic concept of women's rights," rather than the rigid ideology of equal rights.[44] "Equal rights does not challenge the structure of the economy or the role of the government," says Mason. "Asking to be treated as men are treated is a fundamentally conservative position that asks for no special support from the government or special consideration from employers for working mothers."[45]

Mason would not abandon the goal of equal rights entirely; rather, she argues that it is not the only goal for all women. Equal rights, she maintains, is an appropriate strategy for the many women who, like men, "live to work" and wish access to the careers and circles of the male elite. But it is not helpful to the many more millions of women who "work to live," and who are clustered in low-paying, female-dominated occupations.

For this reason, Mason believes, Title VII of the Civil Rights Act of 1964, which forbids discrimination on the basis of race or sex, should not be the sole model of rights for women. "Sex" was added to the language of Title VII at the last minute, as a joke, by Southern congressmen who were hoping to defeat the Civil Rights Act entirely. But if a Woman's Rights Act had been passed at the time, Mason argues, it would have looked quite different. "A bill written for the needs of working women," Mason says, "would not have stressed equal competition, but would address the issues of government-subsidized child care, paid maternity leaves, a higher minimum wage (since 65 percent of all minimum-wage workers are women), medical care and pension rights for part-time workers, affirmative action, and reentry rights. It would also require some form of pay equity between male-dominated occupations and female-dominated occupations. Instead, women have trapped themselves into a competitive model that leaves no room for the special needs of women who are the primary child-rearers."[46] . . .

In general, I share the widespread concern that any legal policy that celebrates or implies that women have a special edge in the maternal, nurturing, . . . connectedness front is bound to be bad for women. Yet, overall, I have been persuaded by a flexible new approach that Christine Littleton calls "equality as acceptance" rather than "equality as sameness."

Equality as acceptance means that instead of regarding cultural and reproductive differences as problems to be eliminated, we would aim to eliminate *the unequal consequences that follow from them.* We would ask how to achieve equality *despite* gender differences, not how to achieve equality by getting rid of (or pretending to ignore) gender differences. We would no longer accept the prevailing male norm as always the legitimate one, while trying to find special circumstances to accommodate women or minorities who are trying to measure up to it. We would stop labeling women's experiences as the deviant ones.

This approach is more complicated than equality as sameness, and it does not generate clear, simple right answers. It is easier to try to squeeze human diversity into one universal, "normal" way of doing things. But equality as acceptance offers new strategies for old problems, even as it unmasks our silent assumptions about whose ways are normal and whose are deviant.

In this view, for example, women and men could achieve equality in athletics without requiring football teams to add a few physically powerful females. Equality as acceptance would require, instead, that equal resources be allocated to male and female sports programs in schools, regardless of whether or not the sports themselves are similar. In this way, sports would *accept* women's athletic skills on their own terms; equality would not depend on the ability of individual women to fit in to the male game or vice versa.

Or consider the gadget maker whose employees must meet a minimum 5′9″ height requirement because of the height of the conveyor belt used to assemble the gadgets. Let's assume that this is an inherent requirement of the job, and not a conscious effort to exclude women (or Asians, Hispanics, and other groups whose average height is shorter than that of Caucasians). Some women and minorities will meet that requirement, but many, because of average height differences between groups, will not. A policy of equality as sameness would lead to two unsatisfactory results: either failing to hire many women, or lowering the standards of gadget-assembly in order to assimilate women.

But a policy based on equality as acceptance offers other solutions. Perhaps the height of the conveyor belt could be modified. Perhaps a second, lower belt could be added for assembling other gadgets. Perhaps jobs could be established

at the plant that do not have height requirements. The resulting de facto sex segregation would be acceptable, says Littleton, "but *only* if the predominantly male and predominantly female jobs have equal pay, status, and opportunity for promotion into decisionmaking."[47] That "only" is the heart of it: Currently, most practices of de facto segregation are not separate and equal; the segregated group pays for it in lower status and opportunity to advance.

In short, equality as acceptance evaluates policies by directing attention to their results rather than their intentions. What is the result of a law that treats divorcing husbands and wives as if they were economically equal? What are the consequences for women of taking off a few years from the work force in order to care for children or elderly parents? What are the consequences for men, women, and families, if men do not get paternity leave? If the results are disastrous for women, as they now are, more equitable remedies must be sought. . . .

Consider again the situation at Mills College. Under an equality-as-sameness umbrella, the students of Mills must accept the admission of men to their college; if women want admission to male schools, they must allow men into theirs. An equality-as-acceptance perspective, however, leads to a different conclusion. Because of existing differences between the sexes in power, opportunities, and resulting self-confidence, on the average young women do better in their intellectual development when they have at least a few years to learn and study with one another than when they are in co-ed environments. In contrast, co-ed education is beneficial for males. However, when males are admitted to female colleges, the traditional patterns of male conversational dominance, in class and out of it, quickly return even when everyone tries to avoid them. In education, what's good for the gander isn't always so good for the goose.

Further, men's and women's single-sex institutions are not equal in the amount of power, prestige, and access to the establishment they provide; thus, the consequences of *not* being admitted to them differ for men and women. Men as a group will not suffer in any way by being excluded from Mills; but females (like minorities) have suffered by being excluded from most male institutions. This is why legal challenges to male-only institutions have had to establish that these institutions are not merely social clubs or private gatherings, but places where business is done, the business of America, the business that for so many years excluded outsiders. If Mills were the only school, say, of veterinary medicine in the United States, or if joining the elite alumnae of Mills represented the only access to the prestige career of, say, banking, then of course men must be admitted.

These considerations convince me that it is neither hypocritical nor necessary to support coeducation at Mills in the name of equality. Of course, I know that these young women will one day be working with men, and some may want to learn how to do that sooner rather than later. That is why they should have the opportunity to do so by going to co-ed schools. But, until males and females are equal in power and status—until, for example, men listen to women as often as women listen to men—there is a legitimate place for all-women schools if they give young women a stronger shot at achieving self-confidence, intellectual security, and professional competence in the workplace. . . .

Notes

1. T. Lang, *The Difference Between a Man and a Woman* (New York: The John Day Co., 1971), pp. 203–204.
2. Le Bon quoted in Gould, 1981, pp. 104–105.
3. Sperry, 1982.
4. Quoted in Gina Kolata, "Math Genius May Have Hormonal Basis," *Science,* 222 (December 23, 1983), p. 1312.
5. Ibid., p. 1312.
6. Smalley and Trent, p. 36.
7. Levy, 1983.
8. The discussion and critique of Geschwind and Behan, 1982, is from Bleier, 1988.
9. Ruth Bleier, "Sex Differences Research in the Neurosciences." Paper presented at the annual meeting of the American Association for the Advancement of Science, Chicago, 1987.
10. The study of the corpus callosum is from de Lacoste-Utamsing and Holloway, 1982.
11. Hyde and Linn, 1986, 1988. Males are more likely to have speech problems, such as stuttering, and to be referred for treatment for dyslexia—though not more likely to actually be dyslexic (see Shaywitz et al., 1990). See also Feingold (1988), who found that gender differences in SAT scores have "declined precipitously" in the last forty years. In 1950, school-age boys and girls differed markedly in verbal ability (girls excelled), abstract reasoning (boys excelled), and "clerical ability" (girls excelled). By 1980, boys had completely caught up with girls in verbal ability. Girls had completely caught up in verbal and abstract reasoning and numerical ability, and halved the difference in mechanical reasoning and space relations. The only exception to the rule of "vanishing gender differences," Feingold found, was the gender gap at the highest levels of math performance.
12. Hyde, Fennema, and Lamon, 1990.
13. Caplan, MacPherson, and Tobin, 1985. Researcher quoted on p. 786.
14. Kinsbourne, 1980, p. 242.
15. Fairweather quoted in Bleier, 1988, p. 154.
16. Fishman, 1983; Lakoff, 1990; McConnell-Ginet, 1983, 1984; Tannen, 1990 (esp. pp. 75–76).
17. McGlone, 1980, p. 226.
18. The story of Myra and Jim is from Mason, 1988, pp. 32–34.
19. Quoted in "News: Body/Mind," *Self,* February 1990, p. 64.
20. *The New York Times,* May 10, 1988, p. 27.
21. Quoted in Laqueur, 1987, p. 2.
22. Giacomini, Rozée-Koker, and Pepitone-Arreola-Rockwell, 1986. Quote, p. 418.
23. Perri Klass and Lila Wallis, "Macho Medicine," *Lear's,* October 1989, pp. 65, 67.
24. Margrit Eichler, Anna Lisa Reisman, and Elaine Borins, "Gender Bias in Medical Research." *Women and Therapy,* September 1992. Authors may be reached at Ontario Institute for Studies in Education. Toronto, Ontario, Canada.
25. Perri Klass, "Bearing a Child in Medical School," *The New York Times Magazine,* November 11, 1984, pp. 120–125.
26. Tobin et al., 1987; Khan et al., 1990.
27. Rosenberg, Palmer, and Shapiro, 1990. The researchers also found, by the way, no reduced risk

of heart attack in women who smoke low-nicotine cigarettes. "The estimated risks did not vary according to the nicotine or carbon monoxide yield of the cigarette," they concluded. (See Palmer, Rosenberg, and Shapiro, "'Low Yield' Cigarettes and the Risk of Nonfatal Myocardial Infarction in Women," *New England Journal of Medicine,* June 15, 1989.)

28. Quoted in Eisenstein, 1988, p. 218.
29. West, 1988, pp. 58–59.
30. Ibid., p. 60.
31. Littleton, 1987, p. 1282.
32. Quoted in Littleton, 1987, p. 1292.
33. Littleton, 1987, p. 1292.
34. Ibid., p. 1302.
35. Judicial Council of California, "Achieving Equal Justice for Women and Men in the Courts: The draft report of the Judicial Council Advisory Committee on gender bias in the courts." The report, which was released in March 1990, is available from the Judicial Council of California, San Francisco. So far twelve states have issued reports on gender bias in the legal system, and another dozen or so have studies in progress.
36. Rothman, 1989, p. 248.
37. Littleton, 1987, p. 1306.
38. Caroline Whitbeck originated the "flowerpot theory of pregnancy"—the view that men have the seeds and women provide the pot for them to grow in. Quoted in Rothman, 1989, p. 248.
39. Ibid., p. 21. On this issue, see also Corea, 1985.
40. Ibid., p. 107.
41. Littleton, 1987, p. 1304.
42. Dworkin, 1977, p. 227.
43. Littleton, 1987, p. 1337.
44. Mason, 1988, p. 45.
45. Ibid., p. 25.
46. Ibid., pp. 41–42.
47. Littleton, 1987, p. 1326.

BIBLIOGRAPHY

Bleier, Ruth (1988). Sex differences research: Science or belief? In R. Bleier (Ed.), *Feminist approaches to science.* New York: Pergamon.

Caplan, Paula J.; MacPherson, Gael M.; & Tobin, Patricia (1985). Do sex-related differences in spatial abilities exist? *American Psychologist,* 40, 786–799.

Corea, Genoveffa (1985). *The mother machine.* New York: Harper & Row.

de Lacoste-Utamsing, Christine, & Holloway, Ralph L. (1982). Sexual dimorphism in the human corpus callosum. *Science,* 216, 1431–1432.

Dworkin, Ronald (1977). *Taking rights seriously.* Cambridge, MA: Harvard University Press.

Eisenstein, Zillah R. (1988). *The female body and the law.* Berkeley, CA: University of California Press.

Feingold, Alan (1988). Cognitive gender differences are disappearing. *American Psychologist,* 43, 95–103.

Fishman, Pamela M. (1983). Interaction: The work women do. In B. Thorne, C. Kramarae, & N. Henley (Eds.), *Language, gender and society.* Rowley, MA: Newbury House.

Geschwind, Norman, & Behan, Peter (1982). Left-handedness: Association with immune disease, migraine, and developmental learning disorder. *Proceedings of the National Academy of Sciences,* 79, 5097–5100.

Giacomini, M.; Rozé-Koker, P.; & Pepitone-Arreola-Rockwell, F. (1986). Gender bias in human anatomy textbook illustrations. *Psychology of Women Quarterly,* 10, 413–420.

Gould, Stephen J. (1981). *The mismeasure of man.* New York: W. W. Norton & Co.

Hyde, Janet S.; Fennema, Elizabeth; & Lamon, Susan J. (1990). Gender differences in mathematics performance: A meta-analysis. *Psychological Bulletin,* 107, 139–155.

Hyde, Janet S., & Linn, Marcia C. (Eds.) (1986). *The psychology of gender: Advances through meta-analysis.* Baltimore, MD: Johns Hopkins University Press.

Khan, Steven S.; Nessim, Sharon; Gray, Richard; Czer, Lawrence S.; Chaux, Aurelio; & Matloff, Jack (1990). Increased mortality of women in coronary artery bypass surgery: Evidence for referral bias. *Annals of Internal Medicine,* 112, 561–567.

Kinsbourne, Marcel (1980). If sex differences in brain lateralization exist, they have yet to be discovered. *The Behavioral and Brain Sciences,* 3, 241–242.

Lakoff, Robin T. (1990). *Talking power: The politics of language.* New York: Basic Books.

Laqueur, Thomas (1987). Orgasm, generation, and the politics of reproductive biology. In C. Gallagher & T. Laqueur (Eds.), *The making of the modern body.* Berkeley, CA: University of California Press.

———— (1990). *Making sex: Body and gender from the Greeks to Freud.* Cambridge, MA: Harvard University Press.

Levy, Jerre (1983). Language, cognition, and the right hemisphere: A response to Gazzaniga. *American Psychologist, 38,* 538–541.

Littleton, Christine A. (1987). Reconstructing sexual equality. *California Law Review, 75,* 1279–1337.

Mason, Mary Ann (1988). *The equality trap.* New York: Touchstone.

McConnell-Ginet, Sally (1983). Intonation in a man's world. In B. Thorne, C. Kramarae, & N. Henley (Eds.), *Language, gender and society.* Rowley, MA: Newbury House.

———— (1984). The origins of sexist language in discourse. In S. J. White & V. Teller (Eds.), *Discourses in reading and linguistics (Annals of the New York Academy of Sciences, vol. 433).* New York: New York Academy of Sciences.

McGlone, Jeannette (1980). Sex differences in human brain asymmetry: A critical survey. *The Behavioral and Brain Sciences, 3,* 215–263.

Rosenberg, L.; Palmer, J. R.; & Shapiro, S. (1990, January 25). Decline in the risk of myocardial infarction among women who stop smoking. *New England Journal of Medicine, 322,* 213–217.

Rothman, Barbara K. (1989). *Recreating motherhood: Ideology and technology in a patriarchal society.* New York: W. W. Norton & Co.

Shaywitz, S. E.; Shaywitz, B. A.; Fletcher, J. M.; & Escobar, M. D. (1990, Aug. 22–29). Prevalence of reading disability in boys and girls. Results of the Connecticut Longitudinal Study. *Journal of the American Medical Association, 264,* 998–1002.

Smalley, Gary and John Trent (1988). *The Language of Love.* Pomona, Calif: Focus on the Family Publishing.

Sperry, Roger W. (1982). Some effects of disconnecting the cerebral hemispheres. *Science, 217,* 1223–1226.

Tannen, Deborah (1990). *You just don't understand.* New York: William Morrow.

Tobin, J. N.; Wassertheil-Smoller, S.; Wexler, J. P.; Steingart, R. M.; Budner, N.; Lense, L.; & Wachspress, J. (1987). Sex bias in considering coronary bypass surgery. *Annals of Internal Medicine, 107,* 19–25.

West, Robin (1988). Jurisprudence and gender. *The University of Chicago Law Review, 55,* 1–72.

Homosexuality

From Sin to Sickness to Life-Style

Peter Conrad and Joseph W. Schneider

MORAL FOUNDATIONS: THE SIN AGAINST NATURE

. . . It is, of course, too simple to claim that homosexual conduct has been always and everywhere despised and prohibited. At the same time, it is essentially accurate to argue that at least in the West, the overwhelming pattern has been one of disapproval if not condemnation (Bullough, 1976, 1977). This is true not only for same-sex conduct but for virtually all sexual behavior; indeed, Western culture has been called "sex negative" (Churchill, 1967).

Some historical evidence suggests that even before it became a sin, same-sex conduct was disapproved because it might interfere with fulfilling one's reproductive responsibility to the community. This included ensuring oneself of care during old age, continuing the family line, and the proper performance of ritual responsibilities (Bullough, 1976). In the Mesopotamian culture of the Tigris-Euphrates valley, dated about 3000 BC, anal intercourse was apparently common (involving both male-male and male-female partners). This tolerance, however, depended on such activities neither precluding progeny nor being exploitive.

The connection between heterosexual reproduction and species-community survival became a kind of practical standard against which other forms of sexual as well as nonsexual conduct might be judged. This biological premise for attitudes toward homosexuality (and other forms of nonprocreative sex) is one important foundation for the common reference to such behavior as "unnatural," with heterosexual, especially reproductive, sex being "natural." . . .

Ancient Origins: The Persians and Hebrews

By the time the Persians conquered the Egyptians and established their culture about the sixth century BC, negative attitudes toward nonprocreative sex outside marriage were common. The Persians, influenced by Zoroastrian religious doctrines, believed that although sexual activity should not be forbidden (eliminating vital progeny), it harbored great potential for social disruption if not carefully controlled and channeled toward "higher" virtues. Doctrines of divine preordination and prescription became superimposed on evolutionary arguments supporting heterosexual conduct as the norm. The Persians believed that male sperm or "seed" had particularly unique and wondrous generative powers (an idea that continued to influence thinking on sex for centuries). To "waste" or "spill" it voluntarily outside the nurturing body of a woman was repudiation of a divine gift. To do so in homosexual conduct was to mock both "Nature" and its creator. It was, in short, an abomination assuring damnation.

The Hebrews were by far the most influential of the ancient Middle Eastern peoples in shaping Western attitudes toward sex. They were a male-centered society (which was typical of that and subsequent historical periods). Women enjoyed perhaps certain marital (including sexual) and family prerogatives, but outside their roles as wives and mothers they received little attention. Marriage was expected of everyone who had reached puberty, and remarriage on the death of a spouse was assumed. Children, and especially males, were important assurance of social and religious continuity.

Sexual liaisons between women were regarded as considerably less significant than those involving men. Doctrines of male supremacy in procreation made what women might do together irrelevant to the reproductive potential of the community. This indifference toward female same-sex conduct is reflected not only in historical records of the ancients but for all societies. Although we speak of homosexual conduct in this chapter, both the historical and contemporary writing on homosexuality concentrates overwhelmingly on males. Regardless of the reasons, same-sex conduct among women simply has not engendered the same social reaction as similar conduct among men.* As long as women's behavior did not interfere with carrying, bearing, and rearing children, it received comparatively little attention.

Condemnation of such behavior among males, however, has been rarely ambiguous. Vern Bullough (1976, p. 82) locates the first specific biblical prohibition in Leviticus 18:22, dating probably from before the seventh century BC: "Thou shalt not lie with mankind, as with womankind: it is abomination"; and later: "If a man also lie with mankind, as he lieth with a woman, both of them have committed an abomination: they shall surely be put to death; and their blood shall be upon them" (Leviticus 21:13). This biblical prophecy was to be interpreted subsequently as a religious sanction for capital punishment and torture.

By far the most influential of all biblical stories used to condemn homosexual conduct is the Old Testament story of Sodom, from which comes the term "sodomy." According to Genesis 19:1–11, God vows to destroy Sodom and several other cities because of the sins of their inhabitants. Abraham pleads with God to spare the innocent who would perish unjustly. God sends two angels into Sodom to determine the true state of affairs. The angels (presumably male figures) are met by Abraham's nephew, Lot, who invites them to his house. During their stay, the men of the city assemble outside and call on Lot to present his guests to them so that they might "know them." Lot refuses but offers to present his daughters instead. The crowd, however, persists and is struck blind by the visiting angels. The next morning Lot and his fam-

---

*It is important to remember that those who made male same-sex conduct so important a transgression—a sin, a crime, and later a sickness—were themselves males. This dearth of information on lesbians has only recently begun to give way to popularly available works and public discussion of the topic.

ily are led from Sodom, after which God destroys it by fire.

The common interpretation is that the foremost sin of the Sodomites was homosexual conduct and that such behavior brings damnation and destruction both to those who pursue it and those who tolerate it. The irony of this interpretation is that the Sodom story contains no specific references to homosexual acts. Indeed, the sins for which the city was destroyed are specified as wickedness, inhospitality, pride, slothfulness, and "abomination"—interpreted most accurately as idolatry rather than same-sex conduct (Bailey, 1955, pp. 9–10). The linguistic justification for the homosexual interpretation turns on the two meanings of the Hebrew word *yadha* (to know). Beyond its conventional usage, meaning to become acquainted with, the word also can be used to mean "to have sexual knowledge of" or sexual relations with. Presuming that both the angels and those outside Lot's house were males, selecting the latter usage implies that the Sodomites were interested in homosexual acts. Such an interpretation, however, would have to be chosen *against* the conventional and more likely one. Given the historic popularity of the homosexual interpretation, it is important to speculate on its source.

Biblical scholar Derrick Bailey (1955, pp. 9–28) and historian Vern Bullough (1976, pp. 82–85) review the historical record carefully and conclude that such interpretation was added by the ancient Hebrews some considerable time after the original story was written, probably some time around the first century AD. The story, as elaborated and used by the Jews of this period, may be in large part a reaction against the rise of paganism and Greek culture. Bailey (1955) argues that Sodom became a "symbol for every wickedness which offended the devout Jewish spirit—pride, inhospitality, adultery, forgetfulness of God and ingratitude for his blessings" (p. 27). As the ancient Hebrews felt more threatened by the expansion of Greek culture, the content of this symbol changed to reflect that which they found most heinous in the Hellenic world. The homo-

sexual interpretation has become so entrenched that it is accepted uncritically not only by Christians and Jews but also by generations of historians, philosophers, and scholars. It has become, in effect, part of the revealed wisdom of the West, providing an almost unimpeachable condemnation of same-sex conduct.

Contributions of the Greeks

The actual prevalence of homosexual conduct in ancient Greece is impossible to determine, the distinction between Greek values and practice forever obscure. There is, however, evidence sufficient to conclude that certain forms of such behavior were institutionalized firmly in Greek culture and practice, and to speculate with some confidence that certain kinds of same-sex liaisons between males were common, particularly between the eighth and second centuries BC (Dover, 1978). This acceptance derived from two cultural ideals: male superiority and an ideal of love that was believed to uplift the human spirit and strengthen community solidarity. To the extent that practice approximated these ideals, the Greeks believed such sexual conduct was neither unnatural nor bad. . . .

This distinction between "natural" and "unnatural" homosexual conduct became irrelevant in Rome. Indeed, the rarefied spiritual and philosophical distinctions that supported Greek pederasty were lost on the Romans, for they regarded such conduct as a shameful aspect of Greek life . . . Although Roman fighting units were pervaded by a strong sense of companionship and loyalty, this did not include intimate fraternization. Homosexual conduct between both men and women probably occurred, but the Romans either gave official and legal disapproval or chose to ignore it. Their sexual ideal was staunchly heterosexual.

FROM SIN TO CRIME: EARLY CHRISTIANITY AND THE MIDDLE AGES

By the time Roman influence began to wane, a new asceticism was being reflected in a variety of religious and civil prohibitions. In the ensuing centuries of the Middle Ages the "naturalness" of heterosexual reproductive sex within marriage was reaffirmed with a vengeance. At the hands of clerics such as the fifth-century figure St. Augustine, Western Christianity defined sex of any sort as base at best. The "goodness" of marital sex was contingent on conception—the promise of progeny redeeming an essentially lustful act. "Unnatural" sexual urges were clearly beyond the bounds of membership in the official Christian community—even though actual practice and this ideal, from Rome to 16th-century England, were rarely aligned.

Christian fathers and sympathetic rulers often cited homosexual conduct throughout this period as posing a serious threat to community welfare. Harsh prohibitions and formal civil penalties for the guilty resulted. Celibacy and chastity, particularly in Western Europe, became the ideal and most spiritually pure state. This remained largely unchallenged until Martin Luther's 16th-century reforms held out heterosexual marriage as an even greater good. It was this general cultural prescription of asceticism, control, and the denial of pleasure that became the centerpiece of developing Christianity and particularly its Western Catholic and Protestant forms. . . .

. . . Given St. Augustine's narrow definition of natural sex, the "sin against nature" variously included anal intercourse, masturbation, bestiality (sex with animals), mouth-genital contact involving either sex, and even heterosexual intercourse in positions other than face-to-face with the man on top. St. Thomas Aquinas attempted to clarify this somewhat in the 13th century. He insisted that a distinction was necessary between same-sex and cross-sex sins. In effect, Aquinas argued that homosexual "unnatural" sex was more heinous than heterosexual "unnatural" sex, such as fornication and adultery (Bullough, 1976, pp. 380–381). These confusions about the precise nature and moral seriousness of "unnatural" sex during the medieval period were enshrined in what came to be known as canon, or Church, law.

This separate system of rules and punishments emerges from the penitential writings of English and Welsh clerics about the sixth century. These penitentials were practical manuals by which clergy-confessors could determine proper penance for people's sins. Explicit attention was given to sexual transgressions. Such writings offer insight into how the early Western Church judged homosexual acts. Interestingly, although there is great variety in seriousness and penance, there is little distinction made between so-called natural and unnatural sexual sins. Fornication and adultery (and other heterosexual sins) and sodomy, including fellatio, kissing, and interfemoral intercourse, were often regarded as of roughly equal seriousness (Bailey, 1955, pp. 100–110). In short, canon law incorporated a good deal of ambiguity not only about the moral seriousness of such conduct but indeed about what such conduct actually entailed.

This confusion was later translated into civil statutes when the vague "sin against nature" became the equally vague but more consequential "crime against nature." This developing criminalization of same-sex conduct throughout the medieval period culminated in the 1533 English statute, enacted under the reign of Henry VIII, making the "crime against nature" a capital offense. It was through this statute, along with its subsequent versions, that the moral condemnation of such behavior common in the Middle Ages came to exert such an important influence on Western social and legal definitions (Gigeroff, 1968, pp. 1–7).

Church punishments, however, were directed toward spiritual renewal rather than corporal sanctions. Variously long periods of atonement including prayer, self-imposed isolation, special diet, and introspection were common. The ultimate punishment was excommunication, banishing the nonrepentant sinner to eternal damnation. There is apparently no evidence that the medieval Church ever executed anyone for anything—including homosexual acts. What did happen, and particularly during the 11th and 12th centuries, is that the accused would be tried by the ecclesiastical court and, if found guilty, turned over to the state for proper secular punishment. . . .

NEW MORAL CONSENSUS: SIN BECOMES SICKNESS

Medicine and Moral Continuity in the 18th Century

The Enlightenment affected sexual attitudes and behavior in important ways. Increasingly the Church had to contend with secular authority; a growing popular interest in sex and sexuality is evidenced in literary and pornographic materials and more specifically in the numerous and highly popular sex manuals available, most notably those bearing the name of the great philosopher, Aristotle*; there was probably also an increase in the incidence of variant sexual practice, although it remained largely covert, and systematic documentation is impossible. London and Paris sported brothels supplying homosexual favors for pay (Bullough, 1976, p. 480). This tolerance toward sexual variety even received the official sanction of the French government under Napoleon in the famed but short-lived 1810 criminal statutes bearing his name. The Napoleonic Code decriminalized homosexual conduct between consenting adults in private.

We must not, however, overstate the scope of Enlightenment tolerance or the extent to which traditional moral principles—particularly regarding sex—were swept aside. This new beacon of tolerance on the continent was only a faint glimmer in England. English thought and laws on deviant sexual conduct—those most influential in America—continued until the latter half of the 19th century to define homosexual acts as inherently detestable crimes punishable, at least in principle, by death. Sexual "excess"—indeed, excess of any sort—was soundly disapproved as

beyond reason and order. The particular forms of sexual behavior that came to be defined as excessive were inevitably those which had been morally disapproved. . . .

The new theories of health and illness that emerged in the 18th century made this distrust of moral excess their scientific centerpiece. Early in that century and throughout the next, a handful of physicians and their popularizers promoted conceptions of health and illness that viewed the body as a closed system of vital nervous energy. Health was defined vaguely in terms of nervous system stability, balance, and equilibrium, which, in turn, were thought to be products of the individual's integration with (read "conformity to") the larger moral and social environment. To the extent that one's activities in the latter realm were "healthy," that is, morally proper, internal physiological and nervous system function would follow accordingly. Conversely, activities that made repeated, unusual, and "unhealthy" (immoral) demands on one's body would lead inevitably to its depletion, debility, wasting, and disease (Rosenberg, 1977). Thus immorality, as evidenced by social behavior, was believed causal of sickness and disease.

Sexual behavior became immediately a focus for such explanation. As had been clear for centuries, sexual orgasm expends energy and is followed by a period that might be described as mild fatigue. These observations, coupled with the new medical theories, yielded the conclusion that too much sexual activity, and particularly deviant sexual activity, could be detrimental to one's health (see Graham, 1834/1837. p. 49).

Proponents of these theories were not, of course, prepared to prescribe abstinence. Arguments that sex was a natural part of life had become too firmly entrenched. In addition, some medical theories warned that retention of "seed" in the male could itself be harmful to health. The solution was to recommend a course of careful moderation. This reflected clearly the traditional moral heritage of Christianity. Procreative sex, judiciously pursued, was somehow believed to be less debilitating to one's nerves than sex for its own sake. It followed that those forms of sexual

---

*Otho Beall (1963) has analyzed these enormously popular works and concludes that virtually none of them were faithful either in letter or spirit to Aristotle's work. Although his name lent them credibility and moral legitimacy, Beall concludes they were clearly products of 17th-century thought.

activity which had been and continued to be sins—including homosexual conduct—were even more threatening.

Sexual activity, and most particularly deviant sex, became medicalized precisely at the time in history when religious prohibitions were becoming less dominant. Medicine, although only beginning to emerge as an efficacious technology, became a new system of social control for sexual behavior (Bullough, 1976; Bullough & Bullough, 1977; Comfort, 1967; Haller & Haller, 1974; Smith-Rosenberg, 1978). . . .

Masturbation and Threatened Manhood: A Crusade in Defense of Moral Health

The rallying point for this medicalization of variant sexual activity in the 18th and particularly 19th centuries was masturbation, variously called "onanism" (after the biblical story of the sin of Onan), the "solitary vice," "secret sin," "self-pollution," and "self-abuse." Throughout this period, and particularly during the Victorian era in America, masturbation was defined by both medical and popular writers as a major cause of physical and particularly mental illness. One especially threatening consequence was feared to be a "morbid interest" in others of one's own sex. These claims against masturbation became so foreboding and consensual among the rising middle class that today's historians of sexuality have named the period the "age of masturbatory insanity" (Bullough, 1976; Comfort, 1967; Englehardt, 1974).

By the middle of the 19th century, middle-class champions of purity and the Christian life (Pivar, 1973) began organizing a crusade to save the youth of America from the physical and moral consequences of improper sexual activities; a prime focus of these guardians of social and political stability was the male youth, the "hope for tomorrow." Although homosexual conduct was mentioned only rarely, its existence and alleged link to masturbation and sexual excess were used to nurture a widespread fear that the one indulgence would lead inevitably to the other.

The warriors in this battle consisted mainly of middle-aged, middle-class medical men and popular medical writers of the mid-19th century (Smith-Rosenberg, 1978). Their audience was the postpubescent-to-young adult male of the middle class, as the titles of some of these works attest: *The Young Man's Guide* (Alcott, 1833), *Lectures to Young Men on Chastity* (Graham, 1834/1837), and *Hints to Young Men on the True Relations of the Sexes* (Ware, 1850/1879). An important theme in this writing was that masturbation could easily lead to homosexual experimentation and subsequent involvement. . . .

CONSOLIDATING THE MEDICAL MODEL: THE INVENTION OF HOMOSEXUALITY

Hereditary Predisposition

By the turn of the century the idea that "immoral" behavior might make people sick was losing support among both popular and medical audiences. Subsequent research on the physiology of human sexuality has, of course, undermined these notions completely.* As physicians turned away from masturbation as the primary cause of sexual deviance, they turned increasingly toward the principles of heredity and evolution. These ideas had gained wide currency among the American middle and upper classes of the latter 19th century in the form of social Darwinism. Physicians who addressed the "problem" of same-sex conduct proposed that it was the product of a hereditary predisposition, "taint," or congenital "degeneration" in the central nervous system. Sexual deviance was somehow produced by the operation of physiological mechanisms largely impervious to environmental influence, although masturbation, reading "dirty books," and association with those already accustomed to such practices were still thought unwise, if not dangerous, to

---

*William Masters and Virginia Johnson (1966, p. 210), in their pathbreaking research on human sexuality, however, report that a significant number of men expressed concern about the possibility that excessive masturbation might affect their mental functioning. Twenty-six percent of a 1970 United States sample of adults said they believed masturbation was "wrong" (Levitt & Klassen, 1974, p. 30).

one's sexual normality. Even in cases where such behavior appeared to be acquired, it was explained commonly as due to the hereditary weakness of the individuals in question; they did not have the constitutional stamina sufficient to withstand environmental pressures. . . .

Criminalization and Medicalization

The late 19th century was also a time of renewed criminalization of same-sex conduct in Germany, England, and the United States. In the late 1860s in Germany, the Second Reich proposed a considerably more harsh penal code against men found guilty of mutual sexual activity. This particular section of the code was called "Paragraph 175" (Lauritsen & Thorstad, 1974). When sodomy was removed from the list of capital offenses in England in 1861, prosecutions of same-sex conduct increased. With less harsh penalties, convictions were more common (Bullough, 1976, p. 569). . . .

The simultaneous medicalization and criminalization of same-sex conduct may appear contradictory; we suggest that these two historical processes represent the rise to dominance of different institutions of social control. It is important, however, to remember that religion, law, and medicine are all systems of morality. The rise of one in any particular historical period is not necessarily accompanied by the decline of another. In fact, as the preceding discussions attest, they are commonly superimposed on and concurrent with one another.

Such is the case with same-sex conduct. In fact, the rise of legal-criminal definitions toward the end of the 19th century may well have stimulated medicalization. The logic of this argument derives from the therapeutic alternative that medical definitions and interventions represent over more punitive, legal mechanisms of control. As same-sex conduct was attributed to biological-genetic roots, blame was lifted from the actors' wills and relocated in their biology and heredity. The concept of free choice and its attendant responsibility was believed applicable only in persons whose wills were healthy and mature. If same-sex conduct were the consequence of hereditary or congenital degeneration, such persons became less likely candidates, as Kittrie (1971) has argued, for criminalization.

In the face of movements toward increased prosecution and arrest in late 19th-century England and America, medical definitions and interventions offered a particularly viable intellectual and philosophical alternative. It is probable that this criminalization, given the growing promise of medicine, produced a strong supportive climate for medicalization of same-sex conduct.* Indeed, it appears that it was precisely at this time that homosexuality as a medical diagnosis began to emerge.

Homosexuality as a Medical Pathology

The term "homosexuality" was invented in 1869 by Hungarian physician K. M. Benkert, who wrote (presumably for his own protection) under the pseudonym of Kertbeny (Lauritsen & Thorstad, 1974). He argued against the growing legal repression of same-sex conduct and the harsh punishments contained in the Prussian legal code, Paragraph 175. Such treatment, he insisted, was both unjust and ineffective inasmuch as homosexuality was congenital rather than acquired. . . .

In the same year, Berlin psychiatrist Karl von Westphal published a case history of a young woman he examined in a local asylum. The woman reported a fondness for boys' games when growing up, liked to dress as a boy, pro-

---

*We speculate that this was particularly true for male homosexual conduct. It appears that the late 19th- and early 20th-century repressive laws against such behavior were aimed primarily, if not exclusively, at men rather than women. This may well have contributed to a greater medical interest in and subsequent medicalization of such conduct among men. American physicians at the turn of the century were perhaps primed to concentrate on problems of male rather than female sexuality, given the crusade against male masturbation. Virtually all those charged under the new laws were males. Physicians may simply have assumed that men were most commonly afflicted with this condition. Finally, those "criminals" which physicians defended as "patients" were in fact men.

fessed strong physical and emotional attractions for certain other women, and said that she had been successful in realizing these desires on a number of occasions. She indicated virtually no sexual interest in men. The patient expressed anxiety and sorrow over this condition and "wished to be free of it." Westphal reported that the woman appeared to be a physically normal female, evidenced no delusions or hallucinations, and displayed no notable peculiarities other than her sexual desires and activities (Shaw, J. C., & Ferris, 1883). He concluded that the problem was congenital, did not necessarily indicate insanity, and should not be considered a vice, since it was not a consciously chosen preference. He called the condition "contrary sexual feelings." Westphal's treatment of this case is important in that it gave a certain degree of medical legitimacy to the topic. Several similar cases were contributed to European medical literature over the next decade.

In 1883 American physicians J. C. Shaw and G. N. Ferris published an important article in *The Journal of Nervous and Mental Disease* entitled "Perverted Sexual Instinct." Shaw and Ferris, stimulated by a patient who had come to the former for help, reviewed all the published medical cases of this condition they could find. Most of these were in German or French, and their review introduced to their American colleagues an area of medical study neither common nor understood widely in this country. The moral tone of the review is decidedly more neutral than the earlier medical writings on masturbation, but there is no doubt that the authors considered the condition undesirable, describing it as "a most interesting pathological sexual phenomenon" typified by "abnormal desires."

The most important physician-psychiatrist whose cases Shaw and Ferris discussed is the late 19th-century German student of deviant sexuality, Richard von Krafft-Ebing. More than any other physician of the period, Krafft-Ebing established same-sex conduct and the mental states from which it was presumed to flow as a physiologically based psychiatric pathology. His most influential work, *Psychopathia Sexualis,* was pub-

lished first in 1886 and contained many case histories of various "sexual abnormalities." Written primarily for his medical colleagues, the work enjoyed an enormous success and ran into many printings and editions. Each successive edition seemed to include more case histories of sexual pathology collected from associates, his own practice, and police and court records. By the 11th edition, published in 1894, they numbered over 200 in all (Bullough, 1977). Krafft-Ebing's book became the definitive source of descriptive material on sexual variety and may well continue to be "the most comprehensive collection of case histories of sexual deviation available" (Van Den Haag, 1965, p. 12). A gauge of this popularity with medical and subsequently lay audiences (much to the author's chagrin) is that it is still in print today.

Krafft-Ebing has been called a pivotal and transitional figure between 19th- and 20th-century medical study of sexuality (Bullough, 1976; Robinson, P., 1976). The 19th-century face of his work is seen in his allegiance to a Victorian moral code that defined heterosexual procreative sex as a standard. Sexual acts and intimate emotional attachments between members of the same sex were considered unequivocally abnormal in Krafft-Ebing's work. In addition, although he gave greatest causal emphasis to a "hereditary taint," a congenital weakness of the nervous system, he agreed that repeated masturbation and sexual excesses of various types could excite or precipitate this condition. In all cases of "sexual inversion," however, physicians were instructed to presume the existence of a constitutional susceptibility. Krafft-Ebing regarded sex as the most powerful and potentially devastating force with which human beings had to cope; to overcome the desires of sexual lust required a vigilant fight.

At the same time, however, he previsions a 20th-century approach to variant sexuality in his willingness to address it openly and directly. This was not, as we have noted, common at the first publication of *Psychopathia Sexualis,* and some of his medical colleagues chided him for what they considered unnecessary frankness on such morally detestable practices (Bullough, 1976, p. 643). He brought attention to what had been up to then, at least in the West, a submerged and dark corner of human experience. Aside from whether he approved or disapproved of such behaviors (and he did disapprove), his work effectively broke this Western, Christian, and middle-class conspiracy of silence about unconventional sexual behavior. At minimum, he enlightened both medical and lay audiences to the incredible variety of sexual expression of which human beings are capable. Having done so, there was no denying this diversity; thereafter it had at least to be recognized.

He is also a specifically pivotal figure in the medicalization of homosexuality. In the face of late 19th-century criminalization of variant sexual practices, physicians (e.g., Benkert and, more significantly, Krafft-Ebing) were called on often to give expert testimony. The latter testified that homosexuals could not change the direction or the expression of their sexual desires and that such persons were sick and therefore should be treated therapeutically rather than punitively. He called not for sympathy but understanding. Finally, Krafft-Ebing's case histories and analyses contributed to the emergence of homosexuality as a medical entity and the homosexual as a distinctive kind of person. . . .

RISE OF THE PSYCHIATRIC PERSPECTIVE

Contribution of Freud

Freud embedded his discussion of homosexuality in a more general theory of psychosexual development that eschewed both biological and environmental determinism—the two common explanatory contenders to that date. He argued that adult sexuality was a complex product of the dynamic tension between physiological sexual desires—the "libido," or sexual appetite—on the one hand and social and cultural prescriptions and proscriptions on the other. A distinctive feature of Freud's theory was that the most crucial period for adult sexuality was childhood. All people

were believed born with a "polymorphous perverse" sexual capacity that included the potential for stimulation by and attraction to same-sex others. Indeed, Freud posited that as children we all pass through a stage of sexual "latency" during which these homoerotic desires and attachments are perfectly normal yet largely covert. He characterized such sexuality as "infantile." As children pass through puberty, however, they typically transfer their sexual attentions to peers of the opposite sex and thereafter pursue the goal of heterosexual reproductive sexuality. This was "mature" and "complete" sexual development in the Freudian scheme. It was not, however, the product of any predisposition other than that imposed by cultural rules and socialization. Such cultural influences were usually effective in "making" heterosexuals, but Freud argued that all "normal" adults retained the "latent" remnants of their homosexual desire. These were "repressed" into the unconscious mind from which they were then expressed in "sublimated" or disguised forms consistent with conventional sexual standards (e.g., same-sex "best friends," poker clubs, sports).

Homosexual adults were described as persons who had not fully completed this sexual development or who had "regressed" to an immature stage. They were depicted as casualties of the various "complexes" and conflicts typical of the Freudian childhood. Among the most important of these is the Oedipus complex wherein children, during puberty, must manage socially prohibited and threatening incestuous desires for opposite-sex parents. Difficulties in relationships with one or both parents almost always assume great importance in Freudian discussions of homosexual conduct. Whereas the sexually mature adult weathers these traumas on the way to heterosexuality, the homosexual's attention to same-sex others represents an inappropriate and immature solution to such crises. Although clearly undesirable, homosexuality under Freud became intimately linked with the sexually "normal."

As part of his criticism of past congenital explanations, Freud attempted to counter the negative image of homosexuals conveyed by the notion of "hereditary degeneration." He insisted that

> inversion is found in people who otherwise show no marked deviation from the normal. It is found also in people whose mental capacities are not disturbed, who on the contrary are distinguished by especially high intellectual development and ethical culture (Freud, 1905/1938, p. 556)*

Neither was homosexuality a monolith; homosexuals were not all alike. There were, for example, the "absolutely inverted" (exclusively homosexual in feelings and action), those whose sexual object choice could be either male or female (the "psychosexually hermaphroditic"), and the "occasionally inverted," who engaged in same-sex conduct because of environmental isolation or limited access to cross-sex others (those we might call "situational homosexuals"). Freud reported that inverts' feelings about their "condition" ranged from matter-of-fact defense and demands for equal treatment to a consuming struggle against what was seen as a "morbid compulsion."

Linked closely to the proposition of "polymorphus perverse" sexuality was Freud's idea of a universal biological predisposition to bisexuality. He believed that people were not simply "masculine" or "feminine," but that *both* men and women displayed such qualities and characteristics:

> there is no pure masculinity or femininity either in the biological or psychological sense. On the contrary, every individual person shows a mixture of his own biological sex characteristics with the biological traits of the other sex and a union of activity and passivity; this is the case whether these psychological characteristic features depend on biological elements or whether they are independent of them. (Freud, 1905/1938, p. 613)

This confounded further the traditional simplicity that depicted "normal" heterosexuality as clearly distinct from "sick" homosexuality. If the sub-

jects and objects of sexual attraction were themselves blurred, how could one be sure which behaviors and feelings were normal and which perverse? Indeed, the very notion that there were physical and psychological dimensions of sexuality that could be distinct and contrary opened up an entirely new realm of study and debate.*

In 1935, Freud unwittingly made one of his most famous statements on the nature of homosexuality. In a letter to a mother who had written to him regarding her son, Freud (1935/1960) summarized the major themes in his writing on the subject:

> I gather from your letter that your son is a homosexual. I am more impressed by the fact that you do not mention this term yourself in your information about him. May I question you, why you avoid it? *Homosexuality is assuredly no advantage but it is nothing to be ashamed of, no vice, no degradation, it cannot be classified as an illness;* we consider it to be a variation of the sexual function produced by a certain arrest of sexual development. Many highly respectable individuals of ancient and modern times have been homosexuals, several of the greatest men among them. . . . It is a great injustice to persecute homosexuality as a crime and cruelty too. . . . (pp. 423–424, emphasis added)

We must reiterate. Freud here argues that homosexuality is a *variation* rather than a deviation; it is not something particularly "bad" but rather something that is merely "different." One would search long for such an unequivocally nonjudgmental statement on this topic among physicians before, during, or after Freud.[†] . . .

---

*Robert Stoller (1968) suggests that Freud's distinction between biological and psychic sexuality represents the origins of the idea of gender as distinct from sex as a physiological condition. Although this idea existed prior to Freud's specification of it, the location of homosexuality as primarily a problem of gender identity rather than genetic or physiological predisposition became the official psychiatric as well as popular position in subsequent decades.

[†]The paradoxical nature of Freud's ideas on homosexuality are evident, however, by Stephen Mitchell (1978). He asserts that the concept of pathology is itself inherent in the very theory and therapy that Freud proposed: psychoanalysis.

---

*Quotation from Freud (1905/1938) reprinted by permission of Gioia Bernheim and Edmund Brill.

Most influential in supporting the pathology-treatment definition of homosexuality have been practicing clinical psychiatrists who have adopted various psychodynamic versions of the Freudian scheme. Charles Socarides was among the most influential American advocate. . . .

Charles Socarides. An important psychoanalytic advocate of the disease view of homosexuality at midcentury is Charles Socarides. A student of homosexuality and other "perversions" for more than two decades, Socarides began publishing professional discussions of the former in the early 1960s. He was instrumental in initiating discussion of homosexuality in 1958 at the first panel held on the topic by the American Psychoanalytic Association and subsequently was a major participant in various interdisciplinary and medical study groups on homosexuality that supported the disease view (New York Academy of Medicine, 1964; Socarides et al., 1973). He subsequently became one of the staunchest defenders of the definition of homosexuality as a serious medical pathology and, along with Bieber, the premier medical "expert" on this topic.* . . .

In 1970 Socarides published an article titled "Homosexuality and Medicine" in *The Journal of the American Medical Association.* He challenges what he and others perceive as a spreading and grievous misperception of homosexuality on the part of some in the medical profession, certain lay groups defending the "normality" of the condition, and many homosexuals themselves. It is a call to action and a defense of expert medical authority. He begins by asserting that homosexuality is publicly abhorrent and that "the majority of the public" favors legal punishment for such

conduct, even if private.[†] At the core of the confusion about homosexuality is the fact that some have lost sight, or refuse to recognize, that it is first and foremost a "medical problem." In unmistakably turf-defending remarks, Socarides[‡] (1970) writes: "Only in the consultation room does the homosexual reveal himself and his world. No other data, statistics, or statements can be accepted as setting forth the true nature of homosexuality" (p. 1199). The well-meaning but "unqualified" defender of homosexual normality is "misguided" because of the absence of clinically trained medical insight necessary to "discern the deep underlying . . . disorder" homosexuality represents. Rather than their being subjected to harsh punishments based on a moral-criminal model, Socarides insists such true homosexuals be helped by medical treatment. Although he supports decriminalization, Socarides believes that without simultaneous medicalization such measures are dangerous. Such legislation should always include unequivocal statements that homosexuality is an emotional illness that "may cause such grave disruption to the . . . individual that all meaningful relationships in life are damaged from the outset and peculiarly susceptible to breakdown and destruction" (1970, p. 1201). . . .

A final piece of evidence for the dominant status of the pathology definition of homosexuality comes from the official classification of psychiatric disorders of The American Psychiatric Association, its *Diagnostic and Statistical Manual of Mental Disorders* (DSM), and its parent document, the World Health Organization's *Interna-*

---

*Dr. Socarides has asked that, in conjunction with our discussion of his work, we point out that, to quote his correspondence, he has "never been against the decriminalization of homosexual acts occurring between consenting adults" and that he "was in the vanguard of promoting this, even before 'gay rights' became an issue in this country." He cites the 1973 Task Force Report of the New York County District Branch, American Psychiatric Association (Socarides et al., 1973) as a reference.

*The sense in which any such therapy for homosexuality is "voluntary" is of course clouded considerably by the widely negative cultural definitions that attach to such conduct and persons. The choice here is rather clearly not free of strong predisposition in favor of treatment.

[†]A 1970 survey of the United States adult population found that approximately 59% of the representative sample thought that "homosexuality is a social corruption that can cause the downfall of a civilization" (Levitt & Klassen, 1974, p. 34).

[‡]Quotation from Socarides from *J.A.M.A.* 1970. 1, 1199–1202. Copyright 1970. American Medical Association.

tional Classification of Disease (ICD). These manuals, and particularly the former, represent the professionally approved diagnostic labels for virtually all mental disorders with which American psychiatrists are concerned. It is, so to speak, the "blue book" of mental illness and not only serves for statistical and operational classification but also provides the official list of what is and what is not considered a psychiatric condition. By reviewing the place of homosexuality in this manual, we can determine the extent of professional organizational support for the notion that it is a bona fide mental illness.

The first edition of DSM was published by The American Psychiatric Association in 1952 and was patterned after ICD-6, the sixth edition of the *International Classification*. This and subsequent editions are the work of a special committee within the association called the Committee on Nomenclature and Statistics. In DSM-1 the diagnostic label "homosexuality" is identified as one of several forms of "sexual deviation" and falls under the more general psychiatric category "Sociopathic Personality Disturbance." The more clinically distinct and medically significant conditions are assigned individual numbers according to a systematic scheme. In DSM-1, homosexuality was one of many unnumbered conditions under this larger sociopathic umbrella.

The second edition of DSM was published in 1968 and is a reflection of ICD-8. In DSM-11, homosexuality assumed new significance as a medical pathology. Under the major category "Personality Disorders and Certain Other Non-Psychotic Mental Disorders" (301–304), and specifically under "Sexual Deviation" (302), we find "Homosexuality" (302.0) (American Psychiatric Association, 1968, p. 10). In a section of the manual on definitions of terms, no specific definition of homosexuality is offered beyond that for "sexual deviations": "This category [302] is for individuals whose sexual interests are directed primarily toward objects other than people of the opposite sex. . . . It is not appropriate for individuals who perform deviant sexual acts because normal sexual objects are not available to

them" (American Psychiatric Association, 1968, p. 44). This reaffirms the important distinction in the psychoanalytic literature between "true" homosexuals and homosexuality and those who, for a variety of "normal" reasons, engage in homosexual conduct. According to both DSM-1 and DSM-11, as well as the manuals of the World Health Organization, homosexuality is a mental disorder, a psychopathology. A 1970 survey of public attitudes toward homosexuality found that about 62% of American adults agreed, calling it a "sickness that can be cured" (Levitt & Klassen, 1974).

DEMEDICALIZATION: THE CONTINUING HISTORY OF A CHALLENGE

. . . In about 100 years' time, from the closing decades of the last century in Germany to the early 1970s in the United States, we have witnessed this growing (although not linear) attack on negative definitions of homosexual conduct and preference. The church and state both have been arenas for such challenges. In the latter half of the 20th century, medicine remained not only steadfastly opposed to "normalization" but in fact, as we have shown, advocated an even stronger sickness view. It is not surprising, then, to find psychiatry as the prime target of such attacks. As we will show, the most successful battle was fought in 1973–1974, but the war had been declared a century before. These first salvos, however, could hardly be considered grave, since they came from a friendly source: other physicians.

The Armor of Pioneering Defense: "Nature," Knowledge, and Medicine

The earliest physician-proponent of the view that homosexuality was not pathological was the Hungarian Benkert, whom we identified earlier as the inventor of the term "homosexuality." He spoke out publicly as early as 1869 against the growing Prussian repression of males found guilty of homosexual acts. In an open letter to state jurists, he criticized imprisonment and fines for such persons as not only a contradiction of the most basic principles of human justice but scientific knowledge as well. He named a long list of important historical figures who were homosexuals as evidence of its nonpathological nature (Lauritsen & Thorstad, 1974).

An important nonphysician advocate of this congenital-variation argument was German jurist Karl Heinrich Ulrichs, himself a homosexual, who authored a wide range of polemical, analytic, and theoretical discussions on the topic for over a decade beginning in 1864. Most significantly, he proposed a congenital theory that homosexuals, or "Urnings" as he called them, were persons whose physical sex simply did not correspond with their own sexual instinct. Urnings were men who had a "feminine soul enclosed in a male body"; later medical writers adapted this to a "female brain in a male body." They were a "third sex" midway between males and females. Ulrichs insisted that the condition was not pathological and that legal repression was both unfair and irrational (Bullough, 1976; Symonds, 1931). His ideas were widely influential in medical circles, and many physicians (e.g., Krafft-Ebing) cited his work.

The most consequential medical defender of the period was German physician Magnus Hirschfeld. Hirschfeld (1936b, p. 318) theorized that the "sexual urge, normal and abnormal, is the result of a certain inborn goal-striving constitution, influenced by the glands of secretion." He reiterated Ulrich's notion that homosexuals were "sexual intermediates." Like Benkert and Ulrichs before him, Hirschfeld vigorously opposed legal and moral persecution of homosexuals and argued that the cool wisdom of science be used to direct a more just and socially useful policy. He often testified in trials involving sex crimes and is credited with "saving" many from prison and even death. Hirschfeld founded what might be called the first homosexual civil rights organization in 1897, the Scientific Humanitarian Committee. This body, whose motto was "Justice through Science," published an annual *Yearbook for Intermediate Sexual Types* that contained a wide variety of information about homosexuality and other forms of variant sex. The committee's goals were (1) to influence legislatures to repeal the repressive Paragraph 175 of the German Penal Code; (2) public education about homosexuality; and (3) "interesting the homosexual himself in the struggle for his rights" (Lauritsen & Thorstad, 1974, p. 11). Aside from his reputation as a scientist, Hirschfeld—and the committee itself— was known widely as devoted to political action. The most vigorous example was a 25-year campaign that gained wide medical and popular support to repeal Paragraph 175. Signed by more than 6000 leading figures of the day, it was finally presented to the Reichstag in 1922, from where it never emerged. The rise of Nazism in Germany signaled an even greater repression, and the movement for homosexual normalization was brought to a standstill during this period.

Hirschfeld put great stock in the assumption that knowledge was the key to progressive and humane attitudes toward homosexuals and sexuality in general. He conducted what was the first nonclinical study of sexual attitudes and practices in which he sent questionnaires to over 10,000 men and women (Hirschfeld, 1936b, p. 318). The diversity of the responses convinced him even more firmly that the metaphors of sickness and pathology were, more often than not, inappropriate descriptions of sexually variant behavior and caused him to question whether, indeed, there was even something that could be defined unequivocally as sexually "normal." Hirschfeld founded the Institute for Sexual Science in Berlin in 1918, which, until it was destroyed by the Nazis in 1933, was a world center for information and study of sex.

All Hirschfeld's colleagues in the Scientific Humanitarian Committee did not agree with his etiological theory of homosexuality. One of the most vocal critics, Benedict Friedländer, established a splinter group in 1907 called The Community of the Special. Friedländer rejected Hirschfeld's theory of the biological origins of homosexuality, and considered it "degrading and beggarly . . . pleading for sympathy" (quoted in

Lauritsen & Thorstad, 1974, p. 50). He cited anthropological evidence to support a more culturally relative view of sexual practice in opposition to what he saw as the prison of biological determinism proposed by Hirschfeld and others. The involvement of medical authorities as experts on homosexuality offended Friedländer, and he warned that congenital arguments brought with them more than a protection from political oppression: to be biologically "different" from the majority precluded equality. Friedländer's fear was indeed realized during roughly this same period. When medical treatments for homosexuality proved repeatedly unsuccessful, the congenital theory was used as the foundation for the pessimistic notion of "hereditary degeneration." Treatment based on this view tended toward confinement and control. This concept came to assume major explanatory significance in the work of Krafft-Ebing and other physicians supporting the pathology view.

The last major turn-of-the-century challenger to medical pathology (with the exception of Freud) was English physician Henry Havelock Ellis, described as the first truly modern thinker on sexuality in the 20th century (Robinson, 1976). Ellis sought first and foremost to describe sexuality rather than to judge it. He was confident that homosexuality or "sexual inversion" was a congenital, inherited condition, and although he admitted the possibility of "exciting" environmental events, he rejected the weight placed on such experiences by Freud and psychoanalysis. His medical training is reflected in the taken-for-granted descriptions of inversion as "unfortunate," "abnormal," and an "anomaly." Ellis insisted, however, that it was not itself a "morbid" condition, except insofar as social hostility could render it so. He found the doctrine of organic bisexuality a plausible but crude explanation of the emergence of homosexuality. It would give way ultimately, he believed, to a more precise hormonal theory. True inversion was not amenable to medical treatment aimed at cure. The physician served best as a counselor who encouraged patients toward restraint and self-discipline

in a negatively predisposed social world. It was "outside the province of the physician to recommend his inverted patients to live according to their homosexual impulses. . . ." (Ellis, 1936, p. 1936, p. 342).*

Ellis appreciated the influence of context and intellectual-political predisposition in the definition of inversion. After enumerating various such definitions ranging from vice to benefit, and from disease to "sport," Ellis (1936) concludes insightfully:

> There is probably an element of truth in more than one of these views. Very widely divergent views of sexual inversion are largely justified by the position and attitude of the investigator. It is natural that the police-official should find that his cases are largely mere examples of disgusting vice and crime. It is natural that the asylum superintendent should find that we are chiefly dealing with a form of insanity. It is equally natural that the sexual invert himself should find that he and his inverted friends are not so very unlike ordinary persons. We have to recognize the influence of professional and personal bias and the influence of environment. (p. 302)

He might have added that physicians are also predisposed to "discover" inversion as a condition emerging from the body and that that is itself an additional kind of "bias"—but such comment would have perhaps dulled the intended theme of moral tolerance for "natural abnormalities" that he hoped to convey.

Like his medical colleagues, Ellis used the case history to present data on the condition of sexual inversion. Unlike virtually all other such medical case histories, however, Ellis chose to display people who, quite aside from their homosexuality, were generally healthy, happy, successful, intelligent, and sensitive human beings rather than the tortured and neurotic figures that emerged from Krafft-Ebing's work. The people Ellis described were not, on the average, consumed with the goal of "cure," that is, of becom-

---

ing heterosexual, and they defended their moral character as equal—if not superior—to that of so-called normals. Ellis pointed out that the generally positive picture of the inverts in his cases was probably due to the fact that none of them had come from police files or psychiatrists' offices. They were drawn, in effect, from that "other" population of homosexuals who rarely if ever become known to the variety of "experts" charged with their control. This contrast served to emphasize the highly selective and unrepresentative nature of the clinical case history as the basis for knowledge about larger populations.

These early medical apologists for homosexuality were important advocates of social and political reform. Their argument that homosexuality was a congenital condition, however, was used by opponents as the basis for increased legal and medical controls. Ellis himself recognized this problem, although he attempted to mitigate the evaluations inherent in such medical terminology. "All . . . organic variations," he noted, "are abnormalities" (Ellis, 1936, p. 318). The argument that homosexuals are organic anomalies but not pathological simply did not win the favor of those in charge of official legal and medical definitions. As medicine expanded its boundaries to include a variety of deviant behaviors, the optimistic hopes of these sympathetic reformers were sacrificed (just as were Freud's ideas on pathology) in the name of "treatment," "cure," and the "protection" of "normal" society.

Spreading Skepticism: Social Change and Social Science Research

Physicians were not the only ones speaking about homosexuality in the early decades of the 20th century, although their voices were the loudest and increasingly most respected. Gradually, literary figures and historians not only raised questions about homosexual civil rights but also presented images of such persons that questioned the tenets of pathology and congenitality. Paul Brandt in Germany, Edward Carpenter and John Symonds in England, and Irenaeus Stevenson (also known as Xavier Mayne) in the United States addressed homosexuality sympathetically in their work (Bullough, 1976, pp. 643–644; 1977).

Public as well as professional interest in sexuality increased dramatically in the first third of the century, and a series of social changes created a growing awareness that sexual activity need not always be linked to procreation. Vern Bullough (1977) suggests the following as providing particularly important arenas in which this independence could be seen and debated: developments and applications of contraceptive techniques and ideology; serious scientific, and gradually popular, study and appreciation of the virtually ignored sexual interests and capacities of women; even more dramatic scientific discoveries about the nature and control of venereal disease (syphilis, in particular); and an appreciation of the ominous implications of overpopulation. In light of this, Bullough suggests the stage was set historically for more serious consideration and tolerance of alternatives to traditional sexual values and activities.

The Kinsey Studies. It was against the background of these developments that Alfred C. Kinsey and associates Wardell Pomeroy, Clyde Martin, and, later, Paul Gebhard, published their monumental and sensational studies of sexual behavior in America. The first volume, *Sexual Behavior in the Human Male,* appeared in 1948, followed 5 years later in 1953 by *Sexual Behavior in the Human Female.* These publications have had (and in many regards, continue to have) an enormous impact on what Americans think about sex. Although similar research had been conducted before Kinsey,* nothing of its scope or detail had been attempted. Kinsey and associates collected data from 16,392 men and women through an interview and survey (statistical analysis was done on only 11,240—5300 males and 5940 females). Although Kinsey was criti-

---

*See Kinsey et al. (1948, pp. 21–34) for a review and evaluation of previous studies on sexual practices and attitudes.

cized subsequently because his sample was not completely representative of the American adult population (Cochran et al., 1954), never before had so many people provided so much information about their sexual lives outside the clinic or the church. Even the authors of these studies were unprepared for the incredible variation in and incidence of sexual practice that they found. Indeed, this theme of the infinite variety in human sexual response became central to their work. Kinsey (1948, pp. 638–639) argued that the traditional categories "heterosexual," "homosexual," and "bisexual" were but synthetic mental constructs that covered an infinite variety of actual behavior.

Kinsey was first and foremost a scientist committed to painstakingly careful description and classification. He believed that there was an unbridgeable gap between statements of fact and statements of value. He was particularly disdainful of the traditional medical categories "normal," "abnormal," and "pathological" and their effects on scientific understanding:

> Nothing has done more to block the free investigation of sexual behavior than the almost universal acceptance, even among scientists, of certain aspects of that behavior as normal, and of other aspects of that behavior as abnormal . . . and the ready acceptance of those distinctions among scientific men may provide the basis for one of the severest criticisms . . . of the scientific quality of nineteenth and early twentieth century scientists. *This is first of all a report on what people do, which raises no question of what they should do, or what kinds of people do it.* (Kinsey et al., 1948, p. 7, emphasis added)*

It is this nonjudgmental spirit of the Kinsey research that was such a dramatic break not only from Freud and other psychoanalysts but even from his predecessor Ellis. The medical heritage

of pathology was simply inappropriate to understand the variation in social behavior. . . .

The Kinsey research addressed a variety of sexual activities, but the data and conclusions about homosexual conduct were among the most consequential (their discussions of masturbation and female sexuality might follow in a close second and third place). They rejected the mysterious psychic processes and sexual "identities" that were the stock-in-trade of psychiatry: homosexual conduct is any physical sexual contact that involves a person of the same sex (Kinsey et al., 1948, pp. 615–617). To their own admitted surprise, they found such behavior considerably more common than they had expected. On the basis of the white male sample, Kinsey (1948, pp. 650–651) concluded that 37% of the adult male population of the United States had "some overt homosexual experience to the point of orgasm between adolescence and old age"; that 50% of the males who were still unmarried at age 35 had had such experience; and that 4% of the white adult male population is "exclusively homosexual throughout their lives." That means, Kinsey (1948, p. 623) interpreted, more than one male in every three that one passes on the street has had an adult homosexual experience. Predictably, the incidence data for women were lower: 13% had had such an adult experience to orgasm; 26% still single at age 45 reported a homosexual orgasm, and less than 3% of the women were exclusively homosexual throughout their lives (Kinsey et al., 1953, p. 487). The immediate effect of these data was, of course, to hail such conduct as a fact of sexual life; quite aside from cultural ideals, homosexual behavior clearly was not rare.

Having documented such incidence, Kinsey offered what he considered to be the only legitimate explanation: it was a perfectly natural phenomenon. Human beings possess, like their mammalian relatives, the biological capacity for sexual stimulation. The particular source of that stimulation (e.g., male, female, animal, self) in no way precludes and is biologically independent of that capacity. The fact that we develop strongly held ideas about the proper nature of this source

---

*Paul Robinson (1976) points out that Kinsey did labor under a few preconceptions, some of which were clear (e.g., a commitment to tolerance, the norm of biologic naturalism, and science itself) and others that were less so (e.g., Kinsey occasionally displays his own preference for the heterosexual norm).

of stimulation is a testimony not to nature but to culture and social values. Through learning cultural proscriptions, we effectively come to deny the suitability of certain of these sources. Kinsey's data showed that this cultural learning and socialization was not foolproof. Contrary to age-old social norms, a significant number of people, and apparently without dire psychological consequences, had engaged in a variety of such forbidden, homosexual conduct.

Following directly from this explanation was one of Kinsey's most startling conclusions about homosexuality: it simply did not exist. There were only homosexual acts and homosexual relationships; as an "identity" or a disease entity—as a "thing" independent of those who constructed it as a category—it did not exist (Kinsey et al., 1948, pp. 616–617). It was (in particular) a medical artifact rather than either a congenital or psychic condition of the human species. It followed directly that if homosexuality did not exist either in people's heads or bodies, it certainly could not be a problem for explanation, unless such explanation would be of its origins and rise as a diagnosis or of social and cultural reactions to the conduct involved. What did exist was same-sex behavior, which one could attempt to explain.* Kinsey summarized what he and his colleagues (1953) believed to be the most important factors in such an explanation:

> (1) the basic physiological capacity of every mammal to respond to any sufficient stimulus; (2) the accident which leads an individual into his or her first sexual experience with a person of the same sex; (3) the conditioning effects of such experience; and (4) the indirect but powerful conditioning which the opinions of other persons and social codes may have on an individual's decision to accept or reject this type of sexual contact. (p. 447)

In short, homosexual conduct was learned and therefore a question of "choice" (Kinsey et al., 1948, p. 661). The fact that we are called on to provide an "explanation" of it is more a reflection of these larger social and cultural constraints than a testimony to its inherent pathological nature.

The conclusions of the Kinsey research did not stand alone. By midcentury a growing body of social science research took up the challenge to the traditional morality of medicine. Support was gathering for the proposition that sexual behavior on the one hand, and the way people choose to construe or define it on the other, are independent questions. Anthropological research, in particular by Devereaux (1937/1963), Ford and Beach (1951), Malinowski (1932, 1955), and Margaret Mead (1949), demonstrated that homosexual conduct both was more common than had been suspected and, in some cases, was an institutionalized part of social life. It became clear that such behavior was "bad," "criminal," or "sick" only when judged so by certain sets of cultural or dominant subcultural values and norms.

In 1956 clinical psychologist Evelyn Hooker (1956, 1957) directly addressed the question of the psychological normality of homosexuals compared to heterosexuals. Using results from psychological tests and life histories, a panel of psychiatrists was unable to distinguish the homosexuals from the heterosexual controls in terms of their emotional health. Hooker concluded tentatively that homosexuality may be "within the normal range psychologically" of human sexual behavior. Chang and Block (1960) drew similar conclusions using scores from a self-acceptance inventory. They concluded that homosexuals were not suffering a psychiatric pathology.*

---

*Kinsey himself, however, had difficulty avoiding usage of the terms "homosexuality" and "homosexual" as typifications of individuals. His well-known seven-point continuum ranging from "exclusively heterosexual" to "exclusively homosexual" (Kinsey et al., 1948, pp. 636–641) also contributes to what he elsewhere tried to avoid—the characterization of persons as types of sexual beings rather than reserving the use of such terms as adjectives to describe behaviors.

*This tradition of social science research on homosexuality has been extended significantly by recent work from The Institute for Sex Research (source of the Kinsey studies). Weinberg and Williams (1974) and Bell and Weinberg (1978) draw on an enormous amount of observation and interview data to nullify the simplistic assumptions inherent in traditional medical descriptions and explanations of such behavior and its authors.

The 1950s also witnessed the famous Wolfenden Report in England. The report was presented to Parliament in 1957 as the result of a special committee called to investigate homosexual "offenses" and prostitution. After meeting for over 2 months, hearing over 200 "expert" witnesses, and considering the extant scientific research, the committee concluded that "legislation which covers . . . [homosexual acts in private between consenting adults] goes beyond the proper sphere of the law's concern" (Wolfenden Report, 1963, p. 43). The committee added, significantly, that whatever homosexuality might be, it most probably is not a disease and that it fails to meet standard medical criteria for such designation (Wolfenden Report, 1963, p. 31). Although the essence of the committee report was not adopted officially for about 13 years,* its moral tone signified and contributed to a gradual redefinition of such conduct and how it should be regarded by the state. At about this same time, the progressive American Law Institute issued its Model Penal Code that recommended similar decriminalization of private consensual adult homosexual conduct.

The seeds of a new, more tolerant, and popular rather than expert-controlled definition of homosexual conduct had been sown and were growing in America. They were about to emerge into the sunlight and fresh air of public view in the form of a political movement that demanded not only respect and equality before the law but also an official repudiation of what its advocates saw increasingly as the last barrier to normalization: the medical argument that *to be* a "homosexual" is itself a pathological condition. It is to the origins and development of this political movement that we now turn.

---

*Decriminalization of private consensual homosexual acts between adults became law in England on July 21, 1967. See Alex Gigeroff (1968, pp. 82–95) for a detailed recapitulation of the political life of this committee recommendation and the debate that surrounded it.

Rise of Gay Liberation: Homosexuality as Identity and Life-style

. . . Origins of the "Homophile Movement" The first groups of self-proclaimed homosexuals in America were small, secret, and self-help oriented. They used euphemistic names to protect their real purposes. Although some of these existed in the United States before 1945, they were short-lived. Between 1945 and 1950 several organizations dedicated to helping people arrested for homosexual conduct were founded that provided counsel and support. The membership of these service organizations was not exclusively homosexual but included various professional and religious persons committed to helping those in need. A social-recreational group of homosexuals (something then considered dangerous) existed in New York beginning in 1945. It was called The Veterans Benevolent Association, had a total membership of about 75, and lasted for roughly 9 years. The West Coast witnessed similar developments, the first being the "Friendship Circle" in 1947. This group consisted of a few women who circulated a mimeographed paper called *Vice Versa* in the Los Angeles area. A somewhat larger and more diverse organization, The Knights of the Clock, formed in 1949 and was committed both to homosexual and black equal rights (Humphreys, 1972).

The early 1950s might be called the beginning of "homosexual consciousness." In 1950 five men established The Mattachine Foundation in Los Angeles. They chose the name "Mattachine" in reference to medieval court jesters who spoke the truth to the royalty of the court from behind masks that protected their identities (Humphreys, 1972). Such secrecy was indeed important, for it was the period of the Cold War, anti-Communism, and Senator Joseph McCarthy. Persons who engaged in homosexual acts were considered serious security risks by the government and prime targets for Communist manipulation. The House Un-American Activities Committee scrutinized carefully the past records of those suspected of such conduct. . . .

These and similar kinds of activities throughout the United States became characterized as the "homophile" (meaning love of same) movement. The first popular (although somewhat apologetic) attempt to describe the conditions faced by homosexuals in the United States was published in 1951. *The Homosexual in America: A Subjective Approach,* by Donald Webster Cory (pseudonym of Edward Sagarin who later became a sociologist expert on homosexuality and sexual deviance). Psychologist Evelyn Hooker (1967) and sociologists John Gagnon and William Simon (1967) contributed additional detailed portraits of the "homosexual community." Edwin Schur (1965), in his highly popular and influential *Crimes Without Victims,* argued forcefully that the criminalization of homosexual conduct in America led not only to personal tragedies but also to police corruption and a general lack of respect for the law. The topic of homosexuality was becoming an increasingly salient one among the American middle class.

Representatives of established religious denominations such as the Episcopal and Unitarian churches lent their support to the movement for respect and equal rights for the homosexual. The Council on Religion and the Homosexual was formed in San Francisco in 1965, and by the end of the decade some of these religious leaders became the strongest external advocates of legal and social reform (Bullough, 1976; Martin & Lyon, 1972). . . .

. . . Although the homophile movement, not unlike most social movements, was by no means without internal dissension (see Humphreys, 1972; Teal, 1971), there was agreement at least on a highly positive, new definition of what it meant to be a homosexual. Franklin Kameny (1969), a respected leader in the movement, captures the essence of this new socially constructed identity:

it is time to open the closet door and let in the fresh air and the sunshine; it is time to doff and to discard the secrecy, the disguise, and the camouflage; it is time to hold up your heads and to look the world squarely in the eye as the homosexuals that you are,

confident of your equality, confident in the knowledge that as objects of prejudice and victims of discrimination you are right and they are wrong, and confident of the rightness of what you are and of the goodness of what you do; it is time to live your homosexuality fully, joyously, openly, and proudly, assured that morally, socially, physically, psychologically, emotionally, and in every other way: *Gay is good.* It is. (p. 145)*

The change from "homosexual" to "gay" in Kameny's passage is instructive. It represents a larger change in meaning and definition that was taking place. "Gay" was used increasingly to refer to a total life-style and a way of thinking about oneself and others (Teal, 1971, p. 44). Not unlike the change in usage from "Negro" to "black," and from "lady" to "woman," "gay" was intended to deemphasize the one-dimensional image imposed by traditional and particularly medical definitions. In many regards, "homosexual" could be seen as itself an oppressive term that grew out of a need to defend rather than assert one's human rights. It was the eve of a new, considerably less deferential, and more militant struggle for normalization. Although this mood did not begin suddenly at the end of the decade, one particular event is cited frequently as the dramatic crucible in which this new militancy was forged: the "Stonewall rebellion" in New York's Greenwich Village.

Politics of Confrontation. The Stonewall Inn was a small gay bar on Christopher Street off Sheridan Square in Greenwich Village, sometimes called the "Mecca" for homosexuals on the East Coast. On June 27, 1969, police conducted a raid on the Stonewall premised on alleged liquor code violations. It was generally believed in the gay community that such raids were in fact to harass and frighten homosexuals (Teal, 1971).

---

*Franklin E. Kameny, "Gay is good," *The same sex: an appraisal of homosexuality,* ed. Ralph W. Weltge (New York: The Pilgrim Press, 1969), p. 145. Copyright © 1969 United Church Press. Used by permission.

The typical scenario was for the management to be arrested, liquor confiscated, and the patrons unceremoniously and sometimes violently ushered out. Also typical was the patrons' passive cooperation. The reaction of those in the Stonewall that night was dramatically different. They, quite literally, fought back in the face of what they perceived as unfair, corrupt, and inhumane treatment. In a battle of fists, rocks, bottles, fire, and even a parking meter used as a battering ram, homosexuals forced police to barricade themselves inside the bar until reinforcements arrived. It was a resistance for which police were clearly unprepared. Over the course of the next several nights, street demonstrations and some violence between police and homosexual protesters and their allies filled Sheridan Square. To the cheers of "Gay Power!" a new, aggressive, politically attuned, and youthful homosexual presence in America was born. . . .

Official Death of Pathology: the American Psychiatric Association Decision on Homosexuality

Challenging Professional Control. With effective challenges to traditional religious and legal definitions of homosexual conduct underway, gay activists began to focus attention on the "helping" professions—those who for so long had attempted to "cure" this illness. Pursuing its dramatic strategy of public confrontation, or "zapping" as it came to be called, gay activists "liberated" (a movement term meaning to disrupt and reconstitute in "more appropriate" form) a session of formal papers at the annual meeting of the American Psychiatric Association on May 14, 1970, in San Francisco (Teal, 1971). The particular target of this attack was a presentation on "aversion therapy," a popular form of behavior control used in the clinical treatment of homosexuals. This treatment in effect punishes emotional responses toward same-sex others (typically, with electric shock) and rewards positive responses toward opposite-sex others. In a later session at the same meeting, a gay activist shouted from the audience at Irving Bieber and his colleagues:

> You are the pigs who make it possible for the cops to beat homosexuals: they call us queer; you—so politely—call us sick. But it's the same thing. You make possible the beatings and rapes in prisons, you are implicated in the torturous cures perpetrated on desperate homosexuals. (Quoted in Teal, 1971, p. 295)

This initial challenge to the medical establishment view of homosexuality was clearly not to be on its own "rational," scientific terms.

Similar confrontations were staged that year at meetings of the American Medical Association against Dr. Charles Socarides, a nurses' seminar on the East Coast, the national convention of American psychologists held in Los Angeles, and a conference on behavior modification (Teal, 1971). Donn Teal, in his book *The Gay Militants,* gives a detailed account of the closing of the "liberated" session at this last conference. A gay activist addressed the behaviorists, pointing up the significance of what had happened:

> large meetings such as the one you have had here today happen in Los Angeles each year. Most of them come and go and nobody but the families of those involved know that they came . . . [but] we noticed you—and the Associated Press and United Press noticed you, and this little episode that we had with you this morning is going out on the wires right now, and everybody in the country is being told that psychologists and homosexuals were *talking* together and we think that's news. I would like to thank . . . the kind people who had the good sense to send the police away. It would have been . . . inconvenient for us to have been in jail this weekend, but we were prepared to do so. . . . We would, in turn, have charged you with disturbing our peace, as you have disturbed our peace lo these many years. Because we cannot and will not allow it to be disturbed any more. This is the unique thing that the Gay Liberation Front does. We no longer apologize because we have nothing to apologize for. When we say "We're Gay and We're Proud," we *mean* it. We *are* proud! (Quoted in Teal, 1971, p. 300)

These challenges continued and were focused on the major spokesmen of the pathology view. . . .

As a result of the 1970 American Psychiatric Association (APA) confrontation, five homosexual activists were invited to participate in the panel "Life-Styles of Nonpatient Homosexuals" at the annual meeting the following year in Washington, D.C. Coordinated by Kent Robinson, a Baltimore psychiatrist, the panel consisted of Frank Kameny of the Washington Mattachine Society; Jack Baker, newly-elected (and homosexual) president of the student body at the University of Minnesota; Larry Littlejohn, past president of the Society for Individual Rights (SIR); Lilli Vencenz, active in lesbian organizations on the East Coast; and Del Martin, a founder of the Daughters of Bilitis and representing the Council on Religion and the Homosexual (Martin & Lyon, 1972, p. 249). In addition to the panel, which as expected produced stinging denunciations of the pathology and cure doctrines, gay activists made their presence known in a discussion of a paper by Dr. Bieber, a seizure of the podium by Kameny at a general session at which time he outlined the implications for homosexuals of the disease view, and an attack on a company advertising and selling its aversion therapy technology (Martin, 1971). . . .

After the 1971 meetings of the American Psychiatric Association, vice-president Judd Mannor began to raise informally the question of dropping the diagnosis of homosexuality as a psychiatric condition from the *Diagnostic and Statistical Manual.* The 1972 annual meetings of the association brought a dramatic event: a gay psychiatrist, masked to protect his identity, spoke at a session on homosexuality. That fall two important developments began that were aimed directly at removing homosexuality from the APA nomenclature (Spector, 1977).

Politics of Official Nomenclature. The Social Concerns Committee of the Massachusetts Psychiatric Society, a committee that routinely had been considering such issues as drugs, the war in Vietnam, and abortion met to consider the question of homosexuality. Dr. Richard Pillard, a counselor of homosexuals who had just recently announced his own homosexuality to colleagues (Brown, 1976, p. 205), urged the committee to adopt a statement in strong support of homosexual civil rights that, in addition, stipulated: "Homosexuality per se should not be considered an illness and APA nomenclature on this subject should therefore be altered" (Spector, 1977, p. 54). The Massachusetts Society approved the committee's resolution early in 1973, as did a regional association, clearing the way for its appearance before all regional representatives at the national meeting in May. At that time a controversy about wording arose, and the resolution was withdrawn for more work. Sponsors, however, discovered a simultaneous but independent development aimed in the same direction.

Robert Spitzer, psychiatrist-member of the APA Committee on Nomenclature and Statistics, had attended a Fall, 1972, meeting of behavior therapists at which a session was disrupted and "liberated" by members of the Gay Activist Alliance, including a man named Ronald Gold. As the result of an encounter with Gold after the meeting, Spitzer began a series of discussions that culminated in a presentation to nomenclature committee members by a contingent of gay activists, including Gold, in February, 1973. It is important to note that this presentation was tailored for its audience: it was based on a careful and thorough review of existing medical and scientific research and writing; it was sensitive—even empathetic—to the increased 20th-century demand on psychiatry to solve a broad range of personal problems (the medicalization of personal troubles as well as deviance), and it was offered in a polite but critical manner (see Silverstein, 1976). In what must have been a rather embarrassing situation for the APA committee members. GAA representative and psychologist Charles Silverstein (1976) catalogued the flaws in scientific methodology of most past medical research. The psychiatric disease theories simply had not been supported by systematic evidence, and treatment technologies, ranging from standard psychotherapy to aversive conditioning*, had not been evaluated critically. In a plea couched in the language of reason and science itself, Silverstein (1976) concluded:

> I suppose what we are saying is that you must choose between the undocumented theories [and treatments] that have unjustly harmed a great number of people, and which continue to harm them, or the controlled scientific studies cited here and in our previous report to you. It is no sin to have made an error in the past, but surely you will mock the principles of scientific research upon which the diagnostic system is based if you turn your backs on the only objective evidence we have. (pp. 157–158)

These gay claims-makers were playing sophisticated politics. By deciding to use not their own but rather their opponents' rules, that is, reason, science, and data, they risked being challenged as amateurs in a professional world. The fact that their strategy was successful can be understood, we think, as a result of two conditions that characterized psychiatric definition and treatment of homosexuals at the time.

First, the scientific evidence for psychiatric disease theories was indeed sketchy and inconsistent. With the focus on this fundamental criterion of scientific evaluation and judgment—evidence—the challengers knew their psychiatric audience would have to listen. When they pointed out the morally based nature of the medical diagnosis of homosexuality, this imbalance between facts and values became painfully clear. Second, although they did not address it specifically, we believe that an important key to the successful challenge to psychiatric diagnosis was the lack of any notably effective treatment. Although the dis-

ease proponents we discussed along with others had cited various "cure" rates as "significant," rarely did such rates approach or exceed 50% of those treated. Psychiatrists were, compared to their medical colleagues, relatively ineffective in solving the problem of homosexuality, even when it was presented to them by guilt-ridden, unhappy patients. Gay activists knew this, if only intuitively, and their keen political judgment is seen in the brand of politics they chose to play with APA officials. It was the politics of science. Their strategy is a good example of how the medicalization of deviance is political in both an obvious sense (e.g., lobbying, "log rolling," the use of influence) and in a more subtle, "expert" sense (e.g., adherence to the rules of scientific evidence, winning the approval of an audience of scientific peers, and success in the practical task of solving people's problems). The ultimate success of gay critics may have been much more in doubt if the challenge could have been launched only on the former, more "crass" political plane.* But their comments had been directed to and heard by medical ears and, apparently, taken to heart. After the nomenclature committee meeting, chairman Henry Brill reportedly agreed that indeed some change seemed in order (Spector, 1977). . . .

When the APA Board of Trustees met in December, 1973, to consider the nomenclature committee's resolution they voted to adopt it with slight but important modifications, the most significant being that they simply deleted [the] word "irregular" in describing homosexuality. The final text of the approved change of DSM-11 read as follows:

> This category is for individuals whose sexual interests are directed primarily toward people of the

---

*Gerald Davison and G. Terence Wilson (1973) found in a 1971 study that among behavior therapists (who in general are not physicians), some form of aversion therapy was the most preferred technique in attempting to change "homosexuals in the direction of heterosexuality."

---

*We speculate that if there were some highly effective medical technology by which the deviance of homosexuality could be changed into heterosexuality, gay activists would have been forced into a contest of much less specialized and influence-dominated politics that they probably would have lost. In addition, they would have been faced with the popular conclusion that if physicians could cure it, homosexuality must then be a disease.

same sex and who are either disturbed by, in conflict with, or wish to change their sexual orientation. This diagnostic category is distinguished from homosexuality which by itself does not necessarily constitute a psychiatric disorder. Homosexuality per se is one form of sexual behavior and, like other forms of sexual behavior which are not by themselves psychiatric disorders, is not listed in this nomenclature of mental disorder. . . . (Quoted in Spector, 1977, p. 53)

References

Alcott, W. *The young man's guide.* Boston: Marvin, 1833.

American Psychiatric Association. *Diagnostic and statistical manual of mental disorders* (2nd ed.). Washington, D.C.: American Psychiatric Association, 1968.

Bailey, D. S. *Homosexuality and the Western Christian tradition.* London Longmans, Green & Co., 1955.

Beall, O. T., Jr. Aristotle's master piece in America: a landmark in the folklore of medicine. *William Mary Quarterly,* 1963, 20(2), 207–222.

Brown, H. *Familiar faces, hidden lives.* New York: Harcourt Brace Jovanovich, Inc., 1976.

Bullough, V. I. *Sexual variance in society and history.* New York: John Wiley & Sons, Inc. 1976.

Bullough, V. L. Challenges to societal attitudes toward homosexuality in the late nineteenth and early twentieth centuries. *Soc. Sci. Quarterly,* 1977, 58, 29–44.

Bullough, V., & Bullough, B. *Sin, sickness and sanity.* New York: The New American Library, 1977.

Chang, J., & Block, J. A study of identification in male homosexuals. *J. Consult, Psychol.,* 1960, 24, 307–310.

Churchill, W. *Homosexual behavior among males: a cross-cultural and cross-species investigation.* New York: Hawthorn Books, Inc., 1967.

Cochran, W. G., Mosteller, F., & Tukey, J. W. *Statistical problems of the Kinsey Report.* Washington, D.C.: U.S. Government Printing Office, 1954.

Comfort. A. *The anxiety makers.* London: Thomas Nelson & Sons, 1967.

Davison, G. C., & Wilson, G. T. Attitudes of behavior therapists toward homosexuality. *Behav. Ther.,* 1973, 4, 686–696.

Devereaux, G. Institutionalized homosexuality of the Mohave Indians. In Hendrik M. Ruitenbeck (Ed.).

The problem of homosexuality in modern America. New York: E. P. Dutton & Co., Inc., 1963. (Originally published, 1937.)

Dover, K. J. *Greek homosexuality.* Boston: Harvard University Press, 1978.

Ellis, H. *Studies in the psychology of sex.* (Vol. 1), New York: Modern Library, 1936.

Englehardt, H. T., Jr. The disease of masturbation values and the concept of disease. *Bull. Hist. Med.,* 1974, 48, 234–248 (Summer).

Ford, C. S., & Beach, F. A. *Patterns of sexual behavior.* New York: Harper & Row, Publishers, 1951.

Freud, S. Three contributions to a theory of sex. In A. A. Brill (Ed.). *The basic writings of Sigmund Freud.* New York: Random House, Inc., 1938. (Originally published, 1905).

Freud, S. [Letter to the mother of a homosexual son] In E. L. Freud (Ed.); J. Stern and T. Stern (trans.), *Letters of Sigmund Freud,* 1873–1939. New York: Basic Books, Inc., 1960. © 1960 by Sigmund Freud Copyrights Ltd. London. (Originally published, 1935.)

Gagnon, J. & Simon, W. *Sexual deviance.* New York: Harper & Row Publishers, Inc., 1967.

Gigeroff, A. *Sexual deviations in the criminal law.* Toronto: University of Toronto Press, 1968.

Graham, S. *Lecture to young men on chastity.* (3rd ed.). Boston: George W. Light, 1837. (originally published, 1834.)

Haller, J. S., Jr., & Haller, R. M. *The physician and sexuality in Victorian America.* Urbana: University of Illinois Press, 1974.

Hirschfeld, M. Magnus Hirschfeld. In Victor Robinson (Ed.), *Encyclopaedia sexualis.* New York: Dingwall-Rock, 1936. (b)

Hooker, E. A preliminary analysis of group behavior of homosexuals. *J. Psychol.,* 1956, 42, 217–225.

Hooker, E. The adjustment of male overt homosexuals. *J. Project. Techniques,* 1957, 21, 18–31.

Hooker, E. The homosexual community. In J. Gagnon & W. Simon (Eds.). *Sexual deviance.* New York: Harper & Row Publishers, Inc., 1967, (originally published, 1961)

Humphreys, L. *Out of the closets: the sociology of homosexual liberation.* Englewood Cliffs, N.J.: Prentice-Hall, Inc., 1972.

Kameny, F. E. Gay is good. In R. W. Weltge (Ed.), *The same sex: an appraisal of homosexuality.* Philadelphia: United Church Press, 1969.

Kinsey, A. C., Pomeroy, W. B., & Martin, C. E. *Sexual behavior in the human male.* Philadelphia: W. B. Saunders Co., 1948.

Kinsey, A. C., Pomeroy, W. B., Martin, C. E., & Gebhard, P. H. *Sexual behavior in the human female.* Philadelphia: W. B. Saunders Co., 1953.

Kittrie, N. *The right to be different: deviance and enforced therapy.* Baltimore: Johns Hopkins University Press, 1971. Copyright The Johns Hopkins Press, 1971.

Lauritsen, J. & Thorstad, D. *The early homosexual rights movement (1864–1935).* New York: Times Change Press, 1974.

Levitt, E. E., & Klassen, A. D., Jr., Public attitudes toward homosexuality. *J. Homosex.,* 1974, 1(1), 29–43.

Malinowski, B. *The sexual life of savages.* (3d ed.). London: George Routledge & Sons, 1932.

Malinowski, B. *Sex and repression in savage society.* New York: Meridian Books, 1955 (Reprint.)

Martin, D. "Sexual Perverts" is the new homosexual classification but psychiatrists let gay people rap. *Vector,* 1971, 7, 34–35.

Martin, D. & Lyon, P. *Lesbian/woman.* San Francisco: Glide Publications, 1972.

Masters, W. H., & Johnson, V. E. *Human sexual response.* Boston: Little, Brown & Co., 1966.

Mead, M. *Male and female: a study of the sexes in a changing world.* New York: Wm. Morrow & Co., Inc., 1949.

Mitchell, S. A. Psychodynamics, homosexuality, and the question of pathology. *Psychiatry.* 1978, 41. 254–263 (Aug.).

New York Academy of Medicine. The problem of homosexuality. *Bull. N. Y. Acad. Med.,* 1964, 40, 576–580.

Pivar, D. J. *Purity crusade: sexual morality and social control 1868–1900.* Westport, Conn. Greenwood Press, 1973.

Robinson, P. *The modernization of sex.* New York: Harper & Row, Publishers, 1976.

Rosenberg, C. E. The therapeutic revolution: medicine, meaning, and social change in nineteenth-century America. *Perspect. Biol. Med.,* 1977, 20, 485–506 (Summer).

Schur, E. M. *Crimes without victims: deviant behavior and public policy.* Englewood Cliffs, N.J. Prentice-Hall, Inc., 1965.

Shaw, J. C., & Ferris, G. N. Perverted sexual instinct *J. Nerv. Ment. Dis.,* 1883, 10, 185–204.

Silverstein, C. Even psychiatry can profit from its past mistakes. *J. Homosex.,* 1976, 2(2), 153–158.

Silverstein, C. Homosexuality and the ethics of behavioral intervention. *J. Homosex.,* 1977, 2(3), 205–211.

Smith-Rosenberg, C. Sex as symbol in Victorian purity: an ethnohistorical analysis of Jacksonian America. In J. Demos & S. S. Boocock (Eds.), *Turning points: historical and sociological essays on the family,* supplement to *Am. J. Sociol.,* Vol. 84. Chicago: The University of Chicago Press, 1978.

Socarides, C. W. Homosexuality and medicine, *J.A.M.A.,* 1970, 1199–1202.

Socarides, C. W., Bieber, I., Bychowski, G., Gershman, H., Jacobs, T. J., Myers, W. A., Nackenson, B. I., Prescott, K. F., Rifkin, A. H., Stein, S., & Terry, J. Homosexuality in the male a report of a psychiatric study group. *Int. J. Psychiatry,* 1973, 11, 460–479.

Spector, M. Legitimizing homosexuality. *Society,* 1977, 14(5), 52–56.

Stoller, R. J. *Gender and sex: on the development of masculinity and femininity.* New York: Science House, 1968.

Symonds, J. A. *Studies in sexual inversion.* Privately published, 1931.

Teal, D. *The gay militants.* New York: Stein & Day Publishers, 1971.

Van Den Haag, E. Introduction. In R. von Krafft-Ebing, *Psychopathia sexualis.* New York: G. P. Putnam's Sons, 1965.

Ware, J. *Hints to young men on the true relations of the sexes.* Boston: Tappan, Whittemore & Mason, 1879. (Originally published, 1850.)

Wolfenden Report. *Report of the Committee on Homosexual offenses and prostitution.* New York: Stein & Day Publishers, 1963.

READING 31

The Health of Black Folk: Disease, Class, and Ideology in Science

Nancy Krieger and Mary Bassett

Since the first crude tabulations of vital statistics in colonial America, one stark fact has stood out: black Americans are sicker and die younger than whites. As the epidemic infectious diseases of the nineteenth century were vanquished, the black burden of ill health shifted to the modern killers: heart disease, stroke, and cancer. Today black men under age 45 are ten times more likely to die from the effects of high blood pressure than white men. Black women suffer twice as many heart attacks as white women. A variety of common cancers are more frequent among blacks—and of cancer victims, blacks succumb sooner after diagnosis than whites. Black infant mortality is twice that of whites. All told, if the mortality rates for blacks and other minorities today were the same in the United States as for whites, more than 60,000 deaths in minority communities could be avoided each year.

What is it about being black that causes such miserable odds? One answer is the patently racist view that blacks are inherently more susceptible to disease—the genetic model. In contrast, environmental models depict blacks as victims of factors ranging from poor nutrition and germs to lack of education and crowded housing. Initially formulated as an alternative to the genetic model by liberals and much of the left, the environmental view has now gained new support from the right. . . . Instead of blaming the victims' genes, these conservatives blame black lifestyle choices as the source of the racial gap in health.

We will argue that these analytic models are seriously flawed, in essence as well as application. They are not the product of a racist use of allegedly "neutral" science, but reflect the ways in which ideology and politics penetrate scientific theory and research. Typically, they deny or obscure that the primary source of black/white health disparities is the social production of disease under conditions of capitalism and racial oppression. The "facts of being black" are not, as these models suggest, a genetically determined shade of skin color, or individual deprived living conditions, or ill-informed lifestyle choices. The facts of being black derive from the joint social relations of race and class: racism disproportionately concentrates blacks into the lower strata of the working class and further causes blacks in all class strata to be racially oppressed. It is the left's challenge to incorporate this political reality into how we approach racial differences in health.

THE GENETIC MODEL

Despite overwhelming evidence to the contrary, the theory that "race" is primarily a biological category and that black-white differences in health are genetically determined continues to exert profound influence on both medical thinking and popular ideology. For example, an editorial on racial differences in birth weight (an important determinant of infant mortality) in the January 1986 *Journal of the American Medical Association* concluded: "Finally, what are the biologic or genetic differences among racial or ethnic groups? Should we shrink from the possibility of a biologic/genetic influence?" Similarly, a 1983 handbook prepared by the International Epidemiologic Association defined "race" as "persons who are relatively homogeneous with respect to biological inheritance." Public health texts continue to enshrine "race" in the demographic triad of "age, race, and sex," implying that "race" is as biologically fundamental a predictor of health as aging or sex, while the medical literature remains replete with studies that examine racial differences in health without regard to class.

The genetic model rests on three basic assumptions, all of which are flawed: that "race" is a valid biological category; that the genes which determine "race" are linked to the genes which affect health; and that the health of any community is mainly the consequence of the genetic constitution of the individuals of which it is composed. In contrast, we will argue that the health of the black community is not simply the sum of the health of individuals who are "genetically black" but instead chiefly reflects the social forces which create racially oppressed communities in the first place.

It is of course true that skin color, hair texture, and other visible features used to identify "race" are genetically encoded—there *is* a biologic aspect to "race." The importance of these particular physical traits in the spectrum of human variation, however, has been determined historically and politically. People also differ in terms of stature and eye color, but these attributes are rarely accorded significance. Categories based primarily on skin color correlate with health because race is a powerful determinant of the location and life-destinies of individuals within the class structure of U.S. society. Ever since plantation owners realized that differences in skin color could serve as a readily identifiable and permanent marker for socially determined divisions of labor (black runaway slaves were easier to identify than escaped white indentured servants and convicts, the initial workforce of colonial America), race and class have been inextricably intertwined. "Race" is not a neutral descriptive category, but a social category born of the antagonistic relation of white supremacy and black oppression. The basis of the relative health advantage of whites is not to be found in their genes but in the relative material advantage whites enjoy as a consequence of political perogative and state power. As Richard Lewontin has pointed out, "If, after a great cataclysm, only Africans were left alive, the human species would have retained 93 percent of its total genetic variation, although the species as a whole would be darker skinned." The fact that we all know which race we belong to says more about our society than about our biology.

Nevertheless, the paradigm of a genetic basis for black ill health remains strong. In its defense, researchers repeatedly trot out the few diseases for which a clear-cut link of race is established: sickle cell anemia, G&PD deficiency, and lactose intolerance. These diseases, however, have a tiny impact on the health of the black population as a whole—if anything, even less than those few diseases linked to "whiteness," such as some forms of skin cancer. Richard Cooper has shown that of the tens of thousands of excess black deaths in 1977, only 277 (0.3 percent) could be attributed to diseases such as sickle cell anemia. Such uncommon genetic maladies have become important strictly because of their metaphorical value: they are used to support genetic explanations of racial differences in the "big diseases" of the twentieth century—heart disease, stroke, and cancer. Yet no current evidence exists to justify such an extrapolation.

Determined nonetheless to demonstrate the genetic basis of racial health differences, investigators today—like their peers in the past—use the latest techniques. Where once physicians compared cranial capacity to explain black/white inequalities, now they scrutinize surface markers of cells. The case of hypertension is particularly illustrative. High blood pressure is an important cause of strokes and heart attacks, contributing to about 30 percent of all deaths in the United States. At present, the black rate of hypertension in the United States is about twice that of whites. Of over five hundred recent medical journal articles on the topic, fewer than a dozen studies explored social factors. The rest instead unsuccessfully sought biochemical/genetic explanations—and of these, virtually none even attempted to "define" genetically who was "white" and who was "black," despite the alleged genetic nature of their enquiry. As a consequence of the wrong questions being asked, the causes of hypertension remain unknown. Nonetheless, numerous clues point to social factors. Hypertension does not exist in several undisrupted hunter/gatherer tribes of different "races" but rapidly emerges in these tribes after contact with industrial society; in the United States, lower social class begets higher blood pressure.

Turning to cancer, the authors of a recent major government report surmised that blacks have poorer survival rates than whites because they do not "exhibit the same immunologic reactions to cancerous processes." It is noteworthy, however, that the comparably poor survival rates of British breast cancer patients have never elicited such speculation. In our own work on breast cancer in Washington state, we found that the striking "racial" difference in survival evaporated when we took class into account: working-class women, whether black or white, die sooner than women of higher social class standing.

To account for the persistence of the genetic model, we must look to its political significance rather than its scientific content. First used to buttress biblical arguments for slavery in a period when science was beginning to replace religion as sanction for the status quo, the genetic model of racial differences in health emerged toward the end of the eighteenth century, long before any precise theory of heredity existed. In well-respected medical journals, doctors debated whether blacks and whites were even the same species (let alone race), and proclaimed that blacks were intrinsically suited to slavery, thrived in hot climates, succumbed less to the epidemic fevers which ravaged the South, and suffered extraordinary rates of insanity if allowed to live free. After the Civil War effectively settled the argument about whether blacks belonged to the human species, physicians and scientists began elaborating hereditarian theories to explain the disparate health profiles not only of blacks and whites, but of the different white "races"—as defined by national origin and immigrant status. Virtually every scourge, from TB to rickets, was postulated to be inherited. Rheumatic fever, now known to be due to strep bacteria combined with the poverty which permits its expression in immunocompromised malnourished people, was long believed to be linked with the red hair and pale complexions of its Irish working-class victims. Overall, genetic explanations of differences in disease rates have politically served to justify existing class relations and excuse socially created afflictions as a result of immutable biology.

Nowadays the genetic model—newly dressed in the language of molecular genetics—continues to divert attention from the class origin of disease. Genetic explanations absolve the state of responsibility for the health profile of black America by declaring racial disparities (regrettably) inevitable and normal. Intervention efforts based on this model founder for obvious reasons: short of recombinant DNA therapies, genetic screening and selective reproduction stand as supposed tools to reduce the racial gap in health.

Unfortunately, the genetic model wields influence even within the progressive health movement, as illustrated by the surge of interest in sickle cell anemia in the early 1970s. For decades after its initial description in 1925, sickle cell anemia was relegated to clinical obscurity. It occurs as often in blacks as does cystic fibrosis in whites. By linking genetic uniqueness to racial pride, such groups as the Black Panther Party championed sickle cell anemia as the number one health issue among blacks, despite the fact that other health problems—such as infant mortality—took a much greater toll. Because the sickle cell gene provides some protection against malaria, sickle cell seemed to link blacks to their African past, now three centuries removed. It raised the issue of racist neglect of black health in a setting where the victims were truly blameless: the fault lay in their genes. From the point of view of the federal government, sickle cell anemia was a uniquely black disease which did not raise the troubling issues of the ongoing oppression of the black population. In a period of political turmoil, what more could the government ask for? Small wonder that President Nixon jumped on the bandwagon and called for a national crusade.

THE ENVIRONMENTAL MODEL

The genetic model's long history and foundations in the joint race and class divisions of our society assure its continued prominence in discussions on the racial gap in health. To rebut this model, many liberals and progressives have relied upon environmental models of disease causation—only to encounter the right on this turf as well.

Whereas the rise of slavery called forth genetic models of diseases, environmental models were born of the antagonistic social relations of industrial capitalism. In the appalling filth of nineteenth-century cities, tuberculosis, typhus, and infant diarrhea were endemic in the newly forming working class; periodically, epidemics of yellow fever and cholera would attack the entire populace. A sanitary reform movement arose, advocating cleaner cities (with sewer systems and pure water) to protect the wellbeing of the wealthy as well as the poor, and also to engender a healthier, more productive workforce.

In the United States, most of the reformers were highly moralistic and staunchly procapitalist, seeing poverty and squalor as consequences of individual intemperance and ignorance rather than as necessary correlates of capital accumulation. In Europe, where the working-class movement was stronger, a class-conscious wing of the sanitary reform movement emerged. Radicals such as Frederick Engels and Rudolph Virchow (later the founder of modern pathology) argued that poverty and ill health could only be eliminated by resolving the antagonistic class relations of capitalism.

The early sanitary reform movement in the United States rarely addressed the question of racial differences in health per se. In fact, environmental models to explain black/white disparities emerged only during the mid-twentieth century, a consequence of the urban migration of blacks from the rural South to the industrial North and the rise of the civil-rights movement.

Today's liberal version of the environmental model blames poverty for black ill health. The noxious features of the "poverty environment" are catalogued and decried—lead paint from tenement walls, toxins from work, even social features like discrimination. But as in most liberal analyses, the unifying cause of this litany of woes remains unstated. We are left with an apparently unconnected laundry list of problems and no explanation of why blacks as a group encounter similar sickening conditions.

The liberal view fetishizes the environment: individuals are harmed by inanimate objects, physical forces, or unfortunate social conditions (like poverty)—by *things* rather than by people. That these objects or social circumstances are the *creations* of society is hidden by the veil of "natural science." Consequently, the "environment" is viewed as a natural and neutral category, defined as all that is external to individuals. What is not seen is the ways in which the underlying structure of racial oppression and class exploitation—which are relationships among people, not between people and things—shape the "environments" of the groups created by these relations.

The debilitating disease pellagra serves as a concrete example. Once a major health problem of poor southern farm and mill laborers in the United States, pellagra was believed to be a genetic disease. By the early 1920s, however, Joseph Goldberger had proved that the disease stemmed from a dietary deficiency in niacin and had also demonstrated that pellagra's familial nature existed because of the inheritance of nutritional options, not genes. Beyond this, Goldberger argued that pellagra, in essence, was a *social* disease caused by the single cash-crop economy of the South: reliance on cotton ensured seasonal starvation as food ran out between harvests, as well as periodic epidemics when the cotton market collapsed. Southern workers contracted pellagra because they had limited diets—and they had limited diets *because* they were southern workers. Yet governmental response was simply to supplement food with niacin: according to this view, vitamin deficiency—not socially determined malnutrition—was the chief cause of pellagra.

The liberal version of the environmental model also fails to see the causes of disease and the environment in which they exist as a historical product, a nature filtered through, even constructed by, society. What organisms and chemicals people are exposed to is determined by both the social relations and types of production which characterize their society. The same virus may cause pneumonia in blacks and whites alike, just as lead may cause the same physiologic damage—but *why* the death rate for flu and pneumonia and *why* blood lead levels are consistently higher in black as compared to white communities is not addressed. While the liberal conception of the environment can generate an exhaustive *list* of its components, it cannot *comprehend* the all-important assemblage of features of black life. What explains why a greater proportion of black mothers are single, young, malnourished, high-school dropouts, and so on?

Here the right is ready with a "lifestyle" response as a unifying theme: blacks, not racism, are the source of their own health woes. . . . The Reagan administration [was a] chief promoter of this view—made evident by the 1985 publication of the Report of the Secretary's Task Force on Black and Minority Health. Just one weapon among many in the government's vicious ideological war to justify its savage gutting of health and social service programs, the report shifts responsibility for the burden of disease to the minority communities themselves. Promoting "health education" as a panacea, the government hopes to counsel minorities to eat better, exercise more, smoke and drink less, be less violent, seek health care earlier for symptoms, and in general be better health-care consumers. This "lifestyle" version of the environmental model accordingly is fully compatible with the genetic model (i.e., genetic disadvantage can be exaggerated by lifestyle choices) and echoes its ideological messages that individual shortcomings are at the root of ill health.

In focusing on individual health habits, the task force report ironically echoes the language of many "health radicals," ranging from iconoclasts such as Ivan Illich to counterculture advocates of individually oriented self-help strategies. United in practice, if not in spirit, these apparently disparate camps all take a "holistic" view, arguing that disease comes not just from germs or chemicals but from lifestyle choices about food, exercise, smoking, and stress. Their conflation of lifestyle choices and life circumstance can reach absurd proportions. Editorializing on the task force report, the *New York Times* agreed that: "Disparities may be due to cultural or lifestyle differences. For example, a higher proportion of blacks and hispanics live in cities, with greater exposure to hazards like pollution, poor housing, and crime." But what kind of "lifestyle" causes pollution, and who chooses to live in high-crime neighborhoods? Both the conservative and alternative "lifestyle" versions of the environmental model deliberately ignore or distort the fact that economic coercion and political disenfranchisement, not free choice, locate minority communities in the most hazardous regions of cities. What qualitatively constrains the option of blacks to "live right" is the reality of being black and poor in the United States.

But liberals have had little response when the right points out that even the most oppressed and impoverished people make choices affecting their health: it may be hard to eat right if the neighborhood grocer doesn't sell fresh vegetables, but teenage girls do not have to become pregnant. For liberals, it has been easier to portray blacks as passive, blameless victims and in this way avoid the highly charged issue of health behaviors altogether. The end result is usually just proposals for more health services *for* blacks, bandaids for the gaping wounds of oppression. Yet while adequate health services certainly are needed, they can do little to stem the social forces which cause disease.

Too often the left has been content merely to trail behind the liberals in campaigns for health services, or to call only for social control of environmental and occupational exposures. The right, however, has shifted the terrain of battle to the issue of individual behavior, and we must respond. It is for the left to point out that society does not consist of abstract individuals, but rather of people whose life options are shaped by their intrinsic membership in groups defined by the social relations of their society. Race and class broadly determine not only the conditions under which blacks and whites live, but also the ways in which they can respond to these conditions and the political power they have to alter them. The material limits produced by oppression create and constrain not only the type of housing you live in, but even the most intimate choices about what you do inside your home. . . .

Popular Culture

Backlash

Susan Faludi

The first action of the new women's liberation movement to receive national front-page coverage was a protest of the Miss America pageant.[1] Many feminist marches for jobs, pay equity, and coeducation had preceded it, but they didn't attract anywhere near the media attention. The reason this event got so much ink: a few women tossed some padded brassieres in a trash can. No one actually burned a bra that day—as a journalist erroneously reported. In fact, there's no evidence that any undergarment was ever so much as singed at any women's rights demonstration in the decade. (The only two such displays that came close were both organized by *men,* a disc jockey and an architect, who tried to get women to fling their bras into a barrel and the Chicago River as "media events." Only three women cooperated in the river stunt—all models hired by the architect.[2]) Yet, to read the press accounts of the time, the bonfires of feminism nearly cremated the lingerie industry.

Mostly, editors at the nation's reigning publications in the late '60s and early '70s preferred not to cover the women's movement at all. The "grand press blitz," as some feminists jokingly called the media's coverage of the movement, lasted three months; by 1971, the press was already declaring this latest "fad" a "bore" or "dead."[3] All that "bra burning," the media perversely said of its own created myth, had alienated middle-American women. And publications where editors were forced to recognize the women's movement—they were under internal pressure as women on staff filed sex discrimination suits—often deployed reporters to discredit it. At *Newsday,* a male editor assigned reporter Marilyn Goldstein a story on the women's movement with these instructions: "Get out there and find an authority who'll say this is all a crock of shit."[4] At *Newsweek,* Lynn Young's 1970 story on the women's movement, the magazine's first, was rewritten every week for two months, then killed.[5] Finally, *Newsweek* commissioned a freelancer for the job, the wife of a senior editor and a self-professed antifeminist. (This tactic backfired when she changed her mind after "my first interview" and embraced the movement.[6])

By the mid-'70s, the media and advertisers had settled on a line that served to neutralize and commercialize feminism at the same time. Women, the mass media seemed to have decided, were now equal and no longer seeking new rights—just new lifestyles. Women wanted self-gratification, not self-determination—the sort of fulfillment best serviced at a shopping mall. Soon periodicals and, of course, their ad pages, were bristling with images of "liberated single girls" stocking up on designer swimsuits for their Club Med vacations, perky MBA "Superwomen" flashing credit cards at the slightest provocation. "She's Free. She's Career. She's Confident," a Tandem jewelry ad enthused, in an advertorial tribute to the gilded Tandem girl. Hanes issued its "latest liberating product"—a new variety of pantyhose—and hired a former NOW officer to peddle it.[7] The subsequent fashion show, entitled "From Revolution to Revolution: The Undercover Story," merited feature treatment in the *New York Times.* SUCCESS! was the stock headline on magazine articles about women's status—as if all barriers to women's opportunity had suddenly been swept aside. UP THE LADDER, FINALLY! *Business Week* proclaimed, in a 1975 special issue on "the Corporate Woman"—illustrated with a lone General Electric female vice president enthroned in her executive chair, her arms raised in triumph.[8] "More women than ever are within striking distance of the top," the magazine asserted—though, it admitted, it had "no hard facts" to substantiate that claim.

The media's pseudofeminist cheerleading stopped suddenly in the early '80s—and the press soon struck up a dirge. Feminism is "dead," the banner headlines announced, all over again.[9] "The women's movement is over," began a cover story in the *New York Times Magazine*.[10] In case readers missed that issue, the magazine soon ran a second obituary, in which Ivy League students recanted their support for the women's movement and assured readers that they were "not feminists" because those were just women who "let themselves go physically" and had "no sense of style."[11]

This time around, the media did more than order up a quiet burial for the feminist corpse. They went on a rampage, smashing their own commercial icons of "liberated" womanhood, tearing down the slick portraits that they themselves had mounted. Like graffiti artists, they defaced the two favorite poster girls of the '70s press—spray-painting a downturned mouth and shriveled ovaries on the Single Girl, and adding a wrinkled brow and ulcerated stomach to the Superwoman. These new images were, of course, no more realistic than the last decade's output. But their effect on live women would be quite real and damaging.

*　　　*　　　*

The press first introduced the backlash to a national audience—and made it palatable. Journalism replaced the "pro-family" diatribes of fundamentalist preachers with sympathetic and even progressive-sounding rhetoric. It cosmeticized the scowling face of antifeminism while blackening the feminist eye. In the process, it popularized the backlash beyond the New Right's wildest dreams.

The press didn't set out with this, or any other, intention; like any large institution, its movements aren't premeditated or programmatic, just grossly susceptible to the prevailing political currents. Even so, the press, carried by tides it rarely fathomed, acted as a force that swept the general public, powerfully shaping the way people would think and talk about the feminist legacy and the ailments it supposedly inflicted on women. It coined the terms that everyone used: "the man shortage," "the biological clock," "the mommy track" and postfeminism." Most important, the press was the first to set forth and solve for a

mainstream audience the paradox in women's lives, the paradox that would become so central to the backlash: women have achieved so much yet feel so dissatisfied; it must be feminism's achievements, not society's resistance to these partial achievements, that is causing women all this pain. In the '70s, the press had held up its own glossy picture of a successful woman and said, "See, she's happy. That must be because she's liberated." Now, under the reverse logic of the backlash, the press airbrushed a frown into its picture of the successful woman and announced, "See, she's miserable. That must be because women are too liberated."

"What has happened to American women?" ABC asked with much consternation in its 1986 special report.[12] The show's host Peter Jennings promptly answered, "The gains for women sometimes come at a formidable cost to them." *Newsweek* raised the same question in its 1986 story on the "new problem with no name."[13] And it offered the same diagnosis: "The emotional fallout of feminism" was damaging women; an "emphasis on equality" had robbed them of their romantic and maternal rights and forced them to make "sacrifices." The magazine advised: " 'When the gods wish to punish us, they answer our prayers,' Oscar Wilde wrote. So it would seem to many of the women who looked forward to 'having it all.' " (This happens to be the same verdict *Newsweek* reached when it last investigated female discontent—at the height of the feminine-mystique backlash. "American women's unhappiness is merely the most recently won of women's rights," the magazine reported then.[14])

The press might have looked for the source of women's unhappiness in other places. It could have investigated and exposed the buried roots of the backlash in the New Right and a misogynistic White House, in a chilly business community and intransigent social and religious institutions. But the press chose to peddle the backlash rather than probe it.

The media's role as backlash collaborator and publicist is a familiar one in American history.

The first article sneering at a "Superwoman" appeared not in the 1980s press but in an American newspaper headline at the turn of the century.[15] Feminists, according to the late Victorian press, were "a herd of hysterical and irrational she-revolutionaries," "fussy, interfering, faddists, fanatics," "shrieking cockatoos," and "unpardonably ridiculous."[16] Feminists had laid waste to the American female population; any sign of female distress was surely another "fatal symptom" of the feminist disease, the periodicals reported. "Why Are We Women Not Happy?" the male-edited *Ladies' Home Journal* asked in 1901—and answered that the women's rights movement was debilitating its beneficiaries.

As American studies scholar Cynthia Kinnard observed in her bibliography of American antifeminist literature, journalistic broadsides against women's rights "grew in intensity during the late 19th century and reached regular peaks with each new suffrage campaign." The arguments were always the same: equal education would make women spinsters, equal employment would make women sterile, equal rights would make women bad mothers. With each new historical cycle, the threats were simply updated and sanitized, and new "experts" enlisted. The Victorian periodical press turned to clergymen to support its brief against feminism; in the '80s, the press relied on therapists.

The 1986 *Newsweek* backlash article, "Feminism's Identity Crisis," quoted many experts on women's condition—sociologists, political scientists, psychologists—but none of the many women supposedly suffering from this crisis. The closest the magazine came was two drawings of a mythical feminist victim: a dour executive with cropped hair is pictured first at her desk, grimly pondering an empty family-picture frame, and then at home, clutching a clock and studying the hands—poised at five minutes to midnight.

The absence of real women in a news account that is allegedly about real women is a hallmark of '80s backlash journalism. The press delivered the backlash to the public through a series of "trend stories," articles that claimed to divine sweeping shifts in female social behavior while providing little in the way of evidence to support their generalizations. The trend story, which may go down as late-20th-century journalism's prime contribution to its craft, professes to offer "news" of changing mores, yet prescribes more than it observes. Claiming to mirror public sentiment, its reflections of the human landscapes are strangely depopulated. Pretending to take the public's pulse, it monitors only its own heartbeat—and its advertisers'.

Trend journalism attains authority not through actual reporting but through the power of repetition. Said enough times, anything can be made to seem true. A trend declared in one publication sets off a chain reaction, as the rest of the media scramble to get the story, too. The lightning speed at which these messages spread has less to do with the accuracy of the trend than with journalists' propensity to repeat one another. And repetition became especially hard to avoid in the '80s, as the "independent" press fell into a very few corporate hands.[17]

Fear was also driving the media's need to dictate trends and determine social attitudes in the '80s, as print and broadcast audiences, especially female audiences, turned to other news sources and advertising plunged—eventually falling to its lowest level in twenty years.[18] Anxiety-ridden media managements became preoccupied with conducting market research studies and "managing" the fleeing reader, now renamed "the customer" by such news corporations as Knight-Ridder.[19] And their preoccupations eventually turned up in the way the media covered the news. "News organizations are moving on to the same ground as political institutions that mold public opinion and seek to direct it," Bill Kovach, former editor of the *Atlanta Journal-Constitution* and the Nieman Foundation's curator, observed.[20] "Such a powerful tool for shaping public opinion in the hands of journalists accustomed to handling fact is like a scalpel in a child's hands: it is capable of great damage."

Journalists first applied this scalpel to American women. While '80s trend stories occasionally considered the changing habits of men, these articles tended to involve men's latest hobbies and whimsies—fly fishing, beepers, and the return of the white shirt. The '80s female trends, by contrast, were the failure to find husbands, get pregnant, or properly bond with their children. NBC, for instance, devoted an entire evening news special to the pseudotrend of "bad girls," yet ignored the real trend of bad boys: the crime rate among boys was climbing twice as fast as for girls.[21] (In New York City, right in the network's backyard, rape arrests of young boys had jumped 200 percent in two years.) Female trends with a more flattering veneer surfaced in women's magazines and newspaper "Style" pages in the decade, each bearing, beneath new-and-improved packaging, the return-to-gender trademark: "the New Abstinence," "the New Femininity," "the New High Monogamy," "the New Morality," "the New Madonnas," "the Return of the Good Girl." While anxiety over AIDS has surely helped fuel promotion of these "new" trends, that's not the whole story. While in the '80s AIDS remained largely a male affliction, these media directives were aimed almost exclusively at women. In each case, women were reminded to reembrace "traditional" sex roles—or suffer the consequences. For women, the trend story was no news report; it was a moral reproach.

The trends for women always came in instructional pairs—the trend that women were advised to flee and the trend that they were pushed to join. For this reason, the paired trends tended to contradict each other. As one woman writer observed wryly in an *Advertising Age* column, "The media are having a swell time telling us, on the one hand, that marriage is 'in' and, on the other hand, that women's chances of marrying are slim. So maybe marriage is 'in' because it's so hard to do, like coal-walking was 'in' a year ago."[22] Three contradictory trend pairs, concerning work, marriage, and motherhood, formed the backlash media's triptych: Superwomen "burnout" versus New Traditionalist "cocooning"; "the spinster boom" versus "the return of marriage"; and "the infertility epidemic" versus "the baby boomlet."

Finally, in female trend stories fact and forecast traded places. These articles weren't chronicling a retreat among women that was already taking place; they were compelling one to happen. The "marriage panic" . . . didn't show up in the polls until after the press's promotion of the Harvard-Yale study.[23] In the mid-'80s, the press deluged readers with stories about how mothers were afraid to leave their children in "dangerous" day care centers. In 1988, this "trend" surfaced in the national polls: suddenly, almost 40 percent of mothers reported feeling fearful about leaving their children in day care; their confidence in day care fell to 64 percent, from 76 percent just a year earlier—the first time the figure had fallen below 70 percent since the survey began asking that question four years earlier.[24] Again, in 1986 the press declared a "new celibacy" trend—and by 1987 the polls showed that the proportion of single women who believed that premarital sex was acceptable had suddenly dropped six percentage points in a year; for the first time in four years, fewer than half of all women said they felt premarital sex was okay.[25]

Finally, throughout the '80s the media insisted that women were fleeing the work force to devote themselves to "better" motherhood. But it wasn't until 1990 that this alleged development made a dent—a very small one—in the labor charts, as the percentage of women in the work force between twenty and forty-four dropped a tiny 0.5 percent, the first dip since the early '60s.[26] Mostly, the media's advocacy of such a female exodus created more guilt than flight: in 1990, a poll of working women by Yankelovich Clancy Shulman found almost 30 percent of them believed that "wanting to put more energy into being a good homemaker and mother" was cause to consider quitting work altogether—an 11 percent increase from just a year earlier and the highest proportion in two decades.

The trend story is not always labeled as such, but certain characteristics give it away: an absence of factual evidence or hard numbers; a tendency to cite only three or four women, typically anonymously, to establish the trend; the use of vague qualifiers like "there is a sense that" or "more and more"; a reliance on the predictive future tense ("Increasingly, mothers will stay home to spend more time with their families"); and the invocation of "authorities" such as consumer researchers and psychologists, who often support their assertions by citing other media trend stories.

Just as the decade's trend stories on women pretended to be about facts while offering none, they served a political agenda while telling women that what was happening to them had nothing to do with political events or social pressures. In the '80s trend analysis, women's conflict was no longer with her society and culture but only with herself. Single women were simply struggling with personal problems; they were "consistently self-destructive" or "overly selective."

The only external combat the press recognized was woman on woman. THE UNDECLARED WAR, a banner headline announced on the front page of the *San Francisco Examiner*'s Style section[27]: "To Work or Not Divides Mothers in the Suburbs." *Child* magazine offered THE MOMMY WARS and *Savvy*'s WOMEN AT ODDS informed readers that "the world is soon to be divided into two enemy camps and one day they may not be civil toward each other."[28] Media accounts encouraged married and single women to view each other as opponents—and even confront each other in the ring on "Geraldo" and "Oprah." IS HE SEPARABLE? was the title of a 1988 *Newsday* article that warned married women to beware the husband-poaching trend; the man shortage had driven single women into "brazen" overtures and wives were advised to take steps to keep "the hussy" at bay.[29]

Trend journalists in the '80s were not required to present facts for the same reason that ministers aren't expected to support sermons with data. The reporters were scripting morality plays, not news stories, in which the middle-class woman played the Christian innocent, led astray by a feminist serpent. In the final scene, the woman had to pay—repenting of her ambitions and "selfish"

pursuit of equality—before she could reclaim her honor and her happiness. The trend stories were strewn with judgmental language about the wages of feminist sin. The ABC report on the ill effects of women's liberation, for example, referred to the "costs" and "price" of equality thirteen times.[30] Like any cautionary tale, the trend story offered a "choice" that implied only one correct answer: Take the rocky road to selfish and lonely independence or the well-paved path to home and flickering hearth. No middle route was visible on the trend story's map of the moral feminine universe. . . .

NEW LABELS, OLD STORY

[In one celebrated trend story a] 1986 *Fortune* cover story entitled "Why Women Are Bailing Out,"[31] [concluded that "A third of all the female MBA's of 197[6] have already returned home]. The article, about businesswomen trained at elite schools fleeing the corporate suite, inspired similar "bailing out" articles in *Forbes, USA Today,* and *U.S. News & World Report,* among others.[32]

The *Fortune* story left an especially deep and troubling impression on young women aspiring to business and management careers; after all, it seemed to have hard data. A year later at Stanford University's Graduate School of Business, women were still talking about the article and the effect it had had on them.[33] Phyllis Strong, a Stanford MBA candidate, said she now planned to look for a less demanding career, after reading how "you give up too much" and "you lose that sense of bonding and family ties" when you take on a challenging business job. Marcia Walley, another MBA candidate, said that she now understood "how impossible it is to have a successful career and a good family life. You can't have it all and you have to choose." . . . . The year after *Fortune* launched the "bailing out" trend, the proportion of women applying to business schools suddenly began to shrink—for the first time in a decade.[34]

Fortune's 1986 cover photo featured Janie Witham, former IBM systems engineer, seated in her kitchen with her two-year-old daughter on her lap. Witham is "happier at home," *Fortune*'s cover announced.[35] She has time now to "bake bread." She is one of "many women, including some of the best educated and most highly motivated," wrote the article's author, *Fortune* senior writer Alex Taylor III, who are making "a similar choice" to quit work. "These women were supposed to lead the charge into the corridors of corporate power," he wrote. "If the MBAs cannot find gratification there [in the work force], can *any* [his italics] women?"

The *Fortune* story originated from some cocktail chatter at a *Fortune* editor's class reunion. While mingling with Harvard Business School classmates, Taylor's editor heard a couple of alumnae say they were staying home with their newborns. Suspecting a trend, he assigned the story to Taylor. "He had this anecdotal evidence but no statistics," Taylor recalls.[36] So the reporter went hunting for numbers.

Taylor called Mary Anne Devanna, research coordinator at Columbia Business School's Center for Research in Career Development. She had been monitoring MBA women's progress for years—and she saw no such trend. "I told him, 'I don't believe your anecdotes are right,'" she recalls. "'We have no evidence that women are dropping out in larger numbers.' And he said, 'Well, what would convince you?'" She suggested he ask *Fortune* to commission a study of its own. "Well, *Fortune* apparently said a study would cost $36,000 so they didn't want to do one," she says, "but they ended up running the story anyway."[37]

Instead of a study, Taylor took a look at alumni records for the Class of '76 from seventeen top business schools. But these numbers did not support the trend either: in 1976, the same proportion of women as men went to work for large corporations or professional firms, and ten years later virtually the same proportion of women and men were still working for these employers.

Nonetheless, the story that Taylor wrote stated, "After ten years, significantly more women than men dropped off the management track." As evidence, Taylor cited this figure: "Fully 30 percent of the 1,039 women from the class of '76 reported they are either self-employed or unemployed, or they listed no occupation." That would seem newsworthy but for one inconvenient fact: 21 percent of the *men* from the same class also were self-employed or unemployed. So the "trend" boiled down to a 9 percentage-point difference. Given that working women still bear primary responsibility for child care and still face job discrimination, the real news was that the gap was so *small*.

"The evidence is rather narrow," Taylor concedes later. "The drop-out rates of men and women are roughly the same."[38] Why then did he claim that women were fleeing the work force in "disquieting" numbers? Taylor did not actually talk to any of the women in the story. "A [female] researcher did all the interviews," Taylor says. "I just went out and talked to the deep thinkers, like the corporate heads and social scientists." One woman whom Taylor presumably did talk to, but whose example he did not include, is his own wife. She is a director of corporate communications and, although the Taylors have two children, three years old and six months old at the time of the interview, she's still working. "She didn't quit, it's true," Taylor says. "But I'm struck by the strength of her maternal ties."

The *Fortune* article passed lightly over political forces discouraging businesswomen in the '80s and concluded that women flee the work force because they simply would "rather" stay home. Taylor says he personally subscribes to this view: "I think motherhood, not discrimination, is the overwhelming reason women are dropping out." Yet, even the ex-IBM manager featured on the cover didn't quit because she wanted to stay home. She left because IBM refused to give her the flexible schedule she needed to care for her infant. "I wish things had worked out," Witham told the magazine's interviewer. "I would like to go back."

Three months later, *Fortune* was back with more of the same. "A woman who wants marriage and children," the magazine warned, "realizes that her Salomon Brothers job probably represents a choice to forgo both."[39] But *Fortune* editors still couldn't find any numbers to support their retreat-of-the-businesswoman trend. In fact, in 1987, when they finally did conduct a survey on business managers who seek to scale back career for family life, they found an even smaller 6 percent gender gap, and 4 percent *more* men than women said they had refused a job or transfer because it would mean less family time.[40] The national pollsters were no help either: they couldn't find a gap at all; while 30 percent of working women said they might quit if they could afford it, 30 percent of the men said that too.[41] And contrary to the press about "the best and brightest" burning out, the women who were well educated and well paid were the least likely to say they yearned to go home. In fact, a 1989 survey of 1,200 Stanford business-school graduates found that among couples who both hold MBAs and work, the husbands "display more anxiety."[42] . . .

THE SPINSTER BOOM: THE SORROW AND THE PITY

"In all respects, young single American women hold themselves in higher regard now than a year ago," the *New York Times* noted in 1974.[43] Single women are more "self-assured, confident, secure." The article concluded, "The [women's] movement, apparently, is catching on."

Such media views of single women were certainly catching on in the '70s. *Newsweek* quickly elevated the news of the happy single woman to trend status. "Within just eight years, singlehood has emerged as an intensely ritualized—and newly respectable—style of American life," the magazine ruled in a 1973 cover story.[44] "It is finally becoming possible to be both single and whole." In fact, according to *Newsweek,* the single lifestyle for women was more than "respectable"; it was a thrill a minute. The cover photo featured a grinning blonde in a bikini, toasting her good fortune poolside. Inside, more singles beamed as they sashayed from sun decks to moonlit dances. "I may get married or I just

may not," a flight attendant, who described her single status as "pretty groovy," told the magazine. "But if I do, it will be in my own time and on my own terms. . . . I see nothing wrong with staying single for as long as you please." And even *Newsweek*'s writers, though betraying some queasiness at such declarations, ultimately gave a round of applause to these spunky new singles who weren't "settling for just any old match."

The many features about giddy single women in the early '70s left the impression that these unwed revelers rarely left their beach towels. The stereotype got so bad that one bachelor grumbled in a 1974 *New York Times* article, "From reading the press, you'd think that every girl is 36-24-36 . . . and every guy lounges by a poolside and waits for the beautiful blondes to admire his rippling muscles."[45]

Married life, on the other hand, acquired a sour and claustrophobic reputation in the early '70s press. "Dropout Wives—Their Number Is Growing," a 1973 *New York Times* trend story advised, asserting that droves of miserable housewives were fleeing empty marriages in search of more "fulfilled" lives.[46] The *Times*'s portrait of the wedded state was bleak: it featured husbands who cheat, criticize and offer "no communication," and wives who obsessively drink and pop pills. According to *Newsweek,* married couples were worse than troubled—they were untrendy: "One sociologist has gone so far as to predict that 'eventually married people could find themselves living in a totally singles-oriented society.'"[47]

A dozen years later, these same publications were sending out the opposite signals. *Newsweek* was now busy scolding single women for refusing to "settle" for lesser mates, and the *New York Times* was reporting that single women are "too rigid to connect" and suffer from "a sickness almost."[48] Single women were no longer the press's party girls; with a touch of the media's wand, they were turned back into the scowling scullery maids who couldn't go to the ball. TOO LATE FOR PRINCE CHARMING? the *Newsweek* headline inquired sneeringly, over a drawing of a single woman sprawled on a lonely mattress, a teddy bear her only companion.[49] The magazine now offered only mocking and insincere pity for women shut out of the marital bedroom, which '80s press accounts enveloped in a heavenly, and tastefully erotic, glow. On the front page of the *New York Times,* the unwed woman stalked the empty streets like Typhoid Mary; though "bright and accomplished," she "dreads nightfall, when darkness hugs the city and lights go on in warm kitchens."[50] It's clear enough why she fears the dark: according to the '80s press, nightmares are a single girl's only bedmate. *New York* magazine's 1984 cover story on single women began with this testimony from "Mary Rodgers," which the magazine noted in small print was not her real name: "Last night, I had a terrible dream. The weight of the world was on my shoulders, and it was pressing me into the ground. I screamed for help, but nobody came. When I woke up, I wanted somebody to hold me. But it was just like the dream. There was no husband. No children. Only me."[51]

"Mary" was an executive in a garment firm. Like most of the ailing single women that the '80s media chose to pillory, she was one of the success stories from the women's movement now awakening to the error of her independent ways. She was single because, as the story's own headline put it, she was one of those women who "expect too much."

The campaign for women's rights was, once more, identified as the culprit; liberation had depressed single women. "Loveless, Manless: The High Cost of Independence," read one women's magazine headline.[52] "Feminism became a new form of defensiveness" that drove men away, explained a 1987 *Harper's Bazaar* article, entitled "Are You Turning Men Off?; Desperate and Demanding."[53] *New York*'s story on grim-faced single women summoned an expert, psychotherapist Ava Siegler, who said the women's movement should be blamed for "failing to help women order their priorities."[54] Siegler charged, "It [the women's movement] didn't outline the consequences. We were never told, 'While you're climbing up the corporate ladder, don't forget to pick up a husband and child.'"

ABC's 1986 special, "After the Sexual Revolution," also told single women to hold feminism responsible for their marital status.[55] Women's success has come "at the cost of relationships," co-host Richard Threlkeld said. Even married women are in danger, he advised: "The more women achieve in their careers, the higher their chances for divorce." Co-host Betsy Aaron concurred: Feminists never "calculated *that* as a price of the revolution, freedom and independence turning to loneliness and depression." It wasn't a trade-off Aaron could have deduced from her own life: she had a successful career and a husband—co-host Threlkeld.

The media's preoccupation with single women's miseries reared up suddenly in the mid-1980s. Between 1980 and 1982, as one study has noted, national magazines ran only five feature articles about single women; between 1983 and 1986, they ran fifty-three—and almost all were critical or pitying.[56] (Only seven articles about single men ran in this same period.) The headlines spoke bleakly of THE SAD PLIGHT OF SINGLE WOMEN, THE TERMINALLY SINGLE WOMAN, and SINGLE SHOCK.[57] To be unwed and female was to succumb to an illness with only one known cure: marriage.

The press contributed to single women's woes as much as it reported on them, by redefining single women's low social status as a personal defect. The media spoke ominously of single women's "growing isolation"—but it was an isolation that trend journalism helped create and enforce. In the '70s, the media's accounts featured photos and stories of real single women, generally in groups. In the '80s, the press offered drawings of fictional single women and tales of "composite" or "anonymous" single women—almost always depicted alone, hugging a tear-stained pillow, or gazing forlornly from a garret window. *McCall's* described the prototype this way: "She's the workaholic, who may enjoy an occasional dinner with friends but more likely spends most of her time alone in her apartment, where she nightly retreats as her own best friend."[58]

Just as the press had ignored the social inequalities that cause career women to "burn out," it depoliticized the situation of single women. While '70s press reports had chipped away at the social stigma that hurt single women, the '80s media maintained, with the aid of pop psychologists, that single women's troubles were all self-generated. As a therapist maintained in the *New York Times* story on single women, "Women are in this situation because of neurotic conflicts." This therapist was even saying it about herself; she told the *Times* she had entered "intensive analysis" to cure herself of this singular distaff disorder.

The media's presentation of single women as mental patients is a well-worn backlash tradition. In the late Victorian press, single women were declared victims of "andromania" and "marriage dread."[59] After briefly rehabilitating single women as sprightly "bachelor girls" in the early 1900s, the press condemned them to the mental ward once more for the duration of the Depression. In the '30s, *Good Housekeeping* conducted a poll of single career women that looked for signs of psychic distress. When the single women all said they were quite satisfied with their lives, the magazine inquired hopefully, "May not some of them have hidden a longing that hurt like a wound . . . as they bent above some crib and listened to the heavy sleeping breath that rhythmed from rosy lips?"[60] And yet again in the '50s, a parade of psychoanalysts led by Marynia Farnham and Ferdinand Lundberg, authors of the 1947 leading manual, *Modern Woman: The Lost Sex*, marched through the women's magazines, declaring single women "defeminized" and "deeply ill."

When the backlash press wasn't labeling single women mental misfits, it was busy counting the bodies. Not only were single women sick, the media pundits warned, they were outnumbered—a message that only helped to elevate anxiety levels. The late Victorian press was obsessed with calculating the exact number of "excess" or "redundant" single women; national periodicals printed graphs and tables listing the overabundance of unaccounted-for women. "Why Is Single Life Becoming More General?" *The Nation* pondered in 1868, noting that the issue "is fast getting into the category of topics of universal discussion."[61] The ratio was so bad, *Harper's Bazar* exclaimed in 1874, that men could get "wives at discount," and "eight melancholy maids" clung to the same bachelor's arm at parties.[62] "The universal cry is 'No husbands! No husbands!'" (Feminist ideas, the magazine was quick to add, were to blame for this "dreadful" situation: "Many 'advanced women' forgot that there can be no true progress for them save in the company of, not in opposition to, men.")

By the mid-1980s, the media was busy once more counting heads in the single-woman pool and issuing charts that supposedly proved a surplus of unattached women, which the press now called "the spinster boom" and "hypermaidenism."[63] The most legendary tally sheet appeared in *Newsweek*. "If You're a Single Woman, Here Are Your Chances of Getting Married," the headline on *Newsweek's* June 2, 1986 cover helpfully announced. The accompanying graph plunged like the north face of the Matterhorn, its color scheme changing from hot red to frigid blue as it slid past thirty—and into Old Maid free-fall. "The traumatic news came buried in an arid demographic study," *Newsweek's* story began, "titled innocently enough, 'Marriage Patterns in the United States.'[64] But the dire statistics confirmed what everybody suspected all along: that many women who seem to have it all—good looks and good jobs, advanced degrees and high salaries—will never have mates."

Newsweek took the flawed and unpublished Harvard-Yale marriage study and promoted it to cover-story celebrity status. A few months later, the magazine received the more comprehensive U.S. Census Bureau marriage study and shrank it to a two-paragraph item buried in the "Update" column.[65] Why? Eloise Salholz, *Newsweek's* lead writer on the marriage study story, later explains the showcasing of the Harvard-Yale study in this way: "We all knew this was happening before that study came out. The study summarized impressions we already had."[66]

The *New York Times* assigned a staff writer to the Harvard-Yale study and produced a lengthy story.[67] But when it came time to cover the Census Bureau study, the *Times* didn't even waste a staff writer's time; it just used a brief wire story and buried it.[68] And almost a year after demographers had discredited the Harvard-Yale study, the *New York Times* ran a front-page story on how women were suffering from this putative man shortage, citing the Harvard-Yale study as proof.[69] Asked to explain this later, the story's author, Jane Gross, says, "It was untimely, I agree."[70] But the story was assigned to her, so she made the best of it. The article dealt with the fact that the study had been invalidated by dismissing the entire critique as "rabid reaction from feminists."[71]

Some of the press's computations on the marriage crunch were at remedial levels. The *Newsweek* story declared that single women "are more likely to be killed by a terrorist" than marry.[72] Maybe *Newsweek* was only trying to be metaphorical, but the terrorist line got repeated with somber literalness in many women's magazines, talk shows, and advice books. "Do you know that . . . forty-year-olds are more likely to be killed by a terrorist than find a husband?"[73] gasped the press release that came with Tracy Cabot's *How to Make a Man Fall in Love with You*. A former *Newsweek* bureau intern who was involved in the story's preparation later explains how the terrorist analogy wound up in the magazine: "What happened is, one of the bureau reporters was going around saying it as a joke—like, 'Yeah, a woman's more likely to get bumped off by a terrorist'—and next thing we knew, one of the writers in New York took it seriously and it ended up in print."[74]

Newsweek's "marriage crunch" story, like its story on a "mother's choice," was a parable masquerading as a numbers report. It presented the "man shortage" as a moral comeuppance for independent-minded women who expected too much. *Newsweek*'s preachers found single women guilty of at least three deadly sins: Greed—they put their high-paying careers before the quest for a husband.[75] Pride—they acted "as though it were not worth giving up space in their closets for anything less than Mr. Perfect." And sloth—they weren't really out there beating the bushes; "even though they say they want to marry, they may not want it enough."

Now came judgment day. "For many economically independent women, the consequences of their actions have begun to set in," *Newsweek* intoned.[76] "For years bright young women single-mindedly pursued their careers, assuming that when it was time for a husband they could pencil one in. They were wrong." *Newsweek* urged young women to learn from the mistakes of their feminist elders: "Chastened by the news that delaying equals forgoing, they just may want to give thought to the question [of marriage] sooner than later."

For the further edification of the young, *Newsweek* lined up errant aging spinsters like sinners before the confessional grate and piously recorded their regrets: "Susan Cohen wishes she had been able to see her way clear to the altar.[77] 'Not being of sound mind,' she refused several marriage proposals when she was younger." Pediatrician Catherine Casey told the magazine's inquisitors, "I never doubted I would marry, but I wasn't ready at twenty-two. I was more interested in going to school. . . . Now my time clock is striking midnight."

Parading the penitent unwed became a regular media tearjerker, and it was on the network news programs that the melodrama enjoyed its longest run. "CBS Morning News" devoted a *five*-day special in 1987 to the regrets of single women.[78] Just like the timing of the *Newsweek* story, the show was graciously aired in the wedding month of June. "We thought we were going to be dating for twenty-five years," one woman moaned. "We'll be sitting here in our forties and our biological clocks will have stopped," wailed another. The relentless CBS newscaster behaved as if she were directing an on-air group therapy session.

"Have you always been this way?" she pressed her patients. "What are you scared of?" "Do you all have strong relationships with your dads?" "Did you learn to talk as kids?"

ABC took television psychiatry one step further in its three-hour special in 1986.[79] Not only did the network hire a psychiatrist to serve as a behind-the-scenes consultant, the newscaster managed to badger one of the program's subjects into an on-camera breakdown. Laura Slutsky, thirty-seven and single, the president of her own company, tried to explain that while living alone could be a "difficult challenge," she was determined to "make my life work." "I'll do it," she said, "I'll be classy about it, at times." But the interviewer would have none of it and kept at her. Finally:

Interviewer: Face that fear a minute for me.

Slutsky: Wait a second, this is not easy stuff. [starts to cry] The fear of being alone is not—I don't like it. I'll do it though. Why am I crying? I don't know why I'm crying. . . . These are hard questions. . . . But I'll do it. I'll do it. I don't want to do it. I don't want to do it.

Apparently still not sated, ABC aired another special the following year, this one the four-day "Single in America."[80] Co-anchor Kathleen Sullivan set the tone in the opening segment: "Well, when I first heard that we were going to do this," she announced on the air, "I said, so what? I mean, who cares about singles? They don't have responsibilities of family. They're only career-motivated." But, she added generously, she's learned to pity them: "I at first wasn't compassionate, but now I am.". . .

Despite the title "Single in America," the network program never addressed the status of single men. The omission was typical. The promotional literature for ABC's "After the Sexual Revolution" actually promised to discuss the impact on men. But it never did. Asked to explain the omission later, co-host Richard Threlkeld says, "There wasn't any time. We only had three hours."[81]

When the press did manage to fit the single man into its busy schedule, it was not to extend condolences. On the cover of the *New York Times* Sunday magazine, a single man luxuriated in his well-appointed bachelor pad. Reclining on his parquet floor, his electric guitar by his side, he was casually reading a book and enjoying (much to the joy of the magazine's cigarette advertisers, no doubt) a smoke. WHY WED? was the headline.[82] Inside, the story's author Trip Gabriel clucked patronizingly about the "worries" of "the army of single women in their thirties." Of single men, however, he had this to say: "I was impressed by the men I talked with" and "I came away thinking bachelorhood a viable choice." Even the men who seemed to be avoiding women altogether earned his praise. He saw nothing wrong, for example, with a thirty-year-old man who recoiled from Saturday night dates because "Sunday's my game day." Nor did he wonder about a thirty-five-year-old single sports photographer who told him, "To me, relationships always seemed very stifling." Instead, Gabriel praised his bachelorhood as a "mature decision."

Having whipped single women into high marital panic—or "nuptialitis," as one columnist called it—the press hastened to soothe fretted brows with conjugal tonic.[83] In what amounted to an enormous dose of free publicity for the matchmaking and bridal industries, the media helped peddle exorbitant miracle cures for the mentally, and statistically, handicapped single women—with scores of stories on $1,000 "How to Marry the Man of Your Choice" workshops, $4,600 dating service memberships that guaranteed marriage within three years, and $25,000 matchmaking consultations.[84] "Time is running out for single people," a *San Francisco Chronicle* columnist (himself an aging bachelor) advised, and then turned his column over to a dating service owner who was anxious to promote her new business: "There's a terrific scramble going on now," she alerted single women, "and in two years there just isn't going to be anyone left out there. There aren't going to be all these great surplus older guys."[85] The media even offered their own coaching and counseling assistance. *New York* trotted out inspirational role models—single women who managed to marry after forty. "When they really decided to set their sights on a marriageable man," the article, entitled "Brides at Last," declared, "they found one."[86] *USA Today* even played doctor, offering a special hot line for troubled singles—with psychologists working the phones.[87] The telephone monitors confessed to being "startled" at the results: lovelorn male callers outnumbered women—by two to one.

Women's magazines rose most grandly to the occasion. Nuptialitis was, after all, their specialty. *Cosmopolitan*'s February 1989 issue offered an eleven-page guide to oiling the husband trap, under the businesslike title "How to Close the Deal."[88] The magazine lectured, "You've read the statistics: More women than men practically everywhere but San Quentin. . . . You have to tidy up your act. *Starting right now.*" Its get-married-quick pointers were all on loan from the last backlash's advice books. Among them: pretend to be less sexually experienced than you are, play up your knitting and cooking skills, let him do most of the talking, and be "extremely accepting." At *Mademoiselle,* similar 1950s-style words of wisdom were on tap: the magazine promoted "The Return of Hard-to-Get," advised women to guard their "dating reputation," and reminded them, "Smart Cookies Don't Phone First."[89] And a *New Woman* cover story by Dr. Joyce Brothers offered some old advice for gold-band hunters: "Why You Shouldn't Move In With Your Lover."[90]

While the press was busy pressing single women into marriage, it was simultaneously ordering already married women to stay put. One effective holding action: spreading fear about life after divorce. In 1986, NBC ran a special report that focused exclusively on "the negative consequences of divorce." *Cosmopolitan* offered a four-page feature wholly devoted to divorce's drawbacks. "Singlehood seems so tempting when you're wrangling bitterly," it instructed.[91] "But be forewarned: More and more marital veterans and experts in the field are cautioning potential divorcées to be wary—extremely wary—of eight common, dangerous delusions [about divorce]." For women, the press reported over and over again,

broken wedding vows lead to severe depression, a life of loneliness, and an empty bank account.

To stave off divorce, the media once more came to the rescue with friendly advice and stern moral lectures. CBS revived "Can This Marriage Be Saved?"—the old *Ladies' Home Journal* feature—as a nationwide talk show in 1989, offering on-air reconciliation for couples with rocky relations.[92] "How to Stay Married" was *Newsweek*'s offering—a 1987 cover story replete with uplifting case studies of born-again couples who had gone "right to the edge" before finding "salvation," usually through a therapist's divine intervention.[93] Several marital counselors made promotional appearances in these pages, one hawking a sixteen-week marital improvement program—for newlyweds.

"How times have changed!" *Newsweek* wrote.[94] "Americans are taking marriage more seriously." The magazine had no evidence that a marital boom was in progress. All it could produce was this flimsy statistic: an insignificant 0.2 percent drop in the divorce rate.

INFERTILITY ILLNESS AND BABY FEVERS

"Is this surge in infertility the yuppie disease of the '80s?" NBC correspondent Maria Shriver asked in a 1987 special report.[95] Could it be, she worried, turning to her lineup of experts, that barren wombs have become "The Curse of the Career Woman"? Her experts, infertility doctors hawking costly experimental cures, were only too happy to agree.

By now, the trend journalists had it down; they barely needed an expert to point out the enemy. If it was a woman's problem, then they knew women's quest for independence and equality must be to blame. In the case of the "curse of the career woman," the witch casting the spell must be carrying her own wallet—with, doubtless, a NOW membership card inside. The headlines made it clear why women's wombs were drying up: "Having It All: Postponing Parenthood Exacts a Price"[96] and "The Quiet Pain of Infertility: For the Success-Oriented, It's a Bitter Pill."[97] As a *New York Times* columnist asserted, the infertile woman today is "a walking cliché" of the feminist generation, "a woman on the cusp of forty who put work ahead of motherhood."[98]

Newsweek devoted two cover stories to the "trend of childlessness."[99] Between shots of lone career women in corner offices and lone teddy bears in empty cribs, *Newsweek* warned that as many as 20 percent of women in their early to mid-thirties will end up with no babies of their own—and "those numbers will be even higher for women with high-powered careers, the experts say."[100] The expert that *Newsweek* used to support this point was none other than Harvard economist David Bloom, co-author of the infamous Harvard-Yale marriage study.[101] Now he was saying that 30 percent of all female managers will wind up childless.

Not to be upstaged in the motherhood department, *Life* issued its own special report, "Baby Craving," which said that "millions" of career women will "pay a price for waiting."[102] *Life* produced photographic evidence: Mary Chase, a forty-two-year-old writer and producer, who stared contritely at an empty bassinet. In subsequent snapshots, Mary was examined by an infertility specialist, bared her back to an acupuncturist attempting to "stimulate the energy," sought counsel from a male psychic claiming to have inspired one pregnancy, stood on her head in her underwear after having sex, and opened her mouth wide for husband Bill, who peered in and tried "to uncover early traumas that might block Mary's ability to conceive." The couple didn't know the cause of their fertility troubles, so it was just as likely that Bill's "early traumas" were the problem. (Infertility odds are the same for both sexes.) But the *Life* story never dealt with that possibility.

As in all trend stories, the data supporting the infertility epidemic were nonexistent, so the magazines had to fudge. "It's hard to tell, but infertility may be on the rise," *Newsweek* said.[103] "There are few good statistical measures of how infertility has overtaken our lives," *Life* said.[104] Of course, plenty of good statistical measures existed; they just didn't uphold the story of the "curse of the career woman." Some magazine articles got around the lack of proof by simply shifting to the future tense. *Mademoiselle,* for example, offered this prediction—in upper-case type: THE INFERTILITY EPIDEMIC IS COMING.[105] And a 1982 feature in the *New York Times* just cast aspersions on all skeptics.[106] Women in their thirties who don't believe their infertility odds are high must be suffering "on an emotional level" from "a need to deny the findings."

The week that this *New York Times* feature ran, women who subscribed to both the *Times* and *Time* magazine must have been bewildered. While the *Times* was busy bemoaning the empty wombs of thirty-plus professional women—it ran, in fact, two such stories that week—*Time* was burbling about all the inhabited ones. The newsweekly was pushing the other half of the trend pair: a baby boomlet. "Career women are opting for pregnancy and they are doing it in style," the magazine cheered in its cover story entitled "The New Baby Bloom."[107] Once again, federal Census numbers didn't bear *Time* out; the birthrate had not changed for more than a decade. But that was beside the point. The baby-boomlet trend was only a carrot for the infertility epidemic's stick. *Time* made that clear when it complemented its boomlet story with this cautionary sidebar article: "The Medical Risks of Waiting."[108]

To get around the lack of data, *Time* resorted to the familiar trend euphemisms: "More and more career women," it asserted, "are choosing pregnancy before the clock strikes twelve."[109] Then it quickly directed readers' attention to a handful of pregnant movie stars and media celebrities. Former "Charlie's Angels" actress Jaclyn Smith and Princess Diana were expecting, so it must be a national phenomenon.

Time wasn't the only publication to substitute a few starlets for many numbers. *McCall's* gushed over "Hollywood's Late-Blooming Moms."[110] *Vogue*'s story on "baby fever" exulted over still another mom from the "Charlie's Angels" set: "Motherhood is consuming Farrah Fawcett. All she wants to talk about is breast-feeding."[111] Reaching even farther afield for evidence of baby mania, the press made much of this bulletin from a zoo official claiming to communicate with a primate: "Koko the Gorilla Tells Keeper She Would Like to Have a Baby."[112] And, just as it had done with single women, the media sought to induce pregnancy with counseling and even prizes. Radio stations in Iowa and Florida sponsored "Breeder's Cup" contests—a $1,000 savings bond, six months' diaper service, and a crib to the first couple to conceive.[113]

The mythical "baby bloom" inspired even more florid tributes on the press's editorial pages. The *San Francisco Chronicle* waxed eloquent:

> In our personal life, we must observe, we have noted an absolute blossoming of both marriages and of births to many women who seemed, not all that long ago, singlemindedly devoted to the pursuit of personal careers. It's nice to hear again the sound of wedding bells and the gurgles of contented babies in the arms of their mothers.[114]

In less purply prose, the *New York Times* conveyed the same sentiments:

> Some college alumnae answered 25th reunion questionnaires with the almost-guilty admission that they were "only" wives and mothers. But before long, other women found that success at jobs traditionally held by men doesn't infallibly produce a fulfilling life. Motherhood started to come back in style.[115]

If the articles didn't increase the birthrate, it did increase women's anxiety and guilt. "You can't pick up a magazine without reading about another would-be-mom with a fertility problem that might have been less complicated if she had just started at an earlier age," a young woman wrote in an op-ed essay in the *New York Times,* entitled "Motherhood's Better Before Thirty."[116] She was upset, but not with the media for terrorizing women. She was mad at the older women who seemed to think it was safe to wait. "I believe it is my birthright to follow a more biologically sound reproductive schedule," she sniffed, sounding suspiciously MBA-ish under those maternity clothes.

Simply being able to recognize the media onslaught put that young writer ahead of a lot of other women readers who, wondering why they suddenly felt desperate, unworthy, and shameful for failing to reproduce on the media's schedule, decided the signals were coming exclusively from their bodies, not their newspapers. "I wasn't even thinking about having a child, and suddenly, when I was about thirty-four, it gripped me like a claw," a woman confided in *Vogue.*[117] "It was as if I had nothing to do with it, and these raging hormones were saying, 'Do what you are supposed to do, which is reproduce.' It was a physical feeling more than a mental feeling."

In the end, this would be the press's greatest contribution to the backlash: not only dictating to women how they should feel, but persuading them that the voice barking orders was only their uterus talking. . . . .

Notes

1. The first action of the . . .: Klein, *Gender Politics,* pp. 23–24.
2. (The only two such . . .): Joanna Foley Martin. "Confessions of a Non-Bra Burner," *Chicago Journalism Review,* July 1971, 4:11.
3. The "grand press blitz" . . . : Jo Freeman, *The Politics of Women's Liberation: A Case Study of an Emerging Social Movement and Its Relation to the Policy Process* (New York: David McKay, 1975) p. 148; Edith Hoshino Altbach, *Women in America* (Lexington, Mass.: D.C. Heath and Co., 1974) pp. 157–58. For an example of the media using the "bra-burning" myth to invalidate the women's movement, see Judy Klemesrud, "In Small Town USA, Women's Liberation Is Either a Joke or a Bore," *New York Times,* March 22, 1972, p. 54.
4. At *Newsday,* a male . . . : Sandie North, "Reporting the Movement," *The Atlantic,* March 1970, p. 105.
5. At *Newsweek,* Lynn . . . : *Ibid.*
6. (This tactic backfired . . .): "Women in Revolt," *Newsweek,* March 23, 1970, p. 78. Helen Dudar, the *Newsweek* editor's wife, confessed that after having "spent years rejecting feminists without bothering to look too closely at their charges," she had become a convert and wrote that she now

felt a "sense of pride and kinship with all those women who have been asking all the hard questions. I thank them and so, I think, will a lot of other women."

7. Hanes issued its . . . : Veronica Geng, "Requiem for the Women's Movement," *Harper's,* Nov. 1976, p. 49.

8. UP THE LADDER . . . : "Up the Ladder, Finally," *Business Week,* Nov. 24, 1975, p. 58.

9. Feminism is "dead" . . . : See, for example, Sally Ogle Davis, "Is Feminism Dead?" *Los Angeles,* Feb. 1989, p. 114.

10. "The women's movement is over . . .": Betty Friedan, "Feminism's Next Step," *The New York Times Magazine,* July 5, 1981, p. 14.

11. In case readers . . . : Susan Bolotin, "Voices from the Post-Feminist Generation," *The New York Times Magazine,* Oct. 17, 1982, p. 29.

12. "What has happened to . . .": "After the Sexual Revolution," *ABC News Closeup,* July 30, 1986.

13. *Newsweek* raised . . . : Eloise Salholz, "Feminism's Identity Crisis," *Newsweek,* March 31, 1986, p. 58.

14. (This happens to be . . .): *Newsweek,* March 7, 1960, cited in Friedan, *Feminine Mystique,* pp. 19–20.

15. The first article sneering . . . : "Superwoman," *Independent,* Feb. 21, 1907, cited in Kinnard, *Antifeminism,* p. 214.

16. Feminists, according to the . . . : *Ibid.,* pp. 55–61, xiii–ix.

17. And repetition . . . : In 1982, fifty corporations controlled over half the media business; by the end of 1987, the number was down to twenty-six. See Ben H. Bagdikian, *The Media Monopoly* (Boston: Beacon Press, 1990), pp. xix, 3–4; *Media Report to Women,* Sept. 1987, p. 4.

18. Fear was also driving . . . : After 1985, profit margins fell steadily at papers owned by publicly traded communications companies. Women, who make up the majority of newspaper readers and network news viewers, were turning to specialty publications and cable news programs in mass numbers, taking mass advertising dollars with them. See Alex S. Jones, "Rethinking Newspapers," *New York Times,* Jan. 6, 1991, III, p. 1; "Marketing Newspapers to Women," *Women Scope Surveys of Women,* 2, no. 7 (April 1989): 1–2.

19. Anxiety-ridden . . . : In a typical media strategy of the decade, Knight-Ridder Newspapers launched a "customer-obsession" campaign to give readers what management imagined they wanted, rather than what was simply news.

20. "News organizations are . . .": Bill Kovach, "Too Much Opinion, at the Expense of Fact," *New York Times,* Sept. 13, 1989, p. A31.

21. NBC, for instance . . . : "Bad Girls," *NBC News,* August 30, 1989.

22. "The media are having . . .": "The Next Trend: Here Comes the Bribe," *Advertising Age,* June 16, 1986, p. 40.

23. The "marriage panic" . . . : "Women's Views Survey: Women's Changing Hopes, Fears, Loves," *Glamour,* Jan. 1988, p. 142.

24. In 1988, this "trend" . . . : Mark Clements Research, Women's Views Survey, 1988.

25. Again, in 1986 . . . : *Ibid.*

26. But it wasn't until . . . : Amy Saltzman, "Trouble at the Top," *U.S. News & World Report,* June 17, 1991, p. 40.

27. THE UNDECLARED WAR . . . : Carol Pogash, "The Undeclared War," *San Francisco Examiner,* Feb. 5, 1989, p. E1.

28. *Child* magazine offered . . . : Sue Woodman, "The Mommy Wars," *Child,* Sept.-Oct. 1989, p. 139; Barbara J. Berg, "Women at Odds," *Savvy,* Dec. 1985, p. 24.

29. IS HE SEPARABLE?" . . . : Kate White, "Is He Separable?" *Newsday,* May 15, 1988, p. 25.

30. The ABC report . . . : Transcript, "After the Sexual Revolution."

31. Popcorn borrowed . . . : Alex Taylor III, "Why Women Are Bailing Out," *Fortune,* August 18, 1986, p. 16.

32. The article about . . . : *USA Today's* story was, in fact, a report on the *Fortune* "findings": "1 in 3 Management Women Drop Out," *USA Today,* July 31, 1986, p. 1.

33. A year later at Stanford . . . : Personal interviews with a group of female Stanford MBA students, Summer 1988.

34. The year after *Fortune* . . . : Laurie Baum, "For Women, the Bloom Might Be Off the MBA," *Business Week,* March 14, 1988, p. 30.

35. Witham is "happier . . .": Taylor, "Bailing Out," pp. 16–23.

36. "He had this anecdotal evidence . . .": Personal interview with Alex Taylor III, 1988.

37. "I told him . . .": Personal interview with Mary Anne Devanna, 1988.

38. "The evidence is . . .": Personal interview with Taylor, 1988. (Subsequent quotes are from personal interview with Taylor unless otherwise noted.)

39. "A woman who wants marriage . . .": Stratford P. Sherman, "The Party May Be Ending," *Fortune,* Nov. 24, 1986, p. 29.

40. In fact, in 1987, . . . : F. S. Chapman, "Executive Guilt: Who's Taking Care of the Children?" *Fortune,* Feb. 16, 1987. A later review of the alumni records at Columbia University's Graduate School of Business for the class of '76 (the same class that Taylor's story focused on) found no significant female defection from the corporate world and no differences in the proportion of men and women leaving to start their own businesses. See Mary Anne Devanna, "Women in Management: Progress and Promise," *Human Resource Management,* 26, no. 4 (Winter 1987): 469.

41. "The national pollsters were . . . : The 1986 Virginia Slims Opinion Poll; Walsh, "What Women Want," p. 60. A survey conducted jointly by *Working Woman* and *Success* magazines also found that men were more concerned about family life than women and less concerned about career success than women. See Carol Sonenklar, "Women and Their Magazines," *American Demographics,* June 1986, p. 44.

42. In fact, a 1989 survey . . . : Margaret King, "An Alumni Survey Dispels Some Popular Myths About MBA Graduates," *Stanford Business School Magazine,* March 1989, p. 23.

43. "In all respects, young . . .": Philip H. Dougherty, "Women's Self Esteem Up," *New York Times,* May 15, 1974, p. 71.

44. "Within just . . .": "Games Singles Play," *Newsweek,* July 16, 1973, p. 52.

45. The stereotype got so bad . . . : Susan Jacoby, "49 Million Singles Can't All Be Right," *The New York Times Magazine,* Feb. 17, 1974, p. 12.

46. "Dropout Wives . . .": Enid Nemy, "Dropout Wives—Their Number Is Growing," *New York Times,* Feb. 16, 1973, p. 44.

47. According to *Newsweek* . . . : "Games Singles Play," p. 52.

48. *Newsweek* was now . . . : Eloise Salholz, "The Marriage Crunch: If You're a Single Woman, Here Are Your Chances of Getting Married," *Newsweek,* p. 54; Jane Gross, "Single Women: Coping With a Void," *New York Times,* April 28, 1987, p. 1.

49. "TOO LATE FOR . . .": Salholz, "Marriage Crunch," p. 54.

50. On the front page . . . : Gross, "Single Women," p. 1.

51. *New York* magazine's . . . : Patricia Morrisroe, "Born Too Late? Expect Too Much? You May Be Forever Single," *New York,* Aug. 20, 1984, p. 24.

52. "Loveless, Manless . . .": "Loveless, Manless: The High Cost of Independence," *Chatelaine,* Sept. 1984, p. 60.

53. "Feminism became a new form . . .": Tricia Crane, "Are You Turning Men Off? Desperate and Demanding," *Harper's Bazaar,* Sept. 1987, p. 300.

54. *New York*'s story . . . : Morrisroe, "Born Too Late?" p. 30.

55. ABC's 1986 special . . . : ABC News, "After the Sexual Revolution."

56. Between 1980 and 1982 . . . : Trimberger, "Single Women and Feminism in the 1980s."

57. The headlines spoke . . . : "The Sad Plight of Single Women," *Philadelphia Inquirer,* Nov. 30, 1980; Kiki Olson, "Sex and the Terminally Single Woman (There Just Aren't Any Good Men Around)," *Philadelphia Magazine,* April 1984, p. 122.

58. *McCall's* described . . . : Peter Filichia, "The Lois Lane Syndrome: Waiting for Superman," *McCall's,* Aug. 1985, p. 55.

59. In the late Victorian . . . : Kinnard, *Antifeminism,* p. 202.

60. "May not some . . .": Kessler-Harris, *Out to Work,* p. 255.

61. "Why Is Single Life . . .": "Why Is Single Life Becoming More General?" *The Nation,* March 5, 1868, pp. 190–91.

62. The ratio was so bad . . . . "Wives at Discount," *Harper's Bazar,* Jan. 31, 1874, p. 74.

63. By the mid-1980s . . . : Billie Samkoff, "How to Attract Men Like Crazy," *Cosmopolitan,* Feb. 1989, p. 168.

64. "The traumatic news . . . ": Salholz, "Marriage Crunch," p. 25.

65. A few months later . . . : David Gates, "Second Opinion," Update, *Newsweek,* Oct. 13, 1986, p. 10.

66. "We all knew . . .": Personal interview with Eloise Salholz, July 1986.

67. The *New York Times* . . . : William R. Greer,

"The Changing Women's Marriage Market," *New York Times,* Feb. 22, 1986, p. 48.

68. But when it came time . . . : AP, "More Women Postponing Marriage," *New York Times,* Dec. 10, 1986, p. A22.

69. And almost a year after . . . : Gross, "Single Women," p. 1.

70. "It was untimely . . .": Personal interview with Jane Gross, 1988.

71. The article dealt with . . . : Gross, "Single Women," p. 1.

72. The *Newsweek* story . . . : Salholz, "Marriage Crunch," p. 55.

73. "Do you know that . . .": Promotional letter from Dell Publishing Co., from Carol Tavoularis, Dell publicist, Dec. 5, 1986.

74. A former *Newsweek* bureau . . . : Personal interview, Oct. 1986.

75. *Newsweek*'s preachers . . . : Salholz, "Marriage Crunch," pp. 61, 57.

76. "For many economically . . .": *Ibid.,* pp. 61, 55.

77. "Susan Cohen wishes . . .": *Ibid.,* p. 57.

78. "CBS Morning News" devoted . . . : "CBS Morning News," "What Do Single Women Want," Nov. 2–6, 1987.

79. ABC took television . . . : ABC News, "After the Sexual Revolution."

80. Apparently still not . . . : ABC, "Good Morning America," "Single in America," May 4–7, 1987.

81. "There wasn't any time . . .": Personal interview with Richard Threlkeld, 1988.

82. "WHY WED?" . . . : Trip Gabriel, "Why Wed?: The Ambivalent American Bachelor," *The New York Times Magazine,* Nov. 15, 1987, p. 24.

83. Having whipped . . . : Brenda Lane Richardson, "Dreaming Someone Else's Dreams," *The New York Times Magazine,* Jan. 28, 1990, p. 14.

84. In what amounted to . . . : See, for example, Barbara Kantrowitz, "The New Mating Games," *Newsweek,* June 2, 1986, p. 58; James Hirsch, "Modern Matchmaking: Money's Allure in Marketing Mates and Marriage," *New York Times,* Sept. 19, 1988, p. B4, Ruthe Stein, "New Strategies for Singles," *San Francisco Chronicle,* March 29, 1988, p. B1.

85. "Time is running out . . .": Gerald Nachman, "Going Out of Business Sale on Singles," *San Francisco Chronicle,* Dec. 1, 1987, p. B3.

86. "When they really decided . . .": Barbara

Lovenheim, "Brides at Last: Women Over 40 Who Beat the Odds," *New York,* Aug. 3, 1987, p. 20.

87. *USA Today* even . . . : Marlene J. Perrin, "What Do Women Today Really Want?" *USA Today,* July 10, 1986, pp. D1, D5; Karen S. Peterson, "Men Bare Their Souls, Air Their Gripes," *USA Today,* July 14, 1986, p. D1. And the women who called weren't all pleading for a man: "How do you get people to stop asking why I'm not married yet?" was the question posed by one thirty-two-year-old woman from Virginia. See Peterson, "Stop Asking Why I'm Not Married," p. D4.

88. *Cosmopolitan*'s February . . . : Samkoff, "How To Attract Men," pp. 163–73.

89. At *Mademoiselle* . . . : Personal interview with *Mademoiselle* editors, 1988; Cathryn Jakobson, "The Return of Hard-to-Get," March 1987, p. 220.

90. And a *New Woman* . . . : Dr. Joyce Brothers, "Why You Shouldn't Move in With Your Lover," *New Woman,* March 1985, p. 54.

91. "Singlehood seems so . . .": Jeffrey Kluger, "Dangerous Delusions About Divorce," *Cosmopolitan,* Sept. 1984, p. 291.

92. CBS revived . . . : Sue Adolphson, "Marriage Encounter, Tube Style," *San Francisco Chronicle,* Datebook, Jan. 22, 1989, p. 47.

93. "How to Stay Married" . . . : Barbara Kantrowitz, "How To Stay Married," *Newsweek,* August 24, 1987, p. 52.

94. "How times have . . .": *Ibid.*

95. "Is this surge . . .": NBC News Special, "The Baby Business," April 4, 1987.

96. "Having It All . . .": "Having It All: Postponing Parenthood Exacts a Price," *Boston* magazine, May 1987, p. 116.

97. "The Quiet Pain . . .": Mary C. Hickey, "The Quiet Pain of Infertility: For the Success-Oriented, It's a Bitter Pill," *Washington Post,* April 28, 1987, p. DO5.

98. As a *New York Times* . . . : Fleming, "The Infertile Sisterhood," p. B1.

99. *Newsweek* devoted two . . . : Matt Clark, "Infertility," *Newsweek,* Dec. 6, 1982, p. 102; Barbara Kantrowitz, "No Baby on Board," *Newsweek,* Sept. 1, 1986, p. 68.

100. *Newsweek* warned . . . : Kantrowitz, "No Baby," p. 74.

101. The expert that *Newsweek . . .* : *Ibid.*

102. Not to be upstaged . . . : Anna Quindlen, "Special Report: Baby Craving: Facing Widespread Infertility, A Generation Presses the Limits of Medicine and Morality," *Life,* June 1987, p. 23.

103. "It's hard to tell, but . . .": Clark, "Infertility," p. 102.

104. "There are few . . .": Quindlen, "Baby Craving," p. 23.

105. *Mademoiselle,* for example . . . : Laura Flynn McCarthy, "Caution: You Are Now Entering the Age of Infertility," *Mademoiselle,* May 1988, p. 230.

106. And a 1982 . . . : Georgia Dullea, "Women Reconsider Childbearing Over 30," *New York Times,* Feb. 25, 1982, p. C1.

107. "Career women are opting . . .": J. D. Reed, "The New Baby Bloom," *Time,* Feb. 22, 1982, p. 52.

108. *Time* made that . . . : Claudia Wallis, "The Medical Risks of Waiting," *Time,* Feb. 22, 1982, p. 58.

109. "More and more . . .": Reed, "New Baby Bloom," p. 52.

110. *McCall's* gushed . . . : "Hollywood's Late-Blooming Moms," *McCall's,* Oct. 1988, p. 41.

111. "Motherhood is consuming . . .": Leslie Bennetts, "Baby Fever," *Vogue,* Aug. 1985, p. 325.

112. Reaching even farther afield . . . : AP, "Koko the Gorilla Tells Keeper She Would Like to Have a Baby," *San Francisco Chronicle,* March 12, 1988, p. A3.

113. And, just as it had done . . . : Roger Munns, "Couples Race to Get Pregnant," *San Francisco Examiner,* Nov. 19, 1990, p. B5.

114. "In our personal life . . .": "The Marriage Odds Improve," *San Francisco Chronicle,* May 1, 1987, p. 38.

115. "Some college alumnae . . .": "Mothers a la Mode," *New York Times,* May 8, 1988, p. E28. The *Times* editorial writers appeared to have forgotten their own words. Only two months earlier, they had noted that there was no change in the birth rate: "New Baby Boom? No, Just a Dim Echo," *New York Times,* March 30, 1988, p. A26.

116. "You can't pick up a magazine . . .": Kim C. Flodin, "Motherhood's Better Before 30," *New York Times,* Nov. 2, 1989, p. A31.

117. "I wasn't even thinking . . .": Bennetts, "Baby Fever," p. 326.

PERSONAL ACCOUNT

JUST SOMETHING YOU DID AS A MAN

In a class we had discussed the ways men stratify themselves in terms of masculinity. I decided I would put that discussion to the test at work.

As I sat at a table, one of my coworkers approached me with a copy of a popular men's magazine, which portrays nude women. He said, "Frank, there is this bitch in here with the most beautiful big tits I have ever seen in my life." I told him that I wasn't interested in looking at the magazine because I had decided I did not agree with the objectification of women. His reply was, "What's the matter, are you getting soft on us?" I joked that it was not a matter of getting soft, it was simply a decision I had made due to a "new and improved consciousness."

At my job, talk about homosexuals, the women who walk by, and graphic (verbal) depictions of sexual aggression toward women abound, but on this occasion I either rejected the conversation or said nothing at all. By the end of the day I was being called, sometimes jokingly and sometimes not, every derogatory homosexual slur in the English language. I was no longer "one of the boys." I did not engage in the "manly" discourse of the day so therefore I was labeled (at best) a "sissy."

My coworkers assumed that I had had or was about to have a change of sexual orientation simply because I did not engage in their conversations about women and homosexuals. Since men decide how masculine another man is by how much he is willing to put down women and gays, I was no longer considered masculine.

This experience affected me as much as it did because it opened my eyes to a system of stratification in which I have been immersed but still had no idea existed. Demeaning women and homosexuals, to me, was just something you did as a man. But to tell you the truth, I don't think I could go back to talking like that. I am sure that my coworkers will get used to my new thinking, but even if they don't I believe that it is worth being rejected for a cause such as this. I had not thought about it, but I would not want men talking about my sisters and mother in such a demeaning way.

Francisco Hernandez

BASKETBALL

I frequently watch my boyfriend play basketball at an outdoor court with many other males in pick-up games. One time when I was there, there was a new face among the others waiting to play—a female face, and she was not sitting with the rest of the women who were watching. She was dressed and ready to play. I had never seen her in all the time I'd been there before, nor had I ever seen another women there try to play.

For several games, she did not play. The guys formed teams and she was not asked to join. It was almost like there was a purposeful avoidance of her, with no one even acknowledging that she was there. Finally, she made a noticeable effort and with some reluctance she was included in the next team waiting to play the winner of the current game. There were whispers and snickers among the guys, and I think it had a lot to do with the perception that she was challenging their masculinity. A "girl" was intruding into their area. My guess is that they were also somewhat nervous about the fact that she really might be good and embarrass some of them.

Anyway, the first couple of times up and down the court she was not given the ball despite the fact that she was wide open. The other guys on the team forced bad shots and tried super hard in what seemed like an effort to prove that she was not needed. The guy who was supposed to guard her on defense really didn't pay her much attention and that same guy who she was guarding at the other end made sure he drove around her and scored on two occasions.

Finally, one time down the court she called for the ball and sank a shot from at least 16 feet. A huge feeling of relief and satisfaction came over me. Being a basketball player myself, I figured she was probably good or would not be there in the first place, but being a woman I was also happy to see her *first* shot go in. I found out later she had played basketball for a university and she had a great outside shot.

Even after she made one more shot off a rebound that ended up in her hands, she was not given the ball again. I suppose after some of the loud comments from some of the guys on the sidelines, that she was beating the male players out there, she wasn't going to get the ball again. I was kind of shocked that she wasn't *more* accepted even after she showed she was talented. I haven't seen her there since.

Andrea M. Busch

A Field Trip to Straight America

Marshall Kirk and Hunter Madsen

UP AGAINST IT

Consider what gays are up against: the wall. It stretches high and broad, like the Great Wall of China, across the full expanse of American society. Today there is almost no social interaction between straights and gays wherein the latter can safely ignore the barricade of dislike and fear which separates them from the rest. Here we seek to understand exactly what that wall is made of, so that . . . we can proceed to tear it down.

For our purposes, homohatred and homophobia are best viewed from a detached, even unfamiliar distance (if one can manage it), because that's the best way to see the situation clearly—perhaps the way the Great Wall of China can be seen in its entirety only from outer space, or the way a visiting anthropologist would disinterestedly record the folkways of a primitive culture.

The goal here is to develop a list of negative things that straights believe and feel about gays—summarized as seven deadly myths—and harmful things that straights do to gays in consequence of those myths. *This list of prejudices and harmful actions [can] stand as our specific agenda for change.* . . .

WHAT STRAIGHTS THINK OF GAYS

1. They Don't.

"[Homosexuals are] the filthiest, dirtiest human beings on the face of the earth," asserted a town commissioner from Traverse City, Michigan, to the *New York Times* in 1987. He then explained, in defense, that his opinions were based on something he once read about gays. "They are not my opinions because I don't know anything about homosexuals, and I don't want to know anything."

This is the first point for gays to understand: *straights know very little about homosexuality and would prefer to know even less.* Because they find the subject distasteful and disturbing—in any but titillatingly small doses—most heterosexuals simply put it out of their minds with a shudder or a shrug of indifference. They go about their lives as though the issue had no bearing on themselves or anyone they know. Their meager fund of knowledge about homosexuality is constructed from hoary myths, rumors, jokes from their school days, and lurid news stories; and, for most straights, that is enough. . . .

Straight indifference to, or avoidance of, the subject is hard for gays to bear in mind, since they perforce must think about their sexual and social predicament daily. Still, gays who come out to their family or straight friends often experience such shunning of the subject firsthand. After the initial brutal or tearful confrontations with loved ones, the topic of homosexuality somehow has a way of slipping silently, awkwardly off the menu of discussable subjects. "You're homosexual?," said a straight friend, "O.K., that's your business. But I'd rather not hear the details, if you don't mind. And *please* don't invite me to visit a gay bar with you; I'm not ready for that." (And as the years went by, this friend was never to prove ready.)

Observing American society as a whole, its refusal to think too much about homosexuality takes on the appearance of deliberate collusion in what we [call] the Big Lie—the nationwide public pretense that in America there are really no gays to speak of.

Avoidance of Gay News Events and Issues
One sees, for example, blackouts of, or deliberate inattention to, gay news events, in ways both small and big—everything from the tearing down of gay speakers' posters on college campuses to the refusal by the *Washington Post* to cover a large Gay Pride Day celebration in the nation's capital some years back.

One sees efforts to minimize the significance of gay public events. The *New York Times* and other newspapers, for example, evidently underestimated by half the number of gays participating in the momentous Gay & Lesbian March on Washington during October 9–12, 1987. If, as the most reliable gay-news sources maintained, the number of demonstrators totaled roughly half a million, then the event rivaled the largest civil rights marches of the sixties. At least the *Times* put the news of "200,000 protesters" on page one: not a single word about the event appeared in the nation's two largest newsweeklies, *Time* and *Newsweek.* Theirs was so blatant a breach of reporting standards that, had any other minority's mass demonstration been likewise neglected, the omission itself would have become the big news story.

While the press's coverage of gay news is inadequate, even this scant attention is more than enough for most Americans. In an ABC News survey conducted in 1984, for instance, fully half of the public felt that the broadcast press gives altogether *too much* attention to gays. As a conservative columnist has complained acidly, homosexuals have always been around, of course, but, like children, should be seen and not heard.

One also observes the profound *reluctance of society to engage in public discussion of issues that concern gays,* such as homohating violence and AIDS. Indeed, there can be only one reason why it took President Ronald Reagan four years of epidemic to utter the word 'AIDS' for the first time in public—years during which twelve thousand citizens fell ill and some six thousand died: Reagan knew that broaching the subject would require that he acknowledge publicly the existence of a large and growing number of gay Americans suffering from a sexually related disease. Homosexuality remains such a ticklish subject that, as late as 1987, Vice-President Bush felt compelled to confess that there was still a "giggling factor" about AIDS within the administration. . . .

Willful Perpetuation of Ignorance About Homosexuality America is not only reluctant to recognize news events or address public issues concerning gays; it also *refuses to educate citizens on the nature of homosexuality itself.* Prodded by the AIDS crisis, a few school boards have gritted their teeth and begun to teach schoolchildren the meaning of words such as 'homosexual' and 'bisexual.' But, apparently mindful of George Orwell's warning that words have the power to stimulate dangerous thoughts and deeds, most educators have not been eager to expand their pupils' vocabulary. "I've talked to school superintendents around the country," one educator from Montgomery, Alabama, told the *New York Times* "and they don't want AIDS education to broach homosexuality or safe sex practices. As far as they are concerned, that's unconscionable." . . .

Just as the American public will not educate its children, neither will it educate itself about homosexuality. *Straight Americans do not care to read serious treatments of gay life.* This also holds true for straight literary critics, who have little good to say about the burgeoning genre of 'gay literature.' Reviewing a gay novel, one book critic for the *Wall Street Journal* recently carped that the love that dare not speak its name has become "the love that can't shut up."

Not that it really matters whether gay writers scream or shut up about their lives, since few straights are listening in any case. You may convince yourself of this by visiting the deserted Gay Studies aisle of your local bookstore or library. The Gay Studies aisle (or, more likely, shelf) is seldom hard to find: it's usually near the Psychology/Therapy section, even though Gay Studies may include works of fiction, history, sociology, or political science, as well as psychology.

Even straights who are curious do not wish to be seen showing interest in that aisle, for fear of what others may conclude about their sexual proclivities. In contrast, no emotionally normal white male would harbor fears of venturing into the Black Studies or Women's Studies aisle; no one is likely to conclude that he's secretly black or female.

Neglect of Gays in Mass Culture   Indeed, if straights were to learn anything about gays, it would not be in schoolrooms or from serious books: it would be from mass entertainments like television shows, films, and plays. *But heterosexuals do not want to watch homosexuality portrayed in their mass entertainments with any frequency.* Most straights haven't the patience to watch sustained portrayals of gay characters in television series, for example, even though such portrayals could provide genuine education, and help counteract the two-dimensional cardboard stereotypes one usually sees whenever gays are introduced briefly on TV shows and in films.

Of course, there have always been public entertainments which featured clownish homosexual men (but, significantly, seldom lesbians) for comic effect. Homosexuals are least frightening to straights when portrayed, like Step 'N Fetchit, as harmless, childish eunuchs. The film and Broadway hit *La Cage aux Folles* followed this hoary formula and prospered in the 1980s. . . .

But the public has shown mixed interest in the recent spate of TV shows and movies with more serious gay themes. These have featured two subjects: (1) young men dying of AIDS, and/or (2) confused gay women or men who must agonize over their 'choice' to become straight or gay. . . .

These shows have been produced partly because gay Hollywood itches to indulge itself; partly because straight Hollywood understands that sexual exotica clad in the diaphanous fig leaf of social relevance is always a sure bet to attract jaded viewers. (Surely this was one motive behind low-rated ABC's abrupt—and encouraging—addition of gay characters to three of its prime-time dramas in the late 1980s.) Yet the public's interest in such productions is ambivalent and basically prurient. Most straights watch stories about 'gays in crisis' with the lurid, reluctant, peekaboo fascination that attends a bloody roadside car wreck. . . .

There Are No Gay Heroes   Which brings us to the matter of Rock Hudson and other all-American heroes who happen to be gay. Just as straights don't like to see homosexuality portrayed in their mass entertainments, neither do they wish to contemplate it among their celebrities and heroes. *Straights who have come to admire closeted heroes refuse to accept their homosexuality, even when it seems a fact beyond dispute.*

The Rock Hudson scandal provides a classic case of public self-delusion, and even collusion in the Big Lie. Hudson had been actively homosexual throughout his career as Hollywood's ultra-macho leading man, but, like so many other famous gay actors, had hidden the fact from the public, and even entered an arranged marriage for a few years to protect his reputation. When Boze Hadleigh asked him confidentially, in 1982, how many top actors in Hollywood were homosexual, Hudson replied, "Whew! Too many for me to name. If you mean gay, or 'bisexual' . . . then maybe most . . . Trust me, . . . America does not want to know."

As it turned out, Rock was right: America did *not* want to know. Shortly before his death from AIDS in 1985, Hudson contracted with a publisher and coauthor to tell the story of his life, homosexuality and all. When the book (like its subject) came out, the coauthor, Sara Davidson, went on promotional tour and was appalled by her book's incredulous and resentful reception. Writing in the *New York Times Magazine* about her experiences on tour, Davidson said she had "underestimated how devastating it would be for many to learn that a star they had cherished as a symbol of manliness was gay." She was astounded when asked repeatedly by reproachful reporters across the country, "Do we need to know the truth about Rock Hudson?" Davidson said that the low point in her tour came during a talk show stint in Detroit, when an entertainment columnist implied that "the book was 'fiction' and that Rock wasn't gay . . . The audience cheered." . . .

2. There Aren't Many Homosexuals in America

. . . Gays must understand that, just as straights decline to think deeply about homosexuality, *straights also refuse to believe there are many homosexuals around for them to think about.*

This is not, of course, the case. During 1938–63, Alfred Kinsey and his colleagues at the Institute for Sex Research gathered nationally representative data, drawn from many thousands of indepth interviews, on the incidence of homosexual experience among American men and women. Their survey method had minor flaws and the results are now, in any case, dated, since their research ended years before the 'sexual revolution' of the '60s and '70s got under way. Still, the Kinsey surveys provide the most reliable data yet available on this sensitive topic. The Institute found that quite a large proportion of the public— roughly one in three men and one in five women—have had at least *some* overtly homosexual experience between their teen years and middle age; and, for many of these, such experience has been rather more than incidental. Some 21% of white college-educated men and 7% of white college-educated women report having had sex with two or more persons of their own gender, and/or having had gay sex six or more times. Percentages for noncollege white men and women are 28% and 5%, respectively. Fewer blacks report such extensive gay experience; e.g., only 16% of black college men and 3% of black college women. Across the board, for some reason, homosexually inclined males seem to outnumber their female counterparts by two or three to one.[1] . . .

Are all of these homosexually experienced individuals 'gay'? In our society, where getting caught in the act *just once* can brand a person for life as a 'homo,' it is tempting to say yes. Certainly, anyone who repeatedly engages in gay sex, or seeks out multiple partners, displays strong homosexual proclivities. On the other hand, as Kinsey explained, sexual orientation isn't an either/or situation: people array themselves along a spectrum ranging from exclusive heterosexuality to exclusive homosexuality. If we must draw the line somewhere and pick a specific percentage for propaganda purposes, we may as well stick with the solidly conservative figure suggested by

Kinsey decades ago: taking men and women together, *at least 10% of the populace has demonstrated its homosexual proclivities so extensively that that proportion may reasonably be called 'gay.'* But we stress that this figure is, if anything, an *under*estimate. When the *Los Angeles Times* conducted a national poll by telephone in December 1985, fully 10% of those who answered the question described themselves as "gay"; one can only imagine how many more actually saw themselves as gay but declined to admit this to a complete stranger, under suspicious circumstances, on the telephone. . . .

. . . But straights show no real understanding of what '10%' actually means. Although it implies that one out of every ten people they know well is predominantly homosexual, *more than half* of all straight Americans continue to believe (according to the *L.A. Times* poll we just mentioned) that they are not personally acquainted with *any* gays. It's a case of "Ten percent, maybe—but not of *my* friends." Many if not most straights would undoubtedly find it hard to believe—ten percent or no—that there are very nearly as many gays as blacks in America today, half again as many as Hispanics, and more than three times as many as Jews.

Straights do not appreciate that, with at least one tenth of the public extensively involved in it, the practice of homosexuality may be a more commonplace activity in America than, say, bowling (6%), jogging (7%), golfing (5%), hunting (6%), reading drugstore romance novels (9%), or ballroom dancing (2%) on a regular basis.[2] (Ballroom dancing—now *that's* abnormal.)

Nor, we suppose, do straights understand what '10%' means in absolute numbers: that there are some 24 million to 25 million homosexual Americans of both sexes, all ages, races, and creeds. That's a whooping big number—as big, in fact, as the total population of California. It means there are as many gays in the United States as there are Swedes in Sweden, Danes in Denmark, Austrians in Austria, and Irish in Ireland—combined. . . .

When we further point out that the social trauma of gay orientation directly touches the lives of more than one third of the American populace (25 million gays, their 50 million parents, plus countless siblings), our friends look downright queasy.

And no wonder this is news to straights: the fact that there are teeming millions of American gays has been suppressed to corroborate the Big Lie. We've noticed that this fact is spookily absent from all kinds of discussions of gay politics and lifestyle in the mainstream press; nor is it to be found even in textbooks on American history, culture, or demography. Sometimes this omission is conscious and deliberate, as when, for example, a major Boston publishing house recently excised from a new high school history text the neutral observation that there are "millions" of homosexual citizens in the United States. The publisher feared that inclusion of this mild statement would cause the entire text to be rejected by incredulous school boards across the South. Thus the Big Lie perpetuates itself. . . .

3. 'All Gays Are Easy To Spot: There Are Telltale Signs!'

The Big Lie that there are not many gays in America is further supported by the myth that all gays are easy to identify by their outward appearance and manner. 'Fags' and 'dykes,' it is believed, can be identified by a short checklist of telltale signs so simple, blatant, and unambiguous that most kids know them before they leave grade school. That relatively few gay people actually exhibit those 'telltale' signs—Kinsey's institute has estimated that only one in seven male and one in twenty female homosexuals are recognizable as such to the general public—reinforces straight America's misconception that its gay neighbors are very few in number.

Once, while showering in the communal bathroom of his graduate school dormitory, one of the authors was cornered by a Mormon friend in what appeared, for an instant, to be a sexual advance: stepping unnervingly close to the (closeted) author, the young man smiled knowingly and whispered, "Hunter, I've got something to tell you. I think Jerry's a queer." Jerry was an ordinary-looking resident of the dorm who nonetheless exhibited, on occasion, vaguely effeminate mannerisms. When the author demanded evidence of Jerry's homosexuality, our Latter-Day Saint shrugged and replied, "Well, of course, he hasn't *admitted* anything, but I can always tell a queer when I see one; there's just something about them that gives them away."

In a similar tale, a gay Manhattan police officer told the *New York Times* about the time when he and another officer had broken up a fight between two men. On the way back, his partner observed, "That younger man—he's a homo." "How can you tell?" asked the covertly gay officer. "I can always spot them," came the confident reply.

This blackly comic scenario, *mutatis mutandis,* has been experienced innumerable times by those many homosexuals who are not recognizably gay: sooner or later some straight friend will pull them aside and disgustedly point out a third person as a homosexual.

How can straights be so sure—and so wrong—so much of the time? Because their confident assessments are never checked against reality: there is no external authority to step in from the wings and affirm or repudiate their suspicions, nor is there anyone to point out when they have *failed* to recognize a gay person.

The only evidence straights have to go on is the accumulated American folk wisdom about homosexuals. This amounts to a lengthy checklist of surefire, telltale signs which are, for the most part, misleading, silly, and irrelevant. Consider the following mythology of gay attributes, culled from what we've overheard in the straight world. One is struck by the richness and complexity of the gay caricature that emerges. If a 'social myth' is defined as 'what the public is dreaming'—as the mythologist Joseph Campbell has suggested—then it is apparent from the highly developed myths about gays that the shadow of homo-sexuality has haunted the public's dreams for a very long time.

Telltale Signs: Gay Names Let's ease into more serious matters of stereotype by dispensing, first, with the most patently preposterous one: name-calling. Many straights grow up believing that you can identify gay males by their pansy-ish first names. (Significantly, the same is not true for lesbians, to whom no particular names have become linked; and whose detection and chastisement have historically been of far less interest to our male-oriented society.) The names that parents give their male infants fix their sexual destinies—or at least predestine the amount of harassment they'll suffer from classmates for being fags. Hardly a lad in America, straight or gay, doesn't wince inwardly and thank his parents that at least he is not, as the old Johnny Cash song put it, "A Boy Named Sue."

Fatedly homosexual names include those which sound a bit too fancy (for example, Byron, Miles, or Guy), or those which lend themselves to derisive pronunciation with a 'gay' lisp, such as Percy or Bruce (pronounced 'brooth' or 'broothee'). Pretty much any blueblood name, unless shortened sportily by its owner, is asking for trouble. Cyril, Neville, Maxwell, and Christopher, for instance, will conjure up in some minds the prissy young men who staff the fragrance counter at Bloomingdale's. . . .

Telltale Signs: Gay Voices, Bodies, and Demeanors We will leave aside, for the most part, the diverse array of signals of (male) homosexuality that children devise among themselves in grade school—even though they have only the dimmest notion of what homosexuality itself might be. There is no limit to the list of silly criteria, and kids rewrite that list weekly. Generally speaking, however, children will say that others are 'fags' and 'homos' if they:

- Show signs of unusual intelligence (i.e., are eggheads or teacher's pets);

- Speak a certain way;
- Dress a particular way (e.g., wear white socks or boxer shorts, or button their shirts up to the top button, or fail to remove the 'fairy hook' or 'fruit loop' found on the back of some dress shirts);
- Move in specific ways (e.g., 'all fags cross their legs like girls');
- Fail designated tests of manly courage (e.g., if they flinch when socked in the shoulder);
- Participate voluntarily in certain school activities (e.g., sing in the chorus or show an interest in school plays).

These childhood indicia certainly show us where the telltale checklists compiled by straight grownups get their start. . . .

In physique, gay males are still widely perceived to be either ectomorphs or endomorphs, seldom solidly muscled mesomorphs (except in California, where a new 'narcissistic body-builder' stereotype is developing). That is, gay men are either frail, willowy, nervous creatures ('neurasthenic,' psychologists used to say), or else they are larger, but with the pudgy contours of a woman. Put these two types side by side and you have a duo resembling Laurel and Hardy.

When gay male bodies move, according to myth, their joints swivel smoothly—too smoothly—particularly at the languid wrist, and sometimes in the wayward pinky. Where other men put their feet down firmly and clomp along heavily, homosexual men are said to be 'light of foot' and to flounce or mince gaily forward. At the same time, their unconscious body language is recognizably prim, tight and constrained, not free and open in the manner of Real Men. In films and plays, one discerns something tentative, even fearfully cautious, about the movements of gay characters. Except for their handshake, which is always bonelessly limp, gay men grasp objects the way weak people do: with a delicacy, deliberate precision, and unmanly grace that suits them for their inevitable careers as antique dealers and floral designers. . . .

In countenance, the gay youth is often supposed to be tellingly pretty, endowed with small features and full lips. He grooms with particular care, wears bracelets and earrings, has unnaturally smooth skin that hints of makeup (!), and he takes fashion risks with his clothing. In manner and attire, he is an extravagant fop. . . .

Now a few words about the less well-developed stereotype of lesbians. They are pictured—when American straights bother to picture them at all—as just the opposite of gay males. They are supposed to have 'butch' voices: low and gravelly. Their speech is abrupt, monosyllabic, profane, and tough. Who knows whether they ever actually cry, or just take everything like a man.

Where gay male bodies are either birdlike or as diffuse and soft as jellyfish, lesbian bodies are reputed to be stout, broad-shouldered, thunder-thighed, and athletic. Their body movements are graceless and abrupt. Their handshake—as well as their vaginal grip, according to William Burroughs—could crush a lead pipe. They have no breasts (having cut them off, Amazon style), but they may have noticeable mustaches. For that matter, according to the old joke, their armpit hair is long enough to braid, and they need to shave their legs daily but don't. No wonder they never wear anything but pants. As a matter of fact, they seem to dress like men in all regards and keep their coiffures cropped short. (A straight friend insists that butch-cut hair *with long dangling earrings* is a sure sign.)

In countenance, the lesbian is thought to be homely and humorless—rather like Picasso's appalling portrait of Gertrude Stein. The lesbian never wears makeup, both because she is acne-prone and because she hates all men, who might find such artifice attractive. (Many straights will suspect from these supposed traits that the lesbian is merely an unhappy heterosexual *femme manquée* who has ultimately sought the affection of other women because she couldn't get a man. . . .

No myth specifies how a lesbian's countenance and demeanor change as she gets older, primarily because she is not thought to change much at all, unless she goes bald. Ironically, it is the aging straight woman—with her thickening skin, coarsened features, and resort to pants and short-cropped gray hair—who eventually evolves to resemble the stereotypic lesbian.

Telltale Signs: Work, Play, and Property As for myths about gay occupations, let's make this simple: all gay men (except for the fungus-covered ones who live in alleyways and abduct boys) are florists, hairdressers, interior decorators, waiters, clothing-store sales clerks, librarians, ballet dancers, or nurses. All lesbians are gym teachers, physical therapists, East European swimmers, masseuses, teamsters, or the headmistresses of girls' boarding schools.

Gay men supposedly live their solitary lives in the city (may we suggest San Francisco or New York?), in homes decorated in the French Provincial style. Their apartments are cluttered with precious, breakable knickknacks and oval photographs of their mothers—who may, in fact, be living on the premises. There are flowers, fresh cut or dried. And slipcovers on the furniture, which is good because there is lots of beloved cat hair everywhere. . . .

The hobbies of gay men are reputed to be strictly domestic: they garden if they can, naturally, and collect toys, butterflies, glass things, and (hidden) male erotica. Big art books, too. Gay men absolutely love to cook, but on the nights when they want to cut loose and get out of the kitchen, they go to the opera or ballet. On their vacations, they travel, alone or in small groups, to Fire Island, southern Europe, or in search of Haitian youths.

Lesbians, on the other hand, are supposedly communal animals, always living together in large prairie-dog towns (a.k.a. 'women's collectives') in either urban or rural communities. Housing, as they do, the full defensive line-up of the NFL, lesbian homes purportedly lack the 'feminine touch' and are not particularly clean. . . .

According to their caricature, lesbians are too glum to have much fun. Still, they do enjoy donating their free time to run local V.D. clinics or shelters for battered women. They also attend militantly anti-American demonstrations, and go to feminist poetry readings. Dykes drink too much and get into barroom brawls. Where gay men have strictly domestic, indoor kinds of hobbies, lesbians mostly entertain themselves outside. They may be seen every Saturday afternoon in their driveways, contentedly overhauling the engines of their Harley Davidson 1200cc motorcycles, or of the gargantuan 18-wheel rigs that so many of them drive for a living.

Telltale Signs: AIDS! These days, gays are even easier to spot than usual, many straights believe, because *they're the ones with AIDS.* Over the past few years, a bit of vicious graffiti has been scrawled repeatedly across the public bathroom walls of America: "GAY = *Got Aids Yet?*" This equation does not even distinguish, as it ought, between gay men (the group at highest risk for AIDS) and lesbians (least at risk). So whether you are male or female, if *you* get AIDS—or begin to lose weight for any other reason—don't be surprised if others jump to conclude that you must be gay. One sex education instructor who worked for the St. Paul, Minnesota, school system told a *Newsweek* reporter in 1987 that many young people are "terrified of getting AIDS and being labeled homosexual. That's the issue—they are more afraid of having people call them gay than they are of dying."

As it happens, the social concern is reversed for most homosexuals: their fear is that people who find out they're gay will assume that they must have AIDS and will shun them. . . .

4. Gays Are Kinky, Loathsome Sex Addicts

Straights tend to group homosexuals into a broad class of 'sexually depraved' types. You should appreciate how important this perception is to the mainstream's revulsion toward gays. Almost by definition, homosexuals are thought to be sex maniacs.

The well-adjusted homosexual comes to view her or his romantic feelings and sexual practices as perfectly *natural*—just a mirror image of straight love and sex. After all, when it comes to the mechanics of sex, most gays make love the way straights do: with petting, kissing, intercourse, and oral-genital stimulation. Compared to more exotic and specialized forms of sexual desire, the flavor of conventional homosexuality is strictly vanilla.

It is easy to forget, then, that most straights lump homosexuality into the 'creepy weirdo' class—alongside necrophilia, bestiality, pedophilia, feces fetishism, and snuff sex. To straights unused to thinking about such things, even the most conventional homosexual practices are shocking, sickening, ludicrous—in a word, completely *perverse*. . . .

. . . Gays begin to resemble sexual monsters, the more so after the press has printed indelible news stories about sociopaths whose demented tastes happen to have been homosexual rather than heterosexual. Who could forget the gruesome torture-murders of twenty-seven boys in Houston in the early '70s, by Elmer Wayne Henley and two other deranged men?; or replays of the same horror show, 'starring' John Wayne Gacey in Chicago, Juan Corona in California, and Wayne Williams in Atlanta?

As these stories mount up, the distinction between normal, victimless homosexuality and psychopathy begins to blur: in December 1987, United Press International disseminated a lurid story about a California professor charged with shooting to death a young male prostitute, then dismembering his body with a chain saw in what prosecutors described as a "homosexual rage"— as though this were a specific kind of rage, a particularly *sordid* rage. Such crimes-*qua*-media events seal and re-seal the reputation of gays as sex fiends of the first order.

In the days before AIDS, libertines deliberately compounded the gay community's wild, felonious reputation with public paeans to sexual liberation, experimentation, and the virtues of promiscuity. Then, as the AIDS disaster unfolded, nightly newscasts shocked ordinary citizens with their reports that the disease was surfacing first among those gays who had had *five hundred or more* sexual partners, those who had been infected repeatedly with venereal diseases, and those for whom drugs and alcohol were an integral part of their hard-driving sex lives. To the happily married Lutheran couple in Ohio, watching TV with the kids at dinnertime, this didn't look like your typical sexual appetite; it looked more like a manic and deadly eating disorder, a kind of sexual bulimia. No wonder one third of all respondents in a 1985 Gallup poll acknowledged that AIDS had worsened their opinion of homosexuality.

Alas, it turns out that, on this point, public myth is supported by fact. There *is* more promiscuity among gays (or at least among gay men) than among straights. . . . Correspondingly, the snail trail of promiscuity—sexually transmitted disease—also occurs among gay men at a rate five to ten times higher than average. Even so, outsiders have often exaggerated the extent of gay promiscuity far beyond what is known from sex research. To get a more accurate perspective, Alan Bell and Martin Weinberg conducted a large survey, published as *Homosexualities: A Study of Diversity Among Men and Women,* in the mid-1970s, at the height of the 'free love' era. They found that, among their sample, roughly one in four gay men and one in six lesbian women had little or no sex with anyone. One in seven men and two-fifths of the women were involved in stable, completely monogamous gay relationships. Altogether, that means that roughly four in ten gay males, and over half of all lesbians, were found to be leading decidedly *un*promiscuous sex lives. The rest ranged from the most typical pattern—singles who occasionally dated and had sex, just as straight singles do—to the most exotic: hungry male adventurers who sought out multiple, anonymous sexual encounters on a daily basis.

In the years since that survey was done, AIDS has thinned out the number of eager sexual wantons: there is reason to think that the proportion of sexually restrained gay men has risen dramatically. But this news has not spread among straights. As the old saying goes, a lady's reputation is unlikely to improve. What is remembered, instead, is the dramatic evening news report about an airline steward named Gaetan Dugas—the infamous 'Patient Zero' blamed for triggering the AIDS epidemic—who was reported to have made some twenty-five hundred homosexual contacts over a ten-year period.

Not only has the reported *quantity* of gay sex alienated straight America, so has its *quality*. The health crisis has confirmed publicly what had only been rumored before: that homosexual men (and, for all the masses know, lesbians as well) have been groping one another's naughty bits anonymously and furtively, two by two and in larger orgies, in the filth of gas station toilet stalls, in public parks, in steamy red-lighted bathhouses, at highway rest stops, in tawdry porn theaters, in 'vaseline alleys' behind bus stations, on the dunes of county beaches in broad daylight, and beneath the coastal piers at midnight. . . .

Just as most straights do, the vast majority of gays wince to hear such a list, and have had little or no personal experience with the activities it proscribes. But because ignorant heterosexuals have no way of knowing which gay behaviors are common and which rare, they seem inclined to assume that the grossest, kinkiest practices they've heard about are enjoyed nightly by *all* gay people. . . .

All this paints a grisly image of gay sex and smears homosexuals as dissolute outlaws. But it does something still more damaging: it compels straights to think in terms of homo*sexuality* instead of homo*philia*: "Homosexuality Is Lust, Not Love," screamed one placard at an antigay demonstration in 1984. Events since that time have only reinforced the impression that homosexuality is all about sex and nothing but. There is little appreciation that homosexuality is also about love, intimacy, and romance—the possibility of which seems to unnerve some straights more than any other term in the equation. Our public image suggests that the gay experience consists of wanton promiscuity, not fidelity and bonding. . . .

5. 'Gays Are Unproductive and Untrustworthy Members of Society'

If gays are good at having sex, reportedly they're not good for much else: *many straights believe that homosexuals lead dissolute and unaccomplished lives.* This is supposedly true for two reasons.

First, because gays are sex maniacs, they cannot discipline their unruly impulses and devote their energies to more worthy endeavors. . . .

Second, gay males do not accomplish much in life (and this myth generally concerns gay males more than females) because they have a basically feminine disposition, and we all know how debilitating *that* can be. This feminine disposition is thought to make them oversensitive and constitutionally unstable—"emotional derelicts," as someone once put it—causing them to be as giddy and overwrought as lovestruck teenage girls. . . .

This is hogwash, of course. In the New York area alone, one can attend regular meetings of FLAG (Federal [Government] Lesbians and Gays), Gay People in Medicine, GovernMen, Lesbians in Government, the Bar Association for Human Rights, the Gay Officers Action League, the Greater Gotham Business Council, Gaytek (for lesbian and gay engineers and scientists), and the Wall Street Lunch Club, to name but a few. Alas, the local gay hotline has no listing for a jewelrymakers league.

Not only are gays believed to be relatively unproductive members of American society, *some straights even think they're untrustworthy citizens.* Part of this indictment is personal and part is political. On the personal side, homosexuality itself is often taken as a sign that its bearers have *other* degenerate defects of character—cowardice, perfidy, selfishness, malevolence, cruelty—which make them unreliable company, if not an actual menace to oneself and society. Some filmmakers have even incorporated homosexuality into their melodramatic, black-and-white symbolism for good and evil: you can readily pick the bad guys out of the story's lineup from the very start, because they're the ones whose sleazy, faggy mannerisms or gay leer make the audience want to hiss. . . .

Nor are they trustworthy citizens on political grounds. The insult 'commie-pinko-faggot' rolls the two most reviled adversaries of right-wing yahoos into a single hate object—the imaginary object, in fact, of Senator Joseph McCarthy's assault on the Department of State during the early 1950s. Although sociological studies have shown gays to be only moderately less conservative than straights on most political and religious issues, much of the public continues to regard them as godless radicals.[3] Indeed, a Texan political scientist may as well have spoken for the entire nation when, in 1985, he observed, "Down here, homosexuals rank in overall public opinion with atheists and communists." . . .

Too many Americans share this mistrust of gay citizens. . . . One in three straights considers gay people to be so subversive in sexual/political/religious terms that they should be denied freedom to speak in public and teach in universities. Not surprisingly, this is about the same proportion who would oppose free speech for other untrustworthy Americans, such as fascists and communists.

Another reason why homosexuals are distrusted as a class is that they are believed to act like a self-interested ethnic group, one that sticks together and favors its own whenever possible. Such special membership groups have traditionally been regarded with resentment and suspicion by Americans. . . .

What makes gays particularly suspect as a special interest group is their conspiratorial invisibility. They seem to constitute a secret society whose members can be as collusive as spies, or guerrillas. Straights can never be entirely sure whether gays are up to something behind their backs, because they're never entirely sure who—telltale signs notwithstanding—might be gay.

Even identifiable gays can be suspiciously reticent. When a straight ventures into gay environs, she may be treated as a distrusted outsider. She may feel like a tourist invading a small Sicilian village: the clamor subsides and the intimate conversation dies away just ahead of her, as she proceeds under watchful eyes. Heterosexuals resent being shut out this way. . . .

Some straights—those inclined to such paranoia—come away from their exposure to the gay world with the impression that a devious plot or well-organized rebellion is taking shape among the downtrodden. . . . Some allege that the gay mafia is expanding its base of operation beyond the ghetto, that it is deliberately inserting its pink tentacles into the nation's chambers of power, intent upon a hidden agenda of social upheaval that poses a serious threat to the fabric of the nation. AIDS, in turn, makes this imagined threat seem more insidious than ever: conservatives have charged the gay lobby with cowing or manipulating both the media and the medical profession to block the exposure and quarantining of gay AIDS-carriers. As Richard Goldstein has observed, homohatred is now being validated by "the myth of the powerful homosexual, first cousin to the myth of the powerful Jew."

Thus, in January 1987, when Roper asked the public to rate which of twenty-two "special interest groups" wield *too much influence* in America today, 48% said "gay rights groups." The only group whose purported influence aroused more hostile concern than did gays—on a list which included big business, pro- and anti-abortion movements, fundamentalist church groups, left-wingers, and the military—was labor unions (52%).[4]

The public's fearful perception of gay power is, then, outlandishly inflated: if the gay movement actually loomed as large as the shadow it casts in straight minds, the era of gay rights would be at hand. . . .

6. 'Gays Are Suicidally Unhappy Because They Are Gay'

Straights are inclined to believe that all gays are—by dint of their emotionally unstable nature and the intrinsic horribleness of their vice—dreadfully unhappy. . . .

. . . The modern blueprint for gay misery was drawn up in 1968, in Mart Crowley's controversial and 'sympathetic' play, *The Boys in the Band;* and again in the 1970 film version directed by William Friedkin. At the end, after the other sorry fairies attending a melancholy birthday party have gone their solitary ways to ponder the dead-end hopelessness of their lives, the central character dissolves into tears and utters a pathetic prayer that he and all other homosexuals might, one day, learn to hate themselves just a little bit less. "It's not always like it happens in plays," he insists, with little heart. "Not all faggots bump themselves off at the end of the story." Maybe not, but faggots certainly do so in movieland; go watch *Advise and Consent.* The same lachrymose stream runs through more recent films having gay characters and subplots, such as *Ode to Billy Joe, That Certain Summer,* and *Another Country.* . . .

Now, the most distressing thing about this American myth of the unhappy homosexual is that it does have some basis in fact. Studies suggest that, while most gays are remarkably well adjusted in light of their stigma, on the whole, gay men (and to a lesser extent lesbians) are more prone to feelings of loneliness, anxiety, paranoia, depression, and unhappiness than are straights. This comes as no surprise. More straights would react likewise, no doubt, if *they* were compelled to live their lives estranged, in constant fear of exposure and attack, and with a clear-eyed comprehension of their bleak predicament. As someone once observed, even a paranoid man can have real enemies. And when his enemies proceed to persecute him on the novel ground that he *is* a bit paranoid—or is socially maladjusted in some other way—then the cycle becomes as vicious as can be. And in the end, the poor maligned fellow is seen hurling himself off a skyscraper ledge in a desperate effort to escape his tormentors once and for all. Did he jump or was he pushed?

We say he was pushed. Gay suicide is America's prescription for preserving the Big Lie. The prospect of homosexuality makes most heterosexuals unhappy; their answer is to make homosexuals, in turn, so *very* unhappy that they just go away, self-destruct, vanish. . . .

So it turns out that, while a majority of gays are as well adjusted and content as straights, a sizable minority of homosexuals *are* deeply unhappy. Straights generally suppose that homosexuality itself is to blame for this. Gays, on the other hand, insist quite rightly that what makes them unhappy is the way straights treat them. . . .

PERSONAL ACCOUNT

A WHITE MALE RESCUED ME

There was one incident where a white male came to my rescue when I was being discriminated against for being a woman, a black woman, and a black-gay woman.

I was on the metro with my friends on the way to a club when two black men started making derogatory, disgusting statements about us. All of a sudden I heard this voice saying, "You need to leave those girls alone. They're college people and they're trying to experience life. This is the '90s. People have the right to express how they are no matter what you think about it." I turned around and it was a *white man.* I was shocked. Another gay person might have stood up for us, but I would never have expected a white, middle-aged man to do that. They all started to get in a fight, but when the train came to a stop the security guard got on and escorted the two harassers off. I thought it was very nice of the man to come to our rescue. I would like for people to stand up for those who are either in a minority status in society or just for those people who are in need of help. But I would also like to thank the man, regardless of his race, for coming to my rescue. Gay people are human beings too, and we also have rights. But a special thanks goes out to this gentleman for seeing me and my friends as people with feelings first, and gay women second. Thank you.

Meticia Watson

NOTES

1. P. H. Gebhard and A. B. Johnson, *The Kinsey Data: Marginal Tabulations of the 1938–1963 Interviews Conducted by the Institute for Sex Research* (W. B. Saunders, 1979). For a smaller, but more recent, survey that produced much the same results as Kinsey's, see M. G. Shively and J. P. DeCecco, "Sexual Orientation Survey of Students on the San Francisco State University Campus," *Journal of Homosexuality,* 4/1 (Fall 1978): 29–39.

2. Statistics about America's participation in various recreational activities come from the Roper Organization's *Roper Reports* 1987–1, 17.

3. In their 1978 study, *Homosexualities* (363–68), Bell and Weinberg found that, among their sample, gays were only slightly more liberal and Democratic, and somewhat less religious, than their straight counterparts. They obtained, for instance, the following comparisons between gay white males and straight white males:

	Gay	Straight
Democrat	36%	36%
Republican	17%	21%
Liberal	75%	69%
Conservative	20%	29%
Not at all/not very religious	51%	44%
Moderately/very religious	22%	26%

4. Roper Organization, *Roper Reports* 1987–2, 49 (Question 14x, y).

YOU CAN'T FORGET HUMILIATION

People who are considered minorities hardly ever forget times when they encounter a bigot. You can't forget being humiliated by the look in their eyes. Instead, you grow long, bitter memories and a defensive stance spurred by anger and fear that someone, someday, will say or do something, and you won't be able to protect yourself. So you are always on guard.

I'll never forget when I was fourteen and my mother shook and screamed at me in a 7–11 parking lot for giving a flower to my best friend because everyone would think I was a lesbian. Or the time that I watched my baby niece, Katie, one afternoon weeks after I told her mom that I was gay.

I had accidently dropped my car keys on the bed when I laid the baby down for a nap. When she woke up, it was time to take her back to my sister. My roommate (who is also gay) and I searched furiously for my keys with no luck. We were locked out of the car so my sister had to come to our apartment to pick up the baby. My roommate found the keys on the bed when he went to make a phone call, and said "Oh! Here they are. They were on the bed. They must have dropped when you put Katie down for her nap." And my sister said, "What were you doing in bed with my child!" At first, I was stunned that she would say that, but then I started to protest and so did my roommate. She told me she was "just kidding." I told her she was gross. After she left with Katie I cried.

I guess I'm angry now because I'm no longer ashamed to be gay. And when things happen to you, you just get angry because it is not fair. And anger stems from something else—something I never had my entire life until now. And that's pride. I didn't grow up with the same pride as an African American or Jewish kid does, hearing stories of how their ancestors survived. My pride was given to me. I got it much later in life than those kids because I didn't have proud parents who had the same "blood" as me or any role models to emulate. I was raised straight, and worse than that, I was raised with hate for the people I now call family. I earned my pride slowly and gently after I came out to myself. I paid for it with many years of self-denial, and many tears, until I found decent and wonderful gay friends that I could love and know that they went through the same trials I did. Now that pride I can share with my "family" and pass it on to some kid who needs it right now as much as I did when I didn't even know it existed.

Amy L. Helm

Language

Racism in the English Language

Robert B. Moore

LANGUAGE AND CULTURE

An integral part of any culture is its language. Language not only develops in conjunction with a society's historical, economic and political evolution; it also reflects that society's attitudes and thinking. Language not only *expresses* ideas and concepts but actually *shapes* thought.[1] If one accepts that our dominant white culture is racist, then one would expect our language—an indispensable transmitter of culture—to be racist as well. Whites, as the dominant group, are not subjected to the same abusive characterization by our language that people of color receive. Aspects of racism in the English language that will be discussed in this essay include terminology, symbolism, politics, ethnocentrism, and context.

Before beginning our analysis of racism in language we would like to quote part of a TV film review which shows the connection between language and culture.[2]

> Depending on one's culture, one interacts with time in a very distinct fashion. One example which gives some cross-cultural insights into the concept of time is language. In Spanish, a watch is said to "walk." In English, the watch "runs." In German, the watch "functions." And in French, the watch "marches." In the Indian culture of the Southwest, people do not refer to time in this way. The value of the watch is displaced with the value of "what time it's getting to be." Viewing these five cultural perspectives of time, one can see some definite emphasis and values that each culture places on time. For example, a cultural perspective may provide a clue to why the negative stereotype of the slow and lazy Mexican who lives in the "Land of Manana" exists in the Anglo value system, where time "flies," the watch "runs" and "time is money."

A SHORT PLAY ON "BLACK" AND "WHITE" WORDS

Some may blackly (angrily) accuse me of trying to blacken (defame) the English language, to give it a black eye (a mark of shame) by writing such black words (hostile). They may denigrate (to cast aspersions; to darken) me by accusing me of being blackhearted (malevolent), of having a black outlook (pessimistic, dismal) on life, of being a blackguard (scoundrel)—which would certainly be a black mark (detrimental fact) against me. Some may black-brow (scowl at) me and hope that a black cat crosses in front of me because of this black deed. I may become a black sheep (one who causes shame or embarrassment because of deviation from the accepted standards), who will be blackballed (ostracized) by being placed on a blacklist (list of undesirables) in an attempt to blackmail (to force or coerce into a particular action) me to retract my words. But attempts to blackjack (to compel by threat) me will have a Chinaman's chance of success, for I am not a yellow-bellied Indian-giver of words, who will whitewash (cover up or gloss over vices or crimes) a black lie (harmful, inexcusable). I challenge the purity and innocence (white) of the English language. I don't see things in black and white (entirely bad or entirely good) terms, for I am a white man (marked by upright firmness) if there ever was one. However, it would be a black day when I would not "call a spade a spade," even though some will suggest a white man calling the English language racist is like the pot calling the kettle black. While many may be niggardly (grudging, scanty) in their support, others will be honest and decent—and to them I say, that's very white of you (honest, decent).

The preceding is of course a white lie (not intended to cause harm), meant only to illustrate some examples of racist terminology in the English language.

OBVIOUS BIGOTRY

Perhaps the most obvious aspect of racism in language would be terms like "nigger," "spook," "chink," "spic," etc. While these may be facing increasing social disdain, they certainly are not dead. Large numbers of white Americans continue to utilize these terms. "Chink," "gook," and "slant-eyes" were in common usage among U.S. troops in Vietnam. An NBC nightly news broadcast, in February 1972, reported that the basketball team in Pekin, Illinois, was called the "Pekin Chinks" and noted that even though this had been protested by Chinese Americans, the term continued to be used because it was easy, and meant no harm. Spiro Agnew's widely reported "fat Jap" remark and the "little Jap" comment of lawyer John Wilson during the Watergate hearings, are surface indicators of a deep-rooted Archie Bunkerism.

Many white people continue to refer to Black people as "colored," as for instance in a July 30, 1975 *Boston Globe* article on a racist attack by whites on a group of Black people using a public beach in Boston. One white person was quoted as follows:

> We've always welcomed good colored people in South Boston but we will not tolerate radical blacks or Communists. . . . Good colored people are welcome in South Boston, black militants are not.

Many white people may still be unaware of the disdain many African Americans have for the term "colored," but it often appears that whether used intentionally or unintentionally, "colored" people are "good" and "know their place," while "Black" people are perceived as "uppity" and "threatening" to many whites. Similarly, the term "boy" to refer to African American men is now acknowledged to be a demeaning term, though still in common use. Other terms such as "the pot calling the kettle black" and "calling a spade a spade" have negative racial connotations but are still frequently used, as for example when President Ford was quoted in February 1976 saying that even though Daniel Moynihan had left the U.N., the U.S. would continue "calling a spade a spade."

COLOR SYMBOLISM

The symbolism of white as positive and black as negative is pervasive in our culture, with the black/white words used in the beginning of this essay only one of many aspects. "Good guys" wear white hats and ride white horses, "bad guys" wear black hats and ride black horses. Angels are white, and devils are black. The definition of *black* includes "without any moral light or goodness, evil, wicked, indicating disgrace, sinful," while that of *white* includes "morally pure, spotless, innocent, free from evil intent."

A children's TV cartoon program, *Captain Scarlet,* is about an organization called Spectrum, whose purpose is to save the world from an evil extraterrestrial force called the Mysterons. Everyone in Spectrum has a color name—Captain Scarlet, Captain Blue, etc. The one Spectrum agent who has been mysteriously taken over by the Mysterons and works to advance their evil aims is Captain Black. The person who heads Spectrum, the good organization out to defend the world, is Colonel White.

Three of the dictionary definitions of white are "fairness of complexion, purity, innocence." These definitions affect the standards of beauty in our culture, in which whiteness represents the norm. "Blondes have more fun" and "Wouldn't you really rather be a blonde" are sexist in their attitudes toward women generally, but are racist white standards when applied to third world women. A 1971 *Mademoiselle* advertisement pictured a curly-headed, ivory-skinned woman over the caption, "When you go blonde go all the way," and asked: "Isn't this how, in the back of your mind, you always wanted to look? All wide-eyed and silky blonde down to there, and innocent?" Whatever the advertising people meant by this particular woman's innocence, one must remember that "innocent" is one of the definitions of the word white. This standard of beauty when preached to all women is racist. The statement "Isn't this how, in the back of your mind, you always wanted to look?" either ignores third world women or assumes they long to be white.

Time magazine in its coverage of the Wimbledon tennis competition between the black Australian Evonne Goolagong and the white American Chris Evert described Ms. Goolagong as "the dusky daughter of an Australian sheepshearer," while Ms. Evert was "a fair young girl from the middle-class groves of Florida." *Dusky* is a synonym of "black" and is defined as "having dark skin; of a dark color; gloomy; dark; swarthy." Its antonyms are "fair" and "blonde." *Fair* is defined in part as "free from blemish, imperfection, or anything that impairs the appearance, quality, or character; pleasing in appearance, attractive; clean; pretty; comely." By defining Evonne Goolagong as "dusky," *Time* technically defined her as the opposite of "pleasing in appearance; attractive; clean; pretty; comely."

The studies of Kenneth B. Clark, Mary Ellen Goodman, Judith Porter and others indicate that this persuasive "rightness of whiteness" in U.S. culture affects children before the age of four, providing white youngsters with a false sense of superiority and encouraging self-hatred among third world youngsters.

ETHNOCENTRISM OR FROM A WHITE PERSPECTIVE

Some words and phrases that are commonly used represent particular perspectives and frames of reference, and these often distort the understanding of the reader or listener. David R. Burgest[3] has written about the effect of using the terms "slave" or "master." He argues that the psychological impact of the statement referring to "the master raped his slave" is different from the impact of the same statement substituting the words: "the white captor raped an African woman held in captivity."

Implicit in the English usage of the "master-slave" concept is ownership of the "slave" by the "mas-

ter," therefore, the "master" is merely abusing his property (slave). In reality, the captives (slave) were African individuals with human worth, right and dignity and the term "slave" denounces that human quality thereby making the mass rape of African women by white captors more acceptable in the minds of people and setting a mental frame of reference for legitimizing the atrocities perpetuated against African people.

The term slave connotes a less than human quality and turns the captive person into a thing. For example, two McGraw-Hill Far Eastern Publishers textbooks (1970) stated, "At first it was the slaves who worked the cane and they got only food for it. Now men work cane and get money." Next time you write about slavery or read about it, try transposing all "slaves" into "African people held in captivity," "Black people forced to work for no pay" or "African people stolen from their families and societies." While it is more cumbersome, such phrasing conveys a different meaning.

PASSIVE TENSE

Another means by which language shapes our perspective has been noted by Thomas Greenfield,[4] who writes that the achievements of Black people—and Black people themselves—have been hidden in

the linguistic ghetto of the passive voice, the subordinate clause, and the "understood" subject. The seemingly innocuous distinction (between active/passive voice) holds enormous implications for writers and speakers. When it is effectively applied, the rhetorical impact of the passive voice—the art of making the creator or instigator of action totally disappear from a reader's perception—can be devastating.

For instance, some history texts will discuss how European immigrants came to the United States seeking a better life and expanded opportunities, but will note that "slaves *were brought* to America." Not only does this omit the destruction of African societies and families, but it ignores the role of northern merchants and southern slaveholders in the profitable trade in human beings. Other books will state that "the continental railroad *was built*," conveniently omitting information about the Chinese laborers who built much of it or the oppression they suffered.

Another example. While touring Monticello, Greenfield noted that the tour guide

> made all the black people at Monticello disappear through her use of the passive voice. While speaking of the architectural achievements of Jefferson in the active voice, she unfailingly shifted to passive when speaking of the work performed by Negro slaves and skilled servants.

Noting a type of door that after 166 years continued to operate without need for repair, Greenfield remarks that the design aspect of the door was much simpler than the actual skill and work involved in building and installing it. Yet his guide stated: "Mr. Jefferson designed these doors . . ." while "the doors **were installed** in 1809." The workers who installed those doors were African people whom Jefferson held in bondage. The guide's use of the passive tense enabled her to dismiss the reality of Jefferson's slaveholding. It also meant that she did not have to make any mention of the skills of those people held in bondage.

POLITICS AND TERMINOLOGY

"Culturally deprived," "economically disadvantaged" and "underdeveloped" are other terms which mislead and distort our awareness of reality. The application of the term "culturally deprived" and third world children in this society reflects a value judgment. It assumes that the dominant whites are cultured and all others without culture. In fact, third world children generally are bicultural, and many are bilingual, having grown up in their own culture as well as absorbing the dominant culture. In many ways, they are equipped with skills and experiences which white youth have been deprived of, since most white youth develop in a monocultural, monolingual environment. Burgest[5] suggests that the term "culturally deprived" be replaced by "culturally dispossessed," and that the term "economically disadvantaged" be replaced by "economically exploited." Both these terms present a perspective and implication that provide an entirely different frame of reference as to the reality of the third world experience in U.S. society.

Similarly, many nations of the third world are described as "underdeveloped." These less wealthy nations are generally those that suffered under colonialism and neo-colonialism. The "developed" nations are those that exploited their resources and wealth. Therefore, rather than referring to these countries as "underdeveloped," a more appropriate and meaningful designation might be "over exploited." Again, transpose this term next time you read about "underdeveloped nations" and note the different meaning that results.

Terms such as "culturally deprived," "economically disadvantaged" and "underdeveloped" place the responsibility for their own conditions on those being so described. This is known as "Blaming the Victim."[6] It places responsibility for poverty on the victims of poverty. It removes the blame from those in power who benefit from, and continue to permit, poverty.

Still another example involves the use of "non-white," "minority" or "third world." While people of color are a minority in the U.S., they are part of the vast majority of the world's population, in which white people are a distinct minority. Thus, by utilizing the term minority to describe people of color in the U.S., we can lose sight of the global majority/minority reality—a fact of some importance in the increasing and interconnected struggles of people of color inside and outside the U.S.

To describe people of color as "non-white" is to use whiteness as the standard and norm against which to measure all others. Use of the term "third world" to describe all people of color overcomes the inherent bias of "minority" and "nonwhite." Moreover, it connects the struggles of third world people in the U.S. with the freedom struggles around the globe.

The term third world gained increasing usage after the 1955 Bandung Conference of "non-aligned" nations, which represented a third force outside of the two world superpowers. The "first world" represents the United States, Western Europe and their sphere of influence. The "second world" represents the Soviet Union and its sphere. The "third world" represents, for the most part, nations that were, or are, controlled by the "first world" or West. For the most part, these are nations of Africa, Asia and Latin America.

"LOADED" WORDS
AND NATIVE AMERICANS

Many words lead to a demeaning characterization of groups of people. For instance, Columbus, it is said, "discovered" America. The word *discover* is defined as "to gain sight or knowledge of something previously unseen or unknown; to discover may be to find some existent thing that was previously unknown." Thus, a continent inhabited by millions of human beings cannot be "discovered." For history books to continue this usage represents a Eurocentric (white European) perspective on world history and ignores the existence of, and the perspective of, Native Americans. "Discovery," as used in the Euro-American context, implies the right to take what one finds, ignoring the rights of those who already inhabit or own the "discovered" thing.

Eurocentrism is also apparent in the usage of "victory" and "massacre" to describe the battles between Native Americans and whites. *Victory* is defined in the dictionary as "a success or triumph over an enemy in battle or war; the decisive defeat of an opponent." *Conquest* denotes the "taking over of control by the victor, and the obedience of the conquered." *Massacre* is defined as "the unnecessary, indiscriminate killing of a number of human beings, as in barbarous warfare or persecution, or for revenge or plunder." *Defend* is described as "to ward off attack from; guard against assault or injury; to strive to keep safe by resisting attack."

Eurocentrism turns these definitions around to serve the purpose of distorting history and justifying Euro-American conquest of the Native American homelands. Euro-Americans are not described in history books as invading Native American lands, but rather as defending *their* homes against "Indian" attacks. Since European communities were constantly encroaching on land already occupied, then a more honest interpretation would state that it was the Native Americans who were "warding off," "guarding" and "defending" their homelands.

Native American victories are invariably defined as "massacres," while the indiscriminate killing, extermination and plunder of Native American nations by Euro-Americans is defined as "victory." Distortion of history by the choice of "loaded" words used to describe historical events is a common racist practice. Rather than portraying Native Americans as human beings in highly defined and complex societies, cultures and civilizations, history books use such adjectives as "savages," "beasts," "primitive," and "backward." Native people are referred to as "squaw," "brave," or "papoose" instead of "woman," "man," or "baby."

Another term that has questionable connotations is *tribe*. The Oxford English Dictionary defines this noun as "a race of people; now applied especially to a primary aggregate of people in a primitive or barbarous condition, under a headman or chief." Morton Fried,[7] discussing "The Myth of Tribe," states that the word "did not become a general term of reference to American Indian society until the nineteenth century. Previously, the words commonly used for Indian populations were 'nation' and 'people.'" Since "tribe" has assumed a connotation of primitiveness or backwardness, it is suggested that the use of "nation" or "people" replace the term whenever possible in referring to Native American peoples.

The term *tribe* invokes even more negative implications when used in reference to American peoples. As Evelyn Jones Rich[8] has noted, the term is "almost always used to refer to third world people and it implies a stage of development which is, in short, a put-down."

"LOADED" WORDS AND AFRICANS

Conflicts among diverse peoples within African nations are often referred to as "tribal warfare," while conflicts among the diverse peoples within European countries are never described in such terms. If the rivalries between the Ibo and the Hausa and Yoruba in Nigeria are described as "tribal," why not the rivalries between Serbs and Slavs in Yugoslavia, or Scots and English in Great Britain, Protestants and Catholics in Ireland, or the Basques and the Southern Spaniards in Spain? Conflicts among African peoples in a particular nation have religious, cultural, economic and/or political roots. If we can analyze the roots of conflicts among European peoples in terms other than "tribal warfare," certainly we can do the same with African peoples, including correct reference to the ethnic groups or nations involved. For example, the terms "Kaffirs," "Hottentot" or "Bushmen" are names imposed by white Europeans. The correct names are always those by which a people refer to themselves. (In these instances Xhosa, Khoi-Khoin and San are correct.[9])

The generalized application of "tribal" in reference to Africans—as well as the failure to acknowledge the religious, cultural and social diversity of African peoples—is a decidedly racist dynamic. It is part of the process whereby Euro-Americans justify, or avoid confronting, their oppression of third world peoples. Africa has been particularly insulted by this dynamic, as witness the pervasive "darkest Africa" image. This image, widespread in Western culture, evokes an Africa covered by jungles and inhibited by "uncivilized," "cannibalistic," "pagan," "savage" peoples. This "darkest Africa" image avoids the geographical reality. Less than 20 percent of the African continent is wooded savanna, for example. The image also ignores the history of African cultures and civilizations. Ample evidence suggests this distortion of reality was developed as a convenient rationale for the European and American slave trade. The Western powers, rather than exploiting, were civilizing and christianizing "uncivilized" and "pagan savages" (so the rationalization went). This dynamic also served to justify Western colonialism. From Tarzan movies to racist children's books like *Doctor Dolittle* and *Charlie and the Chocolate Factory,* the image of "savage" Africa and the myth of "the white man's burden" has been perpetuated in Western culture.

A 1972 *Time* magazine editorial lamenting the demise of *Life* magazine, stated that the "lavishness" of *Life*'s enterprises included "organizing safaris into darkest Africa." The same year, the *New York Times'* C. L. Sulzberger wrote that "Africa has a history as dark as the skins of many of its people." Terms such as "darkest Africa," "primitive," "tribe" ("tribal") or "jungle," in reference to Africa, perpetuate myths and are especially inexcusable in such large circulation publications.

Ethnocentrism is similarly reflected in the term "pagan" to describe traditional religions. A February 1973 *Time* magazine article on Uganda stated, "Moslems account for only 500,000 of Uganda's 10 million people. Of the remainder, 5,000,000 are Christians and the rest pagan." *Pagan* is defined as "Heathen, a follower of a polytheistic religion; one that has little or no religion and that is marked by a frank delight in and uninhibited seeking after sensual pleasures and material goods." *Heathen* is defined as "Unenlightened; an unconverted member of a people or nation that does not acknowledge the God of the Bible. A person whose culture or enlightenment is of an inferior grade, especially an irreligious person." Now, the people of Uganda, like almost all Africans, have serious religious beliefs and practices. As used by Westerners, "pagan" connotes something wild, primitive and inferior—another term to watch out for.

The variety of traditional structures that African people live in are their "houses," not "huts." A *hut* is "an often small and temporary dwelling of simple construction." And to describe

Africans as "natives" (noun) is derogatory terminology—as in, "the natives are restless." The dictionary definition of *native* includes: "one of a people inhabiting a territorial area at the time of its discovery or becoming familiar to a foreigner; one belonging to a people having a less complex civilization." Therefore, use of "native," like use of "pagan" often implies a value judgment of white superiority.

QUALIFYING ADJECTIVES

Words that would normally have positive connotations can have entirely different meanings when used in a racial context. For example, C. L. Sulzberger, the columnist of the *New York Times,* wrote in January 1975, about conversations he had with two people in Namibia. One was the white South African administrator of the country and the other a member of SWAPO, the Namibian liberation movement. The first is described as "Dirk Mudge, who as senior elected member of the administration is a kind of acting Prime Minister. . . ." But the second person is introduced as "Daniel Tijongarero, an intelligent Herero tribesman who is a member of SWAPO. . . ." What need was there for Sulzberger to state that Daniel Tijongarero is "intelligent"? Why not also state that Dirk Mudge was "intelligent"—or do we assume he wasn't?

A similar example from a 1968 *New York Times* article reporting on an address by Lyndon Johnson stated, "The President spoke to the well-dressed Negro officials and their wives." In what similar circumstances can one imagine a reporter finding it necessary to note that an audience of white government officials was "well-dressed?"

Still another word often used in a racist context is "qualified." In the 1960s white Americans often questioned whether Black people were "qualified" to hold public office, a question that was never raised (until too late) about white officials like Wallace, Maddox, Nixon, Agnew, Mitchell, et al. The question of qualifications has been raised even more frequently in recent years as white people question whether Black people are "qualified" to be hired for positions in industry and educational institutions. "We're looking for a qualified Black" has been heard again and again as institutions are confronted with affirmative action goals. Why stipulate that Blacks must be "qualified," when for others it is taken for granted that applicants must be "qualified."

SPEAKING ENGLISH

Finally, the depiction in movies and children's books of third world people speaking English is often itself racist. Children's books about Puerto Ricans or Chicanos often connect poverty with a failure to speak English or to speak it well, thus blaming the victim and ignoring the racism which affects third world people regardless of their proficiency in English. Asian characters speak a stilted English ("Honorable so and so" or "Confucius say") or have a speech impediment ("roots or ruck," "very solly," "flied lice"). Native American characters speak another variation of stilted English ("Boy not hide. Indian take boy."), repeat certain Hollywood-Indian phrases ("Heap big" and "Many moons") or simply grunt out "Ugh" or "How." The repeated use of these language characterizations functions to make third world people seem less intelligent and less capable than the English-speaking white characters.

WRAP-UP

A *Saturday Review* editorial[10] on "The Environment of Language" stated that language

> . . . has as much to do with the philosophical and political conditioning of a society as geography or climate. . . . people in Western cultures do not realize the extent to which their racial attitudes have been conditioned since early childhood by the power of words to ennoble or condemn, augment or detract, glorify or demean. Negative language infects the subconscious of most Western people from the time they first learn to speak. Prejudice is not merely imparted or superimposed. It is metabolized in the bloodstream of society. What is needed is not so much a change in language as an awareness of the power of words to condition attitudes. If

we can at least recognize the underpinnings of prejudice, we may be in a position to deal with the effects.

To recognize the racism in language is an important first step. Consciousness of the influence of language on our perceptions can help to negate much of that influence. But it is not enough to simply become aware of the affects of racism in conditioning attitudes. While we may not be able to change the language, we can definitely change our usage of the language. We can avoid using words that degrade people. We can make a conscious effort to use terminology that reflects a progressive perspective, as opposed to a distorting perspective. It is important for educators to provide students with opportunities to explore racism in language and to increase their awareness of it, as well as learning terminology that is positive and does not perpetuate negative human values.

NOTES

1. Simon Podair, "How Bigotry Builds Through Language," *Negro Digest,* March 1967.
2. Jose Armas, "Antonio and the Mayor: A Cultural

Review of the Film," *The Journal of Ethnic Studies,* Fall, 1975.
3. David R. Burgest, "The Racist Use of the English Language," *Black Scholar,* Sept. 1973.
4. Thomas Greenfield, "Race and Passive Voice at Monticello," *Crisis,* April 1975.
5. David R. Burgest, "Racism in Everyday Speech and Social Work Jargon," *Social Work,* July 1973.
6. William Ryan, *Blaming the Victim,* Pantheon Books, 1971.
7. Morton Fried, "The Myth of Tribe," *National History,* April 1975.
8. Evelyn Jones Rich, "Mind Your Language," *Africa Report,* Sept./Oct. 1974.
9. Steve Wolf, "Catalogers in Revolt Against LC's Racist, Sexist Headings," *Bulletin of Interracial Books for Children,* Vol. 6, Nos. 3&4, 1975.
10. "The Environment of Language," *Saturday Review,* April 8, 1967.

Also see:

Roger Bastide, "Color, Racism and Christianity," *Daedalus,* Spring 1967.

Kenneth J. Gergen, "The Significance of Skin Color in Human Relations," *Daedalus,* Spring 1967.

Lloyd Yabura, "Towards a Language of Humanism," *Rhythm,* Summer 1971.

UNESCO, "Recommendations Concerning Terminology in Education on Race Questions," June 1968.

Gender Stereotyping in the English Language

Laurel Richardson*

Everyone in our society, regardless of class, ethnicity, sex, age, or race, is exposed to the same language, the language of the dominant culture. Analysis of verbal language can tell us a great deal about a people's fears, prejudices, anxieties,

*Adapted from Laurel Richardson, *The Dynamics of Sex and Gender: A Sociological Perspective* (New York: Harper & Row, 1987), by permission of the author.

and interests. A rich vocabulary on a particular subject indicates societal interests or obsessions (e.g., the extensive vocabulary about cars in America). And different words for the same subject (such as *freedom fighter* and *terrorist, passed away* and *croaked, make love* and *ball*) show that there is a range of attitudes and feelings in the society toward that subject.

It should not be surprising, then, to find differential attitudes and feelings about men and women rooted in the English language. Although the English language has not been completely analyzed, six general propositions concerning these attitudes and feelings about males and females can be made.

First, in terms of grammatical and semantic structure, women do not have a fully autonomous, independent existence; they are part of man. The language is not divided into male and female with distinct conjugations and declensions, as many other languages are. Rather, *women* are included under the generic *man.* Grammar books specify that the pronoun *he* can be used generically to mean *he* or *she.* Further, *man,* when used as an indefinite pronoun, grammatically refers to both men and women. So, for example, when we read *man* in the following phrases we are to interpret it as applying to both men and women: "man the oars," "one small step for man, one giant step for mankind," "man, that's tough," "man overboard," "man the toolmaker," "alienated man," "garbageman." Our rules of etiquette complete the grammatical presumption of inclusivity. When two persons are pronounced "man and wife," Miss Susan Jones changes her entire name to Mrs. Robert Gordon (Vanderbilt, 1972). In each of these correct usages, women are a part of man; they do not exist autonomously. The exclusion of women is well expressed in Mary Daly's ear-jarring slogan "the sisterhood of man" (1973:7–21).

However, there is some question as to whether the theory that *man* means everybody is carried out in practice (see Bendix, 1979; Martyna, 1980). For example, an eight-year-old interrupts her reading of "The Story of the Cavemen" to ask how we got here without cavewomen. A ten-year-old thinks it is dumb to have a woman post*man.* A beginning anthropology student believes (incorrectly) that all shamans ("witch doctors") are males because her textbook and professor use the referential pronoun *he.*

But beginning language learners are not the only ones who visualize males when they see the word *man.* Research has consistently demonstrated that when the generic *man* is used, people visualize men, not women (Schneider & Hacker, 1973; DeStefano, 1976; Martyna, 1978; Hamilton & Henley, 1982). DeStafano, for example, reports that college students choose silhouettes of males for sentences with the word *man* or *men* in them. Similarly, the presumably generic *he* elicits images of men rather than women. The finding is

so persistent that linguists doubt whether there actually is a semantic generic in English (MacKay, 1983).

Man, then, suggests not humanity but rather male images. Moreover, over one's lifetime, an educated American will be exposed to the prescriptive *he* more than a million times (MacKay, 1983). One consequence is the exclusion of women in the visualization, imagination, and thought of males and females. Most likely this linguistic practice perpetuates in men their feelings of dominance over and responsibility for women, feelings that interfere with the development of equality in relationships.

Second, in actual practice, our pronoun usage perpetuates different personality attributes and career aspirations for men and women. Nurses, secretaries, and elementary school teachers are almost invariably referred to as *she;* doctors, engineers, electricians, and presidents as *he.* In one classroom, students referred to an unidentified child as *he* but shifted to *she* when discussing the child's parent. In a faculty discussion of the problems of acquiring new staff, all architects, engineers, security officers, faculty, and computer programmers were referred to as *he;* secretaries and file clerks were referred to as *she.* Martyna (1978) has noted that speakers consistently use *he* when the referent has a high-status occupation (e.g., doctor, lawyer, judge) but shift to *she* when the occupations have lower status (e.g., nurse, secretary).

Even our choice of sex ascription to nonhuman objects subtly reinforces different personalities for males and females. It seems as though the small (e.g., kittens), the graceful (e.g., poetry), the unpredictable (e.g., the fates), the nurturant (e.g., the church, the school), and that which is owned and/or controlled by men (e.g., boats, cars, governments, nations) represent the feminine, whereas that which is a controlling forceful power in and of itself (e.g., God, Satan, tiger) primarily represents the masculine. Even athletic teams are not immune. In one college, the men's teams are called the Bearcats and the women's teams the Bearkittens.

Some of you may wonder whether it matters that the female is linguistically included in the male. The inclusion of women under the pseudo-generic *man* and the prescriptive *he*, however, is not a trivial issue. Language has tremendous power to shape attitudes and influence behavior. Indeed, MacKay (1983) argues that the prescriptive *he* "has all the characteristics of a highly effective propaganda technique": frequent repetition, early age of acquisition (before age 6), covertness (*he* is not thought of as propaganda), use by high-prestige sources (including university texts and professors), and indirectness (presented as though it were a matter of common knowledge). As a result, the prescriptive affects females' sense of life options and feelings of well-being. For example, Adamsky (1981) found that women's sense of power and importance was enhanced when the prescriptive *he* was replaced by *she*.

Awareness of the impact of the generic *man* and prescriptive *he* has generated considerable activity to change the language. One change, approved by the Modern Language Association, is to replace the prescriptive *he* with the plural *they*—as was accepted practice before the 18th century. Another is the use of *he or she*. Although it sounds awkward at first, the *he or she* designation is increasingly being used in the media and among people who have recognized the power of the pronoun to perpetuate sex stereotyping. When a professor, for example, talks about "the lawyer" as "he or she," a speech pattern that counteracts sex stereotyping is modeled. This drive to neutralize the impact of pronouns is evidenced further in the renaming of occupations: a policeman is now a police officer, a postman is a mail carrier, a stewardess is a flight attendant.

Third, linguistic practice defines females as immature, incompetent, and incapable and males as mature, complete, and competent. Because the words *man* and *woman* tend to connote sexual and human maturity, common speech, organizational titles, public addresses, and bathroom doors frequently designate the women in question as *ladies*. Simply contrast the different connotations of *lady* and *woman* in the following common phrases:

Luck, be a lady (woman) tonight.

Barbara's a little lady (woman).

Ladies' (Women's) Air Corps.

In the first two examples, the use of *lady* desexualizes the contextual meaning of *woman*. So trivializing is the use of *lady* in the last phrase that the second is wholly anomalous. The male equivalent, *lord,* is never used; and its synonym, *gentleman,* is used infrequently. When *gentleman,* is used, the assumption seems to be that certain culturally condoned aspects of masculinity (e.g., aggressivity, activity, and strength) should be set aside in the interests of maturity and order, as in the following phrases:

A gentlemen's (men's) agreement.

A duel between gentlemen (men).

He's a real gentleman (man).

Rather than feeling constrained to set aside the stereotypes associated with *man,* males frequently find the opposite process occurring. The contextual connotation of *man* places a strain on males to be continuously sexually and socially potent, as the following examples reveal:

I was not a man (gentleman) with her tonight.

This is a man's (gentleman's) job.

Be a man (gentleman).

Whether males, therefore, feel competent or anxious, valuable or worthless in particular contexts is influenced by the demands placed on them by the expectations of the language.

Not only are men infrequently labeled *gentlemen,* but they are infrequently labeled *boys*. The term *boy* is reserved for young males, bellhops, car attendants, and as a putdown to those males judged inferior. *Boy* connotes immaturity and powerlessness. Only occasionally do males "have a night out with the boys." They do not talk "boy talk" at the office. Rarely does our language legitimize carefreeness in males. Rather, they are expected, linguistically, to adopt the responsibilities of manhood.

On the other hand, women of all ages may be called *girls*. Grown females "play bridge with the girls" and indulge in "girl talk." They are encouraged to remain childlike, and the implication is that they are basically immature and without power. Men can become men, linguistically, putting aside the immaturity of childhood; indeed, for them to retain the openness and playfulness of boyhood is linguistically difficult.

Further, the presumed incompetence and immaturity of women are evidenced by the linguistic company they keep. Women are categorized with children ("women and children first"), the infirm ("the blind, the lame, the women"), and the incompetent ("women, convicts, and idiots"). The use of these categorical designations is not accidental happenstance; "rather these selectional groupings are powerful forces behind the actual expressions of language and are based on distinctions which are not regarded as trivial by the speakers of the language" (Key, 1975:82). A total language analysis of categorical groupings is not available, yet it seems likely that women tend to be included in groupings that designate incompleteness, ineptitude, and immaturity. On the other hand, it is difficult for us to conceive of the word *man* in any categorical grouping other than one that extends beyond humanity, such as "Man, apes, and angels" or "Man and Superman." That is, men do exist as an independent category capable of autonomy; women are grouped with the stigmatized, the immature, and the foolish. Moreover, when men are in human groupings, males are invariably first on the list ("men and women," "he and she," "man and wife"). This order is not accidental but was prescribed in the 16th century to honor the worthier party.

Fourth, in practice women are defined in terms of their sexual desirability (to men); men are defined in terms of their sexual prowess (over women). Most slang words in reference to women refer to their sexual desirability to men (e.g., *dog, fox, broad, ass, chick*). Slang about men refers to their sexual prowess over women (e.g., *dude, stud, hunk*). The fewer examples given for men is not an oversight. An analysis of sexual slang, for example, listed more than 1,000 words and phrases that derogate women sexually but found "nowhere near this multitude for describing men" (Kramarae, 1975:72). Farmer

and Henley (cited in Schulz, 1975) list 500 synonyms for *prostitute*, for example, and only 65 for *whoremonger.* Stanley (1977) reports 220 terms for a sexually promiscuous woman and only 22 for a sexually promiscuous man. Shuster (1973) reports that the passive verb form is used in reference to women's sexual experiences (e.g., *to be laid, to be had, to be taken*), whereas the active tense is used in reference to the male's sexual experience (e.g., *lay, take, have*). Being sexually attractive to males is culturally condoned for women and being sexually powerful is approved for males. In this regard, the slang of the street is certainly not countercultural; rather it perpetuates and reinforces different expectations in females and males as sexual objects and performers.

Further, we find sexual connotations associated with neutral words applied to women. A few examples should suffice. A male academician questioned the title of a new course, asserting it was "too suggestive." The title? "The Position of Women in the Social Order." A male tramp is simply a hobo, but a female tramp is a slut. And consider the difference in connotation of the following expressions:

It's easy.

He's easy.

She's easy.

In the first, we assume something is "easy to do"; in the second, we might assume a professor is an "easy grader" or a man is "easygoing." But when we read "she's easy," the connotation is "she's an easy lay."

In the world of slang, men are defined by their sexual prowess. In the world of slang and proper speech, women are defined as sexual objects. The rule in practice seems to be: If in doubt, assume that *any* reference to a women has a sexual connotation. For both genders, the constant bombardment of prescribed sexuality is bound to have real consequences.

Fifth, women are defined in terms of their relations to men; men are defined in terms of their relations to the world at large. A good example is seen in the words *master* and *mistress.* Originally these words had the same meaning—"a person who holds power over servants." With the demise of the feudal system, however, these words took on different meanings. The masculine variant metaphorically refers to power over something; as in "He is the master of his trade"; the feminine variant metaphorically (although probably not in actuality) refers to power over a man sexually, as in "She is Tom's mistress." Men are defined in terms of their power in the occupational world, women in terms of their sexual power over men.

The existence of two contractions for Mistress *(Miss* and *Mrs.)* and but one for Mister *(Mr.)* underscores the cultural concern and linguistic practice: women are defined in relation to men. Even a divorced woman is defined in terms of her no-longer-existing relation to a man (she is still *Mrs. Man's Name*). But apparently the divorced state is not relevant enough to the man or to the society to require a label. A divorced woman is a *divorcee,* but what do you call a divorced man? The recent preference of many women to be called *Ms.* is an attempt to provide for women an equivalency title that is not dependent on marital status.

Sixth, a historical pattern can be seen in the meanings that come to be attached to words that originally were neutral: those that apply to women acquire obscene and/or debased connotations but no such pattern of derogation holds for neutral words referring to men. The processes of *pejoration* (the acquiring of an obscene or debased connotation) and *amelioration* (the reacquiring of a neutral or positive connotation) in the English language in regard to terms for males and females have been studied extensively by Muriel Schulz (1975).

Leveling is the least derogative form of pejoration. Through leveling, titles that originally referred to an elite class of persons come to include a wider class of persons. Such democratic leveling is more common for female designates than for males. For example, contrast the following: *lord-lady (lady); baronet-dame (dame); governor-governess (governess).*

Most frequently what happens to words designating women as they become pejorated, how-

ever, is that they come to denote or connote sexual wantonness. *Sir* and *mister,* for example, remain titles of courtesy, but at some time *madam, miss,* and *mistress* have come to designate, respectively, a brothelkeeper, a prostitute, and an unmarried sexual partner of a male (Schulz, 1975:66).

Names for domestic helpers, if they are females, are frequently derogated. *Hussy,* for example, originally meant "housewife." *Laundress, needlewoman, spinster* ("tender of the spinning wheel"), and *nurse* all referred to domestic occupations within the home, and all at some point became slang expressions for prostitute or mistress.

Even kinship terms referring to women become denigrated. During the 17th century, *mother* was used to mean "a bawd"; more recently *mother (mothuh f——)* has become a common derogatory epithet (Cameron, 1974). Probably at some point in history every kinship term for females has been derogated (Schulz, 1975:66).

Terms of endearment for women also seem to follow a downward path. Such pet names as Tart, Dolly, Kitty, Polly, Mopsy, Biddy, and Jill all eventually became sexually derogatory (Schulz, 1975:67). *Whore* comes from the same Latin root as *care* and once meant "a lover of either sex."

Indeed, even the most neutral categorical designations—*girl, female, woman, lady*—at some point in their history have been used to connote sexual immorality. *Girl* originally meant "a child of either sex"; through the process of semantic degeneration it eventually meant "a prostitute." Although *girl* has lost this meaning, *girlie* still retains sexual connotations. *Woman* connoted "a mistress" in the early 19th century; *female* was a degrading epithet in the latter part of the 19th century; and when *lady* was introduced as a euphemism, it too became deprecatory. "Even so neutral a term as *person,* when it was used as substitute for *woman,* suffered [vulgarization]" (Mencken, 1963: 350, quoted in Schulz, 1975:71).

Whether one looks at elite titles, occupational roles, kinship relationships, endearments, or age-sex categorical designations, the pattern is clear.

Terms referring to females are pejorated—"become negative in the middle instances and abusive in the extremes" (Schulz, 1975:69). Such semantic derogation, however, is not evidenced for male referents. *Lord, baronet, father, brother, nephew, footman, bowman, boy, lad, fellow, gentleman, man, male,* and so on "have failed to undergo the derogation found in the history of their corresponding feminine designations" (Schulz, 1975:67). Interestingly, the male word, rather than undergoing derogation, frequently is replaced by a female referent when the speaker wants to debase a male. A weak man, for example, is referred to as a *sissy* (diminutive of *sister*), and an army recruit during basic training is called a *pussy.* And when one is swearing at a male, he is referred to as a *bastard* or a *son-of-a-bitch*—both appellations that impugn the dignity of a man's mother.

In summary, these verbal practices are consistent with the gender stereotypes that we encounter in everyday life. Women are thought to be a part of man, nonautonomous, dependent, relegated to roles that require few skills, characteristically incompetent and immature, sexual objects, best defined in terms of their relations to men. Males are visible, autonomous and independent, responsible for the protection and containment of women, expected to occupy positions on the basis of their high achievement or physical power, assumed to be sexually potent, and defined primarily by their relations to the world of work. The use of the language perpetuates the stereotypes for both genders and limits the options available for self-definition.

REFERENCES

Adamsky, C. 1981. "Changes in pronominal usage in a classroom situation." *Psychology of Women Quarterly* 5:773–79.

Bendix, J. 1979. "Linguistic models as political symbols: Gender and the generic 'he' in English." In J. Orasanu, M. Slater, and L. L. Adler, eds., *Language, sex and gender; Does la différence make a differ-ence?* pp. 23–42. New York: New Academy of Science Annuals.

Cameron, P. 1974. "Frequency and kinds of words in various social settings, or What the hell's going on?" In M. Truzzi, ed., *Sociology for pleasure,* pp. 31–37. Englewood Cliffs, N.J.: Prentice-Hall.

Daly, M. 1973. *Beyond God the father.* Boston: Beacon Press.

DeStefano, J. S. 1976. Personal communication. Columbus: Ohio State University.

Hamilton, N., & Henley, N. 1982. "Detrimental consequences of the generic masculine usage." Paper presented to the Western Psychological Association meetings, Sacramento.

Key, M. R. 1975. *Male/female language.* Metuchen, N.J.: Scarecrow Press.

Kramarae, Cheris. 1975. "Woman's speech: Separate but unequal?" In Barrie Thorne and Nancy Henley, eds., *Language and sex: Difference and dominance,* pp. 43–56. Rowley, Mass.: Newbury House.

MacKay, D. G. 1983. "Prescriptive grammar and the pronoun problem." In B. Thorne, C. Kramarae, and N. Henley, eds., *Language, gender, and society,* pp. 38–53. Rowley, Mass.: Newbury House.

Martyna, W. 1978. "What does 'he' mean? Use of the generic masculine." *Journal of Communication* 28:131–38.

Martyna, W. 1980. "Beyond the 'he/man' approach: The case for nonsexist language." *Signs* 5:482–93.

Mencken, H. L. 1963. *The American language.* 4th ed. with supplements. Abr. and ed. R. I. McDavis. New York: Knopf.

Schneider, J., & Hacker, S. 1973. "Sex role imagery in the use of the generic 'man' in introductory texts: A case in the sociology of sociology." *American Sociologist* 8:12–18.

Schulz, M. R. 1975. "The semantic derogation of women." In B. Thorne and N. Henley, eds., *Language and sex: Difference and dominance,* pp. 64–75. Rowley, Mass.: Newbury House.

Shuster, Janet. 1973. "Grammatical forms marked for male and female in English." Unpublished paper. Chicago: University of Chicago.

Stanley, J. P. 1977. "Paradigmatic woman: The prostitute." In D. L. Shores, ed., *Papers in language variation.* Birmingham: University of Alabama Press.

Vanderbilt, A. 1972. *Amy Vanderbilt's etiquette.* Garden City, N.Y.: Doubleday.

To Be and Be Seen: The Politics of Reality*

Marilyn Frye

. . . Reality is that which is.

> The English word 'real' stems from a word which meant *regal,* of or pertaining to the king.
>
> 'Real' in Spanish means *royal.*
>
> Real property is that which is proper to the king.
>
> Real estate is the estate of the king.
>
> Reality is that which pertains to the one in power, is that over which he has power, is his domain, his estate, is proper to him.
>
> The ideal king reigns over everything as far as the eye can see. His eye. What he cannot see is not royal, not real.
>
> He sees what is proper to him.
>
> To be real is to be visible to the king.
>
> The king is in his counting house.

I say, "I am a lesbian. The king does not count lesbians. Lesbians are not real. There are no lesbians." To say this, I use the word 'lesbian', and hence one might think that there is a word for this thing, and thus that the thing must have a place in the conceptual scheme. But this is not so. Let me take you on a guided tour of a few standard dictionaries, to display some reasons for saying that lesbians are not named in the lexicon of the King's English.

If you look up the word 'lesbian' in *The Oxford English Dictionary,* you find an entry that says it is an adjective that means *of or pertaining to the island of Lesbos,* and an entry describing at length and favorably an implement called a lesbian rule, which is a flexible measuring device used by carpenters. Period.

Webster's Third International offers a more pertinent definition. It tells us that a lesbian is a homosexual female. And going on, one finds that 'homosexual' means *of or pertaining to the same sex.* The elucidating example provided is the phrase 'homosexual twins' which means *same-sex twins.* The alert scholar can conclude that a lesbian is a same-sex female.

A recent edition of *Webster's Collegiate Dictionary* tells us that a lesbian is a woman who has sex, or sexual relations, with other women. Such a definition would be accepted by many speakers of the language and at least seems to be coherent, even if too narrow. But the appearance is deceptive, for this account collapses into nonsense, too. The key word in this definition is 'sex': having sex or having sexual relations. But what is having sex? It is worthwhile to follow this up because the pertinent dictionary entries obscure an important point about the logic of sex. Getting clear about that point helps one see that there is semantic closure against recognition of the existence of lesbians, and it also prepares the way for understanding the connection between the place of *woman* and the place of *lesbian* with respect to the phallocratic scheme of things.[1]

Dictionaries generally agree that 'sexual' means something on the order of *pertaining to the genital union of a female and a male animal,* and that "having sex" is having intercourse—intercourse being defined as the penetration of a vagina by a penis, with ejaculation. My own observation of usage leads me to think these accounts are inadequate and misleading. Some uses of these terms do fit this dictionary account. For instance, parents and counselors standardly remind young women that if they are going to be sexually active they must deal responsibly with the possibility of becoming pregnant. In this context, the word 'sexually' is pretty clearly being used in a way that accords with the given definition. But many activities and events fall under the rubric 'sexual', apparently without semantic deviance, though they do not involve penile penetration of the vagina of a female human being. Penile penetration of almost anything, especially if it is accompanied by ejacula-

---

*This is a very slightly revised version of the essay which appeared in *Sinister Wisdom 17* with the title, "To Be And Be Seen: Metaphysical Misogyny."

tion, counts as having sex or being sexual. Moreover, events which cannot plausibly be seen as pertaining to penile erection, penetration and ejaculation will, in general, not be counted as sexual, and events that do not involve penile penetration or ejaculation will not be counted as having sex. For instance, if a girlchild is fondled and aroused by a man, and comes to orgasm, but the man refrains from penetration and ejaculation, the man can say, and speakers of English will generally agree, that he did not have sex with her. No matter what is going on, or (it must be mentioned) *not* going on, with respect to female arousal or orgasm, or in connection with the vagina, a pair can be said without semantic deviance to have had sex, or not to have had sex; the use of that term turns entirely on what was going on with respect to the penis.

When one first considers the dictionary definitions of 'sex' and 'sexual', it seems that all sexuality is heterosexuality, by definition, and that the term 'homosexual' would be internally contradictory. There are uses of the term according to which this is exactly so. But in the usual and standard use, there is nothing semantically odd in describing two men as having sex with each other. According to that usage, any situation in which one or more penises are present is one in which something could happen which could be called having sex. But on this apparently "broader" definition there is nothing women could do in the absence of men that could, without semantic oddity, be called "having sex." Speaking of women who have sex with other women is like speaking of ducks who engage in arm wrestling.

When the dictionary defines lesbians as women who have sex or sexual relations with other women, it defines lesbians as logically impossible.

Looking for other words in the lexicon which might denote these beings which are non-named 'lesbians', one thinks of terms in the vernacular, like 'dyke', 'bulldagger' and so on. Perhaps it is just as well that standard dictionaries do not pretend to provide relevant definitions of such terms. Generally, these two terms are used to denote women who are perceived as imitating, dressing

up like, or trying to be men. Whatever the extent of the class of women who are perceived to do such things, it obviously is not coextensive with the class of lesbians. Nearly every feminist, and many other women as well, have been perceived as wishing to be men, and a great many lesbians are not so perceived. The term 'dyke' has been appropriated by some lesbians as a term of pride and solidarity, but in that use it is unintelligible to most speakers of English.

One of the current definitions of 'lesbianism' among lesbians is *woman-loving*—the polar opposite of misogyny. Several dictionaries I checked have entries for 'misogyny' (hatred of women), but not for 'philogyny' (love of women). I found one which defines 'philogyny' as *fondness for women,* and another dictionary defines 'philogyny' as *Don Juanism.* Obviously neither of these means *love of women* as it is intended by lesbians combing the vocabulary for ways to refer to themselves. According to the dictionaries, there is no term in English for the polar opposite of misogyny nor for persons whose characteristic orientation toward women is the polar opposite of misogyny.

Flinging the net wider, one can look up the more Victorian words, like sapphism and sapphist. In *Webster's Collegiate,* 'sapphism' is defined just as *lesbianism.* But *The Oxford English Dictionary* introduces another twist. Under the heading of 'sapphism' is an entry for 'sapphist' according to which sapphists are those addicted to unnatural sexual relations between women. The fact that these relations are characterized as unnatural is revealing. For what is unnatural is contrary to the laws of nature, or contrary to the nature of the substance of entity in question. But what is contrary to the laws of nature cannot happen: that is what it means to call these laws the laws of nature. And I cannot do what is contrary to my nature, for if I could do it, it would be in my nature to do it. To call something "unnatural" is to say it cannot be. This definition defines sapphists, that is lesbians, as *naturally* impossible as well as *logically* impossible. . . .

Lesbian.
One of the people of the Isle of Lesbos.

It is bizarre that when I try to name myself and explain myself, my native tongue provides me with a word that is so foreign, so false, so hopelessly inappropriate. Why am I referred to by a term which means *one of the people of Lesbos?*

The use of the word 'lesbian' to name us is a quadrifold evasion, a laminated euphemism. To name us, one goes by way of a reference to the island of Lesbos, which in turn is an indirect reference to the poet Sappho (who used to live there, they say), which in turn is itself an indirect reference to what fragments of her poetry have survived a few millenia of patriarchy, and this in turn (if we have not lost you by now) is a prophylactic avoidance of direct mention of the sort of creature who would write such poems or to whom such poems would be written . . . assuming you happen to know what is in those poems written in a dialect of Greek over two thousand five hundred years ago on some small island somewhere in the wine dark Aegean Sea.

This is a truly remarkable feat of silence.

. . . I think there is much truth in the claim that the phallocratic scheme does not include women. But while women are erased in history and in speculation, physically liquidated in gynocidal purges and banished from the community of those with perceptual and semantic authority, we are on the other hand regularly and systematically invited, seduced, cajoled, coerced and even paid to be in intimate and constant association with men and their projects. In this, the situation of women generally is radically different from the situation of lesbians. Lesbians are not invited to join—the family, the party, the project, the procession, the war effort. There is a place for a woman in every game. Wife, secretary, servant, prostitute, daughter, assistant, babysitter, mistress, seamstress, proofreader, nurse, confidante, masseusse, indexer, typist, mother. Any of these is a place for a woman, and women are much encouraged to fill them. None of these is a place for a lesbian.

The exclusion of women from the phallocratic scheme is impressive, frightening and often fatal, but it is not simple and absolute. Women's existence is both absolutely necessary to and irresolvably problematic for the dominant reality and those committed to it, for our existence is *presupposed* by phallocratic reality, but it is not and cannot be *encompassed* by or countenanced by that reality. Women's existence is a background against which phallocratic reality is a foreground.

A foreground scene is created by the motion of foreground figures against a static background. Foreground figures are perceptible, are defined, have identity, only in virtue of their movement against a background. The space in which the motion of foreground figures takes place is created and defined by their movement with respect to each other and against the background. But nothing of the background is *in* or is *part of* or is *encompassed* by the foreground scene and space. The background is unseen by the eye which is focused on foreground figures, and if anything somehow draws the eye to the background, the foreground dissolves. What would draw the eye to the background would be any sudden or well-defined motion in the background. Hence there must be either no motion at all in the background, or an unchanging buzz of small, regular and repetitive motions. The background must be utterly un*event*ful if the foreground is to continue to hang together, that is, if it is to endure as *a space* within which there are discrete *objects* in relation to each other.

I imagine phallocratic reality to be the space and figures and motion which constitute the foreground, and the constant repetitive uneventful activities of women to constitute and maintain the background against which this foreground plays. It is essential to the maintenance of the foreground reality that nothing within it refer in any way to anything in the background, and yet it depends absolutely upon the existence of the background. It is useful to carry this metaphor on in a more concrete mode—thinking of phallocratic reality as a dramatic production on a stage.

The motions of the actors against the stage settings and backdrop constitute and maintain the existence and identities of the characters in a play. The stage setting, props, lights and so forth are created, provided, maintained and occasionally rearranged (according to the script) by stagehands. The stagehands, their motions and the products of those motions, are neither in nor part of the play, are neither in nor part of the reality of the characters. The reality in the framework of which Hamlet's actions have their meaning would be rent or shattered if anything Hamlet did or thought referred in any way to the stagehands or their activities, or if that background blur of activity were in any other way to be resolved into attention-catching events.

The situation of the actors is desperately paradoxical. The actors are absolutely committed to the maintenance of the characters and the characters' reality: participation as characters in the ongoing creation of Reality is their *raison d'etre*. The reality of the character must be lived with fierce concentration. The actor must be immersed in the play and undistracted by any thought for the scenery, props or stagehands, lest the continuity of the characters and the integrity of their reality be dissolved or broken. But if the character must be lived so intently, who will supervise the stagehands to make sure they don't get rowdy, leave early, fall asleep or walk off the job? (Alas, there is no god nor heavenly host to serve as Director and Stage Managers.) Those with the most intense commitment to the maintenance of the reality of the play are precisely those most interested in the proper deportment of the stagehands, and this interest competes directly with that commitment. There is nothing the actor would like better than that there be no such thing as stagehands, posing as they do a constant threat to the very existence, the very life, of the character and hence to the meaning of the life of the actor; and yet the actor is irrevocably tied to the stagehands by his commitment to the play. Hamlet, of course, has no such problems; there are no stagehands in the play.

To escape his dilemma, the actor may throw caution to the wind and lose himself in the character, whereupon stagehands are unthinkable, hence unproblematic. Or he may construct and embrace the belief that the stagehands share exactly his own perceptions and interests and that they are as committed to the play as he—that they are like robots. On such a hypothesis he can assume them to be absolutely dependable and go on about his business single-mindedly and without existential anxiety. A third strategy, which is in a macabre way more sane, is that of trying to solve the problem technologically by constructing actual robots to serve as stagehands.[2] Given the primacy of his commitment to the play, all solutions must involve one form or another of annihilation of the stagehands. Yet all three require the existence of stagehands; the third, he would hope, requiring it only for a while longer.

The solution to the actor's problem which will appear most benign with respect to the stagehands because it erases the erasure, is that of training, persuading and seducing the stagehands into *loving* the actors and taking actors' interests and commitments unto themselves as their own. One significant advantage to this solution is that the actors can carry on without the guilt or confusion that might come with annihilating, replacing or falsely forgetting the stagehands. As it turns out, of course, even this is a less than perfect solution. Stagehands, in the thrall of their commitment, can become confused and think of themselves as actors—and then they may disturb the play by trying to enter it as characters, by trying to participate in the creation and maintainance of Reality. But there are various well-known ways to handle these intrusions and this seems to be, generally speaking, the most popular solution to the actor's dilemma.

. . . The king is in his counting house. The king is greedy and will count for himself everything he dares to. But his greed itself imposes limits on what he dares to count.

What the king cannot count is a seer whose perception passes the plane of the foreground Reality and focuses upon the background. A seer whose eye is attracted to the ones working as stagehands—the women. A seer in whose eye the woman has authority, has interests of her own, is not a robot. A seer who has no motive for wanting there to be no women; a seer who is not loyal to Reality. We can take the account of the seer who must be unthinkable if Reality is to be kept afloat as the beginning of an account of what a lesbian is. One might try saying that a lesbian is one who, by virtue of her focus, her attention, her attachment, is disloyal to phallocratic reality. She is not committed to its maintenance and the maintenance of those who maintain it, and worse, her mode of disloyality threatens its utter dissolution in the mere flick of the eye. This sounds extreme, of course, perhaps even hysterical. But listening carefully to the rhetoric of the fanatic fringe of the phallocratic loyalists, one hears that they do think that feminists, whom they fairly reasonably judge to be lesbians, have the power to bring down civilization, to dissolve the social order as we know it, to cause the demise of the species, by our mere existence.

Even the fanatics do not really believe that a lone maverick lesbian can in a flick of her evil eye atomize civilization, of course. Given the collectivity of conceptual schemes, the way they rest on agreement, a maverick perceiver does not have the power to bring one tumbling down—a point also verified by my own experience as a not-so-powerful maverick. What the loyalists fear, and in this I think they are more-or-less right, is a contagion of the maverick perception to the point where the agreement in perception which keeps Reality afloat begins to disintegrate.

The event of becoming a lesbian is a reorientation of attention in a kind of ontological conversion. It is characterized by a feeling of a world dissolving, and by a feeling of disengagement and re-engagement of one's power as a perceiver. That such conversion happens signals its possibility to others.

Heterosexuality for women is not simply a matter of sexual preference, any more than lesbianism is. It is a matter of orientation of attention, as is lesbianism, in a metaphysical context controlled by neither heterosexual nor lesbian women. Attention is a kind of passion. When one's attention is on something, one is present in a particular way with respect to that thing. This

presence is, among other things, an element of erotic presence. The orientation of one's attention is also what fixes and directs the application of one's physical and emotional work.

If the lesbian sees the women, the woman may see the lesbian seeing her. With this, there is a flowering of possibilities. The woman, feeling herself seen, may learn that she *can be* seen; she may also be able to know that a woman can see, that is, can author perception. With this, there enters for the woman the logical possibility of assuming her authority as a perceiver and of shifting her own attention. With that there is the dawn of choice, and it opens out over the whole world of women. The lesbian's seeing undercuts the mechanism by which the production and constant reproduction of heterosexuality for women was to be rendered *automatic.* The nonexistence of lesbians is a piece in the mechanism which is supposed to cut off the possibility of choice or alternative at the root, namely at the point of conception.

The maintenance of phallocratic reality requires that the attention of women be focused on men and men's projects—the play; and that attention not be focused on women—the stagehands. Woman-loving, as a spontaneous and habitual orientation of attention is then, both directly and indirectly, inimical to the maintenance of that reality. And therein lies the reason for the thoroughness of the ontological closure against lesbians, the power of those closed out, and perhaps the key to the liberation of women from oppression in a male-dominated culture.

My primary goal here has not been to state and prove some rigid thesis, but simply to *say* something clearly enough, intelligibly enough, so that it can be understood and thought about. Lesbians are outside the conceptual scheme, and this is something done, not just the way things are. One can begin to see that lesbians are excluded by the scheme, and that this is *motivated,* when one begins to see what purpose the exclusion might serve in connection with keeping women generally in their metaphysical place. It is also true that lesbians are in a position to see things that cannot be seen from within the system. What lesbians see is what makes them lesbians and their seeing is why they have to be excluded. Lesbians are woman-seers. When one is suspected of seeing women, one is spat summarily out of reality, through the cognitive gap and into the negative semantic space. If you ask what became of such a woman, you may be told she became a lesbian, and if you try to find out what a lesbian is, you will be told there is no such thing.

But there is.

NOTES

1. The analysis that follows is my own rendering of an account developed by Carolyn Shafer. My version of it is informed also by my reading of "Sex and Reference," by Janice Moulton, *Philosophy and Sex,* edited by Robert Baker and Frederick Elliston (Prometheus Books, Buffalo, New York, 1975).

2. This solution is discussed in *The Transexual Empire: The Making of the She-Male,* by Janice G. Raymond, (Beacon Press, Boston, 1979).

PERMISSIONS